CORPORATE OWNERSHIP AND CONTROL

Corporate Ownership and Control

British Business Transformed

BRIAN R. CHEFFINS

S.J. Berwin Professor of Corporate Law, Faculty of Law,
University of Cambridge

OXFORD
UNIVERSITY PRESS

OXFORD
UNIVERSITY PRESS

Great Clarendon Street, Oxford OX2 6DP

Oxford University Press is a department of the University of Oxford.
It furthers the University's objective of excellence in research, scholarship,
and education by publishing worldwide in

Oxford New York

Auckland Cape Town Dar es Salaam Hong Kong Karachi
Kuala Lumpur Madrid Melbourne Mexico City Nairobi
New Delhi Shanghai Taipei Toronto

With offices in

Argentina Austria Brazil Chile Czech Republic France Greece
Guatemala Hungary Italy Japan Poland Portugal Singapore
South Korea Switzerland Thailand Turkey Ukraine Vietnam

Oxford is a registered trade mark of Oxford University Press
in the UK and in certain other countries

Published in the United States
by Oxford University Press Inc., New York

British Library Cataloguing in Publication Data

Data available

Library of Congress Cataloging in Publication Data

Data available

Typeset by Newgen Imaging Systems (P) Ltd., Chennai, India
Printed in Great Britain
on acid-free paper by
CPI Antony Rowe, Chippenham, Wiltshire

ISBN 978–0–19–923697–8

1 3 5 7 9 10 8 6 4 2

Outline Contents

Detailed Contents

Preface

During the opening years of the current decade I wrote a number of papers in which I drew on historical developments in the UK to critique theories that had been advanced to explain why ownership splits (or does not split) from control in large companies, pointing out that the theories did not fit the facts in Britain. After I had presented one of these papers, a US law professor asked, 'Why, then, did ownership separate from control in Britain?' This book is the extended answer to that question.

The book is much more than a synthesis of previous research I have done on ownership and control in the UK. It covers a considerably longer time span than my earlier work and offers fresh evidence on numerous topics I have previously considered. Nevertheless, I generously acknowledge the insights I gained from John Armour, Steve Bank, Marc Goergen and David Skeel, co-authors of papers I have written on various themes the book discusses. Marc also provided valuable assistance with various graphs set out in the text.

I would also like to thank the John Simon Guggenheim Memorial Foundation for financial support in the form of a fellowship in 2002–03 for work on 'Foundations of the Anglo-American Corporate Economy'. It was while working under the auspices of this fellowship that I began sketching out plans for this project.

I am also in debt to Ken Thurstans and Joanna Cheffins for their careful reading of the manuscript.

Finally, I would like to express my gratitude for the invaluable support my family, both in Canada and Britain, has shown, not only during the writing of this book but more generally throughout my academic career.

Two housekeeping points are in order. First, monetary amounts are referred to frequently in the book. To give the reader a sense of the value of money in current terms historical currency conversions are provided periodically. The conversions have been done with <http://measuringworth.com/calculators/ukcompare/>, using the retail price index measure.

Second, cross-referencing between various aspects of the book has been done by citing the relevant Chapter, Part, Section and Sub-section, rather than by pinpoint footnote references. To illustrate, a reference in the text or a footnote to 'Chapter Five, Part I' (abbreviated to Ch. Five, Pt I in the case of footnotes) is intended to draw the reader's attention to matters discussed in Part I of Chapter V, and 'Chapter Six, Part III.B.1' (abbreviated to Ch. Six, Pt III.B.1) is a cross-reference to Part III.B.1 of Chapter Six. In circumstances where there is a cross-reference to discussion elsewhere in the same chapter, the text or footnote simply identifies the Part, Section and Subsection, as applicable. For instance, where Part II.A of the same chapter is cited, 'Part II.A' will appear in the text (abbreviated to Pt II.A in the case of a footnote) without any mention of a chapter.

Brian R. Cheffins

June 2008

Table of Cases

Table of Legislation

SUBORDINATE LEGISLATION

UNITED STATES

ONE

Setting the Scene

I. The Separation of Ownership and Control as a Source of Concern

In 2006, a British financial journalist remarked 'Full divorce between ownership and control is a British obsession.'[1] The 'obsession' is understandable. Companies traded on the stock market are a crucial part of the UK economy, with the ratio of the aggregate market capitalization of publicly traded companies to gross domestic product being nearly three times the global average and with the ratio of equity issued by newly listed companies to gross domestic product being nearly four times the global average.[2] The typical British publicly traded company has widely dispersed share ownership and is run by professionally trained managers who collectively own an insufficiently large percentage of shares to dictate the outcome when shareholders vote. As a result there is a separation of ownership (in the sense of ownership of shares) and control (in the sense of having authority to manage). This serves to distinguish Britain from most countries. Not only are publicly traded companies less common elsewhere, but it is also standard for those companies that have distributed shares to the public to have a shareholder controlling a large block of shares rather than fully diffuse share ownership.

A shareholder who owns a dominant block of shares typically has a strong financial incentive to keep a careful watch on what is going on and the leverage to orchestrate the removal of disloyal or ineffective managers. In contrast, when share ownership is widely dispersed, shareholders will tend to have little appetite to intervene actively. Executives thus will potentially have substantial latitude to act in an ill-advised or self-serving manner and impose, in economic parlance, 'agency costs' on investors. In a sense, then, it is surprising companies with dispersed ownership exist at all, whether in Britain or elsewhere. As Jensen and Meckling have remarked, '(h)ow does it happen that millions of individuals

---

[1] 'Plc is Ready to Join Mutuals in Land of the Dodo', Times, April 21, 2006, (column by Graham Searjeant).

[2] Simeon Djankov, Rafael La Porta, Florencio López-de-Silanes and Andrei Shleifer, 'The Law and Economics of Self-Dealing', (2005) NBER Working Paper 11883, Table VI ('Stock Market Development').

are willing to turn over a significant fraction of their wealth to organizations run by managers who have so little interest in their welfare?'[3]

There have long been concerns in the UK that shareholder apathy and insufficient managerial accountability plague large business enterprises. Adam Smith, in his 1776 classic *The Wealth of Nations*, said of the balance between what was then known as the general court (the shareholders) and the court of directors (the board)

This court, indeed, is frequently subject, in many respects, to the control of a general court of proprietors. But the greater part of those proprietors seldom pretend to understand anything of the business of the company, and when the spirit of faction happens not to prevail among them, give themselves no trouble about it, but receive contentedly such half-yearly or yearly dividend as the directors think proper to make to them.[4]

Herbert Spencer, the noted philosopher and political economist, similarly said of mid-19th-century railways:

Proprietors (shareholders), instead of constantly exercising their franchise, allow it to become on all ordinary occasions a dead letter; retiring directors are so habitually re-elected without opposition, and have so great a power of insuring their own re-election without opposition, and have so great a power of insuring their own re-election when opposed, that the board becomes practically a close body; and it is only when the misgovernment grows extreme enough to produce a revolutionary agitation among the shareholders that any change can be effected.[5]

More recently, a 1947 commentary on British corporate law reform argued 'The disproportionate power...vested in a management divorced from ownership makes imperative the most enlightened supervision and regulation.'[6] The Labour government of the day justified the introduction of a major reform of company law that same year on the basis that there was a need to strengthen the relationship between ownership and control, which had become 'more and more shadowy'.[7] In the 1990s, concerns about managerial accountability in UK public companies were sufficiently serious to prompt the establishment of a trilogy of committees—Cadbury, Greenbury and Hampel—to review corporate governance practices and make recommendations on how to improve matters.[8]

---

[3] Michael C. Jensen and William H. Meckling, 'Theory of the Firm: Managerial Behaviour, Agency Costs and Ownership Structure' (1976) 3, Journal of Financial Economics 305, 330.

[4] Adam Smith, *Wealth of Nations*, 5th edn, Book V, ch. 1 (Edwin Cannan, ed., 1904, originally published 1776), 107.

[5] 'Railway Morals and Railway Policy', (1854) 100 Edinburgh Review 420, 420. Spencer is not identified specifically as the author, but the article is nevertheless attributed to him. See, for example, Bishop Carleton Hunt, *The Development of the Business Corporation in England* (1936), 135–36.

[6] 'British Corporate Law Reform', (1974) 56 Yale Law Journal 1383.

[7] Quoted in Josephine Maltby, 'Was the Companies Act 1947 a Response to a National Crisis?', (2000) 5 Accounting History, #2, 31, 53.

[8] Cadbury Committee, *Report of the Committee on the Financial Aspects of Corporate Governance* (hereinafter Cadbury Report) (1992); Greenbury Committee, *Directors' Remuneration: Report of a Study Group Chaired by Sir Richard Greenbury* (1995); Hampel Committee, *Report of the Committee on Corporate Governance* (1998).

The same theme continues to influence heavily debates about British corporate governance today.[9]

II. The Relevant Historical Literature

Since a divorce between ownership and control is not the norm globally and implies insufficient managerial accountability, how has a divorce between ownership and control come to characterize corporate governance in the UK? The purpose of this book is to answer this question. The enquiry is strongly historical in orientation. The book examines how ownership and control evolved from the seventeenth century through to the present so as to explain how this aspect of British business was transformed.

The book's historical orientation provides a fresh twist because the configuration of ownership and control has only been considered tangentially in the relevant historical literature.

Much valuable work has been done on UK business history but share ownership patterns have been a sideshow.[10] Numerous company histories of important UK firms have been published. These are typically wide-ranging affairs, covering topics from marketing to labour relations, and usually only offer brief details on how the share ownership structure changed over time.[11] The pattern has been much the same with various case studies done on the historical development of particular industries.

More generally oriented work on UK business history has also failed to address systematically the issue of corporate ownership and control.[12] For instance, Hannah's *Rise of the Corporate Economy*, which traces the rise of large-scale enterprise in UK manufacturing, offers insights concerning the displacement of family ownership but is concerned primarily with the technical factors and market forces that fostered the economic growth of large firms.[13] Likewise, Chandler and Lazonick argue that the relative economic decline from which Britain suffered from the late 19th century through much of the 20th century was largely attributable to the dominant personalities in owner-managed firms being unable

---

[9] Derek Higgs, *Review of the Role and Effectiveness of Non-Executive Directors* (2003), 11–12; Department of Trade and Industry, 'Rewards for Failure' Directors' Remuneration—Contracts, Performance and Severance: A Consultative Document' (2003), URN 03/652, 5–7.

[10] Coleen A. Dunlavy, 'Social Conceptions of the Corporation: Insights from the History of Shareholder Voting Rights', (2006) 63 Washington & Lee Law Review 1347, 1351–52 (discussing a similar trend in US business history).

[11] Geoffrey Jones and Keetie E. Sluyterman, 'British and Dutch Business History' in Franco Amatori and Geoffrey Jones (eds), *Business History Around the World* (2003), 111, 114–15.

[12] On the contrast between scholarship that analyzes business history on a generalized basis and research on particular companies and industries, see Leslie Hannah, 'New Issues in British Business History', (1983) 57 Business History Review 165, 166.

[13] Leslie Hannah, *The Rise of the Corporate Economy*, 2nd edn (1983).

to cope with the growing complexity of production but offer only perfunctory details on the structure and ownership of the companies involved.[14]

With studies of the history of finance and investment in the UK, there have been some intriguing case studies of patterns of share ownership in particular contexts. The topics include early 19th-century railways, mid-19th-century industrial companies, late 19th-century banks and investment in shares by women in the late 19th and early 20th centuries.[15] Generally, however, research on the history of finance and investment in the UK treats the ownership of shares in business enterprises as merely one subject among many to merit attention.[16] Overall, then, while the divorce between ownership and control may be a British 'obsession', the literature on UK business and economic history does not explain adequately why the split occurred.

III. Ownership, Control and Corporate Governance in a Comparative Context

While the relevant historical literature offers few direct clues concerning the transformation of patterns of corporate ownership and control, recent research on comparative corporate governance provides a potentially fruitful line of enquiry. Corporate governance, which is concerned with the systems by which companies are directed and controlled, first achieved prominence in the business world only a couple of decades ago.[17] There is now a voluminous literature on the topic and a whole sub-field has developed comparing the main features, strengths and weaknesses of corporate governance systems in different countries.[18] Among comparative corporate governance researchers ascertaining the determinants of ownership and control of large companies has proved a popular field of endeavour. The relevant literature in turn provides a promising departure point for examining the British case.

Broadly speaking, and at the risk of over-simplification, corporate governance systems in particular countries divide into two categories: 'outsider/

[14] Alfred D. Chandler, *Scale and Scope: The Dynamics of Industrial Capitalism* (1990); William Lazonick, *Business Organization and the Myth of the Market Economy* (1991).

[15] See M.C. Reed, *Investment in Railways in Britain, 1820–1844: A Study of the Development of the Capital Market* (1975); P.L. Cottrell, *Industrial Finance 1830–1914* (1980) (chapter on companies taken public by mid-19th-century promoter David Chadwick); Charles R. Hickson and John D. Turner, 'The Trading of Unlimited Liability Bank Shares: The Bagehot Hypothesis', (2003) 63 Journal of Economic History 931; Josephine Maltby and Janette Rutterford, '"She Possessed Her Own Fortune": Women Investors from the Late Nineteenth Century to the Early Twentieth Century', (2006) 48 Business History 220.

[16] David Kynaston, *The City of London* (in four vols, 1994, 1995, 2000, 2002); Ranald C. Michie, *The London Stock Exchange: A History* (1999), E. Victor Morgan and W.A. Thomas, *The Stock Exchange: Its History and Functions* (1969).

[17] On the definition, see Cadbury Report, *supra* n. 8, para. 25; <http://www.berr.gov.uk/bbf/corp-governance/page15267.html> (last visited February 7, 2008). On when the topic achieved prominence, see Christine A. Mallin, *Corporate Governance* (2004), 9.

[18] Marco Becht, Patrick Bolton and Ailsa Röell, 'Corporate Governance and Control' in George M. Constantinides, Milton Harris and René M. Stulz (eds), *Handbook of the Economics of Finance*, vol. 1A, (2003), 7, 41–42.

arm's-length' and 'insider/control-oriented'.[19] In countries in the former camp, large business enterprises are most often traded on the stock market, have a sizeable shareholder register and lack a 'core' shareholder capable of exercising 'inside' influence. As for countries in the latter cohort, stock market listings are less common and those companies that have publicly traded shares usually have 'blockholders', a single shareholder or a cohesive alliance of shareholders owning a sufficiently sizeable fraction of the voting shares to exercise considerable influence over management.

The received wisdom is that Britain and the United States both have an outsider/arm's-length system of ownership and control.[20] In contrast, insider/control-oriented corporate governance predominates in continental Europe, with most countries having considerably fewer publicly traded companies per capita than Britain and companies traded on the stock market being much more likely to have blockholders.[21] Capitalist economies in East Asia and India also fall into the insider/control-oriented camp because 'core' shareholders are very much the norm in large business enterprises.[22] Japan is something of a special case, where blockholders are rare but share ownership is characterized by networks (now increasingly fragile) of stable shareholders (e.g. other corporations in the same business group, major creditors and key customers/suppliers).[23] Insider/control-oriented corporate governance predominates elsewhere, with the norm being for even the largest companies to lack a divorce between ownership and control.[24] Australia

[19] Erik Berglöf, 'A Note on the Typology of Financial Systems' in Klaus J. Hopt and Eddy Wymeersch (eds), *Comparative Corporate Governance: Essays and Materials* (1997), 152; Colin Mayer, 'Financial Systems and Corporate Governance: A Review of the International Evidence', (1998) 154 Journal of Institutional and Theoretical Economics 144, 145–47, 159–60.

[20] M. Becht and C. Mayer, 'Introduction' in Fabrizio Barca and Marco Becht (eds), *The Control of Corporate Europe* (2001), 1–2, 20, 36–37; Christoph van der Elst, 'The Equity Markets, Ownership Structures and Control: Towards an International Harmonization?' in Klaus J. Hopt and Eddy Wymeersch (eds), *Capital Markets and Company Law* (2003), 3, 4–5. On the US, see, however, Clifford G. Holderness, 'The Myth of Diffuse Share Ownership in the United States', Review of Financial Studies, forthcoming.

[21] On ownership patterns see Becht and Mayer, *supra* n. 20, 18–26; Mara Faccio and Larry H.P. Lang, 'The Ultimate Ownership of Western European Corporations', (2002) 65 Journal of Financial Economics 365. On other statistics, see Djankov *et al*, *supra* n. 2, Table VI; van der Elst, *supra* n. 20, 7–11.

[22] Stijn Claessens, Simeon Djankov and Larry H. P. Lang, 'The Separation of Ownership and Control in East Asian Corporations', (2000) 58 Journal of Financial Economics 81; Tarun Khanna and Krishna G. Palepu, 'The Evolution of Concentrated Ownership in India: Broad Patterns and a History of the Indian Software Industry' in Randall K. Morck (ed.), *A History of Corporate Governance Around the World: Family Business Groups to Professional Managers* (2005), 283, 284–94.

[23] On the traditional pattern, see Takeo Hoshi, 'Japanese Corporate Governance as a System' in Klaus J. Hopt, Hideki Kanda, Mark J. Roe, Eddy Wymeersch and Stefan Prigge (eds), *Comparative Corporate Governance—The State of the Art and Emerging Research* (1998), 847, 860; Randall K. Morck and Masao Nakamura, 'A Frog in a Well Knows Nothing of the Ocean: A History of Corporate Ownership in Japan' in Morck, *supra* n. 22, 367, 438. On changes occurring, see Curtis J. Milhaupt, 'In the Shadow of Delaware? The Rise of Hostile Takeovers in Japan', (2005) 105 Columbia L. Rev. 2171, 2184–85; 'Going Hybrid: A Special Report on Business in Japan', Economist, December 1, 2007, 8.

[24] Rafael La Porta, Florencio López-de-Silanes, Andrei Shleifer and Robert Vishny, 'Corporate Ownership Around the World', (1999) 54 Journal of Finance 471, 474–75, 491–505.

and Canada are a close call because they have stock market-oriented economies but blockholders continue to exercise considerable influence in both countries.[25]

The fact that 'outsider/arm's-length' corporate governance is the exception to the rule in global terms is a fairly recent revelation. Traditionally, the received wisdom was that the modern large corporation, wherever located, would follow American norms, in the sense that share ownership would be diffuse and managerial functions would be carried out by professionally trained executives owning only a small percentage of the shares.[26] Empirical work carried out during the 1990s changed perceptions markedly, revealing that a separation of ownership and control was the exception worldwide rather than the rule.[27]

At the same time as there was growing awareness that a divorce of ownership and control was not the norm outside the US, American economic prosperity cast its stock market-oriented version of capitalism in a favourable light.[28] In particular, its rich and deep securities markets were thought to be an important source of innovation and economic dynamism.[29] Academics and policymakers thus sought to uncover the variables that determine the system of ownership and control a country is likely to have, with the sub-text of identifying policies that could be adopted to introduce beneficial features of US corporate governance.[30] A combination of a share price slump in the wake of the 'dot-com' stock market frenzy of the late 1990s and a series of major corporate governance scandals (e.g. fEnron, Tyco and WorldCom) took some of the lustre off the American version of capitalism. The intellectual energy devoted to explaining why ownership does (or does not) separate from control has nevertheless been sustained.

Various theories have been advanced to account for global variations in patterns of ownership and control. The most widely cited and influential explanation offered has been that 'law matters',[31] in the sense that the extent to which corporate and securities law within a particular country protects minority shareholders dictates whether large business enterprises will have diffuse or concentrated share ownership. Another law-oriented theory focuses on 'legal origin', with the premise being that widely held firms are more likely to become dominant

---

[25] Alan Dignam, 'The Role of Competition in Determining Corporate Governance Outcomes: Lessons From Australia's Corporate Governance System', (2005) 68 Modern Law Review 765, 770–71; Randall K. Morck, Michael Percy, Gloria Y. Tan and Bernard Yeung, 'The Rise and Fall of the Widely Held Firm: A History of Corporate Ownership in Canada' in Morck, *supra* n. 22, 65, 98–101.

[26] La Porta, *et al, supra* n. 24, 471.

[27] See, for example, Becht and Mayer, *supra* n. 20, 1, 2–3, 18–35; Claessens, *et al, supra* n. 22; La Porta *et al, supra* n. 24.

[28] Rafael La Porta, Florencio López-de-Silanes, Andrei Shleifer and Robert Vishny, 'Investor Protection and Corporate Governance', (2000) 58 Journal of Financial Economics 3, 18; 'Rise and Fall', Economist, May 5, 2001, Survey of Global Equity Markets, 35–36.

[29] Mark J. Roe, 'Political Preconditions to Separating Ownership from Corporate Control', (2000) 53 Stanford Law Review 539, 542; John Plender, *Going Off the Rails: Global Capital and the Crisis of Legitimacy* (2003), 4–11.

[30] Plender, *supra* n. 29, 12–13; Henry Hansmann and Reinier Kraakman, 'The End of History for Corporate Law', (2001) 89 Georgetown Law Journal 439, 450–55.

[31] Mark J. Roe, 'Corporate Law's Limits', (2002) 31 Journal of Legal Studies 233, 236–37; Luca Enriques, 'Do Corporate Law Judges Matter? Some Evidence from Milan', (2002) 3 European Business Organization Law Review 756, 766–67.

in countries with a legal system based on the 'common law' rather than 'civil law'. Political ideology has also been identified as a determinant of ownership structures in large business enterprises, with the underlying assumption being that a left-wing political milieu provides an inhospitable environment for widely held companies. Another theory is that regulations discouraging financial institutions from becoming key shareholders in major business enterprises do much to explain whether ownership and control becomes divorced in large companies. It has also been suggested that national political stability or lack thereof (e.g. being on the losing side in a war or suffering from domestic mass violence) does much to determine a country's level of financial and stock market development.

Each of the theories just summarized has an explicit cross-border orientation, as they seek to account for how corporate governance arrangements differ between countries. One would therefore expect the theories to have traction historically, in the sense they should explain why in particular countries an outsider/arm's-length system of ownership and control emerged and why in others insider/control-oriented governance predominated. The comparative corporate governance literature indeed has a marked historical flavour. Roe, who first argued financial services regulation was a determinant of ownership structure, made his case largely on the basis of historical evidence from the US, Germany and Japan.[32] Rajan and Zingales have relied extensively on history to explain why stock market-oriented capitalism flourished in some countries and failed to take root in others.[33] A 2005 conference volume entitled *A History of Corporate Governance Around the World* offered historically oriented case studies to explain how ownership and control arrangements reached their current state in ten major industrialized countries.[34]

Given that analysis of comparative corporate governance has a strong historical dimension, one might assume that explaining the divorce between ownership and control in Britain would be a straightforward task. All one seemingly needs to do is test the various theories against the known historical facts and discern which ones 'work' best. Matters turn out not to be so simple. As Chapter Two discusses, the emergence of Britain's outsider/arm's-length system of ownership and control cannot be explained adequately by reference to corporate and securities law, legal origin, political orientation, financial services regulation or political stability. Chapter Two also shows that from an efficiency perspective, companies characterized by a divorce between ownership and control do not have a decisive advantage over companies with blockholders, meaning there is no market imperative that the former dominate. Thus, while the comparative corporate governance literature seemingly provides a helpful departure point as one seeks to account for the divorce between ownership and control in the UK, a fresh analytical framework is in fact required.

[32] Mark J. Roe, *Strong Managers, Weak Owners: The Political Roots of American Corporate Finance* (1994).
[33] Raghuram G. Rajan and Luigi Zingales, *Saving Capitalism from the Capitalists: How Open Financial Markets Challenge the Establishment and Spread Prosperity to Rich and Poor Alike* (2003).
[34] Morck, *supra* n. 22.

IV. Explaining Why Ownership Separated from Control: The Questions to Ask

Since none of the various theories offered in the comparative corporate govern-ance literature to explain patterns of corporate ownership and control account satisfactorily for the British case, a broader investigation, encompassing a series of potential determinants of ownership structure, is in order. This is not a unique insight. Morck and Steier have said of the major theories advanced to account for cross-country differences in corporate control, '(i)t would be wonderful for econo-mists if we could conclude that one is correct and discard the others, but economics is rarely so simple'.[35] Gilson has observed similarly, 'Thus, a more complete expla-nation for the distribution of shareholdings must incorporate politics, law and efficiency, together with the serendipity of each country's initial conditions.'[36]

While a single variable is unlikely to account for the divorce between ownership and control in the UK, it is counterproductive to multiply hypotheses unnecessar-ily. A helpful way to keep the enquiry manageable is to focus on three questions one needs to address to explain why ownership will separate from control. These are:

1) Why might those owning large blocks of shares want to exit or accept dilution of their stake?
2) Will there be demand for shares available for sale?
3) Will the new investors be inclined to exercise control themselves?

This book explains how ownership became divorced from control in large UK business enterprises by addressing each of these questions in historical terms.

The answer to each question is by no means obvious. Consider question 1. Blockholders, due to influence associated with their voting power, can benefit from their status in ways unavailable to other shareholders, with the term of art being they can secure 'private benefits of control'.[37] For instance, blockholders can arrange one-sided transactions that divert profits from the publicly traded company they merely dominate to companies they own outright. They can also potentially treat a publicly traded company as a personal fief, bestowing upon themselves generous manage-rial pay, lavish offices, luxurious business travel and other desirable corporate perks. Given the advantages associated with being a blockholder, why stand down?

As for question #2, it is not self-evident why amongst those with capital available to invest there will be significant demand for shares in publicly traded companies. Due to information asymmetries, investors are likely to struggle to distinguish 'high-quality' companies from less meritorious counterparts.[38] For those investors

[35] Randall K. Morck and Lloyd Steier, 'The Global History of Corporate Governance: An Introduction' in Morck, *supra* n. 22, 29.
[36] Ronald J. Gilson, 'Controlling Shareholders and Corporate Governance: Complicating the Comparative Taxonomy', (2006) 119 Harvard Law Review 1641, 1645.
[37] *Ibid.*, 1651.
[38] Peter Blair Henry and Peter Lombard Lorentzen, 'Domestic Capital Market Reform and Access to Global Finance: Making Markets Work', (2003) NBER Working Paper No. 10064, 16.

prepared to take 'a pig in a poke', if they buy shares in a company with a block-holder, they can fall victim to extraction of private benefits of control. Due to the agency cost problem, matters are not necessarily any better in a company characterized by a separation of ownership and control. So why do investors buy shares?

Finally, with question #3, one might anticipate that where there is sufficient demand for shares to facilitate exit by incumbent blockholders, the new shareholders, apprehensive of agency costs, would be inclined to exercise 'hands on' control over potentially wayward managers. In the UK, shareholders in companies with diffuse share ownership theoretically have the necessary clout, since company law currently authorizes a 'general meeting' of the 'members' (shareholders) to dismiss incumbent directors at any time with a simple majority vote.[39] However, for the most part outside investors in the UK have adopted a 'hands-off' approach to corporate governance and refrained from stepping forward to exercise control to protect their interests. Why has this been the case?

In addressing these three questions, the book uses as shorthand two terms most often used to describe key elements of the fund management industry, these being the 'sell side' (the issuance and distribution of securities) and the 'buy side' (the investment of clients' money). For present purposes, the 'sell side' encompasses the factors that can prompt blockholders to dilute their ownership stake or sell their shares outright. The 'buy side' involves factors that motivate investors to buy equities and deter new shareholders from themselves exercising control.

Both must be activated in order for ownership to separate from control in a particular company. On the 'sell side' blockholders must be prepared to unwind control, whether by selling gradually into the market, by acquiescing as the company issues shares in a manner that dilutes their block or by liquidating their entire stake all at once (e.g. in a takeover by another company). Nothing, in turn, can happen, unless the 'buy side' is in play. A blockholder might be prepared (even eager) to exit but will find this impossible to do unless there is demand for the shares, either from someone buying the company (or at least a controlling interest) outright or from stock market investors prepared to purchase shares as they are made available to the public. The effect of a match between the sell side and the buy side was captured evocatively in an 1898 article discussing a wave of company 'promotions' involving the initial distribution of shares to the public: '(W)ith business men anxious to "capitalise their interest", to sell out on good terms, to take money, capital which they will keep, instead of income they will lose; with moneyed people exposed to a veritable investment famine; with promoters always on the alert, there is alas! little hope that we shall see a cessation of company promoting.'[40]

An additional key element on the buy side is that the new owners of the shares must not be inclined to exercise control themselves. Otherwise, insider/control-oriented corporate governance will continue unabated. A situation where new

---

[39] Companies Act 2006, c. 46, ss. 165 (authorizing removal of directors by ordinary resolution), 282 (defining ordinary resolution).

[40] S.F. Van Oss, 'The "Limited Company" Craze', The Nineteenth Century, May 1898, 731, 734.

owners are particularly likely to take a 'hands on' approach is where the block-holder is bought out in a takeover, since the buyer of the company will typically seek to generate a positive return by exercising close control over the relevant assets. This implies insider/control-oriented corporate governance, but if the purchaser is itself a company lacking a blockholder, outsider/arm's-length corporate governance in effect results.

Chapter Three provides a detailed overview of the sell side and Chapter Four does likewise with the buy side. In brief, incentives blockholders have to exit can include:

- A desire to spread investment risks through diversification
- Generational considerations (e.g. lack of an obvious heir)
- Sustained erosion of profit margins due to competition from rivals and other economic and regulatory trends (e.g. taxation of profits)
- Needing to issue shares to carry out mergers or finance expansion
- Exit terms on offer that are too good to pass up (e.g. buoyed by a rapidly rising stock market)
- Explicit constraints imposed on company insiders to curtain 'self-dealing' (e.g. by company law or by 'self-regulation', such as stock exchange listing rules)
- Reduction of 'free cash flow' available for extraction by blockholders due to market pressures to distribute cash to shareholders in the form of dividends.

On the buy side, contingencies affecting demand for shares can include:

- The supply of spare capital available for investment
- Incentives parties orchestrating public offerings of shares have to build up and maintain a sound business reputation
- The quality of disclosure dictated by regulation
- Dividend policy operating as a 'signalling' mechanism
- Performance of shares in comparison with alternate investment choices
- Periodic surges in investor enthusiasm for shares unrelated to past or current performance
- Reassurance provided by merger activity (e.g. potential exploitation of available economies of scale).

As for factors affecting the willingness of buyers of shares to exercise control, these can include:

- Company law (e.g. the scope for 'insiders' to take advantage of the system for shareholder voting to secure desired majorities).
- Expertise concerning corporate policy-making (or lack thereof).
- The temptation to 'free ride' on the efforts of those prepared to take the time and trouble to adopt a 'hands on' approach.
- Diversification (ownership of shares in numerous companies will diminish the impact of any one company on overall returns and thus discourage intervention).

Chapters Five to Eleven of the book, which analyze matters chronologically, draw on these various elements of the sell side and buy side to outline how ownership and control were transformed and to explain why a divorce between the two became, and is likely to remain, the norm in Britain.

V. Empirical Data

The various sell side and buy side factors that influenced the configuration of ownership and control in large UK companies did not operate in the same manner over time. For instance, on the sell side, the constraints that company law imposed on blockholders evolved from being modest at the beginning of the 20th century to substantial by the end. The buy side was radically transformed in the decades following World War II as ownership of publicly traded shares shifted wholesale from private individuals to institutional investors. Thus, in order to ascertain why ownership became divorced from control in the UK, coming to grips with the relevant chronology is a necessary preliminary step.

There are currently two contrasting schools of thought on the chronology. One emphasizes that Britain was a 'first mover' and implies an early separation of ownership from control.[41] Here the focus is on London's long tradition as a dominant financial centre and the early accumulation of capital available for investment as a beneficial economic spin-off from Britain's 19th-century emergence as the world's first industrial nation. With this combination, the thinking goes, a stock market-oriented corporate economy 'locked in' early and provided a natural platform for a divorce between ownership and control.

The second characterization focuses on a debilitating 'corporate lag'.[42] According to this account, at the close of the 19th century and the beginning of the 20th century corporate 'first movers' from the United States and Germany established themselves as global leaders in key manufacturing industries by adopting sophisticated managerial hierarchies dominated by professionally trained, salaried executives. In Britain, in contrast, family owners resisted ceding control over the enterprises they had either created or inherited and this counterproductive commitment to 'personal capitalism' left leading companies organizationally backward and ill equipped to compete.[43] A belated willingness to accept new methods of corporate organization was too late to correct matters and Britain was condemned to decline relative to its major industrial rivals.

[41] See, for example, Colin Crouch, 'Co-operation and Competition in an Institutionalised Economy: The Case of Germany' in Colin Crouch and David Marquand (eds), *Ethics and Markets: Co-operation and Competition Within Capitalist Economies* (1993), 80, 94–95; Will Hutton, *The State We're In* (1995), 132–35, 144–46, 154; Peter A. Gourevitch, 'The Politics of Corporate Governance Regulation', (2003) 112 *Yale Law Journal* 1829, 1862–63.

[42] On the terminology see T.R. Gourvish, 'British Business and the Transition to a Corporate Economy: Entrepreneurship and Management Structures', (1987) 39(4) *Business History* 18, 20; M.W. Kirby, 'The Corporate Economy in Britain: Its Rise and Achievements Since 1900', in Maurice W. Kirby and Mary B. Rose (eds), *Business Enterprise in Modern Britain: From the Eighteenth to the Twentieth Century* (1994), 139, 141.

[43] The term was first used in this particular context by Chandler. See, for example, *supra* n. 14, 12.

An understandable reaction to the different characterizations of what occurred in Britain is to ask about the empirical data. There is, however, a dearth of statistical evidence, due in large part to data collection difficulties. Traditionally, the only 'raw material' available for statistical analysis of share ownership was an alphabetical list of shareholders and their shareholdings which every company had to supply as part of an annual return to be filed with the companies registry.[44] The information was open to public inspection at a nominal charge, but as Parkinson, who coordinated a 1951 study of share ownership based on such information, said of a person investigating, '[T]he company registers with which he is concerned are dismayingly lengthy documents. The register of a single big company runs to several volumes.'[45] Collection of data became somewhat easier when the Companies Act 1967 required shareholders owning 10 per cent or more of a company's shares (reduced to 5 per cent in 1976 and 3 per cent in 1989) to disclose this to the company, and required companies to keep a register of such shareholdings that was open to public inspection.[46]

The earliest empirical evidence on ownership blocks in publicly traded UK industrial and commercial companies dates back to 1920.[47] Franks, Mayer and Rossi, examining a random cross-section of 53 companies quoted on the London Stock Exchange, found the largest shareholder typically owned a sizeable block and that the ten biggest shareholders owned a large but not controlling percentage of shares (Table I). Next is data from 1936, compiled by Florence, for 'very large' industrial and commercial companies. He found full-scale ownership dispersion was not yet the norm in big UK public companies.

A study by Channon of the largest 100 UK manufacturing companies as of 1970 found a majority of the companies were under 'family control' as of 1950. Franks, Mayer and Rossi did another cross-sectional study for 1950, focusing on 55 companies. Though, on average, the percentage of equity owned by the ten largest shareholders was slightly larger than in 1920, the stake held by the largest shareholder was smaller, implying ownership had become somewhat more diffuse. Data Florence compiled for 'very large' companies as of 1951 suggested the same, as he reported blockholding was prevalent in only a minority of 'very large' industrial and commercial companies (Table I).

---

[44] P. Sargant Florence, 'The Statistical Analysis of Joint Stock Company Control', (1947) 110 Journal of the Royal Statistical Society 1, 5; Hargreaves Parkinson, *Ownership of Industry* (1951), 6. On legislative requirements to file information on shareholders, see, for example, Companies Act 1862, c. 25 & 26 Vict., s. 26; Companies Act 1929, 19 & 20 Geo., c. 23, ss. 108(2), 110(1); Companies Act 1948, 11 & 12 Geo., c. 38, sch. 6, ¶6.

[45] Parkinson, *supra* n. 44, 6.

[46] Companies Act 1967, 15 & 16 Eliz. 2, c. 81, ss. 33–34; Companies Act 1976, c. 69, ss. 26(1), (2); Companies Act 1989, c. 40, s. 134.

[47] A.B. Levy, *Private Corporations and Their Control*, vol. 1 (1950), 237 ('For Great Britain only scattered particulars are available.')

Table I: 'Snapshot' studies of ownership concentration in UK, 1920–51

Author(s), (publication date)	Data Year(s)	Sample	Findings
Franks, Mayer and Rossi (2006)[48]	1920	53 quoted companies (unidentified).	The largest shareholder held, on average, 21% of the shares and the largest 10 shareholders owned 43% (Chapter Eight, Part III.B).
Florence (1953)[49]	1936	82 manufacturing and commercial companies qualifying as 'very large' (Chapter Eight, Part III.B).	59% of the companies had a 'dominant ownership interest', 32% were 'marginal' and 9% had no dominant ownership interest (Chapter Eight, Part III.B).
Parkinson (1951)[50]	1941/42	30 major UK publicly quoted companies.	The average shareholding in each company was small; shareholders owning equity with a nominal value of £10,000 or more held 33% of the shares (Chapter Eight, Part III.B).
Channon (1973)[51]	1950	The 92 companies that were among the 100 largest UK manufacturers as of 1970 and were operating in 1950.	50 of the 92 companies were under family control (Chapter Nine, Part II.A; on the definition of control, see Part VIII, this chapter).
Franks, Mayer and Rossi (2006)	1950	55 quoted companies (unidentified).	The largest shareholder held, on average, 15% of the shares and the largest 10 owned 49%.
Florence (1961)[52]	1951	98 manufacturing and commercial companies qualifying as 'very large'.	41% of the companies had a 'dominant ownership interest', 42% were 'marginal' and 17% had no dominant ownership interest. In 64% of the companies, the largest single shareholder owned a stake of less than 10% (Chapter Nine, Part II.A).

[48] Julian Franks, Colin Mayer and Stefano Rossi, 'Ownership: Evolution and Regulation' (2006) ECGI Fin. Working Paper No. 09/2003, 19–20, Table 2.

[49] P. Sargant Florence, *The Logic of British and American Industry: A Realistic Analysis of Economic Structure and Government* (1953), 187–90, 194.

[50] Parkinson, *supra* n. 44, 16–19.

[51] Derek F. Channon, *The Strategy and Structure of British Enterprise* (1973).

[52] P. Sargant Florence, *Ownership, Control and Success of Large Companies: An Analysis of English Industrial Structure and Policy 1936–1951* (1961).

There is then an unfortunate data gap. Various observers have identified the 1950s and 1960s as the decades when 'family capitalism' was eclipsed in the UK.[53] There was, however, during this period no 'snapshot' study equivalent to Florence's identifying ownership patterns in leading companies across a range of industries to test this claim. Channon's analysis of the 100 largest manufacturing companies as of 1970 stands out as the next attempt to offer an analysis of ownership and control in a wide range of companies, and his findings confirm that 'family capitalism' was on the wane. Three other studies based on 1970s data present a somewhat mixed picture, but show generally that large ownership blocks were becoming the exception to the rule (Table II).

Table II: 'Snapshot' studies of ownership concentration in the UK, 1970s data

Author(s), (publication date)	Data year(s)	Sample	Findings
Channon (1973)	1970	100 largest manufacturing companies.	There was 'family control' in 30% of the companies (Chapter Nine, Part II.A).
Royal Commission on the Distribution of Income & Wealth (1975)[54]	1975	A sample of 30 of the 100 largest public companies in the UK.	Found 19 instances where a shareholder owned 5+% of the shares; insurance companies, which rarely had ownership stakes much larger than this, held nine of these blocks.
Nyman and Silberston (1978)[55]	1975	224 largest companies as measured by net assets/sales.	56% of the companies were found to be 'owner-controlled' on the basis they had a 5+% shareholder or a 'family' chairman of the board. Only 24% of the companies that were publicly traded had a shareholder owning 20% or more of the shares (Chapter Nine, Part II.A).
Scott (1985), (1990)[56]	1976	200 largest industrial companies and 50 largest financial businesses.	Of the 191 of the 250 companies that were not state-owned, were not owned by depositors or policyholders and were not wholly owned subsidiaries, 100 (52%) lacked a shareholder owning 10%+ of the shares.

[53] Jones and Sluyterman, *supra* n. 11, 117; John F. Wilson, *British Business History, 1720–1994* (1995), 190–91; Mary B. Rose, 'Families and Firms: The Culture and Evolution of Family Firms in Britain and Italy in the Nineteenth and Twentieth Centuries', (1999) 47 Scandinavian Economic History Review 24, 40–41.

[54] Royal Commission on the Distribution of Income & Wealth (Lord Diamond, chairman), *Report No. 2: Income from Companies and its Distribution*, Cmnd. 6172 (1975), 10–12.

[55] Steve Nyman and Aubrey Silberston, 'The Ownership and Control of Industry', (1978) 30 Oxford Economic Papers (N.S.), 74, 84–85.

[56] John Scott, *Corporations, Classes and Capitalism*, 2nd edn, (1985), 77–78; John Scott, 'Corporate Control and Corporate Rule: Britain in an International Perspective', (1990) 41 British Journal of Sociology 351, 361–65.

Between the 1980s and the present there have been numerous studies of ownership structure in publicly traded UK companies, notable examples of which are summarized in Table III. These confirm that a divorce between ownership and control had become the norm in larger UK companies as the 20th century drew to a close. Each study found some companies with blockholders and studies covering smaller publicly traded enterprises reported that blockholding is relatively common in such firms. Generally, however, large ownership stakes were found to be the exception to the rule.

Table III: 'Snapshot' studies of ownership concentration in UK, 1980–mid-2000

Author(s), (publication date)	Data year(s)	Sample	Findings
Cosh *et al* (1989)[57]	1982	Largest 600 non-financial UK companies by market value.	267 5+% ownership blocks held by non-directors; among the top 100 companies there were 29 ownership blocks of this nature.
Leech and Leahy (1991)[58]	1983–85	470 UK quoted companies from a wide range of industries, including 325 listed in the *Times 1000*.	34% of the companies had a shareholder owning 20+% of the shares and 61% had a shareholder owning a stake of 10% or larger.
Scott (1990), (1997)[59]	1988	200 largest industrial companies and 50 largest financial businesses.	Of the 173 of the 250 companies that were not state-owned, were not owned by depositors or policyholders and were not wholly owned subsidiaries, 113 (65%) lacked a shareholder owning 10%+ of the shares.
Cosh and Hughes (1997)[60]	1981/1996	22 companies in the top 55 of the *Times 1000* companies as of 1981 still operating as of 1996.	21 ownership blocks of 3+% as of 1981; median size 4.1%. 40 ownership blocks of 3+% as of 1996; median size 4.9%.
La Porta, López-de-Silanes and Shleifer (1998)[61]	Early 1990s	20 largest UK publicly quoted companies by market capitalization.	None of the 20 had a shareholder owning 20+% of the shares and two had a shareholder owning a 10+% stake.

[57] A.D. Cosh, A. Hughes, K. Lee and A. Singh, 'Institutional Investment, Mergers and the Market for Corporate Control', (1989) 7 International Journal of Industrial Organization 73, 77.

[58] Dennis Leech and John Leahy, 'Ownership Structure, Control Type and Classifications and the Performance of Large British Companies', (1991) 101 Economic Journal 1418, 1421–23, 1435.

[59] Scott, 'Corporate', *supra* n. 56, 362–67; John Scott, *Corporate Business and Capitalist Classes* (1997), 83, 89–90.

[60] Andy Cosh and Alan Hughes, 'The Changing Anatomy of Corporate Control and the Market for Executives in the United Kingdom', (1997) 24 Journal of Law Society, 104, 107, 117.

[61] La Porta *et al*, *supra* n. 24, 474, 492–93. The authors do not explicitly identify the timing of their data collection.

Table III: (*Cont.*)

Author(s), (publication date)	Data year(s)	Sample	Findings
Goergen and Renneboog (2001)[62]	1992	Random sample of 250 quoted companies.	85% of sample companies lacked a shareholder owning 25+% of the shares; the largest block, on average, was 15%.
Van der Elst (2003)[63]	1994	1,333 publicly traded UK companies.	25% of the companies lacked a shareholder owning 10+% of the shares; 68% lacked a shareholder owning 25+% of the shares.
Faccio and Lang (2002)[64]	1996	1,953 publicly traded UK companies.	63% of the companies were widely held, in the sense they lacked a shareholder controlling at least 20% of the votes.
ISS Europe *et al* (2007)[65]	Mid-2000s	20 'large size' publicly quoted companies and 20 recently listed companies.	15% of 'large size' companies and 45% of recently listed companies had a shareholder owning 20+% of the shares.

A limitation with the empirical work that has been done on ownership and control in UK companies is that the studies generally offer only a series of 'snap-shots', indicating the ownership structure of a cross-section of UK companies at a particular instant, rather than giving a sense of trends over time. Also, comparability between studies is problematic since the sample populations have differed and numerous different benchmarks have been used to measure ownership concentration. In addition, the methodology used to uncover ownership patterns has varied, with earlier studies relying on searches of share registers and later studies generally focusing on compulsory disclosure of sizeable stakes. Franks, Mayer and Rossi have sought to address these methodological shortcomings by measuring changes in ownership structure on a decade-by-decade basis for a panel of 60 companies throughout the 20th century, consisting of a sample of 40 companies incorporated around 1900 and a sample of 20 companies incorporated around 1960.[66]

---

[62] Marc Goergen and Luc Renneboog, 'Strong Managers and Passive Institutional Investment in the UK' in Fabrizio Barca and Marco Becht (eds), *The Control of Corporate Europe* (2001), 259, 268.

[63] van der Elst, *supra* n. 20, 41–42.

[64] Faccio and Lang, *supra* n. 21, 379 (Table 3).

[65] I.S.S. Europe, European Corporate Governance Institute and Shearman & Sterling, *Report on the Proportionality Principle in the European Union* (2007), 80 available at <http://ec.europa.eu/internal_market/company/docs/shareholders/study/final_report_en.pdf> (last visited Oct. 4, 2007). The authors do not explicitly identify the timing of their data collection.

[66] On aspects of the research discussed here, see Franks, Mayer and Rossi, *supra* n. 48, 6, 24, 27–29, Table A1.

Fifty-eight of the 60 companies in Franks, Mayer and Rossi's sample ended up being traded on the stock market, so not surprisingly they found that the collective ownership stake held by the directors of their companies fell over time (e.g. in companies incorporated around 1900, the percentage of shares held by the directors fell from 94 per cent in 1900 to 49 per cent in 1920). They also report that the issuance of shares to carry out takeovers was the single most important cause of share blocks unwinding. These results, however, have to be treated with care due to sample bias, since tracking the evolution of ownership patterns in the same companies over a number of decades meant Franks, Mayer and Rossi had to focus on firms of exceptional longevity. Twenty of the companies incorporated around 1900 survived the entire 20th century and 17 of the others survived until at least 1950. All of the companies incorporated around 1960 were still in operation as of 2001. To put this track record into perspective, among the 100 largest global companies as of 1912—presumably a population that should exhibit greater durability than pretty much any other—48 had disappeared by 1995.[67] Franks, Mayer and Rossi's findings thus provide at best a partial picture of how ownership and control evolves over time across companies.

VI. Chronological Overview/Plan of the Book

Chapters Two to Four of the book address in general terms factors liable to prompt transformations of corporate ownership and control. Chapter Two outlines theories that have been advanced in the comparative corporate governance literature to explain why patterns of ownership and control differ across countries and indicates they do not account for what occurred in Britain. Chapters Three and Four, focusing on the sell side and buy side respectively, identify the variables that in fact influenced the configuration of share ownership in UK public companies. Fully untangling, however, the interrelationship of potential determinants of ownership structure is intractable without some form of chronological sub-division. As a result, the remainder of the book examines in detail for various periods particular trends that influenced patterns of ownership and control.

'Periodization' (the breaking up of time into smaller units) has been called one of the more elusive tasks of historical scholarship.[68] Shortcomings with the relevant empirical evidence complicate the task with respect to the divorce of ownership and control in the UK. Nevertheless, eras with sufficiently stable characteristics can be identified to divide the analysis satisfactorily into discrete periods. The relevant periods—and the chapters that discuss them—are as follows.

---

[67] Leslie Hannah, 'Marshall's "Trees" and the Global "Forest": Were "Giant Redwoods" Different?' in Naomi Lamoreaux, Daniel M. G. Raff and Peter Temin (eds), *Learning by Doing in Markets, Firms and Countries* (1998), 253, 259.

[68] Jerry H. Bentley, 'Cross-Cultural Interaction and Periodization in World History', (1996) 101 American History Review 749, 749.

Up to 1880 (Chapter Five). By the early 18th century all of the institutional structures that characterize an effective market for the trading of securities were in place in London, and Britain experienced the world's first industrial revolution between 1700 and 1850. Conditions thus seemed propitious for the widely held company to emerge early as a dominant form of business organization. This did not occur, as the firms that were at the epicentre of the industrial revolution were typically sole proprietorships or partnerships operating on a modest scale.

There were spasmodic outbursts of company promotion dating back to the 1690s but these were followed by market reversals that prompted the disappearance of many of the companies taken public. Despite the pattern, by the 1830s a sizeable number of enterprises, operating in fields such as utilities, transport, banking, insurance and mining, had publicly traded shares. The firms lacked, however, a modern-style divorce of ownership and control, since the shareholder base was usually small and localized in orientation. Railway companies were soon to become a different proposition. By the mid-19th century the largest ones were complex business enterprises characterized by sophisticated managerial hierarchies, diffuse share ownership and a nationally oriented shareholder register.

1880–1914 (Chapters Six and Seven). During the late 19th and early 20th centuries there were various potential deterrents to buying shares in UK companies, such as companies legislation that offered little protection to outside investors, promising overseas investment options and company 'promoters' of varying ethical standards. Nevertheless, the strong performance of shares relative to obvious investment alternatives, the inferences investors were able to draw from dividend policies companies adopted and periodic surges in investor optimism underpinned demand for shares. With resistance to the unwinding of control simultaneously diminishing among industrialists, numerous industrial and commercial companies made the move to the stock market.

By international standards, the UK had a sizeable number of large companies and a well-developed stock market on the eve of World War I. Ownership had become separated from control in large banks as well as in railway companies. Otherwise, however, a modern-style divorce of ownership and control generally remained the exception to the rule.

1914–1939 (Chapter Eight). During the interwar years changes to tax law provided fresh incentives for companies to carry out public offerings of shares and helped to foster significant growth in the number of people investing in shares. Regulatory and market factors deterring investment in foreign assets and improved quality control by intermediaries organizing public offerings of shares fortified demand for equity. In this milieu, the number of industrial and commercial companies quoted on the London Stock Exchange rose threefold and various contemporaries began referring to 'the widening divorce between ownership and management'.[69] Nevertheless, the available evidence,

---

[69] 'The Changing Capital Market', Economist, September 11, 1937, 507, 508.

particularly Florence's findings for 1936 (Table I), suggests blockholding remained prevalent in large industrial and commercial enterprises on the eve of World War II.

1940–1990 (Chapters Nine and Ten). In the decades following World War II, the UK's ownership and control arrangements coalesced in accordance with the outsider/arm's-length pattern that currently predominates. On the sell side, tax, declining profits and tighter regulation of companies provided blockholders with incentives to exit. On the buy side, the rise of institutional investors—particularly pension funds and insurance companies—was crucial. Personal investors, who dominated share registers prior to World War II, were net sellers of corporate equity thereafter. Robust institutional demand, fostered partly by tax, filled the gap. If this had not occurred, the unwinding of share blocks in larger UK companies could have stalled or even gone into reverse.

Whereas the rise of institutional shareholders helped to ensure that ownership continued to separate from control, the trend also created an intriguing hypothetical opportunity for the re-concentration of share ownership. Once prominent institutional investors held stakes sufficiently large to mean they could not sell out without creating significant downward pressure on share prices, collaborating to add value by dictating corporate policy became, at least theoretically, a sensible corporate governance strategy. However, the potential for intervention went largely unfulfilled, meaning that corporate governance arrangements were firmly 'outsider/arm's-length'.

1990 to the present (Chapter Eleven). Various trends emerging over the past few years suggest the future of the UK's outsider/arm's-length system of ownership and control is not guaranteed. Intervention by traditionally dominant institutional shareholders—again pension funds and insurance companies—reached unprecedented levels in the opening years of the 2000s, implying that control-oriented investment could become commonplace. A new breed of intervention-minded shareholder appeared on the scene, minded to accumulate 'offensively' an appreciable but by no means controlling stakes in publicly traded companies with the express intention of agitating for changes in corporate policy. The emergence of high-profile private equity buyouts which involve the acquisition and taking private of publicly traded enterprises, seemingly implied the marginalization of stock market trading in shares.

In fact, none of these trends is likely to disrupt existing arrangements fundamentally. Pension funds and insurance companies are currently scaling back considerably their investment in shares of publicly quoted companies, 'offensive' shareholder activists are likely to struggle to persuade other shareholders to back their plans and private equity buyouts are unlikely to become anything more than a 'minority sport' in Britain. Thus, for the foreseeable future a separation of ownership and control will remain a hallmark of UK corporate governance.

VII. Caveats

This book covers significant ground, investigating an important but under-explored corporate governance topic by reference to roughly four centuries' worth of history. The analysis is, however, characterized by three key limitations. First, the book explains how ownership became divorced from control in large UK companies rather than offering a normative assessment of the end result. The merits of Britain's stock market-oriented corporate economy have been the subject of intense debate. Defenders of the status quo concede that shareholder-oriented capitalism does not work perfectly, but contend that stock market companies benefit from liberal access to deep pools of investment capital and from the salutary disciplinary mechanisms a falling share price activates.[70] Critics, on the other hand, contend that Britain has been ill served by a market-oriented financial system that provided insufficiently sustained backing for industrial enterprise.[71]

This book does not stake out a position on the merits of Britain's system of ownership and control. Chapter Two indicates that no particular form of ownership structure offers decisive advantages in terms of efficiency, making the point to show the dominance of outsider/arm's-length corporate governance is not economically pre-ordained (Part I). An additional inference one could draw is that the manner in which ownership patterns evolved in the UK did not have major consequences in terms of economic welfare, but the book does not press this claim.

Second, the hypotheses advanced in the book to account for the separation of ownership and control are not tested by means of rigorous quantitative analysis. Numerical evidence is offered throughout the book to support the arguments made and detailed case studies are provided that show ownership had generally not separated from control by 1914 and that merger activity helped to foster the divorce of ownership and control in the decades following World War II. However, due to inadequacies with the available data, full-scale statistical testing is currently not feasible.

If perfect information were available, the obvious statistical test to run would be a time-series regression designed to find correlations between year-by-year fluctuations in ownership structure (the dependent variable) and plausible independent or explanatory variables (the potential determinants of ownership and control). Conducting such a test is not possible for the purposes of this book. Various potential explanatory variables considered cannot be properly expressed in numerical terms, such as the extent to which generational considerations come into play on the sell side and incentives to develop a sound business reputation

---

[70] See, for example, Elaine Sternberg, *Corporate Governance: Accountability in the Marketplace* (1998).

[71] For an overview of the debate, see David J. Jeremy, *A Business History of Britain* (1998), 316–20.

on the buy side. More fundamentally, the data on ownership patterns that is currently available is inadequate for running time-series regressions. There are insufficient data points, particularly before the 1970s, and the samples used and methodologies adopted have varied too widely for the results to be combined properly into a single data set.

Third, the book does not adopt a single 'bright line' test of concentrated versus dispersed ownership that is applied throughout. Since directors of UK companies are elected and dismissed by the shareholders by way of majority vote, in any circumstance where the shareholder with the largest stake owns less than an absolute majority, the dominant shareholder cannot be certain of dictating who will serve on the board and have responsibility for managing the company.[72] However, because voter turnout in shareholder meetings of publicly traded companies virtually never reaches 100 per cent and because many shareholders as a default rule support incumbents—the fact they own shares indicates they have a measure of faith and confidence in those in charge—there is a high probability a shareholder owning a sizeable minority block can dictate the outcome of shareholder votes.[73]

To illustrate the point, while as of 1951 a nominee company apparently controlled by J. Arthur Rank was Odeon Theatre's largest shareholder with less than a majority of the shares (38 per cent) (Chapter Nine, Part II.A), the *Economist* said in 1947 'the outside shareholders of Odeon will reflect…when it came to a vote there could be little doubt of the result'.[74] Cole said more generally in a 1935 paper on share ownership in Britain: '[T]he owner of a large concentrated block of shares usually finds himself confronted not by other shareholders capable of common action, but by a number of scattered individuals who are most unlikely to interfere in a concerted way with the operation of the company.'[75] Mindful of the pattern, Florence suggested that 'the "resolute" person or a small coherent "resolute" group of persons determined on a certain policy or certain key appointments such as that of directors can win even with a concentration of a minority of voting shares as low as, say, 10%'.[76]

As ownership of a majority of shares is not required for a blockholder to exercise disproportionate influence, those carrying out empirical studies of share ownership patterns have been prepared to designate companies as owner-controlled in the absence of a majority shareholder. Beyond this, there

[72] John Cubbin and Dennis Leech, 'The Effect of Shareholding Dispersion on the Degree of Control in British Companies: Theory and Measurement', (1983) 93 Economic Journal 351, 355–56 (making the point more generally rather than focusing merely on the election of directors). On directors being selected by way of majority vote, see Derek French, Stephen W. Mayson and Christopher L. Ryan, *Mayson, French & Ryan on Company Law*, 24th edn (2007), 410.

[73] Adolf A. Berle and Gardiner C. Means, *The Modern Corporation & Private Property* (1997, originally published in 1932), 75 (referring to this scenario as 'working control').

[74] 'The Odeon Affair', Economist, December 20, 1947, 1012, 1014.

[75] G.D.H. Cole, 'The Evolution of Joint Stock Enterprise' in G.D.H. Cole (ed.), *Studies in Capital and Investment* (1935), 51, 85.

[76] Florence, *supra* n. 49, 194.

has been little consensus. Thresholds used to identify shareholders as influential blockholders in empirical studies of ownership structure in the UK have varied from 5 per cent up to 25 per cent of the shares.[77] Also, in some instances, the test has incorporated additional facts. For instance, Channon only classified the manufacturing companies he studied as 'family controlled' if the founder family continued to own 5 per cent or more of the shares, if there had been at least two generations of family involvement and if a family member was serving in the top managerial job.[78] Florence, in contrast, drew on the notion of 'a small coherent "resolute" group' to extend the notion of owner control beyond the largest single shareholder to encompass the collective holding of the top 20 shareholders. He maintained that so long as there was no equally potent opposition group likely to form and some of the shareholders in the group exercised control as directors or executives, ownership of 20 per cent or more of the voting capital by the top 20 shareholders constituted 'minority owners' control'.[79]

The approach Florence adopted was appropriate for the purposes of the studies he conducted for 1936 and 1951. At these points in time, individuals continued to dominate share registers. An individual owning the tenth largest stake in a publicly quoted company with, say, 1 per cent of the shares would be a good candidate to be part of 'a small coherent "resolute" group' in control as he would likely be well-known to the directors and would be minded to keep a close watch on what was going on because of having a substantial fraction of his personal wealth tied up in the company. The dramatic rise of institutional share ownership after World War II changed the equation significantly. As Rose said in 1965, 'Twenty years ago a 1 per cent holding might well have been significant; today it would probably represent in many cases little more than a run-of-the-mill holding by an insurance company or pension fund.'[80] Institutional shareholders in the UK have typically refrained from taking a 'hands on' approach to corporate governance, even when they have held a sizeable percentage of the shares in particular companies (Chapter Ten, Part V.B). As a result, other than in circumstances where institutional investors own an uncharacteristically large stake (say, 15 per cent or more of a company), treating them as part of 'a small coherent "resolute" group' that 'controls' a company will typically be inappropriate.

An example helps to illustrate the point. Florence, for the purposes of his study of the ownership structure in 'very large' industrial and commercial companies as of 1951, deemed Morgan Crucible to be owner controlled. Table IV sets out the shareholder profile of this manufacturer of ceramics, carbon 'brushes' used in the electricity industry and other advanced materials:[81]

---

[77] See Tables I, II and III. Varying definitions is a general pattern with studies of this nature: Becht, Bolton and Röell, *supra* n. 18, 61–62; Cubbin and Leech, *supra* n. 72, 352.

[78] Channon, *supra* n. 51, 16.

[79] Florence, *supra* n. 44, 4–5.

[80] Harold Rose, *Disclosure in Company Accounts*, 2nd edn (1965), 42.

[81] Florence, *supra* n. 52, 251; see also at 211; Peter Pugh, *A Global Presence: The Morgan Crucible Story* (2006), 13–14, 21–22, 183–84, 230–31.

Table IV: Ten largest vote-holders, Morgan Crucible, 1951

Shareholder	% of votes held	Shareholder	% of votes held
L. Hooper (director)	6.4	C. Spiers (former director)	2.5
G. Edward (director)	3.2	P. Lindsay (chairman)	1.8
A. Bosman (director)	2.9	H. Mills (director)	1.7
H. Adams	2.6	Prudential Assurance	1.6
G. Peto (former director)	2.6	L. Emms	1.6

As nine of the top ten shareholders were individuals, seven of the ten were directors or former directors who owned 20 per cent of the shares between them and other Morgan Crucible directors held at least 4 per cent of the shares, Florence's categorization was appropriate. Two or three decades later, seven or eight of the ten largest vote-holders in a company Morgan Crucible's size would probably have been institutional investors. Under such circumstances, the absence of a single investor owning 10 per cent or more of the shares would have meant the company could appropriately be treated as one characterized by a separation of ownership and control.[82]

Given the lack of consensus on the numerical thresholds that signify a separation of ownership and control and given that drawing appropriate inferences from data available is at least to some extent historically contingent, it should now be evident why the book refrains from adopting a single 'bright line' test of concentrated versus dispersed ownership. Certain parameters are in fact assumed. There will clearly be owner control if a single shareholder owns a majority of the voting shares. Conversely, a modern-style divorce between ownership and control implies a sizeable register of shareholders and a liquid market for shares. A firm lacking these features will, regardless of the stake held by the largest owner, in effect be a huge partnership with numerous 'sleeping' partners rather than the functional equivalent of the managerially dominated companies associated with outsider/arm's-length corporate governance. Otherwise, by necessity rather than by preference, for the purposes of the book, a separation of ownership and control will be a somewhat fluid notion defined by reference to the particular historical era under consideration.

VIII. Key Insights

As this book does not test statistically potential determinants of ownership and control and does not employ a single, precise definition of an

---

[82] Contrary to the analysis presented here, Franks, Mayer and Rossi stress continuity on the basis of findings that in cross-sectional samples of publicly quoted companies for 1920, 1950 and 1990 the ten largest shareholders held respectively 43 per cent, 49 per cent and 41 per cent of the shares: *supra* n. 48, 20. Assuming individuals dominated share registers in 1920 and 1950 and institutional investors dominated in 1990, based on the analysis presented here, the appropriate inference to draw is that a separation of ownership and control was the exception to the rule in 1920 and 1950 and the norm in 1990.

ownership/control split, its treatment of the relevant issues cannot be definitive in nature. Nevertheless, the book offers numerous insights for those interested in comparative corporate governance, for those engaged in the study of British business and economic history and for those intrigued by the relationship between law and markets. Four deserve emphasis before the discussion switches to the main body of the text.

First, while there were examples of companies characterized by a divorce between ownership and control from at least the mid-19th century onwards, Britain's outsider/arm's-length system of ownership and control only became fully entrenched in the latter half of the 20th century. Additional empirical work may justify amendments to the chronology. In the meantime, however, the verdict the book offers can be squared fairly readily with existing characterizations of events. Since there were examples of business enterprises with publicly traded shares extending back more than three centuries and because the UK had, in comparative terms, a well-developed stock market by the opening of the 20th century, in key respects Britain was a 'first mover'. As for the notion of 'corporate lag', though it is by no means clear that ownership structure is a determinant of business success, there is sufficient evidence of blockholding during the late 19th and early 20th centuries to indicate 'family capitalism' retained considerable vitality.

Second, no single variable accounts for how, when and why ownership separated from control in the UK. Instead, numerous factors, varying in importance over time, served to transform matters. This likely was not a pattern isolated to Britain. Historical work covering other countries is just beginning, but the evidence available thus far suggests that in each a variety of determinants of ownership structure needs to be taken into account to gauge what happened.[83] This book, in order to marshal the relevant evidence effectively, employs an analytical scheme based around the 'buy side' and the 'sell side'. Since the framework is not UK-specific in orientation it should be suitable for assessing developments elsewhere, though the manner in which it is applied would no doubt need to be tailored to address local circumstances.

Third, law contributed to changes in ownership structure, though the relationship was not straightforward. Company law stands out as an obvious potential determinant of ownership patterns in large firms, as laws that protect outside investors from exploitation by corporate insiders should encourage blockholders to contemplate exit and foster demand for shares by reassured buyers. However, when ownership began to separate from control UK company law did not impose major constraints on corporate insiders or offer substantial protection to outside investors. Tax law was probably a more potent agent of change. From the interwar years through to the 1980s the tax treatment of corporate profits and personal

---

[83] See Morck and Steier, *supra* n. 35, 27–56 (identifying 'common threads' spanning chapters on the evolution of ownership and control in ten countries).

income encouraged blockholders to exit and accelerated institutional investment in shares, particularly by insurance companies and pension funds.

Fourth and finally, the separation of ownership and control that currently characterizes large companies in the UK is likely to be durable. As Chapter Eleven explains, interventions by major institutional shareholders, 'offensive' shareholder activism and private equity buyouts do not pose any sort of fundamental challenge to current arrangements and may even fortify the buy side by enhancing managerial accountability. Also, since UK company law now regulates self-dealing closely and provides substantial protection to outside investors, blockholders are unlikely to stay put to try to extract private benefits of control and investors can buy shares with confidence that they are unlikely to be subjected to dishonest, self-serving uses of corporate control. Thus, the insights this book offers concerning the transformation underlying Britain's outsider/arm's-length system of control should remain salient for some time to come.

TWO

The Determinants of Ownership and Control: Current Theories

I. Separating Ownership from Control: Economic Implications

This chapter outlines the leading theories that have been advanced in the comparative corporate governance literature to account for why patterns of ownership and control differ across borders. It shows that they have limited explanatory power in the British context. To place matters in context, we will begin with an economically oriented primer that reveals the lack of strong efficiency-driven momentum in favour of a divorce between ownership and control.

Through to the 1990s, the received wisdom was that the typical modern large business corporation was characterized by professionalized management and dispersed share ownership (Chapter One, Part III). The implicit orthodoxy was seemingly supported by economic logic.[1] Dispersed ownership offers advantages over more traditional arrangements—primarily firms dominated by first-generation entrepreneurs or families—in a couple of crucial ways.

First, the widely held company has a presumptive financial edge since amassing large amounts of capital is easier to do with equity claims carved up into small units than it is when recourse must be had to a handful of individuals, no matter how wealthy.[2] Second, a widely held company can benefit from higher quality management. In companies where ownership and control are separated, executives can be hired purely on the basis of their managerial credentials rather than by reference to their ability to finance the firm or family connections with dominant shareholders.[3] Companies with dominant blockholders are unlikely to be as well positioned, as Sampson's 1961 harsh indictment of British 'family firms' reveals:

---

[1] Mark J. Roe, *Strong Managers, Weak Owners: The Political Roots of American Corporate Finance* (1994), ch.1; Gregory A. Mark, 'Realms of Choice: Finance Capitalism and Corporate Governance', (1995) 95 Columbia Law Review 969, 973–74.

[2] Margaret Blair, *Ownership and Control: Rethinking Corporate Governance for the Twenty-First Century* (1993), 96; Robin Marris, *Managerial Capitalism in Retrospect* (1998), 6–7.

[3] Henry N. Butler, 'The Contractual Theory of the Corporation', (1989) 11 George Mason University Law Review 99, 107.

Not many families…are ruthless enough to exclude nitwits from the succession, or fecund enough to produce enough first-class managers. The drawing room privilege which hangs about the boardroom can easily act as a disincentive to ambitious outsiders. The chairman (of the board) himself, who must be moderately efficient to survive, is not the main obstacle: it is the periphery of nephews, cousins and particularly sons-in-law who so often clog the wheels of management, and by the assumption of privilege damage the dignity of professional managers.[4]

Although the widely held public company has advantages that seemingly leave it well-positioned to prevail in a contest between different forms of corporate structure, it suffers from a significant potential downside. So long as the executives who manage a widely held company own only a small percentage of the equity, they will receive only a tiny fraction of the returns derived from the profit-enhancing activities they engage in on behalf of shareholders. As a result, they have an incentive to further their own interests at the expense of those who own equity. The conduct of John Blunt, managing director of the South Sea Company as it rose and then collapsed spectacularly in 1719 and 1720 on the strength of a scheme to convert government debt into the company's shares, provides an early example. He dealt heavily, confidentially and profitably in the company's stock, amassing a fortune of £187,000, equivalent to many millions of pounds today, which he soon lost due to legislation enacted to punish the company's directors.[5] He justified his (temporary) self-enrichment to colleagues on the basis that 'in any other nation but this, they would have given him a reward of £500,000 for the service he had done to his country' but as such a reward was not in the offing 'he thought he might take the opportunities to reward himself'.[6]

The potential divergence of interest between managers and shareholders has been long recognized, with various observers offering a description of what are now commonly referred to as managerial 'agency costs'. The *Banker* magazine did so in 1860 to explain why numerous newly incorporated companies of the time failed:

Companies are always managed by a board of directors, a secretary, a manager, a manager's deputy, and a host of officers, none of whom has any interest in the concern beyond their immediate shares, nor any interest in doing the work in the most economical manner…Wherever, therefore, the business of a company is of such a nature that it can be carried on by private individuals, personally managing their own business, as well as by a company, the company has no more chance against them than the bricklayer with one hand tied behind him…would have against the bricklayer using both his hands.[7]

The Railway Service Gazette complained in 1877 that directors of railway companies had accumulated 'a remarkable power administering railways

---

[4] Anthony Sampson, *The Anatomy of Britain* (1961), 477.
[5] Richard Dale, *The First Crash: Lessons from the South Sea Bubble* (2004), 98, 151–52.
[6] *Ibid.*, 97, quoting John Toland's 1726 *Secret History of the South Sea Company*.
[7] 'Failure of Ordinary Joint-Stock Companies', (1860) 20, Banker's Magazine 409, 410–11.

unchecked by Shareholders', meaning, '[T]he Railway Autocracy is impelled by no extraneous influences and has, therefore, no healthy stimulus towards any specific goal.'[8] An 1898 article analyzing a buoyant market for public offerings of shares lamented, 'The old generation of solid, sturdy business men is practically gone', replaced by 'men who depend for their living upon salaries paid for them by their companies'. The author observed, 'And those who know human nature need not be told what that means', but nevertheless elaborated, saying, 'Instead of people who think of and work for the business day and night we have people who as it were stand outside the business they govern, who take things easy, meet once a week or once a fortnight, and leave the rest to hirelings who, though may do their best, must in the nature of things be less efficient than direct owners...'[9]

If executives in a widely held company had truly untrammelled discretion to benefit themselves at the expense of shareholders, this form of business enterprise would have never achieved the pre-eminence it currently enjoys. Executives in fact do not enjoy this sort of latitude since there are various checks on wayward or self-serving management. These currently include monitoring by 'non-executive' directors, 'incentivized' executive pay, the possibility of a takeover offer by a bidder who anticipates creating value by installing new managers and, at least in competitive industries, pressure from rival companies.[10] These market-oriented constraints on management do not, however, entirely eliminate agency costs. Instead, those in charge retain scope to pursue their own agenda at the expense of shareholders, as a series of major corporate governance scandals occurring in the US a few years ago (Enron, Tyco and WorldCom) starkly illustrated.

Empirical evidence confirms that there are costs as well as benefits associated with dispersed share ownership. Research on the relationship between ownership structure and firm performance spans several decades.[11] If a divorce between ownership and control were in fact a recipe for corporate success, the superiority of the widely held company should by now be clearly apparent. Instead, the available empirical evidence is mixed, with some studies indicating companies with dispersed share ownership deliver better financial results than other firms, others indicating the opposite, and still others failing to offer a statistically significant result.[12] Since companies characterized by a separation of ownership and control

---

[8] 'Helpless Proprietors', reprinted in Edwin Phillips, *The Railway Autocracy: A Question of Vital Importance to Shareholders and Directors, Hitherto Overlooked* (1877), 23, 24–25.

[9] S.F. Van Oss, 'The "Limited Company" Craze', *The Nineteenth Century*, May 1898, 731, 734.

[10] Brian R. Cheffins, *Company Law: Theory, Structure and Operation* (1997), 117–23.

[11] Helen Short, 'Ownership, Control, Financial Structure and the Performance of Firms', (1994) 8 Journal of Economic Surveys 203, 206.

[12] For surveys see *Ibid.*; Klaus Gugler, 'Direct Monitoring and Profitability: Are Large Shareholders Beneficial?' in Klaus Gugler (ed.), *Corporate Governance and Economic Performance* (2001), 12; Clifford G. Holderness, 'A Survey of Blockholders and Corporate Governance', Federal Reserve Bank of New York Economic Policy Review, April 2003, 51.

do not systematically outperform companies with blockholders, there does not appear to be a market imperative that the former dominate.

Even if a shift to dispersed ownership would be economically advantageous for a particular company, it cannot be taken for granted the shift will occur. Assume, by way of a highly stylized example, a company has 100 shares with the founding family owning 50 and the remainder being publicly traded.[13] The total value of the company's shares is £100, but the shares traded publicly fetch a price of 80p per share, meaning the outsiders' equity is worth £40 collectively, whereas the family's equity is worth £60, or £1.20 per share. The 40p differential per share constitutes what is known as the 'control premium', partly reflecting the 'private benefits of control' the dominant faction can extract at the expense of outside investors.[14]

The control premium is a potential deterrent to the unwinding of control. To see why, assume that if ownership were separated from control the company would be worth £1.10 per share, or £110 overall (e.g., because of better management). The increase in overall firm value seemingly implies that a shift to dispersed ownership is on the cards, but this cannot be taken for granted. If the family unwound its stake by selling its shares on the stock market, the control premium would no longer be in play. This would mean the most the family could hope to receive for its shares would be £1.10 per share, which assumes the anticipated increase in firm value under new management is fully priced in. The family would not sell out even under these favourable circumstances because it would only receive £55 (50 x £1.10), or £5 less than the value of its shares under current arrangements. The differential potentially creates a 'controller's roadblock' that could preclude a shift towards a more efficient ownership structure.[15]

II. Company Law

Whereas a 'controller's roadblock' might be a feature of companies where there is a dominant shareholder faction, the fact that there are currently numerous large companies characterized by a divorce between ownership and control demonstrates there are circumstances where blockholders will exit or acquiesce as their

[13] The departure point for this example is a scenario set out by Lucian A. Bebchuk and Mark J. Roe, 'A Theory of Path Dependence in Corporate Ownership and Governance', (1999) 52 Stanford Law Review 127, 143–45.

[14] On the contribution which extracting private value makes to the control premium, see Alexander Dyck and Luigi Zingales, 'Private Benefits of Control: An International Comparison', (2004) 59 Journal of Finance 537, 540–41; Diane K. Denis and John J. McConnell, 'International Corporate Governance', (2003) 38 Journal of Financial and Quantitative Analysis 1, 24–25.

[15] On the terminology, see Bebchuk and Roe, *supra* n. 13, 143. The family might consider other alternatives (e.g., replacing the current managers or selling out to another blockholder) but these need not be dealt with here because they imply continued blockholding.

stake is diluted. Why is there variation on the extent to which this occurs in countries around the world (Chapter One, Part III)? Differences in company law stand out as a plausible candidate.

Company law merits attention in the present context for two reasons. First, it governs how control is allocated within companies and regulates the voting rights of the investors who own shares. Second, company law is, in theoretical terms, an excellent candidate as a determinant of patterns of ownership and control. To explain why ownership separates from control it is necessary to account for why blockholders will exit, why investors will be willing to buy shares and why those who invest in equities will opt not to exercise control themselves (Chapter One, Part IV). Company law can do all three.

A. Allocation of Managerial and Voting Control

In many jurisdictions companies legislation specifically allocates managerial authority to the board of directors and uses an 'appointment rights strategy' to empower shareholders by giving them the right to select the directors.[16] UK company law, in contrast, has never dictated who will have managerial authority in a company or the method by which managers are selected. This has instead been left to the internal governance rules of companies, most typically the 'articles of association', the contents of which the shareholders determine.[17] The standard practice has been for the articles to authorize a company's board of directors to manage the company and to stipulate the shareholders elect the directors at shareholder meetings.[18] As a legal matter, then, a shareholder or coalition of shareholders that can secure a majority of votes at shareholder meetings can dictate who sits on the board, and thus who manages the company. As a 1909 text on investment said after describing the legal arrangements, 'The shareholder, therefore, although he surrenders the control of his capital to his directors, is still in a position to exercise a very effective control over his directors...'[19]

Under UK company law the presumptive rule is that all of a company's shares (or at least its 'ordinary' or 'common' shares) have equal rights and restrictions attached to them,[20] which implies a 'one share/one vote' rule will apply. Under such circumstances, owners of a majority of ordinary shares will have, via the

[16] Reinier R. Kraakman *et al, The Anatomy of Corporate Law: A Comparative and Functional Approach* (2004), 33–38.

[17] R.C. Nolan, 'The Continuing Evolution of Shareholder Governance', (2006) 65 Cambridge L.J. 92, 99–101.

[18] Companies Act 1862, 25 & 26 Vict., c. 89, sch. 1, Table A, arts. 55, 61; Companies (Consolidation) Act 1908, 8 Edw. 7, c. 69, Table A, arts. 71, 81; A.B. Levy, *Private Corporations and Their Control*, vol. II (1950), 683, 686.

[19] Henry Lowenfeld, *Investment Practically Considered* (1908), 406.

[20] *Birch v Cropper* (1889) 14 App. Cas. 525, 543.

directors they elect, control of the company. It is possible, however, for voting power to be allocated by means other than one share/one vote. This can occur in two basic ways.

First, the voting power of blockholders can be enhanced. For instance, they can be issued shares with multiple voting rights attached, thus ensuring they can outvote other shareholders on contentious matters. Alternatively, a company can adopt a policy of issuing to outside investors 'non-voting' or 'low voting' equity which has exactly the same rights as ordinary shares to the cash flow the company generates but has no voting rights attached or has only a tiny fraction of the voting power attributable to ordinary shares. When companies use such differential voting schemes, minority shareholders can face an unpalatable outcome: insiders will retain control of a firm without having substantial ownership of outstanding equity.[21] In addition, since the voting power will rest in the hands of the incumbent blockholder, an outside investor will be only be able to move into a dominant position by dealing directly with that blockholder.

Marcus Samuel, the driving force behind the establishment of the petroleum giant 'Shell' Transport and Trading Company in 1897, was an early example of an individual associated with a publicly traded company who secured for himself voting rights out of proportion to share ownership. He retained control of Shell until 1919 by means of shares held by himself and his brother that had special voting rights of five-to-one over all other ordinary shares.[22] During the same period, founders of various shipping companies similarly relied on 'owners' shares' with special voting rights attached to maintain a dominant influence.[23]

Somewhat more recently, numerous companies preserved the voting power of incumbent blockholders through the issuance of ordinary shares lacking full voting rights. During the mid-1950s some 7 per cent of the market value of the industrial and commercial sector of the UK equity market took the form of 'non-voting' ordinary shares and the *Economist* suggested that 'the non-voting ordinary share threatens to become too popular'.[24] This in fact proved to be the heyday for this method of guaranteeing blockholder control. Institutional shareholder opposition to non-voting or low voting shares became increasingly vociferous, discouraging their future use (Chapter Nine, Part II.B). Moreover, companies that had adopted unequal voting arrangements in the 1950s usually ended up

[21] Rafael La Porta, Florencio López-de-Silanes, Andrei Shleifer and Robert Vishny, 'Law and Finance', (1998) 106 Journal of Political Economy 1113, 1126–27.

[22] Robert Henriques, *Marcus Samuel: First Viscount Bearsted and Founder of The 'Shell' Transport and Trading Company* (1960), 198.

[23] Gordon Boyce, *Information, Mediation and Institutional Development: The Rise of Large-Scale Enterprise in British Shipping, 1870–1919* (1995), 231.

[24] 'Shares Without a Say', Economist, April 14, 1956, 167; John Littlewood, *The Stock Market: 50 Years of Capitalism at Work* (1998), 134.

fully enfranchising all investors, albeit sometimes nearly four decades later.[25] Currently it is extremely rare for a UK publicly traded company to have shares that provide outside investors with inferior voting rights or offer blockholders multiple votes per share.[26]

Second, voting power can be 'capped', either by restricting the number of shares any one investor can own or by imposing limits on the number of votes particular owners can exercise, regardless of share ownership. Either way, the effect is to preclude investors holding a large percentage of shares from exercising the voting power they would be entitled to under a one share/one vote regime.[27] An important implication is that an outside investor who buys up a big stake cannot determine corporate policy on the strength only of the shares owned. Instead, dictating the outcome of shareholder votes will be contingent upon appealing directly and successfully to numerous smaller shareholders. This gives incumbent directors a big advantage, because only if the board has completely lost shareholder confidence is it likely to lose on a shareholder vote.[28]

Currently only a tiny minority of publicly traded companies in the UK preclude a shareholder from voting more than a prescribed number of shares or have 'ownership ceilings' preventing the accumulation of large holdings of shares.[29] However, capped voting arrangements have a long historical pedigree in Britain. During the mid-1690s the country experienced its first flurry of company promotions and the companies established—most notably the Bank of England—often imposed a ceiling on the votes any one proprietor could cast (Chapter Five, Part I). During the early 19th century, many joint stock banks and numerous canal companies had capped voting rights.[30] Railway companies at this time generally did not have such limitations in place, but 'graduated' voting (i.e., arrangements where the number of votes increase with the number

---

[25] Ch. Nine, Pt II.B; 'Enfranchise—and Watch Those Shares Rise', Financial Times, February 1, 1992; 'Whitbread Puts End to Two-Tier Voting Structure', Independent, October 7, 1993; 'Why It's High Time to Play Fair Over Votes', Evening Standard, October 20, 1993.

[26] ISS Europe, European Corporate Governance Institute and Shearman & Sterling, *Report on the Proportionality Principle in the European Union* (2007), 23, 26–28 (of a sample of 40 UK companies, 3 per cent had shares with multiple voting rights and none had non-voting shares).

[27] Coleen A. Dunlavy, 'Social Conceptions of the Corporation: Insights from the History of Shareholder Voting Rights', (2006) 63 Washington & Lee Law Review 1347, 1354–57.

[28] Leslie Hannah, 'The Divorce of Ownership from Control from 1900: Re-calibrating Imagined Global Historical Trends', (2007) 49 Business History 404, 409.

[29] ISS Europe et al, supra n. 26, 30–32, 78 (of a sample of 40 UK public companies, 7 per cent capped the number of votes a shareholder could cast and 5 per cent had 'ownership ceilings').

[30] Mark Freeman, Robin Pearson and James Taylor, ' "A Doe in the City": Women Shareholders in Eighteenth- and Early Nineteenth-Century Britain', (2006) 16 Accounting, Business & Financial History 265, 275 (banks); George H. Evans, *British Corporation Finance 1775–1850: A Study of Preference Shares* (1936), 27–30 (canals).

of shares owned, but more slowly than with a one-share/one-vote regime) were common in the late 19th century.[31]

For a number of decades company law even provided a capped voting default rule. UK company legislation has traditionally had a statutory set of articles of association known as 'Table A' that govern if a company lacks its own set of articles.[32] From 1862 to 1906, Table A contained a clause imposing restrictions on voting rights when a shareholder owned 10 or more shares and again when a shareholder owned 100 or more shares.[33] Nevertheless, this arrangement was not the norm in publicly traded UK companies. The Table A regime has always been 'facultative' in the sense that company participants have had freedom to adopt articles that depart from the statutory 'standard form'.[34] With respect to 'capped' voting rights this is what companies typically did. According to data compiled by Campbell and Turner, as of 1883, only 23 per cent of UK companies with publicly traded shares imposed voting caps, and those incorporated before 1862 were more likely to do so than those incorporated after.[35]

Campbell and Turner report that not quite one-half of publicly traded companies had arrangements in place that allocated voting power in accordance with the number of shares owned.[36] One-share/one-vote arrangements were, however, quickly becoming standard.[37] For instance, of 95 UK-based 'commercial and industrial' companies listed in the *Stock Exchange Official Intelligencer for 1899* that had a nominal or authorized share capital of £500,000 or over, 84 had a one-share/one-vote rule rather than some form of capped voting rights.[38]

B. Company Law as a Determinant of Ownership Structure

Company law, in addition to allocating managerial authority and governing shareholder voting arrangements, can influence decisions investors make about whether to buy shares and decisions blockholders make about exit. Assume a

[31] Hannah, *supra* n. 28, 409; Gareth Campbell and John D. Turner, 'Protecting Outside Investors in a Laissez-faire Legal Environment: Corporate Governance in Victorian Britain' (2007), unpublished working paper, Table 2 (providing data for 1883).

[32] This arrangement is scheduled to end in 2009, when distinctive sets of model articles for 'private' companies and for companies eligible to have publicly traded shares are introduced: Companies Act 2006, c. 46, s. 20; <http://www.berr.gov.uk/files/file42847.doc> (last visited March 17, 2008).

[33] Companies Act 1862, sch. 1, Table A, art. 44; Dunlavy, *supra* n. 27, 1360.

[34] Nolan, *supra* n. 17, 99–101.

[35] Campbell and Turner, *supra* n. 31, Table 2.

[36] See *ibid.*, ('Anti-Minority Voting' heading). 35 per cent had straightforward one-share/one-vote arrangements and the others had multiple votes per share.

[37] Francis Gore-Browne and William Jordan, *Handy Book on the Formation, Management and Winding Up of Joint Stock Companies*, 24th edn (1902), 274.

[38] Share and Loan Department (ed.), *The Stock Exchange Official Intelligencer for 1899* (1899), 1052–1536.

country has laws that protect minority shareholders effectively against over-reaching by dominant shareholders, regulate closely transactions between companies and their 'insiders' (directors and key shareholders) and impose comprehensive disclosure requirements on companies that offer shares for sale to the public. Under such circumstances, blockholders should have little scope to extract private benefits of control, which should encourage them to exit. Concomitantly, investors, aware that the law circumscribes exploitation of out-side shareholders and knowing disclosure regulation will help to address infor-mational asymmetries associated with public offerings of shares, should feel 'comfortable' buying equity.

There is empirical evidence that supports the conjecture that company law constitutes a determinant of ownership structures in large companies. In research carried out in the 1990s, La Porta, López-de-Silanes, Shleifer and Vishny (com-monly abbreviated to LLSV) used a six-element 'anti-director rights' index to measure the extent to which company law in a wide range of countries protected minority shareholders from abuse by those controlling companies. They then tested whether there was a statistical correlation between the percentage of com-panies lacking a blockholder and the 'quality' of corporate law as measured by their index and found there was.[39] The inference typically drawn from these find-ings has been that the extent to which corporate law protects outside investors is a determinant of patterns of ownership and control.

LLSV's anti-director index findings have not proved strongly robust in sub-sequent testing. Follow-up studies have revealed coding errors and suggest that once these are corrected many of the correlations LLSV found—including those involving share ownership patterns—disappear.[40] La Porta, López-de-Silanes and Shleifer have, however, extended their empirical investigation beyond anti-director rights. In a 2006 working paper co-authored with Djankov they con-ceded their index of anti-director rights was 'based on an ad hoc collection of variables' and correspondingly constructed a new index of corporate law focus-ing specifically on self-dealing.[41] Their self-dealing index measures both private enforcement (civil remedies) and public enforcement (fines and other criminal sanctions). Their private enforcement component is in turn divided into two parts, *ex ante* (regulation of the process by which there could be validation of a hypothetical transaction where the majority shareholder of a public com-pany was on both sides of the deal) and *ex post* (the ease with which aggrieved minority shareholders could prove wrongdoing with the same hypothetical

[39] La Porta *et al, supra* n. 21; Rafael La Porta, Florencio López-de-Silanes, Andrei Shleifer and Robert Vishny, 'Corporate Ownership Around the World', (1999) 54 Journal of Finance 471.

[40] Holger Spamann, 'On the Insignificance and/or Endogenity of La Porta *et al*'s 'Anti-Director Rights Index' Under Consistent Coding', (2006) Harvard John M. Olin Center for Law, Economics and Business Discussion Paper No. 7, 61–62.

[41] Simeon Djankov, Rafael La Porta, Florencio López-de-Silanes and Andrei Shleifer, 'The Law and Economics of Self-Dealing', (2005), NBER Working Paper 11883, 5.

transaction). Djankov *et al* found there were statistically significant correlations between their public enforcement and private enforcement self-dealing indices on the one hand and various indicators of the development of stock markets on the other. However, only *ex post* private control of self-dealing was correlated with ownership concentration in a statistically significant fashion.

La Porta, López-de-Silanes and Shleifer have also extended their research beyond mainstream company law to securities law, which encompasses legal rules and regulations relating to the marketing and trading of shares. They focused on disclosure rules governing public offerings of shares, testing whether laws favouring enforcement by government regulators and by aggrieved private investors were correlated with the size of national stock markets and the configuration of share ownership.[42] They found no such correlation in the case of public enforcement but did find strong securities markets and diffuse share ownership were associated with laws facilitating private enforcement for misdisclosure.

Given the tenets of the 'law matters' thesis, given that numerous companies joined the stock market in the UK in the late 19th and early 20th centuries and given that dispersed share ownership became increasingly prevalent thereafter, one would anticipate the law would have provided significant protection to minority shareholders in Britain from at least the late 19th century onwards. This was not the case. Instead, UK company law traditionally offered scant protection to outside investors, at least by current standards.[43]

A rough and ready way to illustrate this is by tracking historically the UK's scores on the indices La Porta, López-de-Silanes and Shleifer used as the departure point in their empirical work. LLSV gave Britain a score of '5' out of '6' on their anti-director index, with the only '0' occurring because UK companies legislation did not provide for 'cumulative' voting on the election of directors.[44] Historically matters were much different, with the UK only moving in 1980 above the average (3.00) for the 49 countries LLSV examined (Table I).[45]

---

[42] Rafael La Porta, Florencio López-de-Silanes and Andrei Shleifer, 'What Works in Securities Laws?', (2006) 61 Journal of Finance 1.

[43] Julian Franks, Colin Mayer and Stefano Rossi, 'Ownership: Evolution and Regulation' (2006) ECGI Fin. Working Paper No. 09/2003, 11–17; Brian R. Cheffins, 'Does Law Matter?: The Separation of Ownership and Control in the United Kingdom', (2001) 30 Journal of Legal Studies 459.

[44] La Porta *et al*, *supra* n. 21, 1130. The UK's score remains the same under a revised anti-director index compiled by La Porta, López-de-Silanes and Shleifer with Simeon Djankov. See Djankov *et al*, *supra* n. 41, Table XII.

[45] For full footnotes and discussion, see Brian R. Cheffins, 'Dividends as a Substitute for Corporate Law: The Separation of Ownership and Control in the United Kingdom', (2006) 63 Washington & Lee Law Review 1273, 1289–92.

Table I: Historical evolution of UK company law, as measured by LLSV's Anti-Director Index

	Anti-director index score	Explanation
Mid-19C–1900	1	British companies legislation has never required shareholders to deposit their shares with the company or a financial intermediary prior to a shareholder meeting and thus has always scored at least one out of six on the anti-director index.
1900–1948	2	A 1900 amendment authorized shareholders owning 10% of the shares to call a shareholders' meeting (Chapter Four, Part IV.B).
1948–1980	3	The Companies Act 1948 created a statutory right for shareholders to vote by proxy (Chapter Four, Part IV.B, Chapter Nine, Part III.C).
1980–present	5	Companies issuing new shares were required to make the equity available on a pro-rata basis to existing shareholders in accordance with the percentage of shares already owned (Chapter Nine, Part III.C).The judiciary was authorized to grant a remedy to a shareholder who had been unfairly prejudiced by a company's actions (Chapter Nine, Part III.C).

Anti-director index elements: 1) the ability of a shareholder to cast votes at a shareholders' meeting by mailing in a proxy form; 2) a possible requirement to deposit shares before a proxy vote; 3) the availability of cumulative voting, which permits minority shareholders to 'bundle' their votes and thereby increases the likelihood they can elect their representatives to the board of directors; 4) mechanisms offering relief to oppressed minority shareholders; 5) rules obliging a company to give existing shareholders a right of first refusal when new shares are issued ('pre-emptive' rights) and 6) the ability of shareholders owning up to 10% of the shares to call, on their own initiative, a shareholders' meeting.

The story is the same with regulation of company transactions involving a corporate insider. Again, Djankov *et al* found strong *ex post* private control of self-dealing correlated with the dispersion of share ownership, and, as one would anticipate with a country characterized by a separation between ownership and control, Britain scored highly on this corporate law metric. Djankov *et al* measured *ex post* private control of self-dealing by averaging scores awarded for disclosure in periodic filings (they gave the UK the maximum score of 1.00 here) and for ease of proving wrongdoing (they scored Britain 0.71). The UK therefore scored 0.85 out of 1.00, above the average for common law countries (0.76) and well above the average for civil law countries (0.44) (Table II).

While there seems to be a good 'fit' between Djankov *et al*'s *ex post* private control of self-dealing index and Britain's corporate ownership structure, it is unlikely the relevant rules acted as a catalyst for the separation between ownership and control. One reason is the chronology. With disclosure in periodic filings, Djankov *et al* score this on the basis of whether a country's corporate legislation obliges companies to divulge publicly the existence of large share blocks and to report material facts about transactions in which directors have a personal interest. The UK only introduced such requirements in 1967, therefore raising the country's disclosure score from 0 to 1.00 and boosting the overall *ex post* private control of self-dealing grade by 0.50.[46] Since the separation of ownership and control in UK companies was well under way by this point (Chapter One, Part V) the amendments could not have played anything more than a supporting role in shaping ownership structure.

Another difficulty with Djankov *et al*'s analysis is that they likely awarded the UK a score that was too high for ease of proving wrongdoing. One of the five variables they rely upon to calculate this figure is the ability of a minority shareholder to obtain standing to sue the controlling shareholder in their hypothetical transaction. Djankov *et al* gave the UK a '1' when, at least until the law was amended by the Companies Act 2006 in ways they do not purport to take into account, the score should have been '0'.[47] A second variable Djankov *et al* relied on was the ease of obtaining judgment against the controlling shareholder and they gave the UK a '0.50' when '0' was correct.[48] Similarly, with a third variable—ease of holding the approving body (the board of directors) liable—Djankov *et al* gave the UK a '0.50' when a score of '0' would have been appropriate.[49] Assuming they were correct in awarding Britain a 0.33 and 1 for the other two ease of proving wrongdoing variables they rely upon (the

[46] See Companies Act 1967, c. 81, ss. 16(1)(c) (requiring disclosure of directors' interests in contracts with the company), 33–34 (requiring companies to have a publicly accessible register of shareholders owning 10 per cent or more of the shares).

[47] As Djankov *et al* note, in order for a shareholder to launch 'derivative' proceedings under English law (i.e., sue on a company's behalf) there traditionally had to be 'fraud on the minority' (*supra* n. 41, 14). What they fail to take into account is that there could not be 'fraud on the minority' if shareholders were permitted to ratify the impugned misconduct (*Burland v Earle* [1902] A.C. 83), which they could do with interested party transactions (*North-West Transportation Co. v Beatty* (1887) 12 App. Cas. 589). The Companies Act 2006 has overhauled the law relating to ratification and derivative litigation; see ss. 239, 260–63.

[48] Under Djankov *et al*'s index, a score of 0.50 is appropriate if the individual in question could be held liable if he influenced the transaction or was negligent (*supra* n. 41, Table I). Under UK company law prior to the enactment of the Companies Act 2006, the 'fraud on the minority' doctrine would have precluded an individual shareholder from suing the controlling shareholder—in his capacity as a director—derivatively. Only the company involved would have standing and it would not sue in Djankov *et al*'s hypothetical scenario, given the majority stake of the controlling shareholder.

[49] Djankov *et al* give Britain a score of 0.50 on the basis that the directors could be held liable if they acted negligently (*supra* n. 41, Table III). This was highly unlikely to occur in the hypothetical. Under the law at the time, companies suffering from a breach of the duty of care could sue the director, but a shareholder could not launch such proceedings on behalf of a company because such misconduct would be ratifiable by shareholders: *Pavlides v Jensen* [1956] Ch. 565.

right to seek rescission of the transaction and 'access to evidence', respectively), the UK's ease of proving wrongdoing score should have been 0.27 rather 0.71 (Table II).[50]

If the UK's correct ease of proving wrongdoing score in fact was 0.27, its overall ex-post control of self-dealing grade would have been 0.14 (the average of 0.00 and 0.27) before 1967 and 0.64 thereafter. A score of 0.14 would have placed Britain near the very bottom of the list of countries Djankov *et al* surveyed.[51] Assuming the revised score is correct and their index is a reliable proxy for regulation of self-dealing, it is unlikely the law governing this topic played a significant role in prompting the separation of ownership and control in the UK.

Table II: Historical evolution of *ex post* control of self-dealing in the UK, as measured by Djankov *et al's* Index

	Disclosure in public filing	Standing to sue	Recission	Ease of controlling shareholder liable	Ease of holding approving body liable	Access to evidence	Ease of proving wrong doing	*Ex post* private control of self-dealing
Mid-19C–1967	0[52]	1.00	0.33	0.50	0.50	1.00	0.71	0.35
1967–2006	1.00	1.00	0.33	0.50	0.50	1.00	0.71	0.85
Mid-19c–1967 (revised)	0	0	0.33	0	0	1.00	0.27	0.14
1967–2006 (revised)	1.00	0	0.33	0	0	1.00	0.27	0.64
English Origin average	0.78	0.90	0.62	0.64	0.74	0.73	0.73	0.76
Civil Law average	0.63	0.63	0.10	0.34	0.39	0.46	0.39	0.44

[50] To be more precise, .00 + .33 + .00 + .00 + 1 = 1.33, divided by 5 is 0.27.

[51] Only Russia (0.06), Venezuela (0.09) and Panama (0.13) would have scored lower: Djankov *et al, supra* n. 41, Table III.

[52] From 1929 onwards, a director with an interest in contracts with the company was obliged to disclose the interest, but only to fellow directors at a board meeting (Ch. Eight, Pt I.C).

The story is much the same with securities law. Again, La Porta, López-de-Silanes and Shleifer found strong securities markets and diffuse share ownership correlated with robust private enforcement of prospectus regulation.[53] One would therefore expect that the UK would have scored well on this count as ownership separated from control. As with company law, this was not the case. La Porta *et al* measured private enforcement of prospectus regulation with two components: 1) the extent of disclosure required, and 2) the burden of proof an investor had to meet to sue a company, its directors and its accountants successfully for misdisclosure. During the decades when the ownership structure of larger public companies was unwinding, the UK's scores on both counts were lower than would have been anticipated if securities law was a determinant of share ownership patterns. In particular, Britain's scores were generally inferior to those currently attributed to countries of German legal origin and French legal origin, where blockholders are a hallmark of corporate governance (Table III).[54]

Though in their empirical work on the relationship between law and ownership structure La Porta *et al* examined only a small sample of provisions in corporate and securities law and though doubts have been cast on some of the coding they did, the basic historical trend just identified holds up more generally. For instance, in the UK it has always been very difficult for outside shareholders to launch lawsuits on behalf of their companies to enforce breaches of directors' duties (Chapter Four, Part IV.B). In addition, Parliament was slow to regulate insider dealing. In the absence of legislation directly prohibiting the practice, due

Table III: Historical evolution of prospectus regulation, as measured by a cumulative private enforcement index

	Disclosure requirements	Burden of proof
1867–1890	0.33	0.22
1890–1948	0.33	0.33
1948–1986	0.33	0.44
1986–1995	0.75	0.66
1995–present	0.83	0.66
English legal origin (average)	0.78	0.60
French legal origin (average)	0.45	0.39
German legal origin (average)	0.60	0.42

Source: Cheffins, *supra* n. 45, 1298.

[53] La Porta *et al, supra* n. 42.
[54] On countries where blockholders predominate, see Ch. One, Pt III. On how the UK's historical scores were calculated, see Cheffins, *supra* n. 45, 1294–97.

to a ruling in a 1902 case, it was 'generally assumed that directors (had), legally, *carte blanche* to put to personal advantage their inside information in dealing in their company's securities'.[55] Correspondingly, as Cole claimed in a 1935 paper on share ownership, '[I]n the ceaseless buying and selling of stocks and shares, and above all in the flotation and disposal of new capital issues, the insiders are obviously at an enormous advantage over the general investing public.'[56] While companies became obliged in 1948 to prepare and have available for inspection information regarding share transactions of directors, the legality of insider dealing remained unquestioned until the practice was criminalized in 1980 (Chapter Nine, Part III.C).

While UK companies legislation was not highly protective of shareholders (at least by current standards) as ownership separated from control this does not mean law was irrelevant. Company law reforms introduced in 1948 and 1967 did in various ways provide a more congenial environment for dispersed share ownership (Chapter Nine, Part III.C, Chapter Ten, Part IV.D). In addition, as we will see in Chapters Eight to Ten, other types of legal regulation (e.g., tax law and competition law) had a significant role to play.

Stock Exchange listing rules, with which companies seeking to have their shares traded on an exchange must comply, were relevant as well. Listing rules were often a step ahead of company law in imposing constraints on insiders and providing investors with protection that would have eased concerns they might otherwise have had about purchasing shares (Chapter Three, Part VIII, Chapter Four, Part III.C). However, the compilation of the UK's historical company law scores set out above was generally prepared without taking into account stock market regulation. This is because La Porta *et al* coded only provisions backed by the force of law and stock exchanges in the UK traditionally were purely private associations with rule books supported merely by common law principles of contract and agency.[57] Only from the mid-1980s onwards did stock exchange listing rules acquire the force of law, because at that point financial services reforms vested the London Stock Exchange's listing rules with the status of subordinate legislation (Chapter Ten, Part IV.D). However, even if stock exchange listing rules did not qualify as 'law' for the purposes of coding before the mid-1980s, they regulated companies in various ways that potentially encouraged investors to buy shares and provided blockholders with incentives to exit.

---

[55] L.C.B. Gower, *The Principles of Modern Company Law* (1954), 139, discussing *Percival v Wright* [1902] 2 Ch. 421.

[56] G.D.H. Cole, 'The Evolution of Joint Stock Enterprise' in G.D.H. Cole (ed.), *Studies in Capital and Investment* (1935), 51, 64.

[57] Ch. Ten, Pt IV.D; A.C. Page, 'Self-Regulation: The Constitutional Dimension', (1986) 49 Modern Law Review 141, 145.

III. Trust

Franks, Mayer and Rossi report, based on historical analysis of ownership patterns in various of small samples of UK public companies, that the unwinding of control blocks began before corporate and securities law provided extensive protection to investors.[58] As they recognize, their findings pose the question: How did this occur when the law offered little in the way of explicit protection for those buying equities?[59] The answer they offer is 'trust', with the underlying premise being that this underpinned demand for shares on the part of outside investors.[60] In so doing, they echo claims made by various academics that, as between different countries, higher levels of trust improve economic performance, increase stock market participation and decrease the percentage of stock market capitalization that is closely held.[61] Chambers and Dimson have also invoked the notion of trust to explain why the 'underpricing' of initial public offerings (the differential between the price at which shares are offered for sale and the price at which they subsequently trade) was greater in the UK after 1945 than before, saying that the post-1945 capital market was characterized by lower levels of trust for which stronger regulation did not adequately compensate.[62]

The notion of trust is a decent fit with the analytical approach this book adopts, since it addresses directly one of the 'core' questions, namely 'Why did outside investors buy shares?' Nevertheless, focusing on trust to explain what occurred in Britain is ultimately unhelpful because doing so tends to crowd out more useful lines of thought.[63] The root of the problem is that trust is similar to other major catch-all theoretical terms such as power, equality and justice, in the sense that its meaning varies depending on the context and once the context is known, it is analytically reducible to other more precise concepts.[64] As Williamson, a noted economist, has argued, 'trust is irrelevant to commercial exchange and... reference to trust in this connection promotes confusion' since the behaviour in question

---

[58] Franks, Mayer and Rossi, *supra* n. 43.

[59] *Ibid.*, 3, 31.

[60] *Ibid.*, 31–32; 'The Right Conditions for Trust Between Businesses', Financial Times, June 19, 2006 (column by Franks and Mayer).

[61] Rafael La Porta, Florencio López-de-Silanes, Andrei Shleifer and Robert W. Vishny, 'Trust in Large Organizations', (1997) 87 American Economic Review (Papers and Proceedings), 333, 336; Paul J. Zak and Stephen Knack, 'Trust and Growth', (2001) 111 Economic Journal 295; Luigi Guiso, Paola Sapienza and Luigi Zingales, 'Trusting the Stock Market', (2005) Centre for Economic Policy Research Discussion Paper No. 5288.

[62] David Chambers and Elroy Dimson, 'IPO Underpricing Over the Very Long Run' (2006), unpublished working paper, 20–22.

[63] Timothy W. Guinnane, 'Trust: A Concept Too Many', Economic History Yearbook 2005/1, 77, 80 (discussing generally this feature of trust).

[64] Russell Hardin, *Trust and Trustworthiness* (2002), 56–57.

can be interpreted purely in terms of efficiency.[65] Decisions made by investors to purchase equity in business enterprises large and successful enough to carry out public offerings of shares fall firmly into the commercial rather than the personal realm. It should therefore be possible to rely on analytical concepts more precise than trust to explain why there was sufficient demand for shares to permit ownership to separate from control in larger UK companies.

Unpacking a couple of examples Franks, Mayer and Rossi use to describe trust in action illustrates this is indeed the case. They investigated the shareholder records of 26 companies incorporated around 1900 and found as of 1910 that 56 per cent of ordinary shareholders lived within six miles of the city's headquarters and that the median distance between that city and the shareholders' addresses was 15.4 miles. The highly localized nature of share ownership they found was by no means unique; capital markets in the UK retained a distinct regional orientation through to World War II.[66]

Franks, Mayer and Rossi say their findings show 'relations of trust flourished as a consequence of (the) close proximity of investors to firms'.[67] What occurred can be explained plausibly, however, in more specific and precise terms. When a company's shares were distributed among investors on a highly localized basis, the informational asymmetries potentially afflicting investments in shares would have been reduced because many investors would have had personal knowledge of the proprietors and their business or would at least have been personally familiar with the business environment in which the company is operating. The proprietors, for their part, would have known that failing to deliver expected returns or, more seriously, exploiting minority shareholders, could ruin whatever reputation they had built up in their own city as honest, responsible businessmen. As and when a company went public, feedback through reciprocal dealings (e.g. regular payment of dividends by the company) would have reinforced the belief among investors that the company's shares were a worthwhile investment.[68] One could characterize all this by saying local investors who bought shares in the company did so because they 'trusted' the proprietors.[69] However, other than providing convenient short-hand in this particular context, doing so adds nothing to our understanding of what investors were doing.

A second example Franks, Mayer and Rossi rely upon involves terms offered to shareholders in companies being acquired in merger transactions. In the event of a bid to buy the outstanding equity of a publicly traded company, in

---

[65] Oliver E. Williamson, 'Calculativeness, Trust, and Economic Organization', (1993) 36 *Journal of Law and Economics* 453, 469.

[66] Franks, Mayer and Rossi, *supra* n. 43, 33; on other eras see Ch. Five, Pt V.B.4, Ch. Six, Pt III.C.2, Ch. Eight, Pt II.B.4.

[67] Franks, Mayer and Rossi, *supra* n. 43, 32.

[68] Hardin, *supra* n. 64, 145–50 (discussing feedback and trust).

[69] On this formulation of trust, see Partha Dasgupta, 'Economic Progress and the Idea of Social Capital' in Partha Dasgupta and Ismail Serageldin (eds), *Social Capital: A Multifaceted Perspective* (1999), 325, 332.

an unregulated environment a shareholder (or a tight coalition of shareholders) owning a substantial minority of the shares in a target company stands in a potentially privileged position since the bidder might well be prepared to offer a 'control premium' to persuade such a key investor to sell. This, however, was not the practice in Britain. Franks, Mayer and Rossi report, based on an analysis of 27 mergers occurring between 1919 and 1939, that it was standard for the same price to be offered to all shareholders and characterize the equal treatment of shareholders as a manifestation of 'trust' in British financial affairs.[70]

Given that a majority of Britons answers 'no' when asked whether most people can be trusted, one might wonder how trust was such an important element of interwar takeover dealings in the UK.[71] Perhaps British people are less trusting now than they were during the years between World War I and World War II; surveys indicate that the percentage of Britons who 'trust' others declined from 56 per cent in 1959 to 44 per cent in 1990.[72] There is in fact no need to speculate along these lines because the equal treatment pattern can be explained in more pragmatic terms.

Companies carrying out acquisitions during the interwar years typically aimed to buy up 100 per cent of the shares in the target company and most often succeeded in acquiring all or virtually all of the outstanding equity.[73] In those instances where a small minority would not accept, likely either due to a desire to extract better terms or simple passivity,[74] the acquirer could cash out the minority by purchasing the assets of the target company and winding up the company.[75] This, however, was a tax-inefficient procedure that could destroy the goodwill of the target.[76] In response Parliament enacted in 1929 a provision stipulating that if holders of 90 per cent or more of the shares in a company being acquired accepted a takeover offer, the acquirer could compulsorily purchase the remaining shares on the same terms as were accepted by the majority.[77]

For bidders the most reliable way to convince minority shareholders who might otherwise hold out that the offer on the table was worthwhile accepting was to negotiate with the directors of the target and have the directors recommend

---

[70] Franks, Mayer and Rossi, *supra* n. 43, 35, 38.

[71] See <http://www.worldvaluessurvey.org/> (last visited March 15, 2008); see the listing for Britain under 'Surveys'; data available under question A165.

[72] David Sunderland, *Social Capital, Trust and the Industrial Revolution* (2007), 209.

[73] Franks, Mayer and Rossi, *supra* n. 43, Table A7 (in 29 of 50 mergers occurring in the first half of the 20th century the acquirers ended up owning 100 per cent of the shares and in 10 others they ended up owning between 96 per cent and 99.9 per cent); *Report of the Company Act Committee 1925–26* (chaired by Wilfred Greene) (1926), para. 84.

[74] *Report, supra* n. 73, para. 84; A.E. Cutworth, *Methods of Amalgamation and the Valuation of Businesses for Amalgamation & Other Purposes* (1931), 79.

[75] See, for example, Companies (Consolidation) Act 1908, s. 192.

[76] *Report, supra* n. 73, paras 81–84.

[77] Companies Act 1929, 19 & 20 Geo. 5, c. 23, s. 155; Les Hannah, 'Takeover Bids in Britain Before 1950: An Exercise in Business Pre-History', (1974) 16 Business History, 65, 71, n. 2.

acceptance of an offer where all shareholders received the same price.[78] The logic
was that minority shareholders were apt to reason a bid was fairly priced when
they knew the directors, as those who knew the company best, were prepared
to cash out on the basis of the offer on the table. The directors of the target company, when they agreed to sell out on the same terms as other shareholders, were
not doing so selflessly. Instead, they were typically rewarded with a place on the
board of the new company or a cash payment for loss of office that could amount
to one-tenth of the purchase price.[79] For instance, Franks, Mayer and Rossi specifically draw attention to the 1920 acquisition of steelmakers Alfred Hickman
by rivals Stewart and Lloyds, citing the fact the chairman of Alfred Hickman
said the directors did not receive 'one farthing' in excess of the price offered to
other shareholders.[80] In fact, the Alfred Hickman directors were promised three
seats on the Stewart and Lloyds board as and when the deal went through.[81]
The merger therefore illustrates why it is worthwhile going beyond the label of
'trust' to find out how the market for shares functioned in the UK as ownership
separated from control.

IV. Regulation of Financial Institutions

In 1932 Berle and Means famously proclaimed in *The Modern Corporation &
Private Property* that America's 'corporate system' was characterized by a 'separation of ownership and control'.[82] The definitive historical account of
the evolution of ownership and control in large US companies remains to be
written.[83] Roe nevertheless addressed an important part of the story in his 1994
book *Strong Managers, Weak Owners*.[84] Roe largely took for granted two of the
three questions that need to be taken into account to explain why ownership
separates from control, implicitly assuming blockholders had good reasons to
exit and that there were sound reasons for investors to buy shares in public companies. What he sought to explain is why investors capable of exercising control
over public companies—powerful financial institutions such as banks, insurance
companies, mutual funds and pension funds—failed to follow through.

According to Roe, at several points in the 20th century, major US financial
institutions were poised to take substantial block positions in American business

---

[78] Hannah, *supra* n. 77, 70–71.   [79] *Ibid.*, 72.

[80] Franks, Mayer and Rossi, *supra* n. 43, 36, n. 35.

[81] 'Alfred Hickman Limited: The Amalgamation Proposal', Times , August 30, 1920.

[82] Adolf A. Berle and Gardiner C. Means, *The Modern Corporation & Private Property* (1997,
originally published in 1932), 5.

[83] See Marco Becht and Bradford de Long, 'Why Has There Been so Little Blockholding in
America?' in Randall K. Morck, *A History of Corporate Governance Around the World: Family
Business Groups to Professional Managers* (2005), 613, 651 (conceding in their historical survey of
developments in the US, 'How important were other factors? We wish we knew.').

[84] Roe, *supra* n. 1.

firms but politicians, mindful of a deeply ingrained popular mistrust of concentrated financial power, enacted various laws that derailed the process. In the UK financial institutions were potentially more promising candidates to take 'hands on' responsibility than their US counterparts since throughout the post-World War II era levels of institutional ownership were considerably higher in Britain than in the US.[85] Nevertheless, a hallmark of the UK's outsider/arm's-length system of ownership and control is that institutional shareholders have generally been reluctant to step forward in this way. Roe's analysis of the US implies the corporate governance passivity of British institutional shareholders should be attributable to regulation. This turns out not to have been the case.

Consider deposit-taking banks, which allocated negligible amounts of capital for investment to company shares and adopted 'arm's-length' lending arrangements rather than seeking to cement relations by owning shares in their corporate borrowers.[86] Until the enactment of the Banking Act 1979, the banking industry was characterized by 'self-regulation', albeit under the careful watch of the Bank of England.[87] UK clearing banks thus were entitled to own equity in publicly traded companies if they wished.[88] By the 1970s, a bank was expected to inform the Bank of England of any exposure to a non-bank exceeding 10 per cent of the bank's capital base.[89] Only in the late 1980s, however, did disclosure of large exposures to borrowers become statutorily mandated, with the relevant legislation explicitly ensuring such exposures could include ownership of shares in the borrower.[90]

The story is much the same with the institutional investors that in fact did come to dominate share ownership in the UK in the second half of the 20th century, pension funds, insurance companies and, to a lesser extent, investment trusts and unit trusts (Chapter Four, Part I). Their reticence to adopt an activist posture with respect to the publicly traded companies in which they invested cannot be attributed to regulation, since they faced considerably fewer constraints than their US equivalents.[91] For instance, whereas US securities law traditionally imposed various restrictions on shareholders minded to work together to pressure managers

---

[85] John Armour and David A. Skeel, 'Who Writes the Rules for Hostile Takeovers and Why? The Peculiar Divergence of US and UK Takeover Regulation', (2007) 95 Georgetown Law Journal 1727, 1768–69.

[86] Michael Collins, *Banks and Industrial Finance in Britain 1800–1939* (1991), 48–50, 70–71, 75, 80–81; Forrest Capie and Michael Collins, *Have the Banks Failed British Industry? An Historical Survey of Bank/Industry Relations in Britain, 1870–1990* (1992), 34–35, 50–51, 67.

[87] Capie and Collins, *supra* n. 86, 68–69; Maximilian J.B. Hall, *Handbook of Banking Regulation and Supervision in the United Kingdom* (1989), 3; Banking Act 1979, c. 37.

[88] Herbert Jacobs, *Grant on the Law Relating to Bankers and Banking Companies* (1923), 579; Frank Allen and Douglas Gale, 'Corporate Governance and Competition', in Xavier Vives (ed.), *Corporate Governance: Theoretical and Empirical Perspectives* (2000), 23, 31, 35.

[89] Hall, *supra* n. 87, 19–20 (disclosure of large exposures).

[90] *Ibid.*, 24, 99.

[91] Bernard S. Black and John C. Coffee, 'Hail Britannia?: Institutional Investor Behavior Under Limited Regulation', (1994) 92 Michigan Law Review 1997, 2001–2, 2024–5, 2064–6.

of a publicly traded company, in the UK communication between institutional investors was largely unregulated.[92] In addition, in contrast to their US counterparts, British insurance companies were generally free to invest as they saw fit; even the acquisition of large blocks of shares was unregulated.[93] As far as pension funds were concerned, while from 1961 onwards there was an explicit statutory onus on trustees to have regard for the need to diversify, so long as an investment was of a defensibly prudent sort, pension fund trustees had full discretion to build up a dominant stake in a publicly traded company.[94] As for investment trusts and unit trusts, the spreading of investment risk was unregulated until 1965, when certain tax advantages were denied to a unit trust or investment trust with more than 15 per cent of its investments tied up in a single company.[95] This change to the law had little impact however, since prior to 1965 few unit trusts or investment trusts had portfolio allocations that violated this benchmark.[96]

While regulation did little to deter UK financial institutions from becoming control-oriented investors in publicly traded companies as Britain's outsider/arm's-length system of ownership and control took shape, government policy shaped institutional involvement in corporate governance in other ways. Tax explains in large measure the strong institutional orientation of share ownership in the UK in the decades following World War II, since individuals diverted investment capital to pensions and insurance policies due to tax breaks associated with these forms of saving (Chapter Ten, Parts I.D, III). Also, fears on the part of institutional investors that attempts to influence business policy might expose them to intrusive government oversight and even nationalization helped to deter active intervention in the affairs of UK public companies (Chapter Ten, Part V.C). Still, even if regulation did influence the approach institutions took, Roe's regulation-driven theory of shareholder passivity does little to explain the split of ownership and control in large UK businesses.

V. Politics

Roe, in addition to arguing financial services regulation is a potential determinant of patterns of ownership and control, has put the spotlight on politics. He argues 'left-wing' social democracies will have fewer publicly traded firms and

[92] Cheffins, *supra* n. 10, 639; Paul Myners, *Institutional Investment in the UK: A Review* (2001), 91.

[93] Rose *supra* n. 1, 60, 80–83 (the US); Committee to Review the Functioning of Financial Institutions (Sir Harold Wilson, chair), *Report*, Cmnd. 7937 (1980), 46; Mae Baker and Michael Collins, 'The Asset Portfolio Composition of British Life Insurance Firms, 1900–1965', (2003) 10 Financial History Review 137, 142–43 (the UK).

[94] Trustee Investments Act 1961, ss. 6(1), (2); Pensions Act 1995, ss. 36(2)–(4); John Mowbray, Lynton Tucker, Nicholas de Poidevin and Edwin Simpson, *Lewin on Trusts*, vol. 2, 17th edn (2000), 944.

[95] C.O. Merriman, *Mutual Funds and Unit Trusts: A Global View* (1965), 51–54 (pre-1965 position); Finance Act 1965, c. 25, ss. 67–68, discussed by H. Burton and D.C. Corner, *Investment and Unit Trusts in Britain and America* (1968), 147–48.

[96] Burton and Corner, *supra* n. 95, 150, 291.

significantly higher levels of ownership concentration than 'right-wing' countries where there is little or no tradition of social democracy.[97] He reasons that in social democracies governments favour employees over investors and correspondingly use regulation to increase the leverage workers possess. Corporate executives in turn tend to cater to employee preferences and give shareholders short shrift. This bias, Roe maintains, exacerbates underlying conflicts of interest between managers and shareholders, thereby increasing substantially the disadvantages associated with being a shareholder with a stake insufficiently large to influence corporate policymaking. A split between ownership and control therefore is less likely to occur in a social democracy than it is in a country lacking a strong socialist tradition, such as the United States.

Roe's politics theory, as with his financial services regulation theory, does not fit the facts well in the UK. Whereas left-wing government allegedly 'fits' with blockholding, UK politics in fact swung significantly leftwards as ownership structures unwound. Lowenfeld, a prolific author on investment matters, relied in a 1907 article on the growing power of employees to make a case in favour of readers diversifying by investing abroad, saying 'it is quite clear that the present outlook for British investments is by no means reassuring; for Labour's demands are likely to cause infinite trouble in the future...'[98] Such concerns were exaggerated and premature but a political shift to the left had already begun. The Liberal government of 1905–15 laid the foundations for Britain's modern welfare state by introducing old age pensions, unemployment benefits and state financial support for the infirm. The attendant increase in spending was financed in part by a controversial 1909 'People's Budget' that increased taxation of estates ('death duties') and introduced a 'super tax' (surtax) on incomes over £5,000, thereby establishing a precedent for income tax being 'progressive' in the sense the tax rate rises as the amount to which the rate is applied increases.[99]

As for the interwar years, there was a general consensus among political leaders—Conservative and Labour—that a balanced budget was sensible public policy.[100] However, this has been labelled an era of 'creeping collectivism' due to the state becoming involved in the provision of welfare in a manner unthinkable before 1914 and moving from relatively low to relatively high involvement with industry.[101] The Conservatives, or the Conservative-dominated

---

[97] Mark J. Roe, *Political Determinants of Corporate Governance* (2003).

[98] Henry Lowenfeld, 'The Investor's Defence Against Labour's Attack Upon Capital', Financial Review of Reviews, June 1907, 13, 20.

[99] John Davis, *A History of Britain 1885–1939* (1999), 81–103; Martin Pugh, *State and Society: A Social and Political History of Britain 1870–1997*, 2nd edn (1999), 134–38; 'The Results of the 1909 Budget', Economist , April 26, 1913, 976.

[100] Andrew Thorpe, *Britain in the 1930s: The Deceptive Decade* (1992), 71.

[101] Roger Middleton, *Government versus the Market: The Growth of the Public Sector, Economic Management and British Economic Performance, c. 1890–1979* (1996), Pt III; see also W.G. Runciman, 'Has British Capitalism Changed Since the First World War?' (1993) 44 British Journal of Sociology, 53, 57; James Foreman-Peck and Robert Millward, *Public and Private Ownership of British Industry 1820–1990* (1994), 277.

National Government, were in office throughout much of the interwar period. Nevertheless, government policy lacked a strong *laissez-faire* orientation as Conservative politicians captured the middle ground of British politics by adopting sufficiently left-wing policies to ensure swing voters did not defect to Labour.[102] Government spending illustrates the trend. Government expenditure (central and local), which rose dramatically from 12 to 13 per cent of annual Gross National Product in 1910–13 to over 50 per cent during World War I, never fell below 24 per cent during the interwar years and rose well above this level between 1929 and 1932 and again in the late 1930s.[103]

Much of the additional spending was for the provision of social services, as there was among governing parties a consensus that the state should provide jobs and support when business could not.[104] Indeed, in a famous 1942 report that formed the basis for an ambitious package of social-reform legislation introduced by the Labour government of 1945–51, William Beveridge (later 1st Baron Beveridge of Tuggal) proclaimed that provision against want in Britain was 'on a scale unsurpassed and hardly rivalled in any other country in the world'.[105] The growth in spending was paid for in large measure by increased revenue derived from income tax and surtax, with dramatic tax hikes imposed during World War I remaining largely in place for those in top income brackets.[106]

Regulation of industry also betrayed an increasingly left-wing political orientation. A study of the approach taken by the Conservative party to a wave of nationalization activity carried out by Labour after it swept to power in 1945 suggested 'many of the devices and precedents for Socialist action in Great Britain in 1945–51 were created by the Conservative and Conservative-dominated governments of the inter-war years…'[107] Examples included the establishment of the London Passenger Transport Board, which took control of London's tramway, bus and underground railway services, and the creation of the Central Electricity Board, which purchased the entire output of local authorities and private companies producing power and resold it to the various distributing concerns. Also notable were the Railways Act of 1921, which provided that the charges imposed by railway companies should be regulated so the companies would earn only a 'standard' revenue, and the Coal Mines Act of 1930, which

---

[102] Sean Glynn and Alan Booth, *Modern Britain: An Economic and Social History* (1996), 47–52; Edmund Dell, *A Strange Eventful History: Democratic Socialism in Britain* (2000), 80–82.

[103] Peter Dewey, *War and Progress: Britain 1914–1945* (1997), 66.

[104] 'Appraisal of Britain's Welfare State', New York Times, September 25, 1949.

[105] Quoted in Rodney Lowe, 'Riches, Poverty, and Progress' in Keith Robbins (ed.), *The British Isles 1901–1951* (2002), 197, 223; for a similar verdict, see Runciman, *supra* n. 101, 57.

[106] Ch. Eight, Pt I.F; Dewey, *supra* n. 103, 71.

[107] Deryck Abel, 'British Conservatives and State Ownership', (1957) 10 Journal of Politics 227, 227. See also G.C. Allen, *British Industry* (1944), 23–24; William Ashley, *The Economic Organisation of England: An Outline History*, 3rd edn (with three supplementary chapters by G.C. Allen) (1949), 222–23.

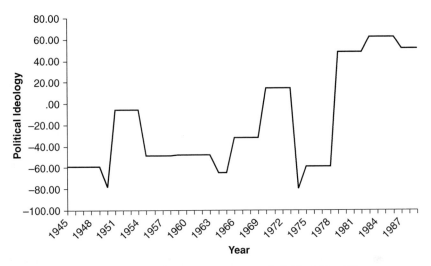

Figure I: Political orientation of governing parties in the UK, 1945–1989

Source: Compiled using data from Cusack and Engelhardt, *supra* n. 109.

established a machinery for fixing prices and controlling output under a quota scheme.[108]

The swing to the left continued after World War II. According to a data set covering 24 OECD countries that scores each from 1945 onwards as 'left wing' (–100 to 0) or 'right wing' (0 to 100) on the basis of positions adopted in the party platform of the governing party in relation to a wide range of social and economic issues, Britain had a left-wing government all but three years between 1945 and the election of Margaret Thatcher's Conservatives in 1979 (Figure I).[109] The upshot is that, contrary to what Roe's political theory predicts, ownership split from control in Britain as politics moved steadily to the left.

Gourevitch and Shinn agree with Roe that worker-oriented social democracy is likely to derail dispersed share ownership but argue that an additional political configuration will do likewise, namely a cross-class 'corporatist' alliance between workers and those who run companies, including family blockholders.[110] In contemporary terms, the situation in Britain is a good fit with Gourevitch and Shinn's conjectures, as the country has dispersed share ownership and scores low

[108] Railways Act 1921, 11 & 12 Geo. 5, c. 55, s. 30; Coal Mines Act 1930, 20 & 21 Geo. 5, c. 33, s. 1.

[109] Marc Goergen calculated and tabulated the data when working with the author on a project on dividends, relying on Thomas R. Cusack and Lutz Engelhardt, 'Parties, Governments and Legislatures Data Set', available at <http://www.wz-berlin.de/mp/ism/people/misc/cusack/d_sets.en.htm#data>(last visited July 2005).

[110] Peter A. Gourevitch and James J. Shinn, *Political Power and Corporate Control: The New Global Politics of Corporate Governance* (2005), 132–38, 157–59.

on tests of 'corporatism'.[111] However, as with Roe's political theory, history tells a different story, since UK politics took on an increasingly corporatist orientation as ownership was separating from control.

'Corporatism' reached its peak in Britain during the 1960s and 1970s,[112] the decades when family-oriented capitalism was in terminal decline. Some doubt whether UK politics was truly corporatist in this era, since formal responsibilities for consultation and policy implementation were not imposed on business or labour.[113] Nevertheless, there was a tripartite orientation to economic policy-making as post-World War II British governments liaised constantly with unions and provided representatives of the UK business community with ample opportunity to confer with civil servants and politicians.[114]

During the 1960s, under both Conservative and Labour governments, the *de facto* tripartite relationship between state, business and organized labour was particularly well developed as public officials successfully encouraged employers and unions to participate directly in national economic planning.[115] The Labour government of 1974–79 treated relations with unions as being the top priority, exemplified by a 'Social Contract' under which union leaders were to exercise strong control over wage demands in return for a policymaking partnership with the state, but continued to engage in continuous consultation with business leaders.[116] Margaret Thatcher's Conservative government then abruptly departed from orthodoxies that had been generally accepted by post-World War II governments, leaving no room for consultation with unions as part of an ambitious economic reform agenda.[117]

The corporatism of the 1960s and 1970s had strong historical antecedents. Corporatist elements—labelled by Middlemas a 'corporate bias'—can plausibly

---

[111] *Ibid.*, 154–55.

[112] See, for example, Trevor Smith, *The Politics of the Corporate Economy* (1979), 163–78; John Dearlove and Peter Saunders, *Introduction to British Politics: Analysing a Capitalist Democracy* (1984), 276–86.

[113] See, for example, Andrew Cox and Joe Sanderson, 'The Political Economy of Britain Since 1939', in Andrew Cox, Simon Lee and Joe Sanderson (eds), *The Political Economy of Modern Britain* (1997), 1, 8–10, 20–24, 26–32; John McIlroy and Alan Campbell, 'The High Tide of Trade Unionism: Mapping Industrial Politics' in John McIlroy, Nina Fishman and Alan Campbell (eds), *British Trade Unions and Industrial Politics, Volume Two: The High Tide of Unionism, 1964–79* (1999), 93, 94–96.

[114] Alan Campbell, Nina Fishman and John McIlroy, 'The Post-War Compromise: Mapping Industrial Politics, 1945–64', in Alan Campbell, Nina Fishman and John McIlroy (eds), *The Post-War Compromise, 1945–64* (1999), 69, 78–80; Robert Taylor, *The Trade Union Question in British Politics, Volume One: Government and Unions Since 1945* (1993), 81–85, 93, 103–5, 329 (unions); Wyn Grant and David Marsh, *The Confederation of British Industry* (1977), 109–10, 120–31, 138–45; Michael Useem, *The Inner Circle: Large Corporations and the Rise of Business Political Activity in the US and the UK* (1984), 184–92 (business).

[115] Cox and Sanderson, *supra* n. 113, 20–22; Colin Crouch, *Class Conflict and the Industrial Relations Crisis* (1977), 41–44, 51–54.

[116] Smith, *supra* n. 112, 165–66; Crouch, *supra* n. 115, 85–86.

[117] Dearlove and Saunders, *supra* n. 112, 286; J. Fulcher, 'British Capitalism in the 1980s: Old Times or New Times?', (1995) 46 British Journal of Sociology 325.

be traced back to the early 20th century.[118] With employers' federations and unions both gaining strength, politicians recognized there were significant benefits to be gained by drawing leaders of business and the unions into policy-making to cope with logistical challenges posed by World War I and ensuing social and political unrest.[119] Thus, earlier than any other industrial country, the UK government was prepared to invoke a tripartite political structure to ameliorate social and political conflict.[120] During the interwar years, the government was not prepared to introduce directly any sort of system of industrial 'self-government' along corporatist lines, but did encourage on an *ad hoc* basis 'planning' efforts of a tripartite nature, involving consultation with business leaders and unions in particular industries.[121] Hence, the Conservative reforms of the 1980s reversed a corporatist trend that had been taking shape over a number of decades, meaning in turn that Britain only definitively abandoned corporatism when ownership was already divorced from control in large businesses.

While events in Britain do not fit well with Roe's or Gourevitch and Shinn's theories, left-wing politics nevertheless did influence the evolution of ownership structure in publicly traded companies. As mentioned, fears of being nationalized helped to deter activism by institutional investors. Also, Labour's 1945–51 nationalization programme and tax policies designed to 'soak the rich' were catalysts for blockholder exit (Chapter Three, Part X). Ironically, then, left-wing politics may have helped to accelerate rather than preclude the divorce of ownership and control in the UK.

VI. Legal Origins

Various academics claim the legal 'family' to which a country belongs does much to explain the presence or absence of strong securities markets.[122] England and many of its former colonies are members of the common law family, the origins of which can be traced back to 11th-century English legal history. The common law system is characterized by 'judge-made' case law, independent judges appointed

---

[118] Keith Middlemas, *Politics in Industrial Society: The Experience of the British System Since 1911* (1979), 374.

[119] *Ibid.*, 57–60, 119, 123–26, 158–65.

[120] Alan Booth, 'Corporatism, Capitalism and Depression in Twentieth-Century Britain', (1982) 33 British Journal of Sociology 200, 202, 206.

[121] Larry G. Gerber, 'Corporatism in Comparative Perspective: The Impact of the First World War on American and British Labor Relations', (1988) 62 Business History Review 93, 126; Daniel Ritschel, 'A Corporatist Economy in Britain? Capitalist Planning for Industrial Self-Government in the 1930s', (1991) 106 English History Review 41, 58.

[122] See, for example, John C. Coffee, 'The Rise of Dispersed Ownership: The Roles of Law and the State in the Separation of Ownership and Control', (2001) 111 Yale Law Journal 1, 59–64; Edward L. Glaeser and Andrei Shleifer, 'Legal Origins', (2002) 117 Quarterly Journal of Economics 1193; Thorsten Beck, Asli Demirüç and Ross Levine, 'Law and Finance: Why Does Legal Origin Matter?', (2003) 31 Journal of Comparative Economics 653.

from the ranks of the legal profession rather than a government bureaucracy and an 'adversarial' mode of trial. The main alternative to common law is civil law, a legal tradition rooted in continental Europe exemplified by written legal codes, 'career' civil servant judges and an 'inquisitorial' trial model.[123]

According to La Porta, López-de-Silanes, Shleifer and Vishny common law countries have, on various measures, more robust stock markets than civil law jurisdictions, including having a higher proportion of companies with diffuse share ownership.[124] They also claim common law countries have company laws that are more highly protective of outside investors than civil law jurisdictions, from which they infer 'legal origins' shape the legal rules that dictate whether countries will have strong securities markets.[125] Other research indicates legal origins are associated with other cross-country differences in financial development, including corporate valuations, access to external finance and the informational efficiency of stock prices.[126]

Why might legal families matter so much, with the common law system apparently offering a more promising foundation for thriving securities markets? One potential explanation is that the common law emphasizes protection of private property rights against state interference to a greater degree than the civil law, with beneficial implications for investment and financial development.[127] Adaptability is also potentially important, in the sense that the common law, by embracing case law, judicial discretion and private dispute resolution, is more responsive to changing financial and economic circumstances than code-based civil law.[128] Another potential explanation is decentralization, with the idea being that, since common law courts had greater independence from the state than their civil law counterparts, there was in common law countries a congenial environment for the growth of private law-making and robust market-based self-regulatory institutions (e.g., the London Stock Exchange) lacking in civil law countries.[129]

Since Britain's leading financial markets have traditionally been based in England (primarily London) and since this was where the common law originated, legal origins theory would predict that the UK would have strong securities markets and diffuse share ownership in large business enterprises. This indeed is what one finds. Nevertheless, for various reasons the common law is an unlikely determinant of corporate governance structures with respect to the UK and more generally.

---

[123] Brian R. Cheffins, 'Our Common Legal Heritage: Fragmentation and Renewal', (1999) 30 Law Librarian 3, 4.

[124] La Porta *et al*, *supra* n. 39, 505.

[125] Rafael La Porta, Florencio López-de-Silanes, Andrei Shleifer and Robert Vishny, 'Investor Protection and Corporate Governance', (2000) 58 Journal of Financial Economics 3, 9.

[126] For an overview of this research, see Beck *et al*, *supra* n. 122, 654.

[127] *Ibid.*, 654–58; La Porta *et al*, *supra* n. 125, 12.

[128] Beck *et al*, *supra* n. 122, 658–61, 672.

[129] Coffee, *supra* n. 122, 61–62.

First, the distinctions between civil law and common law likely are not as stark as is assumed in the comparative corporate governance literature. There is evidence suggesting the two systems have been converging, which implies the particular legal family to which a country belongs should do little to explain current cross-national differences in corporate governance arrangements.[130] More specifically, levels of protection for shareholders apparently differ less than legal origins theorists have assumed. Efforts made to recode the anti-director index LLSV used in their research on the association between corporate law and legal families indicate common law countries were graded too high and civil law countries too low.[131] Legal origins thus may do less to shape corporate law— and by extension capital markets and corporate governance—than was originally hypothesized.

Second, whatever the extent of the differences between common law and civil law, stock markets can flourish in civil law countries. Historical data on the ratio between aggregate stock market capitalization and gross domestic product and on the number of listed companies per million people bears this out. According to these statistical measures, as of 1913 and 1929 several European civil law countries had stock markets that were well developed in relative terms, including in comparison to the United Kingdom and to the United States, the two countries currently characterized as exemplars of dispersed share ownership.[132]

Third, even if in theoretical terms the common law provides a better foundation for robust financial markets than the civil law, there are large disparities within the common law family. Around the world, approximately 40 countries are members of the common law family, and in only two of these—the UK and the US—has the widely held company clearly emerged as dominant.[133] In addition, potentially key features of the common law system are not shared universally by common law countries. Glaeser and Shleifer, two proponents of the legal origins thesis, have argued that the legal systems in England and France diverged fundamentally in the 12th and 13th centuries, ensuring that through to modern times the common law and civil law represented very different strategies for law enforcement and adjudication. The pivotal departure point, they say, was that France opted for adjudication by royally dominated professional judges, whereas

---

[130] Mark Roe, 'Legal Origins and Modern Stock Markets', (2006) 120 Harvard Law Review 460, 475–79.

[131] Spamann, *supra* n. 40, 50–51, 53, 70. See, however, John Armour, Simon Deakin, Prabirjit Sarkar, Mathias Siems and Ajit Singh, 'Shareholder Protection and Stock Market Development: An Empirical Test of the Legal Origins Hypothesis', (2007), Centre for Business Research Working Paper 358, 19–22 (finding a legal origin effect using a different corporate law dataset).

[132] Raghuram G. Rajan and Luigi Zingales, 'The Great Reversals: The Politics of Financial Development in the Twentieth Century', (2003) 69 Journal of Financial Economics 5, 14–17.

[133] Ch. One, Pt III; Simeon Djankov, Rafael La Porta, Florencio López-de-Silanes and Andrei Shleifer, 'Courts' (2003) 118 Quarterly Journal of Economics 453, 478–79 (categorizing 42 of 109 jurisdictions as 'common law'); Simon Djankov, Caralee Macliesh and Andrei Shleifer, 'Private Credit in 129 Countries' (2005), NBER Working Paper 11078 (categorizing 36 of 129 countries as 'common law').

England 'decentralized' matters by leaving cases to be resolved by independent juries.[134] As Roe has pointed out, 'For the jury story to resonate with the overall legal origin story, Britain would have had to have generally transferred the jury system to its colonies.' Roe says, however, 'many, perhaps most, former British colonies do *not* use juries for civil trials and perhaps a majority do not for criminal trials'.[135]

Fourth and finally, to the extent that distinctions between the common law and civil law have affected the development of financial markets, these were as much a product of English politics as the common law *per se*. Again Glaeser and Shleifer argue that the introduction of juries created momentum in favour of the decentralization that in turn was provisionally congenial to the flourishing of securities markets. This account is, however, seriously incomplete.[136] The common law was in fact the product of reforms adopted by English monarchs to increase central control of administration of justice, not to devolve matters. Also, during the 12th and 13th centuries, the period Glaeser and Shleifer treat as crucial, the jury trial was just emerging as one of several accepted trial procedures rather than becoming entrenched as a guaranteed liberty.

Courts in fact only became powerful symbols of decentralization, in the sense they were independent from state influence, a number of centuries later. Key changes were the abolition of 'prerogative courts' (courts allowing the Crown to enforce directly its proclamations) at the end of the 17th century and the enactment of a series of 18th-century statutes that increased judicial salaries and insulated judges from removal at the King's pleasure.[137] The catalyst for change was the displacement of James II of the Catholic House of Stuart from the throne in the 'Glorious Revolution' of 1688. His forced exit opened the way for a stable balance of power between the Crown and Parliament, with the latter clearly being dominant even if it was not exercising exclusive authority.[138] The enshrining of the independence of the courts was an integral element of the new institutional arrangement, as influential players sought to ensure their economic affairs would not be encroached upon by government fiat, whether the source was Parliament or the Crown. Hence, to the extent that English courts exhibit distinctive features that provide a congenial platform for financial markets, these resulted from 17th- and 18th-century political history more than from a common law legacy extending back to the 12th and 13th centuries.[139] More generally, whereas legal origins

---

[134] Glaeser and Shleifer, *supra* n. 122, 1194.

[135] Mark J. Roe, 'Juries and the Political Economy of Legal Origin', (2007) 35 Journal of Comparative Economics 294, 300.

[136] Daniel Klerman and Paul G. Mahoney, 'Legal Origin?' (2007) USC Center in Law, Economics and Organization Research Paper No. C07–5, 6–16.

[137] *Ibid.*, 23; Douglass C. North and Barry R. Weingast, 'Constitutions and Commitment: The Evolution of Institutions Governing Public Choice in Seventeenth Century England', (1989) 69 Journal of Economic History 803, 816.

[138] North and Weingast, *supra* n. 137, 815–19.

[139] Roe, *supra* n. 135, 302; Klerman and Mahoney, *supra* n. 136, 27, 29.

theory implies England's common law heritage should do much to explain the system of ownership and control that arose in Britain, in fact other variables were likely of considerably greater importance.

VII. Path Dependence/'History Matters'

Legal origins theory, to the extent it explains financial development, can be characterized as an example of 'path dependency' in action, in the sense that a country's departure down the common law or civil law 'path' did much to dictate whether vibrant securities markets would emerge.[140] Path dependency is a recurring theme within the comparative corporate governance literature, where academics frequently invoke the notion of path dependence to explain differences in systems of ownership and control across countries.[141] With respect to Britain, certain historical contingencies influenced the development of corporate ownership patterns. Generally, however, analyzing what happened in terms of path dependence obscures more than it reveals.

A key reason the concept has limited explanatory power in the British context is ambiguity concerning path dependence's parameters.[142] Often, the term is employed simply to convey the general notion that initial starting points are important, meaning in turn 'history matters' or 'the past influences the future'.[143] Path dependence can also be defined more narrowly by reference to economic efficiency, with path dependence only being analytically significant where a choice made results in an inferior economic outcome and a market-induced reversal cannot be taken for granted due to substantial switching costs.[144] From this perspective, instances where historical contingencies cause a departure down a particular path when the alternate choices were equally efficient or where the

---

[140] Markus Berndt, 'Global Differences in Corporate Governance Systems' (2000), Harvard Olin Center for Law Economics and Business Discussion Paper No. 303, 5; Charles W. Calomiris, 'Financial History and the Long Reach of the Second Thirty-Years' War' in Timothy W. Guinnane, William A. Sundstrom and Warren C. Whately (eds), *History Matters: Essays on Growth, Technology and Demographic Change* (2004), 115, 117–18.

[141] See, for example, Mark J. Roe, 'Chaos and Evolution in Law and Economics', (1996) 109 Harvard Law Review 641, 644–46, 653–60; Ronald J. Gilson, 'Corporate Governance and Economic Efficiency: When Do Institutions Matter?', (1996) 74 Washington University Law Quarterly 327, 329–34; John C. Coffee, 'The Future as History: Prospects for Global Convergence in Corporate Governance and its Implications', (1999) 93 Northwestern University Law Review 641, 646–47, 660–61.

[142] On the lack of consensus see Paul Pierson, 'Increasing Returns, Path Dependence, and the Study of Politics', (2000) 94 American Political Science Review 251, 252.

[143] Stephen E. Margolis and S.J. Liebowitz, 'Path Dependence' in Peter Newman (ed.), *The New Palgrave Dictionary of Economics and the Law*, vol. 3 (1998), 17, 19; James Mahoney, 'Path Dependence in Historical Sociology', (2000) 29 Theory and Society 507, 507.

[144] Roe, *supra* n. 141, 647–53; S.J. Liebowitz and Stephen E. Margolis, 'Path Dependence, Lock-In and History', (1995) 11 Journal of Law, Economics & Organization 205, 206–7, 214, 223–24.

choice could be reversed easily are treated as uninteresting, even if the alternatives differed from each other in significant ways. This economically oriented version of path dependence correspondingly can only be invoked to account for the existence of a particular set of corporate governance arrangements if what is in place is clearly inefficient compared to obvious alternatives.[145]

The available empirical evidence does not establish clearly the superiority of either dispersed or concentrated share ownership. More generally, debates concerning the merits of the 'Anglo-American' outsider/arm's-length corporate governance model as compared with its insider/control-oriented alternative remain unresolved.[146] Given the absence of clear-cut economic verdicts, from an efficiency perspective it is inappropriate to use path dependence to explain why ownership did or did not separate from control in a particular country. Instead, invoking 'path dependence' terminology involves little more than claiming 'history mattered' in the sense there were critical junctures where a particular choice became progressively more difficult to reverse over time. Accordingly, for the sake of clarity, it is generally best to avoid explaining events in Britain by reference to path dependency and to focus instead on more precise variables that dictated how matters developed.

While the separation of ownership and control in the UK cannot be accounted for readily in terms of path dependence, two instances where history likely 'mattered' merit acknowledgment, these being the early rise of stock market institutions and Britain's political and social stability. In order to rationalize the British case in relation to their political theories Roe and Gourevitch and Shinn invoke path dependency, saying that Britain's strong stock market institutions provided a platform for at least some dispersion of share ownership to occur when the political environment was not congenial and for diffusion to accelerate when conditions changed under Margaret Thatcher's Conservative government.[147]

There is something to this. The stock market indeed was a well-established part of the UK economy as politics swung leftwards. In 1960, when Britain was in the middle of a 35-year stretch of strongly left-wing politics, Wincott said, 'The Stock Exchange is . . . woven into the very texture of our national civilisation and could not be abolished without radically altering our national way of life.'[148] If the London Stock Exchange had lacked this sort of pedigree perhaps the left-wing orientation of British politics following World War II would have undercut the development of strong securities markets in the manner Roe and Gourevitch and Shinn hypothesize.[149] However, the existence of well-established stock

---

[145] Margolis and Liebowitz, *supra* n. 143, 19.

[146] Pt I; Brett H. McDonnell, 'Convergence in Corporate Governance—Possible But Not Desirable', (2002) 47 Villanova Law Review 341, 350–64.

[147] Gourevitch and Shinn, *supra* n. 110, 261; Roe, *supra* n. 130, 508–9; Mark J. Roe, 'Political Preconditions to Separating Ownership from Control', (2000) 53 Stanford Law Review 539, 575–77.

[148] Quoted in R.J. Briston, *The Stock Exchange and Investment Analysis*, 3rd edn (1975), 13.

[149] Roe, *supra* n. 130, 508.

market institutions does not necessarily mean trading in company shares will be sufficiently robust to ensure dispersed ownership can occur. The early history of stock markets in England illustrates the point.

By the early 18th century all of the institutional structures that characterize an effective share market were in place in England, such as rules of guarantee of transfer, professional *arbitrageurs*, freely available price information and a wide range of potentially tradable instruments.[150] Nevertheless, throughout the century only a tiny handful of companies had their shares traded in sufficient volume for prices to be reported (Chapter Five, Part III.B). The basic pattern remained the same for much of the 19th century. The London Stock Exchange was the leading stock market in the world as the century drew to a close.[151] However, railways aside, company shares were little more than a sideshow. For instance, of the £4.9 billion worth of securities traded on the London Stock Exchange as of 1893, most were issued by government (39.5 per cent) or railways (49.4 per cent). Only 5.1 per cent was attributable to shares and debentures issued by banks, insurance companies, commercial and industrial companies, breweries, shipping companies and iron and steel firms.[152]

Throughout the 20th century, as dispersed share ownership became increasingly commonplace in the UK, company shares became an increasingly important part of stock exchange business. Contrary to what Roe and Gourevitch and Shinn imply, however, it could not be taken for granted this would occur. Instead, there were various potential deterrents to investment in shares. As we have seen in this chapter, there was little explicit legal protection offered to outside investors and political conditions for investment in shares were far from optimal. In addition, British companies were not the most promising of investments since the UK was in decline relative to its key industrial rivals throughout the late 19th century and much of the 20th century (Chapter Four, Part II.B). What, given these circumstances, explains the existence of sufficient demand for corporate equity for ownership to separate from control? Chapter Four provides a succinct overview of the topic, and subsequent chapters elaborate.

As for political and social stability, Roe has argued that economic and military devastation during the 20th century (or lack thereof) stands out as a good cross-border predictor of the present strength of securities markets and suggests those countries that avoided military occupation and civil war have a higher degree of separation between ownership and control than those countries that were less fortunate.[153] Political stability, or lack thereof, plausibly is a determinant

---

[150] Philip Mirowski, 'The Rise (and Retreat) of a Market: English Joint Stock Shares in the Eighteenth Century', (1981) 41 Journal of Economic History 559, 566, 576.

[151] Ranald C. Michie, *The London Stock Exchange: A History*, 142.

[152] *Ibid.*, 88–89.

[153] Roe, *supra* n. 130, 498–501; see also Mark Roe and Jordan I. Seigel, 'Political Instability and Financial Development' (2007), unpublished working paper (measuring the impact of political stability from 1960–1982 on a variety of measures of financial development for a wider range of countries).

of the vibrancy of stock markets. In a country handicapped by political and social upheaval mobile financial and human capital will tend to exit, government officials will have priorities other than the protection of property rights and entrepreneurs understandably will be reluctant to invest in sustaining reputations for reliable dealing.[154] Correspondingly, when assessing what occurred in Britain it is appropriate to acknowledge that avoiding defeat in World War I and World War II and the absence of a violent political revolution in its history removed potential obstacles to the rise and ultimate dominance of the widely held company.

Still, although political and social stability may well be a historical contingency that can affect the manner in which a country's system of corporate governance evolves, it is not worthwhile pursuing this line of enquiry any further in seeking to understand what occurred in Britain. To do so it would be necessary to move firmly into the realm of the hypothetical. For instance, to assess the extent to which victory in World Wars I and II mattered, it would be necessary to determine whether strong securities markets would have survived (or been revived) if Britain had lost either conflict. 'Virtual history' is a legitimate field of intellectual enquiry.[155] However, pursuing a World War counterfactual in this instance is too speculative to be productive.

One reason is that the contingencies that would need to be taken into account would be too open-ended to keep the inquiry manageable. For instance, because Britain could not have experienced a separation of ownership and control if market institutions collapsed one would need to take a view on whether Britain would have continued to have a market economy in any meaningful sense if it had lost either of the World Wars. Even if it were assumed that Britain's market economy would have survived defeat, one would need to speculate whether key industrial assets would have been brought under direct control by the victors rather than remaining under private ownership. Moreover, given legal origins theory, one would also want to consider whether the common law would have remained intact after a British defeat.

It is also premature to analyze counterfactuals concerning political and social stability. This chapter has shown existing theories on why systems of ownership and control differ across countries offer, at best, limited insights into the transformation affecting Britain. Since we currently lack a good understanding of why matters turned out as they did even under the conditions that in fact prevailed, it is currently superfluous to speculate in detail about would have happened under hypothetical facts. A more productive line of enquiry is to try to identify the factors that in fact did help to prompt ownership to separate from control in the UK. Chapters Three and Four do this.

---

[154] Roe and Seigel, *supra* n. 153, 8–9.

[155] Niall Ferguson, 'Virtual History: Towards a "Chaotic" Theory of the Past' in Niall Ferguson (ed.), *Virtual History: Alternatives and Counterfactuals* (1997), 1.

THREE

The 'Sell Side'

Given that the divorce of corporate ownership and control in the UK cannot be explained adequately by reference to theories already advanced to account for differing arrangements across countries, a broader enquiry, focusing on what can be termed the 'sell side' and the 'buy side', is in order. This chapter introduces the reader to the sell side, which encompasses the factors that can motivate those owning large blocks of shares to give up their favoured position. As Part II describes, blockholders have incentives to sit tight, as there can be significant benefits associated with owning a large percentage of shares in a company. On the other hand, there are also various reasons why blockholders might prefer to exit or will be content to dilute their holdings. Parts III to X discuss these. The chapter begins, however, by pointing out that the unwinding or dilution of a dominant block of shares is not always required for ownership to separate from control. Instead, companies can be launched without any individual shareholder or coalition of investors qualifying as blockholders.

I. Lack of Blockholding on Formation

Most business enterprises start their life with high insider ownership,[1] with the founders usually being the sole owners of the firm, or majority owners if a few providers of 'start up' capital have been given shares. If ownership separates from control, this occurs at some later stage. Matters can, however, proceed differently, with those launching a business venture seeking wide financial backing immediately by inviting the public to buy shares. For instance, in 1896, Harry Lawson, a well-known company promoter, raised £100,000 by selling ordinary shares of Daimler, an automobile manufacturing venture, before a single automobile had been produced commercially in Britain. He invested only £250 in the company himself and only two out of some 550 original shareholders invested over £1000.[2]

---

[1] Jean Helwege, Christo Pirinsky and René Stulz, 'Why Do Firms Become Widely Held? An Analysis of the Dynamics of Corporate Ownership', (2007) 62 Journal of Finance 995, 995.
[2] S.B. Saul, 'The Motor Industry in Britain to 1914', (1962) 5 Business History 22, 31.

The Daimler pattern was rare for industrial companies of the late 19th and early 20th centuries as most 'flotations' involved offers to the public of shares in established businesses rather than fledgling enterprises (Chapter Six, Part II.A). However, it was commonplace for the businesses that dominated lists of publicly traded firms earlier in the 19th century to be launched without the founders taking up a dominant equity stake. Those proposing to establish companies to build and operate canals, docks, gas lighting schemes and railways usually had no other option. These were infrastructure projects involving a large capital outlay for assets unlikely to yield a return for a number of years. This necessitated tapping a significantly wider reservoir of capital than a few enterprising individuals were typically able or willing to provide, even wealthy ones.[3]

The same pattern was also fairly standard for 19th-century insurance companies. Those launching such enterprises needed to obtain outside backing to accumulate sufficient capital to cope with potentially colossal liabilities, namely disastrous fires in the case of fire insurance, the loss of expensive shipping vessels in the case of marine insurance and, in the case of life assurance, a coincidental set of simultaneous large claims.[4] The failure rate of 19th-century insurance companies illustrates how easily things could go wrong. Between 1844 and 1883, 1186 insurance companies were established, 519 insurance companies were wound up, and only 612 of the 1186 launched ever commenced operations.[5]

Politics provided an additional incentive for those founding 19th-century businesses to secure a broad investment base before commencing operations. Until the mid-19th century, when Parliament enacted legislation streamlining the incorporation process, those seeking explicit authorization to incorporate needed to do so by way of an Act of Parliament or a Royal Charter (Chapter Five, Part IV.A, Part V.B.1). Those establishing canals and railways during the late 18th and early 19th centuries would typically call public meetings in the locality to generate support and obtain subscriptions for shares prior to approaching Parliament. This was sound political tactics because Parliament was more inclined to grant an act of incorporation if a subscriber base reflected strong local support.[6]

Although various prominent 19th-century businesses were launched without blockholders this does not mean that they were characterized by a modern-style division of ownership and control. Outsider/arm's-length corporate governance is associated with large numbers of shareholders and a highly liquid market for

---

[3] Ron Harris, *Industrializing English Law: Entrepreneurship and Business Organization, 1720– 1844* (2000), 99, 108, 183; Phyllis Deane, *The First Industrial Revolution*, 2nd edn (1979), 181; Steven King and Geoffrey Timmins, *Making Sense of the Industrial Revolution* (2001), 118.

[4] Harris, *supra* n. 3, 108.

[5] H.A.L. Cockerell and Edwin Green, *The British Insurance Business: A Guide to its History and Records*, 2nd edn (1994), 102–3.

[6] Ch. Five, Pt III.C; M.C. Reed, *Investment in Railways in Britain, 1820–1844: A Study of the Development of the Capital Market* (1975), 84; Harold Pollins, 'The Marketing of Railway Shares in the First Half of the Nineteenth Century', (1954) 7 Economic History Review 230, 238.

shares—otherwise firms, despite the absence of a dominant owner, are functionally large partnerships (Chapter One, Part VII). As Chapter Five discusses, the large British railway companies of the mid-19th century qualified as pioneers of modern-style dispersed share ownership. Canal companies, on the other hand, typically had only a small shareholder base with a strong local orientation and secondary trading of shares was merely sporadic. Gas light companies resembled canals and insurance companies anticipated from shareholders a level of commitment to the business unknown in today's widely held companies. Given this, and given that during the second half of the 20th century—the period when ownership ultimately separated from control in the UK—it was virtually unknown for fledgling companies to carry out public offerings of shares (Chapter Nine, Part I), for the purposes of determining why a separation of ownership and control occurred it is appropriate to focus primarily on the conventional corporate life cycle where a business enterprise is launched with the founders owning most if not all of the business.

II. The Benefits of Blockholding

When a business enterprise is launched with the founders also being the primary owners, a transition to dispersed ownership can only occur if the dominant faction is prepared to contemplate the unwinding or dilution of its stake. It cannot be taken for granted this will occur. The total return a company's shares yield for investors is a function of the net cash flow the business generates over time. Since all of a company's shares (or at least its 'ordinary' or 'common' shares) generally have equal rights and restrictions attached to them (Chapter Two, Part II.A), the return particular investors receive will be proportionate to the percentage of shares they own. Blockholders, however, can benefit from their status in ways unavailable to other shareholders since they can secure 'private benefits of control'. A desire to retain this favoured position can deter exit even if a transition would increase overall shareholder value (Chapter Two, Part I).

There has long been awareness that dominant shareholders can take advantage of their position. A 1909 text on investment argued buying shares was only a 'fair bargain' if no more than one-third of the voting shares were in the hands of the vendors or the promoters of the company.[7] A 1968 edition of a text on business finance similarly argued that 'the position of a minority shareholder in a subsidiary company is best avoided', citing the fact 'there are many opportunities of arranging the policies and finances of the group so as to increase the profits of the parent company at the expense of any outsider shareholders in one or more of the subsidiaries'.[8]

[7] Henry Lowenfeld, *All About Investment...* (1909), 193.
[8] F.W. Paish, *Business Finance*, 4th edn (1968), 53.

The most obvious forms of private benefits of control are financial in nature. 'Tunnelling' corporate assets by way of one-sided 'sweetheart' deals is a classic means by which blockholders can secure private advantages.[9] The experience of Union International, a food and property conglomerate controlled by the Vestey family, illustrates the point.[10] During the early 1990s the company was more than £400 million in debt and, under pressure from the company's bankers, the Vestey family pumped in an estimated £145 million as part of a rescue effort. The turn-around attempt failed, and in 1995 the company was put into receivership. Before this occurred the Vesteys were able to rely on their family control to exclude alter-native buyers and acquire substantial assets from Union International on advan-tageous terms.

Blockholders can also extract private benefits of control by treating the public companies they dominate as personal fiefs, bestowing upon themselves gener-ous managerial pay, lavish offices, luxurious business travel and other desirable corporate perks. The situation at Marks and Spencer, a successful and widely admired retailer that went public in 1926, is indicative. According to a 2001 history of the company, prior to family control unwinding due to a 1966 'enfran-chising' of the company's non-voting ordinary shares, 'The Sieffs, the Sachers and the Laskis, as big shareholders in the company, came to believe that a luxurious lifestyle both inside and outside the office was their proprietorial right…'[11]

While diverting 'pecuniary' private benefits of control is the most obvious reason why dominant shareholders might want to stay put, there can be other reasons. A charitable explanation is that they can create value for the companies they dominate by using a hard-won reputation for steadfastness and reliability to facilitate contracting with suppliers, customers and capital suppliers.[12] The shipping industry of the late 19th and early 20th centuries might well pro-vide an example. Boyce has said of blockholders in the major shipping groups: '…Inchcape, Furness, Ellerman and the families who ran Cunard, staked large parts of their fortunes and their reputations. The holding company provided a framework for combining public and private capital markets, accommodating transactions in intangible assets, accentuating and concealing leverage and mag-nifying profits. More fundamentally, it preserved asymmetrical information flows and ensured that founders retained access to preferential data.'[13]

---

[9] M. Becht and C. Mayer, 'Introduction', in Fabrizio Barca and Marco Becht (eds), *The Control of Corporate Europe* (2001) 1, 6–7.

[10] 'Vestey in Talks Over £100m Sell-Off', Evening Standard, October 31, 1994; 'Heirs and Disgraces', Guardian, August 11, 1999; Dominic Hobson, *The National Wealth: Who Gets What in Britain* (1999), 751–52.

[11] Judi Bevan, *The Rise and Fall of Marks & Spencer* (2001), 68; on 1966, see Ch. Nine, Pt II.B.

[12] Randall K. Morck and Lloyd Steier, 'The Global History of Corporate Governance: An Introduction' in Randall K. Morck (ed.), *A History of Corporate Governance Around the World* (2005), 1, 36.

[13] Gordon Boyce, *Information, Mediation and Institutional Development: The Rise of Large-Scale Enterprise in British Shipping, 1870–1919* (1995), 239–40.

Blockholders also might be reluctant to depart because their position generates significant 'non-pecuniary' private benefits of control.[14] There can, for example, be a dynastic angle, with a founder or a successor from the same family orchestrating his replacement by his children or other relatives so as to give them a head start in life and to secure his own legacy. Also, there can be the 'buzz' associated with owning a major company and a potential entrée to 'elite' circles occupied by leading politicians and the wealthy. For instance, Simon Marks, who dominated Marks & Spencer until his death in 1964 'enjoyed the trappings of wealth, the influence it gave him with politicians and the allure of film stars and celebrities...'[15]

Despite the situation at Marks & Spencer, in Britain the prestige associated with being the dominant personality in a major post-World War II business was not as great as might have been expected. The *Economist* claimed in 1946 that the 'rewards of success' had 'been poisoned, since commercial success has been turned, in the eyes of wide circles of society, into a positive disgrace'.[16] Faith has said similarly of the 1950s, 'overall the prevailing ethos was deeply uncommercial'.[17] Or, as Florence argued in 1972, '[A] business career failed in Britain to exert the attractive power to which its comparative pecuniary rewards might entitle it because of the non-pecuniary consideration of comparative social disrespect.'[18] Assuming these are correct characterizations of attitudes in Britain, proprietors of successful businesses would have often lacked potent non-pecuniary incentives to retain control.

The logic involved finds support from a popular theory advanced to account for the UK's decline relative to its leading economic rivals between the late 19th and late 20th centuries, namely that Britain lost its way due to an anti-industrial and anti-business cultural bias.[19] The theory is that an aversion to industry and commerce led to a haemorrhage of potential business talent, a weakening of entrepreneurial resolve and tolerance of an educational system ill-suited for training future managers.[20] As Wiener argued in an oft-cited 1981 book, 'For a century and a half the industrialist was an essential part of English society, yet he was never quite sure of his place. The educated public's suspicions of business and industry inevitably colored the self-image and goals of the business community.'[21]

---

[14] Ronald J. Gilson, 'Controlling Shareholders and Corporate Governance: Complicating the Comparative Taxonomy', (2006) 119 Harvard Law Review 1641, 1663–64.

[15] Bevan, *supra* n. 11, 68.

[16] 'The Carrot and the Stick', Economist, June 29, 1946, 1033, 1034.

[17] Nicholas Faith, *A Very Different Country: A Typical English Revolution* (2002), 49.

[18] P. Sargant Florence, *The Logic of British and American Industry*, 3rd edn, (1972), 375.

[19] Keith Robbins, 'British Culture versus British Industry' in Bruce Collins and Keith Robbins (eds), *British Culture and Economic Decline* (1990), 1, 2–3; W.D. Rubenstein, *Capitalism, Culture and Decline in Britain* (1993), 1–3, 5–6.

[20] For summaries of the thesis, see Roger Middleton, *Government Versus the Market: The Growth of the Public Sector, Economic Management and British Economic Performance, c. 1890–1979* (1996), 32; Rex Pope, *The British Economy Since 1914: A Study in Decline?* (1998), 74–76.

[21] Martin J. Wiener, *English Culture and the Decline of the Industrial Spirit, 1850–1980* (1981), 127.

To the extent that the British business community was confronted by a societal anti-industrialist bias, exiting from active commercial life would have held
considerable appeal for blockholders. According to Wiener a 'career pattern
repeated over and over again' was that 'The vigorous unpolished outsider
achieves a business (or professional) triumph, trades his winnings for a knight-
hood...and a country estate, and soon becomes absorbed in the rituals of his
new position, while his business touch slips away...'[22] However, explanations
for Britain's economic decline based on an anti-business bias should not be
taken at face value. Awkwardly, the alleged antipathy towards businessmen
pre-dated the UK's poor economic performance, extending back to the mid-
Victorian era when Britain remained in the ascendancy.[23] The comparative
angle is also troubling, as robust intellectual assaults on capitalism occurred in
countries in continental Europe that gained ground relative to Britain, particularly through the second half of the 20th century.[24] Nevertheless, to the extent
that an anti-industrial and anti-business bias did permeate British society, the
'extra-financial' attractions of retaining a dominant stake in a successful industrial enterprise would have been reduced.

III. Diversification and Liquidity

Negative perceptions of business aside, there are various factors that can
encourage blockholder exit, with one being the investment characteristics of a
big equity stake in a company. Individuals who own a large percentage of the
outstanding shares in a publicly traded company will typically have much of
their wealth tied up in that company. If the company encounters hard times, a
sharp reversal in financial fortunes will likely follow. A desire to spread investment risks through diversification thus can help to induce blockholders, such
as a family, to exit.[25]

Diversification has long been a motive for unwinding control. In 1877, David
Chadwick, a Member of Parliament who had been a successful promoter of companies in the Manchester area, told a committee investigating companies legislation that one factor that induced public offerings of shares in industrial firms was
that 'Men with large interests in some businesses desire to limit that interest and

[22] *Ibid.*, 147.
[23] Peter L. Payne, 'Entrepreneurship and British Economic Decline' in Collins and Robbins,
supra n. 19, 25, 32–33.
[24] Rubenstein, *supra* n. 19, 70–71; Harold James, 'The German Experience and the Myth
of British Cultural Exceptionalism' in Collins and Robbins, *supra* n. 19, 91, 95–106, 122–23;
Leslie Hannah, 'Cultural Determinants of Economic Performance: An Experiment in Measuring
Human Capital Flows' in Graeme Donald Snooks (ed.), *Historical Analysis in Economics* (1993),
158, 159.
[25] Marco Becht and J. Bradford DeLong, 'Why Has There Been So Little Block Holding in
America?' in Morck, *supra* n. 12, 613, 619–20.

the only mode to do it is by forming a joint stock company.'[26] A century later, the family-run foundations that had been the dominant shareholders in the Rank Organisation, a leading entertainment group, lost majority control when the company enfranchised the company's non-voting shares. In short order, the family interests announced they would begin selling out as 'it made little sense for them to keep all of their eggs in one basket'.[27]

In addition to being poorly diversified, blockholders can face liquidity constraints. If a large company has its shares traded on a stock market, its shareholders can typically count on selling their shares promptly at or near the market price. An individual or a coalition of investors owning a large block of equity cannot. If they attempt to cash out quickly, the market might anticipate a panic-driven bail-out is occurring or trading activity in the company's shares may simply be too thin to accommodate a sudden influx of shares available for sale. As a result, they will struggle to sell out via the stock market at a price reflecting the underlying fundamentals of the business. Those blockholders who treat liquidity as a priority thus have a strong incentive to unwind their holdings as and when the opportunity arises.[28]

IV. Generational Issues

One of the 'perks' of blockholding is the scope a dominant owner has to pass along the business in dynastic fashion. If, however, there is no obvious heir or the next generation lacks the appetite, aptitude or determination to carry on the business, this incentive falls away and exit becomes increasingly appealing. A 1970 book on mergers picked up on the point, identifying as promising acquisition targets companies 'whose principal directors and/or shareholders are open to an approach for one or more of a half dozen basic reasons. They may want to retire because they're tired of working twelve hours a day. They have no sons or daughters who can follow them in the job, and they are anxious to enjoy the years left to them...People like these will often agree to a friendly deal, on favourable terms...'[29]

Generational considerations of this sort are of long standing. In Victorian times it was commonplace for aging founders of a successful business enterprise to transfer it outside the family, wind the business down or provide for its disposition in their wills.[30] Sometimes this occurred because there was no

---

[26] Quoted in James B. Jefferys, *Business Organisation in Great Britain 1856–1914* (1997), 82. On Chadwick, see E. Victor Morgan and W.A. Thomas, *The Stock Exchange: Its History and Functions*, 2nd edn (1969), 136.

[27] 'Compensation for the Voters', Times, January 26, 1976; see also Ch. Nine, Pt II.B.

[28] Gilson, *supra* n. 14, 1664.

[29] William Davis, *Merger Mania* (1970), 247.

[30] H.L. Malchow, *Gentlemen Capitalists: The Social and Political World of the Victorian Businessman* (1991), 349–50, 357; David Sunderland, *Social Capital, Trust and the Industrial Revolution* (2007), 180.

younger generation ready to carry on.[31] Also, assuming that the founder of a business followed the norm during the Victorian age and opted not to organize his estate in accordance with primogeniture (passing everything to the eldest son), a sale of the business could be required to generate proceeds to share among his children.[32] In addition, successful industrialists and manufacturers influenced by a societal bias against commercial endeavour may have actively discouraged children from continuing the family business in favour of taking up occupations associated with elite society, such as law, financial services or the civil service.[33] Historians disagree, however, on how pervasive the necessary social attitudes might have been.[34]

Regardless of the precise reason why passing a business through the generations was the exception to the rule in the Victorian era, as the 19th century drew to a close, cashing out by way of a public offering of shares became an increasingly popular strategy for proprietors concerned about succession options. The prospectus issued in 1872 by Scottish metal makers Mercy and Cunningham in support of an initial public offering of shares illustrates the point. The prospectus explained that Mr Cunningham had died and the trustees were compelled to withdraw his capital from the business as soon as possible. It continued: 'Mr. Mercy does not feel disposed to add to the large interest which he already holds in the undertaking and as neither of his sons desires to engage in commercial pursuits he prefers gradually to withdraw from active business. It would be impossible to find private capitalists to contribute the capital necessary for such an enterprise and it has therefore been resolved to place the present proposal before the public.'[35]

The carrying out of public offerings in response to concerns about succession continued in the 20th century. Morgan and Thomas explain a dramatic growth in the number of companies traded on the London Stock Exchange after 1914 partly on the basis that 'the sons and grandsons of successful businessmen, with comfortable fortunes and public school educations...left the family firm in favour of a career in politics or the public service...'[36] Even if there might well have been a suitable heir for a successful business, fate sometimes intervened. The sale of Jaguar, the auto manufacturer, in 1966 to the British Motor Corporation (BMC) illustrates the point. William Lyons co-founded

---

[31] Sunderland, *supra* n. 30, 180; R.S. Sayers, *Lloyds Bank in the History of English Banking* (1957), 248 (describing why the partners of a Rugby-based private bank sold out to Lloyds Bank in 1868).

[32] Malchow, *supra* n. 30, 375; on primogeniture's significance in this context see Marianne Bertrand and Antoinette Schoar, 'The Role of Family in Family Firms', (2006) 20 Journal of Economic Perspectives 73, 79–80.

[33] See, for example, D.C. Coleman, 'Gentlemen and Players', (1973) 26 Economic History Review 92.

[34] John F. Wilson, *British Business History, 1720–1994* (1995), 113–17.

[35] Quoted in Jefferys, *supra* n. 26, 81.

[36] Morgan and Thomas, *supra* n. 26, 204.

the business in the 1920s and managed it largely single-handed throughout its existence as a stand-alone company (Jaguar did not have a proper board meeting until 1965).[37] Nevertheless, Jaguar became publicly quoted and was a market favourite in the 1950s.[38] The company had record profits in 1965 and the company's fate rested squarely in Lyons' hands, as he and his family owned more than half the voting shares.[39] He was, however, 65 years old by then and had lost his only son and heir in an automobile accident a decade earlier.[40] He therefore regarded a merger with a bigger concern as an unavoidable step to safeguard Jaguar's future as a brand. After selling out to BMC (renamed British Motor Holdings after the merger) he managed the Jaguar division until he retired in 1972.

V. Erosion of Profits

Since private benefits of control can motivate dominant shareholders to retain control, concerns about erosion of profits and uncertain business prospects going forward can make exit an attractive proposition. When competitive pressure builds, a blockholder's ability to skim profits might well create at least a partial buffer against hard times. Nevertheless, sustained erosion of earnings due to competition from rivals and other economic trends ultimately constitutes a natural constraint on private benefits of control that can leave a dominant shareholder exposed and welcoming the opportunity to exit.[41]

Even in tough times, a reluctance to walk away from the business may exist, prompted perhaps by a sense of entrepreneurial pride, family loyalty or a desire to maintain social status as a business leader. On the other hand, since a blockholder will have all (or most) of his eggs in a single faltering basket, a pronounced decline in company fortunes will force the blockholder to at least contemplate selling out. Chadwick, in his testimony to the committee reviewing companies legislation in 1877, said 39 of 40 propositions he received to carry out public offerings came from firms 'on the down grade'.[42] Or, with Alfred Hickman, a steel maker acquired in 1920 by Stewart and Lloyds, the directors and their associates owned 40 per cent of the shares and the chairman successfully lobbied in favour

[37] 'Power Play Under Examination', Times, October 25, 1971; <http://www.speedace.info/jaguar.htm> (last visited February 21, 2008).

[38] F.R. Jervis, *The Economics of Mergers* (1971), 93.

[39] 'Jaguars to Join Up With B.M.C.', Times, July 12, 1966.

[40] 'Jaguar's Driving Force', Liverpool Daily Post, October 24, 2001.

[41] Alexander Dyck and Luigi Zingales, 'Private Benefits of Control: An International Comparison', (2004) 59 Journal of Finance 537, 577.

[42] H.A. Shannon, 'The Limited Companies of 1866–1883' (1933) 4 Economic History Review 290, 303; J.H. Clapham, *An Economic History of Modern Britain: Free Trade and Steel 1850–1886* (1932), 360.

of selling out on the basis that '[E]verything to-day is depressed. The threatened coal strike is like a wet blanket over everything.'[43]

Various factors can put pressure on profits and thereby cause blockholders to contemplate exit. To illustrate, companies can face a bleak future due to specific circumstances (e.g. managerial shortcomings) that cause them to lose ground to rivals in the same industry. In other instances, pressure might be industry wide. For instance, with the Alfred Hickman merger, the concern was that a strike by coal miners would jeopardize returns throughout the steel industry. Another possibility is 'excessive' competition within an industry, where due to overcapacity beleaguered proprietors are bedevilled by falling profit margins and unsold inventory. For example, in the opening decade of the 20th century the shipping trade was afflicted by an oversupply of tonnage and declining freight rates and the resulting financial losses induced families dominating a number of shipping firms to sell out.[44]

Broader economic trends can come into play too. Trade liberalization can make exit look enticing if domestic producers struggle to match foreign rivals on the basis of price and quality.[45] Also, economic downturns, such as the ones Britain experienced in the early 1920s, the early 1930s and the mid-1970s, can cause profits to drop sharply across the economic spectrum and put blockholders under uncomfortable pressure. Even without a recession, difficulties can arise for business. For instance, during the 1960s, in what were otherwise reasonably buoyant economic times, the profitability of UK manufacturing companies declined significantly, in large part due to wage growth outpacing productivity increases (Chapter Nine, Part III.A).

Taxation can similarly make exit look like an attractive option. Due to the system of corporate tax the UK has generally had, straightforward taxation of corporate income did not play a major role in this context. In contrast to a 'classical' system of tax where income is taxed both as profits at the corporate level and as dividend income at the shareholder level, UK corporate income tax has traditionally reduced or eliminated the second layer of tax.[46] Under the British version of what has become known as the 'imputation' system of corporate tax, with profits distributed in the form of dividends, companies have operated as *de facto* collecting agencies, nominally paying dividends 'gross' but withholding on behalf of shareholders tax pegged at a prescribed standard rate. Shareholders have been able to then claim a partial or full credit against their dividend income,

[43] 'Alfred Hickman Limited: The Amalgamation Proposal', Times, August 30, 1920.

[44] Boyce, *supra* n. 13, 105–6.

[45] Randall Morck, Daniel Wolfenzon and Bernard Yeung, 'Corporate Governance, Economic Entrenchment and Growth', (2004), NBER Working Paper 10692, 52–53.

[46] For background see Hargreaves Parkinson, *Scientific Investment: A Manual for Company Share and Debenture Holders* (1932), 199; J.A. Kay and M.A. King, *The British Tax System* (1978), 184–185; Steven A. Bank, 'The Dividend Divide in Anglo-American Corporate Taxation', (2004) 30 Journal of Corporation Law 1, 2–3.

depending on their income level, meaning corporate taxation only impinged directly on corporate earnings when profits were retained.

Though the system of corporate tax in UK likely did not erode returns companies generated to an extent sufficient to prompt blockholders to contemplate exit, there have been instances when additional taxes on profits probably had this effect. During both World War I and World War II companies had to pay high taxes on 'excess' profits, defined as profits exceeding prescribed pre-war benchmarks (Chapters Eight, Part I.E, Chapter Nine, Part III.B). The abolition of this form of tax in 1921 coincided with a sharp economic downturn and the re-introduction of a profits tax in 1939 was immediately preceded by a recession. In both eras, the combination of tax and adverse business conditions is likely to have prompted numerous blockholders to contemplate exit.

While it is understandable that blockholders might look for a way out when confronted with difficult business conditions, exiting by way of selling shares on the stock exchange could be problematic since investors would be 'buying into' the adverse trends inducing the blockholders to contemplate exit. Selling out in a merger would be likely to be a more promising possibility. This is because, notwithstanding the pessimism on the part of incumbent blockholders, there might be firms anticipating sufficient returns can be generated to make an acquisition worthwhile. The purchaser might intend to improve returns by trimming excess capacity in the relevant industry and using market dominance to increase profits. Growth by merger could also create economies of scale and distribution, with efficiency gains being enhanced by eliminating redundant plants, clerical facilities and marketing operations. Those running the acquiring company also might believe the contemplated target was inefficiently run and that improvements in managerial performance would generate sufficient additional profits to make the purchase worthwhile.[47] To illustrate, shipping companies bought up weak rivals at the opening of the 20th century in the hopes of making substantial gains by restoring the earning power of the new subsidiaries and the 1950s takeover 'raider', Charles Clore, aimed to profit from leveraging underperforming property assets held by the companies he bought.[48]

Mergers foster abrupt transformations of ownership structure, and can do so in a way that prompts a shift generally towards more diffuse share ownership. One way for this to occur is for firms that are already widely held to buy up companies dominated by family owners, which in effect transfers assets to enterprises where ownership is divorced from control. Banking in England, which by the end of World War I was dominated by a handful of large, widely held banks, provides an early example. The industry was transformed during the late 19th and early 20th centuries by expansion-oriented banks organized as public

---

[47] Bernard S. Black, 'Bidder Overpayment in Takeovers', (1989) 41 Stanford Law Review 597, 609.

[48] Boyce, *supra* n. 13, 152–53 (shipping); George Bull and Anthony Vice, *Bid for Power*, 3rd edn (1961), 119–22; David Clutterbuck and Marion Devine, *Clore: The Man and His Millions* (1987), 71–73, 78, 92–95 (Clore).

companies buying up privately owned banking concerns. The targets often agreed to be acquired due to 'loss of family interest or ability in the business, financial weakness, or even simply loss of faith in the ability of private banks to survive in a world of joint stock banks'.[49]

For blockholders minded to exit a downside with a merger is the finality: control shifts wholesale to the acquiring company. Nevertheless, with returns being eroded by market pressures, tax and so on, this sort of transformation might still be welcomed. As Penrose noted in a 1963 book on the growth of the firm, '[T]he very existence of firms that are not very successful or of firms owned by people who want to leave the business is in itself conducive to merger.'[50] Davis said similarly in 1970 'In bad times, difficult trading conditions and shortage of capital usually make companies aware of the need to consolidate... Faced with a seemingly endless squeeze, as well as stiff competition from large units, family firms are often readier to give up control. Mergers, after all, are preferable to losing money and to being driven out of business.'[51] Large numbers of companies apparently were in precisely this situation in the 1960s. According to Davis, macroeconomic conditions 'played an important role in producing merger mania. It has underlined the fact that, for a very long time now, too many firms have been chasing profits which, in a competitive sellers' market, have been increasingly difficult to come (by).'[52] A merger was therefore welcome relief for many blockholders.

Competition law can affect the receptivity of blockholders to merger offers. In a deregulated setting, when companies are suffering as a result of 'excess' competition it may be possible for industry participants to use anti-competitive alliances to control production and stabilize prices. Proprietors who otherwise would want to exit might then be prepared to persevere. Traditionally Britain offered a congenial legal environment for anti-competitive alliances. Through the first half of the 20th century, the UK lacked any legislation specifically targeting anti-competitive behaviour and rulings in various late 19th-century cases suggested contracts regulating prices or output among competitors might be enforceable if the restraints on competition were 'reasonable'.[53] In 1956, however, anti-competitive agreements were declared by statute to be presumptively illegal and over the following decade companies generally abandoned such arrangements (Chapter Nine, Part III.A). Blockholders under economic pressure from market competition therefore had to consider the merger option more seriously than they did previously, and the change to the law has indeed been

---

[49] Sayers, *supra* n. 31, 248. On bank amalgamations in the late 19th and early 20th centuries, see Ch. Seven, Pt V.

[50] Edith Penrose, *The Theory of the Growth of the Firm* (1963), 159.

[51] Davis, *supra* n. 29, 12. See also 'Clutch of Takeover Bid Situations', Times, December 3, 1965.

[52] Davis, *supra* n. 29, 12.

[53] Ch. Eight, Pt I.E; Tony Freyer, *Regulating Big Business: Antitrust in Great Britain and America 1880–1990* (1992), 123–32.

credited with helping to prompt a surge in acquisition activity between the late 1950s and early 1970s.[54]

VI. Unwinding Ownership Blocks to Finance Mergers/Expansion

Mergers do not necessarily act as a catalyst for dispersed ownership. If an acquiring company has a dominant shareholder, companies it buys become subject to insider/control-oriented corporate governance. Depending on financing, however, mergers can foster diffusion of share ownership among companies carrying out acquisitions.

In a merger transaction, the consideration paid to the selling shareholders will be cash, securities issued by the acquirer or a combination of the two. If target shareholders are paid in cash and the funds were derived from retained earnings or from borrowing, the ownership structure of the acquirer will remain undisturbed. This will also be the case if the acquiring company pays using securities it has issued and these have no voting rights attached (e.g., preference shares, non-voting ordinary shares or debt instruments such as debentures).[55]

The history of Lever Brothers Limited illustrates how a blockholder can retain full control despite carrying out an aggressive acquisition strategy. William Lever (later the first Viscount Leverhulme) started making soap with his brother in 1885 on capital of £27,000. When he died in 1925, Lever Brothers was a multinational conglomerate employing capital of some £64 million that controlled over 140 companies that were not only responsible for 60 per cent of the soap trade in the UK but also included businesses engaged in shipping, coconut and oil-palm planting and the production of margarine, disinfectants, chocolates and canned food.[56]

Lever, from the late 19th century until his death, was in complete control of the ordinary share capital of Lever Brothers (Chapter Seven, Part IX). Lever Brothers, to finance its acquisitions without diluting Lever's command of the ordinary shares, issued debentures, borrowed from banks and relied extensively on the issuance of preference shares and ordinary preferred shares with limited

---

[54] D.C. Elliot and J.D. Gribbin, 'The Abolition of Cartels and Structural Change in the United Kingdom' in A.P. Jacquemin and H.W. de Jong (eds), *Welfare Aspects of Industrial Markets* (1977), 345, 356–65; George Symeonidis, 'The Evolution of UK Cartel Policy and Its Impact on Market Conduct and Structure', in Stephen Martin (ed.), *Competition Policies in Europe* (1998), 55, 68–71.

[55] F.R. Jervis, *The Company, the Shareholder and Growth* (1966), 35.

[56] J. Morgan Rees, *Trusts in British Industry 1914–1921* (1922), 139–40; W.J. Reader, 'Personality, Strategy and Structure: Some Consequences of Strong Minds' in Leslie Hannah (ed.), *Management Strategy and Business Development: An Historical and Comparative Study* (1976), 108, 110–11.

voting rights.[57] As of 1922, the issued capital attributed to ordinary shares was £2.3 million and the issued capital attributed to preference shares and preferred ordinary shares was £44.7 million held by 187,000 shareholders.[58]

If, unlike Lever Brothers, an acquiring company issues new ordinary shares to carry out a share-for-share exchange with the target company's shareholders, executing the merger will inevitably dilute to some degree a blockholder's stake. The result will be the same if the target shareholders are paid in cash raised from a public offering of ordinary shares by the acquirer, assuming the blockholder does not buy a percentage of the shares matching its current holdings. The available evidence suggests merger-driven dilution by whatever means contributed significantly to the divorce of ownership and control in the UK. Of 30 'very large' industrial and commercial companies that Florence deemed 'owner controlled' in his study of share ownership patterns as of 1951, control was reconfigured in 25 over the following three decades and in six instances the dilution associated with undertaking acquisitions was an important cause (Chapter Nine, Part II.B). Likewise, research by Franks, Mayer and Rossi on ownership patterns for 40 long-lived companies incorporated around 1900 and for 20 long-lived companies incorporated around 1960 reveals directors on average collectively owned a sizeable but declining percentage of shares over time, with the single most important cause of dilution being the issuance of shares to carry out mergers.[59]

Companies can issue ordinary shares to raise capital to finance 'internal' investment as well as to carry out mergers, with objectives including refurbishing existing operations, investing in new equipment and reducing outstanding debt. When companies tap capital markets in this way, as with merger transactions, the stake of dominant shareholders will be diluted so long as they do not buy a percentage of the shares matching their current ownership stake.[60] Obtaining access to capital for internal investment has long been a potential motive for industrial and commercial companies to become listed on the stock market.[61] However, this sort of capital-raising apparently had a relatively minor impact on ownership structure in the UK. In Britain, as in all major economies, retained earnings have traditionally been a far more important source of corporate finance than the issuance of equity.[62] Reluctance to turn to external sources of capital has been

---

[57] Preferred ordinary shares were used to acquire firms in similar lines of business to Lever Brothers—'Company Meeting—Lever Brothers Limited', Times, January 10, 1919.

[58] Wilson, *supra* n. 34, 267–69, 290.

[59] Julian Franks, Colin Mayer and Stefano Rossi, 'Ownership: Evolution and Regulation' (2006) ECGI Fin. Working Paper No. 09/2003, 23–24, Tables 4, 5.

[60] Helwege, Pirinsky and Stulz, *supra* n. 1, 997.

[61] John Armstrong, 'The Rise and Fall of the Company Promoter and the Financing of British Industry', in Jean-Jacques van Helten and Youssef Cassis (eds), *Capitalism in a Mature Economy: Financial Institutions, Capital Exports and British Industry, 1870–1939* (1990), 115, 119.

[62] Ch. Five, Pt IVB; Ch. Six, Pt II.B.4; Colin Mayer, 'Financial Systems, Corporate Finance, and Economic Development' in R. Glenn Hubbard (ed.), *Asymmetric Information, Corporate Finance, and Investment* (1990), 307, 310–12; Jenny Corbett and Tim Jenkinson, 'How is Investment

particularly acute when a potential loss of control was implied.[63] As and when companies sold shares to the public, they usually did so to give incumbent share-holders a means by which to cash out rather than seeking to raise fresh capital (Chapter Eight, Part I.B, Chapter Nine, Part I). Hence, acquisitions aside, the financing of corporate expansion generally had little impact on the sell side.

VII. Generous Terms on Offer

To this point, the discussion of motives for exit has focused primarily on down-sides for blockholders, such as lack of a suitable heir and erosion of profit margins. Blockholders, however, can opt to unwind their holdings not so much because their situation has become untenable but because there is a window of oppor-tunity where the firm's shares are advantageously priced.[64] A situation where this is particularly likely to occur is where the stock market is influenced by a wave of investor optimism, a fairly common occurrence with the UK stock market, particularly prior to the mid-20th century (Chapter Four, Part III.F). The surges in investor demand could boost the prices shares were likely to fetch to levels substantially exceeding blockholders' 'shadow valuations'—private estimates of what their companies were worth.[65] Under such circumstances, unwinding control could become too good an option to ignore. A 1930 book on investing in public companies drew attention to the trend in its analysis of public offer-ings of shares, saying, 'In times when much Stock Exchange activity prevails and prices of stocks generally are rising, opportunities for public flotations are excep-tionally favourable. These opportunities are seized with avidity...to sell secur-ities (possibly of very doubtful worth) to the public at inflated prices, the public being, at such times, infected with the general optimism prevailing on the Stock Exchanges, and therefore specially gullible.'[66]

This was a pattern repeated over time. During a share price boom in the early 1870s, numerous proprietors of Yorkshire iron foundries seized the opportunity to carry out public offerings on the Sheffield stock exchange.[67] Investor enthu-siasm for shares in the mid-1890s made exit by way of a public offering appeal-ing for blockholders in numerous industrial and commercial companies. As an 1898 article put it, 'On the one hand we have business men, advancing in years,

Financed? A Study of Germany, Japan, the United Kingdom and the United States', [1997] Manchester School, Supplement, 69, 74–75.

[63] I.C. McGivering, D.G.J. Matthews and W.H. Scott, *Management in Britain: A General Characterisation* (1960), 61.

[64] Helwege, Pirinsky and Stulz, *supra* n. 1, 998.

[65] Leslie Hannah, *The Rise of the Corporate Economy*, 2nd edn (1983), 20, 59.

[66] A.E. Cutforth, *Public Companies and the Investor* (1930), 149.

[67] James Foreman-Peck, 'The 1856 Companies Act and the Birth and Death of Firms' in Philippe Jobert and Michael Moss (eds), *The Birth and Death of Companies: An Historical Perspective* (1990), 33, 37.

perhaps, wishing for rest and retirement, or desirous of going from business into politics, meeting an opportunity of exchanging, on excellent terms, the cares of commerce for private life; on the other hand we have investors, ready to employ their money at a small return; and between them we have the promoter, anxious to bring the two together to mutual advantage and his own.'[68] A 1929 history of financial speculation said similarly of a surge of enthusiasm for shares in 1919 and 1920, 'On top of this came the desire of the very far-seeing to get out of what they felt to be a hollow situation. It was thought, even as late as 1920, that a "bull" position could not be permanent. And the plethora of new issues was taken up.'[69] Likewise, during a surge of investor optimism in the late 1920s public offerings of shares proved to be an attractive way for proprietors of established businesses to cash out on behalf of themselves and their families.[70]

A full-scale division of ownership and control did not necessarily result when blockholders sought to capitalize on generous exit terms. For proprietors not inclined to leave their businesses entirely, a buoyant stock market created the opportunity for them to 'have their cake and eat it too', in the sense they could unwind part of their holdings but retain a dominant role in practical terms. A study of new issues in the London capital market carried out between 1927 and 1933—including the stock market boom at the end of the 1920s—indicates that it was standard for proprietors to use a public offering to take cash out of the business but continue to dominate its affairs.[71] As the authors of the study explained, 'The usual procedure is for a financial group to offer the original owners cash for part of their holding, shares in the new company, acquiring the old, for the balance, and a managerial contract at large salaries, as well as seats on the board. The vendor thereby does well out of the transaction, retaining his job at a high salary, keeping control through shares and directorships...'[72] In such circumstances, although the carrying out of a public offering would be a key step towards diffusion of share ownership, additional steps would be required before a full divorce of ownership and control occurred.

VIII. 'Self-Regulation' in Financial Markets

The opportunity to garner private benefits of control that are unavailable to outside investors can induce blockholders to retain control when concerns about having too many eggs in one basket, fears about succession, adverse business conditions and buoyant stock prices otherwise might well prompt an exit.

[68] S.F. Van Oss, 'The 'Limited Company' Craze', The Nineteenth Century, May 1898, 731, 734.
[69] R.H. Mottram, *A History of Financial Speculation* (1929), 287.
[70] Ranald C. Michie, *The London Stock Exchange: A History* (1999), 258.
[71] A Group of Cambridge Economists, 'Recent Capital Issues' in G.D.H. Cole (ed.), *Studies in Capital and Investment* (1935), 103, 134.
[72] *Ibid.*, 134–35.

A premise underlying the 'law matters' thesis is that company and securities law strongly influences blockholder thinking in this regard, with investor-friendly rules constituting a catalyst for exit. However, UK company law generally did not offer extensive protection to outside investors as ownership separated from control, implying blockholders had an open invitation to exploit minority shareholders (Chapter Two, Part II.B). On the other hand, 'self-regulatory' substitutes for corporate law imposed constraints that could make exit more appealing.

Stock exchange regulation constituted an important market-oriented supplement to corporate law. The London Stock Exchange and stock exchanges formed in a number of larger English 'provincial' (regional) centres during the 19th century each imposed requirements on companies seeking to have shares listed for trading, with the relevant regulations being unified after the exchanges federated in 1965.[73] This constituted market-driven 'self-regulation', in the sense that the stock exchanges were purely private associations and their listing rules were supported by laws of contract and agency rather than via a statutory foundation (Chapter Two, Part II.B). The London Stock Exchange, always the largest and most important of the UK's stock markets, did develop important links to the government during World War II and the decades following.[74] Still, until Parliament overhauled financial services regulation in the mid-1980s and brought the Stock Exchange and its listing rules firmly within a statutorily based regime (Chapter Ten, Part IV.D), UK stock exchanges regulated companies without formal legislative authority.

Through the late 19th and early 20th centuries the approach taken was *laissez-faire* in orientation. The London Stock Exchange did exercise control over whether to grant a security admission to its official list of quoted securities and Stock Exchange officials would decline 'to admit to quotations the questionable enterprises of "shady" promoters'.[75] Otherwise, the Stock Exchange was not concerned with the quality of the securities the market handled, leaving its members free to deal in whatever financial instruments they chose. Exchange officials assumed their sole responsibilities to investors were to provide an effective and well-organized market for dealing in securities and to discipline its members so far as was necessary for that purpose.[76] The rationale was, as the *Economist* said in 1888, to 'avoid the appearance of being a species of public censor, for they have rightly seen that neither they nor any other body could effectually undertake such duties...'[77] Correspondingly, as an 1889 text on the London, New York and Paris stock exchanges said of the London market, '[P]ersons buying issues

---

[73] L.C.B. Gower, *The Principles of Modern Company Law*, 3rd edn (1969), 291.

[74] *Ibid.*; Michie, *London, supra* n. 70, 291–94, 363–68, 416, 423–26, 481, 485–87, 541–42.

[75] George R. Gibson, *The Stock Exchanges of London, Paris and New York: A Comparison* (1889), 37.

[76] Michie, *supra* n. 70, 87; W.T.C. King, *The Stock Exchange* (1947); Francis Hirst, *The Stock Exchange: A Short History of Investment and Speculation* (1948), 214.

[77] 'The Value of Special Settlements on the Stock Exchange', Economist, September 1, 1888, 1102.

that have been "listed" should scrutinize the property and investigate the value for themselves.'[78]

While the London Stock Exchange traditionally shied away from regulating companies closely, a rule it imposed to ensure there was a viable market for quoted securities had important implications for those owning large stakes in companies. From at least the 1850s onwards the London Stock Exchange prohibited the quotation of a class of securities unless two-thirds of the capital had been subscribed for by and was allotted to the public.[79] The two-thirds rule, which was intended to inhibit market manipulation and promote liquidity, could be sidestepped in various ways (Chapter Seven, Part III). Nevertheless, it did put the onus on proprietors of a company wanting a full quotation of the ordinary voting shares to reduce their collective stake to one-third.

The two-thirds rule was repealed in the late 1940s (Chapter Nine, Part III.D). In the meantime, the London Stock Exchange had begun to abandon its *laissez-faire* approach and imposed various restrictions that would have increased corporate transparency and otherwise limited the scope for extraction of private benefits of control.[80] Companies legislation did not require a company to circulate a balance sheet annually to shareholders until 1908, did not oblige directors to disclose a personal interest in a contract with the company until 1929 and has never prohibited directors from voting on any such contract, but by 1902 the Stock Exchange was prepared to deny a quotation to a company if its articles failed to deal with these matters.[81] In addition, while until 1929 UK companies legislation did not require a company to provide annual earnings data to shareholders in the form of a profit and loss account, by 1909 the Stock Exchange was requiring companies seeking a quotation to use their articles to commit themselves to doing so (Chapter Six, Part III.B.3, Chapter Eight, Part II.B.2).

The Companies Act 1948 introduced various provisions that imposed constraints on those controlling companies, including an amendment authorizing the shareholders to dismiss directors by way of an ordinary resolution (i.e., a simple majority vote).[82] Nevertheless, the Stock Exchange listing rules continued in certain ways to be stricter than company law (Chapter Four, Part III.C). Hence, from the beginning of the 20th century until the overhaul of financial services

---

[78] Gibson, *supra* n. 75, 38.

[79] The rule was discussed in '*Robson v Earl of Devon*', Times , June 15, 1857, (describing a lawsuit with 1852 facts); 'Charge of Conspiracy', Times , June 10, 1872 (summarizing a lawsuit with 1858 facts).

[80] On transparency increasing the odds of detection of improper diversion of corporate assets, see Alan Ferrell, 'The Case for Mandatory Disclosure in Securities Regulation Around the World', (2004), Harvard Center for Law, Economics and Business Working Paper No. 492, 13–14.

[81] Ch. Six, Pt III.B.2 (balance sheet); Ch. Two, Pt II.B (contract disclosure); Brenda Hannigan, 'Limitations on a Shareholder's Right to Vote—Effective Ratification Revisited' [2000] Journal of Business Law 493, 507–11 (director voting on contracts); Ch. Six, Pt III.B.3 (listing rules as of 1902).

[82] Companies Act 1948, 11 & 12 Geo. 6, c. 38, s. 184 (director removal); on the Act generally see Ch. Nine, Pt III.C, Ch. Ten, Pt IV.D.

regulation in the mid-1980s, stock exchange listing rules constituted a 'self-regulatory' supplement to company law that may well have encouraged block-holder exit.

IX. Dividends

The managing director of a leading UK fund manager declared in 1994 that dividend policy imposes 'vital discipline on company boards'.[83] By virtue of this feature, dividends, like stock exchange regulation, constituted a market-oriented substitute for company law that provided blockholders with an incentive to exit. The 'agency cost' theory of dividends ascribes to dividends an important role in curbing the potential excesses of insiders controlling public companies. The theory is conventionally discussed with the widely held company as the reference point, postulating that dividends impose constraints on managers otherwise liable to act contrary to the interests of arm's-length shareholders.[84] It is also relevant, however, for companies where a shareholder owns a sufficiently large block of shares to exercise *de facto* control since the regular distribution of earnings to investors reduces the scope of a dominant shareholder to skim or squander corporate profits.[85] It follows that, to the extent that the onus was on UK companies to distribute profits to outside investors in the form of dividends, there would have been a market-oriented incentive for blockholders to unwind their holdings.

British company law has never compelled those managing a company to declare dividends.[86] It has been standard for articles of association to stipulate shareholders must ratify dividends proposed by the board of directors but shareholders have rarely used this right of veto to dictate dividend policy.[87] Given the discretion afforded by company law, the discipline of dividends has been potentially illusory since corporate insiders could simply stop distributing cash to

[83] 'The City Must Defend its Capital Position', Financial Times, April 19, 1994, (the author was Paddy Linaker, managing director of Prudential Assurance).

[84] See, for example, Ronald C. Lease, Kose John, Avner Kalay, Uri Loewenstein and Oded H. Sarig, *Dividend Policy: Its Impact on Firm Value* (2000), 80–81. On the theory generally, see Frank Easterbrook, 'Two Agency-Cost Explanations of Dividends', (1984) 74 American Economic Review 650.

[85] Rafael La Porta, Florencio López-de-Silanes, Andrei Shleifer and Robert W. Vishny, 'Agency Problems and Dividend Policies Around the World', (2000) 55 Journal of Finance 1, 4–5; Mara Faccio, Larry H.P. Lang and Leslie Young, 'Dividends and Expropriation', (2001) 91 American Economic Review 54, 55.

[86] Horace B. Samuel, *Shareholders' Money: An Analysis of Certain Defects in Company Legislation with Proposals for Their Reform* (1933), 145; Alex Rubner, *The Ensnared Shareholder: Directors and the Modern Corporation* (1965), 22.

[87] Brian R. Cheffins, 'Dividends as a Substitute for Corporate Law: The Separation of Ownership and Control in the United Kingdom', (2006) 63 Washington & Lee Law Review 1273, 1310. On the articles, see, for example, Companies Act 1862, 25 & 26 Vict., c. 89, sch. 1, Table A, art. 72; Companies (Consolidation) Act 1908, 8 Edw. 7, c. 59, sch. 1, Table A, art. 95.

shareholders.[88] Dividends could therefore only play the role ascribed to them by agency cost theory if those controlling a company were bound informally but credibly to continue to make regular, ongoing dividend payments.[89] UK public companies conducted themselves as if they were operating under such constraints. The vast majority declared dividends, the dividends paid were a significant fraction of annual earnings and companies sought to avoid reducing or eliminating dividends absent special circumstances (Chapter Six, Part II.B.2, Chapter Eight, Part I.D, Chapter Nine, Part III.A).

A 1966 text on share valuations provides a hint why UK public companies acted as if they felt compelled to pay dividends. As the author acknowledged, some boards were tempted to settle dividend policy by asking 'How little can we pay in order to keep the shareholders quiet?' They did not follow through, however, since they were 'aware of hardships that might be caused by reduction of dividend'.[90] One potential hardship was forsaking the option to return to capital markets to raise funds by issuing shares.

UK companies typically relied on retained earnings as their primary source of finance but used the stock market to raise capital on various occasions, with the driver often being the financing of acquisitions.[91] Dividend policy historically influenced investor assessments of shares available for sale, so preserving the option to return to equity markets gave corporate insiders an incentive to pay dividends and avoid reducing or abandoning payouts to shareholders. Armstrong, in discussing company promoters of the late 19th and early 20th centuries, says, 'The ability to go back to the market depended crucially on the company being profitable, paying anticipated dividends and thus keeping its share price high.'[92] Samuel made the same point in 1933, noting that 'Most companies hope to extend their business, and in fact do so from time to time. For this purpose, fresh money is necessary. Fresh money is usually raised by new issues. But the success and attractiveness of a new issue are to a large extent determined by the earnings and dividend record of the Company during previous years.'[93]

A desire to develop and preserve an active market for shares also created an incentive to pay dividends. Blockholders will often think of the stock market as a source of liquidity rather than capital, taking their companies public to create and retain the option to sell their shares on reasonable terms as and when they

---

[88] Franklin Allen and Roni Michaely, 'Payout Policy' in George M. Constandines, Milton Harris and Rene M. Stulz (eds), *Handbook of the Economics of Finance*, vol.1A, (2003), 337, 384.

[89] Zohar Goshen, 'Shareholder Dividend Options', (1995) 104 Yale Law Journal 881, 881, 889.

[90] T.A. Hamilton Baynes, *Share Valuations* (1966), 84, quoting a pamphlet entitled 'Standard Boardroom Practice'.

[91] Pt VI; Ch. Eight, Pt I, I.; R.F. Henderson, 'Capital Issues' in Brian Tew and R.F. Henderson (eds), *Studies in Company Finance: A Symposium on the Economic Analysis and Interpretation of British Company Accounts* (1959), 64, 69–70.

[92] Armstrong, *supra* n. 61, 129.

[93] Samuel, *supra* n. 86, 145–46.

want or need to.[94] This has been the case in the UK as much as elsewhere, with public offerings often having been carried out to allow incumbent shareholders to cash out at least partially (Part V).

Blockholders eager to preserve the stock market as an exit option will want there to be buyers for the company's equity at an acceptable price as and when a partial unwinding of the block occurs. Investors, in turn, will be looking for evidence the shares will deliver sufficiently good value over time to make a purchase worthwhile. Dividends can then come into play. Once a company has gone public, a blockholder's continuing interest in liquidity can serve as an implicit bond to investors that the company will be run so that dividends will continue to be paid at a rate sufficient to maintain an active market in the company's shares. As Boyce has said of large shipping firms operating in the late 19th and early 20th centuries, 'Founders also influenced the size of dividend payments, and hence the amount of reinvested profits—and their own personal income—subject to constraints imposed by the need to retain outside investors and maintain share values.'[95] Samuel observed similarly in 1933 that directors not only paid dividends to retain the option to raise fresh capital but also to retain the popularity of the company with shareholders.[96] Correspondingly, so long as blockholders were concerned about taking advantage of the liquidity the stock market provided, the onus was on them to ensure that their company continued to pay dividends to outside investors.

The possibility of a 'hostile' takeover bid reinforced the incentives for companies to pay dividends. If those running a company are worried about an unwelcome takeover offer, a defensive tactic they can adopt is to woo investors with higher dividends.[97] Hostile bids first began to take place in the UK in the 1950s and there was much speculation at that point that fears of unwelcome takeover offers induced UK public companies to liberalize their dividend policies.[98] Empirical tests for correlations between the level of acquisition activity and aggregate dividend payouts by UK public companies have yielded mixed results.[99] Nevertheless, at least in companies where blockholders failed to own a sufficiently large percentage of shares to veto an unwelcome takeover offer, the

[94] Helwege, Pirinsky and Stulz, *supra* n. 1, 997; Armando Gomes, 'Going Public Without Governance: Managerial Reputation Effects', (2000) 55 Journal of Finance 615, 634.

[95] Boyce, *supra* n. 13, 250.

[96] Samuel, *supra* n. 86, 145. See also A.R. English, *Financial Problems of the Family Company* (1958), 62–63.

[97] See Daniel R. Fischel, 'The Law and Economics of Dividend Policy', (1981) 67 Virginia Law Review 699, 713–14; Mervyn A. King, 'Corporate Taxation and Dividend Behaviour: A Comment', (1971) 38 Review of Economic Studies 377, 379.

[98] Ch. Ten, Pt IV.E.1; William Mennell, *Takeover: The Growth of Monopoly in Britain, 1951–61* (1962), 34, 131; H.B. Rose, *The Economic Background to Investment* (1960), 231.

[99] Compare King, *supra* n. 97 (finding, using data from 1950–71, a statistically significant link) with Steven Bank, Brian Cheffins and Marc Goergen, 'Dividends and Politics', (2004), ECGI working paper, No. 24/2004 (finding, using data from 1949–2002, takeover activity was inversely correlated with distributions to shareholders).

threat of a hostile takeover bid likely provided an incentive for companies to pay, and perhaps increase, dividend payments.

The upshot is that dividend policy provided a potential catalyst for block-holder exit in the UK. Athough there was discretion to do otherwise, the vast majority of public companies paid sizeable dividends and most shied away from cutting the payout level from the previous year. The cash distributions being made would have reduced the scope for blockholders to skim or squander profits their companies were generating. With private benefits of control thus curtailed, exit would have become a more attractive option.

X. Politics

Politically oriented theories that seek to explain why patterns of corporate ownership and control differ across borders do not fit the British case well because throughout much of the 20th century share ownership became increasingly diffuse as UK politics swung to the left (Chapter Two, Part V). Nevertheless, politics very likely shaped the configuration of ownership and control to some degree. Ironically, given theories advanced in the comparative corporate govern-ance literature, Britain's left-wing politics were in a couple of ways a catalyst for blockholder exit.

Nationalization constituted one channel through which left-wing politics fostered ownership dispersion, admittedly in a circumscribed range of industries. In 1918, the Labour Party adopted a new constitution that incorporated the goal of bringing industry under state ownership.[100] After being elected to office in 1945, Labour followed through by nationalizing coal mining (1946), civil avi-ation (1946), transport (e.g., railways and road haulage) (1947), electricity (1948) and gas (1948). Though nationalization was not exclusively an ideological exer-cise, the Labour Party's programme had a distinct left-wing agenda since state acquisition of key industrial assets fostered the redistribution of economic power and the promotion of governmental economic planning.[101]

Those operating firms in the industries affected by nationalization were forced to exit, either by compulsory acquisition of assets (coal and road haulage) or by way of an exchange of shares for government bonds (railways, electricity, gas and steel, both the 1951 version and a 1967 re-nationalization).[102] When the Conservatives returned to office in 1951, they retained nearly all nationalized

---

[100] Cento Veljanovski, *Selling the State: Privatisation in Britain* (1987), 54. The relevant provi-sion was deleted in the 1990s.

[101] James Foreman-Peck and Robert Millward, *Public and Private Ownership of British Industry, 1820–1990* (1994), 276.

[102] Norman Chester, *The Nationalisation of British Industry 1945–51* (1975), 240, 262–63, 272–76, 284–85, 295–99, 310–12; William Ashworth, *The State in Business: 1945 to the mid-1980s* (1991), 20, 32.

undertakings, with the only major reversals being steel and road haulage.[103] Still, the move to public ownership ultimately served as a precursor to dispersed private ownership in various industries affected since the Conservatives during the 1980s and 1990s carried out an ambitious privatization programme, labelled by one observer as 'the largest transfer of power and property since the dissolution of the monasteries under Henry VIII'.[104]

Under the Conservative privatization programme, the predominant method of selling nationalized assets was the offer of shares to the general public, and privatization became closely associated with the goal of encouraging wider share ownership by individuals.[105] The earliest privatizations (e.g., British Aerospace, Cable and Wireless and British Telecom) left the state as a major shareholder temporarily, as less than half the shares were sold in the first instance.[106] Generally, however, privatized companies had highly diffuse ownership structures, with blockholding being discouraged because the government typically retained a right to veto the accumulation of a voting stake exceeding 15 per cent.[107] As the ceilings on block ownership were lifted, acquisition activity eliminated diffuse share ownership in various privatized companies.[108] Still, the nationalization programme carried out by a left-wing Labour government ironically cleared the decks for diffusion of share ownership during the 1980s and 1990s.

Taxation constituted a second channel through which left-wing politics fostered blockholder exit. We've already seen that wartime taxes on corporate profits likely encouraged blockholders to contemplate selling out (Part V), but taxes can help to prompt the unwinding of control in other ways. When income tax rates are high, individuals tend to increase their consumption of leisure, which for blockholders implies winding down their involvement with the firms they dominate. Also, if taxes cut deeply into the after-tax dividend income blockholders receive from their company, they may will be inclined to exit to benefit from risk-spreading. The incentive to exit will be reinforced if, as compared with direct ownership of shares, there are tax advantages to be derived by investing in other asset classes or by transferring assets to others prior to death.

Throughout much of the 20th century, UK tax policy was configured in a way that brought each of these factors into play.[109] Briefly, taxes on high incomes— which blockholders typically would have earned—were hiked substantially

[103] Ashworth, *supra* n. 102, 26–29; Trevor May, *An Economic and Social History of Britain* (1987), 393–94.

[104] Quoted in Peter Saunders and Colin Harris, *Privatization and Popular Capitalism* (1994), 6.

[105] Veljanovski, *supra* n. 100, 93, 101; Saunders and Harris, *supra* n. 104, 25–26.

[106] Hobson, *supra* n. 10, 415.

[107] *Ibid.*, 415–16; Veljanovski, *supra* n. 100, 104–5, 127–28; Michael Ian Cragg and Alexander J. Dyck, 'Management Control and Privatization in the United Kingdom', (1999) 30 Rand Journal of Economics 475, 480.

[108] Hobson, *supra* n. 10, 419–21.

[109] See Ch. Eight, Pt I.F, Ch. Nine, Pt III.B, Ch. Ten, Pt I.D, Pt III.

during World War I, were only reduced moderately during the interwar years, were increased dramatically during World War II and remained high until Margaret Thatcher's Conservative government reversed the trend in the 1980s. Dividends were taxed either at the same high rate as 'earned' employment income or sometimes at higher rates. For blockholders seeking 'tax friendly' investment alternatives, there were various choices, including exile to gentler tax climes and, for those continuing to reside in Britain, life insurance-based savings schemes, contributions to pension plans, land and works of art. Also, blockholders faced with estate taxes—charges imposed on assets transferred on or shortly prior to death—could largely side-step these by unwinding their ownership stake, at least partially, and investing the proceeds in a trust under which family members would be the beneficiaries. The tax regime also was 'exit-friendly' in that capital gains arising from the sale of a block of shares were untaxed until the mid-1960s and were subsequently taxed at a considerably lower rate than the pre-Thatcher top marginal rates of income tax.

The tax policies that provided incentives for blockholders to exit were motivated partly by a desire to increase revenue, most acutely in response to the financial pressures associated with fighting World War I and World War II. Politics, however, was also part of the story. With the budget of 1909, which introduced for the first time 'progressive' graduation of income tax, the notion that taxation policy should have a redistributional element first began to take hold among politicians in power.[110] The income tax increases introduced during World War I were imposed primarily on those with high incomes. The policy was retained in substantial measure thereafter, with the government consciously opting, to paraphrase Winston Churchill (Chancellor of the Exchequer in the mid-1920s), to leave the very rich 'stranded on the peaks of taxation to which they have been carried by the flood'.[111]

The politics of taxation were most explicit during the Labour administration of 1945–51. Hugh Dalton, Chancellor of the Exchequer, said in Parliament in 1946 that an 'awakened and war scarred generation' was demanding the government to 'close from both ends the gap which separates the standard of living of the great mass of our fellow citizens from that of a small privileged minority'.[112] Labour followed up with a tax-driven attack on 'socially functionless wealth', with primary targets being high incomes, 'unearned' (i.e., investment) income and inherited estates.[113]

---

[110] Ch. Two, Pt V; Martin Daunton, *Wealth and Welfare: An Economic and Social History of Britain 1851–1951* (2007), 472–73 (stressing, though, that the redistributional impulse was weak).

[111] Martin Daunton, *Just Taxes: The Politics of Taxation in Britain, 1914–1979* (2002), 133.

[112] Quoted in G.Z. Fijalkowsi-Bereday, 'The Equalizing Effect of Death Duties', (1950) 2 Oxford Economic Papers (N.S.), 176, 177.

[113] Daunton, *supra* n. 111, 198–99; Richard Whiting, *The Labour Party and Taxation: Party Identity and Political Purpose in Twentieth-Century Britain* (2000), 67–75.

When the Conservatives came to power in 1951, their tax policy was characterized by 'continual movement and little change', due largely to fears that full-scale dismantling of Labour's reforms would have adverse political consequences.[114] Under Labour, which returned to power in 1964 and governed for all but four years up to 1979, the promotion of equality through taxation was again promoted as sound public policy and the tax treatment of income and inherited wealth correspondingly remained highly 'progressive' in orientation.[115] Since promotion of a more egalitarian distribution of wealth and income stands out as a hallmark of left-wing politics, and since the tax policies that encouraged blockholders to exit were at least partly redistributional in orientation, taxation, as with nationalization, constitutes a channel through which left-wing politics fostered ownership dispersion.

There is an additional political dimension to factor in when accounting for the incentives of blockholders to exit, this being the scope they are likely to have to generate advantages for their companies through political means. There are trade-offs between dispersed and concentrated ownership, which means neither offers decisive advantages (Chapter Two, Part I). Politics, however, can tilt the balance in favour of blockholders in certain instances and where such an advantage exists, it should act as a partial brake on the unwinding of control blocks.[116]

Politically well-connected companies can derive various benefits from the influence they wield, such as special tax breaks, relaxed regulatory oversight, preferential status in competition for government contracts and favourable treatment by government-owned business enterprises (e.g. banks or utilities).[117] As compared with widely held firms, companies with blockholders may have the edge in the political arena. While managers of publicly quoted companies engaging in lobbying on behalf of their firm will likely only draw upon the company's resources in so doing, dominant shareholders in major companies should be wealthy enough to up the ante by making side-payments personally.[118] Also, politicians might well think of dominant shareholders as more reliable partners.[119] Widely held companies regularly experience managerial turnover, whereas exit by dominant shareholders will occur only exceptionally. Politicians and bureaucrats will prefer to strike deals with people well-positioned to reciprocate, so, all else being equal, companies with concentrated ownership structures should be able to lobby more effectively for subsidies and other forms of preferential treatment.

[114] Daunton, *supra* n. 111, 233, 277; Whiting, *supra* n. 113, 121.

[115] Daunton, *supra* n. 111, 308, 337; Whiting, *supra* n. 113, 159–61, 241–43.

[116] Marianne Bertrand, Paras Mehta and Sendhil Mullainathan, 'Ferreting Out Tunneling: An Application to Indian Business Groups', (2002) 117 Quarterly Journal of Economics 121, 146–47.

[117] Bertrand and Schoar, *supra* n. 32, 77; Mara Faccio, 'Politically Connected Firms', (2006) 96 American Economic Review 369, 369.

[118] Morck, Wolfenzon and Yeung, *supra* n. 45, 39; Randall Morck and Bernard Yeung, 'Family Control and the Rent-Seeking Society', (2004) 28 Entrepreneurship Theory and Practice 391, 401.

[119] Morck, Wolfenzon and Yeung *supra* n. 45, 39–40; Morck and Yeung, *supra* n. 118, 400–3.

While theoretically bargaining for political rents could provide incentives for blockholders to retain control, in Britain any political advantages blockholders would have had would have been negligible because involvement in politics has not been a particularly promising means of promoting business interests, narrowly defined. There has always been an overlap between business and politics in the UK, with a substantial percentage of Members of Parliament having had a background in manufacturing, trade and commerce.[120] On the other hand, businessmen have not entered politics as a means to get rich. Instead, they have typically generated the wealth first and then sought election to Parliament to consolidate their social success. According to an empirical study of 'elite' political families, as defined by multi-generational Parliamentary representation between 1400 and 1914, 'It is hard to think of an example of someone who made a fortune through electoral influence.'[121]

More generally, the business community has not dominated the British political scene in a way that suggests businessmen have been well situated to secure firm-specific favours. While the business community has been well represented, Parliament has in fact been dominated by party organizations fully prepared to resist pressure from business on issues on which the party has a strong point of view.[122] A 20th-century shift in political influence further reduced the likelihood of blockholders using politics to deliver significant advantages to their companies. The civil service's authority grew progressively at the expense of Parliament's, as 'real decisions' on government policy were increasingly reached behind closed doors by full-time public officials in consultation with cabinet ministers.[123] Civil servants were conscious that meeting with and listening to representatives of the business community could facilitate the process of governing.[124] Nevertheless, as civil servants were eager to preserve their neutrality, they were generally unreceptive to direct pleading in favour of particular firms.[125]

Even to the extent that political rent-seeking was an option in Britain, it is doubtful whether companies with dominant shareholders had a potent advantage over widely held firms. While in family-owned firms aptitude for political networking would simply be fortuitous, in managerially dominated firms this was a criterion that could be and was used in the hiring of top managers.[126]

---

[120] Robert C. Hall, 'Representation of Big Business in the House of Commons', (1938) 2 Public Opinion Quarterly 473; John Turner, 'The Politics of Business' in John Turner (ed.), *Businessmen and Politics: Studies of Business Activity in British Politics, 1900–1945* (1984), 1, 3–4, 15; E.A. Wasson, 'The Penetration of New Wealth into the English Governing Class from the Middle Ages to the First World War', (1998) 51 Economic History Review 25, 39–41.

[121] Wasson, *supra* n. 120, 31.

[122] Turner, *supra* n. 120, 4.

[123] Harold Perkin, *The Rise of Professional Society: England Since 1880* (1989), 327–28.

[124] Wyn Grant and David Marsh, *The Confederation of British Industry* (1977), 109–13; John Fidler, *The British Business Elite: Its Attitudes to Class, Status and Power* (1981), 247.

[125] Fidler, *supra* n. 124, 235.

[126] Michael Useem, *The Inner Circle: Large Corporations and the Rise of Business Political Activity in the US and the UK* (1984), 191.

As the head offices of Britain's largest companies gravitated to London through the 20th century, senior executives of widely held firms had ample opportunity to interact and build up working relationships with key public officials.[127] Also, to the extent widely held companies were concerned about operating at a political disadvantage, they could level the playing field somewhat by appointing a Member of Parliament as a non-executive director, a practice companies adopted quite often.[128] For instance, with railway companies, 19th-century pioneers of dispersed share ownership, there were in the mid-1850s 81 railway directors sitting in Parliament.[129] In sum, even if businesses in the UK could benefit from political connections, blockholders lacked any sort of decisive lobbying edge that would have provided an incentive for them to refrain from exiting.

*   *   *

A willingness on the part of blockholders to unwind their holdings is a necessary condition for a divorce of ownership and control. This chapter has therefore explained why blockholders might have looked for a way out, focusing on concerns about diversification, an apparent lack of prestige associated with business success, potentially problematic generational transitions and various market and regulatory factors limiting the scope to extract private benefits of control. Still, while ownership can only separate from control if blockholders are prepared to exit, there is another side to the story. A dominant block of shares can only be unwound or diluted if the blockholder relies on the stock market to liquidate some of his stake, the company sells additional equity to outside investors or there is a once-and-for-all transformation of the ownership structure by way of a merger. Each scenario hinges crucially on there being demand for the shares (or underlying assets) available for sale. This is something that cannot be taken for granted, given that potential buyers of shares will quite reasonably have concerns about informational asymmetries and the competence and honesty of those running the company. Chapter Four correspondingly identifies the key variables likely to influence investors as they decide whether to buy shares in publicly traded companies.

---

[127] *Ibid.*, 184–92; Anthony Sampson, *The New Anatomy of Britain* (1971), 577–78.

[128] 'The Directors' Liability Bill', Economist, June 28, 1890, 821 (reporting that 26 MPs held six or more directorships of public companies); A. Roth, 'The Business Background of M.P.s', in John Urry and John Wakeford (eds), *Power in Britain: Sociological Readings* (1973), 131, (reporting that as of 1966, the total number of directorships held by MPs, past and present, was 693, whereas in 324 instances an MP had been a chairman of the board or managing director).

[129] 'Railway Morals and Railway Policy', (1854) 100 Edinburgh Review 420, 436.

FOUR

The 'Buy Side'

Chapter Three provided an overview of the 'sell side' of the separation of owner-ship and control, outlining why those owning large stakes in companies might be inclined to accept dilution of their holdings or exit completely. In this chapter, the focus shifts to the 'buy side'. The analysis has two core elements, one of which is to explain why investors in the UK were willing to purchase shares in companies in sufficient volume for control to unwind and the other being to account for why new shareholders refrained from taking a 'hands on' role. To put these matters into context, Part I of the chapter identifies who bought shares in publicly traded UK companies.

I. Who Bought Shares?

There are many potential types of buyers of shares in publicly traded companies. Individual investors, sometimes referred to as 'private' or 'retail' investors, can buy and sell equities for their own personal account. Companies themselves can be shareholders in publicly traded firms, whether as a means of exercising strategic control, fortifying a business alliance or simply as an investment. Governments can own shares in publicly traded companies as well; the UK government had a majority holding in Anglo-Persian Oil (later British Petroleum) until the 1950s and a large minority stake through the 1980s.[1]

There are also various examples of investment intermediaries that buy shares to deploy available capital. Pension funds investing on behalf of pension bene-ficiaries constitute one example. Insurance companies are another. From an investment perspective, life insurance is far more important than 'general' busi-ness (e.g. insurance against accidents and property damage) because the hasty liquidation of investments to meet outstanding commitments associated with

---

[1] R.W. Ferrier, *The History of the British Petroleum Company, vol. I: The Developing Years 1901–1932* (1982), 210, 324; *Times 1000: Leading Companies in Britain and Overseas, 1972–73* (1972), 53; *Times 1000: Leading Companies in Britain and Overseas, 1982–83* (1982), 72.

general insurance is much less likely.[2] Life insurers invest on behalf of policy-holders who buy 'with profits' policies that offer bonuses based on investment returns (Chapter Ten, Part III) and, when organized as companies, invest spare capital in assets in order to improve returns offered to their own shareholders.

Investment trusts and unit trusts, collective investment vehicles akin to what are referred to as mutual funds in the United States, also stand out as potential investors in shares. An investment trust is in fact not a trust at all but a company whose business is to invest money in equities, corporate debt and government bonds on behalf of those owning the investment trust's securities.[3] A unit trust performs the same function but is a fully fledged trust divided into fractions, or units, with an independent trustee holding the assets and a management company making the investment decisions and creating or liquidating units as required to meet public demand.[4]

Individuals investing on their own behalf dominated the buy side in the UK until after World War II (Chapter Six, Part III.A.1; Chapter Eight, Part II.A). Thereafter, the composition of the buy side changed radically as retail investors became persistent net sellers of equity (Chapter Ten, Part I.E). Even a privatization campaign carried out by the Conservative government that increased the number of shareholders from less than three million in 1984 to over 10 million in 1990 made no dent in the trend because most of the new buyers only took up shares in a single privatized company.[5] The total number of individuals owning shares approached 15 million after building society and insurance company de-mutualizations in the 1990s but then slipped back to 11 million, with a large proportion of retail investors continuing to own shares in a single company.[6]

Pension funds and insurance companies largely filled the gap, holding between them more than 40 per cent of the shares of UK public companies by 1981 (Figure I). Investment trusts and unit trusts were of lesser importance but still qualified as the third and fourth legs of the institutional market (Chapter Ten, Part II). Pension funds and insurance companies continued to dominate the buy side thereafter but began winding down their holdings in public companies in the mid-1990s.

---

[2] Committee on the Working of the Monetary System (Lord Radcliffe, Chairman), *Report*, Cmnd. 827 (1959), 82; Committee to Review the Functioning of Financial Institutions (Chairman, Sir Harold Wilson) (hereinafter Wilson Committee), *Report*, Cmnd. 7937 (1980), 46–47.

[3] 'The Financial Institutions', (1965) 5 Bank of England Quarterly Bulletin 132, 138; Dominic Hobson, *The National Wealth: Who Gets What in Britain* (1999), 1035.

[4] C.O. Merriman, *Mutual Funds and Unit Trusts: A Global View* (1965), 13; L.C.B. Gower, J.B. Cronin, A.J. Easson and Lord Wedderburn of Charlton, *The Principles of Modern Company Law*, 4th edn (1979), 266–67.

[5] CBI Wider Share Ownership Task Force, *A Nation of Shareholders* (1990), 14–15.

[6] 'How the BT-led Revolution Fizzled Out', Financial Times, December 4/5, 2004; 'Privatisation Dream Goes Up in Smoke', Telegraph, October 29, 2006.

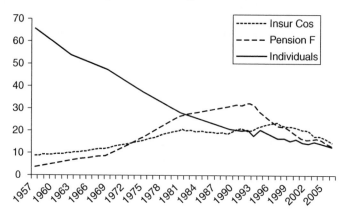

Figure I: Percentage of shares of UK public companies owned by insurance companies, pension funds and individuals, 1957–2006

Sources: Compiled using data from Moyle (cited n. 7) (1957); National Statistics Online, (cited n. 7), (1963–2006), series DEYG, DEYH, DEYI.[7]

Foreign investors, bit players as investors in British companies up to the close of the 20th century, stepped forward as key buyers of shares as pension funds and insurance companies retreated.[8] What have been categorized as 'other financial institutions' for the purpose of statistical studies of the identity of owners of shares of publicly traded companies did likewise (Figure II). Between 1963 and 1989 the percentage of shares owned by 'other financial institutions' was inflated because investment trusts were lumped into this category. Otherwise, their ownership stake was tiny, in part because prominent merchant banks generally refrained from investing directly in shares.[9] However, over the past few years investment vehicles not qualifying as 'authorized' investment trusts under tax law (e.g. hedge funds) and brokers and dealers investing on their account have stepped forward as significant buyers of shares.[10]

---

[7] John Moyle, 'The Pattern of Ordinary Share Ownership', (1971), University of Cambridge Department of Applied Economics Occasional Paper #31, 18; National Statistics Online database: <http://www.statistics.gov.uk/statbase/TSDtables1.asp> (last visited March 19, 2008).

[8] On the position up to and including the interwar years, see 'The Ownership of British Industrial Capital—III', *Economist*, January 1, 1927, 12; 'American Buying of British Securities—I', *Economist*, June 8, 1929, 1292. On recent developments, see Ch. Eleven, Pt I.

[9] Jim Slater, *Return to Go: My Autobiography* (1977), 120. To give an accurate impression, for Figure II the 1957 percentages for investment trusts and other financial institutions have been combined for 1958 even though there was no data for that year.

[10] Ch. Two, Pt IV (tax rules for investment trusts); Ch. Eleven, Pt II (rise of hedge funds etc.); 'Who Owns UK plc as Sell-Off Continues?', The Scotsman, August 24, 2004; Matthew Lynn, 'Power in Different Hands as City of London Goes Global', The Business, August 11, 2007.

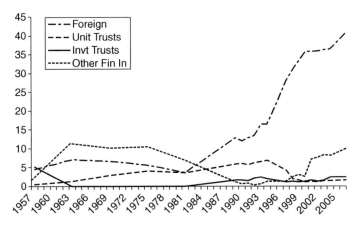

Figure II: Percentage of shares of UK public companies owned by foreign investors, investment trusts, unit trusts and 'other' financial institutions, 1957–2006

Sources: Compiled using data from Moyle, *supra* n. 7 (1957); National Statistics Online, *supra* n. 7, (1963–2006), series DEYF, DEYJ, DEYK, DEYL

Other categories of investors in shares of publicly traded companies that stand out plausibly as significant buyers of shares have been of marginal importance in practice. The government is one example. Public sector owner- ship of business assets has a lengthy pedigree in Britain, with the origins of a state-owned postal service being traceable back to the 17th century and with the country's telegraph network having been nationalized in 1868, followed by the telephone network (1912) and wireless broadcasting (1922).[11] However, Anglo-Persian Oil/British Petroleum aside, it has been rare for the UK gov- ernment to hold stakes in otherwise privately owned companies. For instance, public sector ownership of publicly traded shares never exceeded 4 per cent from 1957 onwards and has been negligible (i.e., 0.1 per cent or below) since the mid-1990s (Figure III).

It has also been rare for the state to own sizeable blocks of shares in individual companies. The fact the government was not identified as a block- holder in any of the 'very large' industrial and commercial companies for which Florence provided a detailed breakdown of share ownership as of 1936 and 1951 illustrates the point.[12] The earliest privatizations in the Conservative government's 1980s privatization campaign did sometimes leave the state as a

[11] James Foreman-Peck and Robert Millward, *Public and Private Ownership of British Industry 1820–1990* (1994), 48, 66–67, 98, 105, 265–66; <http://www.lightstraw.co.uk/ate/main/ telecom1.html> (last visited January 3, 2008).

[12] P. Sargant Florence, *Ownership, Control and Success of Large Companies: An Analysis of English Industrial Structure and Policy 1936–1951* (1961), 196–217.

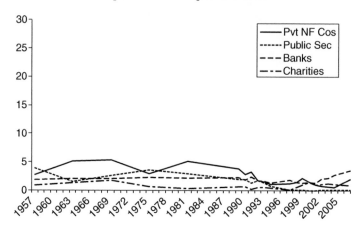

Figure III: Percentage of shares of UK public companies owned by other investors, 1957–2006

Sources: Compiled using data from Moyle, *supra* n. 7, (1957); National Statistics Online, *supra* n. 7, (1963–2006), series DEYM, DEYN, DEYO, DEYP.

major shareholder temporarily (Chapter Three, Part X). However, according to data from the late 1990s, the state owned 20 per cent or more of the voting shares in only 0.08 per cent of UK publicly traded companies, compared with 5 per cent in France, 6 per cent in Germany and over 10 per cent in Finland, Italy and Norway.[13]

Deposit-taking banks have also been minor players as investors in shares. From 1957 through the remainder of the 20th century they never owned more than 2 per cent of the outstanding equity in UK public companies (Figure III). The historical pattern was similar. Though the small private 'country banks' that dominated banking outside London during the late 18th and early 19th centuries sometimes held stakes in large companies concerned with public works (e.g. canals, docks and turnpikes), concerns about the sudden withdrawal of deposits deterred them from tying up capital in potentially illiquid shares.[14] During the late 19th and early 20th centuries a wave of bank amalgamations prompted the replacement of local private banks with large nationwide banking operations (Chapter Seven, Part V). Larger pools of deposits and a greater spread of assets theoretically could have prompted these bigger banks to hold more diversified asset portfolios, including ordinary shares.[15] However, liquidity crises prompting bank failures in 1847, 1857, 1866 and 1878 heightened awareness among

---

[13] Mara Faccio and Larry H.P. Lang, 'The Ultimate Ownership of Western European Corporations', (2002) 65 Journal of Financial Economics 365, 379.

[14] T.S. Ashton, *The Industrial Revolution*, rev. edn (1968), 85; Michael Collins, *Banks and Industrial Finance in Britain 1800–1939* (1991), 29.

[15] Collins, *supra* n. 14, 38.

bankers of how vulnerable their businesses were to a loss of public confidence and reinforced the idea that maintaining a very high proportion of liquid assets was a key means of retaining the faith of customers.[16] Conservative attitudes towards investment became further entrenched as banking practice became increasingly professionalized, with leading bankers and other commentators extolling to the new wave of bank managers the importance of maintaining public confidence by holding a highly liquid asset portfolio.[17]

Beginning around 1890, bank investment in railway, municipal and foreign bonds increased and by the eve of World War I banks were beginning to take up debt securities issued by foreign and domestic private utilities. However, the prejudice against holding assets that could not be readily converted to cash militated against investment in equities and shares remained a major gap in bank portfolios.[18] Matters changed little through the interwar years and beyond. 'Good practice' in banking continued to emphasize the need to maintain liquidity to ensure public confidence and this was translated into 'the cardinal principle of British banking that the resources of the banks should not be locked up in semi-permanent industrial investments or participations'.[19]

What can be termed 'non-financial' companies—companies other than banks, insurance companies and investment trusts—constitute a final category of investor that theoretically could have been an important part of the buy side but in practice was not.[20] In some countries, corporate cross-ownership has been commonplace. The proportion of shares of German public companies held by non-financial companies rose from 18 per cent in 1950 to just over 40 per cent in 1960 and then hovered around that level until the late 1990s, when it fell to around 30 per cent.[21] In Japan, cross-ownership was a corporate

[16] P.L. Cottrell, 'The Domestic Commercial Banks and the City of London, 1870–1939' in Youssef Cassis (ed.), *Finance and Financiers in European History, 1880–1960* (1992), 39, 53; Forrest Capie and Michael Collins, *Have the Banks Failed British Industry? An Historical Survey of Bank/Industry Relations in Britain, 1870–1990* (1992), 41.

[17] Collins, *supra* n. 14, 39; Forrest Capie and Michael Collins, 'Deficient Suppliers? Commercial Banks in the United Kingdom, 1870–1980' in P.L. Cottrell, Alice Teichova and Takeshi Yuzawa (eds), *Finance in the Age of the Corporate Economy: The Third Anglo-Japanese Business History Conference* (1997), 164, 168–69.

[18] C.A.E. Goodhart, *The Business of Banking 1891–1914* (1986), 134–35; Lance E. Davis and Robert E. Gallman, *Evolving Financial Markets and International Capital Flows: Britain, the Americas and Australia* (2001), 120–21; Caroline Fohlin, 'Bank Securities Holdings and Industrial Finance Before World War I: Britain and Germany Compared', (1997) 26 Business and Economic History 463, 464, 472.

[19] 'Credit for Industry', Economist, May 12, 1934, 6; for general background, see Capie and Collins, *supra* n. 16, 50–52, 68–69; Edward Nevin and E.W. Davis, *The London Clearing Banks* (1970), 159.

[20] The National Statistics Online database, *supra* n. 7, uses the label 'private non-financial institutions' but other sources citing the same ownership percentages referred to 'non-financial companies', which is the terminology used here. See Moyle, *supra* n. 7, 18; Wilson Committee, *Progress Report on the Financing of Industry and Trade* (1977), 21.

[21] Caroline Fohlin, 'The History of Corporate Ownership and Control in Germany' in Randall K. Morck (ed.), *A History of Corporate Governance Around the World* (2005), 223, 232–33.

hallmark during the 20th century, both in the pyramidal *zaibatsu* of the 1920s and 1930s and the post-World War II inter-corporate networks referred to as *keiretsu*.[22]

The trend has been different in the UK. According to a study of ownership patterns in 30 major UK public companies as of 1941/42, less than 4 per cent of 'large holdings' (i.e., 10,000 shares or more) were in the hands of 'other companies' (i.e., other than insurance companies and investment trusts).[23] Of 98 industrial and commercial companies Florence categorized as 'very large' as of 1951, there were only 13 companies where the collective ownership stake of corporate shareholders exceeded 5 per cent.[24] Similarly, from 1957 to the present the percentage of shares held by non-financial companies in publicly traded UK companies has never exceeded 5 per cent (Figure III).

The absence of widespread corporate cross-ownership within the public company sector does not mean companies have forsaken share ownership *per se*. Due to amalgamation activity, the shares of many smaller 19th-century railway companies were owned by larger counterparts.[25] During the late 19th and early 20th centuries multi-firm horizontal mergers occurred in various industrial sectors, with a single holding company typically ending up owning the shares of enterprises that otherwise remained administratively autonomous (Chapter Six, Part II.B.4). Throughout much of the 20th century, it was commonplace for large business enterprises to have in place some form of corporate group structure, with the parent company being at the apex of a network of subsidiary companies in which the parent owned the shares.

What has generally been lacking in the UK is companies owning shares in other companies traded on the stock market. The standard pattern in corporate groups has been for the parent to own all of the ordinary shares of the relevant subsidiaries, meaning complex corporate pyramids have been rare.[26] An important reason for this has been that when companies have carried out acquisitions they have usually bought up all or virtually all of the shares, rather than leaving a stake in the hands of the public, a practice that has been quite common in other countries.[27]

---

[22] Randall K. Morck and Masao Nakamura, 'A Frog in a Well Knows Nothing of the Ocean: A History of Corporate Ownership in Japan' in Morck, *supra* n. 21, 367.

[23] Hargreaves Parkinson, *Ownership of Industry* (1951), 46.

[24] Calculated from Florence, *supra* n. 12, 196–217.

[25] François Crouzet, *The Victorian Economy* (1982), 293.

[26] M. Compton and E.H. Bott, *British Industry: Its Changing Structure in Peace and War* (1940), 48 (practice of owning all shares); 'The Odeon Affair', Economist, December 20, 1947, 1012, 1014 (indicating there were 'few parallels in British company finance' to the complex corporate group controlled by J. Arthur Rank); Julian Franks, Colin Mayer and Stefano Rossi, 'Spending Less Time with the Family: The Decline of Family Ownership in the United Kingdom' in Morck, *supra* n. 21, 581, 582 (rarity of pyramids).

[27] Franks, Mayer and Rossi, *supra* n. 26, 606. On the UK practice, see Ch. Two, Pt III; Gower *et al, supra* n. 4, 693, 697; Deborah A. DeMott, 'Current Issues in Tender Offer Regulation: Lessons

There have been exceptions. According to the study of share ownership in 30 major companies as of 1941/42 that showed 'other companies' held only a tiny fraction of 'large holdings', among 'large holdings' the average stake of 'other companies' was the biggest due to 'a few extremely large holdings of tactical significance'.[28] Among Florence's 98 'very large' 1951 industrial and commercial companies there were six instances where a company other than a financial institution owned the largest stake and held 10 per cent or more of the shares.[29] Similarly, Goergen and Renneboog found in a study of ownership patterns in a random sample of 250 UK listed companies as of the late 1980s and early 1990s that industrial companies held far fewer large ownership stakes than directors, pension funds or insurance companies but owned bigger percentages of the equity on average when they were blockholders.[30]

There have also been some examples of complex corporate groups. Throughout much of the 20th century, Imperial Tobacco, which dominated the UK market for tobacco, owned a substantial minority stake in British American Tobacco (BAT), which focused on overseas markets. Each, in turn, had a substantial minority holding in the publicly traded Tobacco Securities Trust, which primarily held ownership stakes in quoted and unquoted subsidiaries of BAT.[31] Also, a business empire built up by Harley Drayton from the interwar years through to the 1960s 'was almost like a Japanese *keiretsu*'.[32] The focal point was 17 investment trusts run by the same clique of directors that collectively held sizeable stakes in numerous companies, including at various points prominent firms such as Consolidated Gold Fields, United Newspapers and British Electric Traction.[33] Subsequent chapters offer some additional analysis of corporate cross-ownership. Given, however, that individual investors and later financial intermediaries (other than banks) dominated the buy side, the remainder of this chapter will analyze matters from their perspective.

from the British' (1983) 58 New York University Law Review 945, 985–87. On takeover practice outside the UK, see Alexander Johnston, *The City Take-Over Code* (1980), 254.

[28] Parkinson, *supra* n. 23, 46–47.

[29] Calculated from Florence, *supra* n. 12, 196–217.

[30] Marc Goergen and Luc Renneboog, 'Strong Managers and Passive Institutional Investment in the UK' in Fabrizio Barca and Marco Becht (eds), *The Control of Corporate Europe* (2001), 259, 271–72.

[31] 'BAT and Imperial Group in Talks on Unscrambling Holdings', Times, October 24, 1973; 'BAT and Trust in Tidying-up Merger', Times, May 1, 1978; 'Imps' BAT Stake Goes for £11m', Times, June 24, 1980.

[32] 'Not Quite Establishment', Financial Times, October 26, 1991. See also Anthony Sampson, *The Anatomy of Britain* (1961), 394–97; 'Mr. Harley Drayton', Times, April 9, 1966; John Newlands, *Put Not Your Trust in Money* (1997), 313–14. On how the Harley Group was reorganized on more conventional lines after the mid-1960s, see 'Provisions, Divisions', Economist, March 19, 1977, 123; Tom Jackson, *The Origin and History of the Drayton Group* (1991), 152–54, 173–219.

[33] On British Electric Traction, see William Mennell, *Takeover: The Growth of Monopoly in Britain, 1951–61* (1962), 95.

II. Deterrents to Investment in Shares

A. In General

Dispersed share ownership hinges on securities markets being sufficiently well developed to accommodate the distribution of equity to and trading among outside investors. However, it is 'almost magical' that such markets exist, as '(i)nvestors pay enormous amounts of money for completely intangible rights, whose value depends entirely on the quality of information that the investors receive and on the honesty of other people, about whom the investors know almost nothing'.[34] A key potential obstacle to the growth of securities markets is that they can constitute a 'market for lemons', based on Akerlof's original example of sub-standard used cars.[35] Circumstances relating to public offerings of shares illustrate the problem.

A reasonable assumption is that among a cohort of public offerings some are destined to deliver excellent value for investors while others are fated to generate disappointing returns (the 'lemons'). To the extent that investors are unable to distinguish higher quality (more valuable) shares from lower quality (less valuable) shares, they will proceed on the assumption that all public offerings are of average quality. Higher quality shares will then sell at lower prices than they would if investors could detect the differences between what was on offer, which in turn will deter better companies from distributing equity to the public. To the extent lower quality shares in fact drive out higher quality equity, investors will be faced with the unappetizing prospect of investing only in the 'lemons'.

As and when companies successfully issue shares to the public, the problems are not over for investors. Since public offerings are irregular occurrences, most dealing in shares is 'secondary trading', meaning that the equity bought and sold has already been made available for sale to the public. Investors, when engaging in secondary trading, will decide whether to buy or sell on the basis of the current price and their assessment of the company's track record and future prospects. The departure point for any such evaluation will be information available at the time. As Berle and Means said in their famous 1932 book *The Modern Corporation and Private Property* about 'a respectable open market appraisal' of corporate securities, 'Appraisal necessarily turns on information. If the open market view was to approximate a judgment of worth, it became essential that some material for such judgment should be provided.'[36] Corporate insiders inevitably know more about

---

[34] Bernard Black, 'The Core Institutions that Support Strong Securities Markets', (2000) 55 Business Lawyer 1565, 1565.

[35] G.A. Akerlof, 'The Market for 'Lemons': Quality, Uncertainty and the Market Mechanism', (1970) 84 Quarterly Journal of Economics 488. For background, see Brian R. Cheffins, *Company Law: Theory, Structure and Operation* (1997), 130–31, 165–66.

[36] Adolf A. Berle and Gardiner C. Means, *The Modern Corporation & Private Property* (1997, originally published 1932), 259.

a company's future prospects than outside shareholders.[37] Nevertheless, investors, once they have bought shares, want a steady flow of information about the companies in question so they can assess whether, given current market prices, to buy more shares, sell what they own or do nothing.

The instinct of those operating companies will generally be the opposite, as they will prefer to keep key corporate intelligence confidential. Fears of rivals gaining access to information on sales figures and other commercially sensitive data will make companies cautious about disclosure, as might concerns about employees using profit numbers to fortify demands for higher pay. Hence, the founding family of textile manufacturers J. & P. Coats, the largest industrial company in Britain as of 1912 and the third largest in the world, regarded the company's shareholders 'as necessary inconveniences, to be as much as possible ignored'.[38]

Companies will not always be secretive. For instance, companies carrying out public offerings have incentives to disclose news about their affairs.[39] If a company makes available information which signals credibly to the market that its prospects are promising, investors will pay more for the equity. This, in turn, will lower the company's financing costs, and, depending on the nature of the public offering and the ownership stake of the company's operators, provide them with a handsome pay-off for shares they sell.

Companies with publicly traded shares that are not in the midst of a public offering also have incentives to engage in at least some voluntary periodic disclosure. Their concern will be that investors will rush wholesale for the exits in the event of a complete information blackout. For instance, while companies in the UK were not compelled to prepare and file a balance sheet publicly until 1908, it was standard practice before this for publicly traded companies to publicize the relevant information.[40] By 1902, companies seeking to have their shares quoted on the London Stock Exchange had to have provisions in their articles of association requiring distribution of the annual balance sheet to shareholders (Chapter Three, Part VIII), but there was market pressure already pushing in the same direction. As a text on investment published the same year disclosure became compulsory under company law said 'It is true that some few companies do not publish their balance sheets. But these 'silent' companies, as they are termed in the city (London's financial district), are so few in number, and they

---

[37] Andrei Shleifer, *Inefficient Markets: An Introduction to Behavioral Finance* (2000), 6–7 (indicating corporate insiders typically earn superior risk-adjusted returns when dealing in their own company's shares).

[38] Dong-Woon Kim, 'From a Family Partnership to a Corporate Company: J. & P. Coats, Thread Manufacturers', (1994) 25 Textile History 185, 195; on Coats' size see Ch. Six, Pt I.

[39] Cheffins, *supra* n. 35, 165–66.

[40] Ch. Six, Pt III.B.2; R.A. Bryer, 'The Late Nineteenth-Century Revolution in Financial Reporting: Accounting for the Rise of Investor or Managerial Capitalism', (1993) 18 Accounting, Organizations and Society 649, 677.

are so obviously to be avoided by the reasonably prudent investor, that they are scarcely worth mentioning.'[41]

Though companies have incentives to engage in voluntary corporate disclosure, there will remain a tendency to be secretive and suppress bad news in the hope that adverse trends correct themselves. For instance, the Rio Tinto Company, a British-based firm which ultimately experienced great success developing mining properties in Spain, issued a prospectus in support of its 1872 initial public offering that 'deliberately understated the degree of risk incurred by the venture, simultaneously over-stating the likely return on capital invested'.[42] Likewise, a study of company promotion in the late 19th and early 20th centuries said, 'Drafting the prospectus was a work of art and often owed more to the novelist than the lawyer.'[43] The experience with UK breweries in this era illustrates the point: 'The quality of information provided for potential investors in prospectuses was often poor. Clearly vendors and promoters were not going to print details that might damage the success of an issue; instead they made use of various devices: none of these were actually fraudulent, but, by the omission of certain details, some probably helped to mislead an optimistic public.'[44] Matters apparently had not improved much by the interwar years. Samuel said in 1933, 'the cold and canny prospectus was, if not the invariable practice, at least quite a prevalent feature in the financial life of the City of London' and cited an estimate by 'shrewd observers that only from 25 per cent to 30 per cent of prospectuses attain the maximum standard of practicable frankness'.[45]

The investing public, or at least more sophisticated elements of it, has long been aware of the tendency of voluntary disclosure to be biased in favour of good news. An 1898 article entitled 'How to Scan a Prospectus' said, 'In dealing with a prospectus we are always justified in assuming there is a reason for the suppression of any relevant information that is withheld.'[46] The *Economist* echoed the sentiment in 1933, saying 'A prospectus, naturally, must always be a species of shop-window, and *caveat emptor* must apply to all goods displayed therein.'[47] Investors, given their awareness of the tendencies of companies, will discount, at least partially, whatever those disseminating information voluntarily say on behalf of a company. Thus, even taking into account voluntary

---

[41] Henry Lowenfeld, *Investment Practically Considered* (1908), 407, see also at 422.

[42] Charles E. Harvey, *The Rio Tinto Company: An Economic History of a Leading International Mining Concern 1873–1954* (1981), 11, 28–32, 45, 103.

[43] John Armstrong, 'The Rise and Fall of the Company Promoter and the Financing of British Industry', in Jean-Jacques van Helten and Youssef Cassis (eds), *Capitalism in a Mature Economy: Financial Institutions, Capital Exports and British Industry, 1870–1939* (1990), 115, 124.

[44] Katherine Watson, 'The New Issue Market as a Source of Finance for the UK Brewing and Iron and Steel Industries, 1870–1913' in Youssef Cassis, Gerald D. Feldman and Ulf Olsson (eds), *The Evolution of Financial Institutions and Markets in Twentieth-Century Europe* (1995), 209, 215.

[45] Horace B. Samuel, *Shareholders' Money: An Analysis of Certain Defects in Company Legislation with Proposals for Their Reform* (1933), 18, 52–53 (italics omitted).

[46] Hartley Withers, 'How to Scan a Prospectus', Cornhill Magazine, July 1897, 105, 107.

[47] 'Prospectus Law', Economist, February 11, 1933, 305.

corporate disclosure, investors can struggle to distinguish 'quality' companies from inferior counterparts, which again could mean a capital market dominated by 'lemons'.

Investing in shares in a publicly traded company is potentially problematic in other respects. In companies with a dominant shareholder, the blockholder might use the leverage the large ownership stake provides to extract private benefits of control at the expense of outside investors (Chapter Two, Part I). For instance, Hugh Matheson, founder of Rio Tinto, resisted suggestions the company should establish wet copper works in new markets and then soon used his knowledge of the process to involve his personal trading company in the erection of such works in France and the US.[48] As for companies that have dispersed shareholdings, executives can impose agency costs through incompetence, dishonesty or ill-advised 'empire-building' (e.g. carrying out mergers that leave executives in charge of a larger business operation but destroy shareholder value in the process) (Chapter One, Part I). As an 1877 pamphlet bemoaning the 'Railway Autocracy' of directors in large railway companies asked, '[W]hat is to hinder them from administering railway affairs as they please... appointing their relatives and friends to lucrative positions over the heads of competent and experienced men, and transforming the higher organisation into a family party, intent mainly on making itself comfortable?'[49]

When executives in widely held companies get sufficiently far enough out of line, corrective action (e.g. replacing them) should yield aggregate net benefits for shareholders. Nevertheless, various practical considerations deter shareholder activism in companies (Part III). The danger correspondingly exists that dishonest, incompetent or otherwise wayward executives will continue to run their companies largely unhindered.

Given all of the potential hazards associated with owning shares in publicly traded companies, why is there ever demand for this form of investment? Company law provides one potential answer. The 'law matters' thesis presupposes investors will buy equity in sufficient volume to permit ownership to separate from control once legal rules offer suitable protection against information asymmetries and potential misconduct by those controlling companies. With disclosures concerning public offerings of shares, even a 19th-century investor who was frequently induced to put chase equity had the right at common law to repudiate the contract or recover damages from those responsible.[50] As Chapter Two discussed, however, until well into the 20th century UK company law generally provided only scant protection to outside investors, at least by contemporary standards. As a result, other (or at least additional) explanations are required to

[48] Harvey, *supra* n. 42, 188.

[49] Edwin Phillips, *The Railway Autocracy: A Question of Vital Importance to Shareholders and Directors, Hitherto Overlooked* (1877), 17.

[50] F. Gore-Browne and W. Jordan, *Handy Book on the Formation, Management and Winding Up of Joint Stock Companies*, 24th edn (1902), 116–21.

account for why UK investors bought shares in sufficient volume for ownership to separate from control.

B. Britain's Economic Decline

Even if outside investors are aware that they lack full information and realize they are vulnerable to being taken advantage of, they might be willing to buy shares because the prospective returns are so good the potential upside outweighs the downside. A 1996 *Financial Times* article captured the logic involved while explaining why investors should buy shares in 'emerging' markets, saying, 'In an economy growing at three times the rate of a Western one, even losing half your profits growth to insiders still leaves you with half as much again as the growth you could get at home. A diversified buy-and-hold strategy in developing markets might expose you to the pitfalls of the local markets, but it will also expose you to the growth. Over the long run, the growth is likely to win out…'[51] Those who 'bought into' this argument would have been sorely disappointed, since the East Asia financial crisis of 1997 prompted a stock market meltdown and a prolonged economic slowdown throughout South East Asia. More generally, recent econometric studies based on historical data cast doubt on the received wisdom that stock market returns are correlated with economic growth.[52] Still, investors acting without the benefit of this form of statistical hindsight would have plausibly surmised that economic success was a 'buy signal' and invested in shares in what otherwise were less than optimal conditions. The experience in the United States illustrates the point.

Large-scale demand for shares in US industrial corporations first emerged in a merger wave occurring in the late 19th and early 20th centuries, lulled somewhat and returned with additional vigour in the 1920s.[53] This all occurred during a period when the legal environment was uninviting for outside investors. Federal securities legislation was not enacted until the mid-1930s and protections for shareholders under state corporate laws were being eroded due to a 'race' ultimately won by Delaware to make available flexible legislation that would be attractive to corporate managers.[54] On the other hand, in the midst of a wave of technological and managerial innovation, successful US companies were emerging as dominant global players in a range of growth industries. The prospect of capturing some of the upside with these dynamic industrial

[51] 'Keeping it all in the Family', Financial Times, May 4/5, 1996.

[52] Jay R. Ritter, 'Economic Growth and Equity Returns', (2005) 13 Pacific-Basin Finance Journal 489; 'LBS Puts No Stock in Economic Growth', Financial Times, March 10, 2008 (discussing research of Elroy Dimson, Paul Marsh and Mike Staunton).

[53] Brian R. Cheffins, 'Mergers and Corporate Ownership Structure: The United States and Germany at the Turn of the 20th Century', (2003) 51 American Journal of Comparative Law 473, 489–92.

[54] Brian R. Cheffins, 'Law as Bedrock: The Foundations of an Economy Dominated by Widely Held Public Companies', (2003) 23 Oxford Journal of Legal Studies 1, 8–10.

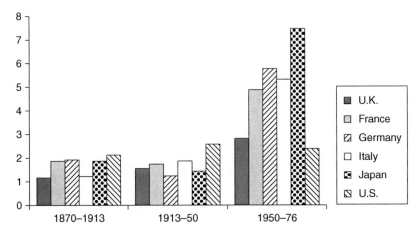

Figure IV: GDP per man-hour, 1870–1976 (average annual compound growth rates)
Source: Compiled using data from Gamble, *supra* n. 56, 17.

enterprises was a powerful lure to share investment and the resulting demand for shares provided a congenial environment for a divorce between ownership and control in numerous large firms.[55]

While investors plausibly will overlook the disadvantages of being outside shareholders to capture broader economic benefits, market trends in Britain were not conducive to this sort of investment as ownership split from control in its major companies. As one study of British 'decline' has characterized matters, from the late 19th century to the late 20th century, the British economy went 'from a position of commanding superiority to a condition where some observers began to speculate whether Britain could be the first developed capitalist economy to become underdeveloped'.[56] In terms of material wealth, the British people grew steadily better off during this period. However, in comparison to other major industrialized countries, the UK was sliding backwards, implying that investors considering whether to buy shares would not have been enticed by the prospect of strong economic growth (Figures IV, V).

The British public were acutely aware of what was going on. As the 19th century drew to a close, there was widespread alarm about Germany and the US eclipsing Britain economically. The fear was that British industry was falling behind due to technological backwardness, failure to exploit adequately

[55] Jonathan Barron Baskin & Paul J. Miranti, Jr, *A History of Corporate Finance* (1997), 170–76; Mary O'Sullivan, *Contests for Corporate Control: Corporate Governance and Economic Performance in the United States and Germany* (2000), 75–77.

[56] Andrew Gamble, *Britain in Decline: Economic Policy, Political Strategy and the British State*, 3rd edn (1990), 12.

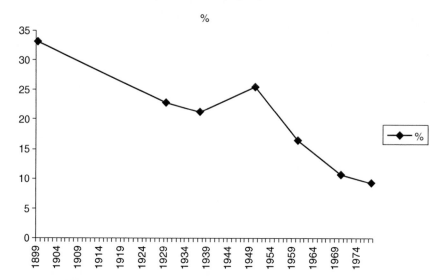

Figure V: UK share in the value of world exports of manufacturing, 1899–1977 (percentages)
Source: Compiled using data from Gamble, *supra* n. 56, 17.

available economies of scale and a basic lack of effort.[57] As the *Daily Mail* newspaper said in 1901, 'At the risk of being thought unpatriotic this journal has persistently...called attention to the numberless blows administered to our commercial supremacy, chiefly by reason of the superior education methods and strenuous life of the American and German.'[58] Such pessimism in turn likely dampened at least to some degree demand for shares in industrial and commercial companies (Chapter Six, Part III.B.1). The *Statist* magazine condemned the trend in 1912:

During recent years there have been many home investments yielding high returns and attaining an improved position every year which have been sadly neglected, because it was foolishly supposed that Great Britain was a played-out country and on the down-grade. The Preference and Ordinary shares of conservatively managed industrial companies operating at home give very handsome returns, and are meantime little appreciated. Most investors are so lazy that they will not trouble to examine things themselves.[59]

In the decades that followed, the UK experienced periods of recovery and advance. Britain's frequent economic reversals nevertheless regularly prompted fresh anxiety about the 'British disease', an economic illness ostensibly rooted

---

[57] *Ibid.*; G.C. Allen, *The British Disease*, Hobart Paper No. 67 (1976), 31.
[58] May 5, 1901, quoted in Gamble, *supra* n. 56, 12–13.
[59] June 29, 1912, quoted in David Kynaston, *The City of London, Volume II: Golden Years* 1890–1914 (1995), 470.

in British culture and attitudes.[60] Pervasive concern about economic 'decline' would have meant that optimism about national economic prospects or the dynamism of British industry would have done little to fortify demand for equity in UK public companies.

Below par management was often cited as an important source of Britain's relative economic decline.[61] To the extent this charge was correct, it is particularly surprising there was sufficient investor demand for shares for ownership to separate from control. From an economic perspective, the potential benefits to be derived from the delegation of decision-making to suitably talented executives help to explain why companies with diffuse share ownership are well positioned to thrive in a competitive economy. As Fama and Jensen have said, '[S]ince decision skills are not a necessary consequence of wealth or willingness to bear risk, the specialization of decision management and residual risk bearing allowed by unrestricted common stock enhances the adaptability of a complex organization to changes in the economic environment.'[62] Or, according to Allen and Gale, 'The major concern for the shareholder is...whether the manager has "the right stuff", the entrepreneurial skills and talents to achieve success for the firm.'[63] To the extent this is correct, and to the extent the quality of British management was sub-optimal, it seems paradoxical that there was sufficient demand for shares among investors for ownership to separate from control.

The thesis that British companies have been hampered by amateurish management has been an enduring one. In 1902 the individuals running Britain's large firms were being condemned on the grounds that they were 'behind the times' and 'plagued by stolid conservatism'.[64] Exactly a hundred years later, the UK's trade and industry secretary observed that 'the average (British manager) lags well behind the best (in the world)'.[65] A study using data from 1960 that showed US subsidiary companies operating in the UK earned higher average profits than similarly situated British competitors offered empirical confirmation of the hypothesis of inferior British management.[66] Sampson explained why the findings reflected poorly on UK executives: 'The managers, confronted with Britain's poor performance, can blame many other factors—the government, the universities, and above all the workers. But the embarrassing fact remains that

---

[60] Gamble, *supra* n. 56, xvii.

[61] Robin Marris, 'Britain's Relative Decline: A Reply to Stephen Blank', in Isaac Kramnick (ed.), *Is Britain Dying? Perspectives on the Current Crisis* (1979), 89, 93; John F. Wilson, *British Business History, 1720–1994* (1995), 115–19, 153–54, 157, 218–23.

[62] Eugene F. Fama and Michael C. Jensen, 'Separation of Ownership and Control', (1983) 26 Journal of Law and Economics 301, 312.

[63] Franklin Allen and Douglas Gale, 'Corporate Governance and Competition' in Xavier Vives (ed.), *Corporate Governance: Theoretical and Empirical Perspectives* (2000), 23, 63.

[64] D.H. Aldcroft, 'The Entrepreneur and the British Economy, 1870–1914', (1964) 17 Economic History Review (N.S.) 113, 114.

[65] Quoted in 'No Simple Cure of UK Management', Financial Times, October 23, 2002.

[66] John H. Dunning, *Studies in International Investment* (1970), 345–400.

American companies in Britain...can produce far better results with the same kind of workers, the same universities, and the same government.'[67]

Such verdicts should have been discouraging to investors contemplating whether to buy shares because they were often counselled to take managerial quality into account before proceeding. As early as 1863, investors were being warned that since companies legislation 'will afford little security to Members (shareholders) of a company' decisions about whether to buy shares 'will (as heretofore) consist of their ascertaining that the Directors and Officers managing its affairs are honest and able men'.[68] A 1909 text targeting investors said of public offerings of shares, 'The directors and managers of the new enterprises are the persons who will create success or failure; hence they should be most carefully considered, not only from the point of respectability, responsibility and social standing, but principally as to their business ability and former business success.'[69] A 1932 book on investment said of two industrial leaders of the period, '[M]en of this calibre will always carry the investment market with them. The demand for first-class industrial brains is greater than the supply, and such men will always attract capital...'[70] The *Times* struck a similar chord in 1963:

Investing in equities is an art, not a science. To master this art, a securities analyst, or an investment manager, must be intelligent concerning the personality of corporate management...The investor is concerned with the quality and competence of the human element which directs and guides the utilization of the physical properties, and establishes or alters the corporation's efforts to profit from an often changing environment.[71]

Why, if investors were counselled to take managerial quality into account when buying shares and UK executives were subject to frequent criticism, was there sufficient demand for shares for ownership to become divorced from control? One possibility is that, even if investors were aware that managerial quality was theoretically important, gauging the capabilities of those running publicly traded companies was too difficult to do to have any sort of decisive influence. For instance, Naish suggested in 1962 if an investor was satisfied 'that a particular management ha(d) an intangible "edge" over its competitors (the company was) likely to be worth following' but conceded the challenge was to make the choice in advance, since once management had 'proved itself...the profits tell the story...and the stock exchange valuation will already discount the further prospects materially'.[72]

---

[67] Anthony Sampson, *The New Anatomy of Britain* (1971), 588.

[68] Quoted in James B. Jefferys, *Business Organisation in Great Britain 1856–1914* (1977), 402.

[69] Henry Lowenfeld, *All About...Investment* (1909), 189.

[70] Hargreaves Parkinson, *Scientific Investment* (1932), 149; see also at 216–17, 221.

[71] 'Judging the Quality of Management', Times, April 16, 1963.

[72] P.J. Naish, *The Complete Guide to Personal Investment* (1962), 125–26. See also T.G. Goff, *Theory and Practice of Investment* (1971), 159–60; 'Velvet Glove Without an Iron Hand', Times, November 17, 1972.

Also, critics' indictments of managerial quality might have been overdone. Defenders of British industrialists of the late Victorian era claim these businessmen generally behaved rationally given the constraints under which they were operating and cite a lack of hard evidence establishing that whatever managerial deficiencies existed in Britain were more pervasive than they were in other countries.[73] Likewise, representatives of the insurance industry explaining in 1977 why insurance companies rarely took an active role in the affairs of companies in which they owned shares partly justified the stance taken on the basis 'by and large British industry is reasonably well managed'.[74] Finally, even if there was unease among investors concerning the capabilities of UK corporate executives, there were other factors that came into play that fortified the buy side sufficiently to permit ownership to split from control. We will now consider various examples.

III. Factors Underpinning Demand for Shares

A. Capital Available for Investment

Unless and until there is a sizeable quantity of capital available for investment, there cannot be sustained demand for shares. On this count, Britain had a solid foundation at an early stage. England suffered plague, war, fire and default on government debt in the 30 years following the restoration of the monarchy in 1660. Nevertheless, there was a great advance in prosperity, with national wealth increasing by a quarter, savings doubling and investment expanding in overseas trade, shipping, building and the agricultural sector.[75] One by-product was the emergence of a still small but expanding cadre of investors based largely in London and composed primarily of the burgeoning merchant and professional classes. They provided a key source of demand as Britain experienced its first wave of company promotions in the 1690s.[76]

Throughout the 18th century the standard of living of rank-and-file workers in Britain was too marginal to accommodate widespread personal saving, let alone investment in shares.[77] On the other hand, with the country generally enjoying stable political and social conditions, technological innovations improving agricultural productivity and overseas trade flourishing, there was significant growth in the number of people with spare capital inclined to save and invest

---

[73] See, for example, S.B. Saul, *The Myth of the Great Depression, 1873–1896*, 2nd edn (1985), 46–47, 67–70.

[74] Wilson Committee, *Evidence on the Financing of Industry and Trade*, vol. 3 (1978), 71, 111.

[75] John Carswell, *The South Sea Bubble*, rev. edn (1993), 7; François Crouzet, 'Editor's Introduction' in François Crouzet (ed.), *Capital Formation in the Industrial Revolution* (1972), 1, 40.

[76] Ch. Five, Pt I; Richard Dale, *The First Crash: Lessons from the South Sea Bubble* (2004), 30.

[77] Phyllis Deane, *The First Industrial Revolution*, 2nd edn (1979), 175.

rather than simply spend or hoard gold or silver.[78] Aggregate savings in turn were ample to provide in theory financial backing for even the largest business enterprise. For instance, investors bought up £440 million of debt instruments issued by the UK government between 1793 and 1815, while the total capital accumulated to construct Britain's canal system in the 70 years following 1750 was only in the neighbourhood of £20 million.[79]

Due to profits accumulating from the industrial revolution and a decline in the proportion of national income absorbed by taxes, the volume of capital available for investment continued to expand during the first half of the 19th century.[80] As the 19th century drew to a close, the rate of growth in general industrial production was declining. Nevertheless, due to falling commodity prices and a declining burden of government debt, the growth in national wealth was sustained (£4.1 billion in 1840 versus £9.4 billion in 1890).[81] An expansion of the investor base occurred in tandem. The number of individuals holding investment securities grew from around 17,000 in the 18th century to about 275,000 in the early 19th century.[82] The total remained much the same through to the 1870s but then increased to around one million by 1914 (Chapter Five, Part V.B.4; Chapter Six, Part III.A.2). Hence, in the UK there was at quite an early stage ample capital available for investment and numerous potential buyers of shares of companies.

B. The Benefits of a Good Business Reputation

An ample supply of capital available for investment is a necessary condition for the buy side for shares to be activated but it is not a sufficient condition. Even if there is the financial wherewithal to invest it cannot be taken for granted that corporate equity will be a popular choice, given that potential purchasers of shares are at an informational disadvantage and run the risk of exploitation or mismanagement at the hands of those controlling companies. In the British context, corporate and securities law traditionally did little to address such concerns since the protection offered was thin by current standards (Chapter Two, Part II.B). There were, however, various factors that operated as at least partial substitutes in the sense they offered reassurance to investors contemplating whether to buy shares in UK companies. One of these was that those who exploited outside investors risked forfeiting commercially valuable reputations they had built up for being able, honest and reliable.

Blockholders who are well known and well regarded by investors have a crucial potential advantage should they seek access to capital markets. A desire

[78] Ashton, *supra* n. 14, 6–7; Peter Mathias, *The First Industrial Nation: An Economic History of Britain 1700–1914*, 2nd edn (1983), 131.

[79] Crouzet, *supra* n. 75, 40–41; see also Mathias, *supra* n. 78, 132.

[80] George W. Edwards, *The Evolution of Financial Capitalism* (1938), 19–20.

[81] *Ibid.*, 34–35, 39.   [82] *Ibid.*, 20.

to acquire and retain a reputation for reliability and business acumen in turn provides an incentive 'to do right' by otherwise vulnerable outside shareholders. The contrasting experiences of two leading shipping owners of the late 19th and early 20th centuries illustrate the point. In the early 1880s, Donald Currie arranged to carry out a public offering of Castle Line and Union Steamship Co. shares at a grossly overvalued price, given the underlying assets and future prospects. While shipping historians have described the terms as 'quite astonishing' and 'one of the more cynical financial exercises perpetrated by a shipowner', the public offering was a success due in part to Currie's personal reputation, forged by building a successful shipping business founded on UK–South Africa mail contracts.[83] Matters had changed by the late 1890s. At that point Currie wanted to find capital to acquire new ships but issuing new shares was not an option because of Castle Line and Union's meagre dividends and because of his tarnished reputation, which was further besmirched by generous commissions Castle Line and Union paid to a company Currie owned.[84]

John Ellerman, a ship owner and financier who went on to become Britain's richest man, fared considerably better.[85] Ellerman, as chairman of Leyland & Co., sold the company in 1901 to International Mercantile Marine, a huge shipping combine formed by J.P. Morgan, the famous American financier. Ellerman secured personally better terms than other shipowners who sold out to Morgan and ensured that outside shareholders in Leyland received those same terms. He emerged with great prestige, and was able to rely on many of Leyland's former shareholders to invest in his future projects, beginning with Ellerman's new shipping concern, the London, Liverpool and Ocean Shipping Co.

Screening by financial intermediaries, reinforced by reputational factors, can also improve the 'comfort level' of investors. Firms that orchestrate public offerings of shares have an incentive to monitor matters carefully since being known as reliable will give them an edge over the competition in securing future business.[86] Over time, those advising UK companies carried out increasingly meaningful 'quality control'. The process, however, took some time to develop.

Prior to World War I, the first-class merchant banks in London's financial district (known as 'the City') had significant reputational capital to protect but they had little appetite for the public offerings that domestic industrial and commercial companies were beginning to carry out. The organization of public offerings in shares of such enterprises was therefore left to 'company promoters' whose standards of integrity varied widely (Chapter Six, Part III.B.4). The protection

---

[83] Gordon Boyce, *Information, Mediation and Institutional Development: The Rise of Large-Scale Enterprise in British Shipping, 1870–1919* (1995), 88–89; Andrew Porter, *Victorian Shipping, Business and Imperial Policy: Donald Currie, the Castle Line and Southern Africa* (1986), 102–8.

[84] Boyce, *supra* n. 83, 93.

[85] *Ibid.*, 103–4, 295; James Taylor, *Ellermans: A Wealth of Shipping* (1976), 17–27.

[86] Black, *supra* n. 34, 1574–75.

financial intermediaries organizing public offerings of shares afforded to outside investors then increased markedly (Chapter Eight, Part II.B.4). By the 1960s, leading merchant banks (e.g. Kleinwort Benson, Baring Brothers and Lazard Brothers) dominated the new-issue market for corporate equity, together with some well-respected issuing houses that gained a foothold by focusing closely on domestic companies as their clients.[87] Eager to build up and protect their reputational capital, these financial intermediaries had powerful incentives to vet carefully the public offerings they were sponsoring.[88]

There were occasions when a reputable merchant bank or issuing house, being keen to obtain profitable business, would let standards slip.[89] Nevertheless, in the great majority of instances, considerable care was taken, with firms attentively checking the credentials of their client companies, addressing accounting and legal matters that could alarm investors and ensuring that share issuances were otherwise made on 'proper terms'.[90] A witness giving evidence in 1977 before a government committee investigating the functioning of financial institutions said of those organizing public offerings of shares:

> They have to judge the market but they know that if they do not get the terms right they push us too far and we are going to say 'We are sorry, you really have got this wrong', and they cannot get it off the ground. In practice, they get it right. It is their job to judge their most favourable terms to their industrial clients on which there is a reasonable chance of the market taking this up, and in practice that works very well.[91]

Hence, despite a hesitant start, reputational dynamics helped to ensure public offerings of shares were subject to 'stringent scrutiny' that helped to ensure what was on offer was 'sound financially as well as legally'.[92]

C. Stock Exchange Regulation

At the same time as financial intermediaries were beginning to provide meaningful quality control in the UK's equity markets, the London Stock Exchange, the dominant stock market in Britain, stepped up its regulation of companies and in so doing likely fortified demand for shares by otherwise apprehensive investors. The scope existed for regulation to occur because the Stock Exchange had to give the go-ahead before dealing in shares issued by a company could

---

[87] Norman Macrae, *The London Capital Market: Its Structure, Strains and Management* (1955), 155; A.J. Merrett, M. Howe and G.D. Newbould, *Equity Issues and the London Capital Market* (1967), 20–28; Gerald B. Newbould, *Business Finance* (1970), 50.

[88] F.W. Paish, 'The London New Issue Market', (1951) 18 Economica 1, 8; F.E. Armstrong, *The Book of the Stock Exchange*, 5th edn (1957), 168.

[89] Richard Spiegelberg, *The City: Power Without Accountability* (1973), 89–90.

[90] Merrett, Howe and Newbould, *supra* n. 87, 17–18; Paish, *supra* n. 88, 8; W.A. Thomas, *The Finance of British Industry 1918–1976* (1978), 178.

[91] Wilson Committee, *supra* n. 74, 113 (evidence of R.H. Peet).

[92] L.C.B. Gower, 'Some Contrasts Between British and American Corporation Law', (1956) 69 Harvard Law Review 1369, 1382.

commence.[93] In addition, once a company's shares were being traded, the Stock Exchange could use the threat to suspend dealing to apply pressure. As the *Economist* said in 1966, 'The Stock Exchange's forte is its power to make rules to which public companies must conform, on pain of losing their quotation. For goading the respectable 99 per cent of public companies along the path towards more enlightened behaviour it is fine.'[94]

The rigour with which the London Stock Exchange exercised its leverage increased over time. Prior to World War I, the Stock Exchange obliged companies seeking a quotation to adopt articles of association that provided shareholders with various protections not afforded by companies legislation. The prevailing orthodoxy nevertheless was '*caveat emptor*' (Chapter Three, Part VIII).

The Stock Exchange stepped up its regulatory efforts after a number of companies that relied on a popular means of launching trading, namely foregoing obtaining a full quotation and securing 'permission to deal', failed dismally in the late 1920s (Chapter Eight, Part II.B.3). A committee set up by the British government to study the reform of company law remarked in its 1945 report that officials at the Exchange 'exercised a beneficial influence in the matter of issues.'[95] By the late 1940s, when the rules for companies seeking permission to deal were combined with those governing quoted companies, Stock Exchange disclosure regulation was characterized as 'exhaustive and even inquisitorial'.[96]

In addition to regulating new issues of shares in a manner that would have been reassuring to investors, the London Stock Exchange carried out 'gap filling' with the regulation of periodic disclosure. The quality of corporate disclosure helps to underpin secondary trading in shares (Part II.A), which means, all else being equal, investor demand for corporate equity should increase with improvements to the sources of information on companies with publicly traded shares. Corporate and securities legislation, by compelling periodic disclosure of financial data by companies with publicly traded shares, can help to supply investors with a continuous flow of information about particular firms. As was the case more generally, however, UK company law was not 'investor-friendly' on this count until well into the 20th century (Chapter Ten, Part IV.D). The London Stock Exchange was somewhat more ambitious.

By virtue of policies adopted during the first decade of the 20th century, companies quoted on the Exchange were obliged to circulate to shareholders a balance sheet and a profit loss account before companies legislation required disclosure of either (Chapter Three, Part VIII). Reforms taking effect in 1948 and 1967 toughened up company law rules concerning periodic disclosure in

---

[93] *Report of the Committee on Company Law Amendment* (Mr Justice Cohen, chair) (hereinafter Cohen Report), Cmd. 6659 (1945), 14.

[94] 'New Watchdogs—or a Longer Leash?', Economist, September 10, 1966, 1037, 1037. See also Wilson Committee, *supra* n. 74, 246.

[95] Cohen Report, *supra* n. 93, 14.

[96] 'S.E. Quotation Rules', Times, May 6, 1947; see further Ch. Eight, Pt II.B.3.

various ways but the legislative requirements only ever concentrated on annual dissemination of audited balance sheets and financial statements.[97] The Stock Exchange went further in various respects. By the late 1940s companies seeking to have shares quoted for trading had to undertake to inform the Exchange of annual net profit figures as soon as these became available, even if the numbers were provisional or subject to audit. In addition, quoted companies were required to keep the market up-to-date with key changes liable to affect their share price, as a quoted company had to promise to pass along to the Stock Exchange any information which shareholders would require to appraise properly the company's position or which was tending to establish a 'false market' in its shares (Chapter Nine, Part III.D). In the mid-1960s the London Stock Exchange introduced requirements that listed companies provide financial results quarterly or half-yearly, rather than simply annually as company law required (Chapter Ten, Part IV.D).

Stock exchange officials in the UK took the regulation of periodic disclosure seriously and tried to ensure those running companies would keep investors appraised of developments that might affect share prices.[98] The threat of a suspension in the dealing in a company's shares was generally sufficient to persuade management to issue explanatory circulars to shareholders when otherwise inexplicable share price fluctuations were occurring.[99] Hence, the London Stock Exchange's efforts to foster disclosure would have offered reassurance to investors who otherwise might have hesitated to buy shares due to gaps in the regulation of periodic disclosure.

D. Dividends

Since disclosure regulation was rudimentary in the UK, particularly prior to World War II, for outside investors information asymmetries were potentially daunting. How could investors acquaint themselves sufficiently with companies to feel 'comfortable' about investing in shares? The London Stock Exchange's efforts offered assistance, if somewhat belatedly. Another possibility was meeting with management. As the 20th century drew to a close, it was commonplace for public company executives to meet with company analysts, who offer advice to institutional clients on which shares to buy and sell, and with fund managers, who make investment decisions on behalf of institutional investors.[100] Such encounters were, however, a marked departure from past practice.

---

[97] Ch. Ten, Pt IV.D; Tom Hadden, *Company Law and Capitalism*, 2nd edn (1977), 305; J.H. Farrar, N. Furey and B. Hannigan, *Farrar's Company Law*, 2nd edn (1988), 440.

[98] 'Misleading Profits Statements', Economist, November 8, 1947, 775; L.C.B. Gower, *The Principles of Modern Company Law* (1954), 437; W.T.C. King, *The Stock Exchange*, 2nd edn (1955), 24–25.

[99] Slater, *supra* n. 9, 61; Wilson Committee, *supra* n. 74, 246.

[100] Cheffins, *supra* n. 35, 481.

The retail investors who dominated the 'buy side' of the stock market until the 1960s had little chance of meeting with those who ran companies. Cole said in 1935 of the 'ordinary investor', 'he is not in a position to acquire any real knowledge of the working of the businesses in which he invests money'.[101] More recently, it has been said of retail investors, 'Try as they might to join a tour round a plant or chat over tea with even one director, they are more likely to see a pig fly.'[102] Company analysts were little better off, at least to start with. A US export, they first became commonplace in Britain during the mid-1950s.[103] Their initial efforts were superficial by present-day standards, as companies denied them direct access to management and hard data was difficult to obtain due to the still undemanding disclosure requirements.[104]

The press also can help to allay investors' concerns about information asymmetries by collecting, selecting and repackaging news and data for readers. A vigilant media can also help to deter insider incompetence and dishonesty by 'naming and shaming' instances of mismanagement and corruption.[105] The 1957 edition of a book on the London Stock Exchange said optimistically of the press, 'The needs of investors and others who follow Stock Exchange price movements are well catered for ... Statistical charts and comparative tables are prepared, past records are examined and paraded, and prospects are diagnosed in a manner so thorough as to be almost embarrassing to directorates themselves.'[106] This might be a fair judgment today, given the extensive coverage of business news by the *Financial Times*, various major daily newspapers and weekly publications such as the *Economist*, the *Business* and the *Investors Chronicle*. However, when private investors dominated the stock market, the financial press generally failed to qualify as a sufficiently reliable source of information to boost demand for shares.

Up to the late 19th century, press coverage of companies was meagre other than for railways (Chapter Five, Part V.B.4). Financial news output proliferated at that point, but the coverage of publicly traded companies generally was insufficiently informative, impartial and timely to address the information asymmetries that existed (Chapter Six, Part III.B.5). Even by the 1950s, while pretty much every company executive felt it a duty to talk with the journalist writing as 'Lex' in the *Financial Times*, the column was viewed as one of the few sources in the press that was both reliable and could influence share prices.[107] Hence, while

[101] G.D.H. Cole, 'The Evolution of Joint Stock Enterprise' in G.D.H. Cole (ed.), *Studies in Capital and Investment* (1935), 51, 84.

[102] 'Always Asking for More', Investors Chronicle, January 14, 1994, 14.

[103] 'Investment Analysts' Society', Times, May 2, 1955; 'Investment Ties Across the Atlantic', Times, July 17, 1967.

[104] 'Investment Ties', *supra* n. 103; B. Mark Smith, *The Equity Culture: The Story of the Global Stock Market* (2003), 164.

[105] Alexander Dyck, Natalya Volchkova and Luigi Zingales, 'Corporate Governance Role of the Media: Evidence from Russia', (2007), unpublished working paper, 7–10.

[106] Armstrong, *supra* n. 88, 120–21.

[107] David Cohen, *Fear, Greed and Panic: The Psychology of the Stock Market* (2001), 105.

there were those who hoped 'the financial press might serve a useful purpose in guiding the inexperienced and unwary through the minefields of the City',[108] coverage in the print media generally did little to compensate for information asymmetries potentially affecting the market for shares.

Although regulation of periodic disclosure, meetings with management and the financial press at best belatedly provided outside investors with the sort of information flow likely to inspire confidence, dividend policy was a long-standing metric the investing public could and did rely upon to assess where matters stood with particular companies. To put matters into context, some general background on the 'signalling' properties of dividends is required.[109] In order for dividend policy to communicate information of value to investors, dividend payments ultimately must impose costs on firms that perform poorly in a way they do not for successful firms.[110] Otherwise, all companies lacking a promising future could adopt a generous dividend policy and deceive investors with impunity, thereby devaluing the dividend signal completely. In contrast, if those responsible for setting dividend policy know a penalty is associated with sending a false signal they will refrain from doing so, at least when the anticipated costs exceed the likely benefit.[111] Decisions to raise, cut or maintain dividend payments can then potentially provide valuable hints concerning a company's prospects.

It can in fact be 'dangerous to lie with dividends'.[112] A company that chooses and adheres to a generous dividend policy without the cash flow to back it up will over time have to resort to external finance to raise the cash required to continue to pay dividends to shareholders and underwrite day-to-day operations. This will be a tough sell due to the company's disappointing track record. If the efforts to raise fresh capital fail and the company continues to pay dividends at the same rate, the company could end up in serious financial difficulty in short order. Assuming lying with dividends is likely to result in this sort of fate, investors can infer sensibly from a company's decision to maintain its dividend payout that those setting dividend policy believe the company's prospects are good enough to support current cash distribution levels for some time to come.

By the same token, a sizeable dividend increase will plausibly constitute good news. Companies lacking a promising future can fairly readily mimic public

---

[108] Dilwyn Porter, ' "A Trusted Guide of the Investing Public": Harry Marks and the *Financial News* 1884–1916', (1986) 28 Business History 1, 12.

[109] For an overview, see Ronald C. Lease, Kose John, Avner Kalay, Uri Loewenstein and Oded H. Sarig, *Dividend Policy: Its Impact on Firm Value* (2000), 102–6.

[110] Jeremy Edwards, 'Does Dividend Policy Matter?', (1984) 5 Fiscal Studies 1, 12–13; Luis Correia da Silva, Marc Goergen and Luc Renneboog, *Dividend Policy and Corporate Governance* (2003), 38–39.

[111] Avner Kalay, 'Signaling, Information Content, and the Reluctance to Cut Dividends', (1980) 15 Journal of Financial and Quantitative Analysis 855.

[112] 'Upending Some Sacred Cows', Financial Times, June 3, 1985; on the theory involved, see Richard A. Brealey and Stewart C. Myers, *Principles of Corporate Finance*, 7th edn (2003), 438.

announcements offering optimistic forecasts.[113] In contrast, given the downside associated with the adoption of an untenably generous dividend policy, companies are unlikely to opt to boost their dividend payout substantially unless those in charge are confident that the company's future is sufficiently bright to sustain matters over time.[114] Conversely, a dividend cut can reasonably be taken to represent bad news, since the decision implies that those running a company are apprehensive about the future and thus are conserving cash to avoid a problematic effort to rely on capital markets to raise funds.[115] In sum, dividends can, as signalling theory implies, offer a valuable profit forecast.

This does not mean dividends are a perfect means of conveying information to investors. As 'A Shareholder' complained in a 1915 letter to the *Economist*, 'The dividend season is nearly over, and it may be interesting to ask, What principles, if any, do boards of directors act upon in recommending and declaring dividends?'[116] One source of potential misapprehension is that a dividend cut conceivably can be good rather than bad news, since the reduction could signify that a company is conserving capital to exploit valuable growth opportunities. Similarly, a dividend increase can be bad rather than good news, as the decision might be an implicit concession by management that their company lacks profitable new ventures to exploit and thus is disinvesting by returning money to shareholders.[117] Still, despite the potential ambiguities or contradictions of dividend action, the language may in fact be clear to those to whom it matters.[118]

There has been little explicit testing of the signalling theory of dividends in the British context, and the first direct evidence available, while supportive of the theory, is from the late 1980s (Chapter Ten, Part IV.D). Nevertheless, there is ample circumstantial evidence indicating that prior to this dividends were conveying information investors valued. For instance, decisions companies take concerning dividends are only apt to have a signalling effect when a change in policy is likely to cause a company to stand out from the crowd, which means cutting or suspending dividend payments tells investors little if a large proportion of publicly fraded companies do not pay dividends.[119] This would not have been

---

[113] Lease *et al*, supra n. 109, 98.

[114] Fischer Black, 'The Dividend Puzzle', (1976) 2 Journal of Portfolio Management 5, 6.

[115] Harry DeAngelo, Linda DeAngelo and Douglas J. Skinner, 'Dividends and Losses', (1992) 47 Journal of Finance 1837, 1838–39.

[116] 'The Principles Governing the Distribution of Dividends', Economist, March 27, 1915, 629.

[117] Victor Brudney, 'Dividends, Discretion, and Disclosure', (1980) 66 Virginia Law Review 85, 109–12; Frank Easterbrook, 'Two Agency-Cost Explanations of Dividends', (1984) 74 American Economic Review 650, 651–52.

[118] Brudney, *supra* n. 117, 113.

[119] G. Chowdhury and D.K. Miles, 'An Empirical Model of Companies' Debt and Dividend Decisions: Evidence from Company Accounts Data', (1987) Bank of England Discussion Paper, No. 28, 8; Yakov Amihud and Kefei Li, 'The Declining Information Content of Dividend Announcements and the Effect of Institutional Holdings', (2006) 41 Journal of Financial and Quantitative Analysis 637 (discussing how dividends lost some of their signaling effect in the US in the 1990s when large numbers of companies refrained from paying dividends).

a problem in Britain. In the UK the vast majority of publicly traded companies paid annual dividends and aimed to keep payouts stable (Chapter Three, Part IX; Chapter Eight, Part II.B.7). As a result, a company that reduced its dividend payment from the previous year or omitted to pay dividends entirely stood out as an exception from the norm, reinforcing the message dividend policy communicated to investors.

A strong link between dividend payouts and share prices further confirms dividends were conveying information valued by investors. There is empirical evidence from the late 19th and early 20th centuries indicating that dividends were closely correlated with share prices (Chapter Six, Part III.C.3). Matters apparently remained much the same following World War II. A study based on 1949–57 data derived from a sample of 165 companies quoted on the London Stock Exchange found the value of shares of UK public companies depended far more on dividend payments than reported earnings.[120] A 1960 text on investment described the price readjustment process: 'If a change in dividend has been fully anticipated, the news of the change will leave the price of the share concerned more or less unaltered . . . If an increase in dividends proves to have disappointed a sufficient number of investors, its announcement will be accompanied by a fall in share prices; and the failure of dividends declared to be reduced as much as had been feared will be accompanied by a rise.'[121]

In purely theoretical terms, dividends should not have been determining share prices. During the late 1950s and early 1960s Miller and Modigliani formulated a series of 'irrelevance' propositions that effectively launched financial economics as a body of knowledge.[122] In so doing they assumed full symmetry of information between managers and investors, no transaction costs and a series of other optimal market conditions. Under such circumstances, a company's share price should reflect fully the information 'in the market', meaning there will be nothing for a company's dividend policy to convey.[123] Investors, however, were in anything but this sort of ideal theoretical position in the UK as ownership separated from control, if only because of the lax regulation of periodic disclosure (Part III.C). As a result, dividends plausibly were a key determinant of share prices.

There is also anecdotal evidence extending far back indicating that shareholders have treated dividends as a key source of information when deciding whether or not to buy shares. During the mid-17th century the East India Company, which had been granted a monopoly by the Crown over trade to the

---

[120] G.R. Fisher, 'Some Factors Influencing Share Prices', (1961) 71 Economic Journal 121.

[121] H.B. Rose, *The Economic Background to Investment* (1960), 456.

[122] Franco Modigliani and Merton H. Miller, 'The Cost of Capital, Corporation Finance and the Theory of Investment', (1958) 48 American Economic Review 261; Merton Miller and Franco Modigliani, 'Dividend Policy, Growth and the Valuation of Shares', (1961) 34 Journal of Business 411. On the significance of Miller and Modigliani's work for the study of corporate finance, see Baskin and Miranti, *supra* n. 55, 12, 18.

[123] See Lease *et al*, *supra* n. 109, 25–27.

Indian sub-continent, shifted from distributing proceeds to investors as liquidations of individual voyages to declaring dividends from net earned income. Dividend declarations, in combination with auction results and the news of fleet arrivals, quickly became closely monitored signals of the company's financial strength.[124]

By the early 18th century, investors had grown accustomed to focusing on the dividend yield when attaching a value to shares.[125] Hence, when the share price of the South Sea Company fell dramatically in the late summer of 1720 after a spectacular rise, a history of this well-known 'bubble' wryly attributed the price decline to '(a)n unhealthy concentration on the real value of South Sea stock in terms of yield and prospects' making people aware the company was unlikely to generate profits sufficient to distribute promised dividends.[126] In the early 1860s, when there was a wave of public offerings by joint stock banks, promoters successfully fuelled demand for shares by pointing to healthy dividends banks had been delivering.[127] More than a century later the *Economist* suggested the 'preoccupation with (dividend) yields can reduce investment analysis to a simple question of whether a dividend is likely to be held or not'.[128]

Investors indeed could over-rely on dividends. A mid-1830s railway share frenzy was an early example.[129] Railway companies of that era promised to pay dividends that far exceeded returns available with alternative forms of investment, with 18 of 29 railway companies that obtained acts of incorporation in 1836 promising dividends of 10 per cent or higher annually. Investors apparently took these predictions at face value as they bought shares eagerly. One optimistic shareholder in the Eastern Counties Railway, which promised an outlandish dividend of 22 per cent, even said the company would meet its target or 'human calculations and expectations can no longer be depended upon'.[130] The optimism proved ill-founded, at least in the short-term. By 1839, the Eastern Counties Railway was paying dividends of merely 1 per cent and only a handful of railway companies were paying more than 4 per cent.

A tendency to over-rely on dividends cropped up for some time thereafter. The *Economist* observed in 1887, 'The shareholders look mainly to the dividend paid and care but little how it may have been earned.'[131] An 1898 article on company promoting similarly accused buyers of shares of going 'for big dividends, ignoring the risk that attends them'.[132] According to a 1930 guide on investment, 'In

---

[124] Baskin and Miranti, *supra* n. 55, 71, 77, 87.

[125] Dale, *supra* n. 76, 38.

[126] Carswell, *supra* n. 75, 147–48; see also Dale, *supra* n. 76, 113–17, 133.

[127] Lucy Newton and Philip L. Cottrell, 'Female Investors in the First English and Welsh Commercial Joint-Stock Banks' (2006) 16 Accounting, Business & Financial History 315, 331–33.

[128] 'To Cut or Not to Cut', Economist, June 9, 1979, 118.

[129] Harold Pollins, *Britain's Railways: An Industrial History* (1971), 27–30, 35.

[130] *Ibid.*, 27.

[131] Quoted in Jefferys, *supra* n. 68, 409.

[132] W.R. Lawson, 'Company Promoting "à La Mode"', National Review, September 1898, 103, 114.

former years, when industrial conditions were more prosperous, it was a fairly general practice to spread money over a number of the biggest and most famous businesses in the country, trusting almost blindly in their reputation and the fact that they had previously paid good dividends.'[133]

Investors were indeed regularly advised it was unwise to focus solely on dividend payouts when assessing companies. In the mid-19th century those contemplating buying railway shares were warned that promises of high dividends had to be assessed in relation to the balance sheets and traffic tables railway companies of the time were obliged to make public.[134] During the late 19th and early 20th centuries investors were counselled to assess the sustainability of dividends in light of conditions in the industry in question and each individual company's dividend track record and future prospects.[135]

Investors in fact did not simply buy and sell shares blindly on the basis of dividend yields. Even in the early 18th century it was standard investment practice to build in a discount to account for the uncertainty relating to the prospective flow of dividends.[136] Also, there were instances where investors simply did not believe that dividends promised were sustainable. The directors of the South Sea Company, eager to prop up the company's share price as investor scepticism began to build in the wake of the speculative frenzy surrounding its shares, announced in 1720 a dividend of 30 per cent accompanied by a promise of an annual dividend of 50 per cent. The plan failed. Instead,

'[T]he effect was not as Blunt (the South Sea Company's managing director) had intended. It was as if someone had thrown a bucketful of cold water over the investors, who had so blindly followed his charismatic financial leadership. They stood blinking and disbelieving at what they saw before them: a company whose proposed dividend implied such extraordinary annual profits that anyone with any sense could now see that it simply could not trade on the multimillion-pound scale which the offer to shareholders suggested . . .'[137]

Later investors also did not treat dividend payouts simply at face value. Bank share prices declined only modestly between 1883 and 1893 despite a significant drop in the dividend yield since investors re-rated the sector on the basis that bank shares were a very sound investment, a welcome change for an industry shaken by numerous bank failures over the previous few decades.[138] The

[133] F.W.H. Cauldwell, *A Practical Guide to Investment* (1930), 93.

[134] Alex Preda, 'The Rise of the Popular Investor: Financial Knowledge and Investing in England and France, 1840–1880', (2001) 42 Sociological Quarterly 205, 222.

[135] 'The Moral of the Coats' Collapse', Economist, November 20, 1897, 1625; Ellis T. Powell, *Mechanism of the City: An Analytical Survey of the Business Activities of the City* (1910), 160–61; Hartley Withers, *The Quicksands of the City and a Way Through for Investors* (1930), 68–69.

[136] Dale, *supra* n. 76, 38.

[137] Malcolm Balen, *A Very English Deceit: The Secret History of the South Sea Bubble and the First Great Financial Scandal* (2002), 147. See also Dale, *supra* n. 76, 136–37.

[138] Pt I above (bank failures); 'A Decade of Home Bank Dividends', Economist, July 14, 1894, 858 (bank shares as a sound investment).

fact that various cycle manufacturing companies were distributing substantial dividends could not forestall the end of a share price boom in 1897 as investors realized price cuts would be required to meet foreign competition.[139] Also, persistent investor unease about the future profitability of railways at the beginning of the 20th century meant that share prices fell 'out of all proportion to the diminution of which has occurred in dividends'.[140] Moreover, in the decades following World War II the importance of dividends as a signal diminished generally as other sources of information improved, primarily due to tighter disclosure regulation and company analysts obtaining better access to management (Chapter Ten, Part IV.D). Nevertheless, throughout the period when ownership separated from control, dividend policy generally acted as a feedback loop between companies and shareholders that gave investors who otherwise may have been apprehensive about buying shares a sufficiently acceptable informational foundation to proceed.

E. Investment Alternatives

It should now be evident that while there were dangers associated with being an outside investor in a publicly traded UK company, there were compensating factors that made shares a plausible investment option. Still, shares in domestic companies constituted only one choice among various alternatives. If other obvious investment options had outperformed equities, this would have dampened considerably demand for shares. In fact, shares generally did well, thus helping to fortify the buy side as ownership separated from control.

It can be difficult to make successful investment decisions about shares by reference to returns competing asset classes are delivering, a fact investors in Britain were sometimes warned about.[141] Nevertheless, in the UK there has over time been acute competition between shares and fixed income securities for investors' money,[142] with returns of fixed interest securities being an important benchmark against which shares have been measured. For instance, a 1720 pamphlet on investment in the South Sea Company said, 'The main principle on which the whole science of stock jobbing is built, viz. that the benefit of a dividend is always to be estimated according to the rate it bears to the price of the stock, because the purchaser is supposed to compare that rate with the profits he might make of money, if otherwise employed.'[143] A 1909 text on investment

---

[139] 'The Fall in Cycle Shares', Economist, January 8, 1898, 43.

[140] 'The Fall in English Railway Securities', Bankers' Magazine, September 1900, 340, 343; see also 'The Yield on Home Railway Ordinary Stocks', Economist, April 20, 1907, 680 (noting that share prices were lower in 1906 than in 1901, even though dividends were higher).

[141] Naish, *supra* n. 72, 53 (cautioning UK investors); Clifford Asness, 'Fight the Fed Model', Journal of Portfolio Management, Fall 2003, 11 (making the point generally).

[142] A.G. Ellinger, *The Art of Investment* (1971), 64.

[143] 'Remarks on the Celebrated Calculations', quoted in Paul Harrison, 'Rational Equity Valuation at the Time of the South Sea Bubble', (2001) 33 History of Political Economy 269, 272.

made the same point, cautioning readers, '[I]t is only wise to hold shares when the income they are likely to produce—be it in the shape of dividends or increasing value—is greater than the fixed rate of income obtainable...'[144] A 1960 text concurred, saying, 'The rate of interest on irredeemable government securities sets a datum for the determination of ordinary-share yields and prices, in that...the rate of interest...appears as a standard, free from risk, by which the merits of an ordinary share can be judged.'[145]

Since investors assessed shares by comparison with other investment alternatives, demand for equities was governed at least partly by their relative performance. The *Economist* observed in 1888:

Of late years (*sic*) there has been a steadily continuing tendency for the yield upon sound investment securities to become lower, and in these circumstances, people with money to invest have looked about them for securities yielding a higher rate of interest than that obtainable on first class stocks, though less absolutely secured. This has had the effect of enhancing the value of second-rate stocks and shares; and so the movement has worked steadily downwards, through industrial enterprises to mining shares.[146]

At the same point in time, the fact the UK's major railway companies were delivering good returns in comparison with other investment options helped to ensure they had a loyal shareholder base. As Alborn has said of railway companies of the era, 'As long as dividends hovered slightly above the 3 per cent they could get from lending to the British state, most shareholders were satisfied to hang on to their stock for dear life.'[147]

Comparisons between the returns offered by industrial securities and government bonds continued to influence decisions about investing in shares throughout the 20th century. In 1926, the *Economist*, after cautioning against an investor simply purchasing 'anything that brings in a higher return' said that the 'excellent practice is growing steadily of a man putting a specified proportion of his capital into gilt-edged securities, and, having made himself safe...utilising the balance in the purchase of stock and shares to which there attaches a more speculative flavour and from which he will gain...in Stock Exchange price movements'.[148] This advice was directed towards retail investors but their institutional counterparts also focused on the relative returns offered by equity and government securities. According to a 1960 article on financial institutions, '[I]n practice investment managers are guided mainly by their assessment of relative yields on different classes of assets.'[149] Or as a

---

[144] Lowenfeld, *supra* n. 69, 77.

[145] Rose, *supra* n. 121, 455.

[146] 'The Growth of Speculation in Mining Shares', Economist, January 12, 1889, 38, 38.

[147] Timothy L. Alborn, *Conceiving Companies: Joint-Stock Politics in Victorian England* (1998), 239.

[148] 'On Changing Investments', Economist, August 21, 1926, 311, 312.

[149] H.B. Rose, 'Financial Institutions and Monetary Policy', Bankers' Magazine, July 1960, 14, 23.

representative of the pension fund industry told the government committee investigating financial institutions in the late 1970s, 'The relative yields of the various types of investment open to us do influence the direction particularly in which new moneys go...'[150] The committee acknowledged the point in a 1977 progress report, saying about pension funds, '(a)s with insurance funds, the yield on gilt-edged (government bonds) is taken as the yardstick against which other investments are judged'.[151]

Events occurring immediately following World War II illustrated how the relative return of shares and government fixed interest securities affected choices made by institutional investors. In the late 1940s, actuary George Ross Goobey orchestrated on behalf of Imperial Tobacco's pension fund a massive shift to shares because he was convinced the 2½ per cent return on government bonds was a 'swindle' when inflation was running at more than 4 per cent and shares were yielding a dividend-driven annual return of about 5 per cent.[152] He found that because investors had been slow to cotton on to the discrepancy deciding which shares to buy was like being 'a child in a sweetshop who discovers everything is for sale at knockdown prices'.[153] Soon others making investment decisions on behalf of pension funds followed suit, helping to launch what became labelled the 'cult of the equity'.[154]

To the extent investors in fact made decisions about whether to buy shares on the basis of performance relative to fixed income securities, market trends should have fortified the buy side. During the late Victorian and Edwardian eras, shares of UK industrial and commercial companies outperformed domestically issued fixed interest securities and during the interwar years shares were a better investment than government bonds and corporate debentures (Chapter Six, Part III.C.1; Chapter Eight, Part II.B.6). The trend continued throughout the entire 20th century, as shares (with dividends reinvested) delivered better annual returns than both 'long dated' government bonds and fixed interest securities issued by the government with short maturity dates ('treasury bills') in every decade but the 1900s and the 1930s (Figure VI).[155] The trend helps to explain why there was substantial demand for shares under circumstances where legal protection for outside investors was modest, political conditions for ownership of shares were not optimal (Chapter Two, Part V) and sources of information on companies left much to be desired.

---

[150] Wilson Committee, *supra* n. 74, 166.

[151] Wilson Committee, *supra* n. 20, 23.

[152] John Plender, *That's the Way the Money Goes: The Financial Institutions and the Nations Savings* (1982), 40–41.

[153] Tony Golding, *The City: Inside the Great Expectation Machine* (2001), 50.

[154] Plender, *supra* n. 152, 41; John Littlewood, *The Stock Market: 50 Years of Capitalism at Work* (1998), 107–8, 122.

[155] Elroy Dimson, Paul Marsh and Mike Staunton, *Triumph of the Optimists: 101 Years of Global Investment Returns* (2002), 153, 303.

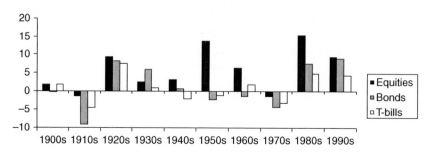

Figure VI: Rates of return for Equity/Government securities, UK 20th Century (inflation-adjusted)

Source: Compiled using data from Dimson, Marsh and Staunton, *supra* n. 155.

While shares generally outperformed domestic fixed interest securities, investors potentially had other options available to them, the most obvious being to look overseas. A well-established fact in the financial economics literature is that, regardless of regulatory constraints, investors hold, on a risk-adjusted basis, too little of their wealth in foreign assets.[156] Reasons for a home-asset preference include exchange-rate risk (currency fluctuations), settlement risk (transactions can fail or be delayed in less advanced markets), liquidity risk (transactions of thinly traded assets may move the market against a major foreign investor) and information asymmetries (an investor will know his own market better than that of another country).[157]

Despite a 'home bias', historically the foreign option was taken up with some enthusiasm in Britain. In the 1850s British investors searching for better investment yields began looking overseas in earnest, and by the middle of the decade overseas portfolio investment amounted to over £200 million.[158] This amount increased more than five-fold during the next twenty years, with the upsurge in overseas portfolio investment entrenching London as the world's leading financial centre.[159] The trend continued up to 1914. More than one-third of UK investment capital was allocated to overseas assets on the eve of World War I, a proportion large enough to imply demand for UK shares was depressed to some degree (Chapter Six, Part I, Part III.C.3).

[156] Ning Zhu, 'The Local Bias of Individual Investors', (2002) Yale ICF Working Paper 02–30, 1; Magnus Dahlquist, Lee Pinkowitz, Rene M. Stultz and Rohan Williamson, 'Corporate Governance, Investor Protection, and the Home Bias', (2003) 38 Journal of Financial and Quantitative Analysis 87, 87.

[157] E. Philip Davis, *Pension Funds: Retirement-Income Security, and Capital Markets—An International Perspective* (1995), 206; see also Dahlquist *et al, supra* n. 156, 87 (noting, though, there is no generally accepted explanation for the home bias).

[158] Newton and Cottrell, *supra* n. 127, 333; E. Victor Morgan and W.A. Thomas, *The Stock Exchange: Its History and Functions* (1969), 88.

[159] Morgan and Thomas, *supra* n. 158, 88.

Whatever handicap foreign investment options imposed on the buy side up to World War I, the trend was of marginal importance for a number of decades thereafter. Capital was instead to varying degrees 'trapped' in the UK due to regulatory constraints and the uneven returns foreign assets delivered (Chapter Eight, Part II.B.1; Chapter Ten, Part IV.B). In the short term, at least, one effect might have been to boost consumption at the expense of saving.[160] However, over time there would have been investment capital seeking a home, meaning constraints on overseas investment would have boosted demand for shares in British companies as the UK outsider/arm's-length system of ownership and control crystallized.

F. Investor Sentiment

UK investors making comparisons with alternative investments, domestic or foreign, did not assess the merits of shares in a fully consistent manner over time. Instead, demand for equity was punctuated periodically by short-lived bursts of optimism concerning shares. The speculation-driven, 18th-century South Sea Company 'bubble' was one example (Part III.D; Chapter Five, Part II). This was preceded by a wave of enthusiasm for shares during the mid-1690s, when investors eagerly agreed to buy stakes in a wide range of proposed companies, including banks, mining enterprises, water supply ventures and manufacturing concerns (Chapter Five, Part I).

At the close of the 18th century, speculative fervour affected canal companies.[161] This was followed by surges in investor enthusiasm for shares during the mid-1820s, mid-1830s and mid-1840s, with the final episode focusing almost entirely on railways (Chapter Five, Part III.B, Part V.A). In the early 1880s, electricity shares captured the imagination of investors, in the mid-1890s there was great enthusiasm for the cycling, automotive and brewing industries and between 1909 and 1911 there was a rubber company fad (Chapter Six, Part III.C.4).

During the interwar years, there were bouts of investor enthusiasm for shares occurring in 1919/20 and the late 1920s. Generally, however, the period lacked the speculative excitement characterizing previous eras (Chapter Eight, Part II.B.8). This was also the case after World War II. A 1954 analysis of the London Stock Exchange suggested it was 'a much steadier market than most overseas stock exchanges', 'an "investment" market as distinct from a "speculative" one'.[162] This assessment proved fairly accurate. There were 'bull' markets between 1953 and 1955, 1958 and 1960 and 1968 and 1972 that belied the fact that the UK was

---

[160] A.L. Levine, *Industrial Retardation in Britain 1880–1914* (1967), 136–37.

[161] Charles P. Kindleberger, *Manias, Panics and Crashes: A History of Financial Crises*, 4th edn (2000), 41.

[162] King, *supra* n. 98, 33.

in relative economic decline in the decades following World War II.[163] On the other hand, only the final one of these bull markets was followed by the sort of plunge in share prices that often characterizes 'bubbles' that have burst.[164] Even the share price decline in 1973 and 1974 was gradual (if inexorable) and was not marked by overt manifestations of investor panic.[165] Indeed, the market's assessment seemed realistic given the gloomy situation, characterized by 'a minority Government hostile to the private sector, unaware or uncaring of the crises faced by many companies, and quite indifferent to the massive loss of institutional and personal wealth suffered in the stock market crash'.[166]

There are various plausible explanations for the reduced intensity of investor exuberance over time. Private investors likely became progressively shrewder due to the process of trial and error. The massive switch from individual to institutional investment from the end of World War II onwards (Part I) probably brought greater resilience to good and bad news.[167] Improvements in the quality of information disseminated to the market due to more rigorous disclosure obligations and improvements in the quality of the analysis provided by the financial press (Part III C.,D.) likely also helped to temper speculative excess.

Mispricing of shares did not become a mere historical artefact. The gyrations of the techMARK 100, a stock market index measuring the stock market performance of larger technology companies traded on the London Stock Exchange, illustrates that fads can still influence UK stock markets. It opened at 2000 in late 1999, peaked at 5753 in March 2000 in the midst of a short-lived 'tech boom' and bottomed out at 577 in March 2003.[168] Nevertheless, the 'buy side' for shares apparently was less prone to surges in investor sentiment after the opening decades of the 20th century than it was previously.

Massive discrepancies between share prices and 'fundamental' value can arise for various reasons.[169] Proprietors of businesses might falsely but credibly claim great prospects for their ventures. Projected future earnings, though based on the best available evidence, may fail to materialize, leaving late buyers feeling foolish as and when a sudden realization that projections were too optimistic causes a sudden drop in price. A possible variant on this scenario is where investors develop not merely incorrect but 'irrationally' upbeat expectations of future profitability. Finally, situations can arise where most investors might understand

---

[163] Littlewood, *supra* n. 154, 120–21, 159–65, 183–84.

[164] Stephen Vines, *Market Panic: Wild Gyrations, Risks and Opportunities in Stock Markets* (2003), 14.

[165] *Ibid.*, 42.   [166] *Ibid.*

[167] Hamish McRae and Frances Cairncross, *Capital City: London as a Financial Centre* (1974), 104.

[168] 'Tech Dream is Over as Index Sinks Below 1000', Evening Standard, May 30, 2002; <http://www.ftse.com/dyn_cache/T1X_hist.csv>, available at <http://www.ftse.com/Indices/FTSE_Techmark_Index_Series/Values.jsp> (last visited Nov. 19, 2007).

[169] Dale, *supra* n. 76, 155–56; Peter M. Garber, *Famous First Bubbles: The Fundamentals of Early Manias* (2000), 88–90; Maureen O'Hara, 'Bubbles: Some Perspectives (and Loose Talk) from History', (2008) 21 Review of Financial Studies 11, 13–16.

companies have little chance of delivering the results necessary to justify current share prices but buy shares, nevertheless confident that the market will continue to rise for the time being and that they will not be in the last unfortunate wave when the game of musical chairs ends.

Discerning why during a particular 'bubble' episode there was a breakdown in the relationship between asset prices and fundamental values is often difficult. For instance, almost 300 years after the South Sea Bubble, commentators disagree whether it was a prime example of irrationality in financial markets, a case of investors acting optimistically but rationally, or some combination of the two.[170] The analysis of various speculative episodes that have influenced share prices in the UK in subsequent chapters draws attention to factors that fuelled investor optimism but does not offer definitive verdicts on why prices temporarily departed from underlying asset values. Going further is unnecessary for present purposes because the waves of investor sentiment are not the subject matter of analysis *per se*. Instead, their significance for present purposes is that they periodically fortified the 'buy side' for shares in ways that could provide a platform for the unwinding of share ownership.

While waves of investor optimism could boost the buy side and foster dispersion of share ownership, there often was a counter-reaction to such 'crazes' that undercut, temporarily at least, investor demand for shares. The decades following the spectacular collapse of the South Sea Bubble were characterized by investor conservatism and '(t)he wings of the stock-market remained clipped, partly as a result of the shock of (1720)'.[171] When mining share prices collapsed after the mid-1820s stock market frenzy ended, there was 'thorough disillusionment of shareholders in this field of investment'.[172] Disappointing results delivered by the electricity companies of the early 1880s and by the cycle and automobile companies of the mid-1890s prompted investor scepticism of these industrial sectors (Chapter Six, Part III.C.4).

Though the downswings in a 'boom and bust' cycle could hamper the 'buy side', for the purposes of share ownership the swings in investor sentiment did not necessarily just cancel out. Instead, optimistic surges tended to have a lasting impact, in the sense that such episodes were net contributors to greater diffusion. For instance, though the 'railway mania' of the mid-1840s reversed in a manner that left investors wary of railway equities for a number of decades thereafter, it served to broaden greatly the investor base for railway companies, which in turn became pioneers of a full divorce between ownership and control (Chapter Five, Part V.A.1). Mergers, discussed next, also illustrate the point.

---

[170] Dale, *supra* n. 76, 156–59, 170–71; Edward Chancellor, *Devil Take the Hindmost: A History of Financial Speculation* (1999), 88–95.

[171] Carswell, *supra* n. 75, 242–43.

[172] Arthur D. Gayer, Anna Jacobson and Isaiah Finkelstein, 'British Share Prices, 1811–1850', (1940) 22 Review of Economic Studies 78, 85.

G. Mergers

Surges in investor optimism concerning company shares are commonly associated with corporate mergers. Merger and acquisition (M & A) activity historically has varied in accordance with the level of the stock market, with M & A booms coinciding with rising stock prices.[173] Plausible explanations for the pattern are that mergers and share prices both spike when growth opportunities are thought to be promising and that high share prices create opportunities for companies to use their highly valued shares as acquisition currency.[174] Regardless of precisely what is going on, since M & A activity is conducive to the unwinding of control in blockholder-dominated companies (Chapter Three, Part VI), waves of investor enthusiasm for shares that prompt mergers should foster the diffusion of share ownership even if there is a temporary market hangover.

Mergers have features that are potentially attractive to buyers of shares independent of the general stock market optimism that accompanies merger waves and thus qualify as an additional factor fortifying demand for shares. The features of mergers that would have been attractive to investors have varied somewhat over time. At the end of the 19th century and the beginning of the 20th century there was a flurry of amalgamations involving multiple firms representing the dominant market share within particular industries. It was standard practice for such mergers to be financed at least partially by the issuance of securities to the public, often including ordinary shares. The pitch typically made to investors, generally with considerable success, was that excess capacity had afflicted the industry in question and the amalgamated company would generate improved profits by using its market power to restore prices to sustainable levels, by closing inefficient plants and by trimming staffing and marketing expenses.[175] Investor receptiveness to such claims was heightened due to much-heralded industrial consolidations occurring in the United States at the same time, such as the formation of industrial giants General Electric, American Tobacco and US Steel.[176]

The multi-firm horizontal mergers that were prevalent at the end of the 19th century and the beginning of the 20th century receded in importance during the

---

[173] See generally Andrei Shleifer and Robert W. Vishny, 'Stock Market Driven Acquisitions', (2003) 70 Journal of Financial Economics 295, 307. On the UK, see Leslie Hannah, *The Rise of the Corporate Economy*, 2nd edn (1983), 59 (discussing the 1920s); Rob Dixon, 'Trends in Takeovers in the UK and International Market and the Reasons for Merger Activity', (1990) 12 British Review of Economic Issues 1, 19 (discussing the 1960s, 1970s and 1980s).

[174] Jarrad Harford, 'What Drives Merger Waves?', (2005) 77 Journal of Financial Economics 529, 534.

[175] Ch. Six, Pt II.B.4; 'The Increasingly Heavy Capitalisation of Industrial Combinations', Economist, April 14, 1900, 532; H.W. Macrosty, 'Business Aspects of British Trusts', (1902) 12 Economic Journal 347, 358–59, 362.

[176] Henry W. Macrosty, *The Trust Movement in British Industry: A Study of Business Organisation* (1907), 174.

interwar years and were virtually unknown following World War II.[177] M & A activity nevertheless had various features that were attractive to investors (Chapter Ten, Part IV.E.1). Shareholders in the companies being bought out could depend on an offer significantly in excess of the pre-bid share price. Mergers also offered the promise of capitalizing on economies of scale and size, exploiting synergies between related businesses and fitting the right managers into the right jobs. Moreover, a new type of merger transaction—a 'hostile' takeover bid where the bidder would by-pass negotiations with the directors of the target—was reassuring for investors because managers quickly deduced the best way to fend off an unwelcome offer was to strive to push the share price beyond the level where a bid would be worthwhile.

Mergers are not always good news for those who invest in shares, since a significant number fail to deliver in the manner promised. UK merger mistakes span from a number of misconceived multi-firm consolidations occurring at the end of the 19th century (e.g. English Sewing Cotton and the Calico Printers Association), to an ill-fated 1968 marriage between British automobile manufacturers Leyland Motor Corporation and British Motor Holdings and to £4 billion worth of acquisitions in 2000/01 by General Electric (renamed Marconi in 2000) that brought what had been one of Britain's leading industrial companies to its knees.[178] Nevertheless, on a net basis merger activity should have reinforced demand for shares as ownership split from control.

IV. Deterrents to Intervention

A. General Considerations

An inclination on the part of blockholders to exit or accept dilution of their stake and willingness on the part of investors to buy shares are necessary but not sufficient conditions for ownership to become divorced from control (Chapter One, Part IV). The additional variable that has to be taken into account is the approach buyers of shares take with companies in which they are investing. If demand for shares is led by investors who take a 'hands on' approach to the operation of the companies incumbent blockholders are exiting, insider/control-oriented corporate governance will remain the norm.

---

[177] M.A. Utton, 'Some Features of the Early Merger Movements in British Manufacturing Industry', (1972) 14 Business History 51, 52, 57–58.

[178] Leslie Hannah, 'Managerial Innovation and the Rise of the Large-Scale Company in Interwar Britain', (1974) 27 Economic History Review 252, 266 (problems with late 19th-century mergers); Roy Church, *The Rise and Decline of the British Motor Industry* (1994), 88–108; Timothy R. Whisler, *The British Motor Industry 1945–1994: A Case Study in Industrial Decline* (1999), 93–121 (Leyland Motor Corporation/British Motor Holdings merger); 'End of the Road for Weinstock's Legacy', Financial Times, October 26, 2005 (General Electric/Marconi).

Private equity firms, which orchestrate buyouts of publicly traded companies in order to generate value by restructuring, constitute present-day examples of control-oriented investors (Chapter Eleven, Part III). The history of Boots, the well-known pharmacy group, provides an earlier illustration.[179] Jesse Boot (later Lord Trent), having built up single-handedly a major manufacturing, wholesaling and retailing organization, was reluctant to pass control to his son John (later the second Lord Trent), whom he felt was not up to the task. As a result, in 1920 he sold his controlling interest in Boots Ltd to Liggett's International Ltd, owned by US chain store magnet Louis Liggett. John Boot aspired to bring Boots back under family control, and in 1923 persuaded Liggett to sell a quarter of his UK shareholdings. Liggett, laid low by the 1929 stock market crash afflicting the US, was then forced to sell out completely. John Boot allied himself with a syndicate led by Tobacco Securities Trust Ltd that won financial control of Boots in 1933. Boot became chairman and managing director and was for the next twenty years the one undisputed authority at Boots.

While there have been instances where those buying shares in a publicly traded company have done so with the intention of exercising control, passivity has long been a hallmark of investment in shares in the UK, thus paving the way for potential outsider/arm's-length corporate governance. An 1854 study of railways, the mid-19th century separation of ownership and control pioneers, said:

> Shareholders elect their directors…Proprietors, instead of constantly exercising their franchise, allow it to become on all ordinary occasions a dead letter; retiring directors are so habitually re-elected without opposition, and have so great a power of insuring their own re-election when opposed, that the board becomes practically a close body; and it is only when the misgovernment grows extreme enough to produce a revolutionary agitation among the shareholders that any change can be affected.[180]

Van Oss observed similarly in 1899 that '[I]n practice shareholders seldom assert their will. They are led and easily led…the rule that shareholders do as they are bidden by their servants (the directors) has very few exceptions.'[181] Lowenfeld, author of a number of investment texts in the first decade of the 20th century, chimed in, saying, 'Shareholders' meetings have long since descended to the level of formal farces', 'the majority of shareholders wholly abdicate the authority which the law and their company's Articles of Association have placed in their hands' and 'only when the directors find themselves compelled to announce the

---

[179] Stanley Chapman, 'Strategy and Structure at Boots the Chemists' in Leslie Hannah (ed.), *Management Strategy and Business Development* (1976), 95, 96–99; F.A. Cockfield, 'The Development and Organisation of Boots Pure Drug Company Limited' in Ronald S. Edwards and Harry Townsend (eds), *Studies in Business Organisation* (1961), 116, 116–19; <http://www.bootsexports.com/main.asp?pid=3040> (Boots' history during the Jesse Boot era) (last visited Aug. 11, 2008); <http://www.bootsexports.com/main.asp?pid=3042> (Boots under US ownership) (last visited Aug. 11, 2008).

[180] 'Railway Morals and Railway Policy', (1854) 100 Edinburgh Review 420, 420.

[181] S.F. Van Oss, 'In Hooley Land', Journal of Finance, January 1899, 1, 11.

steed has been stolen (does)... the generality of shareholders manifest any interest in the fastenings of the stable door'.[182] In 1928, E.M. Griffiths, a vocal critic of the management of Birmingham Small Arms (BSA), an armament, tool and automobile manufacturer, typified British investors as 'patient oxen'.[183] Likewise, the *Economist* said in 1977, 'Shareholders, both private and institutional, are notoriously reluctant to intervene in badly managed companies.'[184]

At first glance the passive stance adopted by those buying shares in UK public companies is perplexing, particularly in companies lacking a blockholder. Shareholders in such companies are confronted with the risk of agency costs and efforts to act collectively cannot be thwarted by a shareholder with a large voting stake. As a result, the way should be clear to address misgivings about management with 'self help', using the powers available to shareholders to arm-twist those in charge to change approach. As Lowenfeld said in 1908, 'But directors who are prepared thus whole-heartedly to devote themselves to their shareholders' interests are the exception; for this reason shareholders in protection of their own capital must, of necessity, exert themselves to follow the vicissitudes of their company's fortunes.'[185]

There have been instances where shareholders who bought shares primarily for investment purposes have subsequently intervened in company affairs. Arnold and McCartney, in their biography of the 1840s 'Railway King' George Hudson, note that '[R]ailway company meetings at this time were often rumbustious and outspoken, and could be marked by insults bordering on the florid...'[186] Hudson himself secured managerial control of a number of the railways he came to dominate by using a combination of skilful oratory and a successful track record to win over shareholder meetings. He subsequently exited the railway business in disgrace after tough questioning at shareholder meetings and investigations by shareholder-appointed investigative committees exposed fraudulent accounting practices and improper personal dealings with the companies he ran.[187] Moving closer to the present, during the 1990s and early 2000s major institutional shareholders became increasingly willing to engage in 'defensive' shareholder activism, challenging companies on controversial topics such as executive pay and periodically orchestrating the removal of underperforming chief executives (Chapter Eleven, Part I).

While there have been instances where investment-oriented shareholders have sought to exercise control, if only temporarily, to protect their interests,

---

[182] Lowenfeld, *supra* n. 41, 407, 419; Lowenfeld, *supra* n. 69, 9.

[183] Roger Lloyd-Jones, Myrddin J. Lewis, Mark D. Matthews and Josephine Maltby, 'Control, Conflict and Concession: Corporate Governance, Accounting and Accountability at Birmingham Small Arms, 1906–1933', (2005), 32 Accounting Historians Journal 149, 174.

[184] 'Year of the Bullock?', Economist, January 29, 1977, 81, 82.

[185] Lowenfeld, *supra* n. 41, 421.

[186] A.J. Arnold and S. McCartney, *George Hudson—The Rise and Fall of the Railway King: A Study in Victorian Entrepreneurship* (2004), 92.

[187] Ch. Five, Pt V.A; Arnold and McCartney, *supra* n. 186, 82–83, 91–92, 96, 112–15, 173–99.

this pattern has been the exception to the rule. The reasons shareholders generally refrained from stepping forward varied depending on the historical period. Private investors dominated the share registers of UK public companies up to the 1960s but, from the end of World War II onwards, institutional shareholders were rapidly displacing them (Part I). The trend created the potential for institutional investors to collaborate to adopt a 'hands on' approach to share ownership and introduce institutionally driven, insider/control-oriented corporate governance, but this potential went largely unfulfilled. Chapter Ten explains why.

B. Private Investors

What about private investors? Why did they adopt a passive approach to the companies in which they bought shares when they dominated the share register? One reason was that most individual shareholders were simply ill-suited to step forward and exercise control. In the UK over the past few years there have been a number of instances where 'activist' investors have built up significant but by no means dominant stakes in target companies and agitated for 'corrective' action (Chapter Eleven, Part II). This form of activism is controversial but these activist shareholders are generally regarded as being sophisticated players who work hard to understand the fundamentals of a target company.[188]

Private investors in the UK were different. As Florence said, they were generally too 'ignorant, business-shy or *too* busy—or any two of them or even all three' to take any sort of active role in the governance of the companies in which they owned shares.[189] For instance, when individual investors dominated share registers of UK public companies, a generous proportion of individuals listed as owners of shares lacked any aptitude or appetite for active intervention. These included children (or trustees for them), older people and women, most of whom were unfamiliar or uncomfortable with the notion of direct involvement in business.[190]

Even among private investors otherwise comfortable with tackling business issues, adopting an activist stance typically made little sense. For example, collective action problems, a widely acknowledged cause of shareholder passivity,[191] would have come into play. A collective action problem exists when individuals

[188] 'Hedge Funds are Very Keen to Exercise Their Secretive Shareholding Muscle', *Financial Times*, August 9, 2005.

[189] P. Sargant Florence, *The Logic of British and American Industry: A Realistic Analysis of Economic Structure and Government* (1953), 179.

[190] Peter L. Payne, 'Industrial Entrepreneurship and Management in Great Britain', in P. Mathias and M.M. Postan (eds), *The Cambridge Economic History of Europe, vol. VII, The Industrial Economies: Capital, Labour and Enterprise, Part I (Britain, France, Germany, and Scandinavia)* (1978), 180, 212.

[191] See, for example, Edward B. Rock, 'The Logic and (Uncertain) Significance of Institutional Shareholder Activism', (1991) 79 Georgetown Law Journal 445, 454, n. 29; J.P. Charkham, 'A Larger Role for Institutional Investors' in Nicholas Dimsdale and Martha Prevezer (eds), *Capital Markets and Corporate Governance* (1994), 99, 105–6.

acting in a rational, self-interested manner fail to take steps that would increase the joint welfare of all involved. Companies with diffuse share ownership are highly susceptible because the disciplining of management is a classic collective good: all shareholders benefit whether or not they contribute to the discipline.[192] Individual shareholders thus will tend to wait for others to step forward and 'free ride' off the efforts of those that happen to do so. As Lowenfeld put it, 'Every shareholder is possessed by the comforting, but erroneous, idea that if anything were radically wrong, some public-spirited person would take the floor at the meeting and openly challenge the policy of the Board.'[193]

The manner in which UK private investors configured their investment portfolios further reinforced the bias in favour of passivity. The Capital Asset Pricing Model, the departure point for financial economists describing diversification and risk, was not developed until the 1960s.[194] However, the practice of spreading capital among numerous investments was being adopted much earlier by UK investors. An 1876 article on speculative investment referred to 'the time-honoured maxim of distributing their eggs in a number of baskets'.[195] By the late 19th century this constituted standard investment advice, often under the label 'scientific investment'.[196]

British investors took the advice to heart. During the mid-19th century, when companies issuing shares to the public commonly called up only a small proportion of the capital, sizeable uncalled liabilities would have discouraged the building up of investment portfolios encompassing large numbers of companies.[197] However, as early as 1877 Bonamy Price, an Oxford political economist, was saying, 'I think persons are becoming accustomed to take shares in various companies rather than have a larger sum in one business.'[198] For late 19th-century followers of advice on 'scientific investment', '"Do not carry all your eggs in one basket" was probably written on the hearts of these investors when they died.'[199] During the opening decades of the 20th century, it was standard practice among individual investors to diversify by buying shares in a variety of different companies.[200]

For most personal investors, diversification would have meant the fate of any one company in which they owned shares should not have had a dramatic impact on their personal financial circumstances. The 'natural and inevitable' result, as

---

[192] Rock, *supra* n. 191, 453–63.

[193] Lowenfeld, *supra* n. 69, 9–10.

[194] William F. Sharpe, 'Capital Asset Prices: A Theory of Market Equilibrium Under Conditions of Risk', (1964) 19 Journal of Finance 425; Peter L. Bernstein, *Capital Ideas: The Improbable Origins of Modern Wall Street* (2005), 191–95.

[195] Alexander Innes Shand, 'Speculative Investments', Blackwood's Edinburgh Magazine, September 1876, 293, 300.

[196] Jefferys, *supra* n. 68, 415–16; Payne, *supra* n. 190, 205.

[197] Jefferys, Business, *supra* n. 68, 172–82.

[198] Quoted *ibid.*, 397.   [199] *Ibid.*, 416.

[200] Cole, *supra* n. 101, 58; Florence, *supra* n. 189 above, 181–182; Payne, *supra* n. 190, 205.

Cole said in 1935, was that those buying shares 'ceased...to regard themselves in any way responsible for the conduct of the enterprises which were legally their property'.[201] Moreover, if shareholders did begin to lose faith in a company's directors, they were still not inclined to rock the boat, since, as Van Oss observed in 1899, '[S]hareholders have an idea that internal strife reduces the value of their shares, and that is of course, the last thing they wish for.'[202] A disgruntled shareholder, as Parkinson suggested in 1932, would instead 'usually cut his loss and sell out'.[203]

For retail investors who, despite collective action problems and the diversification-driven bias in favour of passivity, were inclined to treat their investment in a hands on fashion, there were still various hurdles to surmount. Company law was one deterrent. There was, for instance, little scope for an individual shareholder to use litigation to put pressure on those running a company. As English judges took the view that a director owed duties to the company and the company alone,[204] shareholders generally could not sue personally in the event of a breach by a director. There was a theoretical possibility that an individual shareholder could secure standing to launch 'derivative' litigation and sue on a company's behalf.[205] However, the English judiciary was reluctant to give minority shareholders standing to sue in this way and potential shareholder litigants ran the risk of paying hefty legal fees due to the practice in English courts of ordering losing parties to reimburse the legal expenses of successful parties.[206] As a result, derivative lawsuits have always been rare in practice.[207]

UK company law also did not offer a particularly congenial setting for shareholders seeking to exercise control by acting collectively. The law has always theoretically offered shareholders wide discretion to dictate how a company would be run, since they have been vested with authority to determine the content of the corporate constitution and decide who would serve as the directors (Chapter Two, Part II.A). However, dissident shareholders seeking to exercise 'hands on' control against the wishes of an incumbent board have always faced an uphill

---

[201] Cole, *supra* n. 101, 59; see also Withers, *supra* n. 135, 118.

[202] Van Oss, *supra* n. 181, 12.

[203] Parkinson, *supra* n. 70, 13.

[204] *Percival v Wright* [1902] 2 Ch. 421.

[205] The 'derivative action' label for this sort of litigation was first developed in the United States and was introduced to England in the case of *Wallersteiner v Moir* (No. 2) [1975] Q.B. 373, 391, 406.

[206] Samuel, *supra* n. 45, 150; Gower, *supra* n. 92, 1385.

[207] *Ibid.*; Julian Franks, Colin Mayer and Stefano Rossi, 'Ownership: Evolution and Regulation' (2006) ECGI Finance Working Paper No. 09/2003 12–13 (research on early 1930s); John Armour, Bernard Black, Brian Cheffins and Richard Nolan, 'Private Enforcement of Corporate Law: An Empirical Comparison of the US and the UK', (2008), unpublished working paper (finding only one case filed between 2004 and 2006 alleging a breach of duty by the director of a publicly traded company).

battle. As a 1901 guide to investment said, 'The game is one-sided: the directors hold nearly all the winning cards.'[208]

Currently companies legislation and financial services regulation ensure that publicly traded companies engage in extensive disclosure,[209] thus permitting shareholders planning to mount a challenge to research matters carefully before proceeding. Until well into the 20th century, however, disclosure regulation was rudimentary (Part III.D). Potential insurgents therefore struggled to find out enough about what was going on to mount a plausible challenge to incumbent directors. As the *Economist* said in 1910, '[T]he shareholders' vote, nominally the controlling power, is practically in a fair way to become useless, because the shareholder is kept in a state of more or less complete ignorance.'[210] If shareholders raised their voices to press for relevant financial data the directors could readily rebuff them by arguing that any revelation of 'intimate business details' would threaten future profits by aiding competitors or fostering grumbling by employees.[211] Hence, as Lowenfeld said, 'Even when a shareholder is prompted by his own misgivings, and would like publicly to raise some point which causes him uneasiness, he knows himself to be incapable of doing so. Want of accurate financial knowledge is his stumbling block...'[212]

If shareholders were able to find out enough about a company to mount a credible challenge, the potential insurgents still faced an uphill struggle. Blockholders continued to hold sway in many UK public companies until well into the 20th century (Chapter One, Part VI). If a blockholder held a majority of the outstanding shares, then insurgents had no hope of prevailing in the event of a shareholder vote. Even if a blockholder had merely a sizeable minority holding, insurgents needed to generate overwhelming support among neutral shareholders to prevail.

Company law further hampered mobilization of the shareholder base. At present, the most direct way for insurgent shareholders to gain leverage is to threaten to rely on statutory provisions permitting shareholders owning collectively 10 per cent or more of the shares to call a shareholders' ('general') meeting and propose an ordinary resolution (i.e., a resolution requiring approval by a simple majority of votes cast) dismissing the incumbent directors.[213] UK companies legislation first provided in 1900 shareholders owning 10 per cent or more

---

[208] C.H. Thorpe, *How to Invest and Speculate* (1901), 79.

[209] Companies Act 2006, c. 46, ss. 385–453; Financial Services Authority, Disclosure and Transparency Rules, available at <http://fsahandbook.info/FSA/html/handbook/DTR> (last visited Feb. 18, 2008).

[210] 'The Helplessness of Shareholders', Economist, November 12, 1910, 960, 961.

[211] Payne, *supra* n. 190, 205.

[212] Lowenfeld, *supra* n. 69, 10; see also at 199.

[213] Companies Act 2006, ss. 165 (removal of directors), 282 (defining ordinary resolution), 303 (calling of a general meeting).

of a company's shares with the right to call a general meeting.[214] The right to dismiss directors by ordinary resolution was not introduced, however, until 1948 (Chapter Three, Part VIII). By 1932, the London Stock Exchange listing rules obliged quoted companies to include provisions in their articles of association giving shareholders the option to dismiss incumbent directors but the threshold prescribed was a special resolution, which meant a 3/4s majority vote had to be obtained (Chapter Eight, Part II.B.3).

In the event of a contested vote the relevant ground rules gave an incumbent board a decided advantage in rounding up support among neutral shareholders. As Parkinson observed in 1932 '[T]he great majority of shareholders are prevented by conditions of residence etc., from attending annual (shareholder) meetings, or are insufficiently interested to attend.'[215] Shareholder voting in larger companies was therefore primarily carried out by proxy, which involves a shareholder authorizing another individual to vote on the shareholder's behalf. Here incumbent directors had a significant edge, as they could use proxies artfully to solidify control. An 1855 survey of railways drew attention to the edge railway company boards had:

> How, at half-yearly and special meetings, shareholders should be so readily led by boards, even after repeated experience of their untrustworthiness, seems at first sight difficult to understand. The mystery disappears, however, on inquiry. Very frequently contested measures are carried quite against the sense of the meetings before which they are laid, by means of the large number of proxies previously collected by the directors. These proxies are obtained mostly from proprietors scattered everywhere throughout the kingdom, who are very generally weak enough to sign the first document sent to them.[216]

The law favoured directors as they sought to use the proxy mechanism to their advantage. In the absence of legislative regulation, proxy voting was governed entirely by a company's articles of association.[217] Traditionally, it was standard for company articles to stipulate that only shareholders could be proxies, meaning shareholders inclined to vote against the directors could struggle to find within the notice period set down for a meeting a suitable person to act on their behalf.[218] Also, it was common practice for directors to accumulate votes in their favour by sending out to shareholders proxy forms pre-stamped in favour of the directors or naming themselves or close associates as proxies.[219] Lowenfeld

---

[214] R.C. Nolan, 'The Continuing Evolution of Shareholder Governance', (2006) 65 Cambridge Law Journal 92, 103, discussing Companies Act 1900, 63 & 64 Vict. c. 48, s. 13. The default rule in the Table A articles in the Companies Act 1862 was that one-fifth of the shareholders could call a general meeting: 25 & 26 Vict. c. 89, Sch. 1, Table A, art. 32.

[215] Parkinson, *supra* n. 70, 5–6.

[216] 'Railway Morals', *supra* n. 180, 437–38. See also Phillips, *supra* n. 49, 7–8, 12–16; Jefferys, *supra* n. 68, 398–99.

[217] *Harben v Phillips* (1883) 23 Ch.D. 14, 35 (indicating at common law voting by proxy was only permitted if a company's articles of association authorized the practice).

[218] A.B. Levy, *Private Corporations and Their Control*, vol. II, (1950), 652.

[219] *Ibid.*; 'Proxies at Company Meetings', Economist, September 6, 1930, 453.

correspondingly bemoaned in 1908, 'the injustice of directors, with the aid of proxy-power entrusted to them by their fellow-shareholders, smothering discussion at general meetings'.[220]

Regulation introduced in the 1940s limited to some degree the edge directors had. Companies seeking 'permission to deal' on the London Stock Exchange were required in 1943 to give an undertaking to stipulate clearly in proxy forms they circulated that shareholders could instruct a proxy to vote 'yes' or 'no' on proposed resolutions and in 1947 the requirement was extended to quoted companies.[221] The Companies Act 1948 specifically gave shareholders the right to vote by proxy and in so doing stipulated any person, whether a shareholder or not, could attend and vote on a shareholder's behalf.[222]

Directors still retained a decided advantage with proxy voting, however. So long as a 'yes/no' option was provided they remained fully within their rights to send out at company expense proxy forms naming themselves or close associates as proxies, combined with supporting documentation backing up their case. As a 1950 study of company law observed, 'This inducement to the large mass of inactive members to accept the suggestion was only too often successful. The directors were then in a position to control the majority at the meeting even without having substantial holdings.'[223]

Despite all of the obstacles to shareholder activism it was at least theoretically possible for dissident shareholders to mount a challenge that had to be taken seriously. Interwar events concerning BSA illustrate the point.[224] E.M. Griffiths (Part IV.A) was the most persistent and vocal critic of the company, but other shareholders joined in to contribute to some tense annual shareholder meetings. BSA responded by changing some of its directors and by improving disclosure of the performance of subsidiary companies.

In various ways, however, the facts surrounding BSA indicate what an uphill struggle activism was. The company's performance was genuinely terrible, as between 1922 and 1936 dividends were only declared in four years and shares valued at 59s 6d in 1918 traded in a range between 5s 7d and 15s 9d. Griffiths, somewhat exceptionally, stood out as a natural leader for the dissident shareholders, since he had a significant investment in BSA after it bought his machine tool firm. Finally, the dissidents probably could not have done much more than create an inconvenience since a cohort of influential directors owned a sizeable minority of the shares and thus had a decided edge in the event of a contested vote. Events at BSA correspondingly indicate that, while successful interventions

---

[220] Lowenfeld, *supra* n. 41, 428.

[221] 'Requirements for New Issues', Times, February 23, 1943; Ch. Nine, Pt III.D.

[222] Companies Act 1948, 11 & 12 Geo. 6, c. 38, s. 136.

[223] Levy, *supra* n. 218, 652.

[224] See Lloyd-Jones *et al*, *supra* n. 183; R. Lloyd-Jones, 'Corporate Governance in a Major British Holding Company: BSA in the Interwar Years', (2006) 16 Accounting, Business & Financial History 69.

by individual investors were not impossible, orchestrating any sort of wholesale change was a tall order.

*   *   *

This chapter and Chapter Three have explained in general terms why block-holders in larger UK companies were willing to sell out or accept dilution of their share ownership, why investors were prepared to buy shares made available for sale and why new shareholders were not inclined to exercise control themselves. The reader should therefore now have a general sense of why a separation of ownership and control became a hallmark of UK corporate governance. However, numerous period-specific questions remain unaddressed. For example, with Britain experiencing an industrial revolution in the late 18th and early 19th centuries, why were publicly traded industrial companies very much a sideshow? Was a division between ownership and control the norm in large UK business enterprises by 1914? Why did institutional investors come to dominate the buy side following World War II and why did they remain largely passive despite the potential for them to exercise substantial collective influence? Chapters Five to Eleven take up these and various other questions concerning the transformation of ownership and control in the UK.

FIVE

Up to 1880

Periodic flurries of public offerings of company shares occurred in Britain between the late 17th century and the middle of the 19th century. Corporate enterprise thus generally grew in importance over time and by the mid-19th century large railway companies had emerged as pioneers of 20th-century-style dispersed share ownership. Overall, however, the transformation was erratic, with periodic waves of enthusiasm for shares being followed by market reversals that swept away many of the new businesses. Moreover, prior to the late 19th century few UK manufacturing enterprises moved to the stock market. Those with some familiarity with British economic history might wonder why this was the case. From 1700 to 1850 Britain experienced the world's first industrial revolution. The firms taking the lead would seem to be obvious candidates to distribute shares to the public, a necessary precursor to a split between owner-ship and control. Why, then, did the widely held industrial company not move to the forefront earlier? This chapter addresses that question and provides gener-ally necessary historical context for developments subsequent chapters discuss.

I. The 1690s: The First Wave of Company Promotions

In England, the name 'company' was first used when merchant adventurers were granted a Royal Charter for the purposes of trading overseas.[1] The earliest version was the 'regulated company', where members were admitted upon payment of a designated fee and consented to obey the rules of the company but other-wise traded on their own account and at their own risk.[2] The Russia Company, founded in 1553 to exploit a monopoly over trade with Russian territory, was the first English 'joint stock' company, in the sense that trading occurred on a joint account with a joint stock.[3]

---

[1] L.C.B. Gower, *The Principles of Modern Company Law* (1954), 23.
[2] Adam Smith, *Wealth of Nations*, 5th edn, Book V, ch. 1 (Edwin Cannan, ed., 1904, originally published 1776), 95.
[3] William R. Scott, *The Constitution and Finance of English, Scottish and Irish Joint-Stock Companies to 1720*, vol. 1 (1912), 17–19. All references to Scott are to volume I unless otherwise specified.

Over the next 80 years, numerous additional business corporations were created by Royal Charter and granted monopolistic privileges to engage in overseas
trading. Such corporations relied on the state for their privileges and the state
relied on them as a major source of finance.[4] The essential features of corporate
status became increasingly well established in this period, often by way of express
clauses in the charters. These included perpetual succession, the right to sue and
be sued, the right to own property, governance by way of majority rule rather than
unanimity and limitations on the personal liability of shareholders to creditors.[5]
Clauses stipulating shares were freely transferable and assignable ensured share
dealing was legally feasible, though directors typically were vested with control
over admission to the benefits of stock ownership.[6]

Between the 1630s and the 1690s the trend was one of general decline for
the business corporation, with few new trading companies being established and
with existing companies atrophying or relinquishing their monopoly privileges.[7]
Nevertheless, conditions were becoming propitious for a surge in company formation activity. The last 40 years of the 17th century were marked by increased
prosperity (Chapter Four, Part III.A) and among those with spare capital to
deploy there was growing awareness that good shares or bonds constituted an
attractive substitute for land. Advantages of shares and bonds included not being
subject to a 20 per cent tax that land was, greater liquidity as an investment,
the lack of need for husbandry and qualifying as a form of property married
women could retain as part of their personal estate.[8] These features, combined
with business euphoria prompted by good harvests and the 'Glorious Revolution'
of 1688—the displacement of James II in favour of William and Mary—set the
scene for England's first burst of company formation.[9] Approximately 85 per cent
of the nearly 150 companies in existence in England and Scotland as of 1695 were
launched between 1688 and 1695.[10]

During this first wave of company formation, incorporation solely by Royal
Charter was rare and an Act of Parliament became the more common method
of incorporating. The end of the 17th century also was the first time companies
were established without reference to any form of explicit state endorsement or

---

[4] Ron Harris, *Industrializing English Law: Entrepreneurship and Business Organization, 1720–
1844* (2000), 45.
[5] W.S. Holdsworth, *A History of English Law*, vol. 8 (1956–72), 202–5; Bruce G. Carruthers,
City of Capital: Politics and Markets in the English Financial Revolution (1996), 130.
[6] Carruthers, *supra* n. 5, 130, 134; K.G. Davies, 'Joint Stock Investment in the Later Seventeenth
Century', (1952) 4 Economic History Review 283, 294.
[7] Gower, *supra* n. 1, 25–26; Harris, *supra* n. 4, 46–51.
[8] John Carswell, *The South Sea Bubble*, rev. edn (1993), 8. On the history of legal barriers to
share ownership by married women see Mark Freeman, Robin Pearson and James Taylor, ' "A Doe
in the City": Women Shareholders in Eighteenth- and Early Nineteenth Century Britain', (2006)
16 Accounting, Business & Financial History 265, 267–68.
[9] Edward Chancellor, *Devil Take the Hindmost: A History of Financial Speculation* (1999), 34–35.
[10] Scott, *supra* n. 3, 327–29; on aspects of this wave of company formation discussed here, see
ibid., 326–33, 345–46; Harris, *supra* n. 4, 18, 53; Richard Dale, *The First Crash: Lessons from the
South Sea Bubble* (2004), 33.

involvement. This was facilitated by governmental reluctance to use the preroga-tive writs of *quo warranto* and *scire facias*, which could be invoked to compel those operating enterprises without a charter or statutory authorization to show why their unauthorized companies should not be dissolved.

A lucrative 1688 treasure recovery prompted the launch of various compa-nies declaring an intention to operate in wreck salvaging and treasure-seeking. Company formations then accelerated as promoters sought to take advantage of investor 'euphoria' to market shares in support of new ventures. Investors looked with particular favour on armament enterprises paying large dividends out of hefty profits resulting from a war with France and companies expected to benefit as a result of war-induced restrictions on imports. Some of the enter-prises were established to engage in foreign trading, but many were domestically oriented, proposing to operate in banking and finance (most notably the Bank of England), water supply, mining, fishing and manufacturing (e.g. armaments, fine paper, linen and glass). Scott, in his voluminous 1912 study of pre-1720 joint stock companies, estimates that the issued capital of the joint stock com-panies in existence as of 1695 amounted to £4.25m, or one-tenth of the wealth employed in trade at the time.[11] Trading in shares focused on coffee houses in Exchange Alley, a labyrinth of lanes in the City of London.

The typical governance structure in joint stock companies of the late 17th century involved the general court, an assembly of proprietors akin to shareholders, which elected a court of directors to which conduct of day-to-day business was delegated.[12] The right to vote in the general court was typically determined by the size of proprietors' holdings in the company, in the sense that a substantial financial interest was a pre-requisite to voting. This sort of minimum voting threshold aside, various companies had the modern rule—one share, one vote—in place. Numerous others, organized so as to preclude an undue concentration of control, established capped voting in the form of a low maximum number of votes any one proprietor could cast. For instance, each Bank of England shareholder who owned £500 or more of stock—a medium-sized holding—was entitled to one vote, and the same rule applied with the Million Bank, which operated essentially as an investor in government debt, for those owning £300 or more of stock.

When capped voting rights were in place, key shareholders could not rely directly on their shares to dictate the outcome of matters that came up for a vote (Chapter Two, Part II.A). Directors thus potentially had substantial discretion to conduct business in the manner they saw fit, a feature the famous 18th-century economist Adam Smith cited to cast doubt on the viability of the joint stock company (Chapter One, Part I). This seems to imply a separation of ownership and control had gained a strong foothold, foretelling the later dominance of the

---

[11] Scott, *supra* n. 3, 336–37.
[12] On aspects discussed here, see *Ibid.*, 340; Armand Budington Du Bois, *The English Business Company after the Bubble Act 1720–1800* (1938), 287–88, 291.

widely held company. As Dickson has said of the 1690s, 'In this early period it may well have seemed that the (stock) market would in future centre on company flotations, and that dealings in government securities would gradually decline…'[13] In fact, the roots laid down were far from firm, since a modern-style divorce of ownership and control was largely absent even in the major enterprises of the era and only a tiny number of companies had any staying power.

While capped voting indeed constituted a barrier to an investor minded to rely on a large stake to dictate corporate policy, it was no guarantee of a split between ownership and control. A proprietor with a large holding could evade voting restrictions by 'the splitting of his stock', which involved transferring shares to nominal transferees who held the equity in trust for the owner and voted duly on the owner's behalf at general court meetings.[14] Also, even the largest companies generally lacked diffuse share ownership. According to Scott, £3.23m of the £4.25m capitalization of joint stock companies as of 1695 was accounted for by just six companies, the Bank of England, the Million Bank, the New River Company, a key water supplier for London established in the early 17th century, and three foreign trading enterprises, the East India Company, the Royal African Company and the Hudson's Bay Company.[15] These firms generally resembled large partnerships rather than modern companies characterized by a divorce between ownership and control.

The Bank of England had over 1,500 shareholders as of 1694, with the 170 investors who had 'large' holdings (i.e., a nominal value of £2,000 or more) collectively owning only 48 per cent of the stock.[16] On the other hand, the New River Company, from its incorporation in 1619 through to 1866, never had more than 72 shares, only 29 of which had any form of voting rights.[17] During the 1690s a tiny handful of major investors owned collectively more than one-quarter of the East India Company's shares and they dominated the company's affairs.[18] Even though the Royal African Company apparently lacked a major blockholder (as of 1691 'large' holdings made up only 14 per cent of the total stock) it had barely 200 shareholders, comprised largely of the London mercantile elite.[19] While there apparently was active trading in the Hudson Bay Company's stock, it was even more narrowly held, with only 29 names on its 1690 dividend list and 67 as of 1703.[20]

---

[13] P.G.M. Dickson, *The Financial Revolution in England: A Study in the Development of Public Credit* (1967), 488.

[14] Du Bois, *supra* n. 12, 301.

[15] Scott, *supra* n. 3, 336.   [16] Davies, *supra* n. 6 at 296.

[17] Bernard Rudden, *The New River: A Legal History* (1985), 26–27, 43–44, 92–95.

[18] Davies, *supra* n. 6, 296–97.

[19] *Ibid.*, 296, 298–99.

[20] Ann M. Carlos and Jill L. Van Stone, 'Stock Transfer Patterns in the Hudson's Bay Company: A Study in the English Capital Market in Operation, 1670–1730', (1995) 38 Business History, #2, 15, 19–20.

As for the other companies operating in the 1690s, they were hit hard by a monetary crisis in 1696–97 and by a temporary cessation of hostilities with France, which revived foreign competition and prompted a collapse in demand for armaments.[21] Only 40 of the 140 companies in existence as of 1695 were in a condition to continue to carry on business in 1698. Adverse economic conditions took a further toll in the opening decade of the 18th century, reducing the number of companies still operating to no more than 20.

Share dealing suffered in tandem. For the relevant period, Houghton's weekly *Collection for Improvement of Husbandry and Trade* provided the most comprehensive list of companies with active dealing in shares.[22] The number of companies listed peaked at 64 in 1694, though only 10 had dealings that were sufficiently regular for prices to fluctuate weekly. By 1698, only seven companies in total had prices quoted.[23] In this new more sober milieu company promotion lulled badly, as only four companies were launched between 1700 and 1717.[24] One, however—the South Sea Company—was to play a key role in a new, if again short-lived, burst of company formations.

II. The South Sea Company and the 1719–1720 Bubble

The Glorious Revolution of 1688 set the stage for an English 'financial revolution', as the financing of state activities was fortified by a much improved capacity to issue and service debt backed by the expansion of taxation by Parliament.[25] Though the new arrangements ultimately left England—and Britain after the 1707 Union between England and Scotland—better positioned to finance war than its arch rival France, the transition was not seamless. The South Sea Company played a significant, and controversial, role in the transitional process, helping to launch and bring to a premature end an era where corporate enterprises were viewed as key adjuncts to state finance.

The South Sea Company, pursuant to its formation by an Act of Parliament in 1711, issued stock in exchange for £9 million worth of outstanding irredeemable short-term government debt.[26] To sweeten the deal for holders of the debt, Parliament granted the company the exclusive right to trade with the Spanish

---

[21] Scott, *supra* n. 3, 348, 352–56, 376.

[22] *Ibid.*, 329; Philip Mirowski, 'The Rise (and Retreat) of a Market: English Joint Stock Shares in the Eighteenth Century', (1981) 41 Journal of Economic History 559, 564.

[23] Scott, *supra* n. 3, 360.   [24] Harris, *supra* n. 4, 58.

[25] Dickson, *supra* n. 13 is the leading work on this 'revolution'.

[26] On aspects of the pre-Bubble history of the South Sea Company discussed here, see Dale, *supra* n. 10, 49–50; Dickson, *supra* n. 13, 65–66; Malcolm Balen, *A Very English Deceit: The Secret History of the South Sea Bubble and the First Great Financial Scandal* (2002), 36–38, 90–91; John Micklethwait and Adrian Wooldridge, *The Company: A Short History of a Revolutionary Idea* (2003), 36–37.

colonies in South America, a region that had captured the imagination of the English since the mid-16th century. By 1719, war with Spain was eradicating this business, so The South Sea Company directors turned their attention fully to the market for public debt. The timing was propitious, as the government wanted to reduce the cost of servicing its sizeable war-driven debt burden by restructuring irredeemable government annuities paying fixed interest. In 1719, the South Sea Company vied with the Bank of England to persuade the government to adopt a scheme converting this debt into shares of their companies.

The South Sea Company prevailed, meaning investors holding £30 million of government debt would convert their bonds into South Sea shares. Fortuitously its share price was climbing in value, because the higher the price, the more favourable the conversion terms would be.[27] The South Sea Company directors opted not to leave matters to chance and used means both fair and foul to drive up the market value of the company's stock. These included encouraging newspaper reports exaggerating the company's future profitability, announcing unsustainably generous dividends, arranging for the company to buy its own shares, offering to lend money on generous terms to shareholders and bribing politicians.[28]

A concern the South Sea Company directors had was that a surge in company flotations beginning in 1719 was siphoning off demand for its shares.[29] Investors initially turned their attention to joint stock companies because of disappointing returns from overseas trade and demand was reinforced by speculative capital emanating from Paris, where a plan to convert the national debt into shares of the Mississippi Company had prompted a speculative frenzy among investors.[30] According to Scott, 13 company promotions occurred in 1719.[31] Matters went into full swing in the first six months of 1720, with 179 companies being launched, many with an authorized share capital of £1 million or more.[32]

Matters reached a fever pitch in late May and in June of 1720, with 96 promotions taking place. These were supported by intense investor demand, manifested by dramatic share price increases, with the shares of numerous companies trading as high as five and even ten times par value. The new enterprises were proposing to operate in a wide variety of fields, including insurance, fishing, foreign and colonial commerce, land development and manufacturing (e.g. textiles, paper and glass). Inventors and engineers jostled for financial support for a wide variety of proposed projects, including ventures to supply water to London

---

[27] Harris, *supra* n. 4, 65; Balen, *supra* n. 26, 83–84, 91–92, 113; W.A. Speck, *Stability and Strife: England 1714–1760* (1977), 197–98.

[28] Dale, *supra* n. 10, 100–2; Dickson, *supra* n. 13, 141–42; Balen, *supra* n. 26, 112–18.

[29] Carswell, *supra* n. 8, 119.

[30] *Ibid.*, 84–85; Dickson, *supra* n. 13, 137–38; Balen, *supra* n. 26, 101, 109.

[31] Scott, *supra* n. 3, vol. III, 445.

[32] *Ibid.*, 446–57; for background see also at 409–15, 419–21 as well as Balen, *supra* n. 26, 106–8.

and Liverpool, to produce heat-resistant paint, to make glass bottles and glass coaches and to create a floating pool to bring fresh fish by sea to London.

Many of the schemes were products 'of a vision of material progress in advance of the technical capacity to achieve it'.[33] At the same time, though, a majority were in 'sensible' areas and one historian of the South Sea Bubble has even said the companies represented 'more-or-less the full range of today's *Financial Times* industrial classification excluding modern technology'.[34] However, as the frenzy intensified promoters began to launch companies merely to profit from unloading shares on eager investors at the earliest opportunity and subscribers similarly were frequently aiming to pocket quick capital gains by selling out rather than focusing on dividend yields or probable earning powers.[35] As Mackay said of the companies involved in his classic 1852 text on speculation, 'They soon received the name of Bubbles, the most appropriate that imagination could devise. The populace are often most happy in the nicknames they employ. None could be more apt than that of Bubbles. Some of them lasted for a week, or a fortnight, and were no more heard of, while others could not even live out that short span of existence.'[36]

Viability aside, the legality of many of the newly formed joint stock companies was doubtful since their organizers had not bothered to seek legislation or a Royal Charter authorizing their establishment.[37] Legislation brought into force in June 1720 subsequently labelled 'The Bubble Act' underscored the problematic legal status of such enterprises by explicitly prohibiting undertakings lacking authorization from a Royal Charter or an Act of Parliament from acting as a corporate body or raising capital by the issuance of transferable shares and prescribed penalties and remedies for breach.[38] The legislation has been characterized by some as a public-minded (if imperfectly executed) reaction to the excesses of the South Sea Bubble.[39] Others, analyzing the Bubble Act from a public choice perspective, have suggested the legislation was an effort by lawmakers to protect their ability to raise revenue by authorizing incorporation by legislation or charter.[40] The most widely accepted explanation, however, is that the South Sea Company promoted

---

[33] Carswell, *supra* n. 8, 129.   [34] Dale, *supra* n. 10, 107–8.

[35] *Ibid.*, 108–9; Carswell, *supra* n. 8, 117, 147; C.A. Cooke, *Corporation, Trust and Company: An Essay in Legal History* (1950), 81.

[36] Charles Mackay, *Memoirs of Extraordinary Popular Delusions and the Madness of Crowds* (1852), ch. 2, 15.

[37] Harris, *supra* n. 4, 65.

[38] An Act for better securing certain Powers and Privileges, intended to be granted by His Majesty by Two Charters, for Assurance of Ships and Merchandize at Sea, and for lending Money upon Bottomry; and for restraining several extravagant and unwarrantable Practices, 6 Geo. I, c. 18, ss. 18–21.

[39] Holdsworth, *supra* n. 5, 219–20; Du Bois, *supra* n. 12, 2; H.A. Shannon, 'The Coming of General Limited Liability', (1931) 2 Economic History 267, 268.

[40] Henry N. Butler, 'General Incorporation in Nineteenth Century England: Interaction of Common Law and Legislative Processes', (1986) 6 International Review of Law and Economics 169, 172–73; Margaret Patterson and David Reiffen, 'The Effect of the Bubble Act on the Market for Joint Stock Shares', (1990) 51 Journal of Economic History 163.

the legislation to reduce competition for investment capital.[41] The fact the South Sea Company, together with any other undertaking operating prior to 1718, was exempted from the purview of the Act lends credence to this proposition.

In the latter half of 1720 the company promotion boom subsided, with the number of joint stock companies launched falling to two in July, four in August and three in September before petering out completely.[42] The Bubble Act played a role here, with some contemporaries suggesting Exchange Alley emptied when it came into force in June 1720.[43] However, this check was only temporary, as trading activity apparently revived quickly.[44]

An August 1720 pronouncement by the Treasury, likely prompted by the South Sea Company, that it would apply for a writ of *scire facias* against a series of companies for which charters had in fact been obtained was a further blow to investor optimism.[45] A share price crash ensued over the next few weeks, and some contemporaries identified the issuance of the writs as the proximate cause.[46] However, market factors in all likelihood played a more important role in ending the speculative frenzy.[47] Sceptical assessments of the South Sea Company's prospects began to prompt concerns that the company at the centre of the speculative bubble would be unable to generate promised dividends. A tightening of credit markets meant investors struggled to borrow the funds required to pay deposits on shares they agreed to buy, let alone follow up as and when companies made calls for payment of unpaid share capital. Panicky behaviour by inexperienced investors and a currency crisis prompted by a withdrawal of foreign capital compounded matters.[48]

While particular investors were badly affected, the bursting of the South Sea Bubble did not disrupt the British economy in a major way.[49] The South Sea Company, under new leadership and supported by legislative restructuring of the exchange of government debt for company stock, even survived the 1720 debacle and managed a large portfolio of government securities until its affairs were wound up in 1855.[50] With the exchange of government debt for South Sea stock holding firm, the government's fiscal situation improved and going forward

---

[41] Carswell, *supra* n. 8, 97, 119, 129–30; Cooke, *supra* n. 35, 83; Jonathan B. Baskin and Paul J. Miranti, *A History of Corporate Finance* (1997), 111.

[42] Scott, *supra* n. 3, vol. III, 457–58 (the August figure does not include two transactions listed by Scott since these were offerings of new stock in existing companies).

[43] Carswell, *supra* n. 8, 129–30.

[44] Chancellor, *supra* n. 9, 82; Dickson, *supra* n. 13, 147–48.

[45] Carswell, *supra* n. 8, 138, 141, 144; Chancellor, *supra* n. 9, 83; Balen, *supra* n. 26, 127.

[46] Dale, *supra* n. 10, 135–36; Dickson, *supra* n. 13, 149.

[47] Ch. Four, Pt. III.D; Scott, *supra* n. 3, 422–23, 427–28; Carswell, *supra* n. 8, 161; Dickson, *supra* n. 13, 150–51.

[48] Harris, *supra* n. 4, 79; Chancellor, *supra* n. 9, 83; Peter M. Garber, *Famous First Bubbles: The Fundamentals of Early Manias* (2000), 119–20.

[49] Julian Hoppit, 'The Myth of the South Sea Bubble', (2002) 12 Transactions of the Royal History Society 141, 152–55.

[50] Baskin and Miranti, *supra* n. 41, 116.

those responsible for managing English public finance handled their responsibilities efficiently and competently. The country thus had a system of public borrowing in place that was sufficiently robust to underwrite the military and naval successes that contributed to Britain's global pre-eminence through the latter half of the 18th century and much of 19th century.[51] Given these various circumstances, one might have expected that once the post-1720 hangover passed public investment in companies would have flourished.[52] Matters in fact turned out differently.

III. The Publicly Traded Company, 1721–1844

A. Promising Foundations

In various ways conditions were propitious for the rise of the publicly traded company in the decades following the collapse of the South Sea Bubble. Britain was a wealthy country by contemporary standards, so there were funds available for investment in potentially productive uses of capital (Chapter Four, Part III.A). There seemingly should not have been a shortage of worthwhile industrial projects for investors to back, since Britain experienced what is widely referred to as 'the Industrial Revolution' between 1760 and 1830.[53] Whether the label is appropriate is a hotly debated topic.[54] Nevertheless, with Britain experiencing an unrivalled burst of technological creativity its ability to create and adapt new production methods was unsurpassed and it was the home of a path-breaking mode of production, the factory system.[55] Exploiting the competitive advantage operating in the first industrial nation offered, British business dominated the world's markets, exemplified by grand displays at the Great Exhibition in London's Crystal Palace in 1851.[56]

Matching those with financial wherewithal up with ambitious industrial and commercial proprietors also should not have posed serious problems. By the early 18th century, the key institutional structures that characterize an effective share market were in place in England and through the remainder of the century

---

[51] Dickson, *supra* n. 13, 9–12, 197–98.

[52] Bishop Carleton Hunt, *The Development of the Business Corporation in England* (1936), 9; W.J. Reader, *A House in the City: A Study of the City and of the Stock Exchange Based on the Records of Foster & Braithwaite 1825–1975* (1979), 16.

[53] On the period covered, see Joel Mokyr, 'Editor's Introduction: The New Economic History and the Industrial Revolution' in Joel Mokyr (ed.), *The British Industrial Revolution: An Economic Perspective*, 2nd edn (1999), 1, 3.

[54] For overviews of the debate, see *ibid.*, 3–5, 8–12; David S. Landes, 'The Fable of the Dead Horse; or, the Industrial Revolution Revisited' in Mokyr, British, *supra* n. 53, 128, 130–50.

[55] Mokyr, 'Editor's' *supra* n. 53, 19–23, 36–39; David Landes, 'Technological Change and Innovation in Western Europe, 1750–1914' in H.J. Habakkuk and M. Postan (eds), *Cambridge Economic History of Europe*, vol. VI (1965), 274, 274–75.

[56] John F. Wilson, *British Business History, 1720–1994* (1995), 21.

dealing in transferable securities developed greatly in terms of intermediation and technique.[57] By the end of the 18th century London-based professional brokers and dealers seeking speedy and reliable trading were endeavouring to establish a market where all active participants were ready and willing to deal and possessed a reputation for honouring their bargains. This culminated in the formation of the London Stock Exchange in 1801, which not only functioned as a clearing house for securities trading but also was structured as a closed market, regulated so that those who participated obeyed the rules and paid for its administration. Moreover, while Britain had a regionally oriented economy in the 18th century (e.g. the industrial revolution occurred almost exclusively in the northern and Midland regions of England and in Scotland), the fact government interest rates began correlating more closely with real estate markets and bankruptcy rates outside London implies there were growing inter-regional economic connections.[58]

B. Types of Companies Traded on the Stock Market

While in various ways conditions appeared hospitable for the rise of publicly traded corporate enterprises in the wake of the South Sea Bubble the corporate sector of the economy only grew tentatively and through to the 1840s a modern-style divorce of ownership and control was essentially unknown. Of the 190 or so companies launched in 1720, only four survived and there were only 24 London-based joint stock companies as of 1740.[59] There was then modest growth in the number of companies. The *Course of the Exchange*, a journal issued under the authority of the London Stock Exchange, reported there were 61 companies with shares listed for trading on the Exchange as of 1811 (Figure I). The growth was accounted for largely by canal companies and by other companies in the transport and utility sectors, namely water supply and docks. The public trading of canal shares was largely the result of a surge in promotion activity in the early 1790s that marked the first time canal companies were floated publicly rather than being launched purely by private subscription.[60] The fact that the investment returns on these new canal enterprises were poor as compared with their predecessors helped to deter further public offerings.[61]

---

[57] Ch. Two, Pt. VII; Ranald C. Michie, *The London Stock Exchange: A History* (1999), 26–31, 35–36.

[58] Moshe Buchinsky and Ben Polak, 'The Emergence of a National Capital Market in England, 1710–1880', (1993) 53 Journal of Economic History 1; Julian Hoppitt, *Risk and Failure in English Business 1700–1800* (1987), 132–33; Larry Neal, 'The Finance of Business During the Industrial Revolution' in Roderick Floud and Deidre McCloskey (eds), *The Economic History of Britain, Volume 1: 1700–1860*, 2nd edn (1994), 151, 178–80.

[59] Dale, *supra* n. 10, 107; Balen, *supra* n. 26, 107 (1720 companies); Harris, *supra* n. 4, 171 (1740).

[60] Hunt, *supra* n. 52, 10; Arthur Gayer, W.W. Rostow and Anna Jacobson Schwartz, *The Growth and Fluctuation of the British Economy 1790–1850*, vol. I (1975), 417–18.

[61] Chancellor, *supra* n. 9, 123–24.

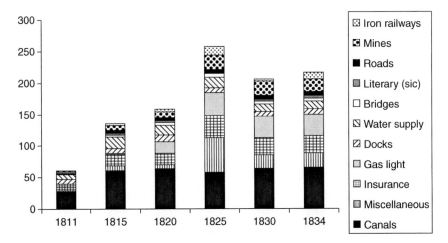

Figure I: Companies listed in the Course of the Exchange (as of May in each of the years listed)

Source: Compiled using data from Harris, *supra* n. 4, 219, Table 8.1.

The number of companies with shares traded publicly, as reported by the *Course of the Exchange*, grew in the opening decades of the 19th century, but progress was fitful (Figure I). A change in editorial policy rather than a flourishing of corporate enterprise accounted for the growth of the list between 1811 and 1815.[62] The increase in 1825 was due to a flurry of company promotions sparked when 'a boom psychology gripped the public's imagination'.[63] The foundations were a growing confidence in the economy, a build-up of spare capital by the mercantile community due to bumper British harvests and a drop in returns offered by government bonds due to reduced borrowing.[64] Promotions of South American mining companies got matters underway, followed by more mining companies, both domestic and foreign. New domestic companies of various types then followed, including gas light concerns, insurers, railways and some more outlandish ventures, such as an umbrella rental concern and a company proposing to pipe seawater to London so its residents could enjoy the benefits of seawater bathing.[65]

The 1824–25 surge in company promotion ended abruptly after a poor harvest necessitated the use of invested funds to import foodstuffs and a national credit squeeze hammered investors who had borrowed to buy shares.[66] Of the

---

[62] Harris, *supra* n. 4, 122, 218, n. 52.

[63] Arthur D. Gayer, Anna Jacobson and Isaiah Finkelstein, 'British Share Prices, 1811–1850', (1940) 22 Review of Economic Studies 78, 87.

[64] R.C. Michie, *Money, Mania and Markets* (1981), 27–28, 30.

[65] Harris, *supra* n. 4, 217–18; Chancellor, *supra* n. 9, 100–6.

[66] Michie, *supra* n. 64, 35.

624 company formations announced in England during the promotion wave, only 127 of these companies were in existence as of 1827.[67] A drop in the number of companies listed by the *Course of the Exchange* between 1825 and 1830 (Figure I) implies few of the survivors lacked sufficient staying power to have their shares publicly traded.

In the early 19th century most enterprises that had distributed shares to the public were 'non-industrial', generally falling broadly into the public utilities category. Publicly traded industrial enterprises were conspicuous by their absence, particularly given the occurrence of the industrial revolution. For the purpose of the *Course of the Exchange* listings manufacturing enterprises were lumped into the 'miscellaneous' category, but this category included a wide variety of enterprises, few of which lasted long and none of which had shares traded with any degree of regularity.[68] By the 1840s it was becoming somewhat more common for manufacturing concerns to operate as joint stock companies, including two dozen operating as woollen mills. However, in this industry, as with other trades representative of the industrial revolution, small common law partnerships remained the dominant form of commercial organization.[69]

The collapse of the share market in the wake of the 1824–25 company promotion frenzy combined with 'runs' on various local banks to prompt what was characterized as 'a torrent of distrust'.[70] Investor enthusiasm for shares nevertheless returned before long, as a company promotion boom occurred in the mid-1830s, dominated by railways and banks. Between 1834 and 1836, 300 companies, with an aggregate nominal capital of £135.2m, were floated.[71] Eighty-eight were railways, with a nominal capital of £69.7m, and 20 were banks, with a nominal capital of £23.8m. Seventy-one of the companies floated were mining enterprises, but their total nominal capital was only £7.0m and they had little staying power. An 1843 statistical survey of Britain said of mining companies: 'For the greater part they are not only complete failures, but are memorable proofs of the folly and cupidity of British capitalists on the one hand, and the knavery of their projectors on the other.'[72]

C. Ownership and Control

Among the corporate enterprises with shares available for trading up to the 1840s, there is little direct evidence of investors owning dominant voting blocks but a modern-style divorce of ownership and control was generally conspicuous

---

[67] Gayer, Rostow and Schwartz, *supra* n. 60, 412–13.

[68] *Ibid.*, 363, 415.

[69] B.C. Hunt, 'The Joint Stock Company in England', (1935) 43 Journal of Political Economy 331, 352–53; P.L. Cottrell, *Industrial Finance 1830–1914* (1980), 9; Pat Hudson, 'Industrial Organisation and Structure' in Roderick Floud and Paul Johnson (eds), *The Cambridge Economic History of Modern Britain, Volume I: Industrialisation, 1700–1860* (2004), 28, 49.

[70] Chancellor, *supra* n. 9, 110–12.   [71] Hunt, *supra* n. 69, 351.

[72] *Ibid.*, 352, quoting W.F. Spackman, *Statistical Tables of the U.K.* (1843).

by its absence. On a general level, the corporate sector was very much a side-show in a stock market dominated by dealing in government debt securities, implying the absence of a liquid market for shares. As of the early 1840s, when the membership of the London Stock Exchange was approaching 800, only four or five brokers and an even fewer 'jobbers' ('marketmakers' who bought and sold shares on a wholesale basis on their own behalf) handled the entire trade in company shares.[73]

The situation with canal companies, the most numerous category of company on the *Course of the Exchange* list (Figure I), also indicates the lack of a modern-style divorce of ownership and control. Evans, relying on his research on two late 18th-century canals showing each lacked a major blockholder, paralleled canal companies with large widely held US corporations of his day (the 1930s).[74] In fact the differences outweighed the similarities. Evans himself found family names appeared on the canal company share registers with sufficient frequency to suggest efforts were being made to circumvent provisions in acts of incorporation designed to preclude the concentration of voting control.[75] More generally, canals generally lacked the widespread, investment-driven shareholder base that became a hallmark of widely held public companies. Share ownership was not geographically dispersed but instead was concentrated primarily in the vicinity of the canal in question, with numerous investors buying shares to provide backing for improved transportation facilities to benefit their business activities.[76] Canal companies also did not have a large number of shareholders. According to data provided by a study of share ownership of canals established between 1755 and the end of the 18th century, the average number of investors taking up shares in such enterprises was 139.[77] Finally, secondary trading for canal shares was rudimentary. Dealing was primarily informal and localized and based on personal connections and newspaper advertisements.[78]

Gas light companies, the second most numerous type of enterprise on the *Course of the Exchange* list from 1825 onwards, resembled canals. Local initiative and local capital played a key role in their launch and operation and backing

---

[73] Gayer, Rostow and Schwartz, *supra* n. 60, 409.

[74] George H. Evans, *British Corporation Finance 1775–1850: A Study of Preference Shares* (1936), 7, 28–29.

[75] *Ibid.*, 30. The Leeds and Liverpool Canal legislation stipulated no individual could own more than 100 shares and the Stroudwater Navigation Company legislation provided that owners of 10 or more shares could not exercise more than five votes.

[76] *Ibid.*, 6, 12–13, 31–33, 38; J.R. Ward, *The Finance of Canal Building in Eighteenth-Century England* (1974), 79, 128–33 (saying, though, that financial considerations were likely more important).

[77] Calculated using data compiled by Ward, *supra* n. 76, 26–74 (providing for 39 canal companies information on the number of proprietors named in the Act of incorporation or the number of shares available for initial subscription and size of the average subscription).

[78] *Ibid.*, 81–82, 97–108, 135; E. Victor Morgan and W.A. Thomas, *The Stock Exchange: Its History and Functions* (1969), 101–2.

for them was motivated partly by a desire to upgrade local infrastructure.[79] Early 19th-century insurance companies, likewise well represented on the list, also were not models of diffuse share ownership. Instead, 'the passive investor was frowned upon'.[80] Insurance companies were typically backed by local networks of wealthy mercantile and industrial families, often interlinked by marriage and business partnerships. Insurance company shares lacked full liquidity since directors carefully controlled access to the share register so as to ensure holders were financially sound. Also, insurance companies generally expected new shareholders to buy insurance from the company and anticipated key shareholders would assist the business by providing intelligence on market conditions and by recruiting and vetting potential customers. These were hardly hallmarks of 'arm's-length' investment.

As for banks and railways, the centrepiece of the company promotion surge in the mid-1830s, they also were not characterized by modern-style diffuse share ownership. In England, it only became possible for banks to develop a sizeable ownership base after legislative amendments in 1826 and 1833 dismantled restrictions on the establishment of banks exceeding a prescribed number of partners.[81] Prior to this deregulation, banking in England was dominated by 'country banks', private banks established outside London, often by merchants and industrialists seeking an outlet for spare capital and to assist the financing of their business ventures.[82] Numerous banks incorporated in the 1830s resulted from conversions of these private banks and the partners typically remained dominant shareholders.[83] As Anderson and Cottrell have said, 'Since, in normal circumstances, the holdings of former partners, together with those of directors and local worthies, were unlikely to be traded, a high concentration of shareownership (sic) usually resulted in a "thin" secondary market for bank shares

---

[79] M.E. Falkus, 'The British Gas Industry Before 1850', (1967) 20 Economic History Review (N.S.) 494, 505; Robert Millward and Robert Ward, 'From Private to Public Ownership of Gas Undertakings in England and Wales, 1851–1947: Chronology, Incidence and Causes', (1993) 35(3) Business History 1, 6.

[80] Robin Pearson, 'Shareholder Democracies? English Stock Companies and the Politics of Corporate Governance During the Industrial Revolution', (2002) 117 English History Review 840, 852. On aspects of insurance companies discussed here, see *ibid.*, 851–52; Clive Trebilcock, *Phoenix Assurance and the Development of British Insurance, vol. I: 1782–1870* (1985), 391, 516; Robin Pearson and David Richardson, 'Business Networking in the Industrial Revolution', (2001) 54 Economic History Review 657 (focusing on investors in fire insurance offices).

[81] Hunt, *supra* n. 69, 337–41.

[82] Stephen Quinn, 'Money, Finance and Capital Markets' in Floud and Johnson, *supra* n. 69, 147, 159; Rondo Cameron, 'England 1750–1844' in Rondo Cameron (ed.), *Banking in the Early Stages of Industrialization: A Study in Comparative Economic History* (1967), 15, 20, 24, 56–58; T.S. Ashton, *The Industrial Revolution*, rev. edn (1968), 83.

[83] B.L. Anderson and P.L. Cottrell, 'Another Victorian Capital Market: A Study of Banking and Bank Investors on Merseyside', (1975) 28 Economic History Review (N.S.), 598, 606 (discussing conversions of Liverpool private banks); R.S. Sayers, *Lloyds Bank in the History of English Banking* (1957), 159 (discussing the conversion of a Nottinghamshire bank where the former partners retained nearly one-third of the shares and 6,000 additional shares were 'left at the disposal of the Directors, for the benefit of the company').

and so restricted the scope for diffusion of ownership.'[84] In addition, share ownership in banks was frequently not an arm's-length investment-driven decision, with a substantial minority of the lending joint stock banks engaged in involving shareholders.[85]

Railway companies were to become mid-19th-century forerunners of the modern widely held company (Part V.A) but remained in a transitional phase as of the late 1830s. The launching of railway companies in the opening decades of the 19th century often resembled the procedure for canals, with local business elites recognizing the need for improved communication in their locality, calling public meetings to arouse support and obtaining subscriptions for shares prior to seeking from Parliament an Act of incorporation.[86] This pattern was unravelling, however, by the 1830s, with the market for railway share capital taking on an increasingly cross-regional character.

Most of the share capital raised between 1835 and 1845 by the 13 companies that became the Lancashire & Yorkshire Railway was subscribed for by residents of 'interested' counties (i.e., counties the railways served).[87] However, investment in other railways of this era was by no means a purely local affair. Instead, Lancashire and London investors often joined local counterparts as initial backers and the investor base of successful railways tended to take on an increasingly cross-regional orientation over time.[88] Trading activity in railway shares was sufficiently robust to provide a platform for the opening of organized stock markets in Liverpool and Manchester in the mid-1830s, the first in Britain outside London.[89] The foundation thus had been laid for railways to become the earliest companies to experience a modern-style divorce between ownership and control.

IV. Why Didn't the Industrial Revolution Act as a Catalyst for Publicly Held Industrial Companies?

A. Law

Why did the industrial revolution fail to yield major industrial corporate enterprises? Many blame the law, arguing full economic development was impossible

[84] Anderson and Cottrell, *supra* n. 83, 599. See also Hudson, *supra* n. 69, 53.

[85] Lucy Newton and Philip L. Cottrell, 'Female Investors in the First English and Welsh Commercial Joint-Stock Banks', (2006) 16 Accounting, Business & Financial History 315, 322.

[86] Evans, *supra* n. 74, ch. 2; François Crouzet, *The Victorian Economy* (1982), 289.

[87] Seymour Broadbridge, *Studies in Railway Expansion and the Capital Market in England 1825–1873* (1970).

[88] M.C. Reed, *Investment in Railways in Britain, 1820–1844: A Study of the Development of the Capital Market* (1975), D. Brooke, 'The Promotion of Four Yorkshire Railways and the Share Capital Market', (1972) 5 Transport History 243.

[89] M.C. Reed, 'Railways and the Growth of the Capital Market' in M.C. Reed (ed.), *Railways in the Victorian Economy: Studies in Finance and Economic Growth* (1969), 162; W.A. Thomas, *The Provincial Stock Exchanges* (1973), 17–18, 21–22.

until the legal setting for business enterprise was more congenial. Hunt says, 'Confusing litigation and the ghosts of 1720 harried the course of the unincorporated joint stock company until the middle of the (19th) century.'[90] Gower maintains similarly 'throughout the (18th) century and beyond the shadow of 1720 retarded the development of incorporated companies'.[91]

'1720' was a reference to the Bubble Act, which again imposed penalties on corporate undertakings lacking due authorization by a Royal Charter or legislation. Incorporation by specific act or charter could be cumbersome, time-consuming and expensive, particularly if commercial rivals lobbied against state authorization. In 1769, the Leeds and Liverpool Canal earmarked £1,300 of its £260,000 subscribed capital for its application to Parliament for incorporation and related expenses.[92] When the founders of the Equitable Assurance petitioned for a charter in 1757 they had to wait four years for a decision, ultimately finding out their application had been refused due to pressure from other insurance companies lobbying to protect their corporate privileges.[93]

Occasionally, manufacturing enterprises incorporated by way of legislation (e.g. the London Flour and Bread Company in 1800). A few others sought Parliamentary authorization and failed (e.g. the Albion Steam Flour Mill in 1784).[94] More often, the thinking goes, the Bubble Act deterred proprietors of industrial and commercial enterprises from attempting to incorporate and thereby inhibited the flow of capital into corporate enterprise.[95] As Holdsworth claimed in his classic *History of English Law*, 'The Act . . . stopped the development of the joint stock system.'[96]

The Bubble Act was repealed in 1825.[97] However, the law arguably still deterred the growth of corporate enterprise. According to Hunt, 'Large partnerships, joint stock and ordinary, still labored under a common law which had long been ill adapted to their inherent necessities.'[98] Partnership law of the time indeed posed various disadvantages for larger business enterprises.[99] Outside investors understandably would have been wary of the unlimited liability associated with being a partner. The conduct of litigation was a potentially burdensome process since all partners theoretically had to be added as parties. The death of any partner implied termination of the partnership, necessitating reorganization

---

[90] Hunt, *supra* n. 52, 21.　　　[91] Gower, *supra* n. 1, 31; see also at 39.
[92] Harris, *supra* n. 4, 133.　　　[93] *Ibid.*, 102–3.
[94] *Ibid.*, 178–80.
[95] Carswell, *supra* n. 8, 129, 243; Cameron, 'England', *supra* n. 82, 35; Peter Mathias, *The First Industrial Nation: An Economic History of Britain 1700–1914*, 2nd edn (1983), 145.
[96] Holdsworth, *supra* n. 5, 221.
[97] An Act to repeal so much of an Act passed in the Sixth Year of His late Majesty King George the First, as relates to the restraining several vagrant and unwarrantable Practices in the said Act mentioned . . . , 6 Geo. 4 c. 91.
[98] Hunt, *supra* n. 52, 82.
[99] Du Bois, *supra* n. 12, 217; Shannon, *supra* n. 39, 270–74; Gary M. Anderson and Robert D. Tollison, 'The Myth of the Corporation as a Creation of the State', (1983) 3 International Review of Law and Economics 107, 110.

of the enterprise. Also, transferability of ownership interests could be problematic since the transfer of partnership stakes was potentially subject to the consent of all partners.

A joint stock company established by way of a 'deed of settlement' under which a body of trustees held the company's property for the benefit of investors could be used to achieve results akin to full-scale incorporation.[100] For instance, after being rebuffed by Parliament, the promoters of the Equitable Assurance persevered and established the company on a mutual basis under a deed of settlement.[101] However, even after the repeal of the Bubble Act, the legality of the unincorporated joint stock company remained in some doubt, with uncertainties including litigation mechanics, the transferability of shares and limited liability.[102] Also, the legislation repealing the Bubble Act specifically declared that undertakings remained subject to the common law, implying companies unauthorized by legislation or charter remained potentially illegal. A series of post-repeal cases yielded conflicting results, so while the trend was in favour of legality of the unincorporated joint stock company,[103] legal advisers could not offer definitive advice to clients on the risks involved with operating in this manner.[104] Hence, even after the repeal of the Bubble Act an inhospitable legal environment potentially hamstrung the development of fully fledged corporate undertakings.[105]

While there were legal impediments to incorporation, the state of the law was in fact not the dominant factor deterring corporate enterprise in the 18th century and the first part of the 19th century. The pattern was set when market conditions did more than the Bubble Act to bring to an end the company promotion boom of 1719/20 (Part II) and continued in the decades following. Du Bois claims that '[I]n the first decades that followed its passage, the Bubble Act was a latent menace in every board room and lawyer's chambers when problems of business organization were deliberated.'[106] However, up to 1808 there was only a single enforcement proceeding brought under the 1720 legislation and this was launched shortly after it came into force.[107] The Bubble Act therefore faded as a concern as businessmen and their advisers treated it as obsolete. As Du Bois himself notes, 'Even in company and legal records references to it were few and far between.'[108] Under the circumstances, those wanting to establish and operate business associations became increasingly willing to risk proceeding through the medium of a deed of settlement to establish an unincorporated joint stock company, refraining even

---

[100] Du Bois, *supra* n. 12, 217; Cooke, *supra* n. 35, 85–88; Anderson and Tollison, *supra* n. 99, 110–11.
[101] Harris, *supra* n. 4, 103.   [102] Du Bois, *supra* n. 12, 219–26.
[103] Gower, *supra* n. 1, 39; Cooke, *supra* n. 35, 106–8.
[104] Harris, *supra* n. 4, 249.
[105] Butler, *supra* n. 40, 176; Hunt, *supra* n. 52, 82.
[106] Du Bois, *supra* n. 12, 11.
[107] Anderson and Tollison, *supra* n. 99, 111; see also Harris, *supra* n. 4, 236–37.
[108] Du Bois, *supra* n. 12, 35; see also Harris, *supra* n. 4, 237; Cooke, *supra* n. 35, 95.

from imposing restrictions on share transfers in response to the Bubble Act's specific targeting of transferable shares.[109] The result was, as the Lord Chancellor said in an 1854 case, joint stock companies 'consonant with the wants of a growing community, [had] forced their way into existence whether fostered by the law or opposed to it'.[110]

The Bubble Act, after being neglected for decades, was pressed into service by the Attorney General and private litigants in a series of six cases between 1808 and 1812.[111] The early rulings construed the Act broadly, implying the demise of the unincorporated joint stock company. In the later decisions a more pragmatic approach was adopted, with the determinative question, to be resolved on a factual basis case-by-case, being whether the business enterprise was prejudicial to the public. This meant the legality of a company not incorporated by charter or under an Act of Parliament was never entirely guaranteed.[112] On the other hand, so long as a skilful draftsman could craft a joint stock company's deed of settlement in a way that demonstrated the company had an object clearly beneficial to the public, the proprietors generally could be confident they were protected from legal challenge.[113] The inconsistent rulings handed down by the courts on the common law status of the joint stock company after the 1825 repeal of the Bubble Act meant the situation remained much the same in the decades following. This suggests that although the law was an inconvenience, it did not have a crucial impact on the organization of industrial and commercial enterprise.[114]

The experience in Scotland illustrates the law was not a decisive impediment to the development of large, publicly traded industrial firms. Shannon has claimed the law governing joint stock companies was 'different and better' in Scotland than in England.[115] While Freeman, Pearson and Taylor contend 'it is not entirely clear how different and how much better',[116] Scots law was generally hospitable to the establishment of business enterprises as unincorporated joint stock companies. A partnership could be established with transferable shares and was recognized as a legal person distinct from the partners of which it was composed.[117]

---

[109] Du Bois, *supra* n. 12, 40.

[110] In re *Sea, Fire and Life Insurance Co.* (Greenwood's Case) (1854) 3 DeG., M. & G. 459, 477, 43 E.R. 180, 187.

[111] *The King v Dodd* (1808) 9 East 51, 103 E.R. 670; *Buck v Buck* (1808) 1 Camp. 547, 170 E.R. 1052; *Metcalf v Bruin* (1810) 12 East 400, 104 E.R. 156; *The King v Webb* (1811) 14 East 406, 104 E.R. 658; *Pratt v Hutchinson* (1812) 15 East 511, 104 E.R. 936; *Brown v Holt* (1812) 4 Taunt. 587, 128 E.R. 460.

[112] Harris, *supra* n. 4, 238–41.

[113] Cooke, *supra* n. 35, 99.   [114] Cottrell, *supra* n. 69, 10.

[115] Shannon, *supra* n. 39, 267, n. 2; see also R.H. Campbell, 'The Law and the Joint-Stock Company in Scotland' in Peter L. Payne (ed.), *Studies in Scottish Business History* (1967), 136, 148.

[116] Mark Freeman, Robin Pearson and James Taylor, '"Different and Better?" Scottish Joint Stock Companies and the Law, *c.* 1720–1845', (2007) 122 English Historical Review 61, 81.

[117] Campbell, *supra* n. 115, 143; David M. Walker, *A Legal History of Scotland*, vol. VI (2001), 715.

This facilitated the conduct of legal proceedings affecting a firm and made it feasible to raise credit on the basis of an enterprise's assets. There also was some case and text authority supporting the proposition shareholders were protected by limited liability, though the extent to which the law in fact afforded this protection is unclear.[118] In addition, while the Bubble Act extended to Scotland, it was a 'dead letter' since it was referred to only twice in Scottish judgments and was never used to challenge successfully the legality of a Scottish joint stock company.[119]

The industrial revolution transformed Scotland in much the same way as it did regions in the north and west of England.[120] If law in fact was a major deterrent to the development of corporate enterprise in the industrial sector in England and Scots law was indeed appreciably 'different and better', the industrial company should have moved to the forefront in Scotland before it did in England. This did not occur. During the 18th century, there were a few attempts to launch industrial joint stock companies in Scotland, but these were generally unsuccessful.[121] The stock promotion boom of 1824–25 (Part III.A) affected Scotland as well as London, but a list of joint stock companies with shares traded regularly on the Edinburgh market as of 1825 and of 'principal' Scottish companies as of 1841 indicates the types of companies that dominated in England (transport, finance and utilities) did the same in Scotland (Table I). The Scottish experience therefore confirms that law was not a major stumbling block to the development of industrial corporate enterprise up to the 1840s.

Table I: Scottish joint stock companies: principal categories, 1825, 1840

Sector	Joint stock companies 'known' on the Edinburgh market, 1825	Joint stock companies in Scotland *c.* 1840
Financial (banks and insurance)	17	55
Transport (railways, canals and shipping)	16	25
Urban utilities	9	23
Industrial and commercial	9	2
Government		1
Total	51	106

Source: Compiled using data from Michie, *supra* n. 64, 45–46.

[118] Walker, *supra* n. 117, 715–17; J. Robertson Christie, 'Joint Stock Enterprise in Scotland Before the Companies Acts', (1909–10) 21 Juridical Review 128, 138–45.

[119] Freeman, Pearson and Taylor, *supra* n. 116, 64; Christie, *supra* n. 118, 137–38.

[120] Rondo Cameron, 'Scotland, 1750–1845' in Cameron, *Banking, supra* n. 82, 60, 62–64; T.M. Devine, 'Scotland' in Floud and Johnson, *supra* n. 69, 388, 399–401.

[121] Michie, *supra* n. 64, 34.

B. Market Dynamics

Though law deterred the progress of the company to some extent, market factors do more to explain why Britain's industrial revolution failed to yield major industrial and commercial corporate enterprises.[122] In 18th-century Britain, which was wealthy in comparative terms, there was a sizeable contingent of investors with the wherewithal to back business ventures. As Postan has put it, '[T]here were enough rich people in the country to finance an economic effort far in excess of the modest activities of the leaders of the Industrial Revolution.'[123] Nevertheless, various institutional and geographical barriers hampered investment in industrial enterprises.

The fractionalized nature of British capital markets was one obstacle. Although during the 18th century economic connections between Britain's regions were strengthening (Part III.A), there was no single national reservoir of capital during the industrial revolution. Instead, 'there was a multiplicity of small disjointed pools' functioning on a regional basis.[124] The iron industry in South Wales was launched by wealthy London and Bristol merchants and a number of hosiers in the Midland textile industry were able to draw on finance provided by London contacts.[125] Nevertheless, since capital markets remained primarily regional in orientation, industrialists minded to raise capital to build up their firms were generally poorly positioned to appeal to investors outside their locality.

The fact industrial enterprises did not stand out as attractive investments was another buy side obstacle. Most industrial firms were either small or of middling size and many had a short lifespan, disappearing a few years after they were set up.[126] Industrial enterprises that were expanding rapidly—the sort of 'growth' businesses that would later become popular among investors—were distrusted. Quick expansion was thought to increase the risk of bankruptcy due to increased reliance on credit, and doubts existed whether sizeable enterprises could exploit effectively economies of scale.[127]

---

[122] Reader, *supra* n. 52, 17; Mokyr, 'Editor's' *supra* n. 53, 51; Peter L. Payne, 'Industrial Entrepreneurship and Management in Great Britain', in P. Mathias and M.M. Postan (eds), *The Cambridge Economic History of Europe, vol. VII, The Industrial Economies: Capital, Labour and Enterprise, Part I (Britain, France, Germany, and Scandinavia)* (1978), 180, 195.

[123] M.M. Postan, 'Recent Trends in the Accumulation of Capital' (1935) 6 Economic History Review 1, 2; see also Ch. Four, Pt. III.A; Phyllis Deane, 'Capital Formation in Britain Before the Railway Age', (1961) 9 Economic Development and Cultural Change 352, 354.

[124] Postan, *supra* n. 123, 4–5. See also François Crouzet, 'Editor's Introduction' in François Crouzet, *Capital Formation in the Industrial Revolution* (1972), 1, 53; Pat Hudson, *The Industrial Revolution* (1992), 104; Steven King and Geoffrey Timmins, *Making Sense of the Industrial Revolution* (2001), 124–25.

[125] Ashton, *supra* n. 82, 79 (Welsh iron industry); King and Timmins, *supra* n. 124, 127 (Midland textile industry).

[126] Katrina Honeyman, *Origins of Enterprise: Business Leadership in the Industrial Revolution* (1982), 122–23; P.L. Payne, *British Entrepreneurship in the Nineteenth Century*, 2nd edn (1988), 24–25; David Sunderland, *Social Capital, Trust and the Industrial Revolution* (2007), 158, 174–75.

[127] Sunderland, *supra* n. 126, 175.

There were also concerns about what is currently characterized as the agency cost problem, in the sense that large industrial enterprises reputedly were likely to suffer as a result of reliance on poorly motivated salaried managers.[128] The fate of the Albion Mill Company, which built in London in the mid-1780s the biggest and most technologically sophisticated mill of the period, reinforced apprehension on this count. This unincorporated joint stock company was backed by James Watt, the steam engine innovator, Mathew Boulton, a leading entrepreneur of the day, as well as members of the London mercantile elite. Nevertheless, due partly to mismanagement by salaried managers, the venture failed within a few years of launch.[129]

For those who became rich through trade, commerce or other means, land was often the first choice as an investment, in part because a landed estate provided an important base for social standing.[130] Otherwise, debt securities issued by the government were popular. Government bonds known as 'Consols' tended to 'crowd out' other forms of investment since they offered security, solid returns, and could almost always be readily converted to cash.[131] Their attraction grew when Britain was at war since the interest rate assigned was higher than in peacetime.[132] This was no small matter, since Britain was engaged in armed conflict for 36 of the 60 years following 1760 and accumulated a large debt to finance its war efforts.[133] Given that government debt was bought, held and traded primarily in London and the surrounding area and the industrial revolution occurred in the north of England and in Scotland, the extent to which government borrowing crowded out industrial investment is unclear.[134] On the other hand, with economic connections between Britain's regions strengthening during the 18th century, the popularity of Consols may well have deterred the deployment of capital to industry to some extent.[135]

The fact industrialists during the industrial revolution were disinclined to seek outside investment also constrained the development of large-scale corporate enterprise. On this count manufacturing firms differed from the transport, utility and insurance enterprises which offered shares for sale to the public. Canals, docks, gas lighting schemes and railways were capital-intensive

---

[128] Sidney Pollard, *The Genesis of Modern Management: A Study of the Industrial Revolution in Great Britain* (1965), 19–23. On managerial agency costs, see Ch. One, Pt. I.

[129] Pollard, *supra* n. 128, 20; O.A. Westworth, 'The Albion Steam Flour Mill', (1932) 2 Economic History 380, 387, 391, 393.

[130] Reader, *supra* n. 52, 12–13.

[131] *Ibid.*, 13, 16 (advantages of investing in government debt); Jeffrey G. Williamson, 'Why Was British Growth So Slow During the Industrial Revolution?' (1984) 44 Journal of Economic History 687, 692–94, 698–700, 712 ('crowding out').

[132] François Crouzet, 'Capital Formation During the Industrial Revolution' in Crouzet, *Capital*, *supra* n. 124, 162, 214–16; Carol E. Heim and Philip Mirowski, 'Interest Rates and Crowding-Out During Britain's Industrial Revolution', (1987) 47 Journal of Economic History 117, 122.

[133] Williamson, *supra* n. 131, 689, 694–98.

[134] Michie, *supra* n. 57, 32–33; Cottrell, *supra* n. 69, 6.

[135] Landes, *supra* n. 55, 296–97; Heim and Mirowski, *supra* n. 132, 130.

infrastructure projects that could not be readily financed by even wealthy individuals. With insurance companies, risk-spreading among numerous investors was sensible as massive liabilities could wipe out even very rich individual backers (Chapter Three, Part I). In mining enterprises, the digging of shafts and the acquisition of pumping equipment associated with exploiting deeper lodes and veins could entail substantial capital outlays exceeding what their proprietors could or would provide.[136]

During the industrial revolution, manufacturing enterprises were in a different financial category.[137] A proprietor could establish a viable operation with modest premises, such as an old farm or cottage, and machinery could be bought quite cheaply, particularly second-hand at post-bankruptcy auction sales. For instance, in the 1830s a power-loom shed could be built and equipped with 50 looms for about £5,000 (£350,000 in 2006 currency).[138] Many operations were considerably smaller, employing a dozen workers or fewer, and therefore cheaper.

The modest scope of manufacturing enterprises was due to minimal economies of scale. Industrial revolution technology, though innovative, was fairly simple and thus cheap to acquire.[139] Rapidly changing production techniques meant expensive machinery could quickly be obsolete. Firms also lacked the accounting tools necessary to measure costs and set prices with sufficient accuracy to exploit whatever scale economies might have existed.[140] For those starting a manufacturing business and lacking cash to buy premises and machinery outright, further capital-economizing measures were available, such as purchasing on credit or renting space and/or machinery.[141] Landlords of bankrupt industrial tenants were usually eager to lease both.

While fixed capital requirements for manufacturing enterprises were rarely substantial, working or 'circulating' capital requirements, arising from mismatches between a firm's outlays and its revenues, could be.[142] Suppliers of raw materials had to be paid and would not grant indefinite credit. Wages had to be paid when due. At the same time, converting raw materials into finished goods could take weeks and months could pass before payment was effected for goods

---

[136] Cottrell, *supra* n. 69, 9, 34; King and Timmins, *supra* n. 124, 107.

[137] Hudson, *supra* n. 124, 25, 36–37; Honeyman, *supra* n. 126, 2; Herbert Heaton, 'Financing the Industrial Revolution', (1937) 11 Bulletin of the Business Historical Society 1, 2–3; Sidney Pollard, 'Fixed Capital in the Industrial Revolution in Britain', (1964) 24 Journal of Economic History 299, 300–3.

[138] As mentioned in the preface, historical currency conversions carried out in this chapter and elsewhere throughout the book have been done with <http://measuringworth.com/calculators/ukcompare/>, using the retail price index measure.

[139] Hudson, *supra* n. 69, 37–38; Peter Mathias, 'Capital, Credit and Enterprise in the Industrial Revolution', (1973) 2 Journal of European Economic History 121, 128–29.

[140] Hudson, *supra* n. 69, 38.

[141] Honeyman, *supra* n. 126, 117–18; Heaton, *supra* n. 137, 3.

[142] Heaton, *supra* n. 137, 4; Pollard, *supra* n. 137, 305. On the definition of working capital, see Neal, *supra* n. 58, 154.

delivered. Still, while finding circulating capital could be fraught with hazards, once industrial enterprises survived the difficult initial stages of operation they could meet the challenge without backing from arm's-length investors.

Revenues in fledgling manufacturing firms were frequently negligible as they had to develop an initial customer base. Correspondingly, there was a high incidence of bankruptcy and failure during the opening years of operation, particularly when there was a downward turn in the trade cycle or working capital requirements were higher than anticipated.[143] Entrepreneurs, to get their businesses off the ground under such challenging conditions, were best situated if they could rely on personal funds and loans from family members and wealthy friends. As Mathias has said, 'Undoubtedly, the first rule for a successful entrepreneur in the eighteenth century, as today, was to choose his parents wisely—or at least the rest of his family.'[144] The financial resources on hand could be expanded further by launching the enterprise as a partnership with the backing of business associates, usually recruited on the basis of mercantile connections or religious affiliations, who could draw similarly on personal funds and family wealth.[145]

Once industrial enterprises were up and running a credit network that became increasingly sophisticated during the industrial revolution could address the cash flow problems circulating capital requirements posed. The most usual way in which businessmen of the time obtained short-term credit was through issuing bills of exchange, documents purchasers would sign acknowledging their obligation to pay on a future date what was owing plus an amount compensating for the delay in payment.[146] In the case of manufacturers, they would provide bills of exchange to their suppliers. The suppliers—typically merchants and wholesalers—could keep the bills of exchange until maturity, thus earning a rate of interest, but they were more likely to pass bills on to their own creditors to settle their own debts. The person receiving a bill would accept it at less than the face value at maturity, again to compensate for the delay in receiving payment. During the industrial revolution, the 'discounting' of bills of exchange was increasingly dominated by country banks and went a long way towards meeting the credit demands of industry.[147]

English country banks, in addition to discounting bills of exchange, would provide overdrafts to industrial enterprises that were formally short-term in orientation but for which the bankers would routinely consent to renewal, creating a form of long-term lending.[148] Otherwise, with the exception of the intermingling of

---

[143] Cottrell, *supra* n. 69, 35; Honeyman, *supra* n. 126, 119–20.

[144] Mathias, *supra* n. 139, 133. See also King and Timmins, *supra* n. 124, 117, 125–26; Honeyman, Origins, *supra* n. 126, 166–68; Heaton, *supra* n. 137, 5.

[145] Hudson, *supra* n. 69, 53; King and Timmins, *supra* n. 124, 119; Heaton, *supra* n. 137, 6.

[146] Cottrell, *supra* n. 69, 22–23; King and Timmins, *supra* n. 124, 120–24.

[147] Crouzet, 'Editor's', *supra* n. 124, 48; King and Timmins, *supra* n. 124, 123; Mathias, *supra* n. 139, 127, 130.

[148] Cameron, 'England', *supra* n. 82, 55; Crouzet, *supra* n. 132, 192–93; Mathias, *supra* n. 139, 136–38.

business operations by industrialists who established their own banking operations (Part III.C), country banks refrained from direct backing of business borrowers (e.g. through share ownership) because they needed their assets in liquid
form to be able to pay depositors on demand.[149] Hence, when industrial firms
had become sufficiently well established to be profitable and contemplate expansion, they would rely primarily on retained earnings to finance investment.[150] As
Ashton says, 'The records of firm after firm tell the same story . . . : restrict the household expenses, and put their profits to reserves. It was in this way that Wedgwood
(the pottery firm) and scores of others built up their great concerns.'[151]

When funding requirements exceeded retained earnings, proprietors would
usually rely on loans from family members and business associates or admit
'sleeping' partners who would inject fresh capital but not take an active role in
running the business.[152] There was little appetite to unwind control, as evidenced
by the fact that owners of larger, successful concerns who relied on outside investment would more often manoeuvre to oust existing backers than to bring in
new investors.[153] Industrialists were biased against outside investment because
they operated in a business culture that stressed self-reliance and scepticism of
outsiders.[154] Given that '(n)early everything depended on personal knowledge
and trust . . . the idea of "going public" would have seemed strange, distasteful,
a betrayal not only of business principles but of family loyalties'.[155] Also, as with
investors, proprietors of industrial enterprises were apprehensive about the agency
costs associated with entrusting business operations to salaried managers. As
Robert Peel, one of the country's leading industrialists, said in 1816: 'It is impossible for a mill at any distance to be managed, unless it is under the direction of a
partner or a superintendent who has an interest in the success of the business.'[156]

Successful industrialists were aware of the dangers of having all of their eggs
in one basket, but instead of responding by unwinding control in the firms they
ran, they achieved diversification by using the wealth generated by their primary
business to invest elsewhere. Land was perceived as a safe choice and was a popular
outlet for excess capital.[157] Another possibility was to open a country bank, which
could provide a platform to deploy funds available for investment. Industrialists
were also often major backers of infrastructure projects, such as canals and railways, motivated partly by a desire to bolster their industrial operations with better
transport links (Part III.C). An additional option was to invest as a 'sleeping' partner in other industrial enterprises, providing capital to active members who focused

---

[149] Ashton, *supra* n. 82, 83–85; Cameron, 'England', *supra* n. 82, 56–58; Crouzet, *supra* n. 124, 46–47.
[150] Cottrell, *supra* n. 69, 23–24, 31, 35; Cameron, 'England', *supra* n. 82, 39; Crouzet, *supra* n. 132, 188–90, 195.
[151] Ashton, *supra* n. 82, 78.   [152] *Ibid.*, 78–79; Crouzet, *supra* n. 132, 191–92.
[153] Crouzet, *supra* n. 132, 191.   [154] *Ibid.*; King and Timmins, *supra* n. 124, 117.
[155] Reader, *supra* n. 52, 18.
[156] Quoted in Pollard, *supra* n. 128, 21. See generally *ibid.* 21–23; Payne, *supra* n. 122, 192.
[157] Mary B. Rose, 'Diversification of Investment by the Greg Family, 1800–1914', (1979) 21 Business History 79, 80–88.

on different entrepreneurial functions in the same industry or even operated in entirely different industrial sectors.[158] A popular way to do this was to finance enterprises launched by members of the younger generation of the family.[159]

What about industrialists using their families to perpetuate the businesses they had established? There were examples of heirs of successful industrialists of the time following the founder and entering the family business.[160] This, however, was apparently the exception to the rule as only a very small proportion of firms created by a deed of partnership in the first half of the 19th century survived more than 30 years.[161] Many of these enterprises would have simply failed but even with successful firms founders commonly sold the firm or provided for its disposition in their wills, often because of a lack of suitable descendants willing to take over the firm or because cash was needed to facilitate an equal distribution of the founder's estate among the children.[162]

Drawing matters together, between the 1720s and the 1840s the legal environment was not particularly congenial for corporate enterprise, with the only foolproof means of obtaining fully fledged corporate status being the expensive and time-consuming enactment of legislation or the obtaining of a charter. Nevertheless, even if the law had provided a congenial platform for corporate activity, the outcome would have been little different. Because industrial enterprises were low in the pecking order for investors and their proprietors generally had little inclination to carry out public offerings of shares, the industrial revolution was not destined to generate large, widely held industrial companies.

V. The mid-1840s–1880

A. Railways

1. Ownership and Control

As of the early 1850s, the directors of the Midland Railway, a major railway company, owned only 2 per cent of the value of the eligible capital between them and there was no evidence of an influential blockholder lacking representation on the board.[163] Otherwise, there is little empirical data available on the share ownership structure of UK railway companies of the mid-19th century.[164] However, it

---

[158] Payne, *supra* n. 122, 192; Mathias, *supra* n. 139, 133–34; see also Crouzet, *supra* n. 132, 168–72 (providing examples).

[159] Mathias, *supra* n. 139, 133.

[160] See, for example, Mary B. Rose, 'The Role of the Family in Providing Capital and Managerial Talent in Samuel Greg and Company', (1977) 19 Business History 37, 41–44.

[161] Payne, *supra* n. 126, 24–25.   [162] Sunderland, *supra* n. 126, 180.

[163] Geoffrey Channon, 'A Nineteenth Century Investment Decision: the Midland Railway's London Extension', (1972) 3 Economic History Review 448, 454.

[164] R.A. Bryer, 'Accounting for the 'Railway Mania' of 1845—A Great Railway Swindle?', (1991) 16 Accounting, Organizations and Society 439, 462; S. McCartney and A.J. Arnold, 'The

appears the largest railways during the mid- and late 19th century were pioneers of the modern-style divorce of ownership and control.[165]

Early railway companies generally had the locally oriented shareholder base characteristic of canal companies (Part III.B). By the 1840s the investment base had expanded significantly. According to returns filed with Parliament, in 1845 more than 20,000 different individuals had subscribed for railway shares for amounts less than £2,000 and 5,000 others had subscribed for amounts exceeding £2,000.[166] A survey of the railway industry published in 1854 suggested 'smaller holders' constituted 'the bulk of the Company' and maintained railway directors dictated company policy by relying on proxies collected 'from proprietors scattered throughout the Kingdom'.[167] As of 1855, the ten largest railway companies in the UK had an average of 7,700 shareholders, with London & North Western Railway (LNWR) leading the way with over 15,000.[168]

Transactions in railway shares became so voluminous by existing standards that the traditional dealing channels proved inadequate.[169] As a result, the number of stock exchanges in Britain increased from 3 to 18 during the mid-1840s.[170] Within a few years, a number of the provincial stock exchanges suspended operations and the number of provincial stockbrokers fell about 20 per cent.[171] The British securities market had nevertheless become multi-centred in orientation, with stock exchanges operating in cities like Birmingham, Bristol, Edinburgh, Glasgow, Liverpool, Leeds and Manchester through the remainder of the 19th century.[172] Railways also became a major presence on the London Stock Exchange, accounting for 16 per cent of the nominal value of all securities quoted as of 1853, and 67 per cent of securities quoted excluding domestic and foreign government bonds.[173]

The large railway companies, in addition to having a sizeable shareholder base, lacked powerful blockholders. The fact the two dominant railway personalities of the 1840s and 1850s were not controlling shareholders of the railways they ran illustrates this. The first, George Hudson, referred to as both the 'Railway King' and the 'Railway Napoleon' of the 1840s, dominated the affairs of four major railway companies, York & North Midland, York, Newcastle & Berwick, and

---

Railway Mania of 1845–1847: Market Irrationality or Collusive Swindle Based on Accounting Distortions?', (2003) 16 Accounting, Auditing and Accountability Journal 821, 827.

[165] Crouzet, *supra* n. 86, 293; Channon, *supra* n. 163, 449; T.R. Gourvish, 'Railways 1830–70: The Formative Years' in Michael J. Freeman and Derek H. Aldcroft (eds), *Transport in Victorian Britain* (1988), 57, 83.

[166] Hunt, *supra* n. 52, 105, n. 67.

[167] 'Railway Morals and Railway Policy', (1854) 100 Edinburgh Review 420, 438, 445.

[168] Gourvish, *supra* n. 165, 83.

[169] Francis W. Hirst, *The Stock Exchange: A Short Study of Investment and Speculation* (1948), 56.

[170] Michie, *supra* n. 57, 63.

[171] *Ibid.*, 64; Thomas, *supra* n. 89, 60–65.

[172] Michie, *supra* n. 57, 64; David Kynaston, *The City of London, Volume I: A World of its Own 1815–1890* (1994), 153.

[173] Michie, *supra* n. 57, 88–89.

Midland & Eastern Counties.[174] These railways, together with other lesser railways Hudson was involved with, controlled almost 30 per cent of the rail track operating in the UK.[175] He quit his major posts in 1849, prompted by damaging revelations of illicit share dealings, accounting fraud and self-serving related-party transactions.[176]

Hudson owned, partly through secretive and improper allotments, nearly 20 per cent of the shares in Newcastle and Berwick Railway Co., which merged in 1847 with York & Newcastle to form York, Newcastle & Berwick.[177] Generally, though, Hudson did not rely on share ownership as a platform for exercising influence. He made his name initially as chairman of the York & North Midland, a post to which he was appointed due to his availability and his political connections rather than his share ownership. He was the largest shareholder upon incorporation but only held £10,000 worth of shares out of a capital of £370,000.[178] By 1845 Hudson owned railway shares worth £320,000, falling to closer to £100,000 by 1849 when railway share prices fell sharply (Figure II, below).[179] These were sizeable sums, but were dwarfed by the combined £8.9 million share capital of the major four railways with which he was associated.[180] A court judgment granted in favour of York & North Midland for misappropriation of shares combined with restitution offered voluntarily to his various companies left Hudson poverty stricken and he lived out his days with the support of an annuity that former friends purchased.[181]

Hudson's fall from grace coincided with the rise of the second railway star, Mark Huish, general manager of the LNWR from 1846 to 1858.[182] Under Huish's leadership, the company became the dominant railway in Britain, with a share capitalization larger than any of its rivals or any other business enterprise of the era. Huish was a pioneer of corporate management, necessitated by the fact the LNWR operated on a massive scale by contemporary standards. Huish enjoyed high social status and his salary peaked at £2,000 per annum, an exceptional

---

[174] Henry G. Lewin, *The Railway Mania and its Aftermath 1845–1852* (1968), 261; A.J. Peacock, *George Hudson 1800–1871: The Railway King* (1988), 107, 165–66.

[175] Sean McCartney and A.J. Arnold, 'George Hudson's Financial Reporting Practices: Putting the Eastern Counties Railway in Context', (2001) 10 Accounting, Business & Financial History 293, 294, 299.

[176] Ch. Four, Pt. IV.A; Sean McCartney and A.J. Arnold, ' "A Vast Aggregate of Avaricious and Flagitious Jobbing?" George Hudson and the Evolution of Early Notions of Directorial Responsibility', (2001) 11 Accounting, Business & Financial History 117.

[177] McCartney and Arnold, *supra* n. 176, 133.

[178] Peacock, *supra* n. 174, 50; A.J. Arnold and S. McCartney, *George Hudson—The Rise and Fall of the Railway King: A Study in Victorian Entrepreneurship* (2004), 35, 47–48 (noting as well that Hudson received in 1844 a controversial 'bonus' of 300 shares 'at his disposal').

[179] On the value of shares owned, see Arnold and McCartney, *supra* n. 178, 217; <http://www.spartacus.schoolnet.co.uk/RAhudson.htm> (last visited March 7, 2008).

[180] Calculated from 'The Railway Interest of the United Kingdom', Times, November 17, 1845.

[181] On the judgment and the annuity, see Arnold and McCartney, *supra* n. 178, 215–17, 222, 234; Hamilton Ellis, *British Railway History: An Outline from the Accession of William IV to the Nationalisation of Railways 1830–1876* (1954), 174–75. On voluntary restitution, see Arnold and McCartney, *op. cit.*, 185, 187, 190, 196; McCartney and Arnold, *supra* n. 176, 131, 133, 136.

[182] On the aspects of Huish's career discussed here, see T.R. Gourvish, *Mark Huish and the London & North Western Railway: A Study of Management* (1972), 53–56, 108, 181–82, 257–63.

sum by the standards of the day. He was not, however, a major shareholder in the LNWR. The board dismissed him in 1858 without a hint of Hudson-style scandal or impropriety, something that would not have been feasible if he had owned a large enough block of shares to influence board elections. His will revealed that upon his death he had a personal fortune of £40,000, large by the standards of the time but trivial in comparison to the aggregate capitalization of LNWR, which exceeded £29 million even in the early 1850s.

2. Railway 'Mania'

How did the separation of ownership and control come about in the large railways of the mid-19th century? One reason was that the question 'Why did blockholders exit?' rarely came into play. With capital requirements being too great for individual wealthy individuals to satisfy, railways generally lacked on incorporation shareholders owning dominant blocks of shares (Chapter Three, Part I). Similarly, the question 'Why didn't buyers of shares exercise control?' was largely moot. Under normal circumstances, personal investors are ill-equipped to exercise 'hands on' control and large railway companies were too big for even rich Victorians to buy a dominant stake in outright.[183]

This leaves open the question why investors bought shares in railway companies in sufficient volume for ownership to separate from control. A railway share 'mania' occurring in the mid-1840s played a significant role. The *Economist* declared in 1845 that 'Everybody is in the Stocks now. Needy clerks, poor tradesmen's apprentices, discarded serving men and bankrupts—all have entered the ranks of the great monied interest.'[184] As for Scottish investors, the poet Wordsworth observed, 'From Edinburgh to Inverness the whole people are mad about railways. The country is an asylum of railway lunatics.'[185] There was an element of exaggeration here, since even as late as the 1870s 'the typical private investor was always a man of wealth'.[186] Nevertheless, enthusiasm for railway shares in the mid-1840s did result in a significant widening of the investor base.[187]

The strong demand for railway shares was sufficient to create in 1845 the impetus for nearly 1,400 applications to Parliament to incorporate new railway companies.[188] A significant increase in the share prices of leading railways (Figure II) also provided evidence of investor enthusiasm.

[183] On investors generally see Ch. Four, Pt. IV.B. An 1845 list of subscribers who had signed subscription contracts for £2,000 or more during the Parliamentary session did reveal a banker and a merchant who subscribed for sums approaching £600,000, but there were probably substantial trustee holdings involved: Thomas, *supra* n. 89, 38.

[184] 'The Stock Mania', Economist June 28, 1845, 601. See also Hunt, *supra* n. 52, 106 (quoting Thomas Tooke and William Newmarch, *A History of Prices*, vol. 5 (1857), 234).

[185] Quoted in Chancellor, *supra* n. 9, 134.

[186] A.K. Cairncross, *Home and Foreign Investment 1870–1913* (1953), 84–85; see also Broadbridge, *supra* n. 87, 171.

[187] T.R. Gourvish, *Railways and the British Economy 1830–1914* (1980), 17.

[188] R.W. Kostal, *Law and English Railway Capitalism 1825–1975* (1994), 28–29.

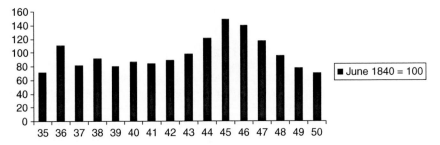

Figure II: Railway share price index for 10 leading companies traded on the London Stock Exchange, 1835–50[189]

Source: Compiled using data from Gayer, Rostow and Schwartz, *supra* n. 60, 437.

Various factors contributed to the surge in demand for railway shares.[190] Supported by a series of excellent harvests, deposits in savings banks were accumulating rapidly and falling interest rates meant there was a dearth of profitable channels for deploying investment capital. Railways stood out as an obvious outlet. The expansion of the railway network was a 'great fact', not merely some sort of proposed venture, so when railway companies rebounded smartly after the collapse of the mid-1830s railway share frenzy they began to acquire 'a reputation for security and profit'.[191]

Dividends were also a lure. While dividend payments disappointed those who had bought shares in the railway boom of the mid-1830s, by the early 1840s a number of railways were delivering dividends of 6 per cent per annum and several others were yielding 10 per cent or more.[192] A government bill introduced in Parliament in 1844 reinforced expectations these generous payouts were sustainable. The bill, which was never enacted, proposed giving the Government the power to purchase railways, with the terms varying depending on whether the return on paid-up capital was 10 per cent or more, which implied lower returns would be the exception rather than the rule.[193]

Investors were also attracted by the possibility of easy capital gains. An expectation quickly built up of securing instant profits by the purchase and prompt resale of railway shares, exemplified by 'stags' who subscribed for unissued shares

---

[189] The index encompassed 14 companies, but from 1836 onwards only 10 companies were included: Gayer, Rostow and Schwartz, *supra* n. 60, 361.

[190] Hunt, *supra* n. 52, 102–4; Michie, *supra* n. 64, 80–81; Bryer, *supra* n. 164, 455–56; Kostal, *supra* n. 188, 28.

[191] Hunt, *supra* n. 52, 102.

[192] *Ibid.*; Ch. Four, Pt. III.D (railways in the 1830s); Harold Pollins, *Britain's Railways: An Industrial History* (1971), 35.

[193] Bryer, *supra* n. 164, 453; Pollins, *supra* n. 192, 36.

in anticipation of selling on the 'scrip' entitling the holder to buy shares at face value.[194] An 1845 letter to the *Times* alleged 'There is not a single dabbler in scrip who does not steadfastly believe—first, that a crash sooner or later is inevitable; and secondly, that he will escape it.'[195]

Finally, investors discounted too readily negative aspects of railway shares. There was a tendency to overlook the fact railway companies were empowered to make capital calls as more cash was needed to build up their railway networks.[196] Also, most investors did not bother to inspect financial statements to determine whether revenues and profits were sufficient to underpin the sizeable dividend payments.[197] Even had investors been more vigilant, they might well have struggled to assess matters properly since various railways had accounts that were misleading or even fraudulent (e.g. George Hudson's Eastern Counties railway).[198]

Investor sentiment concerning railways changed dramatically as the 1840s drew to a close. A drain of bullion arising from massive importing of food due to poor harvests caused the Bank of England to increase the minimum bank rate, thus choking off the cheap credit that had facilitated the buying of shares.[199] Moreover, railway companies began to put the squeeze on shareholders. While in the changing economic environment many railways Parliament authorized in 1845/46 never got off the ground, major railway companies largely built as planned, increasing total track mileage from just over 3,000 to nearly 7,000 between 1846 and 1851.[200] To raise the money required, railways relied heavily on calls against shareholders and collected £182 million between 1844 and 1851, despite many shareholders being squeezed by the credit crunch induced by the agricultural crisis.[201] The pain for shareholders was compounded because the major railway companies, hobbled by ongoing competition among themselves and construction costs, cut dividends substantially (Figure III).[202] Negative sentiment was reinforced by newcomers to railway investment engaging in panicky distress selling.[203] Share prices fell accordingly (Figure II), and the

---

[194] Morgan and Thomas, *supra* n. 78, 108–9; Charles Duguid, *The Story of the Stock Exchange: Its History and Position* (1901), 150–51; Anthony Burton, *The Railway Builders* (1992), 20.

[195] 'The Railway M'ania', Times, July 12, 1845.

[196] Burton, *supra* n. 194, 22.

[197] Bryer, *supra* n. 164, 457.

[198] George Robb, *White-Collar Crime in Modern England: Financial Fraud and Business Morality 1845–1929* (1992), 43–44.

[199] Bryer, *supra* n. 164, 465–67; B. Mark Smith, *The Equity Culture: The Story of the Global Stock Market* (2003), 75–76.

[200] Timothy L. Alborn, *Conceiving Companies: Joint-Stock Politics in Victorian England* (1998), 194, 196–97.

[201] Kostal, *supra* n. 188, 50; Smith, *supra* n. 199, 76; Alborn, *supra* n. 200, 194, 196–97.

[202] Lewin, *supra* n. 174, 365 (supplying dividend data for seven companies in addition to those in Figure III; the trend was the same with each). See also Pollins, *supra* n. 192, 33–34.

[203] Bryer, *supra* n. 164, 469–70.

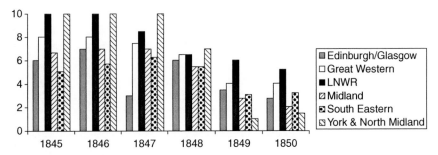

Figure III: Dividend rates (per cent per annum) paid by leading railway companies, 1845–50

Source: Compiled using data from Lewin, *supra* n. 174, 365.

aggregate stock market value of railway capital fell from £54 million in 1847 to £18 million in 1853.[204]

The collapse of the railway share boom and the unpleasant experience with capital calls stigmatized railways as an uncertain class of investment; even the strongest companies were shunned.[205] Low dividends in the 1850s reduced further the attraction of railway investment.[206] Still, with the railway mania of the 1840s providing the obvious departure point, there already was an investor base composed of 'proprietors scattered throughout the Kingdom'.

During the 1850s and 1860s the major railways completed the branch lines, stations and marshalling yards complementing their main lines. The railways financed the construction by issuing preference shares, borrowing from banks and relying on contracting firms willing to undertake work for payment largely in the form of shares.[207] Railway construction stalled temporarily when an 1866 financial crisis hit contracting firms hard.[208] However, in the concluding decades of the 19th century major railway companies achieved financial stability, began to enjoy a favoured position in the domestic capital market as a safe haven for investment and added steadily to their supply of new shareholders with regular

[204] Adrian Vaughan, *Railwaymen, Politics and Money: The Great Age of Railways in Britain* (1997).

[205] Kostal, *supra* n. 188, 49; 'B', 'Facts for the Times. No. 2—Railway Finance', (1867) 122 Quarterly Review 489, 496 (reprinted from Pall Mall Gazette); P.L. Cottrell, 'Railway Finance and the Crisis of 1866: Contractors' Bills of Exchange, and the Finance Companies', (1975) 3 Journal of Transport History 20, 24.

[206] Cottrell, *supra* n. 205, 21; James B. Jefferys, *Business Organisation in Great Britain 1856–1914* (1997), 48–49.

[207] Morgan and Thomas, *supra* n. 78, 110; Cottrell, *supra* n. 205, 21–22, 24; Harold Pollins, 'Railway Contractors and the Finance of Railway Development', (1957–58) 3 Journal of Transport History, 41 (Pt. I), 103 (Pt. II). On the situation in Scotland, see Michie, *supra* n. 64, 142.

[208] Pollins, *supra* n. 192, 52–53; Cottrell, *supra* n. 205, 33.

dividend payments that generally exceeded returns available on government bonds.[209] As *Bankers' Magazine* said in 1901, 'English railway stocks were so persistently absorbed by investors that they came to be exceptionally well held.'[210] There were nearly 260,000 ordinary shareholders listed on railway share registers by 1887 and 550,000 holders of railway securities generally.[211] Though the investor base was in fact not as large as this figure implies—owning shares in more than one railway was commonplace—this was mass investment on a modern scale.

Railway securities also became a popular outlet for early institutional investors, in the form of investment trusts and insurance companies.[212] At the same time, the senior managers of the major railway companies became firmly established as a bureaucratic elite, complete with agency costs. Railway management was mindful of the need to distribute dividends at a level that would appease investors, but otherwise allegedly preferred to maintain investment and employment levels rather than maximize returns to investors.[213] In various respects, then, the larger railway companies of the mid-to-late 19th century pioneered the divorce of ownership and control, with the key transition being traceable back to the wave of share investment occurring during the 1845/46 railway mania.

B. Company Law and the Organization of Industrial/Manufacturing Enterprise

1. Legal Reforms

Though the legal setting for incorporation of industrial firms was less than ideal during the industrial revolution, due to market dynamics affecting industrial enterprises, publicly traded firms would have been very much the exception to the rule regardless of the law (Part III.B). Company law reform occurring between 1844 and 1862 improved the legal climate for corporate enterprise, giving those operating businesses a straightforward and reliable procedure to incorporate a company with full legal personality, transferable shares, limited liability (from 1855 onwards) and other essential corporate attributes (Table II).

---

[209] Michie, *supra* n. 64, 143; Alborn, *supra* n. 200, 239; R.J. Irvine, 'British Railway Investment and Innovation, 1900–1914', (1971) 22 Business History 39, 39.

[210] 'The Fall in English Railway Securities', (1900) 70 Bankers' Magazine 340, 340.

[211] 'Investors' Holdings of British Railway Stocks', Economist, January 22, 1887, 107.

[212] Alborn, *supra* n. 200, 239, 241–42.

[213] P.J. Cain, 'Railways 1870–1914: The Maturity of the Private System' in Freeman and Aldcroft, *supra* n. 165, 92, 112–13; Terence R. Gourvish, 'A British Business Elite: The Chief Executive Managers of the Railway Industry, 1850–1922', (1973) 47 Business History 289, 290.

Table II: Major corporate law reforms, 1844–62[214]

Legislation	Key features	Key omissions
1844: Joint Stock Companies Act, 7 & 8 Vict. c. 110	* Applied to any company formed for commerce or any purpose of profit (including insurance) and to partnerships with more than 25 partners with freely transferable shares * Such firms had to register, with provisional registration permitting the issuance of shares * Full corporate status was achieved with the filing of a deed of settlement * Provided for a model (optional) deed of settlement (Sch. A) * Directors were required to appoint auditors and supply the accounts and balance sheet annually to shareholders * Prospectuses issued had to be registered (repealed 1847)	* Did not provide for limited liability * Did not apply to Scotland * Incorporation procedure not made available to companies incorporated by charter or legislation, pre-1844 joint stock companies and banks (regulated under separate 1844 legislation)
1855: Limited Liability Act, 18 & 19 Vict. c. 133	* Authorized, subject to shareholder approval, satisfaction of minimum capital requirements and the imposition of various rules to protect creditors, companies already formed under the 1844 Act to re-register limiting the liability of shareholders	* Banks and insurance companies excluded
1856: Joint Stock Companies Act, 19 & 20 Vict. c. 47	* Replaced 1844 and 1855 Acts * Dealt with the incorporation, management and winding up of companies * The deed of settlement was replaced by the memorandum and articles of association * Provisional/complete registration procedure in 1844 Act and minimum capital requirements in 1855 Act dropped—filing of a memorandum of association with seven subscribers sufficed * Liability of shareholders could be limited to the par value of the shares they owned * Applied in Scotland	* Did not apply to companies incorporated by charter or legislation or to insurers or banks * Accounting/auditing/prospectus rules in 1844 Act abandoned

[214] For further details, including citation of specific statutory provisions, see Gower, *supra* n. 1, 41–50; Cooke, *supra* n. 35, 136–39, 152–55, 158–75; Hunt, *supra* n. 52, 96–98, 133–44; A.B. Levy, *Private Corporations and Their Control*, vol. I (1950), 64–70, 75–79, 82–84.

Table II: (*Cont.*)

Legislation	Key features	Key omissions
1862: Companies Act, 25 & 26 Vict. c. 89	* Larger than 1856 Act (212 sections vs. 116), primarily due to more detailed drafting and amendments to winding up provisions * Insurance companies included (banks had been brought within the scope of the 1856 Act by reforms in 1857/58)	* Abandoned regulation of accounting/auditing/ prospectuses not revived

Companies legislation enacted in the mid-19th century displaced whatever legal 'shadow' the Bubble Act of 1720 and the common law cast. Industrial enterprises hesitated, however, before picking up on the cue. Hence, the changes to the law did not foster any sort of wholesale transformation of patterns of ownership and control in industrial and manufacturing enterprises by 1880.

2. Incorporation Activity

The legislation adopted between 1844 and 1862 was used with some frequency. An average of 337 applications for incorporation were filed annually under the Joint Stock Companies Act of 1844.[215] There were on average 377 incorporations per year under the Joint Stock Companies Act 1856 and 874 annually in the 15 years following the enactment of the Companies Act 1862.[216] Despite the incorporation activity, through to 1880 founders and their families continued to dominate the ownership structure of industrial enterprises.[217] This was the case in Scotland as well as south of the border, as 'It was not until the 1870s the new laws were seriously resorted to, and even by the mid-1880s the use to which they were put was limited.'[218]

One reason the new statutory framework failed to affect markedly the ownership structure of industrial enterprises was that a substantial proportion of the companies incorporated never commenced operations. Under the Joint Stock Companies Act of 1844, incorporation involved a two-stage process, 'provisional' and 'complete' registration (Table II). Only 24 per cent of companies entering the provisional stage left it to enter complete registration.[219] Though incorporation was streamlined to a one-step procedure under the Joint Stock Companies Act

[215] Leone Levi, 'On Joint Stock Companies' (1870) 33 Journal of the Statistical Society 1, 26.

[216] Calculated from data in Leone Levi, *The History of British Commerce and of the Economic Progress of the British Nation* (1880), 346.

[217] Payne, *supra* n. 122, 195; Mary B. Rose, 'The Family Firm in British Business, 1780–1914' in Maurice W. Kirby and Mary B. Rose (eds), *Business Enterprise in Modern Britain: From the Eighteenth to the Twentieth Century* (1994), 61, 65, 67–68.

[218] Michie, *supra* n. 64, 149–50.

[219] Levi, *supra* n. 215, 6, 26.

of 1856 and the Companies Act 1862, 18 per cent of companies registered up to 1868 were simply abandoned.[220] Among companies that were not 'abortive' in this sense a significant fraction disappeared quickly. Of 'effective' companies incorporated between 1856 and 1883, within five years 17 per cent were wound up on grounds of insolvency and a further 14 per cent were wound up voluntarily.[221] A significant proportion of those companies that were not abandoned right from the start or formally terminated simply became defunct. As of 1877, when there were about 7,000 companies registered, 2,750 had not filed any returns for the previous seven years and many more had defaulted for at least three years.[222]

Among companies that became fully operational after incorporation, often there was no intention of raising capital from the public. Though UK companies legislation only introduced differential treatment for the 'private company' in 1907, there was never any legal requirement that an incorporated company offer shares to the public.[223] There was in the mid-19th century a general sense in the business community that it was inappropriate for firms to incorporate without broadening the investor base.[224] Nevertheless owners of businesses increasingly began to incorporate simply to limit their liability and otherwise operated the business in the same way they would have done as a sole proprietorship or partnership.[225] 'Private limiteds' were on the scene by the mid-1860s in the cotton industry and between 1875 and 1883 at least one-fifth of the companies incorporated were fully 'private'.[226]

Even when companies launched were not intended to be fully 'private', there often was no immediate plan to offer shares to the public. For instance, while 479 companies were incorporated in 1861, only 56 solicited the public to buy shares that year.[227] Between 1863 and 1865, a period characterized by buoyant market conditions hospitable to company promotions, the number of companies making offers of shares to the public increased to an average of 277 per year.[228] However, in the wake of a financial crisis marked by the collapse of bankers Overend Gurney, which itself had incorporated and sold shares to the public in 1865, the number of companies selling shares to the public fell precipitously to 44 in 1866 and 27 in 1867.[229] In 1871, the number of companies offering shares to the public

[220] *Ibid.*

[221] H.A. Shannon, 'The Limited Companies of 1866–1883', (1933) 4 Economic History Review 290, 295, 299.

[222] D.H. MacGregor, 'Joint Stock Companies and the Risk Factor', (1929) 139 Economic Journal 491, 493.

[223] Company Law Amendment Act 1907, 7 Edw. 7, c. 50, s. 37.

[224] Jefferys, *supra* n. 206, 129–30.

[225] Morgan and Thomas, *supra* n. 78, 131–32.

[226] Shannon, *supra* n. 221, 302; D.A. Farnie, *The English Cotton Industry and the World Market* (1979), 240.

[227] Thomas, *supra* n. 89, 118; Levi, *supra* n. 215, 14.

[228] Levi, *supra* n. 216, 462–65; 'Money-Market & City Intelligencer', Times, December 29, 1866.

[229] 'Money-Market', *supra* n. 228 (1866 figure); 'Commercial History and Review of 1867', Economist, March 14, 1868, 39 (1867 figure); Levi, *supra* n. 216, 478–80 (market conditions);

was up to 196 but this was not indicative of a sustained trend because the 1877 figure was 57.[230]

Even if a company managed to offer shares to the public, this only rarely resulted in active trading. Of the companies that went public in 1863, only 14 per cent had a market price at the end of the year and the equivalent figures for 1865 and 1867 were 13 per cent and 3 per cent.[231] Moreover, of the companies that carried out public offerings of shares only a minority were in 'manufacturing and trading' (32 per cent between 1863–66, 23 per cent in 1871 and 40 per cent in 1877). Correspondingly, despite the increase in incorporation activity in the wake of company law reform in the mid-19th century, industrial companies were very much a sideshow on the London Stock Exchange, which had barely 60 manufacturing firms quoted as of the mid-1880s.[232] Even with these companies, there was no guarantee that there would be a liquid market in their shares. Since industrial shares were part of the 'miscellaneous market', no jobbers or brokers specialized in dealing in them and it was often impossible to trade without advertising on a Stock Exchange notice board.[233]

Provincial stock exchanges took up the slack somewhat. The Manchester Stock Exchange was eager to facilitate trading in industrial enterprises based in the area, primarily iron and steel firms, and by 1885, 70 industrial and commercial companies were quoted, including 'many local companies of first-class magnitude'.[234] Sheffield became a centre of dealing in iron and steel company shares in the early 1870s, when iron masters took advantage of rapidly rising share prices to carry out 'sales of private concerns at inflated prices'.[235] Lancashire experienced numerous flotations of cotton spinning, weaving and mill-building companies in the early 1870s and again in the early 1880s.[236]

Oldham was the centre of the action with Lancashire textile pubic offerings.[237] Company promotions in the early 1870s and early 1880s spawned a network of

Geoffrey Elliot, *The Mystery of Overend and Gurney: A Financial Scandal in Victorian London* (2006), 163–66 (on the Overend Gurney share offering).

[230] 'Money-Market & City Intelligencer', Times, December 30, 1871; 'Commercial and History Review of 1876', Economist, March 10, 1877, 32.

[231] 'Commercial History', *supra* n. 229, 39; 'New Joint Stock Companies Brought Out During the Year 1863', Economist, February 20, 1864, 36–39; 'Commercial History and Review of 1865', Economist, March 10, 1866, 35–39.

[232] S.J. Prais, *The Evolution of Giant Firms in Britain: A Study of the Growth of Concentration in Manufacturing Industry in Britain 1909–70* (1981), 90; Leslie Hannah, *The Rise of the Corporate Economy*, 2nd edn (1983), 20.

[233] Cottrell, *supra* n. 69, 149–50; P.L. Cottrell, 'Domestic Finance, 1860–1914' in Roderick Floud and Paul Johnson (eds), *The Cambridge Economic History of Modern Britain, Volume II: Economic Maturity, 1860–1939* (2004), 252, 267.

[234] Thomas, *supra* n. 89, 118, 123, 133; 'The Stock Markets of the United Kingdom', Economist, April 19, 1884, 480.

[235] 'Stock Markets', *supra* n. 234, 480; see also Thomas, *supra* n. 89, 123.

[236] Farnie, *supra* n. 226, 220–25.

[237] See generally Thomas, *supra* n. 89, 145–51; Farnie, *supra* n. 226, 252–53; Shin'ichi Yonekawa, 'Flotation Booms in the Cotton Spinning Industry 1870–1890: A Comparative Study' (1987) 61 Business History Review 551, 552–54.

firms known collectively as 'the Oldham Limiteds' that had shares traded at various Oldham venues. Reportedly, in the 'Oldham share utopia'[238] one-fifth of the population bought shares. With this sort of local support, the information asymmetries potentially afflicting public offerings (Chapter Two, Part II.B) were not a serious problem. Investors buying shares were familiar with the business model, often knew the directors personally or by reputation and could monitor matters closely by examining balance sheets published in the local press and attending quarterly shareholders meetings. Demand for shares was fuelled further by 'hypnotically attractive dividends',[239] the potential for quick capital gains on resale and simply following fashion.

The Oldham Limiteds had some elements of a separation between ownership and control.[240] They displaced in the Oldham area owner-occupier spinner concerns, opening mills of unprecedented size well suited for the introduction of new machinery that enhanced the productivity of labour. The firms generally were not controlled by a single proprietor or family, having instead several shareholders with sizeable but not dominant ownership stakes combined with small holdings held by an investing class—apparently unique to the Oldham area—composed of local traders, mill foremen and even manual labourers. At the same time, though, the number of shareholders in individual companies often was less than 200. Moreover, a local elite drawn from the cotton spinning businesses already in place emerged as leaders in the 'Oldham Limiteds', playing a pivotal role in the formation of such firms and holding directorships on the boards of numerous companies.

Elsewhere, if the manner in which David Chadwick, principal partner in an accounting firm that organized public offerings on behalf of various iron, coal and steel enterprises during the 1860s and 1870s, conducted business reflects wider practice, share ownership generally remained tightly concentrated in the small minority of industrial firms that distributed shares to the public up to 1880. Chadwick's firm was meticulous by the standards of the day, carefully examining a company's accounts before agreeing to carry out a flotation.[241] His firm also encouraged proprietors of enterprises seeking to make public offerings of shares to retain a sizeable equity stake. As he explained at a Parliamentary inquiry in 1877, 'we never allow a vendor, or only in a few cases, to take his hands off the property' and '(t)he directors in our companies have always been among the largest shareholders'.[242] In companies Chadwick's firm promoted in the 1860s the vendors on average took up 23 per cent of the issued shares and the directors often received additionally 10 per cent or more

---

[238] Farnie, *supra* n. 226, 253; the quote is from an 1875 Oldham newspaper.

[239] *Ibid.*

[240] See generally Cottrell, *supra* n. 69, 110; Thomas, *supra* n. 89, 146–48; Jefferys, *supra* n. 206, 86–89, 93; Roland Smith, 'An Oldham Limited Liability Company' (1961) 4 Business History 34, 41–42.

[241] Cottrell, *supra* n. 69, 113, 116; Robb, *supra* n. 198, 99.

[242] Jefferys, *supra* n. 206, 403, n. 3.

of the shares.[243] Chadwick himself estimated that the proportion of shares taken up by outside investors in firms he promoted amounted to only 25 or 30 per cent.[244] The remaining investment presumably was accounted for by friends and acquaintances of the vendors and other directors.

3. Sell Side

The lack of progress towards a separation of ownership and control in the industrial enterprises of the mid-19th century was due to lack of momentum on both the sell side and buy side. On the sell side, during the industrial revolution blockholders were disinclined to exit because factories lacked large fixed capital requirements and a strong sense of individualism prevailed (Part III.B). Matters did not change markedly up to 1880. Factories typically continued to operate on a small scale averaging fewer than 90 employees as of 1871.[245] As a result, there generally was little need for industrialists to go beyond self-financing—retained profits and backing by family and business associates—to meet capital needs.[246] The desire for independence and the strong sense of individual responsibility that militated against public offerings during the height of the industrial revolution was also largely sustained.[247] Proprietors of industrial enterprises were also not minded to carry out public offerings to facilitate retirement from the businesses they ran. Instead, they generally opted to transfer their businesses outside the family or simply wound up their firms.[248]

The sell side obstacles did not fully preclude industrialists from unwinding control. Jefferys, in his study of business organization from 1856 to 1914, quotes language from the prospectuses of the Brittania Iron Works Company (1872), Bilson and Crump Meadow Collieries (1874), Darlington Iron Company (1872), Mercy and Cunningham (an ironworks firm) (1872) and South Cleveland Iron Works (1872) to provide examples of proprietors carrying out public offerings to permit founders to retire or to facilitate exit after the death of a key partner.[249] Growing fixed capital requirements also helped to prompt numerous iron and steel firms to incorporate as the 1870s drew to a close.[250] Nevertheless, as a general matter, up to 1880 there was only weak momentum on the sell side in favour of a move to the stock market by industrial companies.

---

[243] Cottrell, *supra* n. 69, 116.   [244] Jefferys, *supra* n. 206, 79, 108.

[245] Crouzet, *supra* n. 86, 81–82.

[246] Payne, *supra* n. 122, 195; Michael Collins, *Banks and Industrial Finance* (1991), 34–35; Forrest Capie and Michael Collins, 'Deficient Suppliers? Commercial Banks in the United Kingdom, 1870–1980' in P.L. Cottrell, Alice Teichova and Takeshi Yuzawa (eds), *Finance in the Age of the Corporate Economy: The Third Anglo-Japanese Business History Conference* (1997), 164, 176–77.

[247] Payne, *supra* n. 126, 39, 43; S.G. Checkland, *The Rise of Industrial Society in England 1815–1885* (1964), 107.

[248] Ch. Three, Pt. IV; Jefferys, *supra* n. 206, 112.

[249] Jeffery, *supra* n. 206, 79–81.   [250] *Ibid.*, 76–77.

4. Buy Side

As for the buy side, during the 1850s, 1860s and 1870s there was a lack of secure, remunerative investment outlets since returns on government bonds, land and mortgages were weak.[251] Nevertheless, demand for shares in industrial companies was not particularly robust or widespread. In the 1860s and 1870s there were around 250,000 people in Britain who owned investment securities.[252] In order for share ownership in industrial firms to have become dispersed there would need to have been significant demand from such investors, but no more than one-fifth of these individuals owned shares in companies other than railways.[253] Most 'safe' investors, simply looking for a reliable annual return of 4 to 5 per cent on their capital, thought of shares in industrial enterprises as being too risky and steered clear.[254] 'Safe' investors frustrated by lacklustre domestic returns were more inclined to look outside the UK, with overseas borrowers being eager to import capital due to the immaturity of domestic financial markets.[255] The UK's net foreign investment/annual GNP ratio duly rose from 0.76 in the 1840s to 4.00 in the 1870s.[256]

'Safe' investors had good reason to steer clear of shares in industrial enterprises. Between the mid-1850s and the early 1880s overall profit levels in manufacturing enterprises were healthy compared to earlier and later eras.[257] Nevertheless, investing in shares of industrial enterprises was risky. It was standard practice for companies to incorporate with shares having a sizeable nominal capital (very often more than £10 per share) and only requiring subscribers to pay a small portion upon issuance (30 per cent on average), with the remainder being available for the company to call.[258] Directors would sometimes offer reassurances that they had no immediate intention to follow up, but there were numerous instances where companies indeed called up most, if not all, of the unpaid nominal capital.[259] Investors in shares thus faced a residual liability that, while not unlimited, could theoretically bankrupt them in the long run and likely curtailed the marketability of the shares in the meantime.[260]

Lack of reliable information was another deterrent to investing in shares of industrial undertakings. An 1876 article on 'Speculative Investments' said of such enterprises, 'People must invest, but they must form their own opinion on

---

[251] Cottrell, *supra* n. 69, 46–47.

[252] Jefferys, *supra* n. 206, 385.   [253] *Ibid.*, 435.

[254] *Ibid.*, 385, 387, 392–93; John Newlands, *Put Not Your Trust in Money* (1997), 9, 35.

[255] Cottrell, *supra* n. 69, 46; Michael Edelstein, 'Foreign Investment, Accumulation and Empire, 1860–1914' in Floud and Johnson, *supra* n. 233, 190, 197.

[256] Edelstein, *supra* n. 255, 193.

[257] R.A. Church, *The Great Victorian Boom* (1975), 40–41, 51.

[258] Cottrell, *supra* n. 69, 82–86.

[259] Geoffrey Todd, 'Some Aspects of Joint Stock Companies, 1844–1910', (1932) 4 Economic History Review 46, 68–69.

[260] Hunt, *supra* n. 52, 155 (bankruptcy risk); Jefferys, *supra* n. 206, 175, 178 (liquidity).

statements and statistics which may be as honest as they seem, or which may conceal or distort the most material facts.'[261] In various ways ascertaining the merits of industrial companies was much easier said than done, so for 'those with substantial assets ignorance was a great impediment to investment, causing men of substance to prefer security—the sweet simplicity of 3 per cent'.[262]

For investors inclined to do their homework one difficulty was that prospectuses issued in support of public offerings of shares often 'contained lurid promises of success rather than substantive financial data'.[263] Once a company was up and running, shareholders could examine the share register to judge whether those listed had the financial wherewithal to satisfy capital calls, but such inspections were unlikely to be feasible for anyone living any distance from a company's registered office.[264] Reliable financial data was also hard to come by. From 1855 onwards there was no requirement that companies incorporated under general companies legislation file publicly annual financial data (Table II).[265] When directors voluntarily circulated balance sheets and financial reports to shareholders, the information offered was typically meagre and was difficult to interpret since accountancy principles were in their infancy.[266] It was even a struggle to get up-to-date information on elementary matters such as dividend rates and the range of share price fluctuations.[267]

Press coverage did little to fill the data gap. As Kynaston has said, 'It was a situation that prior to 1884 left deans, widows and others badly placed, and considerably mitigated against the natural attraction of holding shares'.[268] From the 1840s onwards there was widespread coverage of railway companies in the leading London and provincial newspapers and weekly journals such as the *Railway Times* and Herpath's *Railway Gazette* regularly published company accounts, reports of shareholder meetings and other investor-related financial information.[269] The situation was bleaker for those seeking to follow industrial companies.[270] There was no general daily financial newspaper until 1870, and the establishment of the *Financier* that year did little to improve matters for the

---

[261] Alexander I. Shand, 'Speculative Investments', Blackwood's Edinburgh Magazine, September 1876, 293, 296.

[262] Checkland, *supra* n. 247, 40.

[263] Robb, *supra* n. 198, 97.

[264] Jefferys, *supra* n. 206, 402–3.

[265] Financial disclosure requirements were more exacting for railways, banks and insurance companies: R.H. Parker, 'Regulating British Corporate Financial Reporting in the Late Nineteenth Century', (1990) 1 Accounting, Business and Financial History 51, 62–64.

[266] Robb, *supra* n. 198, 127–28; P. Barnes and R.J. Firman, 'Difficulties in Establishing a Limited Liability Company During the 1860s and the Role of Financial Information: A Case History', (2001) 8 Financial History Review 143, 145, 154–55.

[267] Hargreaves Parkinson, 'The Stock Exchange' in *The Economist 1843–1943: A Centenary Volume* (1943), 126.

[268] David Kynaston, *The Financial Times: A Centenary History* (1988), 3.

[269] Reed, *supra* n. 89, 171–72.

[270] Kynaston, *supra* n. 172, 266–68.

average investor since it offered little editorial comment or reporting on events. A daily 'money article' in the *Times* that offered assessments of various company promotions was popular but was discredited in 1875 when the editor was found to have accepted large 'donations' from Albert Grant, a flamboyant company promoter.

In addition to 'safe' investors, there were during the mid-19th century two basic categories of investor in investment securities, a 'commercial class' composed of wealthy traders, and merchants, and successful proprietors of industrial enterprises.[271] The commercial class was prepared to buy shares in publicly traded companies. However, these investors largely bypassed industrial enterprises in favour of finance and credit companies, hotels, telegraph operators and transport companies.[272]

Proprietors of successful industrial firms, on the other hand, were prepared to step forward and constituted the primary source of demand for shares in manufacturing enterprises that offered shares to the public.[273] A wide-ranging solicitation effort was rarely used to tap this source of demand. Instead, subscribers were usually recruited through friends of the vendors and through business connections of the promoters. Efforts would be made to solicit investors in regions to where these connections extended, but the primary focus was on local investment.[274] Correspondingly, prior to 1880 the number of shareholders in industrial companies that offered their shares to the public frequently did not exceed 200, a stock market quotation often was not sought or obtained and trading activity in the shares was sporadic.[275]

The regional orientation of investment by the industrialist class meant the informational asymmetries that deterred the 'safe' category from buying shares were not a serious obstacle. Even if formal disclosure was rudimentary, local investors could buy shares on the strength of their knowledge of the directors and the business environment in which the company was operating (Chapter Two, Part III). Once a company was up and running, assuming the vendors retained shares in the manner Chadwick urged, it was reasonable for shareholders to rely on the strong financial and personal interest the directors would have in the success of the company.[276] Industrialist investors were also usually well positioned to keep an eye on things since they normally only bought shares in a handful of companies and since the practice of issuing shares with a large uncalled capital

[271] Jefferys, *supra* n. 206, 101, 388–91; J.B. Jefferys, 'The Denomination and Character of Shares, 1855–1885', (1946) 16 Economic History Review 45, 50.

[272] Jefferys, *supra* n. 206, 388–90.

[273] *Ibid.*, 206, 391; see also Cottrell, *supra* n. 69, 122 (reporting 'manufacturer' was the occupation most often listed for subscribers in companies Chadwick promoted).

[274] Jefferys, *supra* n. 206, 391, 393, 397; for empirical confirmation of the local orientation of share ownership, see Cottrell, *supra* n. 69, 91–95, 118–22.

[275] Jefferys, *supra* n. 206, 391–92.

[276] *Ibid.*, 409–10.

gave them a financial incentive to be vigilant.[277] Still, while industrial companies that offered shares to the public could anticipate at least some demand for the shares, the fact the potential market remained narrowly focused meant that a full blown divorce of ownership and control was not on the cards.

* * *

This chapter's analysis of developments occurring between the mid-1840s and 1880 has focused on railways, manufacturing enterprises and personal investors. There was, however, during this period a sizeable contingent of companies operating in other sectors that offered shares to the public, such as banking, insurance and shipping. Also, the establishment of the first investment trusts in the late 1860s and 1870s at least theoretically broadened the scope for institutional investment in shares.[278] These various 'loose ends' will be taken up in Chapters Six and Seven as they move the story forward to 1914.

[277] *Ibid.*, 172–75.   [278] Newlands, *supra* n. 254, 12–13, 110–12.

SIX

1880–1914

Explaining the relative economic decline from which Britain suffered between the late 19th century and late 20th century has been a major analytical problem within the study of modern British history.[1] This is hardly surprising. The UK was the world's dominant economic power through much of the 19th century, fortified by the industrial revolution and military success. However, Britain then stumbled badly, at least in relative terms. Explanations range over a wide variety of features of the economy and wider society.[2] However, a dominant line of thought is that Britain suffered a late 19th- and early 20th-century 'corporate lag', which caused the country's industrial enterprises to lose ground relative to rivals in the United States and Germany, consigning British firms to also-ran status in pivotal industrial sectors (Chapter One, Part V). Britain's relative economic standing reputedly suffered accordingly. As one study of the decline of industrial Britain has said, 'British businessmen, analysts of the "British disease" have concluded with near unanimity, have typically viewed "their companies as family estates to be nurtured and passed down to their heirs rather than mere money-making machines" and their passion for continuity has placed family control rather than efficiency, profitability, or growth at the center of corporate decision-making.'[3]

The corporate lag thesis implies that the UK's corporate economy was poorly developed, at least relative to its major industrial rivals, by World War I. In fact, as Part I of the chapter will describe, Britain stacked up well in comparative terms. Parts II and III explain how matters reached this point by reference to the 'sell side' and 'buy side'. Part II draws attention to a significant change on the sell side, this being a growing willingness among proprietors of industrial and commercial firms to accept at least partial dilution of their ownership stakes. Part III explains why there was sufficient demand for shares for the UK's corporate

---

[1] Martin J. Wiener, *English Culture and the Decline of the Industrial Spirit, 1850–1980* (1981), 3; M.J. Daunton, '"Gentlemanly Capitalism" and British Industry' 1820–1914' (1989) 122 Past and Present 119, 120.

[2] Nic Tiratsoo, *Industrial Efficiency and State Intervention: Labour 1939–1951* (1993), 1.

[3] Michael Dintenfass, *The Decline of Industrial Britain 1870–1990* (1992), 64–65; the quote in this passage is from Alfred D. Chandler, 'The Emergence of Managerial Capitalism' in Richard S. Tedlow and Richard R. John (eds), *Managing Big Business* (1986), 368, 391. See more generally John Micklethwait and Adrian Wooldridge, *The Company: A Short History of a Revolutionary Idea* (2003), 83–89.

economy to become well developed in comparative terms even though Britain was losing ground to its major economic rivals and company law, financial inter-mediaries and the press offered at best uneven protection to outside investors.

I. Development of the UK's Corporate Economy

Numerous UK companies made the move to the stock market between 1880 and 1914, with the most rapid phase during the mid-1890s.[4] On the London Stock Exchange, the value of securities quoted accounted for by shares and debentures of shipping companies, breweries, iron and steel firms and other commercial and industrial companies increased from 1.2 per cent in 1883 to 3.5 per cent in 1893 and 9.9 per cent in 1903.[5] Likewise, the number of industrial and commercial companies quoted on the London Stock Exchange increased from 70 in 1885 to 571 in 1907.[6] The industrial enterprises joining the stock market generally operated in brewing, iron and coal production, chemicals, textiles and the newly established cycle and automobile industries.[7]

Trading of company shares on provincial stock exchanges also expanded. Stock markets outside London were particularly attractive to smaller industrial and commercial companies since a provincial quotation was cheaper to obtain. In addition, professional traders affiliated with provincial stock exchanges were more likely to invest time and energy 'making a market' in the shares of smaller companies than their busier counterparts in London.[8] Hence, the number of commercial and industrial companies quoted on the Manchester list increased from 70 in 1885 to nearly 220 in 1906.[9] Likewise, by 1900, 196 companies had the main market for their shares on the Glasgow Stock Exchange, as did 182 com-panies on the Edinburgh Stock Exchange.[10] Trading on other provincial stock markets was expanding and the number of provincial stock exchanges operating grew from 11 in 1882 to 22 in 1914.[11]

---

[4] E. Victor Morgan and W.A. Thomas, *The Stock Exchange: Its History and Functions* (1969), 133.
[5] Ranald C. Michie, *The London Stock Exchange: A History* (1999), 88–89.
[6] Julian Franks, Colin Mayer and Stefano Rossi, 'Spending Less Time with the Family: The Decline of Family Ownership in the United Kingdom' in Randall K. Morck (ed.), *A History of Corporate Governance Around the World* (2005), 581, 587–588.
[7] P.L. Cottrell, *Industrial Finance 1830–1914: The Finance and Organization of English Manufacturing Industry* (1980), 168–76; A.E. Harrison, 'Joint-Stock Company Flotation in the Cycle, Motor Vehicle and Related Industries, 1882–1914' in R.P.T. Davenport-Hines (ed.), *Capital, Entrepreneurs and Profits* (1990), 206; T.R. Gourvish and R.G. Wilson, *The British Brewing Industry 1830–1980* (1994), 257–61.
[8] James B. Jefferys, *Business Organisation in Great Britain 1856–1914* (1997), 370–71; W.A. Thomas, *The Provincial Stock Exchanges* (1973), 133.
[9] Thomas, *supra* n. 8, 133.
[10] R.C. Michie, *Money, Mania and Markets* (1981), 196.
[11] Michie, *supra* n. 5, 117–18; Thomas, *supra* n. 8, 129–33, 139 (growth of existing stock mar-kets); Michael Edelstein, *Overseas Investment in the Age of High Imperialism: The United Kingdom* (1982), 56 (increasing number).

Evidence compiled by Grossman illustrates not only the increase in the number of companies traded on the stock market but also their changing nature. He constructed an index of all companies with share information catalogued in the *Investor's Monthly Manual* from 1870 to 1913, which included securities traded on the London Stock Exchange and provincial stock markets.[12] Between 1870 and 1913 the number of companies in Grossman's index rose from 520 to around 1,100 and the proportion of the market capitalization made up by railways fell from 76 per cent to 16 per cent. The slack was taken up mostly by banks (11 per cent of the market capitalization in 1870/19 per cent in 1913), mining (primarily Australian and South African-based companies) (0.6 per cent in 1870, 15 per cent in 1913) and 'miscellaneous'—the sector of the stock market to which industrial and commercial companies were consigned—(1.6 per cent in 1870, 18 per cent in 1913).

A listing on the stock exchange was not synonymous with liquidity. As of 1910, fewer than 15 per cent of securities quoted on British stock exchanges had an official record of actual dealings, and many of these were not dealt in for intervals of many months.[13] Lavington described the situation just after World War I in the following terms:

Even on the London Stock Exchange, as is well known, the quotations of many securities are only nominal; they have no active market and can be dealt in only at a considerable sacrifice in price. Provincial markets are naturally far less effective; many small but sound local industrials can neither be bought nor sold within any reasonable margin of price or period of time; the holders of such securities are often, in this respect, in a position little better than partners in a business.[14]

As Lavington implied, industrial shares were particularly susceptible to market 'stickiness'. While the 'miscellaneous market' grew markedly in the late 19th and early 20th centuries, it remained a 'junior' partner in comparison to the markets for government and railway debt.[15] Liquidity suffered accordingly. As the *Economist* said in 1904, 'For the greater part of the best-known industrial shares Capel Court (the location of the building then housing the London Stock Exchange) still remains the nominal market, but of the score of descriptions that come under that heading an absurdly small proportion can boast ready negotiability.'[16] Ironically, when numerous industrial and commercial

---

[12] Richard S. Grossman, 'New Indices of British Equity Prices, 1870–1913', (2002) 62 Journal of Economic History 121, 124–32. The index encompassed foreign-domiciled companies but excluded shares issued in foreign currencies.

[13] Henry Lowenfeld, 'The Hall-Mark of Official Stock Exchange Quotations', Financial Review of Reviews, November 1910, 3, 13; see also F. Lavington, *The English Capital Market*, 2nd edn (1929), 221–22.

[14] Lavington, *supra* n. 13, 221.

[15] David Kynaston, *The City of London, Volume II: The Golden Years 1890–1914* (1995), 460.

[16] 'Not Negotiable', Economist, August 27, 1904, 1410. See also 'The Position of Leading Industrial Shares', Economist, January 20, 1900, 72.

companies moved to the stock market in the late 19th and early 20th centuries this likely hindered liquidity, with the *Economist* going on to say, 'It may be the very vastness of the field covered by industrial investments which makes, or helps to make, the narrowness of the market in so many.'

Whereas the market for shares was 'sticky' in many instances, in comparative terms the British corporate economy was well developed. Payne, in a 1967 article, reported that the average capitalization of the 50 largest companies resulting from a major merger wave the United States experienced at the turn of the 20th century was nearly four times as large as the average capitalization of the top 50 industrial companies in the UK as of 1905.[17] These figures implied 'big business' was an American rather than a British phenomenon but a 1998 study by Hannah indicated that the corporate sector in Britain did not 'lag' badly. He reports that as of 1912, 15 of the 100 largest industrial (manufacturing and mining) firms, in the world had their headquarters in Britain, ranked by equity market capitalization (Table I). The US had considerably more companies in the top 100 (54) but Britain was ahead of Germany (14), France (6) and all other countries.[18] UK companies in the top 100 were also not dinosaurs afflicted by terminal decline, as they were more likely to survive and be in the top 100 decades later than rivals from the US, Germany and elsewhere.[19]

Table I: UK industrial companies in Global Top 100, 1912

Name of Company	Rank	Industry	1912 Market Capitalization (£m.)[20]
J. & P. Coats	3	Textiles and Leather	59
Royal Dutch Shell (joint HQ in the Netherlands)	5	Petroleum	38
British American Tobacco	11	Branded Products	33
Rio Tinto	13	Nonferrous Metals and Other Mining	30
Imperial Tobacco	17	Branded Products	25
Guinness	20	Branded Products	22
Lever Brothers	27	Branded Products	18
Vickers	51	Iron, Steel and Heavy Industry	11

[17] P.L. Payne, 'The Emergence of the Large-scale Company in Great Britain, 1870–1914', (1967) 20 Economic History Review (N.S.) 519, 539–41.

[18] Derived from Leslie Hannah, 'Marshall's "Trees" and the Global "Forest": Were "Giant Redwoods" Different?' in Naomi Lamoreaux, Daniel M. G. Raff and Peter Temin (eds), *Learning by Doing in Markets, Firms and Countries* (1998), 253, Table 7A.1.

[19] *Ibid.*, 263.

[20] Hannah does not specify clearly whether equity market capitalization encompasses preference shares as well as ordinary shares. Conversion from $US to £s performed using <http://www.measuringworth.com/calculators/exchange/result_exchange.php>.

Table I: *(Cont.)*

Name of Company	Rank	Industry	1912 Market Capitalization (£m.)
Brunner Mond	57	Chemicals	10
Consolidated Goldfields	60	Nonferrous Metals and Other Mining	10
Armstrong, Whitworth	67	Iron, Steel and Heavy Industry	8
Burmah Oil	74	Petroleum	8
Reckitt & Sons	75	Branded Products	8
Fine Cotton Spinners	82	Textiles and Leather	7
Metropolitan Carriage	95	Mechanical Engineering	6

Source: Data from Hannah, *supra* n. 18, Table 7A.1.

Since Hannah focused on industrial companies, his findings actually understate the scale of big business in the UK. According to Cassis, in 1907 Britain had 93 enterprises engaging in trade, finance and industry that were 'large' (i.e. had a paid up capital of £2 million or more) while Germany had 45.[21] The differential becomes even greater if railways are taken into account, since they were Britain's largest private sector enterprises, while the entire German railway network was state-owned.[22] As of 1905, 22 of Britain's largest 50 companies were railways, as measured by market capitalization, including all of the top 10.[23]

In addition to having companies that were big by international standards, Britain had, according to a couple of 1913 statistical measures, an equity market that was large relative to the rest of the economy.[24] Figure I indicates the ratio of companies traded on domestic stock exchanges to the population (in millions) was higher in Britain than in Germany, France, Japan or the United States.

[21] Youssef Cassis, 'Big Business in Britain and France, 1890–1990' in Youssef Cassis, Francois Crouzet and Terry Gourvish (eds), *Management and Business in Britain and France: The Age of the Corporate Economy* (1995), 214, 216.

[22] On state ownership of German railways, see *ibid.*, 217; Alfred D. Chandler, *Scale and Scope: The Dynamics of Industrial Capitalism* (1990), 413.

[23] Peter Wardley, 'The Anatomy of Big Business: Aspects of Corporate Development in the Twentieth Century', (1991) 33 *Business History* 268, 278, 283–85.

[24] Raghuram G. Rajan and Luigi Zingales, 'The Great Reversals: The Politics of Financial Development in the Twentieth Century', (2003) 69 Journal of Financial Economics 5, 17 (Table 5); Raymond W. Goldsmith, *Comparative National Balance Sheets: A Study of Twenty Countries, 1688–1978* (1995), 153. An additional historical measure of the size of the equity market—stock market capitalization/GDP—has not been included because estimates vary widely depending on the methodology used. Compare Rajan and Zingales, *op. cit.*, 15 (Table 3) with Aldo Musacchio, 'Do Legal Origins Have Persistent Effects Over Time? A Look at Law and Finance Around the World *c.* 1900' (2007), unpublished working paper, Appendix A.

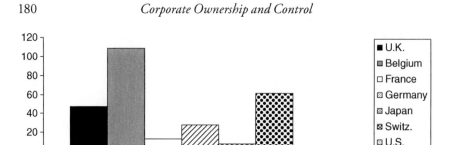

Figure I: Listed companies per million people, 1913

Source: Compiled with data from Rajan and Zingales, *supra* n. 24, Table 5.

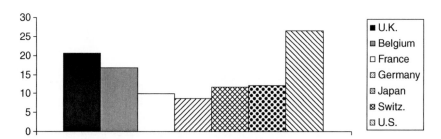

Figure II: Domestic corporate shares as a percentage of financial assets, 1913

Source: Compiled with data from Goldsmith, *supra* n. 24, Table 57.

Figure II shows the value of domestic corporate shares as a percentage of financial assets owned by individuals was high in Britain in relative terms, implying shares were a popular investment choice.

Using statistics to measure the size of the market for corporate equity has to be done with caution, as the data for the United States reveals.[25] As measured by domestic corporate equity as a percentage of financial assets, the US stands out as a leader, whereas, as measured by the number of listed companies per million people, it is very much a laggard. The conflicting data complicates assessment of the American situation but with respect to Britain the statistical evidence indicates that the UK had, in international terms, a well-developed stock market. We will now consider how matters developed in this way, doing so first by reference to the sell side and then the buy side.

---

[25] For further development of this point see Richard Sylla, 'Schumpeter Redux: A Review of Raghuram G. Rajan and Luigi Zingales's *Saving Capital from the Capitalists*' (2006) 44 Journal of Economic Literature 391, 400–2.

II. The Sell Side

A. Companies Launched from Scratch

The founders of a successful business typically dominate share ownership when the enterprise is launched and any unwinding of control will take place at some later stage as the business matures. However, it was commonplace for founders of the businesses that dominated lists of publicly traded firms in the UK through much of the 19th century—canals, docks, gas lighting schemes and railways—to seek financial backing immediately by inviting the public to buy shares and forsake a controlling stake (Chapter Three, Part I). As the 19th century drew to a close, electrical companies were the most prominent type of enterprise where public investment was sought immediately upon launch.

During the early 1880s, there was a flurry of public offerings involving electrical undertakings based on proposals to develop lighting systems and supply electricity for particular localities.[26] A common way for backers of electrical ventures to seek support from investors was to agree to purchase patent rights from an inventor, incorporate a company to acquire the patent rights and then carry out a public offering of the company's shares. A flagship flotation of this sort occurred in 1880 when the Anglo-American Brush Electric Light Corporation was formed to exploit British patent rights to the 'Brush system' of lighting and an independent incandescent lamp patent. A rapid rise in the company's share price prompted the launch of numerous enterprises in the electricity generation field, referred to as 'little Brushes'.

The Anglo-American Brush Electric Light Corporation ultimately was able to thrive on the manufacture of dynamos, motors, switchgears and small transformers.[27] Generally, however, in what became known as 'the Brush Bubble', the electrical undertakings launched in the early 1880s fared badly, with at least half of £16 million invested in electricity companies being lost.[28] The fledgling enterprises were hampered by patents of questionable validity or utility, primitive technology, an economic downturn and 1882 legislation that gave local government authorities the right to purchase compulsorily successful privately owned electricity supply works after a 21-year period.[29]

---

[26] See generally Thomas Parke Hughes, 'British Electrical Lag: 1882–1888', (1962) 3 Technology and Culture 27, 29–30; W.J. Reader, *A House in the City: A Study of the City and of the Stock Exchange Based on the Records of Foster & Braithwaite 1825–1975* (1979), 94–95.

[27] <http://www.brush.eu/aboutus/operationalsites/historybem.html> (last visited Oct. 22, 2007).

[28] Reader, *supra* n. 26, 95–96; Ranald Michie, 'The Finance of Innovation in Late Victorian and Edwardian Britain: Possibilities and Constraints', (1988) 17 Journal of European Economic History 491, 510–11; David Kynaston, *The City of London, Volume I: A World of its Own 1815–1890* (1994), 340–41.

[29] Hughes, *supra* n. 26, 31–32; Leslie Hannah, *Electricity Before Nationalisation: A Study of the Development of the Electricity Supply Industry in Britain to 1948* (1979), 6; Thomas P. Hughes, *Networks of Power: Electrification in Western Society, 1880–1930* (1983), 60–64.

In 1888 legislation was enacted that extended the tenure for private electricity supply companies and redefined the compulsory purchase terms in a manner more favourable to the incumbent owners.[30] Since large electricity generators were becoming relatively much cheaper and more economical methods of transmission were being developed it seemed a good time to launch a new wave of electricity supply ventures.[31] Often it was major municipalities that took up the challenge.[32] They were joined during the first decade of the 20th century by approximately 20 power companies incorporated to generate and sell electricity in various regions throughout Britain. Even though technology had raised the minimum efficient scale of electricity supply since the 1880s, construction costs and delayed revenue flow meant the launching of such ventures remained out of the reach of even rich individuals. Hence, funding was sought immediately by way of public offerings of securities.[33]

During the first decade of the 20th century, rubber production was another area in which numerous companies were promoted without any sort of pre-existing business in place. In the midst of a spectacular rise in rubber prices[34] UK investors enthusiastically backed yet-to-be-built rubber plantations in South-East Asia, Ceylon (now Sri Lanka) and the Amazon. They subscribed for approximately £90 million worth of shares between 1908 and 1910 (£6.45 billion in 2006 currency), as the number of British companies in the rubber business increased from less than 150 to somewhere approaching 500.[35] The experience proved to be an unhappy one. When the investment frenzy subsided, 'Only a miserable fraction of new companies survived to show any record of dividends.'[36] Rarely 'had so many small savings been transferred into less meritorious pockets'.[37]

The Anglo-American Brush Electric Light Corporation was by no means the only company that carried out public offerings on the strength of inventions. The *Economist* reported in 1899 on 34 public offerings launched to exploit patent rights and 33 of the companies were newly incorporated.[38] The *Economist* characterized the companies' collective performance as 'a ghastly record of failure'. The dismal results, together with the difficulties afflicting electricity and rubber

---

[30] Hughes, *supra* n. 26, 37–38.

[31] I.C.R. Byatt, *The British Electrical Industry 1875–1914: The Economic Returns to a New Technology* (1979), 111–13.

[32] Hannah, *supra* n. 29, 8, 42–43; Byatt, *supra* n. 31, 114 (listing major municipal power supply undertakings as of 1912).

[33] Michie, *supra* n. 28, 509; William J. Hausman, Mira Wilkins and John L. Neufeld, 'Multinational Enterprise and International Finance in the History of Light and Power, 1880s–1914', (2007) 58 Revue Economique 175, 177–79.

[34] Barbara Weinstein, *The Amazon Rubber Boom* (1983), 69.

[35] W.R. Lawson, 'The Rubber Madness in the City', Financial Review of Reviews, June 1910, 15, 17–18; The Investment Critic, 'How "Booms" Betray the Investor', Financial Review of Reviews, November 1911, 16, 19; Francis W. Hirst, *The Stock Exchange* (1911), 175–77.

[36] Investment Critic, *supra* n. 35, 19.

[37] Hirst, *supra* n. 35, 177.

[38] 'Inventions as Investments', Economist , December 8, 1899, 1731.

companies, helps to explain why enterprises offering shares to the public during the late 19th and early 20th centuries were mainly established firms converted from private to public concerns rather than ventures launched from scratch.[39]

B. Reasons for Exit—at Least Partially

1. *Individualism in Decline/Diversification*

Up to the 1880s, a strong sense of individualism and modest capital requirements militated against public share offerings by industrial concerns (Chapter Five, Part IV.B, Part V.B.3). Chandler implies not much had changed during the late 19th and early 20th centuries, saying of UK industrial enterprises 'the family wanted to retain and manage its birthright'.[40] Still, the predisposition against accessing public markets apparently did diminish, leaving proprietors more receptive to the idea of unwinding control, at least partially.

One reason for the change in attitude may have been 'the restless strive to maximize profits ceased'.[41] Industrialists of the late Victorian and Edwardian eras are often accused, to quote Landes, of going 'through the motions of entrepreneurship', opting to pursue social advancement rather than dedicate themselves to growing their business.[42] The British, it is said, reacted ambivalently to industrialization, discounting the value of single-minded pursuit of production and profit in favour of the virtues of being 'gentlemen'—enlightened amateurs with due appreciation of the virtues of tradition, gentility and country life. Industrialists, having achieved initial success, thus would continue to run the businesses they founded more as a social duty than to maximize economic opportunities.

It is impossible to measure whether entrepreneurial drive in fact declined generally as the 19th century drew to a close.[43] It is also doubtful whether an innate British cultural bias against business activity fostered any such trend (Chapter Three, Part II). Nevertheless, for proprietors of industrial firms who were inclined to draw back, carrying out public offerings of shares provided an opportunity to realize at least part of their investment in the business and reinvest the proceeds,

[39] Michie, *supra* n. 28, 497; A.R. Hall, 'A Note on the English Capital Market as a Source of Funds for Home Investment before 1914', (1957) 24 Economica (N.S.) 59, 65; A.K. Cairncross, 'The English Capital Market Before 1914', (1958) 25 Economica (N.S.) 142, 143–44.

[40] A.D. Chandler, 'The Growth of the Transnational Industrial Firm in the United States and the United Kingdom: A Comparative Analysis', (1980) 33 Economic History Review (N.S.), 396, 402.

[41] D.H. Aldcroft, 'The Entrepreneur and the British Economy, 1870–1914', (1964) 17 Economic History Review (N.S.) 113, 128.

[42] David Landes, 'Technological Change and Innovation in Western Europe, 1750–1914' in H.J. Habakkuk and M. Postan (eds), *Cambridge Economic History of Europe, vol. VI, The Industrial Revolution and After: Incomes, Populations and Technological Change (I)* (1965), 274, 563–64. See also Wiener, *supra* n. 1, 145–52; H.J. Habakkuk, *American and British Technology in the Nineteenth Century: The Search for Labour-Saving Inventions* (1967), 192–93.

[43] François Crouzet, *The Victorian Economy* (1982), 411.

thereby diminishing their reliance on the firm's financial success. A 1911 text on the London Stock Exchange drew attention to the pattern, discussing a scenario where 'a brilliantly successful manufacturer or merchant, who has built up his business and wishes to retire' would incorporate and carry out a public offering of shares.[44] An 1886 public offering of shares by Guinness, the brewers, provides an illustration. Sir Edward Guinness (later the first Earl of Iveagh) decided to take the business public because of 'his ambition for social position, titles, honours, an impressive life-style, which in turn required a large disposable income and the leisure to employ it advantageously'.[45]

The 1896 flotation of Bovril, manufacturers of a popular hot drink, also fit the pattern.[46] John Lawson Johnston and Andrew Walker, the founders of the business, were both in their mid-50s at that point and their sons were not obvious successors. This made both susceptible to persuasion when company promoter E.T. Hooley offered to buy Bovril for £2 million, cashing out Johnston and Walker. Hooley then re-launched the company by way of a public offering, selling the shares to the public for £2.5 million but retaining Johnston and Walker to run the company, apparently at increased remuneration.

2. Dividends

If a publicly traded company has a shareholder who owns a sufficiently large block of shares to exercise *de facto* control, to the extent there is pressure to distribute earnings to investors in the form of dividends an incentive to unwind the block will exist because the dominant shareholder will have reduced scope to skim or squander corporate profits (Chapter Three, Part IX). These dynamics would have been at work in the UK in the late 19th and early 20th centuries. Companies of the era would have wanted to retain investor confidence to ensure the market for their shares did not dry up and to keep open the option to return to capital markets to finance mergers and internal expansion. The payment of regular dividends was an effective means of keeping investors onside. As Lowenfeld said in 1909, 'The number of Investors who can afford to entirely disregard income, and are ready to wait five or ten years for their stock to develop, is very small.'[47] Correspondingly, 'Prosperous companies, with shareholders numbered by hundreds, find it difficult to form a quorum at General meetings;

---

[44] Hirst, *supra* n. 35, 216–17; see also John Hobson, *The Evolution of Modern Capitalism: A Study of Machine Production* (1906), 248; Leslie Hannah, *The Rise of the Corporate Economy*, 2nd edn (1983), 57; Ranald Michie, *The City of London: Continuity and Change* (1992), 115.

[45] Derek Wilson, *Dark and Light: The Story of the Guinness Family* (1998), 115.

[46] See John Armstrong, 'Hooley and the Bovril Company', (1996) 28 Business History, #1, 18, 21–22, 29–30; 'Results of the Hooley System of Finance', Economist, August 20, 1898, 1213.

[47] Henry Lowenfeld, *All About…Investment* (1909), 46–47. See also Jefferys, *supra* n. 8, 398 (quoting a witness at an 1877 investigation into company law reform); Peter L. Payne, 'Industrial Entrepreneurship and Management in Great Britain', in P. Mathias and M.M. Postan (eds), *The Cambridge Economic History of Europe, vol. VII, The Industrial Economies: Capital, Labour and Enterprise, Part I (Britain, France, Germany, and Scandinavia)* (1978), 180, 205.

whilst so soon as there is a cessation of dividends shareholders attend in large numbers.'[48] Or as a 1901 text on investment observed more caustically, 'Too often shareholders are blindly content so long as the dividends are paid.'[49]

The available evidence suggests UK public companies conducted themselves as if they were bound in a credible way to continue making regular, ongoing dividend payments. Campbell and Turner report that just over 80 per cent of the 820 or so UK-based companies listed in the *Investor's Monthly Manual* and *Burdett's Official Intelligence* as of 1883 were dividend payers.[50] Smaller samples reveal the same pattern. According to an 1893 list of major publicly traded companies, 18 of 19 breweries and distilleries listed paid dividends on their ordinary shares, as did 60 of 69 industrial and commercial companies.[51] An 1898 article on companies traded on provincial stock markets listed 155 companies with ordinary shares quoted in Manchester, Liverpool and Edinburgh and 140 of these were dividend-payers.[52] Of 36 'leading industrial shares' identified by *Economist* as of 1900, 32 were paying dividends.[53] In a 1914 article entitled 'Minor Industrial Securities', the *Economist* provided share price and dividend data for 46 smaller concerns and 43 of these paid dividends on their ordinary shares in 1913.[54]

Most companies not only paid dividends but adopted a generous distribution policy. Chandler reports the ratio of dividends to earnings for six major industrial concerns ranged from 68 per cent to 92 per cent between 1901 and 1906.[55] This evidence is merely suggestive, given the small size of the sample.[56] Nevertheless, according to Grossman and De Long,[57] between 1890 and 1903 the average dividend yield of companies operating in a wide variety of industrial sectors comfortably exceeded the return on 'gilt-edged' government bonds, which never climbed above 3 per cent during this period (Figure III, Part III.C.1). In sum, during the late 19th and early 20th centuries companies with publicly traded shares were under a market-driven onus to distribute sizeable dividends and for those that succumbed the distribution of profits otherwise eligible for extraction as private benefits of control would have provided an incentive for blockholders to unwind their holdings.

---

[48] Henry Lowenfeld, *Investment Practically Considered* (1908), 419.

[49] C.H. Thorpe, *How to Invest and to Speculate* (1901), 84.

[50] Gareth Campbell and John D. Turner, 'Protecting Outside Investors in a Laissez-faire Legal Environment: Corporate Governance in Victorian Britain' (2007), unpublished working paper, Table 7.

[51] *Gregory's Hints to Speculators and Investors in Stocks and Shares*, 9th edn (1894), 187–93.

[52] 'Local Securities as a Field for Investment', Journal of Finance, November 1898, 970.

[53] 'Position of Leading', *supra* n. 16.

[54] 'Minor Industrial Securities', Economist, February 21, 1914, 390.

[55] Chandler, *supra* n. 22, 390, 695 (providing data from Armstrong Whitworth, Bleachers' Association, Bradford Dyes, Brunner Mond, J. & P. Coats and Vickers).

[56] Roy Church, 'The Family Firm in Industrial Capitalism: International Perspectives on Hypotheses and History', (1993) 35 *Business History* 17, 23.

[57] Richard S. Grossman and J. Bradford De Long, 'The British Economic Stock Market and British Economic Growth, 1870–1914' (1996), unpublished working paper, 21.

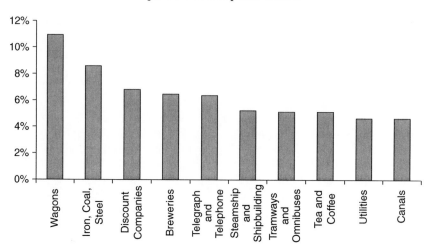

Figure III: Average dividend yield, 1890–1903

Source: Reproduced with permission from Grossman and De Long, *supra* n. 57, 21.

3. *The Price Was Right*

Consistent with the pattern in other eras (Chapter Three, Part VII) the possibility of selling out at an attractive price could prompt proprietors of late 19th- and early 20th-century business enterprises to exit, at least partially. Donald Currie, the driving force behind the Castle Line shipping concern, used an 1881 initial public offering to divest partially since he knew the industry was near the top of a boom in the trade cycle and that his firm would have difficulty renewing a lucrative postal contract.[58] Likewise, when Sir Edward Guinness decided to convert his brewery into a publicly traded company in 1886, 'His business sense told him that with the brewery showing enormous profit growth now was the right time to go public.'[59] He was proved right, as the public offering was highly over-subscribed, with only 6,000 of 19,000 applications receiving allotments. As for the decision by Bovril's founders Johnston and Walker to sell out to Hooley, 'Their resistance was overcome partly by the high price paid for their shares' as well as by Hooley giving existing shareholders the option to buy up to one-third of each class of the shares on offer in the new company on preferential terms when he re-launched it.[60]

An 1899 article on company promoting suggested, 'In a "boom" a promoter can bring out almost anything, because the public will take almost anything.'[61]

---

[58] Andrew Porter, *Victorian Shipping, Business and Imperial Policy: Donald Currie, the Castle Line and Southern Africa* (1986), 102–3; Gordon Boyce, *Information, Mediation and Institutional Development: The Rise of Large-Scale Enterprise in British Shipping, 1870–1919* (1995), 89.

[59] Wilson, *supra* n. 45, 115; see also S.R. Dennison and Oliver MacDonagh, *Guinness 1886–1939: From Incorporation to the Second World War* (1998), 19–20.

[60] Armstrong, *supra* n. 46, 20–21; 'Bovril Limited Prospectus', Times, November 23, 1896.

[61] S.F. Van Oss, 'In Hooley Land', Journal of Finance, January 1899, 1, 8; see also W.R. Lawson, 'Company Promoting "à la Mode" ', National Review, September 1898, 103, 106.

There were during the late 19th and early 20th centuries various surges in investor enthusiasm for shares and for proprietors operating in sectors that captured the fancy of investors, such episodes provided an excellent opportunity to cash out, at least partially, for prices in excess of their private estimates of the value of their firms (Part III.C.3, Chapter Three, Part VII). The *Economist* drew attention to the pattern in 1897 while cautioning readers that, '[T]he worst feature of the recent activity of company promotion is the fact that promoters are no longer satisfied with converting businesses which are offered spontaneously, but insist on touting about among merchants and traders, and endeavouring them to joint-stock.' As the *Economist* suggested, generous terms were the key to winning over proprietors, as '[A]nyone who possesses a business with which he is satisfied and is approached by an eager buyer, naturally demands a price which shall be sufficient to overcome his contentment with the present state of things—in other words, as is necessarily the case when the buyer is urgent and the holder is indifferent, the buyer must give more than the property is worth.'[62]

During the mid-1890s, cycling was one industry very much in a 'boom' phase. With cycling becoming fashionable in Britain for the first time, many came to believe one could make 'a mint of money in the bicycle trade'.[63] Investors and manufacturers took the cue, and the number of cycle companies listed in the *Stock Exchange Official Intelligencer* surged from nine in 1894 (aggregate nominal capital—£1.02 million) to 67 in 1897 (aggregate capital—£19.59 million).[64] For industry incumbents the time could not have been better to use a public offering of shares to take cash out of the business. An 1898 survey of the post-boom cycle industry used the example of industry leader Humber Company to make the point, saying of the company's 1895 public offering, 'One can quite understand the advantage which accrued to the shareholder in the old company who disposed of his equivalent shares at the high prices which ruled during the boom.'[65]

4. Raising Capital

On the 'sell side' public offerings of shares can be carried out to raise capital as well as to facilitate exit (Chapter Three, Part VI). In the UK during the late 19th and early 20th centuries retained profits, bank finance and capital provided by key incumbent shareholders were of much greater importance as sources of finance for industrial development.[66] However, numerous public offerings were carried out to help to finance mergers.

---

[62] 'Public Companies Again', Economist, September 11, 1897, 1288, 1289. See also Hall, *supra* n. 39, 65.

[63] Duncans, 'The Cycle Industry', Contemporary Review, April 1898, 500, 501–2.

[64] *Ibid.*, 502.   [65] *Ibid.*, 507.

[66] Dintenfass, *supra* n. 3, 41–42; Cottrell, *supra* n. 7, 189; Lance E. Davis and Robert E. Gallman, *Evolving Financial Markets and International Capital Flows: Britain, the Americas and Australia* (2001), 163.

Amalgamations of industrial and commercial firms were rare in the UK until near the end of the 19th century, but matters then changed.[67] During the late 19th and early 20th centuries there were numerous 'vertical' mergers designed to bring successive stages of production under the control of a single firm that were financed at least partly by a public offerings of securities, quite often including ordinary shares (Chapter Seven, Table I). There also were between 1888 and 1912 at least 26 'horizontal' amalgamations involving five or more firms operating in the same industry, with sectors affected including textiles, chemicals, metals, cement and tobacco.[68] It was standard practice with such multi-firm mergers for the amalgamated entity to issue securities to the public to help to finance the deal, with ordinary shares quite often being made available where outside investment was sought.[69] The rationale for tapping capital markets was that 'It would have been impossible for a few men in partnership to raise the capital necessary in a combination such as the Salt Union, the first British joint stock industrial combination, with its capital of £4,000,000, or the Fine Cotton Spinners and Doublers Associations with a share and loan capital of £8,000,000.'[70]

Mergers are significant on the sell side not only because they can prompt companies to tap capital markets but also because they provide a once-and-for all solution for proprietors of business enterprises minded to exit. As Clapham said of multi-firm industrial mergers occurring at the turn of the 20th century '[T]he declining vigour and interest of the second or third generation of an industrial family saw in the promoters' schemes the attractions which had long been associated with simple limitation of a family business.'[71] For instance, according to a history of soap and chemical manufacturers Joseph Crosfield & Sons Ltd., the third generation of Crosfields decided to sell the company in 1911 to rival Brunner, Mond because 'The terms offered were financially attractive, and perhaps J.J. and George Crosfield were not too sorry to relinquish the family business...J.J. was "not greatly interested in soap" but was an excellent amateur mechanic [on] lathe work, etc...., [and a] great fisherman. George, too, was a fond sportsman, fond of hunting...'[72]

A situation where exit by merger could be particularly attractive for blockholders was where they were victims of intensifying competition within

[67] J.H. Clapham, *An Economic History of Britain: Machines and National Rivalries (1887–1914) with an Epilogue (1914–1929)* (1938), 212.

[68] M.A. Utton, 'Some Features of the Early Merger Movements in British Manufacturing Industry', (1972) 14 Business History 51, 53. Utton lists 29 mergers in all, but three of these involved serial acquisitions by a single firm rather than a once-and-for all multi-firm amalgamation.

[69] Ch. Seven, Table I; George R. Carter, *The Tendency Towards Industrial Combination* (1913), 186; Hermann Levy, *Monopolies, Cartels and Trusts in British Industry* (1927), 218, n. 2.

[70] Jefferys, *supra* n. 8, 128.

[71] Clapham, *supra* n. 67, 228.

[72] A.E. Musson, *Enterprise in Soap and Chemicals: Joseph Crosfield & Sons Limited 1815–1965* (1965), 244 (also attributing the decision to sell partly to 'the pressure of competition and losses in the soap trade').

their industry. Utton says of multi-firm horizontal industrial amalgamations occurring at the turn of the 20th century, 'The argument which recurs again and again in the prospectuses and reports of preliminary meetings between interested firms is of the need to eliminate severe short term price competition which reduced profits and accentuated the burden of excess capacity... The prime objective of amalgamation was, therefore to stabilize prices at a higher level than had prevailed prior to the merger...'[73] In mergers organized in response to competitive pressures, if the transactions had resulted in extensive centralization of managerial functions, the potential cure for competitive pressures could have been worse than the disease, at least for those not wanting to retire. However, in the horizontal multi-firm mergers of the time, the constituent firms often remained legally and administratively autonomous entities, meaning the former owners had the option to continue working and to exercise significant managerial discretion.[74] The possibility 'to eat the cake and have it' thus paved the way for many of the mergers that occurred, admittedly with a potential cost.[75] In various instances the independence constituent firms enjoyed hampered the exploitation of economies of scale, with examples of firms adversely affected including English Sewing Cotton, the Calico Printers Association and the British Cotton & Wool Dyers Association, though only one major amalgamated firm (the Yorkshire Woolcombers Association) operating in the late 19th and early 20th centuries collapsed entirely.

III. The Buy Side

No matter how eager proprietors of a firm may be to exit, short of liquidating the assets and winding up the firm no transformation in ownership structure can occur unless on the buy side there are investors willing to buy up part or all of the business (Chapter One, Part IV). During the late 19th and early 20th centuries investment in shares was potentially hampered by significant informational asymmetries and the growing popularity of investing abroad. Nevertheless, share ownership was an option taken up by a considerably wider circle of investors. We will consider why there was demand for shares after identifying who the buyers were.

A. Who Bought Shares?

1. Institutional Investors

By default, individual investors dominated the 'buy side' for shares in UK companies in the late 19th and early 20th centuries as institutional investment failed

---

[73] Utton, *supra* n. 68, 54. See also Carter, *supra* n. 69, 156–57, 188–89.

[74] Chandler, *supra* n. 40, 406; Payne, *supra* n. 47, 206–7; Clapham, *supra* n. 67, 228.

[75] Clapham, *supra* n. 67, 228; Utton, *supra* n. 68, 54–55.

to get off the ground in a significant way. Banks were conservative investors and did not build up significant holdings in domestic company securities, railways partially excepted.[76] Late Victorian and Edwardian investment trusts were not under any onus to reveal their holdings and generally did not do so.[77] However, the available evidence suggests that they focused on overseas securities and that shares, whether domestic or foreign, were only a small component of their investment portfolios.[78] In addition, the progress of the investment trust sector was hampered by a financial crisis culminating in the near collapse of the investment bank Barings in 1890 and recessionary conditions in the early 1890s. The consequences were disastrous for all but the most conservatively managed outfits and the establishment of new investment trusts was largely postponed until just prior to World War I.[79]

Insurance companies and pension funds would come to dominate institutional investment in the latter half of the 20th century (Chapter Four, Part I) but they were relatively minor players up to 1914. As a proportion of life assurance assets available for investment, corporate securities increased from 3.5 per cent of total assets in 1885 to 6.2 per cent in 1900 and again to 9.6 per cent in 1913.[80] Insurance companies, however, remained wary of shares, generally preferring to invest in debentures.[81] Industrial equities made up only 3.9 per cent of total invested assets as of 1903 and 3.1 per cent in 1921.[82]

As for pension funds, as the 19th century drew to a close most large railways had established pension plans for their employees, as had a few banks. By the end of World War I, a variety of major industrial and commercial companies had done likewise. Nevertheless, there was negligible pension-oriented investment in company shares, as all the way through to World War II pension plans invested almost entirely in fixed interest securities issued by British and overseas governments and by public utilities.[83]

---

[76] Davis and Gallman, *supra* n. 66, 120–21; C.A.E. Goodhart, *The Business of Banking 1891–1914* (1972), 134–35; Caroline Fohlin, 'Bank Securities Holdings and Industrial Finance Before World War I: Britain and Germany Compared', (1997) 26 Business and Economic History 463, 472.

[77] Percy Ripley, *A Short History of Investment* (1934), 126–27; Youssef Cassis, 'The Emergence of a New Financial Institution: Investment Trusts in Britain, 1870–1939' in J.J. van Helten and Y. Cassis (eds), *Capitalism in a Mature Economy: Financial Institutions, Capital Exports and British Industry, 1870–1939* (1990), 139, 147; John Newlands, *Put Not Your Money* (1997), 138.

[78] Davis and Gallman, *supra* n. 66, 152–53; Hugh Bullock, *The Story of Investment Companies* (1959), 5; Stanley Chapman, *The Rise of Merchant Banking* (1984), 98–99.

[79] Cassis, *supra* n. 77, 142; Newlands, *supra* n. 77, 142; Bullock, *supra* n. 78, 10; 'A Lesson from the Late Trust Companies Mania', Economist, May 2, 1891, 562.

[80] William P. Kennedy, *Industrial Structure, Capital Markets and the Origins of British Economic Decline* (1987), 131–32.

[81] Davis and Gallman, *supra* n. 66, 150; Mae Baker and Michael Collins, 'The Asset Portfolio Composition of British Life Insurance Firms', (2003) 10 Financial History Review 137, 153.

[82] H.A.L. Cockerell and Edwin Green, *The British Insurance Business: A Guide to its History and Records*, 2nd edn (1994), 114.

[83] Leslie Hannah, *Inventing Retirement: The Development of Occupational Pensions in Britain* (1986), 10–12, 18–19, 73.

2. Personal Investors

As for individual investors, the number of people owning shares increased significantly in the late 19th and early 20th centuries, albeit from a low base. According to Michie, the number of 'serious holders of securities' in the UK rose from 250,000 to 1 million between 1870 to 1914.[84] Not all of these investors would have owned equities, but a substantial proportion likely owned at least some. The number of holders of railway securities rose from 546,000 in 1887 to around 800,000 in 1902, with nearly half holding ordinary shares.[85] As for companies other than railways, estimates of the number of people owning shares rose from somewhere approaching 50,000 in the early 1860s to between 250,000 and 500,000 by the first decade of the 20th century.[86]

While the investor base broadened substantially in the late 19th and early 20th centuries, there were significant limits on how far things went. A 1910 study of London's financial markets noted that shareholders of Selfridges, a major department store, included a cabinet maker, a gas collector, a clerk, a nurse, a housekeeper, a school mistress and a governess, saying nearly every one 'represents a class of the community to whom investment was a word of unknown meaning, and the process itself an unprobed mystery, fifty years ago'.[87] Nevertheless, investment in shares remained an activity largely reserved for the wealthy.[88] If Michie's estimate that there were one million 'serious holders of securities' is correct, that would have been only 2.2 per cent of the UK's population.[89] Assuming investments of the deceased are a reliable proxy for holdings of all investors, that small minority would have been the most prosperous sector of society. Aggregate data compiled by the Inland Revenue on wills left by those dying in 1913/14 indicates estates worth over £50,000 (£3.38 million in 2006 currency) held almost 55 per cent of the shares, stocks and funds vested in all estates.[90]

Within the cadre of investors who owned shares, as was the case before 1880, proprietors of prosperous industrial concerns remained an important source of demand, particularly those looking to invest spare capital after exiting, at least partially, from the enterprises they had been running.[91] There also was a movement by wealthy landowners to invest in stock exchange securities (Part III.C.1). A change in approach by 'safe' investors was the most important trend, however, within the investing class.

---

[84] Michie, *supra* n. 5, 72.

[85] 'Investors' Holdings of British Railway Stocks', Economist, January 22, 1887, 107; A.K. Cairncross, *Home and Foreign Investment 1870–1913: Studies in Capital Accumulation* (1953), 85, n. 4.

[86] Ch. Five, Pt V.B.4; Jefferys, *supra* n. 8, 435. Jefferys suggests the figures for the early 20th century were an underestimate, but they were confirmed by a 1901 study finding 445,000 different individuals owned shares in companies other than railways: Michie, *supra* n. 5, 72.

[87] Ellis T. Powell, *Mechanism of the City: An Analytical Survey of the Business Activities of the City* (1910), 127.

[88] Cairncross, *supra* n. 85, 84–88.

[89] Michie, *supra* n. 5, 72.   [90] Davis and Gallman, *supra* n. 66, 195, 197.

[91] Jefferys, *supra* n. 8, 413; Hannah, *supra* n. 44, 57; Davis and Gallman, *supra* n. 66, 196.

As of the 1870s, four-fifths of the 250,000 or so people in the UK who owned securities were 'safe' investors and they largely bypassed shares as an investment (Chapter Five, Part V.B.4). Between 1880 and 1914, this class of investors increased markedly in size, partly because of a rapid growth in the number of professionals and managers earning sizeable salaries.[92] At the same time, the investment horizons of 'safe' investors were expanding.[93] By 1880 a considerable number were already investing in railway securities.[94] Major joint stock banks soon became popular outlets for investment as well (Chapter Seven, Part V). As World War I drew closer, 'safe' investors increasingly turned to securities issued by industrial and commercial enterprises. A predilection for marketability and security meant 'pre-ordinary' securities—debentures and preference shares—were often their first choice.[95] Still, by the end of the opening decade of the 20th century a majority likely held at least some ordinary shares as well.[96]

B. Deterrents to Investing in Shares

1. *The Overseas Option*

In various ways, it is surprising that the buy side for shares in UK companies expanded between 1880 and 1914. One potential deterrent was the availability of overseas investment options. As Lloyd-Jones and Lewis have said of the Edwardian period, there was 'a rentier class which earned vast incomes accruing from interest payments from foreign assets. These earnings created a vast pool of savings but, rather than investing them in domestic industry, and particularly the new technological sectors of industry, they were siphoned abroad...'.[97] There has been intense debate among economic historians as to whether Britain's relative decline in the late 19th and early 20th centuries constituted a form of economic 'failure' or was merely an inevitable transition away from unsustainable pre-eminence.[98] Even if the more optimistic interpretation is correct, the foreign option was attractive to British investors of the late 19th and early 20th centuries because they could potentially benefit from allocating capital to locales growing relative to Britain (Figure IV).[99]

---

[92] Jefferys, *supra* n. 8, 209, 412.

[93] Davis and Gallman, *supra* n. 66, 197–98.

[94] Jefferys, *supra* n. 8, 414.   [95] *Ibid.*, 209–10, 417–21.

[96] Henry Lowenfeld, 'Shares as an Investment', Financial Review of Reviews, February 1911, 5, 8.

[97] Roger Lloyd-Jones and M.J. Lewis, *British Industrial Capitalism Since the Industrial Revolution* (1998), 128; see also Sidney Pollard, 'Entrepreneurship, 1870–1914' in Roderick Floud and Donald McCloskey (eds), *The Economic History of Britain Since 1700*, 2nd edn (1994), 62, 67.

[98] On the debate see Crouzet, *supra* n. 43, 371–401; Michael Dintenfass, 'Converging Accounts, Misleading Metaphors and Persistent Doubts: Reflections on the Historiography of Britain's "Decline"' in Jean-Pierre Dormois and Michael Dintenfass (eds), *The British Industrial Decline* (1999), 7, 7–11.

[99] Edelstein, *supra* n. 11, 232.

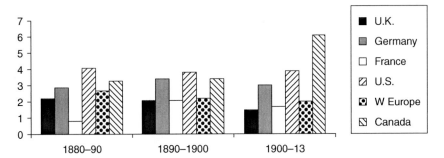

Figure IV: Annual growth rates, major potential destinations for investment 1880–1913 (as measured by GDP, GNP for Canada, Western Europe)[100]

Source: Compiled with data from Pollard, *supra* n. 100, 5; Urquhart, *supra* n. 100, 26.

Plenty of advice was offered to investors that it would be wise to forsake Britain to take advantage of better prospects elsewhere. As the *Economist* said in 1909:

> For the past three or four years politicians and journalists have, in and out of season, been preaching the insecurity of British investments and the wisdom of placing money abroad. This is not the place to discuss the truth of that doctrine, but we can admit that when the newspapers which are most read by investing classes tell their readers every day money invested in Great Britain is money wrongly invested, some of their readers will come to believe them. Whether that has happened we do not profess to say, but we do believe that the industrial market has been rather foolishly neglected.[101]

The *Economist*'s note of caution on exactly why foreign investment might occur was well taken, as investing abroad could have been motivated not so much by the superior economic performance of other countries as by the potential benefits of diversification, an investment strategy many British investors were acquainted with during the late 19th and early 20th centuries.[102] Regardless of precisely why investors might have wanted to invest abroad, the capital flows were substantial, with Davis and Huttenback saying, 'The outflow may well represent the largest absolute voluntary capital transfer in the history of the world.'[103] Estimates of the percentage of total British capital holdings invested

---

[100] On GDP/GNP figures, see Sidney Pollard, *Britain's Prime and Britain's Decline: The British Economy 1870–1914* (1989), 5 (all countries other than Canada); Malcolm C. Urquhart, *Gross National Product, 1870–1926: Derivation of the Estimates* (1993), 26 (Canada, providing data for 1900–10 rather than 1900–13). On Canada's importance as a destination for UK investment, see Lance E. Davis and Robert A. Huttenback, *Mammon and the Pursuit of Empire: The Economics of British Imperialism* (1988), 39; William N. Goetzmann and Andrey D. Ukhov, 'British Investment Overseas 1870–1913: A Modern Portfolio Theory Approach', (2005), Yale ICF Working Paper No. 05–03, 12.

[101] 'Industrial Profits and the Industrial Market', Economist, October 9, 1909, 687, 688.

[102] Goetzmann and Ukhov, *supra* n. 100, 7, 21–26, 30–35.

[103] Davis and Huttenback, *supra* n. 100, 60.

in overseas assets range from 34 per cent to 44 per cent.[104] Investment on this sort of scale implied at least some 'crowding out' of demand for shares of UK-domiciled companies. To quote Davis and Huttenback again, 'Had the British saver chosen to invest these accumulations in a different manner, the course of development in England and abroad would have been very different.'[105]

2. Company Law

Even in purely domestic terms, between 1880 and 1914 there were various deterrents to investment in shares in UK companies. Potential investors in public companies proceed under conditions of asymmetric information, outside shareholders in companies with blockholders face the risk of extraction of private benefits of control and their counterparts in firms characterized by a separation of ownership and control are potential victims of managerial agency costs. The risks involved can be reduced by company law creating substantial rights for outside shareholders, by financial intermediaries performing diligently so as to protect their reputational capital and by press scrutiny of insider misdeeds (Chapter Two, Part I; Chapter Four, Part III). However, up to World War I the protection afforded on each of these counts left much to be desired, which implies a weak foundation for the buy side for company shares.

In the late 19th and early 20th centuries UK company law offered what was, by current standards, minimal protection to outside investors. Chapter Two (Part II) drew attention to the pattern in a general way, and a brief survey of the rules governing disclosure confirms the point. Up to 1900 there was almost no regulation of the contents of prospectuses, and promoters of companies frequently waived statutory requirements that a prospectus disclose contracts between a company and its directors and other contracts likely to influence an investor's decision to purchase shares.[106] Between 1856 and 1900 there was no legislative requirement that a company's financial statements be audited.[107] Until 1908, companies were not required to file publicly their annual balance sheets (a statement of a company's assets and liabilities).[108] This was not merely a technical

---

[104] Goetzmann and Ukhov, *supra* n. 100, 7; Sidney Pollard, 'Capital Exports, 1879–1914: Harmful or Beneficial', (1985) 38 Economic History Review 489, 491–92.

[105] Davis and Huttenback, *supra* n. 100, 60. See also Edelstein, *supra* n. 11, 163–64, 288–311 (acknowledging the effect but saying it diminished over time).

[106] 'The Companies Acts No. 1', Economist, February 11, 1888, 177, 178 (waiver of disclosure requirements); Richard Jordan and Francis Gore-Browne, *A Handy Book on the Formation, Management and Winding up of Joint Stock Companies*, 18th edn (1895), 54 (outlining items that should be included in prospectuses, but noting there was no statutory obligation to discuss them).

[107] J.R. Edwards, *Company Legislation and Changing Patterns of Disclosure in British Company Accounts 1900–1940* (1981), 3, 56.

[108] The requirement was imposed by Company Law Amendment Act 1907, Edw. VII c. 50, ss. 19, 21, which took effect in 1908.

concern, as balance sheets were regarded as a key variable to consider in assessing share values.[109]

The limited protection the law offered to shareholders was evident to contemporaries. An 1894 article headlined 'The Crying Need for Reforms in Our Company Law' claimed, '[T]he carrying out of objects which would be more or less fraudulent, and would be impossible, in the case of a private individual or a partnership is rendered easy by the means of the Companies Acts.'[110] The *Times* remarked the same year upon 'the growing and indiscriminate distrust of investors and new undertakings' and argued '[T]he safeguards which were perhaps sufficient in 1862 seem—especially since the introduction of the (prospectus) "waiver clause"—ridiculously inadequate.'[111] Another critic claimed in 1899, '[T]he shareholder is absolutely defenceless. Provided you do not commit downright larceny or embezzlement you can do anything under suitable Articles of Association.'[112]

The Companies Act 1900 and the Companies Act 1907, the provisions of which became operative in 1908, addressed some perceived deficiencies.[113] Protection of outside investors nevertheless remained scant, with one critic proclaiming in 1917 'our company law is less exacting in its safeguards than that of any other great business community...'.[114] For instance, Parliament opted not to adopt an 1894 recommendation by a Board of Trade company law committee that directors be required by statute to exercise 'reasonable care and prudence', due largely to concerns that respectable individuals would decline to serve as directors.[115] The Companies Act 1900 obliged companies to appoint an auditor but did not require that the auditor be professionally qualified.[116] New prospectus disclosure requirements introduced in 1900 were commonly sidestepped by promoters, who simply distributed shares without a supporting prospectus.[117]

---

[109] Investment Critic, 'How to Select Investments', Financial Review of Reviews, March 1907, 13, 25.

[110] Alfred Emden, 'The Crying Need for Reforms in Our Company Law', Nineteenth Century, June 1894, 1033, 1033.

[111] 'Editorial', Times, November 20, 1894.

[112] Van Oss, *supra* n. 61, 10.

[113] Companies Act 1900, 63 & 64 Vic., c. 48; Company Law Amendment Act 1907; for background, see 'Is the New Companies Act a Failure?', Bankers' Magazine, February 1903, 209; A.B. Levy, *Private Corporations and Their Control*, vol. I (1950), 120–25.

[114] H.S. Foxwell, 'The Financing of Trade and Industry', (1917) 27 Economic Journal 502, 514.

[115] Cottrell, *supra* n. 7, 70–73.

[116] Derek Matthews, Malcolm Anderson and John Richard Edwards, *The Priesthood of Industry: The Rise of the Professional Accountant in British Management* (1998), 101–2. A requirement that an auditor be professionally qualified was introduced by Companies Act 1948, 11 & 12 Geo. 6, c. 38, s. 161.

[117] See Companies Act 1900, s. 10. For background, see 'The Prospectusless Company Scandal', Economist, December 26, 1903, 2196; Francis Gore-Browne and William Jordan, *A Handy Book on the Formation, Management and Winding up of Joint Stock Companies*, 30th edn (1909), 98–108.

In 1908 the prospectus regulation loophole was addressed when companies distributing shares to the public without a prospectus were required to prepare 'a statement in lieu of prospectus' containing much of the same information.[118] Companies also became obliged from this point onwards to file publicly a balance sheet, but little guidance was offered to companies on the format to be used and there was no requirement to file a profit and loss account, meaning that companies were not under a statutory onus to provide data on current earnings.[119] Hence, the *Economist* suggested in 1910, '[I]t is surely not unreasonable to suggest that the proprietors of a company are entitled to rather more information than most boards ever give.'[120] Arnold concurs, saying in a study of the quality of corporate financial disclosure in the opening decades of the 20th century, 'Company law did little to encourage high standards' and 'disclosures were uninformative and misleading'.[121]

3. Stock Exchange Regulation

Throughout the 20th century, the listing rules governing companies traded on the London Stock Exchange provided protection to investors that filled gaps in companies legislation (Chapter Four, Part III.C). Prior to 1914, however, the assistance offered was generally meagre.[122] A key limitation was that companies could have their shares traded without seeking a full quotation. Instead, a 'special settlement' would suffice. Once this was granted, transactions in a company's shares became part of the normal bi-monthly account system of Stock Exchange dealings, enforced by penalties for brokers or jobbers who defaulted.[123] Major companies usually sought a quotation, since having one facilitated transactions in shares, thus potentially boosting the share price.[124] Nevertheless, a special settlement was a popular pre-World War I option, with a member of the Stock Exchange claiming in court testimony in 1910 that '99 per cent of the dealings in the shares of new companies were for the special settlement'.[125]

Even for companies seeking an official quotation, Stock Exchange listing requirements were not rigorous. The London Stock Exchange did make it a condition precedent that a class of securities was of 'sufficient magnitude and importance' and that two-thirds of the class had been allotted to and taken up by

---

[118] Company Law Amendment Act 1907, s. 1, sch. 1; 'The New Companies Bill', Economist, March 16, 1907, 452.

[119] Boyce, *supra* n. 58, 225; Edwards, *supra* n. 107, 4.

[120] 'The Helplessness of Shareholders', Economist, November 12, 1910, 960, 961.

[121] A.J. Arnold, "Publishing Your Private Affairs to the World': Corporate Financial Disclosures in the U.K. 1900–24', (1997) 7 Accounting, Business and Financial History 143, 161.

[122] Morgan and Thomas, *supra* n. 4, 153.

[123] Cottrell, *supra* n. 7, 148.

[124] Jordan and Gore-Browne, *supra* n. 106, 289; 'Unmarketable Securities and Official Quotations', Economist, May 30, 1885, 657.

[125] 'A Deal in Rubber Shares', Times, December 13, 1910, 14. The special settlement procedure was abolished in World War I: 'Vendors' Shares on Stock Exchange', Times, January 24, 1930, 20.

the public.[126] As Chapter Seven discusses, the 'two-thirds' rule had potentially important implications for blockholders since some diffusion of voting control was required if ordinary shares were going to be distributed to the public. Otherwise, the London Stock Exchange generally declined to operate as any form of 'public censor' (Chapter Three, Part VIII).

The primary form of regulation in which the Stock Exchange engaged was to require companies seeking a quotation to have articles of association in a form of which the Committee of the Stock Exchange approved. As early as the 1870s, the Stock Exchange was prepared to deny a quotation if a company's articles failed to preclude a company from buying back its own shares.[127] As of 1895, even though the Stock Exchange was not specifying in its listing rules what the articles should say, it was requiring companies seeking a quotation to have a provision in their articles imposing limits on the borrowing powers of directors.[128] By 1902 the Stock Exchange also required a company's articles to oblige the directors to own a minimum prescribed number of shares, to circulate a balance sheet annually to shareholders and to the Stock Exchange and to require a director to disclose and not vote upon any contract with the company in which he had a personal interest.[129] By 1909, the Stock Exchange listing rules spelled out specifically the provisions the articles should contain, and, in addition to the requirements already mentioned, stipulated the articles should compel annual circulation of the company's profit and loss account to the shareholders and the Stock Exchange.[130] Though in various respects these requirements were more stringent than those company law imposed (Chapter Three, Part VIII), generally the protection offered to investors was not substantial and thus should not have provided a substantial inducement to purchase shares.

4. Financial Intermediaries

Screening by financial intermediaries can improve the 'comfort level' of investors as firms specializing in the organization of public offerings of shares can benefit competitively from having a reputation for reliability, diligence and honesty (Chapter Four, Part III.B). Protection of this sort was generally weak, however, in the late 19th and early 20th centuries. The first-tier merchant banks in London's financial district had significant reputational capital to protect and occasionally helped to organize public offerings of shares by industrial and commercial companies. Examples included the 1886 Guinness public offering (Barings), an amalgamation between Maxim Gun and Nordenfeldt

---

[126] Jordan and Gore-Browne, *supra* n. 106, 290, 293; Gore-Browne and Jordan, *supra* n. 117, 487–88.

[127] Grossman and De Long, *supra* n. 57, 14.

[128] Jordan and Gore-Browne, *supra* n. 106, 290–92.

[129] Francis Gore-Browne and William Jordan, *A Handy Book on the Formation, Management and Winding up of Joint Stock Companies*, 24th edn (1902), 458–60.

[130] Gore-Browne and Jordan, *supra* n. 117, 489.

Ammunition (Rothschilds, 1897) and flotations by Thames Ironworks Shipbuilding and Engineering Co. (Hambro, 1899) and Trollope, Colls & Co., a building and decorating firm (Hambro, 1903).[131] Generally, however, the top merchant banks avoided sponsoring domestic issues of shares.[132] Key personnel in many of these elite firms were foreign, so proposals from UK-based industrial companies lacked any 'home field' advantage.[133] Also, public offerings by industrial enterprises were rarely on a scale large enough to justify the hefty fees merchant banks charged, unlike the transactions they arranged on behalf of governments (domestic and foreign) and foreign railways.[134]

At the other end of the scale, smaller enterprises based outside London would often distribute shares to the public without the assistance of any financial intermediary specializing in offerings of securities, relying instead on a stockbroker or solicitor to assist with the marketing and placement of the shares.[135] In between was what was in the 1880s 'a new genus of business men', company promoters who 'act(ed) as the intermediaries between those who have properties, patents or businesses to sell and the investing public'.[136] These promoters, described somewhat snobbishly as 'fresh arrivals from the provinces (i.e., outside London), from the States, from bouncing Colonies, and from the Continent',[137] did not have the field entirely to themselves. Investment trusts quite commonly organized public offerings but would not have participated often in share issuances by UK-based companies as they largely by-passed domestic shares for investment purposes (Part III.A.1).[138] Established stockbrokers also engaged in some company promotion activity.[139] However, the new arrivals came to dominate the launching of UK-based industrial and commercial enterprises in the late 19th and early 20th centuries.

The identities of numerous promoters have faded into obscurity, probably because they only launched a few schemes before disappearing to the fringes of the financial world.[140] Among promoters who achieved notoriety, there was wide variation in the quality of the work they did on behalf of their clients and

---

[131] Dennison and MacDonagh, *supra* n. 59, 17, 23 (Guinness); Kynaston, *supra* n. 28, 403 (Maxim Gun); Janette Rutterford, 'The Merchant Banker, the Broker and the Company Chairman: A New Issue Case Study', (2006) 16 Accounting, Business & Financial History 45 (Thames Ironworks and Trollope).

[132] Kynaston, *supra* n. 15, 456; Michael Collins, *Banks and Industrial Finance in Britain* 1800–1939 (1991), 43, 52–53.

[133] Chapman, *supra* n. 78, 98.

[134] *Ibid.*, 100–1; Cairncross, *supra* n. 85, 101; Foxwell, *supra* n. 114, 519; S.G. Checkland, 'The Mind of the City', (1957) 9 Oxford Economic Papers 261, 262.

[135] Harrison, *supra* n. 7, 206, 212; Jefferys, *supra* n. 8, 313; Edelstein, *supra* n. 11, 54.

[136] 'Companies', *supra* n. 106, 177.

[137] Van Oss, *supra* n. 61, 4. See also Jefferys, *supra* n. 8, 306–10; Payne, *supra* n. 17, 522.

[138] On investment trusts as promoters, Jefferys, *supra* n. 8, 309–10; 'Trust Companies as Promoters', Economist, August 9, 1890, 1016; 'Trusts as Company Promoters', Economist, December 8, 1894, 1505.

[139] Reader, *supra* n. 26, 89–124 (describing the promotion activities of Foster & Braithwaite).

[140] Morgan and Thomas, *supra* n. 4, 136; Cottrell, *supra* n. 7, 184–85; Payne, *supra* n. 17, 138.

investors. Historians of late 19th- and early 20th-century capital markets often praise the efforts of H. Osborne O'Hagan, the promoter for various breweries, tramways and coal companies and a major amalgamation of cement companies, citing his close investigation of the proposals he received and his insistence that proprietors of businesses he took public continue to be involved closely with the business thereafter.[141]

The fact O'Hagan published an autobiography providing ample detail on promoting practices helps to explain why he features so prominently in secondary accounts.[142] Other promoters, on the other hand, have an enduring legacy due to careers tainted with scandal. Harry Lawson, promoter of numerous cycle and automobile companies in the mid-1890s, was discredited on the grounds that his promotions lacked staying power and that he diverted capital opportunistically to himself and his allies.[143] E.T. Hooley, labelled the 'Napoleon of Finance' after successful public offerings of Bovril and Dunlop, the tyre company, was declared bankrupt in 1898 after other promotions left a string of ruined companies.[144] Whitaker Wright, a flamboyant mining company promoter, committed suicide in court in 1904 after being convicted for issuing false balance sheets.[145]

The incentive structure of 'professional promoters' helps to explain why they achieved notoriety for being makeshift and even dishonest rather than for being diligent and careful.[146] They were aware that if things went wrong they would struggle to gain support from investors in the future.[147] Nevertheless, because they were often newcomers to London's financial district and lacked an accompanying day-to-day business such as stockbroking for which a reputation for probity and honesty was worth building and protecting, they did not make major sacrifices if things went wrong. As Van Oss said in 1899 '(T)hose who bear the direct responsibility for the deterioration of City morals are not our old-fashioned honourable houses, but the newcomers without an honourable reputation to live up to…It is these people who chiefly 'control' the unclean trade in companies…'[148]

With the numerous new entrants joining the promotion business, competition was keen among those prepared to orchestrate public offerings, particularly

---

[141] Cottrell, *supra* n. 7, 185–86; Davis and Gallman, *supra* n. 66, 173–74; Kynaston, *supra* n. 15, 403–5.

[142] Chapman, *supra* n. 78, 100; citing H. Osborne O'Hagan, *Leaves from my Life, in Two Volumes* (1929).

[143] Kynaston, *supra* n. 15, 145–48; George Robb, *White-Collar Crime in England: Financial Fraud and Business Morality 1845–1929* (1992), 104–5.

[144] Kynaston, *supra* n. 15, 142–45, 179–83; Robb, *supra* n. 143, 105–7. On the moniker, see 'The Hooley Failure', Economist, July 30, 1898, 1113.

[145] Robb, *supra* n. 143, 108–9; 'Today's Fraudsters and Taking the Wright Path', Telegraph, June 25, 2006.

[146] Cottrell, *supra* n. 7 at 187; Lavington, *supra* n. 13, 213–14.

[147] Ernest Terah Hooley, *Hooley's Confessions* (1925), 250.

[148] Van Oss, *supra* n. 61, 4.

in buoyant market conditions.[149] As a result, when a deal offered the potential for large one-off profits, the temptation to act opportunistically and ignore the potential benefits of self-sacrifice was strong. Also, it was uncommon for promoters to develop any sort of ongoing relationship with those involved with the companies distributing shares to the public, so that the possibility of repeat business provided little inducement for prudence and honesty. As the *Times* remarked in 1909, '[M]oney for industrial purposes has to be raised through the independent financier, who looks upon the "industrial" as a means of making promotion money or profit on the Stock Exchange, rather than a steady income, and to him a successful flotation is of more importance than a sound venture.'[150] Hooley put the point more directly in his 1925 memoirs, saying, 'I bought a business as cheaply as I could and sold it again for the biggest price it would bring. Some people might say that by this method I robbed the public of millions of pounds, but nevertheless I did not do anything against the law.'[151] With the 'Napoleon of Finance' approaching company promotion in this way, potential investors understandably would have received little reassurance from the financial intermediaries orchestrating public offerings of shares in the late 19th and early 20th centuries.

5. *The Press*

The financial press can improve the 'comfort level' of investors by making pertinent news and data readily accessible and by 'naming and shaming' instances of mismanagement and corruption (Chapter Four, Part III.D). Up to the 1880s, the press was of little assistance to investors (Chapter Five, Part V.B.4). Financial news and commentary proliferated between 1880 and World War I, underpinned by the growing number of serious investors, improved communications technology and rapid growth in the number of business enterprises accessing capital markets.[152] The *Financier*, launched as the UK's first financial daily newspaper in 1870, was soon joined by two rivals, the *Financial News* (1884) and the *Financial Times* (1888). There were also 50 'finance and investment' journals by the mid-1890s and nearly 110 by 1914, supplemented by yearbooks and specialist handbooks.[153] Most of the financial papers were London-based and their combined circulation remained smaller than that of any of Britain's major daily

---

[149] Edelstein, *supra* n. 11, 54–55.

[150] 'The Need for Industrial Banks', Times, October 8, 1909.

[151] Hooley, *supra* n. 147, 12; see also at 73 ('I was never one to concern myself with what happened afterwards').

[152] Dilwyn Porter, "A Trusted Guide of the Investing Public': Harry Marks and the *Financial News* 1884–1916', (1986) 28 Business History 1, 1.

[153] *Ibid.*; P.L. Cottrell, 'Domestic Finance 1860–1914' in Roderick Floud and Paul Johnson (eds), *The Cambridge Economic History of Modern Britain, Volume II: Economic Maturity, 1860–1939* (2004), 253, 269.

newspapers.[154] However, coverage of financial matters in national and provincial 'dailies' also increased up to 1914.[155]

An 1899 article aiming to provide 'Object Lessons for Small Investors' suggested 'the public is gradually becoming more educated', partly due 'to the enlightening influence of the public Press'.[156] A 1910 survey of London's financial district suggested similarly '[I]t is the cheap Press which stimulated the financial education, and fired the imagination, of its readers, and has, in that way, brought into being the vast public which now casts a critical eye upon the daily record of City happenings.'[157] Despite these optimistic verdicts, investors in fact had difficulty finding incisive, timely and trustworthy information from press coverage.

Many of the financial publications of the late 19th and early 20th centuries were merely marketing tools of the stockbrokers or financial agents that published them.[158] Other publications were thoroughly dependent on advertising by promoters and stockbrokers and thus tended to repay ads with warm endorsements rather than objective assessments of shares on offer.[159] Even the founding editor of the *Financial News* was widely suspected of receiving payments in return for providing favourable reviews of company prospectuses.[160] An 1898 article entitled 'The Company Scandal' implied this sort of corruption explained why 'the Press, or a large section of it', was 'mortally afraid of agitation against financial scandals'.[161] Whatever the precise reason, the *Financial News* and the *Financial Times* generally adopted a neutral tone towards new issues, summarizing the main aspects of a prospectus rather than offering a critical assessment.[162] The major daily newspapers similarly were slow to move beyond offering the 'bare record' of basic information on prices, dividend yields and the holding of annual meetings and when they did offer analysis and assessment there was suspicion that there was an unhelpful blurring of editorial content and advertisements.[163]

Readers of the financial press were occasionally offered pointers on how to assess judiciously company prospectuses, such as the need to bear in mind transitory considerations affecting the prosperity of a particular trade and to be

---

[154] Jefferys, *supra* n. 8, 355–56 (London orientation); Lowenfeld, *supra* n. 48, 133–34 (circulation).

[155] Porter, *supra* n. 152, 1.

[156] Ernest E.T. Irons, 'Object Lessons for Small Investors', Journal of Finance, April 1899, 280, 281.

[157] Powell, *supra* n. 87, 117.

[158] Jefferys, *supra* n. 8, 377; David C. Itzkowitz, 'Fair Enterprise or Extravagant Speculation: Investment, Speculation, and Gambling in Victorian England', (2002) 45 Victorian Studies 121, 137.

[159] Itzkowitz, *supra* n. 158, 137; S.F. Van Oss, 'The Limited-Company Craze', Nineteenth Century, May 1899, 730, 742.

[160] Porter, *supra* n. 152, 8–10.

[161] Hugh E.M. Stutfield, 'The Company Scandal: A City View', National Review, December 1898, 574, 575.

[162] David Kynaston, *The Financial Times: A Centenary History* (1988), 67.

[163] Porter, *supra* n. 152, 2; Andrew Still, 'Front Sheet Reflections', Journal of Finance, November 1898, 988, 993; 'The New Financial Journalism—News and Advertisements', Economist, November 1, 1913, 943.

suspicious of valuations not provided by a qualified expert.[164] Particular individuals and financial practices could also be subject to some harsh criticism. The *Journal of Finance* condemned promoters in 1898 as 'a profession in which, unfortunately, the bad characters have the whip hand'.[165] The *Economist* in 1902 warned readers of 'the Electric Construction and Maintenance Company, Limited, which is little more than an *alias* for Henry J. Lawson', noting 'the Lawson companies have a way of sticking very closely to any money they obtain'.[166] In 1906 Lowenfeld assailed investors themselves, saying, '[J]ust as a kitten is unable to restrain itself from eagerly jumping in pursuit of a cork which is steadily drawn away from it, so the average investor finds himself impelled to jump into a market which is steadily rising.'[167]

While financial news coverage could take on a critical tone, there remained significant limits on the benefits investors could derive from the press. Journalists could only work with the subject matter at hand, and because companies faced negligible periodic disclosure requirements (Part III.B.2), there was little scope for the press to offer assessments of companies absent a major change in dividend policy, a dramatic fluctuation in the share price, a contentious shareholders' meeting or involvement in court proceedings.[168] Even when press reports could offer timely assessments of how companies were faring, the investing public remained at a significant disadvantage because those 'in the know' were free to deal on the basis of price-sensitive information before the outside public had had a chance to read up, let alone contact a stockbroker to buy or sell.[169]

Collectively, the various deterrents to investment in shares create a pretty discouraging picture. Indeed, the *Financial Review of Reviews* cautioned readers in 1907 'to the speculator should be left Ordinary Shares' and reiterated the point in 1911, suggesting 'ordinary shares can only be regarded as safe under very exceptional circumstances'.[170] Kennedy offered a similar verdict in 1984, saying of the market for equities in late 19th- and early 20th-century Britain, 'Victorian company promoters, vendors and underwriters were...ludicrously better informed about the prospects of the ventures they were selling than were the vast majority of potential buyers.'[171] Kennedy indeed doubted there could be a viable market for

---

[164] 'Prospectuses and Their Pitfalls', Economist, February 27, 1897, 304.

[165] 'The Idiocy of Investors', Journal of Finance, July 1898, 638, 639.

[166] 'Spurious Company Promotion and its Results', Economist, November 15, 1902, 1762, 1762.

[167] Henry Lowenfeld, 'Investment Crazes', Financial Review of Reviews, March 1906, 161, 161.

[168] See, for instance, 'The Moral of the Coats' Collapse', Economist, November 20, 1897, 1625 (discussing a dividend cut by J. & P. Coats); 'The Aftermath of the Public-House Boom', Economist, August 23, 1902, 1322 (discussing the annual meeting of Allsop and Sons, a troubled brewer); 'British Electric Traction Company', Economist, June 20, 1908, 1295 (discussing a failure to pay the full dividend on preference shares).

[169] Hartley Withers, *The Quicksands of the City and a Way Through for Investors* (1930), 180.

[170] Investment Critic, *supra* n. 35, 21; Investment Critic, *supra* n. 109, 23.

[171] William P. Kennedy, 'Notes on Economic Efficiency in Historical Perspective: The Case of Britain, 1870–1914', (1984) 9 Research in Economic History 109, 118. See also Kennedy, *supra* n. 80, 124–30.

shares in UK domestic companies under such conditions, arguing 'the tendency for the asymmetrical distribution of relevant information between buyers and sellers of investment assets to distort, if not totally destroy, investment markets, creating at an extreme a situation in which *no* trade in investment assets would take place even if the gains flowing from informed trade were large'.[172]

The various difficulties on the buy side likely affected demand for ordinary shares in UK companies. An 1898 article in the *National Review* argued '[T]he dishonesty fostered by our existing limited liability system is ... deterring the public from embarking their money in undertakings which, though possibly speculative, are yet perfectly legitimate and useful.'[173] Kennedy has claimed '[T]he ignorance and mistrust that surrounded the issues of most provincial industrial concerns gave a pronounced foreign orientation to British capital markets.'[174] Despite these gloomy verdicts, the buy side obviously had some vitality, since Britain had, in comparative terms, a well-developed market for domestic company shares by 1914 (Part I). Statistics Kennedy himself cites illustrate how far things changed in the late 19th and early 20th centuries. Whereas as of 1870 securities issued by 'home companies' (i.e., other than railways) made up only 4 per cent by value of all outstanding home and foreign securities held in the UK, by 1913 the figure was 17 per cent.[175] We will consider next why there was significant demand for shares in British companies despite the various deterrents to investment.

C. Factors Promoting Investment in Shares

1. Returns in Comparison with Other Investments

With economic growth apparently being stronger abroad, British investors seemingly had good reason to bypass domestic equities (Part III.B.1). On the other hand, to the extent shares in UK companies delivered competitive rates of return compared with foreign alternatives, the pull from overseas should have weakened and investors should have been prepared to allocate capital to British equity markets. The limited empirical evidence available suggests UK companies indeed delivered competitive returns compared with overseas alternatives between 1880 and 1914, which should have helped to sustain demand for shares throughout the period.

A study by Davis and Huttenback illustrates the point. They examined for the years between 1883 and 1912 the profitability of nearly 500 companies incorporated under UK law operating in Britain, the Empire and foreign jurisdictions.[176] They divided the companies into 12 different sectors (e.g. railroads, commerce and industry, banks, agricultural and extractive and financial trusts) and found that

---

172 Kennedy, *supra* n. 171, 118.   173 Stutfield, *supra* n. 161, 583.
174 Kennedy, *supra* n. 171, 126.   175 Kennedy, *supra* n. 80, 128–29.
176 Davis and Huttenback, *supra* n. 100, 64–83.

companies operating in Britain were more profitable than Empire companies in seven sectors and more profitable than foreign companies in six. Davis and Huttenback summarized their data in a way that suggests investing in domestically based companies could be a sensible strategy for investors: 'Perhaps the single most important conclusion to be drawn from the fiscal history of these firms does not concern the Empire but, rather, the much maligned British domestic economy. Industrial and commercial enterprises performed far better than conventional wisdom has indicated; and while there is evidence of a long-run decline in profits, it is no more rapid than the fall in foreign, and less so than the decline in Empire, returns.'[177]

Research by Edelstein on returns on financial capital reveals a similar pattern. His sample consisted of 566 'first- and second-class' UK and foreign companies listed in the *Investor's Monthly Manual,* meaning companies that between 1870 and 1913 that were traded on a UK stock market, paid dividends regularly, paid interest on debt without interruption, did not suffer long periods of heavy price discounts and had securities available for trading through much if not all of the period.[178] He found that between 1870 and 1913 foreign securities (equity, debentures and preference shares) outperformed domestic securities, on average, 5.72 per cent per annum to 4.41 per cent. Similarly, foreign shares outperformed domestic shares, on average, 8.28 per cent to 6.37 per cent.[179] However, the differential between domestic shares and foreign shares was attributable largely to the poor performance of UK railways, which delivered an average annual return of only 4.33 per cent and made up 13.0 per cent of the database as of 1880 and 9.7 per cent as of 1913.[180] UK-based companies in other sectors fared fairly well in comparison with foreign counterparts. As Edelstein acknowledges, '[A] number of home manufacturing and commercial groupings generated equity returns in the same range as the highest non-domestic equity groupings.'[181]

The chronology also needs to be borne in mind since the 'pull' of foreign investment would have waxed and waned over time. Among Edelstein's companies, there were alternating periods of home and overseas domination, with domestic shares outperforming foreign shares during 1870–76, 1887–96 and 1910–13 and overseas returns being better in other periods. Assuming the availability of better returns abroad impacted on investment in shares in UK companies, the trend should only have operated with any force during periods of 'overseas domination'.

A 1914 article in the *Economist* on 'Investing Abroad and at Home' confirms the point.[182] The *Economist* said of the years 1908–10, 'The fashion for foreign

---

[177] *Ibid.,* 66–67.

[178] Edelstein, *supra* n. 11, 112, 116.

[179] *Ibid.,* 126. For each security Edelstein calculated the return per annum, taking into account dividends distributed or interest paid.

[180] Derived from *ibid.,* 117–18, 123.   [181] *Ibid.,* 124.

[182] 'Investing Abroad and at Home', Economist, January 17, 1914, 113.

bonds had set in, and the investing public was being invited on all hands to keep clear of Great Britain and trust to the foreigner', which is not surprising given Edelstein's data indicates that 1897–1909 was a period of 'overseas dominance' and was the strongest in the absolute size of the gap.[183] On the other hand, 1910–13 was a period of 'home dominance' and the relative attraction of domestic investment options changed accordingly. The *Economist*, in its 'Investing Abroad' piece, remarked upon 'an article recently published by the *Times*, congratulating those who had stood by British securities', argued that 'the fashion of investing abroad was due partly to an unnecessary panic among capitalists' and claimed that 'British industry can raise money more easily and cheaply than that of any foreign country.'[184]

In considering the options investors had open to them in the late 19th and early 20th centuries, domestic alternatives were also important because investors retained a general preference for UK assets. A domestic investment bias is a well-established fact in the financial economics literature (Chapter Four, Part III.E) and it was clearly at work in Britain during this era, since nearly two-thirds of total British capital holdings were invested in domestic assets, despite politicians and journalists advocating investing abroad (Part III.B.1). Lowenfeld, a staunch advocate of the wisdom of international diversification, conceded as much in 1907, saying, 'Naturally enough England is the "pet" investment country of the great majority of English investors.'[185]

To the extent British investors were minded to allocate capital domestically, the returns shares were delivering in comparison with potential alternatives would have helped to underpin demand for equity. The interest rate on governmental 'gilt-edged' securities, which had been above 3 per cent throughout the 19th century, fell below this threshold in 1888, and did not rise above it again until 1907, which forced investors accustomed to higher yields to contemplate alternatives.[186] As Morgan and Thomas have said about the 1890s in their history of the London Stock Exchange, 'Small wonder that investors were eager for better returns and willing to accept some risk in seeking them.'[187] Shares in UK-based companies proved a good choice, outperforming government bonds 34 out of 43 years preceding World War I.[188] Even if an investor bought a range of fixed

---

[183] Edelstein, *supra* n. 11, 147–48.

[184] 'Investing Abroad', *supra* n. 182; see also Kynaston, *supra* n. 15, 470.

[185] Henry Lowenfeld, 'The Investor's Defence Against Labour's Attack Upon Capital', Financial Review of Reviews, June 1907, 13, 18.

[186] Morgan and Thomas, *supra* n. 4, 278–29 (setting out high and low Consol yields for each year between 1800 and 1968).

[187] *Ibid.*, 133. See also Janette Rutterford, 'The World Was Their Oyster: Managing Portfolio Risk pre-World War I' in Janette Rutteford *et al* (eds), *Financial Strategy*, 2nd edn (2006), 5, 12.

[188] J. Bradford De Long and Richard S. Grossman, ' "Excess Volatility" on the London Stock Market, 1879–1990' (1993), unpublished working paper, 3, 22. De Long and Grossman compared one-year returns generated by safe government bonds with the returns an investor would have received by buying an index of industrial shares in one year, holding it for a year and then selling the shares.

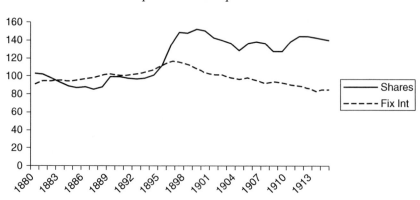

Figure V: Performance of industrial shares versus fixed interest securities, 1880–1914 (mid-1890 = 100)

Source: Compiled with data from K.C. Smith and G.F. Horne, 'An Index Number of Securities, 1867–1914', (1934) Royal Economic Society (Great Britain), Memorandum No. 47, 4–5.

interest securities rather than simply focusing on government bonds, shares were a better bet (Figure V).

Equities also outperformed railway securities (Figure VI). The poor track record of railway securities in turn caused their popularity to diminish relative to other investments. As the *Economist* observed in 1907, 'The fall has been long-continued and extensive, and while it has not been confined to the railway market alone, it would appear, without making exact comparisons that, for various reasons, investors have become specially apprehensive with regard to the future of a group of investments that formerly commanded more confidence than almost any other of a similar class.'[189] Demand among investors adjusted accordingly, with the *Economist* saying in 1909, 'The public may not—and are not—buying Consols and Home Rails, but they are energising markets in other directions.'[190] Shares in other types of companies would have been logical beneficiaries of the shift.

Disappointing returns on agricultural land likely served to fortify further demand for shares in UK-based companies in the late 19th and early 20th centuries.[191] A rising flood of imported foodstuffs combined with bad weather hammered domestic agriculture in the concluding decades of the 19th century.

---

[189] 'The Yield on Home Railway Ordinary Stocks', Economist, April 20, 1907, 680, 680.

[190] 'The Revival in Stock Exchange Securities', Economist, October 9, 1909, 698, 698.

[191] David Spring, 'Land and Politics in Edwardian England', (1984) 58 Agricultural History 17, 22–23; F.M.L. Thompson, *English Landed Society in the Nineteenth Century* (1963), 307–20; M.J. Daunton, 'Financial Elites and British Society, 1880–1950' in Youssef Cassis (ed.), *Finance and Financiers in European History, 1880–1960* (1992), 121, 126. On Scotland, see J.H. Treble, 'The Pattern of Investment of the Standard Life Assurance Company', (1980) 22 Business History 170, 171, 175.

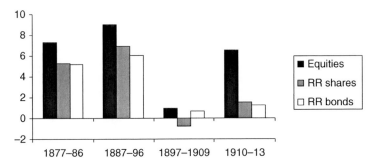

Figure VI: Average annual returns of UK shares (non-railway) and UK railway shares/bonds, 1877–1913

Source: Compiled with data from Edelstein, *supra* n. 11, 148, 153–54.

Rents and land prices fell in turn, with arable farming being particularly hard hit. Landowners responded by trying to reduce their dependence on agriculturally related income and by the 1880s stock market investment had begun in earnest.

The introduction of a new scheme for the taxation of land in a controversial 1909 budget created fresh momentum in favour of exit by major landowners, with tenant farmers often buying the land for sale. Thompson has said of this period '[A] further section of the landed interest began to regard their estates in the cold light of investments, and decided that they would be better off if they sold land, deciding in so doing the social advantages of land ownership had so diminished as to be no longer worth paying for.'[192] Shares in UK companies were in all likelihood a popular outlet for the capital newly available for investment, particularly given the healthy returns they enjoyed in the years just before World War I (Figures V, VI).

2. Means Available for Assessing Public Offerings

While relative investment returns would have made shares in domestically based companies potentially appealing to UK investors, the information asymmetries afflicting the market for equities would have still been a deterrent. There was scant regulation of disclosure in respect of public offerings and ongoing financial performance (Part III.B.2), which meant investors considering whether to buy shares offered directly for sale to the public by a company or in secondary trading were at a potentially serious informational disadvantage. When securities markets are characterized by informational asymmetries, a destructive 'lemons market' can develop (Chapter Four, Part II.A). In UK equity markets of the late 19th and early 20th centuries, there were various corrective features that, while far from perfect, operated sufficiently effectively to sustain a reasonably robust buy side for shares.

---

[192] Thompson, *supra* n. 191, 326; see also Spring, *supra* n. 191, 30–33.

During the late 19th and early 20th centuries applying for shares in public offerings was a potentially cheap and convenient method of investing, well suited for the needs of the smaller investor.[193] Company promoters had various techniques they could use to swing potentially hesitant investors around. While promoters did not put much stock in cultivating reputations for honesty and integrity (Part III.B.4), they realized flamboyant displays of wealth and influence could induce investors to buy shares on the strength of the idea of 'backing a winner'. As Armstrong has said, 'The lavishness of (a promoter's) entertaining, the magnificence of his stables, mansion and cellar showed how successful he had been in making money and helped to overcome investor reluctance. If the promoter could accumulate the capital to live so regally, the logic seemed to be, why should the investor not make similar gains?'[194] Hence, Whitaker Wright's promotional style was described shortly after his downfall as 'Everything was swagger…The whole thing was a gorgeous vulgarity—a magnificent burlesque of business.'[195]

While promoters knew they could capture attention with public displays of success, an ethos of respectability also served their interests. One way to foster this was to appoint titled or famous people to serve on company boards, meaning their names could be put on the prospectuses distributed to market shares. For instance, amidst a flurry of public offerings by cycle, tyre and motor vehicle companies, in 1896 19 companies operating in these industries making public offerings appointed a peer of the realm to their board, only one of whom had substantial business experience.[196] Hooley, when asked in 1898 personal bankruptcy proceedings why he arranged for titled directors to be named in company prospectuses, said 'It was to get the company subscribed.'[197] Why might the 'name bait' have been expected to work? According to an 1898 critic of promoting practice, it was because of a weakness for class and status: 'The average Briton dearly loves a lord, or if he is not to be had, a baronet, knight or hon. will serve, while colonels and majors have their special uses. The investor is *very* average in this respect, and when he sees one of these titles in a prospectus he sends off his application without further enquiry.'[198]

It was also helpful to a promoter to be able to signal there was already investor backing for ventures he was seeking to market. Sometimes promoters would do this by lobbying friends and business associates to subscribe up front for shares, creating the sort of strong advance demand that could capture the attention of outside investors.[199] In other instances matters would be formalized by putting in place underwriting arrangements (i.e. parties guaranteeing for a fee to take up

---

[193] 'Prospectuses', *supra* n. 164.

[194] John Armstrong, 'The Rise and Fall of the Company Promoter and the Financing of British Industry', in van Helten and Cassis, *supra*, n. 77, 115, 126.

[195] Robb, *supra* n. 143, 108, quoting a 1900 article in *Blackwood's Edinburgh Magazine*.

[196] Harrison, *supra* n. 7, 215–16.   [197] *Ibid.*, 217.

[198] Still, *supra* n. 163, 994. For a similar verdict, see Armstrong, *supra* n. 194, 126.

[199] Armstrong, *supra* n. 194, 127.

any unsold shares), though up to 1914 the use of underwriting was not particularly widespread with domestic companies issuing shares.[200]

Promoters could also seek to appeal to investors with optimistic profit projections. The *Economist* remarked in 1897 on 'the way in which estimates of future profits are dangled before the eyes of investors, instead of detailed information with regard to the profits made for a series of years'. The technique appeared to work, at least in some instances. As the *Economist* went on to say, 'If investors would ignore the invitations made to them to subscribe capital on the strength of vague generalisations...we should have fewer companies, no doubt, but we should have much fewer failures.'[201]

From a modern perspective, the marketing methods of company promoters were primitive. Armstrong and Kennedy, among others, have argued that company promoters were a particularly deleterious feature of a flawed capital market system.[202] Kennedy uses the automobile industry to make his point, saying, '[W]hen resources were flung into the market, it was often done without coherence or discipline...waves of money carelessly supplied, mostly to "lemons", followed by an equally unreflective withdrawal when problems appeared, problems magnified by the previous carelessness.'[203] Promoters and their marketing techniques no doubt helped to prompt the misallocation of capital in some instances. However, a number of qualifications are in order.

First, investor demand for shares during the late 19th and early 20th centuries ebbed and flowed (Part III.C.4), and company promoters had to operate within the confines of shifts in market sentiment. The marketing techniques promoters relied on were unlikely to gain traction unless shares were already moving into favour and they had spotted a 'fad' that appealed to investors.[204] As an 1898 critique of promoting said, 'Industrial securities could never have been sold to the extent they have been without a genuine demand for them...By force of sympathy good shares drag bad ones of the same class along with them, and thereby assist the wiles of the unscrupulous promoter. The better the market the easier it is to foist new stuff on it...'[205]

Second, cautious investors were given plenty of 'health warnings' about public offerings they could draw upon if they wanted to assess critically what was available for sale. An 1899 article offered its cautionary message colourfully, saying, '[I]t seems fairly reasonable to assume that even the small country investor, whom the vampire promoters regard as their particular prey, will in the course of time learn to distinguish between wild cats—wild to the point of

---

[200] Jefferys, *supra* n. 8, 350.

[201] 'Some Recent Company Promotions', Economist, July 31, 1897, 1097, 1097–98; see also Hartley Withers, 'How to Scan a Prospectus', Cornhill Magazine, July 1897, 105, 106.

[202] Kennedy, *supra* n. 80, 134; Armstrong, *supra* n. 194, 130; Youssef Cassis, 'British Finance: Success and Controversy' in van Helten and Cassis, *supra* n. 77, 1, 6–7.

[203] Kennedy, *supra* n. 80, 140.

[204] 'Companies', *supra* n. 106; Armstrong, *supra* n. 194, 123.

[205] Lawson, *supra* n. 61, 105–6.

extremest savagery—and sober honest propositions.'[206] The author suggested potentially vulnerable investors could 'sift the chaff of specious promise from the grain of actual fact' by consulting the *Stock Exchange Intelligencer*, which provided detailed information on share capital arrangements of publicly traded companies, a volume listing directors of major companies and a volume reprinting past prospectuses.

For investors lacking the requisite patience, there was plenty of guidance on how to get to much the same point with less effort. A 1901 text on investment said bluntly, 'When a prospectus is "florid" its proper place is usually the wastepaper basket.'[207] An 1897 article entitled 'How to Scan a Prospectus' said, '[I]f the investor will suspect snares in every sentence, and insist on knowing what ought to be told and disregarding what is irrelevant, he will not only avoid many of the pitfalls that beset his footsteps, but will even find prospectuses an interesting study from a purely platonic point of view.'[208] The *Economist* likewise offered in 1897 'a few rough rule-o'-thumb principles for the guidance of those who would prefer to use their own judgment', such as 'Nor are the names of the directors a sure guide, for the most honest and upright of men are liable to be misled.'[209] With 'ornamental' directors, promoters may have deduced this technique was wearing thin with investors, since, at least with public offerings by cycle, tyre and automobile companies, titled individuals were less common on company boards after 1900 than before.[210]

Whether due to such invocations or not, investors did discriminate between public offerings, even in the middle of a wave of enthusiasm for a particular category of shares. Despite the mid-1890s boom in cycle, tyre and motor vehicle shares, only 97 of 306 public offerings involving such companies carried out during the late 19th and early 20th centuries were fully subscribed.[211] Investors tended to discriminate against smaller concerns, but large-scale public offerings could fail as well, even if one of the era's master promoters was involved. For instance, when Hooley tried to capitalize on the successful 1895 flotation of bicycle manufacturer Humber Company by launching four Humber off-shoots, each public offering was undersubscribed.[212]

Third, during the late 19th and early 20th centuries many public offerings of shares were carried out on a largely local basis without promoter involvement. Prior to the 1880s, railways excepted, the market for shares had a strong regional orientation (Chapter Five, Part III.C, Part V.A.2, B.4). According to data compiled by Campbell and Turner, as of 1883 nearly 80 per cent of UK companies with publicly traded shares had their headquarters in the same city as the chief stock market on which their shares were traded.[213] Matters changed somewhat

---

[206] Irons, *supra* n. 156, 281. [207] Thorpe, *supra* n. 49, 123.
[208] Withers, *supra* n. 201, 113. [209] 'Prospectuses', *supra* n. 164, 304–5.
[210] Harrison, *supra* n. 7, 215. [211] *Ibid.*, 219.
[212] *Ibid.*, 220; Armstrong, *supra* n. 194, 128.
[213] Campbell and Turner, *supra* n. 50, 20, Table 1 (noting, though, this figure was inflated by a large number of companies headquartered in London).

as World War I approached, as the London Stock Exchange became an increasingly important market for dealing in industrial and commercial shares and use of the telegraph and the telephone eroded barriers to cross-regional share trading.[214] Still, Cottrell maintains that up to 1914 'there was a "Balkan-like" mosaic consisting of a number of regional bowls of saving which occasionally coalesced under special circumstances'.[215] Davis and Gallman concur, saying 'in Britain there was not one capital market but two', making their point with data showing that among UK-incorporated companies British investors outside London dominated ownership of shares in companies operating domestically, whereas London investors made up a majority of shareholders of companies operating overseas.[216]

When public offerings of shares had a strong local orientation the informational asymmetries that potentially plagued flotations were much less acute. As Lavington said in 1921, 'It might reasonably be expected that in the Provincial markets local knowledge on the part of the investor, both of the business reputation of the vendor and of the prospects of the undertaking, would do a good deal to eliminate dishonest promotion and ensure that securities were sold at prices fairly near their investment values.'[217] Also, whereas reputational constraints on company promoters were generally weak, with companies raising capital locally, those making recommendations to investors had strong incentives to be careful. Mottram said in 1929 of the market for shares in the late 19th and early 20th centuries, 'A great deal of marketing of stocks and shares was done through the medium of [stock]brokers, fed by bankers and lawyers of the county or manufacturing town, all of whom, for the sake of their own reputations... gave increasingly staid and balanced advice to their clients.'[218]

The growth of trading in company shares on the London Stock Exchange during the late 19th and early 20th centuries implies there were numerous instances where proprietors of companies found options for marketing shares in their own part of the country to be inadequate.[219] Nevertheless, local capital markets were sufficiently robust to meet the needs of many companies, including prosperous ones. A 1911 text on the Stock Exchange advised investors, 'It is a good principle to remember that if an enterprise is really very promising, money will somehow be found locally, by those who have seen it with their own eyes.'[220] The *Economist* concurred, suggesting, 'Yorkshire and Lancashire... take care not to send anything really profitable up to London.'[221] Given the continued robustness of local capital markets, the informational asymmetries potentially plaguing the market

---

[214] Michie, *supra* n. 5, 118–19.   [215] Cottrell, *supra* n. 7, 269.

[216] Davis and Gallman, *supra* n. 66, 200–1. See also Davis and Huttenback, *supra* n. 100, 171–73.

[217] Lavington, *supra* n. 13, 208; see also 'Minor Industrial', *supra* n. 54.

[218] R.H. Mottram, *A History of Financial Speculation* (1929), 244.

[219] Edelstein, *supra* n. 11, 59.   [220] Hirst, *supra* n. 35, 245.

[221] 'The Financing of Industry at Home and Abroad', Economist, May 20, 1911, 1059, 1060.

for shares in late 19th- and early 20th-century public offerings were not as acute as they appeared at first glance.

3. Dividends

Although during the late 19th and early 20th centuries investors minded to engage in secondary trading of shares could not depend on legislatively compelled corporate disclosure to provide guidance on what to buy and sell, they could and did rely on dividend policy to judge companies.[222] There was awareness that assessments of companies ideally should go well beyond dividend payments. The *Economist* argued the market had over-reacted to a disappointing 1910 dividend announcement by textile manufacturer J. & P. Coats, saying, 'The prices of shares should be governed less by the dividends paid than by profits earned, for when dividends are paid and not earned, the shareholders are merely receiving their capital back...'[223] Investors were similarly warned not to assume that because a company had paid steady dividends in the past 'such a happy state of affairs is bound to continue indefinitely'.[224] Correspondingly, they were counselled to take into account financial results, potential market pressure from competitors and general trends affecting the relevant business sector.[225] On the other hand, with hard data being scarce, dividend policy was what investors typically fell back on.

In order for dividend policy to constitute a reliable means of conveying information to investors, a change in policy should cause a company to stand out from the crowd (Chapter Four, Part III.D). This would have been the case during the late 19th and early 20th centuries. With most companies paying dividends, often at generous levels (Part II.B.2), a company that cut its dividends or passed entirely was likely to be conspicuous to investors.

Dividends also can only perform a signalling function if there is a penalty associated with sending a false signal (Chapter Four, Part III.D). During the late 19th and early 20th centuries, company law was a potential constraint on imprudent dividend payouts, as dividends could only be paid out of profits.[226] There were, however, ways to sidestep this limitation, at least in the short term, because the profit figure could be adjusted upwards by reducing charges against earnings (e.g. depreciation) and because companies were allowed to distribute profits generated in the current year as dividends even if losses sustained in previous years remained on the books.[227] Also, if cash was short, companies could and did borrow from banks to maintain dividend payments.[228]

---

[222] Pt III.B.2; A.C. Storrar and K.C. Pratt, 'Accountability vs. Privacy, 1844–1907: The Coming of the Private Company', (2000) 10 Accounting, Business & Financial History 259, 273.

[223] 'J. and P. Coats', Economist, November 5, 1910, 918.

[224] Lowenfeld, *supra* n. 47, 77.

[225] *Ibid.*, 79–81; Investment Critic, *supra* n. 109, 22–23; 'Moral', *supra* n. 168; Henry Lowenfeld, *Investment: An Exact Science* (1908), 16.

[226] Jordan and Gore-Browne, *supra* n. 106, 168.

[227] Horace B. Samuel, *Shareholders' Money* (1933), 146–47.

[228] Storrar and Pratt, *supra* n. 222, 273 (adjusting profits); Forrest Capie and Michael Collins, 'Banks, Industry and Finance, 1880–1914', (1999) 41 Business History 37, 53 (borrowing).

Even if company law could be sidestepped temporarily, unless cash distributions were at some point supported by underlying profits, directors could not simply brazen it out. A company suffering trading losses that persisted in distributing cash to shareholders would sooner or later have to carry out a reconstruction at a heavy loss, likely accompanied by unwelcome scrutiny. Various 'dividend cases' alleging cash had been improperly distributed out of capital arose in the courts in the late 19th and early 20th centuries and the deliberations frequently attracted critical press scrutiny.[229] Given the hazards associated with an inappropriately generous dividend policy, investors could sensibly infer from a company's decision to maintain or increase its dividend payout that those setting dividend policy believed the company's prospects were good enough to support current cash distribution levels for some time to come.

Since dividends provided clues about corporate prosperity (or lack thereof) and since there was a dearth of other financial data, investors not surprisingly focused closely on dividend payouts when deciding when to buy and sell shares. A 1901 history of the London Stock Exchange said dividend announcements for 'an active security...are anticipated with intense interest. When the notice is brought into the House (the trading floor of the Stock Exchange) the members crowd around the board upon which it is soon to be posted.'[230] In 1904 the *Economist* argued in favour of 'dividend meetings (being) held at such an hour as precludes the possibility of operations being entered into in advance of the general body of proprietors who take the trouble to keep a look-out for the announcement', suggesting it was good practice for companies to resolve matters outside trading hours and then arrange for the dividend announcement to be made in morning newspapers. The *Economist* acknowledged that this was not a suitable procedure for all company announcements, but 'Dividend declarations, we repeat, stand on another footing...'[231]

Indices compiled by Ayres of share values and of dividends declared by companies in eight industries between 1899 and 1913 provide empirical confirmation of the impact dividends had on investors, revealing a strong correlation in fluctuations between the two (Figure VII).[232] The upshot was that dividend policy provided investors with an adequate departure point to engage in secondary trading in circumstances where hard financial data was scarce.

4. Market Sentiment

According to a 1910 study of the City of London's financial markets, 'No attempt at a fairly comprehensive characterisation of City activities would be even *prima facie* adequate if it ignored the influence of "fashion" in investments.'[233] The

[229] Storrar and Pratt, *supra* n. 222, 273.
[230] Charles Duguid, *The Story of the Stock Exchange: Its History and Position* (1901), 295.
[231] 'The Publication of Dividend Declarations', Economist, October 15, 1904, 1655.
[232] G.L. Ayres, 'Fluctuations in New Capital Issues on the London Money Market', M.Sc., University of London, 1934, 58; on the nature of the indices, see *ibid.* 22, 34, 36.
[233] Powell, *supra* n. 87, 84–85.

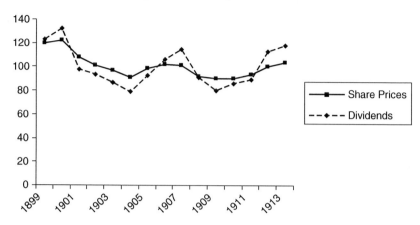

Figure VII: Dividend and share price indices for eight industries, 1899–1913 (100 = average for the entire period)

Source: Constructed using data in Ayres, *supra* n. 232, 53.

Economist observed similarly in 1912, 'It is a matter of common knowledge that the form in which capital can be raised on the London market varies very much from year to year according to whether caution or a spirit of adventure prevails among the investing public.'[234] Fluctuations in market sentiment indeed should be taken into account to have a full picture of the 'buy side' for shares in the late 19th and early 20th centuries, with the caveat that investor demand was not merely the product of psychological whims.

Numerous contemporaries drew attention to the influence of investor sentiment on demand for shares. In 1898 Van Oss suggested that 'an extraordinary mania for speculation, for dabbling in shares, has seized hold of the nation' and Stutfield condemned 'the speculating public' saying, 'If you tell a man that the stock which he is speculating in is worthless trash, he will often reply, "Yes, I know that but" (with a knowing wink which always stamps the complete idiot) "So-and-so is going to put them a good deal higher yet." '[235] Lowenfeld, writing in 1906 about 'investment crazes', said '[T]he public not unnaturally becomes fascinated by the particular topic of the hour, namely the buoyancy of the new market and the sums of money which are being made by those who are fortunate enough to be interested therein.'[236] Hirst, in a discussion of speculative securities in his 1911 book on the London Stock Exchange and other leading stock markets, said 'People think and act in mobs; and the speculative fever always rages in an atmosphere of high prices.'[237]

---

[234] 'The Capital Market in 1911', Economist, February 10, 1912, 283, 283.
[235] Van Oss, *supra* n. 159, 741; Stutfield, *supra* n. 161, 580.
[236] Lowenfeld, *supra* n. 167, 161.
[237] Hirst, *supra* n. 35, 165.

Various academic commentators have subsequently acknowledged waves of investor enthusiasm helped to underpin demand for shares in the UK in the late 19th and early 20th centuries. Cairncross notes, 'At times of great speculative activity, it was possible to float completely new companies in the trades that were booming.'[238] Cottrell has said similarly '[P]romoters, the stock exchanges and investors were prepared to support in some measure "mania" waves of flotations.'[239]

In the years between 1880 and 1914, the first surge of investor optimism influencing demand for shares occurred in 1882 and affected the electricity industry (Part II.A). Next was a flurry of public offerings of breweries following Guinness' successful 1886 flotation (Part II.B.1). According to Cottrell, '[T]he success of the issue was like the firing of a starting pistol; by 1890, 86 other brewery companies had appealed to the public for funds.'[240] Matters then went quiet, with the *Economist* saying in 1893, 'The business of company promoting and underwriting is practically dead.'[241] However, in the mid-1890s public offerings by domestic companies moved into high gear, led by a fresh wave of brewery promotions, and 'the cycle boom', characterized by numerous public offerings by cycle, tyre and automotive companies.[242]

In 1899, in the wake of the collapse of the cycle boom and a trial involving well-known company promoter E.T. Hooley that cast company promoting in a harsh light, the *Economist* noted 'there has been, for the most part, a conspicuous disinclination on the part of the investing public to purchase stocks'.[243] The lull continued for a while, with the *Economist* in 1903 attributing 'the current difficulty in getting the public to subscribe for even good securities' partly 'to bitter experience in connection with company flotations'.[244] However, as 1909 drew to a close this same journal was referring to 'The Revival in Stock Exchange Speculation', noting 'the renewed animation amongst industrial shares of various classes'.[245]

The rubber industry, composed of UK companies engaged, or proposing to engage, in the manufacture of rubber, was affected particularly dramatically. The 'rubber boom' began in 1909 and peaked in 1910 (Part II.A). By the latter half of 1910 doubts were arising, with the disappointing financial news announced by the Malacca Company, one of the bigger and better-respected rubber companies, being 'an unpleasant reminder of the dangers which underlie undiscriminating investment when the public is seized by a mania, and company promoters hastily

---

[238] Cairncross, *supra* n. 39, 144.

[239] Cottrell, *supra* n. 7, 189.   [240] *Ibid.*, 169.

[241] 'Some Results of Latter-Day Financing', Economist, December 2, 1893, 1431, 1432.

[242] Cottrell, *supra* n. 7, 173–74; Harrison, *supra* n. 7, 207–8; 'The Cycle Boom', Economist, May 16, 1896, 618.

[243] 'Nervousness in the Stock Markets', Economist, November 4, 1899, 1556, 1556; see also Van Oss, *supra* n. 61, 1–2; 'The Fall in Cycle Shares', Economist, January 8, 1898, 43.

[244] 'How Not to Encourage the Investor', Economist, November 21, 1903, 1966, 1966.

[245] 'The Revival in Stock Exchange Speculation', Economist, October 9, 1909, 698, 698.

cater for the passion'.[246] By 1911 the giddy expectations had been largely dashed. According to one retrospective,

'The frenzy of speculation had taken the public in its grip. Prospectus after prospectus rolled out, the money rolled in from excited investors, and company after company was formed. No one stopped to consider the consequences, the most apparent one being that even if the mythically rich plantations proved to be real, more rubber would be produced in one year than the market could utilise in a long period of years, in which event there could be very little return in the shape of profits.'[247]

Though waves of investor optimism boosted demand for shares periodically in the UK between 1880 and 1914, the buy side was not purely a product of periodic market 'froth'. Shares of domestic companies outperformed foreign securities, government bonds and railway securities between the mid-1880s and mid-1890s (Part III.C.1), which implies there was a realistic foundation for the market booms affecting the brewery sector in the mid-1880s and the cycle, tyre, automobile and brewing industries in the mid-1890s. The gap between the surges in enthusiasm for shares can plausibly be attributed to financial rectitude instilled by the near-collapse of merchant bank Barings in 1890.[248]

Even in 'boom' conditions investors continued to pay attention to market fundamentals, in the sense dividend policy continued to exercise a strong influence on investors. In 1905 and 1906, investor interest in shares of automobile companies, which had been largely dormant since the end of the mid-1890s cycle boom, was rekindled as for the first time various companies in the sector began declaring dividends.[249] Indeed, according to a 1908 history of the industry, 'Investors lost their heads, and assumed that the motor industry was going to continue to provide handsome dividends.'[250] Generous dividends paid by rubber companies were a powerful lure for investors, with healthy payout figures prompting the *New York Times* to say in 1910 of the UK market for rubber shares, 'These figures show a very real basis for the boom.'[251] Matters began to go into reverse when later that year the Malacca Company announced it was refraining from making its expected dividend payment, leaving investors to wonder 'where were the huge dividends which other companies of less repute had promised'.[252]

Though surges in investor demand during the late 19th and early 20th centuries may have had a foundation in market fundamentals, over the long haul disappointed expectations possibly hampered the buy side. De Long and Grossman report, based on an index of shares of UK public companies covering

[246] 'The Rubber Market and Rubber Shares', Economist, September 17, 1910, 550.

[247] Investment Critic, *supra* n. 35, 18–19.

[248] Kynaston, *supra* n. 28, 426–37; Chapman, *supra* n. 78, 78–81.

[249] Kynaston, *supra* n. 15, 464; Wayne Lewchuk, 'The Return to Capital in the British Motor Vehicle Industry', (1985) 27 Business History 3, 8.

[250] Kynaston, *supra* n. 28, 464.

[251] '$500,000,000 Spent on Rubber Shares', New York Times, April 24, 1910.

[252] 'Rubber Market Hit by Malacca Report', New York Times, August 21, 1910.

from 1870 to 1990, that share prices were lower in relation to dividend yields prior to 1914 than after, implying that pre-World War I investors valued shares more conservatively than their post-World War I counterparts.[253] A possible explanation is that pre-1914 investors adopted a 'once bitten, twice shy' mentality after surges of optimism proved unfounded, thus undercutting demand for shares. As Cottrell says, 'But once fingers had been burnt with watered stocks and shares, and worthless patents, then surviving firms, even those with good profit records, found it difficult to raise finance of sufficient quantity or of the right type…'[254] Or according to Kennedy, '[E]arly and calamitous financial mobilizations severely crippled subsequent development and the funds necessary for expansion, when they did appear, almost invariably did so too slowly to exploit the periodic booms in demand.'[255]

The sub-text here, particularly in Kennedy's case, is to argue that a counterproductive anti-industrial bias in Victorian capital markets was an important reason why the British economy began to 'lag' in the late 19th and early 20th centuries.[256] It is impossible to do justice in this particular context to this contribution to the debate on the causes for Britain's economic decline. However, it is unlikely harsh experiences following short-lived surges in investor sentiment greatly hindered the buy side for shares up to 1914. Consider De Long and Grossman's findings again. If the attitude of investors towards shares was determined by having their fingers burnt, they should have become ever more suspicious of equity over time as they suffered the adverse effects of 'the Brush Bubble', the cycle boom, the rubber mania, etc. De Long and Grossman's findings suggest precisely the opposite occurred, since the higher post-World War I price/dividend ratios imply that investors attached a lower, not higher, risk premium to shares after these various episodes.[257]

The experience with particular industries also casts doubt on the notion that 'calamitous financial mobilizations' following surges in investor optimism had a debilitating impact on the willingness of investors to finance industry. Cottrell and Kennedy both focus on the electricity industry and car production to make their case.[258] Kennedy says of the collapse of the 'Brush Bubble', '[T]he financial assets of the electrical engineering industry were firmly established as "lemons" and, perhaps not coincidentally, Britain was never again to be so prominent in the theoretical development and practical application of electricity as in the

---

[253] Grossman and De Long, *supra* n. 57, 7, 16–19; De Long and Grossman, *supra* n. 188, 5, 7. De Long and Grossman's findings need to be treated with caution, since their results were not derived from a single series of company share prices but several series spliced together and since their pre-World War I sample was small: De Long and Grossman, *op. cit.*, 3–4, 6.

[254] Cottrell, *supra* n. 7, 189.

[255] Kennedy, *supra* n. 80, 135.

[256] *Ibid.*, 120–47; *cf.* Cottrell, *supra* n. 7, 187–91 (saying the problems were greater in some sectors than in others).

[257] De Long and Grossman, *supra* n. 188, 21.

[258] Cottrell, *supra* n. 7, 182–83; Kennedy, *supra* n. 80, 134–40.

decades preceding the early 1880s.'[259] Cottrell says of the early British automobile industry, '[T]he pattern that occurred of early and calamitous issues (of shares) crippling medium-term development was more or less a repetition of the previous experience with the nascent electrical industry.'[260] In neither case, however, was a 'once bitten, twice shy' mentality firmly entrenched.

Developments in the early 1880s likely did cause investors to pause before buying electricity shares again. As the president of the Institute of Electrical Engineers complained in 1894, 'There was a short time of excitement to the public and of profit to the promoters; then the confidence of the public in electricity was almost completely destroyed.'[261] Consistent with this pessimistic verdict, when a series of power companies established at the beginning of the 20th century carried out public offerings of their shares, investors balked. The companies had an aggregate authorized share and loan capital of £21 million, but only raised £3.8 million from the public.[262]

Nevertheless, investors were by no means totally averse to backing electricity ventures. The *Economist*, in an 1898 analysis of electric lighting companies, remarked on an 'extraordinary advance in the market value of the shares that has taken place within the last eighteen months'.[263] Between 1900 and 1905, when investment in domestic industry was otherwise in a lull, new issues made by companies in the electrical lighting industry amounted to £10.24 million, or just over £750 million in 2006 currency.[264]

Moreover, to the extent investors had reservations about investing in companies engaged in electricity supply, they had plenty of reasons other than bad experiences in the early 1880s.[265] The companies involved delivered patchy results, with the *Economist* saying in 1911 the dividend record was 'a melancholy one for shareholders'.[266] Electric supply companies operating in urban areas had to cope with stiff competition from gas companies that were efficient and kept prices down by virtue of municipal management or regulation.[267] The power companies formed at the beginning of the 20th century struggled due to cost overruns, poor engineering and an economic chill brought on by a 1907 financial crisis.[268]

The legislative setting was problematic as well. Statutory amendments in 1888 reduced the risk thrown up by 1882 legislation that local authorities would step in and exercise the right to purchase successful electricity supply companies

---

[259] Kennedy *supra* n. 80, 135.   [260] Cottrell, *supra* n. 7, 189.

[261] Kynaston, *supra* n. 28, 342.

[262] Pt II.A; H.H. Ballin, *The Organisation of Electricity Supply in Great Britain* (1946), 34.

[263] 'Are Electric Lighting Shares Over-Valued?', Economist, March 5, 1898, 349, 349.

[264] Ayres, *supra* n. 232, 44; conversion performed using 1903 as the base year.

[265] Pollard, *supra* n. 100, 21.

[266] 'Electricity Supply Companies', Economist, March 25, 1911, 612, 613.

[267] Hannah, *supra* n. 29, 9; 'Gas and Electrical Lighting Companies', Economist, February 4, 1911, 209.

[268] Byatt, *supra* n. 31, 115; Ballin, *supra* n. 262, 55–57.

(Part II.A). However, achieving economies of scale remained problematic because the companies could only operate under the control of a single local authority, which heavily discouraged potentially beneficial collaboration. The various statutes that authorized the formation of new power companies at the opening of the 20th century permitted these enterprises to operate over a wide area but in practice their market failed to include potentially lucrative cities because local government authorities typically secured and exercised the right to opt out.[269] In 1912, premature and ultimately ill-founded market rumours that a rationalization of electricity supply interests binding private companies and local authorities was in the offing prompted investors to bid up the price of electricity company shares considerably, confirming that, despite the unpleasant experiences of the early 1880s, investors were in no way averse to the electric supply industry *per se*.[270]

As for the automobile industry, to the extent that early experiences with the industry were discouraging, investors nevertheless proved willing on various subsequent occasions to back fledgling automobile manufacturers. Investors had good reason to be sceptical after the public offerings carried out in the mid-1890s worked out badly.[271] However, when investor interest in the automobile sector was rekindled due to various companies becoming sufficiently prosperous to declare dividends, investors eagerly bought up shares in public offerings. New issues by automobile companies amounted to £2.28 million between 1905 and 1907, as compared with just £264,000 between 1899 and 1904.[272]

After a trade depression sideswiped the motor car industry in 1907, some industry observers complained UK investors were unjustly reluctant to back automobile companies.[273] It is not surprising, however, that investors were wary, since the return to financial capital on British motor vehicle shares fell by 50 per cent in 1907 and 28 per cent in 1908.[274] In addition, of 221 automobile manufacturers founded between 1901 and 1905, 112 failed between 1906 and 1910, joining 59 others that had done so between 1901 and 1905.[275]

Despite this rather dismal record, shareholder returns did eventually improve and capital duly started to flow back into the motor car industry, with new issues of shares by automobile manufacturers amounting to £426,000 in 1912 and £1.44 million in 1918.[276] Saul, in his history of the industry up to 1914, draws on such evidence to suggest it gives 'lie to the argument that the industry was held back in its growth by the inadequacy of the facilities provided by the stock exchange or because of public indifference'.[277] Admittedly, the funds raised were

---

[269] Michie, *supra* n. 28, 512–13; Byatt, *supra* n. 31, 113; 'Electricity Supply Shares and Market Rumours', Economist, August 3, 1912, 229.

[270] 'Electricity Supply', *supra* n. 269.

[271] S.B. Saul, 'The Motor Car Industry in Britain to 1914', (1962) 5 Business History 22, 22, 40.

[272] Ayres, *supra* n. 232, 44.   [273] Kynaston, *supra* n. 15, 464–65.

[274] Lewchuk, *supra* n. 249, 15.   [275] Saul, *supra* n. 271, 23.

[276] Ayres, *supra* n. 232, 23, 44; Lewchuk, *supra* n. 249, 15.

[277] Saul, *supra* n. 271, 40; see also Michie, *supra* n. 28, 523–24; Lewchuk, *supra* n. 249, 18; Roy Church, *The Rise and Decline of the British Motor Industry* (1994), 3.

often not allocated particularly effectively. Companies that successfully appealed to the public for financial backing often struggled, at least in the short term (e.g. Daimler and Humber in the mid-1890s) whereas various successful car manufacturers (e.g. Napier, Sunbeam and Vauxhall) were built up by their founders, who obtained finance privately.[278] Still, even if investors made some mistakes, contrary to the 'once bitten, twice shy' characterization, demand for shares in automobile manufacturers retained vitality despite setbacks following surges in demand.

* * *

By international standards, the corporate economy and the market for shares was well-developed in the UK by 1914. The roster of companies with publicly traded shares expanded significantly, with numerous industrial and commercial companies joining railways and other traditional stock market staples, such as banks and insurance companies. The transformation can be explained partly in terms of the sell side, as proprietors of industrial and commercial companies became increasingly willing to accept dilution of their holdings in order to exit, at least partially, or to secure finance for mergers. There were deterrents on the buy side, such as the possibility of investing in foreign assets and the weak protection afforded by company law, financial intermediaries and the press. Nevertheless, the number of stock market investors increased markedly, with inducements to buying shares including good returns in comparison with domestic investment alternatives, the signalling role of dividends and occasional investment fads. Does all this mean that ownership had become divorced from control by the eve of World War I? Chapter Seven takes up this question.

[278] Michie, *supra* n. 28, 523; Saul, *supra* n. 271, 40.

SEVEN

The Separation of Ownership and Control by 1914

While in comparative terms the market for shares was well developed in Britain by 1914 (Chapter Six, Part I), the relevant historical literature generally implies ownership had not become divorced from control by the eve of World War I. Numerous observers indeed cite 'the remarkable tenacity of the family firm in Britain's economy'[1] as a key reason why in the late 19th and early 20th centuries the UK began to decline relative to its key economic rivals. Leslie Hannah has provocatively claimed ownership was in fact divorced from control in large UK companies by the early 20th century, thus inviting re-examination of entrenched assumptions.[2] Nevertheless, as this chapter shows, his bold assertions need careful qualification. By the eve of World War I, there were various companies with modern-style diffuse share ownership, with major deposit-taking banks and perhaps large insurance companies joining railways in this category. Otherwise, however, the transformation to an outsider/arm's-length system of ownership and control still had some distance to go as World War I began.

I. The Received Wisdom on Ownership and Control

It has been said of distinguished business historian Alfred Chandler 'Virtually every work now written on the history of modern, large-scale enterprise must begin by placing itself within the Chandlerian analytical framework.'[3] Chandler outlined, using detailed case examples, how technological advances set the stage for the arrival of 'big business' in the late 19th and early 20th centuries and emphasized that salaried managers—technically proficient executives lacking large ownership stakes in the firms they ran—played a crucial role in ensuring

[1] Peter L. Payne, 'Family Business in Britain: An Historical and Analytical Survey' in Akio Okochi and Shigeaki Yasuoka (eds), *Family Business in the Era of Industrial Growth: Its Ownership and Management* (1984), 171, 173.

[2] Leslie Hannah, 'The Divorce of Ownership from Control from 1900: Re-calibrating Imagined Global Historical Trends', (2007) 49 Business History 404. A companion paper by Hannah, 'Pioneering Modern Corporate Governance: A view from London in 1900' (2007) 8 Enterprise & Society 642 came to the author's attention too late to take into account for present purposes but the analysis offered is similar in various respects to the discussion of the buy side in Ch 6.

[3] Glenn Porter, *The Rise of Big Business 1860–1920*, 2nd edn (1992), 125.

firms exploited effectively newly available economies of scale and scope.[4] Chandler initially focused exclusively on developments in the United States but added an explicit comparative dimension to his research, examining in his 1990 book *Scale and Scope* the beginnings and growth of 'managerial capitalism' in what historically were the world's three leading industrial nations, Britain, Germany and the United States. Among these three, Britain stands out as the laggard: 'the speed with which the output of the United States and Germany surpassed Great Britain, the first industrial nation, was striking'.[5] Hence, for Chandler 'Britain is the place to study enterprises' failures to develop competitive strength.'[6]

Chandler argues the fundamental problem with British business was that a counterproductive adherence to 'personal capitalism' precluded emulation of sophisticated managerial structures US companies pioneered and German companies adopted. In the new capital intensive industries of the late 19th and early 20th centuries, American and German companies benefited greatly by creating extensive managerial hierarchies staffed by professionally trained, salaried executives. In contrast, according to Chandler, in Britain simplistic, primitive managerial structures were the norm. He acknowledges this sort of arrangement could succeed when the production process was straightforward and there were few opportunities for scale economies, as with branded and packaged consumer goods.[7] However, according to Chandler, personal capitalism faltered in key industries such as light and heavy machinery, automobiles, electrical equipment and chemicals. British business did 'catch up' in some sectors in the interwar years, such as oil refining and industrial chemicals. Generally, though, the window of opportunity was brief and once closed proved difficult to reopen. Lacking a 'first mover' advantage, UK firms generally remained laggards, and Britain's relative economic standing suffered accordingly.

Chandler associates the personal capitalism that allegedly afflicted Britain with the continuing prominence of family-run businesses. He maintains that in America's managerially dominated firms the key goals were to build profits and growth over the long haul. In contrast, the primary objective of British firms was to provide a steady flow of cash to shareholders, particularly family owners, thus discouraging investment in new machinery, production techniques and marketing. The fact UK family businesses were reluctant to recruit managers from outside and to bring salaried executives into top managerial jobs compounded the problem. As Chandler says, 'British entrepreneurs continued to view their

---

[4] Alfred D. Chandler, *The Visible Hand: The Managerial Revolution in American Business* (1977); Alfred D. Chandler, *Scale and Scope: The Dynamics of Industrial Capitalism* (1990).

[5] Chandler, *Scale, supra* n. 4, 3.

[6] Alfred D. Chandler, 'Response to the Contributors to the Review Colloquium on *Scale and Scope*', (1990) 64 *Business History Review* 736, 751.

[7] On Chandler's views on this point and those following, see, *Scale, supra* n. 4, 242, 262–68, 274–86, 291–92, 298–304, 355–67, 390–92. See also A.D. Chandler, 'The Growth of the Transnational Industrial Firm in the United States and the United Kingdom: A Comparative Analysis', (1980) 33 Economic History Review (N.S.), 396, 402, 406.

businesses in personal rather than organizational terms, as family estates to be nurtured and passed on to heirs.'[8] This was all acceptable (if deleterious) because '(i)n the United States nepotism had a pejorative connotation. In Britain it was an accepted way of life.'[9]

Chandler, in focusing on the potentially damaging consequences of family capitalism, echoed a persistent theme in British business history. Landes argued in a 1965 survey of technological change in Western Europe between 1750 and 1914 that Britain declined in the industrial sweepstakes due to the complacency of third-generation children of affluence going 'through the motions of entrepreneurship'.[10] Lazonick, in a 1991 historical analysis of capitalism in leading industrial countries, said of Britain at the beginning of the 20th century, 'The British practice of passing on managerial control of the firm to family members from generation to generation, regardless of relevant career credentials, stifled the growth of the enterprise and the development of organizational capability.'[11] Wilson, in a 1995 survey of British business history, concurred, claiming, 'Nepotism and practical training within the context of a family owned and family managed firm were consequently features of British business until the early-twentieth century, inhibiting the opportunities to introduce new ideas on management which both American and German corporations were developing at the time.'[12]

There are various problems with the argument that a legacy of 'personal capitalism' caused Britain to fall behind the United States and Germany economically. The organization of big business is one of only a series of variables likely to influence overall national economic performance.[13] Due to the agency cost problem, it is not self-evident that managerially oriented capitalism is superior to its family oriented counterpart.[14] While personal capitalism was clearly on the wane in Britain by 1950, in terms of worker productivity, the major period of British decline relative to Western Europe was after this date.[15] Finally, the importance of family firms in Britain relative to the United States and Germany

[8] Chandler, *Scale, supra* n. 4, 286.   [9] *Ibid.*, 292.

[10] David Landes, 'Technological Change and Innovation in Western Europe, 1750–1914' in H.J. Habakkuk and M. Postan (eds), *Cambridge Economic History of Europe, vol. VI, The Industrial Revolution and After: Incomes, Populations and Technological Change (I)* (1965), 274, 563–64.

[11] William Lazonick, *Business Organization and the Myth of the Market Economy* (1991), 48.

[12] John F. Wilson, *British Business History, 1720–1994* (1995), 117–18.

[13] Barry Supple, 'Scale and Scope: Alfred Chandler and the Dynamics of Industrial Capitalism', (1991) 44 Economic History Review (N.S.) 500, 511–12.

[14] Ch. Two, Pt I; those making the point specifically in relation to Chandler's work include Roy Church, 'The Limitations of the Personal Capitalism Paradigm', (1990) 64 Business History Review 703, 708; Mary B. Rose, 'Introduction' in Mary B. Rose (ed.), *Family Business* (1995), xiii, xvii; Robert Fitzgerald, 'Ownership, Organization, and Management: British Business and the Branded Consumer Goods Industries' in Youssef Cassis *et al* (eds), *Management and Business in Britain and France: The Age of the Corporate Economy* (1995), 31, 33–38.

[15] Ch. Nine, Pt II.A; Geoffrey Jones, 'Great Britain: Big Business, Management, and Competitiveness in Twentieth-Century Britain' in Alfred D. Chandler, Franco Amatori and Takashi Hikino (eds), *Big Business and the Wealth of Nations* (1997), 102, 105–6.

may have been overdone, which implies family control *per se* should not be blamed for Britain's failings.[16]

Chandler went some way towards conceding this final point, saying in a colloquium on *Scale and Scope* '[T]he critical difference between British and German and US firms was not the size of family holdings.'[17] What really mattered was that, while founders of British industrial enterprises and their heirs stubbornly continued to centralize corporate decision-making, family owners in Germany and the US were willing to cede authority as sophisticated managerial hierarchies were established. Even with this refined assessment, Chandler is not questioning that families dominated industrial capitalism in Britain. He had said in earlier work dealing with Britain that in leading industrial companies prior to World War I 'owners managed and managers owned'[18] and his response to critiques of *Scale and Scope* did not qualify that verdict. Instead, he simply conceded that family ownership blocks may have remained prevalent in the US and Germany as well, with family owners in these two countries crucially being more enlightened than their counterparts in Britain.

Chandler's assessment of corporate ownership and control is consistent with the conventional wisdom.[19] Gourvish has argued 'corporate change in Britain before 1914 was more legal and financial than managerial, with an emphasis on the retention of control by founding family groups.'[20] Blackford says of industrial firms in the UK 'Throughout the nineteenth century and into the twentieth, ownership and management remained united, with business long remaining a personal, not a bureaucratic affair.'[21] Rose concurs, arguing that '[I]n contrast to the experience in the United States, where from the 1880s onwards ownership and control became increasingly divorced, in Britain personal capitalism persisted well into the twentieth century.'[22]

---

[16]   Church, *supra* n. 14, 706; Jones, *supra* note 15, 108.

[17]   Chandler, *supra* n. 6, 747.

[18]   'The Development of Modern Management Structure in the US and the UK', in Leslie Hannah (ed.), *Management Strategy and Business Development: An Historical and Comparative Study* (1976), 24, 40.

[19]   François Crouzet, *The Victorian Economy*, (1982), 406 (summarizing the literature). For examples, see Payne, *supra* n. 1, 172–73; D.H. Aldcroft, 'The Entrepreneur and the British Economy, 1870–1914', (1964) 17 Economic History Review (N.S.) 113, 131; Yousef Cassis, 'British Finance: Success and Controversy' in J.J. van Helten and Y. Cassis (eds), *Capitalism in a Mature Economy: Financial Institutions, Capital Exports and British Industry, 1870–1939* (1990), 1, 5; Forrest Capie and Michael Collins, *Have the Banks Failed British Industry? An Historical Survey of Bank/Industry Relations in Britain, 1870–1990* (1992), 31.

[20]   T.R. Gourvish, 'British Business and the Transition to a Corporate Economy: Entrepreneurship and Management Structures', (1987) 29 Business History 18, 26.

[21]   Mansel G. Blackford, *The Rise of Modern Business in Great Britain, the United States and Japan*, 2nd edn (1998), 62.

[22]   Mary B. Rose, 'The Family Firm in British Business, 1780–1914' in Maurice W. Kirby and Mary B. Rose (eds), *Business Enterprise in Modern Britain: From the Eighteenth to the Twentieth Century* (1994), 61, 67–68.

II. Hannah's Challenge

Hannah, in a 2007 article, has challenged the received wisdom concerning the historical evolution of corporate ownership and control in industrialized countries. His main target was 'the erroneous belief that America led in divorcing ownership from control'.[23] Hannah acknowledges that by the 1930s ownership was separating from control in large US industrial companies, but emphasizes that 'plutocratic' personal capitalism was very much a hallmark of US corporate governance as the 20th century opened, not only in the industrial sector but also with railways, banks and insurance companies.[24] Hannah says that in contrast 'ownership was already substantially divorced from control in leading European businesses' by the early 20th century, with Britain and France exhibiting the largest degree of separation.[25] Thus, it is 'those with faulty memories (who) reconstruct the financial and business past to match the capital market present'.[26]

Despite the forceful rhetoric, Hannah concedes '(t)he evidence on these issues is far from perfect' and the early 20th century is pretty much 'a statistical dark age'.[27] This is correct with the UK as for other countries. Crucially, there is for early 20th-century Britain no equivalent to Florence's evidence on share ownership in 'very large' industrial and commercial companies as of 1936 and 1951 (Chapter I, Table I). Franks, Mayer and Rossi report from a sample of 40 industrial and commercial companies incorporated around 1900 that as of 1910 the directors collectively owned 53 per cent of the shares.[28] This implies ownership was highly concentrated, but it is inappropriate to draw strong inferences from the data since only 13 of the 40 companies were listed on the London Stock Exchange or a provincial stock market as of 1914.[29]

III. The 'Two-Thirds' Rule

Hannah, to compensate for the lack of statistical evidence available to buttress his claims about the separation of ownership and control in the UK, places considerable weight on a listing rule of the London Stock Exchange that made it a condition precedent to an application for an official quotation of a class of securities that two-thirds of the capital was applied for by, and allotted to, the public.[30] By virtue of this rule, if a company sought a quotation of its ordinary shares, the

---

[23] Hannah, *supra* n. 2, 423.   [24] *Ibid.*, 410–14, 417–19.
[25] *Ibid.*, 405, 406.   [26] *Ibid.*, 425.
[27] *Ibid.*, 407, 415.
[28] Julian Franks, Colin Mayer and Stefano Rossi, 'Ownership: Evolution and Regulation', (2006) ECGI Fin. Working Paper No. 09/2003, 23–24.
[29] *Ibid.*, Table A1.
[30] Hannah, *supra* n. 2, 414.

'vendors' (typically the founders or inheritors of a company seeking a quotation) could only retain a one-third stake.

The *Economist* said in 1885 of the two-thirds rule 'this condition is constantly evaded, and always can be when the necessity is sufficient to stimulate the inventive faculty'.[31] Hannah, however, argues based on archival research the rule was strictly enforced.[32] He therefore claims that '[A] substantial majority of large, quoted British industrials had a greatly dispersed shareholding by the early twentieth century, with directors owning no more than 33 per cent and many with less.'[33] The two-thirds rule no doubt fostered share dispersion to some degree. However, the rule's impact was qualified in various ways, which means that it is inappropriate to infer from it that ownership had separated generally from control in the UK's largest companies by the eve of World War I.

One qualification was that proprietors of companies that obtained quotations on the London Stock Exchange and duly arranged for the sale of a two-thirds stake could subsequently fortify their block by buying back shares in the stock market. Hannah suggests the practice was not widespread, citing transaction costs and a general tendency for share prices to rise in the wake of public offerings.[34] However, after the Castle Line, a shipping company, distributed exactly two-thirds of its ordinary shares to the public in 1881, Donald Currie steadily built up his personal holdings from 9 per cent in 1882 to 18 per cent in 1883, 27 per cent in 1886 and peaking at 44 per cent in 1899.[35] Sir Edward Guinness did much the same after his brewery carried out an initial public offering in 1886. Having been allotted the maximum one-third proportion of the ordinary shares permitted by the London Stock Exchange, he bought up equity on the open market and by 1888 held 132,500 of the 250,000 outstanding shares.[36]

Proprietors of a company seeking a quotation for its shares could also comply with the London Stock Exchange listing rules and retain full voting control by issuing only preference shares and debentures. Hannah acknowledges this but claims that, other than breweries, almost all companies seeking a quotation opted to issue two-thirds or more of the ordinary shares to the public.[37] In fact it appears it was standard for vendors to retain a full one-third stake or very close to it, and that they quite often retained all of the ordinary shares.

---

[31] 'Unmarketable Securities and Official Quotations', Economist, May 30, 1885, 657, 658.

[32] Hannah, *supra* n. 2, 415. See also 'Stock Exchange Quotations', Economist, November 30, 1907, 2088.

[33] Hannah, *supra* n. 2, 417.   [34] *Ibid.*, 416.

[35] Andrew Porter, *Victorian Shipping, Business and Imperial Policy: Donald Currie, the Castle Line and Southern Africa* (1986), 104, 109, 222, 290.

[36] T.R. Gourvish and R.G. Wilson, *The British Brewing Industry 1830–1980* (1994), 257–58; S.R. Dennison and Oliver MacDonagh, *Guinness 1886–1939: From Incorporation to the Second World War* (1998), 17, 20–21, 23; Derek Wilson, *Dark and Light: The Story of the Guinness Family* (1998), 115.

[37] Hannah, *supra* n. 2, 416.

Hall has suggested that up to 1914 probably a majority of public offerings by UK companies did not involve the sale of any ordinary shares.[38] Watson reports that with public offerings in the brewing and iron and steel sectors in the late 19th and early 20th centuries the vendors typically retained all of the ordinary shares and that in only one iron and steel company did the proprietors fail to retain at least a one-third stake.[39] Macrosty similarly found that in nearly half of the major horizontal and vertical mergers of industrial companies carried out between 1888 and 1902 that were supported by public offerings of shares the vendors retained all of the voting shares.[40] In a few instances the vendors retained a larger stake than the two-thirds rule prescribed and otherwise it was standard practice for them to retain the one-third stake permitted, or very close to it (Table I).

As for the minority of mergers where Macrosty did not specify the stake retained by the vendors, blockholding apparently remained the norm. He does not list any vendor shares retained with shipping concerns Ellerman Lines Ltd (a 1901 amalgamation/public offering) or Union-Castle Ltd (1900), but John Ellerman was the majority shareholder in the former and Donald Currie held nearly 25 per cent of the shares in the latter.[41] Similarly, Macrosty does not list the retention of any vendor shares with J. & P. Coats (built up by amalgamation

Table I: Retention of ordinary shares by 'vendors' in major mergers supported by public offerings of shares, 1888–1902

Vendor retention of ordinary shares	'Horizontal' mergers	'Vertical' mergers (see Chapter Six, Part II.B.4)	Total
All	13	9	22
More than one-third	2	2	4
One-third	6	3	9
Between one-quarter and one-third	4	0	4
Under 25%	0	1	1
No figure specified	4	7	11
Total	29	22	51

Source: Compiled with data from Macrosty, *supra* n. 40, 351, 353.

[38] A.R. Hall, 'The English Capital Market Before 1914—A Reply', (1958) 25 Economica (N.S.), 339, 342.

[39] Katherine Watson, 'The New Issue Market as a Source of Finance for the UK Brewing and Iron and Steel Industries, 1870–1913' in Youssef Cassis, Gerald D. Feldman and Ulf Olsson (eds), *The Evolution of Financial Institutions and Markets in Twentieth-century Europe* (1995), 209, 235–36.

[40] H.W. Macrosty, 'Business Aspects of British Trusts', (1902) 12 Economic Journal 347.

[41] James Taylor, *Ellermans: A Wealth of Shipping* (1976), 25–27 (Ellerman Lines); Porter, *supra* n. 35, 244, 290; Gordon Boyce, *Information, Mediation and Institutional Development: The Rise of Large-Scale Enterprise in British Shipping, 1870–1919* (1995), 93 (Union-Castle).

in 1896), Armstrong, Whitworth (an 1897 amalgamation/public offering) and Vickers, Sons & Maxim (ditto) but each company was characterized by block-holding (Part IX).

A hallmark of the large horizontal mergers occurring in the late 19th and early 20th centuries was that they brought under a single corporate umbrella numerous firms competing in the same industry, with the predominant objective typically being to reduce inter-firm competition among constituent firms (Chapter Six, Part II.B.4). In mergers of this sort the dominant block retained would be split among the former owners of the constituent companies, creating greater dispersion than if there was a single founder or a family acting as the vendor. Nevertheless, *de facto* blockholding apparently was the typical outcome. According to Payne, '[T]hose who came out on top during the course of the internecine wars of vendor-directors of the new combinations could continue to conduct the affairs of the merged companies as if all that happened was that what had hitherto been their own particular firms had grown larger by the multiplication of units.'[42] Even where there was no first among equals, so long as the former proprietors had not fallen out between themselves they typically would have had sufficient voting power to thwart any kind of shareholder challenge to their authority.

What motivated proprietors of late 19th- and early 20th-century companies seeking quotations to retain sizeable equity stakes or refrain entirely from parting with ordinary shares? A desire to exploit private benefits of control perhaps came into play (Chapter Three, Part II). Market pressures were also a factor. Investors in both shares and debentures treated the retention of a sizeable stake by the original owners of a company carrying out a public offering or amalgamation as a telling demonstration of belief in and commitment to the company's future prosperity. As a 1909 text on investment said, 'If it is found that the Directors are but small shareholders, there is the risk that the management may not display active intelligence . . . In an ideal list of shareholders the Directors should have large personal shareholdings of old standing.'[43] With market expectations being of this sort, when notorious promoter E.T. Hooley took Bovril, the hot drink manufacturer, public in 1896 and the proprietors took up 'only' 16 per cent of the shares, the share register was said to have been 'completely metamorphosed'.[44] Founders of

---

[42] Peter L. Payne, 'Industrial Entrepreneurship and Management in Great Britain', in P. Mathias and M.M. Postan (eds), *The Cambridge Economic History of Europe, vol. VII, The Industrial Economies: Capital, Labour and Enterprise, Part I (Britain, France, Germany, and Scandinavia)* (1978), 180, 206.

[43] Henry Lowenfeld, *All About . . . Investment* (1909), 183. See also Boyce, *supra* n. 41, 90, 232–33 (accounting for a lukewarm investor reaction to an 1890 shipping merger on the basis that the vendors retained only 27 per cent of the ordinary capital); C.H. Thorpe, *How to Invest and to Speculate* (1901), 117; Janette Rutterford, 'The Merchant Banker, the Broker and the Company Chairman: A New Issue Case Study', (2006) 16 Accounting, Business & Financial History 45, 52.

[44] W.R. Lawson, 'Company Promoting "à la Mode"', National Review, Sept. 1898, 103, 111–12.

businesses, or their successors, thus risked breaching powerful market norms by failing to retain a major interest, which could in turn jeopardize the success of a public offering.

An additional important qualification with the two-thirds rule is that it only applied when a company sought a London Stock Exchange quotation. Companies making public offerings of shares often did not go down this route. For instance, prior to World War I companies frequently arranged to have their shares traded on the London Stock Exchange by way of a special settlement rather than by way of a full quotation (Chapter Six, Part III.B.3). To establish a special settlement, a company had to provide the Stock Exchange with a prospectus or equivalent documentation, the particulars of the company's share capital and details on the number of shares allotted to the public and to others.[45] The Stock Exchange sought the information on the number of shares allotted to the public to ensure the market would not be subject to a 'corner', but only exceptionally was an anticipated special settlement refused.[46] Hence, a special settlement provided a means by which the proprietor of a business could realize some of his investment without relinquishing control to the extent required with a full quotation of ordinary shares.[47]

Companies that obtained a special settlement were merely a subset of companies that distributed shares to the public without seeking a quotation on the London Stock Exchange.[48] Various others were floated on provincial stock exchanges, where quotations were occasionally rejected when shares were 'insufficiently in the public hands' but could be granted without compliance with the two-thirds rule.[49] There was a general expectation in the commercial world that when ordinary shares were offered for sale to the public a substantial proportion of the equity should be made available for sale.[50] Still, companies traded on provincial stock exchanges apparently often had a smaller 'free float' than that which the two-thirds rule prescribed. The Manchester Stock Exchange, one of the most important provincial stock markets, objected to a proposal put forward in 1910 that all provincial exchanges adopt the London listing rules for their own purposes on the basis that many local companies could not satisfy the two-thirds requirement.[51]

[45] Francis Gore-Browne and William Jordan, *A Handy Book on the Formation, Management and Winding up of Joint Stock Companies*, 30th edn (1909), 487–88.
[46] 'Stock Exchange Quotations and Settlements—A Note of Warning', Economist, January 5, 1889, 5; 'The Marconi Decision', Times, November 20, 1913, 15.
[47] 'Special Settlements and Public Protection', Economist, September 10, 1910, 508.
[48] F. Lavington, *The English Capital Market*, 2nd edn (1929), 202–3 (between 1911 and 1913 378 companies were formed that issued a prospectus and of these only 165 applied for a special settlement).
[49] W.A. Thomas, *The Provincial Stock Exchanges* (1973), 138–39.
[50] Lowenfeld, *supra* n. 43, 193; 'The Joint Stock Companies Bill', Times, November 19, 1888.
[51] Thomas, *supra* n. 49, 198. On the Manchester Stock Exchange's status, see 'The Provincial Stock Exchanges', Economist, April 16, 1904, 645.

There were also numerous instances where shares were placed privately with parties connected by personal or trade interests without the company securing any sort of trading platform on a stock market.[52] Capital markets retained a regional orientation prior to 1914 (Chapter Six, Part III.C.2), and distributions of shares on a local basis to friends, business associates and clients of well-connected stockbrokers or solicitors occurred with some frequency. The companies would have generally been smaller concerns, but at least some would have been prosperous enterprises offering good investment prospects.[53] As a 1911 study of the London Stock Exchange said, '... there is never any difficulty in raising capital locally or privately for the creation or extension of any business which offers a reasonable probability of large profits. A really good thing from Glasgow, or Yorkshire, or Lancashire, or the Midlands, seldom comes to London to be floated on the public. The insiders naturally keep it to themselves and their friends.'[54]

Drawing matters together, with many companies distributing shares to the public without the two-thirds rule imposing a constraint, with numerous owners of quoted companies retaining all of the ordinary shares and with many others retaining a full one-third stake and sometimes subsequently fortifying it through market purchases, the two-thirds rule does not provide a sufficient factual foundation to support Hannah's contention that prior to World War I dispersed ownership was the norm in larger UK companies. Hence, to assess the extent to which ownership had in fact separated from control up to 1914, further investigation is required. While there is a lack of detailed statistical data on this point, it is possible through the use of contemporary sources, company histories and other secondary literature to gain a good sense of where things stood. The remainder of the chapter considers the evidence on ownership patterns in various key business sectors, namely railways, banking, insurance, shipping companies, electricity companies and industrial companies.

IV. Railways

Hannah correctly cites British railways as examples of companies characterized by dispersed share ownership pre-1914.[55] Ownership was divorced from control in large UK railway companies as far back as the mid-19th century (Chapter Five, Part IV.A) and the situation remained unchanged up to World

---

[52] Lavington, *supra* n. 48, 203–4; James B. Jefferys, *Business Organisation in Great Britain 1856–1914* (1997), 369–73.

[53] Lavington, *supra* n. 48, 203; A.K. Cairncross, *Home and Foreign Investment 1870–1913: Studies in Capital Accumulation* (1953), 96.

[54] Francis W. Hirst, *The Stock Exchange* (1911), 216; see also Sidney Pollard, *Britain's Prime and Britain's Decline: The British Economy 1870–1914* (1989), 94.

[55] Hannah, *supra* n. 2, 409.

War I. The London & North Western Railway (LNWR), the largest railway by equity capitalization, was a model of dispersed share ownership. It had 36,000 shareholders as the 20th century opened and the 23 directors of the LNWR owned between them less than 1 per cent of the company's outstanding shares. The shareholder base of the Midland Railway was even larger (almost 47,000) and as of 1900, eight other UK railways had 10,000 or more shareholders.[56]

V. Banking

Hannah also cites banking as a sector where ownership had separated from control in the UK by 1914.[57] He was on the mark here as well, certainly by the end of World War I. The divorce of ownership and control was the culmination of a half-century of radical change in English banking. Though legislative reforms in the 1820s and 1830s cleared the way for the incorporation of joint stock banks, private 'country banks' organized as partnerships remained an important factor in banking through much of the 19th century.[58] As for banks that were incorporated, many of the early ones were conversions from private banks, which frequently meant share ownership was dominated by the former partners together with wealthy business allies from the same locality (Chapter Five, Part III.C). During the middle decades of the 19th century, the shareholders in a typical English joint stock bank were predominantly local people and customers of the bank (shares were quite often issued to account holders and used as bait to tempt customers to transfer accounts).[59] As of 1860 only two English or Welsh banks had more than 1,000 shareholders.[60]

Attributes of a separation of ownership and control increasingly characterized the banking sector thereafter. Capped voting rights, which hinder the accumulation of influence through ownership of large blocks of shares, were generally waning in popularity generally in UK companies as the 19th century drew to a close (Chapter Two, Part II.A). However, as of the early 1880s almost half of publicly traded banks had this voting structure.[61]

---

[56] *Ibid.*, 408.   [57] *Ibid.*, 412–13.

[58] Ch. Five, Pt III.C; W.F. Crick and J.E. Wadsworth, *A Hundred Years of Joint Stock Banking* (1936), 34 (indicating private banks outnumbered joint stock banks as late as the mid-1880s).

[59] T.E. Gregory, *The Westminster Bank Through a Century* (1936), 384; R.S. Sayers, *Lloyds Bank in the History of English Banking* (1957), 91–92, 160, 221; B.L. Anderson and P.L. Cottrell, 'Another Victorian Capital Market: A Study of Banking and Bank Investors on Merseyside', (1975) 28 Economic History Review (N.S.) 598, 612.

[60] Jefferys, *supra* n. 52, 387.

[61] Gareth Campbell and John D. Turner, 'Protecting Outside Investors in a Laissez-faire Legal Environment: Corporate Governance in Victorian Britain' (2007), unpublished working paper, Table 2.

The shareholder base was also expanding. By 1880, there were 15 British banks with more than 1,000 shareholders, including four with more than 3,000.[62] London and Westminster Bank topped the list, with 4,800 shareholders by the mid-1870s.[63] The bank evidently was characterized by the shareholder apathy commonly associated with a separation of ownership and control. The *Economist* commented that events at an 1887 shareholder meeting showed 'that shareholders look mainly at the dividend paid, and care but little how it may have been earned, the result being that a most valuable check upon management of the bank is thus removed'.[64]

The banking sector nevertheless was not yet characterized by a full-scale divorce of ownership and control. Hickson and Turner's study of the Ulster Banking Company illustrates the point.[65] As of the late 1870s the bank had around 1,000 shareholders and was substantially larger, in terms of branches, assets and number of shareholders, than the average English provincial bank.[66] Despite this, and despite the fact the largest shareholder owned less than 3 per cent of the outstanding equity, ownership was not separated from control in the modern sense. The biggest shareholders all participated actively in the governance of the company as directors or as members of a committee of shareholders that met regularly to deal with bank business. Share ownership also was almost entirely local, with 90 per cent of the shareholders living within 10 miles of a bank branch and only 2.5 per cent being from outside Ireland.

There were some late 19th-century banks with a more diverse share register than the Ulster Banking Companys. For instance, as of 1878, 22 per cent of the Union Bank of London's shareholders were from Ireland and Scotland even though all its branches were in London.[67] On the other hand, bank shares typically lacked the liquidity associated with companies where ownership is divorced from control.[68] The fact bank directors usually had to approve share transfers diminished marketability considerably.[69]

---

[62] *Ibid.*, 4.

[63] Charles R. Hickson and John D. Turner, 'Shareholder Liability Regimes in Nineteenth-Century English Banking: The Impact Upon the Market for Shares', (2003) 7 European Review of Economic History 99, 108–9.

[64] 'The Indifference of Bank Shareholders', Economist, January 22, 1887, 107.

[65] Charles R. Hickson and John D. Turner, 'The Trading of Unlimited Liability Bank Shares in Nineteenth Century Ireland: The Bagehot Hypothesis', (2003) 63 Journal of Economic History 931.

[66] See an earlier version of *ibid.*: Charles R. Hickson and John D. Turner, 'The Trading of Unlimited Liability Bank Shares: The Bagehot Hypothesis', (2002), ESRC Centre for Business Research Working Paper No. 241, 6.

[67] Campbell and Turner, *supra* n. 61, 10.

[68] P.L. Cottrell, 'Finance and the Germination of the British Corporate Economy' in P.L. Cottrell *et al* (eds), *Finance in the Age of the Corporate Economy: The Third Anglo-Japanese Business History Conference* (1997), 5, 17 (discussing problems involved with dealing in shares of the National Provincial Bank even though it was in 1878 one of the two largest commercial banks in England).

[69] Hickson and Turner, *supra* n. 63, 107–8.

The transfer restrictions on bank shares were a legacy of history. English banks were first given the option to introduce limited liability for shareholders in 1858.[70] Many did not do so, deterred partly by concerns that a limitation of liability would impair confidence on the part of depositors and partly by an obligation to publish twice-yearly balance sheets providing a statement of assets and liabilities.[71] For banks where shareholders lacked limited liability, giving the directors the authority to veto share transfers was an important check against exiting shareholders imposing externalities on remaining shareholders by selling out to impecunious buyers. However, to the extent directors took their responsibilities to investigate buyers seriously, delays in share transfers would ensue and the anonymity of potential purchasers would be compromised, thus curtailing liquidity. Hickson and Turner have demonstrated this effect with English banks by showing that in the 1870s share prices of unlimited shares were less likely to fluctuate month-to-month than were shares offering limited liability.[72]

The 1878 collapse of the City of Glasgow Bank, which bankrupted most of its 1,800 shareholders, prompted a wholesale conversion away from unlimited liability.[73] An amendment to companies legislation in 1879 stipulated banks that wanted to convert to limited liability could divide any unpaid capital on issued shares into an amount callable at the discretion of the directors and a remainder callable only in the event of the winding up of the bank.[74] This was good news for shareholders, since not only did they get the benefit of limited liability, there was a less-taxing upper bound on the amount they might be asked to contribute over time, assuming their bank did not fail. The credit standing of banks with this sort of 'reserved' liability was well regarded and during the early 1880s most banks continuing to have unlimited liability re-registered as limited liability companies.[75]

The 1879 legislation, in addition to providing a convenient means of converting to limited liability, supplied a congenial platform for bank amalgamations,[76] a trend that fostered a full divorce of ownership and control in large English banks. Banks that opted to convert to limited liability under the 1879 legislation had to publish their balance sheets,[77] which meant that for a bank seeking to grow

---

[70] 21 & 22 Vict. c . 91; for background, see Gregory, *supra* n. 59, 200.

[71] Crick and Wadsworth, *supra* n. 58, 31–32; Gregory, *supra* n. 59, 204; Sayers, *supra* n. 59, 221–22, 224; T. Balogh, *Studies in Financial Organization* (1947), 5 (reasons banks hesitated to switch).

[72] Hickson and Turner, *supra* n. 63, 107–8, 110–13.

[73] Michael Collins, 'The Banking Crisis of 1878', (1989) 24 Economic History Review (N.S.) 504, 504–5.

[74] Companies Act 1879, 42 & 43 Vict. c. 76, s. 5.

[75] Crick and Wadsworth, *supra* n. 58, 34; Sayers, *supra* n. 59, 222–23; Balogh, *supra* n. 71, 6.

[76] Crick and Wadsworth, *supra* n. 58, 34, 310; Balogh, *supra* n. 71, 6–7.

[77] Companies Act 1879, s. 7.

by way of acquisition it became easier to assess the relative strength and importance of potential targets. Those banks that opted to retain unlimited liability and continued to keep their balance sheets confidential lost influence and popularity, which over time meant for most proprietors an offer to sell out in a merger would have been welcomed.

There were various plausible justifications for acquisitive banks to buy up rivals, particularly outside regions in which they already had a strong base.[78] Individual credit risks could be distributed more widely and therefore reduced. The head office of a major bank could provide expert services to customers that local banks were unlikely to be able to offer. Big corporate borrowers could be catered to more effectively, as a bank with a large capital base could accommodate liabilities too sizeable for a smaller concern to take on prudently. Transaction costs for customers could be reduced once a bank had an extensive branch network because much more remittance business (e.g. transferring cash, bills and documents) could be carried out in-house. Finally, with size becoming an important signal of reliability and prestige in an industry plagued by bank failures through much of the 19th century (Chapter Four, Part I), mergers could enhance an acquisitive bank's reputation for prudence and stability.

These various arguments in favour of merger proved persuasive. The banking sector experienced hectic amalgamation activity through the late 19th and early 20th centuries, dominated by amalgamations between joint stock banks and the acquisition of private banks by joint stock banks (Figure I). Banks could also achieve growth by internal expansion—primarily opening new branches—but if quick action was a priority, amalgamation was the better bet, since acquired banks supplied ready-made premises, business and personnel.[79] In Scotland, banks grew chiefly by way of internal expansion rather than mergers but in England amalgamations were the primary source of growth of leading banks.[80]

The surge in amalgamations in the late 19th and early 20th centuries helped to prompt a dramatic increase in concentration in the banking industry. The

---

[78] On the arguments in favour of bank amalgamations, see 'Amalgamations Among Banks', *Banker's Magazine*, July 1901, 1, 3–4; J.H. Clapham, *An Economic History of Britain: Machines and National Rivalries (1887–1914) with an Epilogue (1914–1929)* (1938), 281–82; Mae Baker and Michael Collins, 'English Commercial Bank Stability, 1860–1914', (2002) 31 Journal of European Economic History 493, 502–3. See also Joseph Sykes, *The Amalgamation Movement in English Banking, 1825–1924* (1926), 64–65, 149–51, 162 (reciting the arguments but expressing doubts about their persuasiveness).

[79] Sykes, *supra* n. 78, 46; C.N. Ward Perkins, 'Book Review', (1959) 12 Economic History Review (N.S.) 295, 296.

[80] Crick and Wadsworth, *supra* n. 58, 333; Gregory, *supra* n. 59, 291–92, 379–81; Forrest Capie and Ghila Rodrik-Bali, 'Concentration in British Banking 1870–1920', (1982) 24 Business History 280, 288–89.

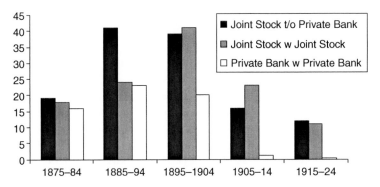

Figure I: Banking amalgamations, England and Wales, 1875–1924

Source: Compiled with data from Sykes (1926), *supra* n. 78, Appendix I.[81]

percentage of total deposits held by the largest five banks grew from 21 per cent in 1890 in the UK (27 per cent in England/Wales) to 36 per cent in 1910 (43 per cent) and 66 per cent (80 per cent) in 1920.[82] By the end of World War I banks soon christened the 'Big Five'—Barclays, Lloyds, the Midland, the National Provincial and the Westminster—were set to dominate English banking for some time to come.[83]

Merger activity, in addition to fostering increased concentration in British banking, prompted dispersal of share ownership in leading banks. Not all bank amalgamations had this effect. If in a merger shareholders of the target company are paid in cash and the funds are derived from retained earnings or borrowing, the ownership structure of the acquirer will remain undisturbed (Chapter Three, Part VI). Some bank acquisitions were of this nature. Most banks Lloyds bought during the 1860s and 1870s were private banks 'in which the families were losing the enthusiasm or the ability of the older generation of bankers', with the terms typically being three years' worth of profits payable in cash.[84] In subsequent decades, 'In taking over the very small banks from family hands, the more powerful joint-stocks could sometimes be persuaded to pay a large proportion, exceptionally the whole, in cash.'[85]

---

[81] There were two instances where private banks absorbed a joint stock company (Sykes, *supra* n. 78, 194); these have not been included in the table. Sykes' figures likely inflate to some degree the number of mergers due to counting all bank disappearances (excluding bankruptcies) as acquisitions: Capie and Rodrik-Bali, *supra* n. 80, 282.

[82] Capie and Rodrik-Bali, *supra* n. 80, 287.

[83] 'The Five Great Banks', Times, November 8, 1927, Supplement, xv; Monopolies Commission, *Barclays Bank Ltd, Lloyds Bank Ltd, and Martins Bank Ltd: A Report on the Proposed Merger* (1968), 9–10.

[84] Sayers, *supra* n. 59, 248.

[85] *Ibid.*, 258.

Generally, as the quote implies, payment in cash was the exception to the rule. For instance, of 24 major amalgamations the Midland Bank carried out up to 1918, in only three instances could the shareholders in the bank being acquired elect for payment in cash. In 14 instances shareholders in the target bank were offered only Midland shares and in seven instances the offer was a combination of shares and cash.[86] When acquiring banks offered a combination of shares and cash the cash element was typically subsidiary, being used to adjust for an odd amount in the price that could not be accommodated by a pure exchange of shares.[87]

When a company uses its own shares as acquisition currency, the company will necessarily experience some diffusion of share ownership (Chapter Three, Part VI). For instance, when in 1902 Union Bank (subsequently part of a 1917 merger that boosted the National Provincial Bank into the Big Five) bought Smith, Payne and Smiths, a leading private bank, Union Bank directors estimated that the dilution for existing Union Bank shareholders would be in a proportion of about one share to five.[88] The effect mergers had on shareholdings was known and accepted in the banking sector. Sayers says of the bank mergers of the late 19th and early 20th centuries: 'The purchasing bank preferred to pay its price by the issue of shares, an enlarged capital being appropriate to its enlarged responsibilities.'[89] Sykes, in a 1926 study of bank mergers, noted similarly, 'Amalgamation has increased greatly the number of shareholders, by reason of the splitting of capital which it has caused.'[90]

The Midland Bank illustrates the effect mergers had on the diffusion of share ownership. By 1908 this acquisitive bank, operating as the London Joint City and Midland Bank, had 14,200 shareholders.[91] As of 1911, the directors collectively owned only 1.2 per cent of the outstanding shares, and it seems unlikely there was a major shareholder who was not represented on the board. While the Midland Bank's general policy with amalgamations was to give shares in payment, it would typically cash out large shareholders of the banks it bought, thereby precluding the accumulation of sizeable blocks of its own shares.[92]

By 1919 the shareholder base of the UK's largest banks had expanded still further, with each of the 'Big Five' banks having 30,000 or more shareholders. Share ownership on this scale implied a full-scale split between ownership and control (Table II).

---

[86] Crick and Wadsworth, *supra* n. 58, 93, 95, 98, 137, 154 158, 161, 165, 193, 234–35, 238, 272–74, 313, 317, 323–24.
[87] Sayers, *supra* n. 59, 258.
[88] 'The Union Bank of London and Messrs. Smith, Payne and Smiths', Times, July 9, 1902.
[89] Sayers, *supra* n. 59, 258.   [90] Sykes, *supra* n. 78, 159, n. 1.
[91] Hannah, *supra* n. 2, 412.
[92] *Ibid.*

Table II: Number of shareholders/branches in the 'Big Five' English banks and leading Scottish banks, 1919

Bank (the name by which 'Big Five' banks were known in the 1920s in **bold**)	Number of Shareholders	Branches/Offices
Lloyds Bank	50,000	1,400
London County **Westminster** and Parrs Bank	50,000	771
London Joint City and **Midland** Bank	47,299	1,359
Barclays Bank	36,000	1,450
National Provincial and Union Bank	30,000	708
Commercial Bank of Scotland	5,175	184
Bank of Scotland	4,210	166
Royal Bank of Scotland	3,928	167
Clydesdale Bank	3,199	157

Source: Compiled with data from Thomas Skinner (ed.), *The Bankers Almanac and Year Book for 1919–20* (1920).

Merger activity played a significant role in the decisive final chapter. By 1919, the largest English banks had far more shareholders than their Scottish counterparts (Table II), which again largely steered clear of amalgamations. The National Provincial Bank was late entering the merger sweepstakes but its 1918 amalgamation with Union of London and Smiths Bank was the deal that moved it into the Big Five.[93] Barclays' inclusion in the Big Five was also a product of merger activity. Barclays only became incorporated in 1896, prompted by an amalgamation of around 20 private banks that formally allied a number of prominent and often inter-married English banking families.[94] Upon incorporation Barclays had only 110 shareholders and much was done to preserve the individuality of the amalgamated banks, such as creating 'Local Directors' and inviting representative partners of the absorbed banks to sit on the main board of directors.[95] Nevertheless, mergers quickly prompted change.

Barclays carried out 13 acquisitions up to 1912, by which point it had 6,800 shareholders.[96] A 1918 merger with the London and Provincial and South Western Bank, a major joint stock bank in its own right, was for Barclays the decisive break from its private banker/family-oriented traditions.[97] Barclays continued to operate on more decentralized lines than its Big Five rivals.[98] However,

[93] Balogh, *supra* n. 71, 18; Sykes, *supra* n. 78, 78.

[94] Clapham, *supra* n. 78, 283; P.W. Matthews and Anthony W. Tuke, *History of Barclays Bank Limited* (1926), 3–6.

[95] Ranald C. Michie, *The London Stock Exchange: A History* (1999), 72; H.S. Foxwell, 'A History of Barclays Bank', (1927) 37 Economic Journal 411, 413–14.

[96] Matthews and Tuke, *supra* n. 94, 10–11 (listing mergers between 1897 and 1912); Michie, *supra* n. 95, 72 (number of shareholders).

[97] Matthews and Tuke, *supra* n. 94, 13–14.

[98] Balogh, *supra* n. 71, 20–21.

with mergers swamping the share ownership pattern of 1896 and increasing the shareholder base to 36,000, by 1919 Barclays had joined its Big Five brethren as a company characterized by a separation of ownership and control.

VI. Insurance

In various ways, the insurance sector stands out as a promising candidate for a pre-World War I divorce of ownership and control. There was a long-standing tradition in the UK of insurers offering shares for sale to the public. The Royal Exchange and London Assurance, two major insurance houses, carried out successful public subscriptions in the midst of the 1720 South Sea Bubble.[99] Capped voting rights and ownership ceilings, which discourage the accumulation of voting control (Chapter Two, Part II.A), were quite common with insurers. Of the 88 UK-based insurance companies listed in the *Stock Exchange Official Intelligencer for 1899*, 49 had such restrictions.[100] There also was little legacy of family ownership. As Westall said of the Provincial Insurance Company, which the Scott family controlled from its inception in 1903 through the opening decades of the 20th century, 'In these ways the Provincial remained unique among significant British insurance companies. While others were dominated by a particular family, as the Mountains controlled Eagle Star, or the Norie-Millers the General Accident, they shared ownership with shareholders whose interests they were bound to serve and they raised funds in the public capital markets.'[101]

Finally, amalgamations, which were a catalyst for dispersed ownership for banks, were also common in the insurance sector. Between 1844 and 1859, the business of 158 insurance companies was either amalgamated or transferred to other companies.[102] In the late 19th and early 20th centuries there were numerous diversification-oriented mergers as leading insurers specializing in fire or life insurance built themselves into 'composite' insurance companies operating not only in more than one of the traditional sectors of fire, life and marine insurance but also in new sectors (e.g. personal accident and employers' liability insurance).[103]

Despite these various hallmarks of dispersed ownership, it is unclear whether a modern-style divorce of ownership and control characterized the insurance

---

[99] H.A.L. Cockerell and Edwin Green, *The British Insurance Business: A Guide to its History and Records*, 2nd edn (1994), 99.

[100] Calculated by analyzing the list of commercial and industrial companies in Share and Loan Department (ed.), *The Stock Exchange Official Intelligencer for 1899* (1899), 1942–79.

[101] Oliver M. Westall, *The Provincial Insurance Company 1903–38: Family, Markets and Competitive Growth* (1992), 41.

[102] Cockerell and Green, *supra* n. 99, 106.

[103] *Ibid.*, 107–10; Takau Yoneyama, 'The Rise of the Large-Scale Composite Insurance Companies in the U.K.', KSU Economic and Business Review, #20, May 1993, 1, 2, 10–14.

sector by the eve of World War I. While the policy acquisitive banks adopted of carrying out amalgamations by way of share-by-share exchanges meant the mergers they executed generally tended to split ownership from control, the practice apparently was different in insurance. Commercial Union, which relied on amalgamations to build itself into Britain's second largest insurer by 1910, issued debentures to shareholders of insurers it bought rather than issuing shares.[104]

In addition, while there were insurers with enviable track records of financial stability—London Assurance paid dividends to shareholders each and every year from 1722 through to the mid-20th century[105]—collectively the 19th-century insurance sector would have been too risky for many arm's-length investors. A large proportion of firms that solicited backing from the public never actually opened their doors, and of those that did, many failed (Chapter Three, Part I). Even the two most acquisitive insurance companies of the mid-19th century, the European (44 amalgamations) and the Albert (26), collapsed.[106] As and when things went wrong, shareholders in insurance companies could be in for a nasty surprise in the form of capital calls. As of 1915, only 32 per cent of the issued capital of insurance companies was paid up.[107]

It also appears the shareholder base of insurance companies was not as large as it was with banks. A 1949 history of the London Assurance said, 'As has always been the practice, the shares tend to be held by a great and varied number of individuals, not for the most part in large sections.'[108] On the other hand, as of 1879, the average number of shareholders in publicly traded insurance companies was only 342.[109] As of 1908, Phoenix Assurance, the fifth largest 'composite' insurer in the UK, had fewer than 1,700 shareholders.[110] The Prudential, which was almost twice as large as any other British insurer as of 1910, had only just over 1,000 shareholders at that point and share ownership was dominated by directors, officers and staff.[111] It did not obtain a quotation on the London Stock Exchange until 1924.[112] If these major insurance companies lacked a large shareholder base, their smaller rivals are unlikely to have experienced a divorce of ownership and control akin to that which characterized the Big Five banks.

[104] Yoneyama, *supra* n. 103, 6 (position as of 1910); Edward Liveling, *A Century of Insurance: The Commercial Union Group of Insurance Companies* (1961), 48–49, 79–83 (acquisition policy).

[105] Bernard Drew, *The London Assurance: A Second Chronicle* (1949), 216.

[106] Cockerell and Green, *supra* n. 99, 106.

[107] Jefferys, *supra* n. 52, 205.

[108] Drew, *supra* n. 105, 225.

[109] Campbell and Turner, *supra* n. 61, 5.

[110] Clive Trebilcock, *Phoenix Assurance and the Development of British Insurance, vol. II: The Era of Insurance Giants* (1998), 124, 360.

[111] Laurie Dennett, *A Sense of Security: 150 Years of Prudential* (1998), 121–22; Josephine Maltby and Janette Rutterford, 'She Possessed Her Own Fortune: Women Investors from the Late Nineteenth to the Early Twentieth Centuries', (2006) 48 Business History 220, 232.

[112] Dennett, *supra* n. 111, 232–33.

VII. Shipping

Shipping companies were providing investors with a significant domestic alternative to railway shares and government bonds as early as the 1830s and were a cornerstone of share trading on the London Stock Exchange and provincial stock markets by the beginning of the 20th century.[113] As a result, they would seem to be promising candidates for a pre-1914 divorce between ownership and control. Matters in fact were much different. Boyce reports that of 73 shipping firms operating out of Britain as of 1914, 14 were unincorporated.[114] Of the 59 companies, 14 were fully private, 24 had issued subordinate securities to the public but not ordinary shares, 21 had issued ordinary shares to the public and only five of these lacked an investor owning enough shares to exert voting control.

Even among the largest shipping firms fully dispersed share ownership was the exception to the rule. Of the five industry leaders, which between them controlled 35 per cent of the British fleet, only one, P. & O., appears to have had fully dispersed share ownership on the eve of World War I.[115] Cunard's directors owned a majority of the company's ordinary shares as of 1911 and by 1919, after share issuances and capital reorganizations arising from a series of acquisitions, associated companies owned 37 per cent of Cunard's shares.[116] As of 1913 John Ellerman owned 59 per cent of the shares of Ellerman Shipping through private ownership and investment trusts he controlled.[117] Stephen Furness, nephew of the founder of the firm, owned 42 per cent of Furness Withy in 1912. After his untimely death in 1914, 30 per cent of the shares were held in trust for family members, 7 per cent were held by management and he was succeeded as chairman of the board by his cousin Lord Furness.[118]

The Royal Mail Steam Packet Co., the final of the five leading firms, seemed prone to dispersed share ownership since it carried out numerous acquisitions and a massive program of fleet renewal between 1903 and World War I. However, the expansion was financed primarily by loan capital and a group of companies chairman of the board Owen Phillips (later Lord Kylsant) and his close

---

[113] Edwin Green and Michael Moss, *A Business of National Importance: The Royal Mail Shipping Group 1902–1937* (1982), 1, 10.

[114] Boyce, *supra* n. 41, 232.

[115] Gordon Boyce, '64thers, Syndicates, and Stock Promotions: Information Flows and Fundraising Techniques of British Shipowners Before 1914', (1992) 52 Journal of Economic History 181, 195 (on the five major groups and their share of the British fleet); Boyce, *supra* n. 41, 236, Table 10.2 (indicating there was no information on P.& O. blockholders).

[116] Francis E. Hyde, *Cunard and the North Atlantic 1840–1973* (1975), 168–69.

[117] Boyce, *supra* n. 41, 236, Table 10.2.

[118] *Ibid.*; <http://portcities.hartlepool.gov.uk/server.php?show=ConNarrative.90> (biography of Stephen Furness, last visited October 9, 2007); 'Furness, Withy and Company, Limited', Economist, July 31, 1915, 186.

associates ultimately came to dominate ownership of the ordinary shares.[119] Outsider/arm's-length corporate governance was therefore the exception to the rule in the shipping sector before 1914.

VIII. Electric Utilities

As with insurance and shipping, a split between share ownership and control plausibly could have characterized companies in the electric utility sector. On the sell side the financial demands involved implied founders could not launch such enterprises without seeking immediate backing from the public and on the buy side investors had an appetite for the electricity shares, most obviously during the 'Brush Bubble' of the early 1880s (Chapter Six, Part II.A, Part III.C.4). However, a divorce between ownership and control apparently was not the norm among electrical utility companies.

Fledgling electricity supply companies of the 1880s raised capital in a manner akin to canals and early railways, selling a large proportion of shares to locals anticipating benefiting directly from the services.[120] Similarly, local industrialists usually put up the initial risk capital for the power companies established at the beginning of the 20th century.[121] Of these only the Newcastle-on-Tyne Electric Supply Company, which was dependent on the engineering, business and financial network of J. Theodore Merz and his son Charles, had any sustained success.[122] By the interwar years, most private electricity supply companies were subsidiaries in larger holding company groups and those that maintained their independence were typically under the control of a local and restricted group of shareholders.[123]

The situation with electric tramways also illustrates the lack of a divorce between ownership and control in electric utility companies up to 1914. The electric tramway business was split between private and municipal operators prior to World War I. On the private side British Electric Traction (BET) was the dominant player, carrying, through companies it controlled, about 60 per cent of the passengers on private sector trams as of 1903.[124] By 1985 BET was a widely held

---

[119] Green and Moss, *supra* n. 113, 33–34; Edwin Green, 'Very Private Enterprise: Ownership and Finance in British Shipping, 1825–1940' in Tsunehiko Yui and Keiichiro Nakagawa (eds), *Business History of Shipping: The International Conference on Business History II: Proceedings of the Fuji Conference* (1995), 219, 232–35.

[120] Ranald Michie, 'The Finance of Innovation in Late Victorian and Edwardian Britain: Possibilities and Constraints', (1988) 17 Journal of European Economic History 491, 510–11. On canals and railways, see Ch. 5, Pt III.C.

[121] I.C.R. Byatt, *The British Electrical Industry 1875–1914: The Economic Returns to a New Technology* (1979), 115–17; Leslie Hannah, *Electricity Before Nationalisation: A Study of the Development of the Electricity Supply Industry in Britain to 1948* (1979), 43.

[122] Thomas P. Hughes, *Networks of Power: Electrification in Western Society, 1880–1930* (1983), 447–55.

[123] Hannah, *supra* n. 121, 223; Hughes, *supra* n. 122, 402–3.

[124] Byatt, *supra* n. 121, 34.

company, though by this time it had been forced out of passenger transport and derived its profit flow from a diverse range of businesses, including broadcasting, publishing, freight and textile maintenance.[125] Matters were different pre-1914. BET was publicly traded with around 2,000 shareholders of its own, and there were numerous small investors interested in its tramway group of securities.[126] Nevertheless, BET was not a model of dispersed share ownership.

The Electric & General Investment Trust was the instrumental force in BET's early development. Electric & General formed BET in 1896 out of various tramway companies it had floated on the stock market, provided a substantial part of BET's capital when BET's initial public offering was not fully subscribed and orchestrated various subsequent public offerings of BET securities.[127] Electric & General's chairman was a large shareholder in BET and responded when asked whether he was a member of the board of directors, 'No, but I am behind it.'[128] BET in turn operated as a holding company, with its profits being derived initially from the promotion and flotation of local tramway companies and then primarily from dividends paid by companies it continued to control or acquired.[129] While it has been standard practice in the UK for parent companies at the apex of corporate groups to own all shares in subsidiary companies (Chapter Four, Part I), BET often merely held a controlling interest in companies that remained independently listed on the London Stock Exchange or provincial stock markets. It therefore was an early example of the sort of complex corporate cross-ownership arrangements that have been prevalent in many countries but rare in Britain.

IX. Industrial Companies

While the received wisdom is that 'personal capitalism' prevailed in pre-World War I British industrial concerns, Hannah contends 'a divorce between ownership and control was the norm in large publicly traded inductrial companies'.[130] Electric Railway & Tramway Carriage Works Co. (ERTCW), a manufacturer of tram bodies that made a public offering of shares in 1898,

[125] Monopolies and Mergers Commission, *The British Electric Traction Company PLC and Initial PLC: A Report on the Proposed Merger*, Cmnd. 9444 (1985), 13–14.

[126] Raphael Schapiro, 'Public Ownership in the British City: Perspectives on Urban Utilities' (2003), D.Phil. thesis, Oxford University, Ch. 8, 6 (BET's shareholder numbers); W.R. Lawson, 'The Investor's Shilling Year Book for 1910', Financial Review of Reviews, December 1909, 18, 20 (small investors' and tramways).

[127] Schapiro, *supra* n. 126, Ch. 8, 5; Roger Fulford, *Five Decades of B.E.T.* (1946), 20–21.

[128] Fulford, *supra* n. 127, 21; see also W.J. Reader, *A House in the City: A Study of the City and of the Stock Exchange Based on the Records of Foster & Braithwaite 1825–1975* (1979), 105–6.

[129] Jefferys, *supra* n. 52, 127, n. 1; Schapiro, *supra* n. 126, Ch. 8, 4; 'British Electric Traction Company', Economist, June 20, 1908, 1295.

[130] Hannah, *supra* n. 2, 417.

was an example of an industrial company characterized by a divorce between ownership and control. Executives of Metropolitan Railway Carriage & Wagon Co. and Dick Kerr, a mechanical and engineering firm, used boardroom influence to dictate ERTCW's overall strategy. However, by 1905 no single shareholder owned more than 2.2 per cent of the shares and the board collectively owned only 8.9 per cent.[131]

But just this how widespread was the pattern? While there is no empirical evidence directly on this point (Part II), Hannah's contention that most large industrial companies were characterized by a divorce between ownership and control can be tested by way of a case study of Britain's largest industrial enterprises as of the eve of World War I. A list Hannah compiled of the world's 100 largest industrial companies as of 1912 included 15 companies based in the UK (Chapter Six, Table I) and there is evidence available for each that permits at least a tentative determination of whether ownership was divorced from control.

To anticipate, contrary to Hannah's argument, a separation of ownership and control was the exception to the rule in the 15 companies. In only one instance (Consolidated Gold Fields of South Africa) is there no evidence of a sizeable concentrated block of shares on the eve of World War I. This implies, in turn, a divorce between ownership and control was generally rare in the industrial sector. Among British industrial companies that had issued securities to the public as of 1910, the average number of shareholders was perhaps 500, far below large concerns such as Guinness (12,000 shareholders) or J. & P. Coats (23,700).[132] Assuming the very largest companies were not characterized by a divorce of ownership and control, this pattern probably prevailed more widely. This is because for various reasons larger companies are more likely to have diffuse share ownership than their smaller counterparts.[133]

First, the attractions of spreading risk through diversification discourages ownership of major blocks of shares in large companies, since a dominant stake of a big firm will take up a larger proportion of an investment portfolio than a dominant stake in a smaller concern. Second, accumulating or purchasing a control block is more likely to be beyond the financial resources of an individual or family if the company is large than if it is small.[134] Third, big companies are more likely to have bought up companies than their smaller counterparts and thus are more likely to have experienced the diffusion of share ownership associated with acquisition activity (Chapter Three, Part V).

---

[131] John Wilson, 'A Strategy of Expansion and Combination: Dick Kerr & Co., 1897–1914', (1985) 27 Business History 26, 30–31.

[132] Lawson, *supra* n. 126, 18 (reviewing *Investors' Shilling Year Book for 1910*, which provided the original figures).

[133] Harold Demsetz & Kenneth Lehn, 'The Structure of Corporate Ownership: Causes and Consequences', (1985) 93 Journal of Political Economy 1155, 1158; Ronald J. Daniels and Edward M. Iacobucci, 'Some of the Causes and Consequences of Corporate Ownership Concentration in Canada' in Randall K. Morck (ed.), *Concentrated Corporate Ownership* (2000) 81, 90.

[134] Leslie Hannah, *The Rise of the Corporate Economy*, 2nd edn (1983), 55.

Turning to Hannah's 15 companies, J. &. P. Coats was the largest and the Coats family dominated its share register.[135] J. &. P. Coats were thread manufacturers that carried out an initial public offering in 1890 and were the lead firm in a highly successful 1896 amalgamation of four family-owned thread-making firms. The Coats family collectively owned 35 per cent of the shares after the 1890 public offering and as of 1910 retained a collective 31 per cent stake.

Royal Dutch Shell, ranked second of Hannah's 15 companies, was the product of a 1907 amalgamation between the Royal Dutch Petroleum Company and the 'Shell' Transport and Trading Company Ltd, based in London. The companies remained separate but united their interests, creating a powerful Anglo-Dutch group domiciled in England under which the risks and rewards were allocated 60 per cent to Royal Dutch and 40 per cent to Shell Transport.[136] Royal Dutch and Shell Transport became holding companies, deriving their income from the operating companies they co-owned on the same 60:40 basis. Shell Transport, the UK side of the group, was a publicly traded company but up to 1919 Marcus Samuel, its founder, and his brother Sam, had full voting control due to owning a large block of ordinary shares vested with five times the voting rights of other ordinary shares (Chapter Two, Part II.A).

British American Tobacco, third on Hannah's list, and Imperial Tobacco, ranked fifth, are most conveniently considered together. Imperial Tobacco, the result of a 1901/02 amalgamation ultimately involving 17 UK-based tobacco firms, was the largest and best-known of various multi-firm horizontal mergers occurring in Britain in the late 19th and early 20th centuries.[137] Imperial Tobacco carried out a public offering of securities in 1902 to help to finance the deal, but 'in many ways the new giant was a glorified family firm'.[138] The vendor companies retained all of the ordinary shares, of which the Wills family, founders of the W.D. & H.O. Wills Ltd, the dominant firm in the merger, ended up with nearly 68 per cent. The family continued to hold 55 per cent of the shares when William Henry Wills (Lord Winterstoke of Blagdon), the founder chairman of Imperial, died in 1911.

Imperial Tobacco was formed in direct response to an attempt by James Duke's American Tobacco Company to enter and dominate the UK market for cigarettes and tobacco. In 1902, Imperial Tobacco and American Tobacco settled their differences by incorporating a UK-domiciled company, British American

[135] Dong-Woon Kim, 'From a Family Partnership to a Corporate Company: J. & P. Coats, Thread Manufacturers', (1994) 25 Textile History 185, 194–95, 197.

[136] Clapham, *supra* n. 78, 275 (Shell's domicile); Stephen Howarth, *A Century in Oil: 'Shell' Transport and Trading Company 1897–1997* (1997), 73–76.

[137] Chandler, *supra* n. 7, 404–5; Bernard W.E. Alford, 'Strategy and Structure in the UK Tobacco Industry' in Hannah, *supra* n. 18, 73, 73.

[138] Gourvish, *supra* n. 20, 25. For further background, see Henry W. Macrosty, *The Trust Movement in British Industry: A Study of Business Organisation* (1907), 230; B.W.E. Alford, *W.D. & H.O. Wills and the Development of the U.K. Tobacco Industry* (1973), 259, 263, 306, 327; Maurice Corina, *Trust in Tobacco: The Anglo-American Struggle for Power* (1975), 83, 87, 90, 124.

Tobacco (BAT), to operate outside Britain.[139] Imperial Tobacco and American Tobacco agreed not to trade in each other's domestic territory and to transfer their export and overseas trade to BAT. American Tobacco was allotted two-thirds of BAT's shares and Imperial one-third. As a result of a 1911 antitrust decree, American Tobacco's shares in BAT were distributed among American Tobacco's shareholders. Imperial Tobacco retained its one-third stake, which it increased when BAT issued new shares in 1919.

The Rio Tinto Company, ranked fourth on Hannah's list, was a British-based mining firm that enjoyed great prosperity in the late 19th and early 20th centuries developing mining properties it bought from the Spanish government in the early 1870s.[140] Hugh Matheson, the driving force behind the launch of Rio Tinto, and his financial associates effectively controlled the company until the late 1880s. Control then passed to N.M. Rothschild and Sons of London and De Rothschild Frères of Paris, with Rothschild interests owning 30 per cent of the company by 1905. The Rothschilds remained the dominant shareholders until after World War I.

Guinness, the Irish brewers, ranked sixth among Hannah's 15 companies. When the firm carried out an initial public offering in 1886, Sir Edward Guinness retained the maximum one-third stake permitted by London Stock Exchange listing rules and then quickly built up a majority stake by buying up shares on the open market (Part III). He controlled the company until his death in 1927, when his estate was assessed for probate at £13.5 million, a record at that time.[141] As late as 1952, the Guinness family owned just over 30 per cent of the company's shares.[142]

William Lever (later the first Viscount Leverhulme) was in complete control of voting power in soap manufacturers Lever Brothers Limited, the seventh largest of Hannah's 15 companies. From the time of Lever Brothers' incorporation in 1890 to Lever's death in 1925 the ordinary shares were held, in Lever's words, 'practically in one hand', namely his.[143] Though Lever Brothers carried out numerous acquisitions, payment was made by the issuance of securities other

---

[139] On events concerning BAT discussed here see Alford, *supra* n. 138, 269; Corina, *supra* n. 138, 72–73, 102, 126–29, 141.

[140] On aspects of Rio Tinto discussed here, see Charles E. Harvey, *The Rio Tinto Company: An Economic History of a Leading International Mining Concern 1873–1954* (1981), 42–46, 103, 107, 188, 219; Robert Vicat Turrell and Jean Jacques Van-Helten, 'The Investment Group: The Missing Link in British Overseas Expansion Before 1914?', (1987) 40 Economic History Review (N.S.) 267, 272; 'Rothschild Banking Company of France' http://en.wikipedia.org/wiki/De_Rothschild_Fr%C3%A8res> (last visited October 15, 2007).

[141] Dennison and MacDonagh, *supra* n. 36, 175; Wilson, *supra* n. 36, 169; Edward Guinness, 1st Earl of Iveagh, <http://en.wikipedia.org/wiki/Edward_Guinness,_1st_Earl_of_Iveagh> (last visited October 15, 2007).

[142] John Vaizey, *The Brewing Industry 1886–1951* (1960), 61.

[143] 'Company Meeting—Lever Brothers Limited', Times, January 10, 1919; see also Charles Wilson, *The History of Unilever: A Study in Economic Growth and Social Change*, vol. I (1954), 45–47, 132, 269.

than ordinary shares, meaning Lever's voting control was not diluted (Chapter Three, Part VI).

While ownership and control remained closely aligned at Lever Brothers up to 1914, matters had moved along quite a bit further with Vickers, eighth on Hannah's list.[144] In 1867 Albert and Thomas Vickers incorporated as Vickers, Sons & Co. the steel-making concern they led. As the 19th century drew to a close, Vickers expanded through acquisition into armaments and shipbuilding, most notably through the 1897 purchase of Maxim Nordenfelts, resulting in the renaming of the company as Vickers, Sons & Maxim Limited. Vickers issued securities to the public, including ordinary shares, to finance the Maxim acquisition. The increase in the share capital meant that while during the 1890s Vickers was 'almost entirely a family firm'[145] by 1898 the Vickers family held a substantial but not controlling 21 per cent block of the ordinary shares.

Vickers, Sons & Maxim increased its ordinary share capital again from £1.5 million in 1899 to £3.7 million through to 1902, partly due to acquisitions and also to meet increased business. This served to dilute further the Vickers family stake to 13 per cent by 1901. The change in share ownership was matched by adjustments in the boardroom. Thomas Vickers stepped down as chairman in 1909 and Albert Vickers, his successor, 'retained supreme gubernatorial power (but) his touch on the reins was light and designed primarily to release the talents and energies of...skilled subordinates'.[146] This all implies the separation of ownership and control had gone some distance, but the Vickers family remained first among equals. They owned 10 per cent of the ordinary shares as of 1913 and when in 1919 Vickers merged with Metropolitan Carriage (15th on Hannah's list), Thomas' son Douglas had become chairman of the company and personally owned 5 per cent of the shares.[147]

Brunner Mond & Co., ninth on Hannah's list,[148] was incorporated in 1881 to operate the business Ludwig Mond and John Brunner founded to make soda ash (sodium carbonate) using a new process developed by Ernest Solvay. Of the authorized capital of 30,000 ordinary shares, Brunner and Mond took up 12,000 shares between them, the Solvay side took up 4,500, and most of the remaining

[144] On aspects of Vickers discussed here, see J.D. Scott, *Vickers: A History* (1962), 41, 44–45; Clive Trebilcock, *The Vickers Brothers: Armaments and Enterprise 1854–1914* (1977), 28, 40, 88–89, 154–57, 163.

[145] Scott, *supra* n. 144, 41.

[146] Trebilcock, *supra* n. 144, 88–89.

[147] *Ibid.*, 163; 'The Vickers-Metro Fusion', Times, March 17, 1919 (indicating Vickers ordinary share capital was £7.4 million, meaning there were 7.4 million shares because the par value was £1); 'Vickers (Limited)', Times, March 25, 1919 (Douglas Vickers indicating he owned 350,000 shares).

[148] On aspects of Brunner Mond discussed here, see W.J. Reader, *Imperial Chemical Industries: A History, vol. I: The Forerunners 1870–1926* (1970), 55, 221, 238–40, 253–54, 371–75, 456, 463–65; Stephen E. Koss, *Sir John Brunner: Radical Plutocrat 1842–1919* (1970), 33–34, 46–47; Jean Goodman, *The Mond Legacy: A Family Saga* (1982), 44, 83.

capital was purchased by investors in Lancashire and Cheshire. Brunner Mond shares became quoted on the London Stock Exchange in 1885.

The Solvay side held much the same proportion of Brunner Mond's share capital until 1926 when the company merged with Nobel Industries, United Alkali Co. and the British Dyestuffs Corporation to form Imperial Chemical Industries Ltd. There is little direct evidence on the size of the ownership stakes held by John Brunner, Ludwig Mond and their respective families up to World War I but ownership likely remained fairly tightly concentrated. Other than the purchase of soap-maker Joseph Crosfields & Sons Ltd. in 1911 (Chapter Six, Part II.B.1), prior to World War I Brunner Mond grew primarily by way of internal expansion, meaning share ownership would not have been diluted to finance acquisitions. John Brunner, chairman of the company from 1891 until just before his death in 1919, told a 1905 shareholders' meeting he was the company's largest shareholder.[149] His successor was his son Roscoe, who also had an active managerial role.

Ludwig Mond relinquished executive responsibilities a decade or so before he died in 1909. His son Alfred Mond (later Baron Melchett of Landford) opted to disengage from the firm to focus on politics. However, the family remained influential. When Roscoe Brunner was compelled to give up the chairmanship in 1926 as a result of a messy dispute with Lever Brothers, Alfred Mond took up the post and, together with Harry Duncan Morgan (later Baron McGowan of Ardeer), managing director of Nobel Industries, orchestrated the massive merger that resulted in the formation of Imperial Chemical Industries.

Consolidated Gold Fields, 10th on Hannah's list, was launched by Cecil Rhodes, the British born South African businessman and politician, and his partner Charles Rudd. The public eagerly bought shares when Gold Fields of South Africa Ltd, a UK-domiciled company, carried out a public offering in 1887.[150] The company had a strongly personal character, with the original 400 or so shareholders essentially providing Rhodes and Rudd with working capital to exploit their mining knowledge. Rhodes and Rudd retained a significant block of shares when in 1892 Gold Fields of South Africa amalgamated with three other companies to form Consolidated Gold Fields.[151] In 1895, by which point Consolidated Gold Fields had 10,000 shareholders, Rhodes and Rudd were forced to reduce their involvement with the company after the much-publicized

---

[149] 'Brunner, Mond, and Co. (Limited)', Times, January 4, 1906.

[150] On Gold Fields, see *The Consolidated Gold Fields of South Africa, Limited, 'The Gold Fields' 1887–1937* (1937), 8–10, 13, 115; Geoffrey Wheatcroft, *The Randlords* (1985), 146–47; Paul Johnson, *Consolidated Gold Fields: A Centenary Portrait* (1987), 21–28.

[151] On the events concerning Consolidated Gold Fields discussed here, see *Consolidated Gold Fields, supra* n. 150, 35–36, 62–74, 127, 129; Johnson, *supra* n. 150, 35–36; Roy Macnab, *Gold, Their Touchstone: Gold Fields of South Africa, 1887–1987: A Centenary Story* (1987), 31–32, 51–52, 63, 66–67, 74–76, 90; Roger T. Stearn, 'Rudd, Charles Dunell (1844–1916)', *Oxford Dictionary of National Biography*, Oxford University Press, online edn, May 2006, <http://www.oxforddnb.com/view/article/65577> (accessed February 25, 2008).

failure of a raid on the Boer-run Transvaal Rhodes had helped to plan. A series of share offerings also would have diluted their ownership stake. Rhodes died in 1902 and Rudd retired from business the same year. Consolidated Gold Fields, which by 1904 had between 20,000 and 30,000 shareholders, lacked equivalent dominant personalities thereafter.

Armstrong Whitworth, ranked 11th among Hannah's 15 companies, specialized in armament manufacturing and shipbuilding. The company lacked a single authority figure equivalent to Marcus Samuel or William Lever, but it was not a model of diffuse share ownership either. W.G. Armstrong (later Lord Armstrong), the driving force behind the engineering and armaments firm W.G. Armstrong & Co., united the business in 1883 with the shipyard operation of Charles Mitchell.[152] W.G. Armstrong, Mitchell & Co. then carried out a public offering, but only 35 per cent of the shares were offered for sale to the public.[153] When Armstrong & Mitchell sought to have its shares quoted on the London Stock Exchange in 1889 without complying with the 'two-thirds' rule, the listing committee balked and in 1891 the quotation went ahead with the vendors' retained stake being one-third.[154]

Armstrong was chairman of the board until his death in 1900, but lost interest in the business in his later years and had no children to continue his legacy.[155] Andrew Noble, recruited by Armstrong to join his business in 1860, became the largest shareholder.[156] In 1900, following an 1897 merger with Whitworth & Co. that resulted in the creation of Armstrong Whitworth, Noble succeeded W.G. Armstrong as chairman, a post he held until Armstrong Whitworth merged with Vickers in 1914.[157]

Noble was reluctant to share the managerial responsibilities he accumulated. He was unable to exercise untrammelled control, however, due to the history of the Armstrong Whitworth. W.G. Armstrong, in addition to recruiting Noble, involved George, Stuart and Hamilton Rendel, sons of a good friend, in his business. Noble over time marginalized the Rendels from managerial duties, but after Armstrong's death Stuart Rendel (later Lord Rendel) was vice-chairman of the company and a major shareholder.[158] Rendel's stake provided him with

---

[152] Scott, *supra* n. 144, 30–31, 34; David Dougan, *The Great Gun-Maker: The Story of Lord Armstrong* (1970), 152–53.

[153] 'Money Market and City Intelligencer', Times, November 18, 1882.

[154] Hannah, *supra* n. 2, 415.

[155] Scott, *supra* n. 144, 34; Dougan, *supra* n. 152, 131, 168–69.

[156] P.W., 'Sir Andrew Noble', Proceedings of the Royal Society of London, Series A, Containing Papers of a Mathematical and Physical Character, August 1, 1918, i, vi.

[157] On aspects of the post-1900 history of Armstrong Whitworth discussed here, see Scott, *supra* n. 144, 46, 90–93; Dougan, *supra* n. 152, 70–71, 99, 154; Stafford M. Linsley, 'Noble, Sir Andrew, first baronet (1831–1915)', *Oxford Dictionary of National Biography*, Oxford University Press, 2004, online edn May 2006, <http://www.oxforddnb.com/view/article/35243> (accessed October 17, 2007).

[158] On Rendel's role as vice-chairman, see 'Company Meetings: Sir W.G. Armstrong, Whitworth and Co. (Limited)', Times, April 20, 1914.

a power base sufficient for him to force a deal in 1911 where new directors were added to the board and Noble ceded day-to-day managerial control.

The Burmah Oil Company, 12th on Hannah's list, was incorporated in 1886 and carried out a public offering of shares in 1889.[159] The directors, including the chairman, David Cargill, held at that point one-quarter of the outstanding equity. David's son John succeeded him as chairman of the company in 1904 at the age of 37, which implies the Cargill family and its allies had sufficient voting power to dictate boardroom structure. The easy defeat of an attempt by dissident shareholders at the 1906 annual general meeting to block the election of two board candidates the company nominated suggests likewise. Corley's otherwise thorough history of Burmah Oil does not provide direct information on the early 20th-century share ownership structure. However, since two-thirds of David Cargill's £943,000 1904 estate represented his stake in Burmah Oil Company and since the authorized ordinary share capital of Burmah Oil was £1.5 million as of 1902, the Cargill family apparently held a sizeable block of the shares as World War I approached.

Reckitt Sons Ltd, 13th on Hannah's list, grew to prominence through the manufacturing and innovative marketing of starch, washing blue (a household product used to improve the appearance of textiles) and boot and metal polish.[160] Reckitt & Sons Ltd carried out a public offering of shares in 1888 but only 2,500 of the 27,500 £10 ordinary shares were offered for sale to the public. In 1899 it was reconstructed to form a new public company with an issued share capital (ordinary and preference shares) of £1.7 million, but the company was still owned mainly by the Reckitt family. Between 1903 and 1912 Reckitt & Sons bought a number of washing blue, boot polish and metal polish firms but did so without any significant dilution of the share capital. The company did not even secure a formal listing of its shares on a stock market until 1911, when its shares began trading on the Leeds stock market.[161] This implies continued family dominance up to World War I, as does the fact that as of 1910 seven of the ten directors were members of the Reckitt family.

The sort of multi-firm merger that resulted in the creation of Imperial Tobacco was common in the textile industry, with the firms involved nearly all

---

[159] On aspects of Burmah Oil discussed here, see T.A.B. Corley, *A History of the Burmah Oil Company* (1983), 30–32, 85–86, 113; T. A. B. Corley, 'Cargill, David Sime (1826–1904)', *Oxford Dictionary of National Biography*, Oxford University Press, Sept 2004; online edn, May 2006, <http://www.oxforddnb.com/view/article/47989> (accessed October 12, 2007); W.H. Marwick, *Scotland in Modern Times: The Outline of Economic and Social Development Since the Union of 1707* (1964), 150.

[160] On events concerning Reckitt and Sons discussed here, see Basil N. Reckitt, *The History of Reckitt and Sons, Limited* (1952), 47, 54–56, 100–1; Roy Church and Christine Clark, 'Product Development of Branded Packaged Household Goods in Britain, 1870–1914: Colman's, Reckitts, and Lever Brothers' (2001) 2 Enterprise & Society 503, 506, 511–12; Roy Church, 'Reckitt, Sir James, first baronet (1833–1924)', *Oxford Dictionary of National Biography*, Oxford University Press, 2004, online edn May 2006 <http://www.oxforddnb.com/view/article/48144> (accessed October 17, 2007).

[161] Franks, Mayer and Rossi, *supra* n. 28, Table A1.

being family businesses.[162] The Fine Cotton Spinners and Doublers Association, ranked 14th among Hannah's 15 companies, was a leading example. It was the by-product of an 1898 consolidation that amalgamated 31 firms specializing in spinning high-quality cotton and supplying the makers of sewing thread and other exacting users of cotton yarn.[163] A hard-driving managing director and an 'executive board' of seven members helped to coordinate management. Generally, though, Fine Cotton Spinners operated on a decentralized basis, with the full board having nearly 30 directors, the constituent companies retaining full control over buying and selling decisions and often continuing a separate stock market listing for their preference shares or debentures.

As with many of the amalgamations of the time (Table I) the Fine Cotton Spinners consolidation was financed partly by a public offering of securities and soon after its 1898 public offering the company had between 5,000 and 6,000 shareholders.[164] By World War I this number had grown to around 30,000.[165] On the other hand, the firms acting as vendors retained a one-third stake in the ordinary shares at the time of the 1898 public offering.[166] When the company issued new shares subsequently, the equity was offered to existing shareholders on advantageous terms.[167] This implies Fine Cotton Spinners' constituent firms retained collectively a dominant block of the shares at least up to World War I. J. & P. Coats was likely among the more influential since it doubled in 1900 its existing holding so as to increase control over the supply of raw materials.[168]

Metropolitan Carriage, Wagon and Finance Company (MCWF), last of the 15 on Hannah's list, was dominated by Dudley Docker, a leading early 20th-century industrialist.[169] Docker orchestrated in 1902 the merger of five Midland rolling stock companies, culminating in the formation of MCWF, of which he became chairman of the board. Davenport-Hines' biography of Docker does not provide any details of the percentage of the company's shares he owned but indicates Docker received a 'vast sum' when Vickers, 8th on Hannah's list, bought MCWF in 1919 (Chapter Eight, Part I.H). This implies Docker qualified as a major blockholder through to World War I.

---

[162] Chandler, *Scale, supra* n. 4, 288–89; Clapham, *supra* n. 78, 227; M.A. Utton, 'Some Features of the Early Merger Movements in British Manufacturing Industry' (1972) 14 Business History 51, 53 (listing 29 multi-firm manufacturing mergers occurring between 1888 and 1912, of which 12 involved textile firms).

[163] Chandler, *Scale, supra* n. 4, 288–89; Clapham, *supra* n. 78, 227; Macrosty, *supra* n. 138, 137–41.

[164] William Ashley, *The Economic Organisation of England: An Outline History*, 3rd edn (1949), 182.

[165] Josephine Maltby, 'Showing a Strong Front: Corporate Reporting and the Business Case in Britain, 1914–1919', (2005) 32 Accounting Historians Journal 145, 161.

[166] Macrosty, *supra* n. 138, 137; 'Fine Cotton Spinners' and Doublers Association, Limited public offering advertisement', Times, May 9, 1898.

[167] See, for example, 'The Fine Spinners Cotton Growing Scheme', Times, May 6, 1911.

[168] Macrosty, *supra* n. 138, 132.

[169] On Docker's involvement with MCWF, see R.P.T. Davenport-Hines, *Dudley Docker: The Life and Times of a Trade Warrior* (1984), 24–32, 163–66. MCWF was initially christened Metropolitan Amalgamated Carriage and Wagon Company; 'Amalgamated' was soon dropped.

Drawing matters together, of the 15 British companies on Hannah's list of the world's 100 largest industrial companies as of 1912, on the eve of World War I only one (Consolidated Gold Fields) lacked any kind of significant blockholder. Two companies stand out as marginal cases, one because the family stake was around 10 per cent (Vickers) and the other because the dominant block of shares was owned collectively by numerous constituent firms (Fine Cotton Spinners). Blockholders apparently dominated share ownership in the other twelve companies, though the evidence is not definitive in some instances (Brunner, Mond, Burmah Oil and Metropolitan Carriage). Given that, due to the size of the enterprises involved, this sample of industrial companies was particularly likely to have dispersed share ownership, Hannah's claim that ownership was 'substantially divorced from control' before 1914 seems incorrect for the industrial sector.

*   *   *

Due to developments on both the sell side and the buy side, the UK's corporate economy was transformed in various ways between 1880 and 1914. The number of publicly traded companies increased significantly and trading of company shares became sufficiently well-developed for the UK to stand out in comparative terms as a country where the market for equity was highly developed. Diffusion of share ownership was also by no means unknown. Banks joined railways as companies where a separation of ownership and control had become the norm and the London Stock Exchange's two-thirds rule prompted at least some blockholders to unwind control to a greater extent than they would have preferred (e.g. Armstrong & Mitchell). Overall, though, the UK lacked an outsider/arm's-length system of ownership and control on the eve of the First World War. Chapters Eight to Ten describe how matters moved in that direction.

EIGHT

1914–1939

While the UK corporate economy was not yet characterized by a divorce of ownership and control up to 1914, factors on the sell side and the buy side provided the impetus for numerous public offerings of shares and for dispersed share ownership in various important companies. As Parts I and II of this chapter describe, there was continued momentum in favour of the diffusion of share ownership between the eve of World War I and the eve of World War II. However, as Part III indicates, the available empirical evidence suggests blockholders remained prevalent in large business enterprises as the 1930s drew to a close. Only after World War II would the transformation to outsider/arm's-length corporate governance become complete.

I. The Sell Side

A. Companies Distributing Shares to the Public

It became increasingly common during the interwar years for business enterprises to incorporate. Most remained fully private concerns, due partly to a preference for independence on the part of many owners.[1] Nevertheless, moving to the stock market was an increasingly popular option. The *Economist* observed in 1937, 'Before the war, the small industrial undertaking obtained a very large proportion of its finance without making a general appeal to the public. From choice or necessity, industrialists now deem it worth their while to turn family businesses into public companies with widely diffused shareholdings.'[2] An increase in the number of companies with securities quoted on the London Stock Exchange from 571 in 1907 to 1,712 in 1939 illustrates the growth in the number of companies with publicly traded shares.[3]

Though most business enterprises start their life with high insider ownership, between the late 18th and early 20th centuries there were in the UK various

---

[1] Derek H. Aldcroft, *The Inter-War Economy: Britain, 1919–1939* (1970), 138–39, 142.

[2] 'The Changing Capital Market', Economist, September 11, 1937, 507, 508.

[3] Julian Franks, Colin Mayer and Stefano Rossi, 'Spending Less Time with the Family: The Decline of Family Ownership in the United Kingdom' in Randall K. Morck (ed.), *A History of Corporate Governance Around the World* (2005), 581, 587–588.

newly founded businesses that carried out public offerings of shares immediately (Chapter Three, Part I). Firms that adopted this approach during the interwar years were typically a wash out. During a stock market boom in 1928, 109 of 277 initial public offerings on the London Stock Exchange were carried out by new or virtually new enterprises. Their performance was dismal, as their collective market valuation declined by 83 per cent by 1931. The market valuation of the most important single grouping—gramophone and radio companies—fell by 99 per cent.[4]

B. Diversification

Interwar blockholders had various incentives to sell out, at least partially, or otherwise accept dilution of their stake. One was a desire to diversify, financed by taking cash out of their businesses.[5] According to a 1935 study of public offerings '[C]areful investigation of new issues reveals that often they are a mere financial operation initiated not by the industrialist in need of fresh capital, but by the financier who tempts the industrialist to capitalise his business...' The study, after noting that a vendor would commonly retain control through shares and directorships, indicated that 'at the same time he has cashed in his profit and has money in the bank'.[6] The study made the point by reporting that among a sample of 29 industrial concerns that carried out initial public offerings in 1928, £7.5 million of the newly subscribed capital of £9.85 million was paid in cash to the vendors, leaving very little for fresh investment after relevant fees and expenses were accounted for.[7] Though the sample is small, it chimes with Grant's assessment of the interwar capital market, as he said, '[T]he Stock Exchange is primarily an institution for imparting marketability to securities; only very secondarily is it an institution for providing new money for enterprise.'[8]

C. Company Law

Although risk-spreading provides an incentive for blockholders to unwind their holdings, they can find it worthwhile to keep most of their eggs in one basket if there are substantial private benefits of control to extract. According to the 'law matters' thesis corporate law can foster blockholder exit by circumscribing

---

[4] R.A. Harris, 'A Re-Analysis of the 1928 New Issue Boom', (1933) 43 Economic Journal 453, 457–58.

[5] Barnard Ellinger, *The City: The London Financial Markets* (1940), 314; Leslie Hannah, *The Rise of the Corporate Economy*, 2nd edn (1983), 57.

[6] A Group of Cambridge Economists, 'Recent Capital Issues' in G.D.H. Cole (ed.), *Studies in Capital and Investment* (1935), 103, 134–35.

[7] *Ibid.*, 136.

[8] A.T.K. Grant, *A Study of the Capital Market in Britain From 1919–1936* (1967), 128.

exploitation of outside investors (Chapter Two, Part II.B). During the interwar years, however, company law would have done little on this front.

Despite amendments taking effect in 1900 and 1908, up to 1914 UK companies legislation placed few constraints on those in a position to control companies (Chapter Six, Part III.B.2). During the interwar years, the only major changes to the legislative framework were introduced by the Companies Act 1929.[9] The 1929 amendments were strongly influenced by recommendations in a 1926 report of a committee struck by the Board of Trade to evaluate company law reform. The underlying philosophy of the committee was that the system of company law was generally working well and that 'the careless speculator' could not expect protection when that would involve 'unwarranted interference with the ordinary honest person'.[10] Given the *status quo* bias, not surprisingly the 1929 Act did not introduce wholesale changes.[11]

The Companies Act 1929 toughened somewhat prospectus disclosure rules, imposed some new periodic disclosure requirements on companies, stipulated directors could be fined if they failed to disclose at a board meeting personal interests in corporate contracts and precluded companies from including provisions in the corporate constitution purporting to excuse directors from liability for a breach of duty.[12] However, the Act continued to leave regulation of transactions between companies and their directors primarily to each company's articles of association, imposed no direct restrictions on insider dealing and offered no procedural assistance to a minority shareholder seeking to enforce breaches of duty by directors.[13] Interwar company law therefore likely did little to erode private benefits of control and create momentum in favour of exit by blockholders.

D. Dividends

While changes to company law probably did little to prompt blockholder exit during the interwar years, pressure to distribute profits as dividends likely did so. Those running interwar public companies, seeking to sustain the liquidity of the shares and to preserve the option to return to capital markets to finance mergers and internal expansion, used dividends as a key means to keep investors

[9] The new provisions were set out in the Companies Act 1928, 18 & 19 Geo. 5, c. 45, which were then embodied in the Companies Act 1929, 19 & 20 Geo. 5, c. 23, and became fully operative in November 1929: Horace B. Samuel, *Shareholders' Money: An Analysis of Certain Defects in Company Legislation with Proposals for Their Reform* (1933), 3.

[10] Samuel, *supra* n. 9, 2, 9–10; A. Wilfred May, 'Financial Regulation Abroad: The Contrasts with American Technique', (1939) 47 Journal of Political Economy 457, 469; Paul Bircher, *From the Companies Act of 1929 to the Companies Act of 1948: A Study in the Law and Practice of Accounting* (1991), 75.

[11] 'The Companies Bill, 1927', Economist, April 23, 1927, 840, discussing the bill that became the Companies Act 1928.

[12] Pt II.B.2; Companies Act 1929, ss.149, 152.

[13] Samuel, *supra* n. 9, 150, 160–70.

onside. The cash payouts would have reduced the private benefits of control available to skim and thus would have created an incentive to exit (Chapter Three, Part IX).

The *Economist*'s June 1934 list of London active security prices, encompassing companies falling into the banking, insurance, shipping, electricity supply and 'miscellaneous' (typically manufacturing) sectors, illustrates companies were under an onus to pay dividends. Of 183 companies on the list, 141 were paying dividends on their ordinary shares.[14] The non-payers were restricted largely to iron and steel, textiles and shipping, all sectors that were under considerable economic strain during the interwar years,[15] and automobile manufacturing, where leading companies struggled to generate profits consistently.[16]

In addition to paying dividends, the payouts UK companies made were typically generous, at least in relation to the profits generated. Banks and insurance companies acquired a reputation for a conservative dividend policy.[17] Most publicly traded companies, however, paid out a large proportion of their reported profits to shareholders. According to data Thomas compiled from the *Economist* for the years between 1919 and 1938, quoted companies (banks and railways excluded) distributed on average 75 per cent of 'net profits' (i.e. after deduction of debenture interest and preference share dividends) as dividends.[18] This figure never fell below 58 per cent and even exceeded 100 per cent in 1921 (Figure I). Since interwar companies commonly shifted profits to 'reserves' in their accounts as insurance against a 'rainy day' (Part II.B.2), these figures likely exaggerate to some degree the proportion of earnings distributed to shareholders. Nevertheless, dividend payments should have been generous enough to erode significantly the 'free cash flow' from which blockholders might otherwise have extracted private benefits of control, thus creating an incentive to exit.

A striking interwar illustration of the pressure companies were under to distribute dividends involved the Royal Mail Steam Packet Company, the centrepiece of the shipping group Lord Kylsant controlled.[19] Royal Mail suffered trading losses

---

[14] 'London Active Security Prices and Yields', Economist, June 23, 1934, 1392. Companies on the list that were clearly foreign-based (e.g. South African Breweries and United States Steel) were excluded in making these calculations.

[15] Sean Glynn and John Oxborrow, *Interwar Britain: A Social and Economic History* (1976), 96–97, 99–100, 104–6.

[16] P.E. Hart, *Studies in Profit, Business Saving and Investment in the United Kingdom, 1920–1962*, vol. I (1965), 81–82; Wayne Lewchuk, 'The Return to Capital in the British Motor Vehicle Industry', (1985) 27 Business History 3, 18.

[17] H.E. Raynes, 'The Place of Ordinary Stocks and Shares (as Distinct From Fixed Interest Bearing Securities) in the Investment of Life Assurance Funds', (1928) 59 Journal of the Institute of Actuaries 21, 29.

[18] On the data, see W.A. Thomas, *The Finance of British Industry 1918–1976* (1978), 88; 'British Industrial Profits: A Survey of Three Decades', Economist, December 17, 1938, 597. On how dividends could exceed profits in 1921 see Thomas, *op. cit.*, 94.

[19] See Pt II.B.2; P.N. Davies and A.M. Bourn, 'Lord Kylsant and the Royal Mail', (1976) 14 Business History 103, 113–17; Edwin Green and Michael Moss, *A Business of National Importance: The Royal Mail Shipping Group 1902–1937* (1982), 65, 71–73; R.K. Ashton, 'The Royal Mail

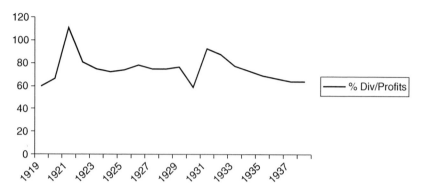

Figure I: Per cent of net profits distributed as dividends by quoted UK industrial companies, 1919–38

Source: Derived from Thomas, *supra* n. 18, 89, Table 4.2.

during most years in the 1920s but finessed its accounts in order to declare profits annually. Lord Kylsant deemed it imperative to retain the confidence of share-holders and debenture-holders through this down cycle, particularly in 1926 and 1927 as the company struggled to cope with the acquisition of White Star, a major rival. His chosen technique was to ensure the company paid dividends on its ordinary shares, combined with modest writing down of the value of Royal Mail's financial assets in its accounts to give the impression of financial recti-tude. The combination worked, at least in the short term, with a leading shipping journal saying in 1927, '[S]tockholders can regard the outlook with confidence in the ability of the Royal Mail Steam Packet Co. to develop their vast shipping undertaking on sound and progressive lines.'[20] The turnaround Lord Kylsant had been hoping for failed to materialize, and his shipping empire collapsed in 1930. Less brazen blockholders may well have treated the pressure to pay dividends as a cue to exit rather than to move to the outer bounds of financial propriety in the manner he did.

E. Erosion of Corporate Profits by Taxation, Recession and Competition

During World War I, companies supplying goods and services to the armed forces (e.g. armaments firms and shipping lines) stood to benefit considerably

Case: A Legal Analysis' (1986) 22 Abacus 3, 13. On the ownership structure of Royal Mail, see Edwin Green, 'Very Private Enterprise: Ownership and Finance in British Shipping, 1825–1940' in Tsunehiko Yui and Keiichiro Nakagawa (eds), *Business History of Shipping: The International Conference on Business History II: Proceedings of the Fuji Conference* (1995), 219, 237–39.

[20] Shipbuilding and Shipping Record, May 19, 1927, 572, quoted in Green and Moss, *supra* n. 19, 72.

from wartime conditions.[21] To preclude 'profiteering' and to help to finance the war effort, between 1915 and 1921 the UK government imposed on all trading concerns an Excess Profits Duty (EPD) on profits above a prescribed pre-war standard, with the rates ranging from a low of 40 per cent in 1918 and 1919 to a high of 80 per cent in 1917. This lucrative tax (it accounted for 25 per cent of the UK government's tax revenue while it was in place) prompted considerable criticism from the business community, which implies it had a significant impact on the 'bottom line'.[22] Arnold's study of archival records of 30 quoted industrial companies covering between 1910 and 1924 confirms the point, showing that while the pre-tax return on equity was significantly higher between 1915 and 1920 than it was between 1910 and 1914, once tax was taken into account, the after-inflation return on equity was lower.[23]

The pressure businesses and their blockholders faced continued in the immediate aftermath of World War I. The abolition of the EPD coincided with the introduction of the Corporation Profits Tax (CPT), a flat 5 per cent levy on all corporate profits.[24] The CPT's launch in 1921 occurred as Britain experienced a severe recession.[25] Due to corporate profits lagging badly, numerous companies contesting their tax bills and difficulties collecting arrears, the tax failed to generate the revenue anticipated.[26] The CPT was repealed in 1924, but the combination of tax and adverse business conditions over the previous decade likely would have prompted numerous blockholders to contemplate exit.

After the CPT was repealed, the UK lacked a tax specifically targeting corporate profits until the eve of World War II (Chapter Nine, Part III.B). Britain also avoided a downturn as deep as that afflicting the country in 1921, experiencing instead a moderate slowdown in 1926, a slump between 1929 and 1932 that was mild in comparison with the depression afflicting other major industrialized countries and a modest recession in 1937–38.[27] Nevertheless, due to large variations in performance across the economy, in particular industries there was acute pressure on firms and, by extension, blockholders.[28] Chemicals, mechanical engineering and steel making were 'slow growth' sectors where

---

[21] Josephine Maltby, 'Showing a Strong Front: Corporate Reporting and the 'Business Case' in Britain, 1914–1919', (2005) 32 Accounting Historians Journal 145, 155–57.

[22] *Ibid.*, 160 (business criticism); J.R. Hicks, U.K. Hicks & L. Rostas, *The Taxation of War Wealth* (1941), 71 (EPT revenue).

[23] A.J. Arnold, 'Profitability and Capital Accumulation in British Industry During the Transwar Period, 1913–1924', (1999) 52 Economic History Review 45.

[24] R.S. Tucker, 'The British Finance Act, 1920', (1920) 35 Quarterly Journal of Economics 167, 170.

[25] On the recession, see Aldcroft, *supra* n. 1, 37.

[26] M.J. Daunton, 'How to Pay for the War: State, Society and Taxation in Britain, 1917–24', (1996) 111 English Historical Review 882, 914; Ursula K. Hicks, *The Finance of British Government 1920–1936* (1938), 238–39.

[27] Aldcroft, *supra* n. 1, 37–45; Glynn and Oxborrow, *supra* n. 15, 90–91; Peter Dewey, *War and Progress: Britain 1914–1945* (1996), 142, 200–1.

[28] Glynn and Oxborrow, *supra* n. 15, 96–100; Dewey, *supra* n. 27, 86–94, 96–99.

declining exports and foreign competition posed potentially serious problems for vulnerable companies. Textiles, coal and shipbuilding were even more troubled, with the problems compounded because each industry was too fragmented for producers to reduce excess capacity when demand declined. In 1929 the *Times* characterized the situation in the cotton industry and other industries similarly afflicted 'as containing a large number of comparatively small and independent units (that) have been forced in the scramble for orders to indulge in an inter-necine form of uneconomic competition which has forced prices in many cases far below a remunerative level, and, by dispersing production instead of concen-trating it on efficient units, has vastly increased costs'.[29]

Anti-competitive arrangements were a common response to excess capacity and related difficulties within particular industries, with practices ranging from 'gentlemen's agreements' to selling agencies and formal trade associations.[30] When British trading policy became overtly protectionist during the early 1930s, the sheltered economic regime made it easier for industrial firms to estab-lish collusive alliances.[31] Such practices, which were unconstrained by statutory regulation during the interwar years, would have offered some relief for com-panies facing competitive pressures and thus made it easier for individualisti-cally minded proprietors to retain control of their businesses going forward.[32] However, combinations in restraint of trade were often hit-and-miss affairs since parties were constantly tempted to cheat or defect so as to maximize their own advantage.[33] As a result, competitive pressures likely created at least some momentum in favour of blockholder exit in numerous industries during the interwar period.

F. Other Taxes

On the tax front, aspects of income tax and estate tax combined with taxation of profits to provide interwar blockholders with incentives to exit. From 1909 to 1973 UK income tax had two elements—taxation on income set at the 'standard rate'

[29] 'Success at Last', Times, January 25, 1929.

[30] On potential methods, see Patrick Fitzgerald, *Industrial Combination in England* (1927), 3–7. On the prevalence of anti-competitive arrangements, see G.C. Allen, *British Industry* (1944), 20–1; J.G. Walshe, 'Industrial Organization and Competition Policy' in N.F.R. Crafts and N.W.C. Woodward (eds), *The British Economy Since 1945* (1991), 335, 338, 342, 361.

[31] John F. Wilson, *British Business History, 1720–1994* (1995), 155.

[32] 'Problems of Rationalisation', (1930) 40 Economic Journal 351, 365 (remarks of Prof. P.S. Florence); David C. Mowery, 'Firm Structure, Government Policy, and the Organization of Industrial Research: Great Britain and the United States, 1900–1950', (1984) 58 Business History Review 504, 517; Leslie Hannah, 'Introduction: Business Development and Economic Structure in Britain since 1880' in Leslie Hannah (ed.), *Management Strategy and Business Development: An Historical and Comparative Study* (1976), 1, 12–13.

[33] Aldcroft, *supra* n. 1, 143; Glynn and Oxborrow, *supra* n. 15, 112; Fitzgerald, *supra* n. 30, 3, 5–7.

and 'supertax', generally known as 'surtax'.[34] Surtax was imposed on taxpayers with incomes exceeding a prescribed level and was levied on a rising scale on successive slices of income above that level. The financial demands of World War I prompted the government to boost the standard rate and surtax sharply, meaning the top rate of tax rose from 8.3 per cent on an income of £5,000 or more in 1913 (£338,100 in 2006 currency) to 52.5 per cent on an income of over £10,000 in 1918 (£334,800).[35]

The end of World War I did not yield significant tax relief for the wealthy. Instead, the Conservative government of the time opted to leave the very rich 'stranded' (Chapter Three, Part X). Labour, during a short spell in office between 1929 and 1931, tightened the screws further, resulting in the taxation of income between £15,000 and £20,000 at a rate of 52.5 per cent and income above £50,000 at 60 per cent.[36] Income tax rates were increased yet again in the late 1930s to finance rearmament, so that in 1938 tax payable on income above £6,000 (£255,000 in 2006 currency) was 50 per cent and the top marginal tax rate, applicable to income greater than £50,000, was 72.5 per cent.[37]

During the interwar years corporate earnings distributed to shareholders in the form of dividends were taxed with both the standard rate and surtax elements built in while undistributed profits were taxed in a company's hands on behalf of shareholders at the standard rate.[38] This meant there was a tax bias in favour of retained earnings and to address the discrepancy the government introduced corrective measures that created incentives for private companies to obtain a stock exchange listing, a stepping stone to ownership dispersion. Beginning in 1922, tax officials were empowered to direct a company failing to distribute 'reasonable' dividends to pay the tax the shareholders would have had to pay as surtax or income tax if such dividends had been paid.[39] Tax legislation exempted a company from such an order if its shares were regularly traded on a stock exchange and the public had a substantial interest, defined from 1927 onwards as a publicly held voting stake of 25 per cent or more (increased to 35 per cent in 1965).[40]

[34] For a nutshell history of 'super tax', see Mervyn Lewis, *British Tax Law—Income Tax: Corporation Tax, Capital Gains Tax* (1977), 14.

[35] Martin Daunton, *Just Taxes: The Politics of Taxation in Britain, 1914–1979* (2002), 47 (Table 2.5).

[36] Derived from Hicks, *supra* n. 26, 234, 246; 'Proposed Changes in Taxation', Times, April 15, 1930.

[37] Extrapolated from 'War Budget/Proposed Changes in Taxation', Times, September 28, 1939.

[38] A. Wilfred May, 'American and European Valuation of Equity Capital: A Comparison', (1939) 29 American Economic Review 734, 736; Steven A. Bank, 'The Dividend Divide in Anglo-American Corporate Taxation', (2004) 30 Journal of Corporation Law 1, 30–31 (discussing Income Tax Act of 1918, 8 & 9 Geo., c. 40, General Rule 20).

[39] Finance Act 1922, 12 & 13 Geo. 5, c. 17, s. 21.

[40] Finance Act 1927, 17 & 18 Geo. 5, c. 10, s. 31; Finance Act 1965, c. 25 sch. 18, para. 1(3) (35 per cent requirement).

Developments concerning William Morris (later Lord Nuffield), founder of Morris Motors, a major interwar auto manufacturer, illustrate that this tax regime could prompt the unwinding of control. Morris Motors became a publicly traded company in 1926, but Morris retained all of the ordinary shares, reflecting the fact that 'what he prized above most things in business was the freedom to do as he liked and to risk only his own money'.[41] Morris had a strict policy of retaining profits so as to grow the business and through the mid-1920s the ratio of distributed to retained profits was 0.06 per cent.[42] Tax officials sought a 'surtax direction' for 'unreasonably' withheld profits against Morris Motors for the tax years 1922 and 1923, and again for 1927 and 1928.[43] Though counsel for Morris Motors successfully opposed both efforts, Morris became convinced that it would soon be impossible for him to continue his policy of keeping back profits if he continued to own all of the shares in Morris Motors and decided to begin placing his equity on the market. He started to implement his plan in 1936, retaining at that point three-quarters of the ordinary shares.[44] By 1951, just prior to a merger with Austin Motor Co. that resulted in the formation of the British Motor Corporation, he had wound down his personal stake to 18.8 per cent.[45]

The structure of estate tax also provided owners of family businesses with an incentive to move to the stock market. From 1930 until 1975, if a company had equity traded on a recognized stock market and there were regular dealings in the shares, for estate tax purposes its shares were valued by reference to the stock market price during the year prior to death.[46] Otherwise, the shares were valued by estimating a company's net assets and allocating a fraction of this amount to the estate in accordance with the percentage of shares the deceased owned at the time of death.

In companies with a dominant shareholder, valuation by the stock market was most often advantageous to the estate.[47] Since an asset-based valuation was conducted on the basis that all shares were equivalent and the share price would typically have incorporated a minority discount due to a major block of shares not being 'in play', all else being equal the share price would have been lower.[48]

---

[41] P.W.S. Andrews and Elizabeth Brunner, *The Life of Lord Nuffield: A Study in Enterprise and Benevolence* (1955), 174.

[42] Calculated for the years 1922 to 1927 from *ibid.*, 341.

[43] On these cases, see *ibid.*, Pt III, Ch. IX.

[44] *Ibid.*, Pt IV, Ch. IV; <http://www.austin-rover.co.uk/index.htm?morrisf.htm> (last visited Dec. 4, 2007).

[45] Roy Church, *The Rise and Decline of the British Motor Industry* (1994), 31–33; P. Sargant Florence, *Ownership, Control and Success of Large Companies: An Analysis of English Industrial Structure and Policy 1936–1951* (1961), 211.

[46] Finance Act 1930, 20 & 21 Geo. 5, c. 28, s. 37; Finance Act 1940, 3 & 4 Geo. 6, c. 29, s. 55(4); John Coombes, *Capital Transfer Tax* (1977), 52 (discussing the 1975 change).

[47] Alex Rubner, *The Ensnared Shareholder* (1966), 125.

[48] 'Shell Kernels', Economist, March 15, 1958, 957; T.A. Hamilton Baynes, *Share Valuations* (1966), 64–65, 115 (noting that an assets value measure did not take into account explicitly the size of the shareholding involved).

Also, while the share price of a publicly traded company would have been determined in an unbiased fashion by the sources of supply and demand, net asset valuations were made by tax officials typically lacking experience in assessing the market value of shares and facing the temptation to do well for the government by ascribing a high price to equity for death duty purposes.[49] Thus, beginning in 1930 owners of large, successful private firms had an incentive to secure a stock market listing and subsequently ensure, most obviously by adopting a reasonable dividend policy, investing in the company was sufficiently attractive to ensure regular trading activity occurred.[50]

G. Generational Considerations

Tax and financial conditions aside, generational considerations can provide an incentive for the unwinding of control (Chapter Three, Part IV), and there were examples of this occurring in the interwar years. The fact Lord Nuffield had no children to pass Morris Motors along to combined with his tax situation to induce him to unwind control.[51] Events occurring at two of Britain's 15 largest industrial companies as of 1912 also illustrate the importance of generational transitions. At Lever Brothers, seventh largest industrial company in Britain at the eve of World War I, Viscount Leverhulme (i.e. William Lever) retained total control of the ordinary shares until his death in 1925 (Chapter Seven, Part IX). Leverhulme had groomed his son, William Hulme Lever, as his successor, but the junior Lever realized the company would fare better if accountant Francis D'Arcy Cooper took over as managing director. According to Wilson, 'The change was to condition the entire future of the company. It signified nothing less than the complete metamorphosis of Lever Brothers from a private empire owned and controlled by one man into a public company administered by a professional management.'[52] In 1929, the business was transformed further by a merger with Dutch margarine producer Margarine Unie, resulting in the establishment of the Anglo-Dutch consumer products giant Unilever.[53]

At J. & P. Coats, the textile maker that was Britain's largest industrial company on the eve of World War I (Chapter Six, Part I), the third generation of the Coats family was eligible to move to the forefront in the opening decades of the

---

[49] 'Family Businesses' (Letter), Times, January 3, 1953.

[50] Brian R. Cheffins, 'Dividends as a Substitute for Corporate Law: The Separation of Ownership and Control in the United Kingdom', (2006) 63 Washington & Lee Law Review 1273, 1317.

[51] Nuffield donated much of his wealth to charity: Andrews and Brunner, *supra* n. 41, Pt V. On the lack of children see <http://en.wikipedia.org/wiki/William_Morris,_1st_Viscount_Nuffield> (last visited Dec. 4, 2007).

[52] Charles Wilson, 'Management and Policy in Large-Scale Enterprise: Lever Brothers and Unilever, 1918–1938' in Barry Supple (ed.), *Essays in British Business History* (1977), 124, 133.

[53] Charles Wilson, *The History of Unilever: A Study in Economic Growth and Social Change*, vol. II (1954), 306–8.

20th century. None of the third generation in fact took up a senior managerial post, preferring instead to focus on their estates, sports and public activities. By 1929 non-family members outnumbered Coats family members on the board and the board had a non-family chairman.[54] The Coats apparently were far from unique. Balogh attributes the growing popularity of public offerings of shares in the interwar years largely 'to the change in the social status and ambitions of the former owning families'.[55]

H. Favourable Exit Terms

While blockholders are often prompted to consider exit due to downsides such as the lack of a suitable heir and erosion of profit margins, there can also be situations where good news can have the same effect, namely where generous terms are on offer (Chapter III, Part VII). Sometimes canny negotiation skills can put a block-holder in this position. This was the case with Dudley Docker, chairman and the dominant personality behind the Metropolitan Carriage, Wagon and Finance Company (MCWF), Britain's 15th largest industrial company as of 1912.[56] By 1918 Docker was anxious to give up executive responsibilities with MCWF due to poor health. Vickers, the armament and shipbuilding company that had just worked together with Docker to buy British Westinghouse (soon renamed the Metropolitan-Vickers Electrical Company) emerged as the potential buyers.

Vickers, which was run by a self-assured board and stood to benefit by diversifying to counteract an anticipated drop in demand for munitions at the end of the First World War, was eager to proceed. Docker relied on Vickers' enthusiasm to secure a generous deal, even putting pressure on by threatening to abandon negotiations. Vickers ended up paying nearly £14 million for MCWF in the form of Vickers' ordinary and preference shares, implying a premium of about 400 per cent on the par value of MCWF's ordinary shares and exceeding by almost £3 million Vickers' finance director's estimate of MCWF's value. A Vickers insider said subsequently that the board 'had been dazzled by Docker's ability, high-level salesmanship, vision and reputation into paying more for the shares than they should have done'. The deal was a winner for Docker as it meant he 'personally received a vast sum of money in preference shares which were almost as good as cash to him. Docker's personal profit from the deal must have been enormous'.[57]

[54] Dong-Woon Kim, 'From a Family Partnership to a Corporate Company: J. & P. Coats, Thread Manufacturers', (1994) 25 Textile History 185, 206, 208.

[55] T. Balogh, *Studies in Financial Organization* (1947), 275.

[56] Ch. Seven, Pt IX; R.P.T. Davenport-Hines, *Dudley Docker: The Life and Times of a Trade Warrior* (1984), 157–66; see also 'Vickers Limited', 'Metropolitan Carriage, Wagon and Finance Company (Limited)', Times, March 25, 1919, 22.

[57] Davenport-Hines, *supra* n. 56, 165 (quoting Terrence Maxwell, director of Vickers, 1934–75).

Share prices inflated by market sentiment can also induce blockholders to exit (Chapter Three, Part VII). Conditions were ideal for this to occur at the end of the First World War, as an economic and financial boom seemed on the cards.[58] Domestically, there was pent-up demand for consumer goods the supply of which had been restricted during the conflict. Exports seemed destined to flourish as wartime restrictions on trade were dropped. Businesses were due to splash out to compensate for wartime disinvestment. The public and banks had accumulated during the war a massive amount of capital in the form of short-term government bonds, cash and bank deposits that could be deployed for investment elsewhere.

The anticipated 'Peace boom' got under way at the beginning of 1919 and ended in mid-1920 as exports fell, interest rates rose and the government cut spending.[59] Before the downturn, investors seeking to benefit from the anticipated profits the economic boom would generate eagerly bought shares.[60] Frantic buying and selling of industrial concerns at highly inflated prices duly followed, matched by numerous public offerings of shares.[61] Perhaps most dramatically, firms responsible for 42 per cent of cotton spinning capacity changed hands at an estimated seven times pre-World War I values, financed largely by the proceeds of new share capital.[62]

For proprietors of industrial concerns, the stock market boom provided a golden opportunity to cash out at premium prices. The *Economist* said of cotton spinning mills at the end of 1919, 'The transfer of these undertakings from their present owners is being arranged only, to put it mildly, at very full values.'[63] The 1920 acquisition of Horrockses, Crewdson & Co., a major cotton spinning and manufacturing concern, by the Amalgamated Cotton Mill Trust (AMCT) illustrates the point. AMCT bought nine cotton spinning firms between 1918 and 1920 and S.B. Joel, the London financier who was the prime mover behind AMCT, justified the acquisition spree on the basis of 'Isn't it better that we should take them over, than that a lot of old fogeys should have charge of them?' Macrosty drew upon this remark to say of AMCT's purchase of Horrockses, Crewdson, '(T)he original capital of Horrockses' was £1,218,000, and the purchase price was reported to be "not less than £5,000,000," so that the "old fogeys" did not do badly out of the smart Londoner.'[64] Improving matters further, most

---

[58] Aldcroft, *supra* n. 1, 31.

[59] *Ibid.*, 36.   [60] Grant, *supra* n. 8, 137.

[61] W.R. Garside, 'Declining Advantage: The British Economy' in Keith Robbins (ed.), *The British Isles 1901–1951* (2002), 163, 175.

[62] Henry W. Macrosty, 'Inflation and Deflation in the United States and the United Kingdom, 1919–23', (1927) 90 Journal of the Royal Statistical Society 45, 71; Derek H. Aldcroft, *The British Economy, Volume 1: The Years of Turmoil, 1920–1951* (1986), 4.

[63] 'Industrial Issues', Economist, December 6, 1919, 1029.

[64] Macrosty, *supra* n. 62, 71. For additional background, see 'The Horrockses Deal', Times, December 2, 1919; 'Death of Sir Frank Hollins', Times, January 28, 1924; R. Robson, *The Cotton Industry in Britain* (1957), 157.

of the directors of Horrockses, Crewdson kept their jobs after the amalgamation, and the chairman became a director of AMCT.

Tax also put some blockholders in a situation where prices on offer would have been sufficiently attractive to justify exit. For those with high incomes tax, taxes on income began to 'bite' from World War I onwards (Part I.F). Those owning major blocks of shares in larger companies typically would have felt the full effects of the change in policy because their sizeable dividend payments and managerial salary (if any) likely would have put them in or near the top income tax bracket. In contrast, as blockholders were no doubt aware, profits derived from a sale of shares, whether unwound via the stock market or in a 'once and for all' disposition in a merger, were tax-free since capital gains remained untaxed through to the 1960s.[65] The tax bias in favour of exit would have been particularly potent for prosperous companies because of the opportunity to 'lock in' the upside tax free rather than continue to pay tax on dividends and managerial income while running the risk of losing the tax windfall due to a reversal of fortunes.

The tax advantages of exit would have been greatly neutralized if former blockholders simply invested the proceeds of sale in assets that generated fully taxable investment income (e.g. shares in UK-based companies). In fact, various tax-friendly options were available. Life insurance-based savings schemes offered potentially significant tax advantages (Chapter Ten, Part III). There also were 'tax-saving' securities issued before World War I at low interest rates but ultimately redeemable on generous terms, thus generating little taxable income but creating scope for sizeable capital gains.[66]

Another option was to purchase as investments durable assets that yielded no annual income, such as antiques, works of art and land with building potential.[67] The absence of income meant fluctuations in the market value of such assets were often capricious but the decision to invest could be worthwhile, particularly if the assets were of aesthetic value.[68] Finally, while British residents were generally taxable for investment income arising overseas, until 1936 assets held on behalf of a UK resident by a foreign company that were not subject to British income tax in the hands of non-residents did not generate tax liabilities for the UK taxpayer until the company was wound up.[69] The upshot is that for interwar blockholders

---

[65] On the tax position, see Hannah, *supra* n. 5, 58; Raymond Frost, 'The Macmillan Gap', (1954) 6 Oxford Economic Papers (N.S.) 181, 184; Ch. Ten, Pt I.D. On interwar awareness of the situation, see 'Taxation and Speculation', Economist, December 27, 1919, 1187; F.W.H. Caudwell, *A Practical Guide to Investment* (1930), 9.

[66] E.D. Kissan and L.D. Williams, *Investment in Stocks and Shares* (1933), 80.

[67] J.A. Kay and M.A. King, *The British Tax System* (1978), 51, 55; Kenneth Midgley and Ronald G. Burns, *Business Finance and the Capital Market*, 3rd edn (1979), 432.

[68] Oliver Stanley, 'Introduction' in Oliver Stanley (ed.), *The Creation and Protection of Capital* (1974), 1, 8.

[69] Finance Act 1936, 26 Geo. 5 & 1 Edw. 8, c. 34, s. 18; Leonard Stein and Herbert H. Marks, *Tax Avoidance: An Interpretation of the Provisions of the Finance Act, 1936* (1936), 2–4.

the combination of untaxed capital gains and significant increases in income tax meant exit was a considerably more attractive proposition in after-tax terms than it was prior to World War I.

I. Financing Mergers and the Growth of the Company

Mergers can foster the dispersion of ownership and control either when a target company with a blockholder is bought by a widely held firm or the manner in which the transaction is structured causes the ownership structure of a participating company to unwind (Chapter Three, Part VI). Brunner Mond, a leading chemical manufacturer during the opening decades of the 20th century, provides an interwar example of the latter scenario.[70] The Brunner, Mond and Solvay families each were major players in the firm. Alfred Mond (later Baron Melchett of Landford) did much to orchestrate the 1926 merger between his firm, Nobel Industries, United Alkali Co. and the British Dyestuffs Corporation that resulted in the formation of Imperial Chemical Industries Ltd (ICI). Since the transaction was carried out by way of a share-for-share exchange, with shareholders in each of the constituent companies exchanging their equity for shares in ICI, the Brunner, Mond and Solvay families were destined to have a significantly smaller stake in ICI than they had in Brunner Mond.[71] Nevertheless, the board of Brunner Mond, together with the boards of the other companies, urged shareholders to accept the deal, saying, 'We feel confident that such an exchange will be beneficial to them, that they will secure, from the wide scope of the new Company's operations, an effective insurance against the fluctuations of prices or trade to which every individual company is subject, and that they will thereby be enabled to participate in the growing trade of the Chemical Industry and the profits of its future developments.'[72]

Events concerning the Bowater paper wholesaling and manufacturing business also illustrate how a merger could prompt at least the partial unwinding of share blocks.[73] In 1927 Eric Bowater, grandson of the founder of the business, became chairman and managing director of W.V. Bowater & Sons as it became a publicly traded company. Bowater's policy when carrying out acquisitions was generally to compensate vendors using debentures, meaning share ownership would remain undiluted. However, to buy Edward Lloyd Ltd, at that point the largest newsprint business in the UK, Bowater made in 1936 a large issuance of ordinary shares, in combination with sizeable offerings of preference shares. The partial unwinding of control was worth it to the Bowater family, as the rechristened

---

[70] For background, see Ch. Seven, Pt IX.
[71] As of 1941, Solvay Et Cie was the largest shareholder in ICI, with a stake of 5¼ per cent: Hargreaves Parkinson, *Ownership of Industry* (1951), 33–34.
[72] 'Imperial Chemical Industries Limited' (advertisement), Times, December 16, 1929.
[73] W.J. Reader, *Bowater: A History* (1981), 60, 82, 117–19.

Bowater-Lloyd Group controlled 60 per cent of the British newsprint market and Bowater interests remained dominant.[74]

Companies can issue shares to raise capital for 'internal' investment as well as to carry out mergers. In the UK, however, organically generated expansion and the refurbishing of existing operations has typically been financed by retained earnings (Chapter Three, Part VI). This remained the case during the interwar years, with a 1932 study estimating that four-fifths of new capital put into industry came from undistributed profits.[75] The balance between internal and external finance in fact became a topic of some controversy, with smaller and medium-sized firms needing cash to modernize or expand to remain competitive being hard hit due to a contraction of locally based risk capital and reluctance on the part of conservatively run deposit-taking banks to provide desired funding. The pattern was christened the 'Macmillan Gap' after discussion of it in the 1931 report of the Committee of Enquiry into Banking, Finance and Credit, chaired by Lord Macmillan.[76]

Few 'Macmillan Gap' companies could feasibly issue shares to the public to finance expansion. Advertising expenses, fees payable to advisers and charges for underwriting were disproportionately large for modest public offerings and thus would have absorbed too much of the proceeds to make the effort worthwhile.[77] Nevertheless, there were some interwar enterprises that turned to the stock market to raise finance for internal expansion. According to Thomas, between World War I and World War II the stock market 'helped to provide much-needed capital for expanding productive capacity, and for funding short-term debt, and it did so not only for large companies but over the period an increasing number of small companies who found that they could not grow without becoming public companies'.[78]

Richard Thomas & Co. was an example of a firm that not only relied on the stock market to expand but experienced an unwinding of control in the process. After a 1917 amalgamation it was the single largest producer of tinplate in the UK.[79] Frank Thomas, the managing director, and his immediate family held between them 73 per cent of the ordinary shares at that time. Thomas ran the firm autocratically but share issuances carried out in the early 1920s to finance

---

[74] The exact identity of those in control is not entirely clear; as of 1936, 58 per cent of the shares were held by nominees, including the largest single stake of 29.6 per cent: Florence, *supra* n. 45, 199.

[75] Henry Clay, 'The Financing of Industrial Enterprise', Transactions of the Manchester Statistical Society, 1931–32 Session, 205, 214, 223–24. See also Ranald C. Michie, *The London Stock Exchange: A History* (1999), 258. On the historical pattern see Ch. Three, Pt VI.

[76] Committee of Enquiry into Banking, Finance and Credit Finance (Lord Macmillan, chair), *Report*, Cmd. 3897 (hereinafter Macmillan Report) (1931), 173. For background, see Balogh, *supra* n. 55, 286–87; Michie, *supra* n. 75, 259–60.

[77] Balogh, *supra* n. 55, 293–97; Clay, *supra* n. 75, 219–20.

[78] Thomas, *supra* n. 18, 34; see also Ellinger, *supra* n. 5, 314.

[79] John Vaizey, *The History of British Steel* (1974), 33–36; Steven Tolliday, *Business, Banking, and Politics: The Case of British Steel, 1918–1939* (1987), 132–37.

expansion of steel-making works and acquire collieries diluted his dominant share block. After Thomas retired as managing director, he attempted to rely on his ownership stake to protect his interests but the new management team was able to outmanoeuvre him and ensure retention of full managerial discretion.

General Electric Company Limited (GEC), which emerged as one of Britain's leading electrical engineering companies in the opening half of the 20th century, was another company where share issuances carried out to finance internal expansion contributed to the unwinding of control.[80] GEC carried out a public offering in 1900, but founders Gustav Byng and Hugo Hirst continued to dominate the share register. Just prior to the introduction of capital controls in World War I, GEC carried out a large public offering of ordinary and preference shares to extend its engineering works and build a new corporate headquarters. The resulting diffusion of share ownership and a sharp rise in profits during World War I meant that by the time the war ended, GEC had 'moved on to a broader plane... out of the family business into the league of big corporations'.[81] Between 1918 and 1922 additional public offerings expanded GEC's issued capital (ordinary shares, preference shares and debentures) from £1.5 million to £8.9 million, with the funds being used to expand almost all sections of a company that prided itself on being 'Everything Electrical' and operated on a scale comparable to any British rival.

II. The Buy Side

A. Who Was Buying Shares?

1. Institutional Investors

The unwinding of control in companies with blockholders is only feasible if there is demand on the buy side (Chapter One, Part IV). What were the potential sources of demand during the interwar period? Up to 1914, institutional investment was very much a sideshow and only became dominant after World War II (Chapter Six, Part III.A.1; Chapter Ten, Part II). It grew in importance during the interwar years, but nevertheless played only a supporting role in comparison to direct investment in shares by individuals. As of the early 1930s, private investors owned upwards of 80 per cent of the securities traded on the London Stock Exchange and were responsible for around the same proportion of trading activity.[82] The *Financial News*' explanation was that 'Investors, on the whole, seem to prefer to have the fun of managing their investments themselves

---

[80] Robert Jones and Oliver Marriott, *Anatomy of a Merger: A History of G.E.C., A.E.I. and English Electric* (1972), 75–78, 85–90.

[81] *Ibid.*, 87.

[82] Michie, *supra* n. 75, 178 (trading activity); ' "Institutional" Investors', Economist, November 11, 1933, 918; John Michael Atkin, *British Overseas Investment 1918–1931* (1977), 110–11.

through their own stockbrokers rather than to entrust their savings to an insurance company, an investment trust or a building society.'[83]

Pension funds, a crucial element in the buy side after World War II, were not important investors in shares during the interwar years.[84] Large employers increasingly considered pension benefits to be an essential element of employee remuneration and concerns about the tax implications of pension benefits yielded legislative concessions in 1921 that would ultimately do much to foster the growth of pension funds. However, the trust deeds governing interwar pension funds usually precluded buying shares and those trustees vested with wide discretion generally shunned 'risky' equity investments.

Insurance companies stepped forward somewhat earlier as investors in shares than pension funds, but still did not become major players during the interwar years. Only a tiny proportion of assets insurance companies had available for investment prior to World War I was allocated to equities (Chapter Six, Part III.A). During the interwar years, various advisers lobbied insurance companies to step up their buying of shares, with famous economist John-Maynard Keynes saying, 'The public joint stock company has taken a tremendous leap forward and now offers a field for investment which simply did not exist even twenty years ago ... [A]ny investment institution which ignores, or is not equipped for handling, their shares is living in a backwater.'[85]

A minority of insurance companies, including two firms Keynes advised, the National Mutual Life Assurance Society and the Provincial Insurance Company, did adopt an 'active investment policy' and reallocated their investment portfolios in favour of equities.[86] A majority of insurers, however, opted for caution and did not invest heavily in shares.[87] The percentage of total assets held in the form of ordinary shares increased from 4 per cent in 1924 to 6 per cent in 1929 and 10 per cent by 1937.[88] These figures, however, overstate the scale of investment in equities since the share portfolios of numerous insurance companies consisted of little more than blocks of railway equities and/or stakes

[83] Quoted in Michie, *supra* n. 75, 179.

[84] For background, see Atkin, *supra* n. 82, 122; Committee on the Working of the Monetary System (Lord Radcliffe, Chairman), *Report*, Cmnd. 827 (1959), 89; Leslie Hannah, *Inventing Retirement: The Development of Occupational Pensions in Britain* (1986), 20, 73–74. On the position after World War II, see Ch. Ten, Pt III, Ch. Eleven, Pt I.

[85] Clive Trebilcock, *Phoenix Assurance and the Development of British Insurance, vol. II: The Era of Insurance Giants, 1870–1984* (1998), 598.

[86] *Ibid.*, 595–99; Oliver M. Westall, *The Provincial Insurance Company 1903–38: Family, Markets and Competitive Growth* (1992), 354–76; Peter Scott, 'Towards the 'Cult of the Equity'? Insurance Companies and the Interwar Capital Market', (2002) 55 Economic History Review 78, 98.

[87] Scott, *supra* n. 86, 98; John Butt, 'Life Assurance in War and Depression: The Standard Life Assurance Company and its Environment, 1914–39' in O.M. Westall (ed.), *The Historian and the Business of Insurance* (1984), 155, 170.

[88] Mae Baker and Michael Collins, 'The Asset Portfolio Composition of British Life Insurance Firms, 1900–1965', (2003) 10 Financial History Review 137, 149, 153. See also Trebilcock, *supra* n. 85, 598; F.W. Paish and G.L. Schwartz, *Insurance Funds and Their Investment* (1934), 66 (providing similar data).

in associated companies.[89] As Trebilcock has said in his history of Phoenix Assurance, a highly conservative interwar investor, 'The really active punters were few.'[90]

Investment trusts also warmed to the idea of investing in equities during the interwar period and by the 1930s some 30 per cent to 40 per cent of investment trust assets were invested in ordinary shares. On the other hand, investment trusts only had assets available for investment totalling about one-third of those possessed by insurance companies.[91] A foreign bias further reduced the prominence of investment trusts on the buy side. Glasgow said in 1930 'on the whole...British concerns are avoided by the investment trusts'.[92] Data from the 1930s confirmed that only 40–45 per cent of investment trust resources were invested in UK assets.[93] Hence, during the interwar years investment trusts, as with pension funds and insurance companies, remained a sideshow as owners of shares in publicly traded UK companies.

2. *Individual Investors*

Through the 19th and early 20th centuries, the number of individuals owning shares in UK companies grew considerably (Chapter Six, Part III.A.2). The trend continued in the interwar years. There was never going to be truly mass investment when, according to probate records for 1936, only one in four people had an estate worth more than £100 (£4,700 in 2006 currency).[94] Nevertheless, contemporaries remarked that investors were becoming 'more and more numerous', that 'investment had been extended and democratized' and that 'After the War there was a great broadening of public interest in Stock Exchange matters.'[95]

These assessments seem correct. Estimates of the total number of individuals owning shares during the interwar years are lacking. However, lists of people owning shares containing as many as 500,000 names compiled from company share registers were available for purchase from specialist outfits during the interwar years.[96] Also, the *Financial Times* reported in 1949 that approximately 1.25 million people held shares in companies quoted on the London Stock Exchange.[97] It seems likely the figure was much the same at the end of the

[89] Raynes, *supra* n. 17, 35 (comments of G.H. Recknell); Trebilcock, *supra* n. 85, 599.

[90] Trebilcock, *supra* n. 85, 599.

[91] See generally Grant, *supra* n. 8, 192; Francis Williams, 'Insurance Companies and Investment Trusts' in Cole, *supra* n. 6, 139, 154; John Newlands, *Put Not Your Money* (1997), 175.

[92] George Glasgow, *The English Investment Trust Companies* (1930), 15.

[93] Ellinger, *supra* n. 5, 271; Atkin, *supra* n. 82, 121.

[94] Adrienne Gleeson, *People and Their Money: 50 Years of Private Investment* (1981), 29.

[95] G.D.H. Cole, 'The Evolution of Joint Stock Enterprise' in Cole, *supra* n. 6, 51, 57, 89; David Finnie, *Capital Underwriting* (1934), 160; Hargreaves Parkinson, 'The Stock Exchange' in *The Economist 1843–1943* (1943), 130.

[96] E. Victor Morgan and W.A. Thomas, *The Stock Exchange: Its History and Functions* (1969), 205; Laurie Dennett, *The Charterhouse Group 1925–1979: A History* (1979), 16.

[97] 'An Association of Investors? (III)—How Many Investors are There?', Financial Times, March 2, 1949.

interwar years, given that capital controls and high rates of taxation would have discouraged investment in shares by individuals during World War II and the years immediately following.[98] Assuming this is correct, by 1939 the number of individuals owning shares in UK companies had more than doubled from approximately half a million at the beginning of the 20th century.

In addition, the composition of the category of individuals owning shares changed. At the beginning of the 20th century, through local business connections or as clients of stockbrokers, wealthy industrialists constituted an integral source of demand for shares and rich landowners were growing in importance (Chapter Six, Part III.A.2). Matters changed after World War I. Withers said in 1930, '[A]s we all know, the high rates of direct taxation—income tax, super tax and death duties—now bite a big slice out of the surplus income of the old investing classes.'[99] Indeed, after World War I the rich often became net sellers of securities to finance their lifestyles and tended to invest safely with surplus capital available for the purpose.[100] This reflected broader trends concerning the distribution of wealth in the UK. Due party to income tax that was very high by pre-World War I standards, the share of wealth held by the top 1 per cent of the population fell from 70 per cent to 55 per cent between 1911/13 and 1936/38.[101] Most dramatically, caught by inflation and falling rents as well as rising taxes, many major landowners broke up their estates and did so at such a rate between 1918 and 1921 there reportedly was a transfer of land 'probably not equalled since the Norman Conquest'.[102]

At the same time the wealthy receded as a source of demand for shares, the middle class, or at least the upper middle class, stepped forward. While the very rich in Britain did poorly relative to others during World War I and the decades following, the merely well-off prospered as the share of wealth held by the top 2 per cent to 10 per cent of the population rose from 23 per cent to 32 per cent between 1911/13 and 1936–38.[103] Things that had generally been the exclusive

[98] On conditions during World War II and immediately thereafter, see Michie, *supra* n. 75, 291–92, 355–56.

[99] Hartley Withers, *The Quicksands of the City and a Way Through for Investors* (1930), 17. See also Lord Piercy, 'The Macmillan Gap and the Shortage of Risk Capital' (1955) 118 Journal of the Royal Statistical Society, Series A, 1, 2.

[100] A.P.L. Gordon, 'The Capital Market of Today', (1939) 102 Journal of the Royal Statistical Society 501, 509.

[101] On tax trends, see Pt I.F. On data see Kathleen M. Langley, 'The Distribution of Capital in Private Hands 1936–1938 and 1946–1947: Part II', (1951) 13 Bulletin of the Oxford University Institute of Statistics 37, 47; Rodney Lowe, 'Riches, Poverty, and Progress' in K. Robbins (ed.), *The British Isles 1901–1951* (2002), 197, 200. For further background, see Dewey, *supra* n. 27, 8, 32, 63, 71, 325.

[102] F.M.L. Thompson, *English Landed Society in the Nineteenth Century* (1963), 333; see also T.O. Lloyd, *Empire, Welfare State, Europe: History of the United Kingdom 1906–2001*, 5th edn (2002), 88–89.

[103] Dewey, *supra* n. 27, 64–65; Lowe, *supra* n. 101, 200; Andrew Thorpe, *Britain in the 1930s: The Deceptive Decade* (1992), 95.

preserve of the rich in turn became dispersed more widely, including ownership of shares.[104] The trend was correctly anticipated by a witness giving evidence in 1918 to a committee investigating company law reform and discussing the large number of people who had invested in bonds the UK government issued to finance World War I:

> We have seen during the War a remarkably widespread diffusion of money, and a wonderful growth in the habit of investment, among classes of the population to whom both are a novelty. It is computed that no less than 13,000,000 people are directly interested in various forms of Government war securities. After the war it may be expected that a large number of people who were never investors before will be willing to entrust their savings to commercial companies...[105]

A 30 per cent inflation-adjusted increase in average earnings between 1914 and the end of the 1930s, supported by significant increases in GDP per capita, contributed significantly to the relative prosperity the upper middle class enjoyed.[106] Tax also played a role, as the Conservative government of the 1920s that opted to leave the very rich 'stranded' sought to give relief to 'professional men, small merchants and businessmen—superior brain workers of every kind'.[107] As the 1920s drew to a close, the top marginal tax rate applicable to incomes up to £5,000 (£209,000) was a fairly modest 31 per cent and a single person earning £5,000 paid under £1,200 in income tax.[108] This meant for the upper middle class tax was not a significant deterrent to investment in shares. As a 1930 guide to investment said, '[A]lthough taxation on unearned income becomes a serious consideration after the £500 income level, it does not render investment for the sake of dividends unattractive till some distance after the Surtax level has been reached.'[109]

Income taxes payable by the upper middle class did rise in the 1930s.[110] However, even as late as 1937 for a single person earning £5,000, his 'take home' pay would have been more than 70 per cent of his income.[111] Given rising earnings, taxation at this sort of level should have left prosperous members of the middle class with sufficient spare funds to invest. Thus, even during the 1930s a reasonably congenial tax environment helped to provide a platform for upper middle class investment in shares.

---

[104] Lloyd, *supra* n. 102, 176; Bentley B. Gilbert, *Britain 1914–1945: Aftermath of Power* (1996), 49–51.
[105] Quoted in Ranald C. Michie, *The City of London: Continuity and Change, 1850–1990* (1992), 117.
[106] Aldcroft, *supra* n. 62, 150; Lowe, *supra* n. 101, 202.
[107] Pt I.F.; Daunton, *supra* n. 35, 133.
[108] 'Income Tax and Surtax', Times, April 15, 1930.
[109] Caudwell, *supra* n. 65, 11.
[110] Glynn and Oxborrow, *supra* n. 15, 48.
[111] Tax would have been £1465: 'Higher Rate of Income Tax', April 27, 1938.

B. Factors Influencing the Decision to Buy Shares

While during the interwar years investment was 'extended and democratized', demand for shares could not be taken for granted given the informational asymmetries involved, the capacity for extraction of private benefits of control by blockholders and the agency cost problem in firms where ownership had separated from control (Chapter Four, Part II.A). However, various pre-World War I deterrents to investment in shares lost some of their potency and factors encouraging the purchase of equities generally remained in play. The result was a more broadly based demand for shares, referred to in 1930 by Withers—albeit generously—as a 'cult of the common stock'.[112]

1. *The Overseas Option*

From the mid-19th century to 1914 a predilection for overseas investment depressed to some degree demand for shares in British companies (Chapter Five, Part V.B.4; Chapter Six, Part III.B.1). From 1914 to 1939 conditions were less favourable for the export of capital, which should, all else being equal, have fostered the buy side with UK equities. As Grant said, 'The explanation of the willingness of the investor in Stock Exchange securities to interest himself in home industry is to be found in the decline, and ultimately disappearance of overseas investment.'[113] The *Economist* made the same 'trapped capital' point in 1934. After outlining various factors ensuring 'domestic savings must be utilised in our own closed community for some period in the future' it said, 'The present willingness of investors to pay gilt-edged prices for equity holdings... testifies to the pressure of available funds seeking investment, for which adequate channels of a "new business" kind are denied them.'[114] It struck the same chord in 1935, arguing that 'the closing valve of foreign investment' had helped to drive the price of UK investment securities, including equities, 'to higher levels than might have obtained under the old regime'.[115]

Basic aggregate data reveals the eclipse of the foreign option after 1914.[116] Between 1915 and 1918, the annual average of overseas issuances on the London Stock Exchange was only 17 per cent the total of such issues in 1913. Annual overseas investment equalled about 8 per cent of national income between 1911 and 1913 but only amounted to about 2.5 per cent between 1925 and 1931. Overseas issues carried out on the London Stock Exchange fell from an average of £93 million per annum between 1918 and 1931 to £32 million between 1932 and 1938.

---

[112] Withers, *supra* n. 99, 28.   [113] Grant, *supra* n. 8, 179.
[114] 'Interest Rates and the Investor', Economist, April 14, 1934, 824.
[115] 'Twenty-Five Years of British Investment', Economist, May 4, 1935, 1019, 1019, 1020.
[116] Atkin, *supra* n. 82, 25, 321, 325.

A decline in investment in foreign assets was inevitable during World War I because the UK government, eager not to be 'crowded out' as it sought to finance the war effort, imposed tight restrictions on foreign capital-raising on the London Stock Exchange and the purchase of securities abroad.[117] State intervention continued to handicap overseas investment through the interwar years. Intermittently between 1919 and 1931 the Treasury and the Bank of England protected the pound by orchestrating unofficial but effective embargoes on the marketing of foreign debt securities on the London Stock Exchange.[118] In the 1930s the Treasury engaged in informal discrimination against capital-raising from countries that were not part of the 'Sterling Area', a group of countries whose trading, financial and political connections with Britain made it prudent for them to peg their currencies to sterling.[119] Arm-twisting intensified with World War II on the horizon, as the UK government secured an undertaking from stockbrokers and bankers to discourage trading in foreign securities.[120]

Market factors also discouraged overseas investment. Amidst a major worldwide economic slump and the tightening of restrictions on trade, it became commonplace during the 1930s for foreign governments, railways and utilities to skip interest or dividend payments.[121] Britain looked a good bet in comparison. As the *Economist* observed in 1935, 'The investor, however, during the last twenty-five years, has probably fared better, on the whole, in Great Britain, than anywhere else in the world, under a stable system of Government, whose policy, though frequently opportunist, like his own, has eschewed extreme measures.'[122] Moreover, in contrast with the late 19th and early 20th centuries, Britain's economic performance stacked up quite well during the interwar years (Figure II). Correspondingly, investors who in the pre-World War I era might have refrained from buying shares in UK companies to benefit from superior economic performance elsewhere would have been less inclined to do so in the interwar era.

2. Company Law

Company law can help to fortify the buy side for shares by addressing concerns investors have about extraction of private benefits of control and by reducing information asymmetries associated with share ownership. However, companies legislation provided scant protection to investors prior to 1914, and the

---

[117] *Ibid.*, 23–26.

[118] *Ibid.*, 28–33, 48–58, 67–68, 163, 321; Bernard Attard, 'Moral Suasion, Empire Borrowers and the New Issue Market During the 1920s' in Ranald Michie and Philip Williamson (eds), *The British Government and the City of London in the Twentieth Century* (2004), 195.

[119] Ellinger, *supra* n. 5, 322–26; Atkin, *supra* n. 82, 325; P.J. Cain, 'Gentlemanly Imperialism at Work: The Bank of England, Canada and the Sterling Area, 1932–1936', (1996) 49 Economic History Review 336, 337 (defining the Sterling Area).

[120] 'British Take Steps to Curb Purchases of US Securities', New York Times, May 18, 1939.

[121] Grant, *supra* n. 8, 152, 179; Balogh, *supra* n. 55, 270–73; Michie, *supra* n. 75, 274, Ernest Davies, 'Foreign Investment' in Cole, *supra* n. 6, 213, 245–50.

[122] 'Twenty-Five', *supra* n. 115, 1019. See also Harold Wincott, *The Stock Exchange* (1946), 76.

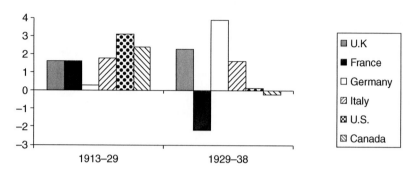

Figure II: Annual growth rates of total output for major potential destinations for investment 1913–38 (as measured by GDP)

Source: Compiled with data from Derek H. Aldcroft, 'Economic Growth in Britain in the Inter-War Years: A Reassessment' in Derek H. Aldcroft and Peter Fearon (eds), *Economic Growth in Twentieth-century Britain* (1969), 34, 37.

Companies Act 1929, influenced by a 1926 report that was deferential to the *status quo*, did little to check blockholder opportunism (Part I.C; Chapter Six, Part III.B.2). The approach to disclosure was much the same, with the changes to the law being fairly modest.

With prospectuses, the Companies Act 1929 introduced requirements that voting rights attached to different classes of shares be disclosed and that a company's auditors had to provide a report on the profits and dividends generated by the company for three years or each year the company had been doing business.[123] The 1929 Act also closed a much-exploited 'offer for sale' disclosure loophole, where an intermediary such as an issuing house would purchase the securities a company was proposing to distribute to the public, carry out the offering itself and in so doing ensure neither the intermediary nor the directors of the company were liable for misstatements in the 'abridged prospectus' supporting the offering.[124] The 1929 legislation also prescribed guidelines on the format of the balance sheet companies were required to prepare and file, obliged directors to prepare and file publicly an annual report on the company's affairs and required companies to present to shareholders annually—but not file publicly—a profit and loss account.[125]

The immediate reaction to the enactment of the Companies Act 1929 was generally favourable and the requirement to disclose three years' worth of financial results in the prospectus has been credited with improving the survival rate of

---

[123] Companies Act 1929, s. 35, sch. 4, Pt I, para. 16, Pt II, para. 1, Pt III, para. 5.

[124] Companies Act 1929, s. 38(1); for background, see Samuel, *supra* n. 9, 42–43; 'Prospectus Law', Economist, February 11, 1933, 305.

[125] Companies Act 1929, ss.110, 123–24.

companies carrying out initial public offerings in the 1930s.[126] However, various market crises soon cast into sharp relief the legislation's limitations and helped to create momentum in favour of further statutory change that would culminate in the enactment of the Companies Act 1948.[127] A stock market reversal and a nascent economic recession cruelly exposed the frailties of companies carrying out public offerings in a new issue boom in 1928, as within three years more than one in three companies involved were wound up or lacked capital of ascertainable value.[128] As 1929 drew to a close, the business empire of prominent financier and company promoter Clarence Hatry collapsed, resulting in Hatry's conviction for forging share certificates and over-issuing shares.[129] In 1930 the Royal Mail Steam Packet Company, which had in 1929 a market capitalization of approximately £100 million (£4.3 billion as of 2006) collapsed, resulting in Lord Kylsant, the company's driving force, being charged with circulating false accounts and convicted for publishing a false prospectus supporting an issuance of debentures.[130]

These investor reverses tarnished the sense of propriety surrounding corporate affairs that had justified the presumption against legislative intrusion informing previous efforts to reform company law, including the Companies Act 1929.[131] In this new context, criticism of certain practices previously targeted was renewed, such as the appointment of 'prestige directors' whose names would appeal to the public and who did not know much about the business.[132] Disclosure-oriented themes were paramount, however. As the *Economist* said in 1931, 'A repetition of the scandals of the 1928 boom in new issues is not impossible if the law continues to allow directors of large established concerns to mislead the public with unintelligible accounts... Somehow or other the confidence of the investor in the industrial merger... must be restored; and an important factor in bringing this about will be more intelligent accounting.'[133] There continued to be complaints about aspects of disclosure in prospectuses, but it was also acknowledged that the Companies Act 1929 had made significant improvements.[134] Considerably more

---

[126] Bircher, *supra* n. 10, 65; J.R. Edwards, *Company Legislation and Changing Patterns of Disclosure in British Company Accounts 1900–1940* (1981), 6 (immediate reaction); David Chambers, 'New Issues, New Industries and Firm Survival in Interwar Britain' (2007), unpublished working paper, at 20 (IPO survival).

[127] Bircher, *supra* n. 10, 79–89.

[128] Samuel, *supra* n. 9, 1. See also Pt I.A; 'The Cost of Boom Finance', Economist, February 15, 1930, 363.

[129] P.S. Manley, 'Clarence Hatry', (1976) 12 Abacus 49; George Robb, *White-Collar Crime in England: Financial Fraud and Business Morality 1845–1929* (1992), 122–24.

[130] 'Sinking Sea Lord', Time, December 23, 1929 (size of Royal Mail group); Ashton, *supra* n. 19 (false accounts); Davies and Bourn, *supra* n. 19, 119; 'Rex v Kylsant—A New Golden Rule for Prospectuses', (1932) 45 Harvard Law Review 1078 (false prospectus).

[131] Bircher, *supra* n. 10, 81, 89, 103–4.

[132] Samuel, *supra* n. 9, 111–18; May, *supra* n. 10, 485; 'The Position of Company Directors', Economist, August 9, 1930, 284.

[133] 'Holding Companies and Their Accounts', Economist, July 4, 1931, 25, 25.

[134] 'Prospectus Law', *supra* n. 124; 'Prospectus Law Reform', Economist, March 21, 1936, 655.

energy was devoted to lobbying for reform of periodic disclosure, particularly the treatment of 'secret reserves' and holding companies.

Samuel observed in 1933 'So far as the majority of the lay investors of the country are concerned, they probably had not the faintest notion what a secret reserve was, until the Royal Mail Steam Packet Co. "flogged the horse to death".'[135] The creation of secret reserves in company accounts generally involved the deliberate underestimating of potential future profits or overestimating of possible losses generated by bad debts, taxation and depreciation.[136] Companies also could set up reserve accounts in the company's internal books that were treated as 'creditors' on the published balance sheet.[137] The attraction for management was that reserves could be deployed to 'even out' fluctuations in earnings and thus function as an insurance policy against unforeseen developments. The justification for leaving shareholders in the dark was that if they knew of large profits in prosperous years, they would demand bigger dividends, jeopardizing the future welfare and prosperity of the company. The creation of secret reserves was by no means a universal practice, but it appears a substantial fraction of sizeable publicly quoted companies made use of this accounting technique at least to some extent.[138]

With Royal Mail, the years 1915 to 1921 had been extremely prosperous and the company, by making provisions for war-time EPD that proved to be excessive, set aside over £2 million in a secret reserve fund that did not appear in the company's published accounts.[139] Royal Mail suffered trading losses through much of the 1920s but drew on the reserves to declare net profits and relied on dividends paid by associated companies using their own reserves (most were trading at a loss themselves) and payments by the government as a result of retrospective EPD allowances to service outstanding debts, pay interest on debentures and distribute dividends. After Royal Mail's collapse, Lord Kylsant and the company's auditor were acquitted of accounting fraud because there was a cryptic indication in the accounts that substantial transfers from reserves were occurring. Nevertheless, the scandal spotlighted a far greater disparity between company accounts and economic reality than investors had contemplated, and in so doing provided the catalyst for numerous recommendations for reform.[140]

---

[135] Samuel, *supra* n. 9, 275.

[136] *Ibid.*, 270–75; 'Secret Reserves', Economist, July 18, 1931, 127; Hargreaves Parkinson, *Scientific Investment: A Manual for Company Share and Debenture Holders* (1932), 120–23.

[137] A.J. Arnold and D.R. Matthews, 'Corporate Financial Disclosures in the UK, 1920–50: The Effects of Legislative Change and Managerial Discretion', (2002) 32 Accounting and Business Research 3, 12.

[138] *Ibid.*, 12–13; A.J. Arnold, '"Publishing Your Private Affairs to the World"' Corporate Financial Disclosures in the UK 1900–24', (1997) 7 Accounting, Business and Financial History 143, 162.

[139] See Green and Moss, *supra* n. 19, 62–65, 72–76; Ashton, *supra* n. 19; Robb, *supra* n. 129, 144–45.

[140] Bircher, *supra* n. 10, 101, 115, 148–49; 'Secret Reserves', *supra* n. 136.

Since Royal Mail relied partly on dividend payments received from associated companies to allow it to continue to operate despite regular trading losses, the Royal Mail scandal also helped to fuel controversy concerning the accounting treatment of holding companies. Holding companies of the interwar era were often products of mergers where the acquiring company would end up owning the shares of target companies which in turn would continue to operate as distinct legal entities so as to preserve the name, goodwill and other intangible assets.[141] By the early 1930s, according to the *Economist*, the holding company had 'penetrated every branch of industry, and scarcely a single large British concern exists to-day which is not a holding company'. The *Economist* illustrated the significance of the pattern in 1931 with data indicating that with nine of fourteen large industrial concerns operating as holding companies, the ratio of investment in subsidiary and associated companies plus net amounts loaned to subsidiaries exceeded two-thirds of the total assets of the holding company.[142]

New provisions in the Companies Act 1929 constituted the first explicit recognition of the holding company pattern in UK companies legislation. The Act defined a 'subsidiary' company as one where the holding company owned 50 per cent or more of the shares, stipulated that a holding company's balance sheet should discuss how the profits and losses of the subsidiaries had been dealt with for the purpose of the holding company's accounts and required a holding company to identify the aggregate value of investments in its subsidiaries.[143] Most holding companies went little further with the disclosures they made.[144] This meant that shareholders could only find what was happening in individual subsidiary companies by carrying out searches of public filings of the subsidiaries, which usually amounted to no more than the sketchy details required of fully 'private' companies.[145]

In the aftermath of the Hatry and Royal Mail scandals, both of which implicated interlocking companies and directorates, the manner in which UK companies legislation dealt with the accounts of holding and subsidiary companies was denounced on the basis that shareholders were being deprived of the informative accounts they were entitled to receive.[146] The remedy generally suggested was to require the preparation and publication of accounts reflecting the aggregate profits or losses of the subsidiaries.[147] The objection to the

---

[141] 'Holding Company Finance', Economist, December 12, 1931, 1131.

[142] *Ibid.*   [143] Companies Act 1929, ss. 125–27.

[144] Edwards, *supra* n. 126, 30; Arnold and Matthews, *supra* n. 137, 6, 10–11; Mary E. Murphy, 'The Profession of Accountancy in England: The Client and the Investor', (1940) 15 Accounting Review 241, 259.

[145] Companies Act 1929, s. 108 (requirement to file annual return); Samuel, *supra* n. 9, 287–88.

[146] Bircher, *supra* n. 10, 84–85, 89, 96–103 (citing numerous contemporary sources); see also Parkinson, *supra* n. 136, 150.

[147] Samuel, *supra* n. 9, 294–95; Bircher, *supra* n. 10, 109, 111, 114, 144–46, 155, 185; 'Holding Companies', *supra* n. 133.

other obvious solution—supplying the accounts of all subsidiary companies to shareholders of the holding company—was that there would be far too much detail to digest. The pressure for reform did not yield immediate tangible results, largely because civil servants at the Board of Trade wanted further experience with the 1929 legislation before undertaking a revision and because there was divided expert opinion on how regulation of holding company accounts should be changed, assuming reform was indeed required.[148] The groundwork never-theless had been laid for a fresh round of company law reform, and when the Board of Trade established in 1943 a new committee under the chairmanship of Mr Justice Lionel Cohen to review the amendment of company law, the form and content of company accounts and relations of holding and subsidiary com-panies were firmly on the agenda.[149]

3. Stock Exchange Regulation

Although the collapse of the new issue boom of 1928 and the Hatry and Royal Mail scandals did not yield company law reform during the interwar period, the London Stock Exchange was responsive to the changing conditions. A consensus developed that, due to the growing number of investors relying on the Exchange's dealing facilities, the Exchange should step up its control over securities involving a high degree of risk and uncertainty.[150] With quoted companies, the increased vigilance manifested itself in more careful scrutiny of applications for quotations and a greater inclination to reject in marginal cases.[151] The applicable rules did not change greatly. As was the case before World War I (Chapter Six, Part III.B.3), the primary technique the Stock Exchange used to regulate quoted companies was to require firms seeking a quotation to have stipulated provisions in their articles of association. The only major additions made during the interwar period were the inclusion of an explicit statement by the Stock Exchange that it reserved the right to take exception to any provision in the articles that would 'be unrea-sonable in the case of a Public Company' and the imposition of a requirement that companies have a provision in their articles authorizing the shareholders to dismiss directors at any time by passing a 'special' resolution requiring support by a 3/4s majority vote.[152]

The London Stock Exchange was much more active in regulating compa-nies seeking to have their shares traded on the Exchange without seeking a full

---

[148] Bircher, *supra* n. 10, 107–29, 141–42.

[149] *Report of the Committee on Company Law Amendment*, Cmd. 6659 (1945) (hereinafter Cohen Report), 112.

[150] Michie, *supra* n. 75, 282.

[151] *Ibid.*, 280; Finnie, *supra* n. 95, 182–83.

[152] London Stock Exchange, Rules and Regulations of the Stock Exchange, Appendix 35B, para. 9, supporting note, set out in R.H. Code Holland and John N. Werry, *Poley's Law and Practice of the Stock Exchange*, 5th edn (1932) 420. On how matters stood as of 1914, see Walter S. Schwabe and G.A.H. Branson, *A Treatise on the Law of the Stock Exchange*, 2nd edn (1914), 374–75, Rules and Regulations for the Conduct of Business on the Stock Exchange, Appendix 36A.

quotation. During World War I the London Stock Exchange began granting permission for dealing to begin in the shares of unquoted companies by adding companies to its 'Supplementary List'.[153] During the interwar years, an 'introduction' was generally used to launch trading in this way, with shares typically being distributed privately to a range of buyers before trading began and the company then seeking 'permission to deal'.[154] Under such circumstances, neither the company nor its blockholders—whose shares might be those that were marketed privately—dealt directly with the public at all and the shares found their way into the public's hands through the ordinary trading machinery of the stock market.[155] Introductions were popular because they were inexpensive, both in terms of fees payable to advisers and advertising, and were subject to less rigorous regulation by the London Stock Exchange than quotations (e.g. the rule requiring two-thirds of capital to be distributed to the public did not apply).[156] Though introductions could be a precursor to the obtaining of a quotation, a company that had obtained 'permission to deal' was not under any explicit onus to take this extra step.

In the 1920s the London Stock Exchange was generally willing to give permission to deal to any security that offered the prospect of generating good business for its members.[157] Matters changed in 1930. The Stock Exchange, mindful that numerous ill-fated 1928 public offerings had encompassed abuses of the share introduction procedure and aware that the Hatry scandal was a blow to the Exchange's credibility, introduced detailed rules governing the circumstances where an introduction would be granted.[158] For instance, a company seeking permission to deal that opted not to issue a prospectus was required to publish an advertisement in two major London daily newspapers providing a summary of the company's most recent audited balance sheet and profit and loss account, the particulars of any material contracts entered into by the company otherwise than in the ordinary course of business in the two years preceding the publication of the advertisement and certain other particulars.[159] The Stock Exchange also required the directors of a company seeking permission for deal to make a 'general undertaking' before granting the necessary authorization, with the focus being on proper documentation of shares distributed.[160]

---

[153] W.T.C. King, *The Stock Exchange*, 2nd edn (1954), 76.

[154] Finnie, *supra* n. 95, 184–85; 'Prospectus or Introduction', Economist, January 15, 1927, 105; Harold W. Batty, *The Issue of Shares, Debentures and Bonds by Joint Stock Companies* (1937), 16, 421.

[155] Oswald M. Brown, *The Routine of a Public Issue* (1932), 9.

[156] See generally Michie, *supra* n. 75, 267, 275; David Kynaston, The *City of London, Volume III: Illusions of Gold 1914–1945* (1999), 421. On the lack of a two-thirds rule, see Code Holland and Werry, *supra* n. 152, 409–17, London Stock Exchange, Rules, Appendix 34B.

[157] Michie, *supra* n. 75, 272.

[158] 'New Rules for the Stock Exchange', Times, August 13, 1930 (motivation for reform); Finnie, *supra* n. 95, 186–87 (abuses of the introduction procedure).

[159] Code Holland and Werry, *supra* n. 152, 409–17, London Stock Exchange, Rules, Appendix 34B.

[160] Code-Holland, and Werry, *supra* n. 152, 375, 410–11, London Stock Exchange, Rule 159, Appendix 34, para. A10.

The London Stock Exchange's reform efforts, no doubt fortified by improving market conditions, apparently helped to restore investor confidence, as capital 'introduced' increased from £9 million in 1931 to £35 million in 1933.[161] The London Stock Exchange nevertheless remained vigilant. The 1945 report of the Cohen Committee said the London Stock Exchange's Share and Loan Department made 'searching' enquiries concerning applications for permission to deal and made its point by noting that between 1929 and 1939 the Stock Exchange refused permission outright in two cases and ordered deferments in 38 instances, of which only 11 had resulted in permission subsequently being granted.[162] In 1936 the London Stock Exchange declared that it preferred companies to rely on full-scale public offerings rather than introductions, though it still left the introduction option open.[163] In 1939, the Stock Exchange indicated that holding companies would only be given permission to deal if they undertook to supply consolidated accounts annually to shareholders.[164] During World War II the Stock Exchange expanded still further the undertakings companies seeking permission to deal had to give and in 1947 eliminated once and for all the option to side-step the rules for quoted companies by merging the Supplementary List into the Official List.[165]

The London Stock Exchange's new approach to enforcement generally received favourable reviews. There were complaints that the introduction procedure remained less than satisfactory because investors could be left empty-handed when there was intense demand for shares and because determination of the initial price was left purely to the market rather than being set in any way in advance.[166] On the other hand, Finnie said the Stock Exchange had 'shown a real determination to check financial abuses that had previously flourished'.[167] The *Times* argued similarly in 1936 that 'One of the best of the latter-day reforms introduced by the Stock Exchange Committee for the protection of all who deal in securities is that permission to deal in stocks and shares is no longer a perfunctory affair, but is granted only after careful investigation.'[168]

The *Economist* remarked the same year on 'the advantage which the Stock Exchange enjoys over Parliament in investment matters, for its policy can be made effective in checking abuses, with far greater expedition and elasticity than the cumbersome machinery of law'.[169] Finnie concurred, saying

[161] 'Stock Exchange "Placings"', Economist, February 15, 1936, 367.
[162] Cohen Report, *supra* n. 149, 14.
[163] Ellinger, *supra* n. 5, 287; Kynaston, *supra* n. 156, 422.
[164] 'Consolidated Accounts and Voting Rights', Times, February 21, 1939; Josephine Maltby, 'Was the Companies Act 1947 A Response to a National Crisis?', (2000) 5 Accounting History 31, 51.
[165] Ch. Nine, Pt III.D; King, *supra* n. 153, 83; 'Obtaining an SE Quotation', Economist, May 10, 1947, 728; F.W. Paish, 'The London New Issue Market', (1951) 18 Economica 1, 4.
[166] May, *supra* n. 10, 471; Kynaston, *supra* n. 156, 421.
[167] Finnie, *supra* n. 95, 190.
[168] 'City Notes', Times, August 15, 1936; see also Grant, *supra* n. 8, 164–65.
[169] 'Stock Exchange', *supra* n. 161, 368.

'Business on the Stock Exchange depends on the confidence of investors' and that the Stock Exchange was 'potentially a far more effective source of protection to the investor than the law'.[170] The underlying logic was that, because the London Stock Exchange made and enforced its own rules rather than having to depend on Parliamentary involvement, it could amend the relevant regulations promptly and waive them judiciously in appropriate circumstances. The Cohen Committee's 1945 report echoed praise of this feature, saying the 'flexibility makes it possible for (rules) to be more stringent and to afford the investor a greater degree of protection than could be achieved by statute except at the cost of hampering legitimate business'.[171] The upshot is that the efforts of the London Stock Exchange should have fortified the buy side for shares in the 1930s even in the absence of an immediate legislative response to blows investors suffered between 1929 and 1931.

4. Market Oriented 'Quality Control'

Between 1880 and 1914, the quality of screening provided by financial intermediaries organizing public offerings of shares left much to be desired but the fact that equity was often distributed on an informal, local basis significantly diminished potential informational asymmetries (Chapter Six, Part III.B.4, C.2). The Macmillan Committee acknowledged the pattern, saying in its 1931 report that industrial enterprises in the UK had traditionally refrained from looking to the London market to meet their financial requirements because 'there had existed for many years in this country a large class of investors with means to invest, who exercised an independent judgment as to what to invest in' and indicated that in many instances 'the most satisfactory method' for arranging smaller issues of shares remained 'through brokers or through some private channel among investors in the locality where the business is situated'.[172]

As the Macmillan Report implies, local capital markets retained some vitality during the interwar years, illustrated by the fact numerous public offerings were carried out on provincial stock exchanges, particularly during the new issue booms occurring in 1919/20 and the late 1920s.[173] There also remained in certain major provincial centres, such as Birmingham and Bristol, ample capital available to finance smaller enterprises with promising track records.[174] Still, the regional orientation of capital markets was fading in importance. Grant observed in the mid-1930s that 'the small issue of purely local interest would appear to be rare', and quoted a report from Liverpool referring to 'the almost complete elimination of the small private capitalist'.[175]

---

[170] Finnie, *supra* n. 95, 182, 183.   [171] Cohen Report, *supra* n. 149, 14.

[172] Macmillan Report, *supra* n. 76, 162, 174.

[173] W.A. Thomas, *The Provincial Stock Exchanges* (1973), 248–51; David Chambers and Elroy Dimson, 'IPO Underpricing Over the Very Long Run', (2006), unpublished working paper, at 7.

[174] Grant, *supra* n. 8, 225–26, 229.

[175] *Ibid.*, 223, 228; see also Ellinger, *supra* n. 5, 315.

The new pattern was due partly to an interwar shift in the geographical distribution of industry that brought firms closer to the London market, which in turn was offering increasingly efficient facilities for public offerings by domestic companies.[176] Also, investment in local industrial enterprises was a significant casualty when, due largely to tax, demand for shares diminished among the rich investors who frequently provided backing for industrial enterprises pre-1914 (Part II, A.2). Sir Josiah Stamp, a business executive, statistician and Bank of England director, made the point when giving evidence to the Macmillan Committee, saying, '[Y]ou cannot expect these private businesses to be financed as they were by people who knew them once the money has left them by high taxation and . . . if (wealthy investors' money) is bid for by home enterprise it goes into the very large concerns.'[177] Balogh, in a 1947 study of financial organization in Britain, concurred, saying of the interwar years 'the incidence of taxation must have impeded the finance of industry by private capitalists'.[178]

While the regional orientation of industrial finance diminished during the interwar period, potential investors in shares were able to draw comfort from improved quality control by the financial intermediaries organizing public offerings of shares. Many imperfections admittedly remained. The 'golden age' of the Hooley-style individual company promoter was over by the interwar years.[179] Nevertheless, there continued to be flamboyant individuals who used the finance houses they established to operate in a similar way, at least in buoyant market conditions. Clarence Hatry was best known in this category, establishing Austin Friars Trust in 1927 and relying on it as the linchpin of a series of ambitious but ill-fated company promotions (Part II.A.1, B.2). Eugen Spier was another example. Through his Lothbury Trust, he organized the flotation of Combined Pulp and Paper Mills Ltd in 1927 to acquire various pulp and paper operations. Spier initially profited handsomely when the public offering was a success and Lothbury Trust sold a large portion of the shares it held in Combined Pulp and Paper at advantageous prices.[180] However, Combined Pulp and Paper soon went bankrupt and Spier, together with a number of other defendants, was held liable for fraudulently misrepresenting the company's first-year profits in support of a follow-up public offering of shares.[181]

On the positive side, reputable financial intermediaries increasingly became involved in the issuance of securities by UK-based companies during the interwar years. One important development was the emergence of a class of issuing

[176] Grant, *supra* n. 8, 223; Balogh, *supra* n. 55, 275.

[177] Quoted in Ranald C. Michie, 'The Stock Exchange and the British Economy, 1870–1939' in J.J. van Helten and Y. Cassis (eds), *Capitalism in a Mature Economy: Financial Institutions, Capital Exports and British Industry, 1870–1939* (1990), 95, 105.

[178] Balogh, *supra* n. 55, 275.

[179] John Armstrong, 'The Rise and Fall of the Company Promoter and the Financing of British Industry', in van Helten and Cassis, *supra*, n. 177, 115, 132.

[180] Samuels, *supra* n. 9, 74–75; Kynaston, *supra* n. 156, 139.

[181] 'Law Report', Times, July 28, 1932.

house that treated the preparation and sponsoring of new issues as their principal business and was inclined to carry out meaningful quality control.[182] The business model of these issuing houses meant a reputation for reliability was a key asset. It was standard practice for them to ask banking houses, insurers, trust companies and rich individuals to underwrite issues. The influence and reputation of an issuing house was pivotal in building up and maintaining a long list of potential underwriters, who usually would agree to participate on the basis of what they knew of the issuing house rather than on the basis of any investigation of the companies the shares of which were being distributed. As Hobson said in 1938, 'The City...pays an enormous regard to the character of the "stable" in which an issue is bred.'[183] That meant, as Grant said of issuing houses, 'The real strength of these institutions is to be found in their reputations and connections with the investing public.'[184]

Issuing houses that treated their reputation as a valuable asset had a potent incentive to carry out quality control. According to a 1930 text on investing in public companies, 'The (high-class) Issuing House has a high conception of its responsibilities towards the investor, and it is anxious to ensure, so far as practicable, that its name should only be associated with sound and respectable undertakings, and that the terms on which the investor is invited to take an interest in these are fair.'[185] As part of the vetting process, reputable issuing houses would require a full description of the business, study the past record of profits earned, determine the general market standing of the firm and ascertain the capabilities of those in charge.[186] Leading examples of issuing houses of operating in this manner were the Charterhouse Investment Trust and Philip Hill & Partners, both of which specialized in sponsoring industrial issues of £200,000 upwards, and the Leadenhall Securities Corporation, set up in the mid-1930s to deal with smaller issues.[187]

Stockbroking concerns also began to play a positive role in the launching of public offerings during the interwar years.[188] Such firms generally specialized in investing on behalf of clients, arranging for the buying and selling of shares already in the market in so doing. However, opportunities to organize public offerings of shares could arise when industrialist clients approached them when first contemplating new issues and stockbrokers could take advantage of their familiarity with the domestic economy and extensive professional contacts to orchestrate matters effectively. Stockbroking concerns had incentives to exercise

---

[182] Thomas, *supra* n. 18, 49; Balogh, *supra* n. 55, 259–60; Stanley Chapman, *The Rise of Merchant Banking* (1984), 102–3.

[183] Oscar Hobson, *How the City Works* (1938), 106.

[184] Grant, *supra* n. 8, 155.

[185] A.E. Cutforth, *Public Companies and the Investor* (1930), 148.

[186] Ellinger, *supra* n. 5, 289.

[187] Thomas, *supra* n. 18, 119; Balogh, *supra* n. 55, 289–90; Chapman, *supra* n. 182, 102–3.

[188] Ellinger, *supra* n. 5, 304–7; Grant, *supra* n. 8, 155–56; Michie, *supra* n. 75, 229–30, 260–61.

quality control akin to well-regarded new issue houses because they wanted to avoid tarnishing the reputation for honesty and reliability they had built up in their core business. Most stockbrokers handled only a few public offerings, but a handful carried out a substantial number, with the best-known being Cazenove.

Growing involvement of London's leading merchant banks (e.g. Barings, Rothschilds and Lazards) in the new issue market further enhanced its credibility.[189] Interwar merchant banks, mindful of their reputational capital, emphasized quality control when they orchestrated a public offering, with a director of Lazards telling the Macmillan Committee, 'If we put our name to... (an issue)... we really say to the public, "We have looked thoroughly into this, we thoroughly believe in it and we can recommend it." '[190] Elite merchant banks largely shunned public offerings of UK companies prior to World War I and even 'in the 1920s, it was often a case of dipping their toes generally into the murky waters of domestic industrial finance...'[191] However, the steep interwar decline in overseas investment forced a rethink, and first-class merchant banks increasingly took on domestic business, at least when large issues were involved. Since their involvement gave an important implicit endorsement to the public offerings they handled and since they watched carefully over issues they launched, their increased participation in the interwar domestic capital market bolstered the market-oriented 'quality control' on which buyers of shares could rely.

5. *Financial Press*

The press can assist with quality control on the buy side by scrutinizing the merits of share offerings companies are carrying out and by publicizing the failures of incompetent and corrupt corporate managers and financial intermediaries (Chapter Four, Part III.D). The editor of the *Investor's Chronicle* said in 1946 that 'Today, in my admittedly partial opinion, the British public is very well served in its financial press.'[192] Nevertheless, the market environment in which the press operated significantly compromised the protection it afforded to investors during the interwar years.

Discussion of the merits of particular investments was highly popular with interwar readers.[193] However, as the *Economist* pointed out in 1933, 'A disappointment... may await investors who look to the modern newspaper for outspoken judgment and, in extreme cases, for scathing condemnation of doubtful prospectuses.' Instead, newspapers took 'a "safe" line by confining (themselves) to non-committal views, or employ(ed) a conventionalised phraseology of under-statement'.[194]

---

[189] Grant, *supra* n. 8, 154–55; Thomas, *supra* n. 18, 48–49.
[190] Quoted in Atkin, *supra* n. 82, 103.
[191] Kynaston, *supra* n. 156, 135; Ch. Six, Pt III.B.4.
[192] Wincott, *supra* n. 122, 95.   [193] *Ibid.*, 98.
[194] 'Prospectus Law', *supra* n. 124, 306.

In some instances, journalists were non-committal because they were poorly informed and had not bothered to check the accuracy of the prospectuses on which they were reporting.[195] Libel laws were another constraint. The editor of the *Financial News* estimated concerns about being sued precluded the press from exposing perhaps half-a-dozen scandals occurring in the midst of the stock market boom of 1928/29.[196] Advertising fees derived from the publication of prospectuses and other documentation relating to share issuances also compromised the frankness of the views expressed. Reputable newspapers maintained that editorial policy was unaffected. However, as even the editor of the *Investor's Chronicle* acknowledged, the fact that damning companies making public offerings could jeopardize advertising business was a 'thorny matter'.[197] The *Economist* suggested in 1933 '[T]he newspaper critic has to take a position of impartiality towards projects from the launching of which his newspaper derives substantial revenue.'[198] The financial press accordingly could offer only limited reassurance to investors and thus likely did not make a major contribution to the buy side in the interwar years.

6. Returns in Comparison with Other Investments

As in other eras (Chapter Four, Part III.E), during the interwar years the performance of shares relative to other investment options influenced decisions investors made about owning shares. H.E. Raynes, an executive at Legal and General, a major insurer, spearheaded debate on asset allocation by insurance companies by showing in 1928 and 1937 academic papers that, as compared with corporate debentures, ordinary shares had delivered higher income in addition to superior capital appreciation, implying ordinary shares were a safe as well as a remunerative investment.[199] Grant explained a surge of new issues by companies in the mid-1930s partly in terms of a fall in returns on gilt-edged securities, saying the decline caused 'investors to turn to new fields in the search for openings bringing in a larger return'.[200] A 1940 text on London's financial district agreed relative performance influenced demand for investments, saying of fixed-interest securities and shares, '[I]nvestors whose main interest is to secure as far as possible the same income under all circumstances will change from one form of investment to the other with changes in the relationship of prices.'[201]

During the interwar period equities stacked up well in comparison with other major investment options. The difficulties from which overseas investments

---

[195] Dennett, *supra* n. 96, 14.

[196] Kynaston, *supra* n. 156, 140. See also 'Prospectus Law', *supra* n. 124, 306.

[197] Wincott, *supra* n. 122, 93.

[198] 'Prospectus Law', *supra* n. 124, 306.

[199] Raynes, *supra* n. 17; H.E. Raynes, 'Equities and Fixed Interest Stocks During Twenty-Five Years', (1937) 68 Journal of the Institute of Actuaries 483. On Raynes and the debate on investment by insurers, see Trebilcock, *supra* n. 85, 597–98; Baker and Collins, *supra* n. 88, 144–45.

[200] Grant, *supra* n. 8, 148, 152.

[201] Ellinger, *supra* n. 5, 341.

suffered have already been noted (Part II.B.1). Raynes' 1937 paper indicated that between 1912 and 1936 the income generated by equities was almost double that of corporate debentures.[202] Shares were also a better bet than government bonds, with the average annual net of tax return on a broadly based portfolio of leading shares being 12.4 per cent between 1919 and 1939 as compared with 6.5 per cent for gilt-edged securities.[203] Given that investors would have been comparing the returns equities delivered in comparison with obvious alternatives, the fact shares performed well in relative terms should have provided support for the buy side for shares during the interwar years.

7. Dividends

Disclosure requirements imposed on UK public companies were generally meagre on the eve of World War I (Chapter Six, Part III.B.2) and legislative amendments coming into force in 1929 made only modest improvements (Part II.B.2). Correspondingly, as Parkinson suggested in 1932, 'the majority of balance sheets (were) distressingly unilluminating'.[204] The *Economist* said likewise in 1934 of the state of corporate disclosure, '[T]he majority of published reports still fail to satisfy all the requirements of reasonably informative documents. Legal stipulations are frequently interpreted in a Puritan spirit, and may well serve only to create a barrier behind which obscurantism may shelter in complete inviolability.'[205] Prior to World War I, investors deciding which shares to buy and sell in secondary trading relied heavily on dividends to compensate for the lack of available financial data and their interwar counterparts apparently did likewise.[206]

Direct UK-based empirical tests of the signalling properties of dividends were not carried out until near the end of the 20th century (Chapter Four, Part III.D). Nevertheless, the manner in which those deciding upon dividend policy on behalf of interwar companies conducted themselves offers strong circumstantial evidence that dividends functioned as an influential informational signal. At the anecdotal level, Lord Kylsant clearly believed dividends 'mattered' since his plan to sustain confidence in Royal Mail hinged largely on ensuring the company paid dividends to ordinary shareholders (Part I.D). The chairman of the board of Dunlop Rubber Company took the same view, saying at a 1931 shareholder meeting there were 'tremendous arguments' in favour of the company declaring an interim dividend to reassure investors, rather than allowing bearish speculation regarding the company to persist.[207]

[202] Raynes, *supra* n. 199, 490–91.
[203] A.J. Merrett and Allen Sykes, 'Return on Equities and Fixed Interest Securities: 1919–1966', District Bank Review, June 1966, 29, 36, 41. See also Scott, *supra* n. 86, 93, relying on data compiled by Barclays de Zoete Wedd to report similar results.
[204] Parkinson, *supra* n. 136, 116.
[205] 'Toward Better Accounting', Economist, December 22, 1934, 1210, 1210.
[206] Ch. Six, Pt III.C.3; Caudwell, *supra* n. 65, 93.
[207] 'Quarterly Earnings' Statements', Economist, June 13, 1931, 1282.

Even more revealing is what Dudley Docker, just named a director of Vickers after it had bought MCWF (Part I.H), said in a 1919 letter to the chairman of Vickers after the Vickers board cut the dividend from 12½ per cent to 11¼ per cent, rather than to 10 per cent as he recommended. He indicated the episode was

'most unsatisfactory, for it has defeated the object which we all had in view, namely to fix the dividend at a sum which could be maintained steadily year by year. The impression now created is that the Board have been unable to maintain the 12½ per cent and have strained to get as near to it as possible... (I)t will be impossible to drop the dividend again next year without creating a bad impression as to the profit-earning capacity of the company.'[208]

The desired policy Docker referred to has been labelled as 'dividend smoothing', which means only making adjustments to dividend payouts in response to substantial and persistent changes in earnings rather than purely in response to annual financial results. Various empirical tests of dividend policy, typically involving US companies, indicate directors in fact do tend to resist cutting dividends in response to a temporary decline in earnings and only increase distributions to shareholders when they are confident higher payments can be maintained.[209] Directors are inclined to 'smooth' dividends because of concerns about a negative investor reaction if they set dividend policy differently. The logic, according to a 1979 text on UK business finance, is that 'shareholders value steadily increasing dividends very highly because they think such a rise would not be implemented unless directors had confidence in being able to maintain it. Hence... (d)irectors try hard not to reduce dividends, resorting if necessary to past undistributed profits to maintain them.'[210]

The available statistical evidence suggests those setting dividend policy in the UK during the interwar years adopted a policy of 'smoothing'. According to a study of a sample of 510 companies operating in a wide range of industrial sectors between 1925 and 1934, directors became somewhat more willing to allow dividend payments to fluctuate in accordance with earnings after the 1929/30 stock market slump but generally were strongly inclined to keep dividend payments stable.[211] This implies in turn those running companies during the interwar years were cognizant dividends had a strong signalling aspect.

Directors were correct in assuming investors thought dividends were important. During the summer of 1926 shares in industrial companies were rising smartly until Courtaulds, a leading manufacturer of rayon, cut its interim dividend by 16.7 per cent from the previous year. Even though the *Economist*

---

[208] Davenport-Hines, *supra* n. 56, 171–72.

[209] For summaries, see Ronald C. Lease, Kose John, Avner Kalay, Uri Loewenstein and Oded H. Sarig, *Dividend Policy: Its Impact on Firm Value* (2000), 128–29; Luis Correia da Silva, Marc Goergen and Luc Renneboog, *Dividend Policy and Corporate Governance* (2003), 41.

[210] Midgley and Burns, *supra* n. 67, 253.

[211] Ronald Hope, 'Profits in British Industry from 1925 to 1935', (1949) 1 Oxford Economic Papers (N.S.) 159, 170–77.

labelled the reduction as 'trifling', it acknowledged the dividend cut 'set in train a good deal of uneasiness among holders of shares of other popular industrial companies. People who had been running after the industrials, and buying the shares more on tips than on sound reasons, became suddenly frightened.'[212] The Stock Exchange itself acknowledged the influence of dividends in the late 1930s when it requested companies to make dividend announcements in accordance with Exchange guidelines and set up 'Trans Lux'—a large screen—to convey dividend news, together with other key announcements, simultaneously to all members of the London Stock Exchange.[213]

By the mid-1920s US investors were increasingly turning their attention from dividends to earnings in valuing shares.[214] Various UK observers argued British investors should do the same, with a 1930 text on investment saying, 'Past dividends naturally are a feature of great interest, but a more illuminating and reliable test of a company's worth is provided by its record of actual earnings, and it is on these chiefly that share prices are, or should be, based.'[215] With mergers carried out in the late 1920s designed to rationalize production in a series of troubled industries, investors did in fact buy shares in public offerings at prices reflecting anticipated future earnings (generously estimated) rather than on the basis of the dividend policies or profitability of the constituent companies.[216] Generally, however, interwar UK investors were less inclined than their US counterparts to forsake dividends in favour of earnings as the chosen metric for evaluating shares.[217]

Differences in the dividend policies UK and US companies adopted constituted one reason for the discrepancy. Publicly traded industrial and commercial companies in the UK distributed most of their earnings as dividends during the interwar years—nearly 75 per cent, on average, according to data from the *Economist* (Part I.D). Their US counterparts were more inclined to retain earnings, with the payout ratio averaging 61 per cent annually between 1915 and 1929.[218] Hence, while a crude assessment of the earning power of UK companies could plausibly begin and end with the dividend payout, in the US, investors were under a greater onus to investigate profits data to make an equivalent determination.

[212] 'The Lull in Speculation', Economist, July 24, 1926, 150, 151.

[213] 'Announcement of Dividends', Times, December 13, 1938, 24 (dividend announcements); F.E. Armstrong, *The Book of the Stock Exchange*, 5th edn, (1957), 123–24 (Trans Lux).

[214] Janette Rutterford, 'From Dividend Yield to Discounted Cash Flow: A History of UK and US Equity Valuation Techniques', (2004) 14 Accounting, Business & Financial History 115, 129.

[215] Caudwell, *supra* n. 65, 98; see also Withers, *supra* n. 99, 142–43; Parkinson, *supra* n. 136, 218–19.

[216] 'The Activity of Industrial Shares', Economist, September 3, 1927, 388; 'The Capitalisation of British Mergers', Economist, July 26, 1930, 182.

[217] Rutterford, *supra* n. 214, 130–36.

[218] Jack W. Wilson and Charles P. Jones, 'An Analysis of the S&P 500 and Cowles' Extensions: Price Indexes and Stock Returns', (2002) 75 Journal of Business 527, 528–29. See also May, *supra* n. 38, 735; P. Sargant Florence, 'The Statistical Analysis of Joint Stock Company Control', (1947) 110 Journal of the Royal Statistical Society 1, 3. During the 1930s, the ratio of dividends to profits was much higher than the previous norm in the US as many companies maintained dividend payments despite profits being crushed by the Depression.

Tax was another factor. Under the UK income tax regime, companies deducted tax 'at source' on behalf of shareholders, who then would typically be liable to pay additional income tax if they were surtax payers since they would only be credited for tax paid on their behalf by the company at the 'standard' rate of income tax (Part I.E). As the tax position of shareholders varied and was unknown to companies, it was impossible for companies to report corporate earnings net of income tax.[219] In contrast, beginning in 1917 companies and individuals in the US were taxed separately, meaning that companies could readily report earnings after corporate taxes, which in turn facilitated investor analysis of profits data.[220]

The quality of accounts was a final reason earnings failed to displace dividends as the dominant factor in the valuation of shares in the UK in the interwar years. In the US, corporate disclosure was far from perfect, illustrated by the fact Ivar Kreuger could rely on a combination of secrecy and dubious accounting practices to build up a $600 million 'match empire' that collapsed largely without warning in 1932.[221] Nevertheless, in a couple of ways American shareholders were better situated during the interwar years to draw inferences on the basis of earnings data than their counterparts in Britain.

First, sales figures, an important accounting metric for investors because the data can be used to discern trends in profit margins,[222] were generally available in the US but not the UK. In the US, the Securities Exchange Act of 1934 required companies that had distributed shares to the public to divulge annual turnover data and prior to this a majority of companies quoted on the New York Stock Exchange provided the figures voluntarily.[223] UK companies were not required to publish turnover figures until 1967 and British companies generally did not reveal such data voluntarily before then.[224]

Second, during the interwar years the New York Stock Exchange's listing rules encouraged leading US public companies to engage in quarterly reporting, whereas neither UK companies legislation nor the London Stock Exchange's listing rules required companies to publish financial data other than annually.[225] The *Economist* remarked on the discrepancy in 1931, saying, 'At a time when earnings are liable to sudden and extensive fluctuations, the advantages enjoyed

---

[219] May, *supra* n. 38, 736.

[220] Bank, *supra* n. 38, 2, 15–22, 30–31; Rutterford, *supra* n. 214, 131.

[221] Paul G. Mahoney, 'The Exchange as Regulator', (1997) 83 Virginia Law Review 1453, 1467 (disclosure quality generally); 'The Match King', Economist, December 22, 2007, 113 (Kreuger).

[222] Rutterford, *supra* n. 214, 131; George J. Benston, 'Required Disclosure and the Stock Market: An Evaluation of the Securities Exchange Act of 1934', (1973) 63 American Economic Review 132, 142; Securities Exchange Act of 1934, 15 USC 78.

[223] Benston, *supra* n. 222, 142.

[224] P.J. Naish, *The Complete Guide to Personal Investment* (1962), 96; Ch. Ten, Pt IV.D.

[225] On the UK, see Pt II.B.2 (company law); Code Holland and Werry, *supra* n. 152, 420, London Stock Exchange, Rules, Appendix 35B, para. 10 (setting out provisions quoted companies had to include in their articles concerning disclosure). On the US, see Mahoney, *supra* n. 221, 1466; Carol J. Simon, 'The Effect of the 1933 Securities Act on Investor Information and the Performance of New Issues', (1989) 79 American Economic Review 295, 297–98.

by American investors—who, on average, are nine months ahead of British investors as regards real knowledge of their position—are self-evident.' The *Economist* went on to say, '[I]t would undeniably be helpful if some British company, of first-class importance, were prepared to break with tradition and get the ball rolling.'[226] This did not happen, as even following World War II it remained uncommon for UK public companies to produce half-yearly statements, let alone quarterly figures.[227] The upshot was that while there was growing awareness in Britain that earnings constituted a significant potential benchmark in valuing equity, investors typically continued to treat dividends as the more trustworthy reference point when deciding which shares to buy and sell.

8. *Market Sentiment*

A 1927 text on UK industrial finance observed 'The public should understand that the Stock Exchange, like every other market, is quite ready to make use of waves of feeling, even if it is irrational feeling.'[228] A 1939 survey of the UK capital market suggested similarly an 'unfortunate feature of the market for new issues of ordinary shares is its dependence on the speculatively minded class of capitalist'.[229] There was plenty of historical precedent to support these claims, since, extending back to the 1690s, there were numerous instances where waves of optimistic market sentiment helped to underpin the buy side for shares (Chapter Four, Part III.F). The pattern was evident again in the interwar years, though it was diminishing in intensity.

The first wave of investor enthusiasm was the 1919/20 'Peace boom', which was fortified by spare capital accumulated during wartime, the relaxation of capital controls and general post-World War I optimism (Part I.H). The *Economist* suggested during the ensuing market downswing that investors had learned their lesson, saying, '[T]he satisfactory part about the present trend of investment is the increasing discrimination shown by the average investor in making his purchases...Financial education is obviously making substantial progress.'[230] However, the educational effect seemingly was short-lived. By '1927–28, the public were avid for investment and speculation,'[231] as the excitement of an epic bull market on Wall Street spilled over to the London Stock Exchange.

Investor enthusiasm in the late 1920s was evidenced by 'the repeated over-subscription of speculative issues, the attraction of whose deferred shares as gambling counters were more regarded by the public than their merits as an investment'.[232] A new element was that the investor class was growing markedly in size (Part II.A.2).

---

[226] 'Quarterly Earnings", *supra* n. 207, 1282.

[227] 'British Companies Urged to Disclose More', Times, February 11, 1964.

[228] A.S. Wade, *Modern Finance and Industry* (1927), 86; see also Kissan and Williams, *supra* n. 66, 82–83.

[229] Gordon, *supra* n. 100, 514.

[230] 'The Investor's Education', Economist, May 14, 1921, 971, 971.

[231] Finnie, *supra* n. 95, 152.

[232] 'The Year's New Capital', Economist, November 10, 1928, 1206, 1208.

At least some of these new investors were speculatively minded. As Finnie said in 1934, 'This young and impetuous public had picked up the jargon of speculation. They were immensely interested in new enterprises, in fresh inventions, in products that had yet to be marketed.'[233] The flourish of investor optimism was met by a flurry of public offerings of shares, nearly 300 in 1928 alone (Part I.A).

While investor sentiment helped to shape the buy side in the UK during the interwar years, it likely was not as potent a factor as it had been in previous eras. Murphy said of securities markets in 1941, '(t)he speculative impulse on the part of the public in England is considered to be held to a minimum level'.[234] She attributed the relative absence of speculative momentum to the careful vetting conducted by financial intermediaries organizing public offerings of shares and the habit of British investors of relying heavily on conservative-minded stockbrokers and family bankers for advice.[235] Regardless of the precise reasons, the new issue boom in the late 1920s may have been exciting for contemporaries but it apparently paled in comparison to prior stock market frenzies in Britain.[236] Markets were also sedate compared with the US. UK share prices never came close to reaching the dizzying heights they did stateside, nor fell as precipitously when matters went into reverse. (Figure III).

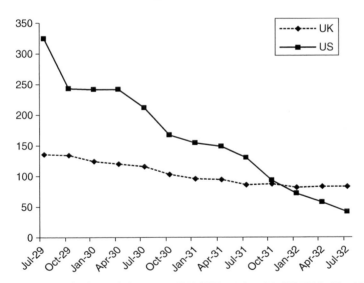

Figure III: Prices of industrial shares, UK/US (UK 1924 = 100; US 1923–25 = 100)
Source: Compiled with data from Paish and Schwartz, *supra* n. 88, 98–99.[237]

[233] Finnie, *supra* n. 95, 161.
[234] Mary E. Murphy, 'The English Approach to the Distribution of Securities', (1941) 14 Journal of Business 372, 373.
[235] *Ibid.*, 379–83.   [236] Parkinson, *supra* n. 95, 129.
[237] Paish and Schwartz only provide three-month averages for the US for 1929 and 1930. For the purposes of the chart, these have been matched with the monthly figures for the UK for July 1929, October 1929, January 1930, April 1930, July 1930 and October 1930.

During the mid-1930s, amidst a strong recovery from the economic slump earlier in the decade, industrial share prices reached their interwar peak.[238] The bull market was accompanied by a surge of new issues, with the aggregate amount of capital raised by industrial companies and public utilities growing from £70.2 million in 1933 to £165.6 million in 1936, which exceeded the 1928 total (£159.4 million).[239] Perhaps because of fresh memories of prior booms gone wrong or increased London Stock Exchange regulation, the swing upwards was unaccompanied by a wave of speculative flotations.[240] Instead, to begin with the public offerings were 'mostly new mining propositions...or established enterprises with a satisfactory record under private auspices', followed by established engineering and manufacturing companies anticipating expansion as Britain began rearmament for the looming conflict with Germany.[241] Correspondingly, there was little adverse fallout when market conditions went sour as the 1930s drew to a close, as only a tiny fraction of the new issues went badly wrong and cost investors the money they put up.[242] This confirms Murphy's assessment of the relative sobriety of the interwar UK share market, which in turn implies market sentiment played a diminished role on the buy side as compared with previous eras.

III. The Pattern of Ownership and Control

While during the late 19th and early 20th centuries there was momentum in favour of blockholders unwinding their stakes and investors buying shares, as of 1914 a divorce between ownership and control remained the exception to the rule (Chapter Seven). Matters conceivably could have changed during the interwar years. Various factors encouraged exit on the sell side and supported demand for shares on the buy side. Moreover, as we will see now, outside investors buying shares were generally not inclined to adopt a 'hands on' approach to corporate governance and there were numerous references by contemporaries to a separation of ownership and control. Nevertheless, the outsider/arm's-length system of ownership and control that came to characterize the UK had yet to take final form by the eve of World War II.

---

[238] Aldcroft, *supra* n. 1, 43–44 (on the economic recovery); London and Cambridge Economic Service, *Key Statistics of the British Economy 1900–1962* (1963), 6 (share price index covering interwar years).

[239] Grant, *supra* n. 8, 149.

[240] Wincott, *supra* n. 122, 128; see also Gordon, *supra* n. 100, 512.

[241] 'Boom Symptoms in the Capital Market?', Economist, September 8, 1934, 450, 450; 'Re-Armament Boom Finance', Economist, October 10, 1936, 71.

[242] Wincott, *supra* n. 122, 128–29.

A. Outside Investors and Control

Outsider/arm's-length corporate governance is contingent upon those buying shares being predisposed towards passivity. Interwar investors generally qualified, since neither individuals nor institutional shareholders were inclined to be activist. Before we consider their position, corporate investment in shares deserves consideration.

Though corporate cross-ownership has been the exception to the rule in the UK (Chapter Four, Part I) corporate blockholders were by no means unknown during the interwar years. Of 62 'very large' industrial and commercial companies for which Florence provides a detailed breakdown of share ownership as of 1936, in six instances the largest shareholder was a company (other than an institutional investor) owning a stake of 20 per cent or more.[243] Also, whereas British-based subsidiaries of US companies typically were wholly owned by the parent, as of 1935 there were 61 instances where the US parent held either a majority or substantial minority stake in a company with equity traded on a UK stock market.[244]

There was potential for considerably greater corporate cross-ownership. Interwar observers characterized the investment portfolios of large UK companies as being 'very considerable' and of 'surprising magnitude' and suggested the potential significance of the investment holdings of 'matured' companies was 'very great'.[245] As of the mid-1930s, Britain's four major railway companies owned between them investment securities worth some £40 million (£1.91 billion in 2006 currency) and 11 of Britain's largest industrial companies had collective investment holdings of £85 million, approximately 35 per cent of their nominal issued capital.[246] Capital available for deployment on this scale created theoretical potential for substantial corporate investment in the shares of publicly traded companies. However, it went largely unrealized because large interwar companies tied up their capital in government bonds and other highly liquid securities, not shares.[247]

Parkinson recommended in 1932 that major companies with sizeable investment portfolios adopt a more adventurous approach to improve returns.[248] However, for various reasons conservatism was sustained.[249] First, companies wanted to have ready access to cash should it be required and fixed interest

---

[243] Amalgamated Metal, Associated Electrical Industries, British American Tobacco, British United Shoe Machinery, Ford Motor Co. and Woolworth F.W.: see Florence, *supra* n. 45, 196–217.

[244] Geoffrey Jones and Frances Bostock, 'US Multinationals in British Manufacturing Before 1962', (1996) 70 Business History Review 207, 239–40.

[245] Grant, *supra* n. 8, 196–97; Parkinson, *supra* n. 136, 129.

[246] Grant, *supra* n. 8, 196–97.

[247] *Ibid.*, 197; Parkinson, *supra* n. 136, 128–29.

[248] Parkinson, *supra* n. 136, 130–32; see also Grant, *supra* n. 8, 197.

[249] Parkinson, *supra* n. 136, 128–29.

investments offered greater liquidity than equities. Second, investments in fixed interest securities could be a beneficial hedge against downswings in the economic cycle.

Third, investor scepticism came into play. UK investors have traditionally disliked messy corporate structures, typified by cross-holdings and minority positions in publicly traded companies.[250] Scepticism of corporate cross-ownership was already present during the interwar years. A 1930 text on investment said 'Groups of companies with interlocking finances present a still worse problem. Stockbrokers and the public are coming to realise that it is not good business to spend a great deal of time puzzling over a company whose affairs are a tangle of intricate accountancy, seeing that there are 34,999 or so other securities available from which to pick.'[251] The Hatry and Royal Mail scandals, which both implicated interlocking companies and directorates and prompted extensive debate about the inadequacies of holding company accounts, heightened investor scepticism of corporate cross-holdings. As a 1972 study of the Royal Mail debacle said, 'The capital market also reacted strongly to (its failure). Fears of "group finance" were reinforced.'[252] This scepticism would have helped to discourage investment in shares by major companies.

Corporate owners aside, there was little inclination on behalf of those buying shares in interwar public companies to exercise influence. The establishment of the Association of Investment Trust Companies (AITC) in 1932 did create some potential for collective intervention by institutional shareholders. The *Times* welcomed its establishment, saying that 'some association was needed for the purpose of representing and protecting the interests of the general body of investors'.[253] The AITC was soon working together with an investor protection committee established by the British Insurance Association, a potentially influential combination.[254] A 1935 study of insurance companies and investment trusts even suggested, '[T]he worldly-wise directorate of a company whose shareholders include one or more of the investment trusts not unnaturally regard it as politic to keep friendly with the trusts, and to consult them in advance regarding any proposals for policy alteration or reorganisation...'[255]

Generally, though, interwar institutional investors had only a peripheral impact on the companies in which they owned shares. Insurance companies and investment trusts grew in prominence as owners of shares between 1914 and 1939 but remained too much of a sideshow as investors to exercise substantial influence over companies in which they owned shares (Part II.A.1). Moreover,

[250] Tony Golding, *The City: Inside the Great Expectation Machine* (2000), 164.

[251] Caudwell, *supra* n. 65, 101; see also 'Parent Finance', Economist, January 19, 1929, 111.

[252] Davies and Bourn, *supra* n. 19, 122.

[253] 'Investment Trusts and Investors', Times, September 24, 1932, 16.

[254] Williams, *supra* n. 91, 157–58; 'The Association of Investment Trusts', Times, November 19, 1935, 22.

[255] Williams, *supra* n. 91, 160.

there was little inclination on their part to be activist. Even when insurance companies moved to the forefront as investors after World War II, they had little appetite for intervening in the affairs of the companies in which they owned shares (Chapter Ten, Part V.B). As for interwar investment trusts, their business model was based around diversified 'hands off' investment, not the accumulation of sizeable stakes in particular companies that would imply intervention as a governance strategy.[256] To the extent institutional activism occurred, it was narrowly focused. The AITC, together with the organizations it cooperated with, channelled its efforts into protecting the rights of preference shareholders in various capital reorganizations that occurred during the economic slump of the early 1930s.[257]

Private individuals owned collectively a much higher percentage of shares than institutional shareholders during the interwar years but they too were disinclined to exercise influence over the companies in which they owned shares. Shareholder interventions prompted reforms at Birmingham Small Arms and generated managerial and boardroom turnover at Rover, an automobile manufacturer, in the late 1920s and early 1930s.[258] Generally, however, individual shareholders adopted a passive stance.

The *Economist* remarked on the bias in favour of passivity in 1926, saying. 'Provided that the mass of shareholders receive their dividends regularly, the directors may hold their power indefinitely.'[259] It made the point again in 1929, indicating 'history afford(ed) certain, though not very numerous, instances of shareholders successfully resisting proposals...which appeared to them undesirable in one way or another'.[260] Parkinson observed similarly in 1932, 'the ownership of the capital of the average company has become diffused among small proprietors, comparable with an army in numbers but not in discipline or organization', with a major obstacle to intervention being that a dissident shareholder could 'look for little support from his fellow proprietors until matters have reached an advanced stage, when remedial measures may be ineffective'.[261] Or as Cole said in 1935, 'The great majority of investors...are mere buyers and sellers of stock market values, to whom it is utterly indifferent in what commodities or forms of production the companies in which their money is placed are engaged or in what manner their capital is employed.'[262]

---

[256] Youssef Cassis, 'The Emergence of a New Financial Institution: Investment Trusts in Britain, 1870–1939' in van Helten and Cassis, *supra*, n. 177, 139, 153.

[257] Newlands, *supra* n. 91, 200–1; 'Preference Share Rights', Times, November 25, 1933, 18; 'De Beers Plan Dropped', Times, July 5, 1935, 21.

[258] Ch. Four, Pt IV.B; J. Foreman-Peck, 'Exit, Voice and Loyalty as Responses to Decline: The Rover Company in the Inter-War Years', (1981) 22 Business History 191.

[259] 'The Ownership of British Industrial Capital—II', Economist, December 25, 1926, 1108, 1109.

[260] 'Shareholders and Control', Economist, March 30, 1929, 691, 692.

[261] Parkinson, *supra* n. 136, 220.   [262] Cole, *supra* n. 95, 84.

The explanations interwar observers offered to account for the bias in favour of passivity are familiar ones. These included the strategic advantage bestowed upon incumbent directors by their control of proxy voting, the 'rational apathy' of shareholders spawned by insufficient time, expertise and firm-specific information and the collective action problem afflicting shareholders otherwise minded to intervene.[263] Parkinson also drew attention to efficiency arguments in favour of shareholder passivity, while at the same time acknowledging what is currently known as the agency cost problem: 'Shareholders' interests, indeed, may be well served by giving a shrewd, skilful and hard-working executive its head. In less able and less scrupulous hands, however, the divorce of control from ownership offers formidable possibilities of abuse.'[264]

As the Parkinson quote implies, various interwar contemporaries, taking as read shareholder passivity, conjectured that a split between ownership and control had become the norm in large UK companies. Parkinson himself said '[I]t is not the banks and great corporate investors which control the supply of industry's capital, but the small investor, who probably knows very little about industries other than his own.'[265] The *Economist* observed similarly in 1931 that 'shareholders, as a body, have become progressively less cohesive and coherent as their numbers have expanded' and referred to 'a virtually complete divorce between ownership and control'.[266] Finnie likewise claimed in 1934 'to-day the divorce of ownership from management is almost complete'.[267] Cole made the same point the following year, maintaining the 'diffusion of share ownership is to a great extent a fact; but it carries with it practically no control by the owners of industry over the use which is made of their property'.[268] Compton and Bott, in a 1940 survey of British industry, concurred, indicating 'To-day, ownership often is divorced from active participation in industry, except in agriculture, and certain sectors of distribution.'[269] The available empirical evidence suggests on balance, however, these claims were exaggerated.

B. Evidence on Share Ownership Patterns

Small-scale empirical studies carried out during the interwar years lent credence to claims that ownership had become divorced from control. In 1926 the *Economist* investigated the share registers of 17 publicly traded companies. Its seven 'large size' companies had, on average, an ordinary/preference share

---

[263] For general analysis of reasons for shareholder passivity, see Ch. Four, Pt IV. On the interwar years, see Kissan and Williams, *supra* n. 66, 157; 'Proxies at Company Meetings', Economist, September 6, 1930, 453 (proxy voting); Cole, *supra* n. 95, 58–59, 84; Withers, *supra* n. 99, 85, 88–89, 118; Parkinson, *supra* n. 136, 13, 220 (other factors).

[264] Parkinson, *supra* n. 136, 11–12.   [265] *Ibid.*, 13.

[266] 'The Responsibilities of Directors', Economist, November 14, 1931, 916, 916.

[267] Finnie, *supra* n. 95, 28.   [268] Cole, *supra* n. 95, 90.

[269] M. Compton and E.H. Bott, *British Industry: Its Changing Structure in Peace and War* (1940), 128.

capital of £19.3 million, 35,400 ordinary shareholders and 98 'large' investors (defined as owners of £10,000+ worth of ordinary shares) holding cumulatively 27.3 per cent of the ordinary shares.[270] Its 10 'moderate size' companies had, on average, a share capital of £2.9 million, 7,900 ordinary shareholders and 10 'large' shareholders owning cumulatively 17.1 per cent of the shares. In 1932 Parkinson reported the results of a similar study for 10 companies, which, on average, had a paid up capital of £15.6 million, 44,300 shareholders and 19 large shareholders (holdings of 50,000+ shares) owning cumulatively 20.3 per cent of the shares.[271]

Parkinson followed up by examining for 1941/42 the share registers of 30 major publicly quoted companies. His results were similar, as the 30 companies had, on average, a total market capitalization (ordinary and preference shares) of £29.2 million, 27,600 ordinary shareholders and 64 large shareholders (holdings of 10,000+ shares) owning cumulatively 33.4 per cent of the ordinary shares.[272] Parkinson, analyzing his results, argued that 'Fragmentation of ownership, therefore, must be reckoned an ineradicable tendency' and that 'there is only one bond of union between shareholders—a common desire to obtain as high a dividend as possible'.[273] This verdict may have been apt at the time of publication of Parkinson's study (1951). However, the various interwar pronouncements that ownership had separated from control were premature.

Franks, Mayer and Rossi, for the purposes of a 2006 paper, examined the share ownership structure of a random sample of 53 unidentified quoted companies as of 1920.[274] In this sample the largest shareholder owned an average of 21 per cent of the shares, meaning it was the norm for companies to have a shareholder owning a sizeable if not controlling block of equity. In addition, the 10 largest shareholders owned collectively, on average, 43 per cent of the shares. Since institutional investors were a sideshow during the interwar years, the shareholders in question likely were individuals well known to the directors and minded to keep a close watch on what was going on because of having a substantial fraction of their personal wealth tied up (Chapter One, Part VII). Franks, Mayer and Rossi's companies therefore were unlikely to be characterized by any sort of full-scale separation of ownership and control.

Data compiled by Florence confirms that even as the interwar period drew to a close a divorce between ownership and control was not the norm. He examined as of 1936 share ownership patterns in the 82 UK manufacturing and commercial

---

[270] 'Ownership of British – II', *supra* n. 259; 'The Ownership of British Industrial Capital—I', Economist, December 18, 1926, 1053. The Economist, as it acknowledged, ignored the British government's 56 per cent holding in one of the companies, the Anglo-Persian Company.

[271] Parkinson, *supra* n. 136, 2–13. Four of the companies (Courtaulds, Cunard, Dunlop, Imperial Tobacco) were also part of the Economist study.

[272] Derived from Parkinson, *supra* n. 71, 17, 19, 41–42.

[273] *Ibid.*, 100.

[274] Julian Franks, Colin Mayer and Stefano Rossi, 'Ownership: Evolution and Regulation' (2006) ECGI Fin. Working Paper No. 09/2003, 19, Table 2.

(e.g. shipping and newspapers) companies qualifying as 'very large', in the sense they had issued share capital of over £3 million. Iron and steel companies and oil producers were excluded from his analysis.[275]

There was, according to Florence, 'no dominant ownership of interest' in only seven of the 82 companies, in the sense the largest 20 shareholders collectively owned less than 10 per cent of the shares.[276] Florence characterized 27 companies as 'marginal cases', these being 11 companies where the largest 20 shareholders owned between them 10 per cent and 20 per cent of the shares and 16 others where the largest 20 shareholders owned 20+ per cent of the shares but some large holders could not be identified. Florence categorized the remaining 48 companies as having a 'dominant ownership interest'. Of these, 13 had a majority shareholder, 12 had a single shareholder owning between 20 per cent and 50 per cent of the shares and lacked another shareholder owning 10 per cent or more of the shares and 23 had 'less concentrated dominance', in the sense the leading 20 shareholders owned 30 per cent or more of the shares. Florence also found that in the 82 companies the largest shareholder, on average, held 10.3 per cent of the shares.[277] Florence's assessment of the evidence was that 'Judging from the comparatively low proportion of companies with no discernible dominance of ownership interest, proclamation of the managerial revolution should perhaps, for the present, be postponed!'[278]

Florence's results were biased against finding a separation of ownership and control because he included neither railway companies nor deposit-taking banks in his sample. Diffuse share ownership was the norm in large railway companies as early as the mid-19th century (Chapter Five, Part V.A.2) and the pattern continued during the interwar years. The Railways Act of 1921 provided for the amalgamation of some 120 separate railway companies into four large groups.[279] Parkinson's 1941/42 data indicates each of the four lacked a major blockholder and had a large number of ordinary shareholders, ranging from 54,000 (the Great Western Railway) to 119,000 (the London & North Eastern).[280] As for banking, the 'Big Five' that moved to the forefront in English banking at the end of World War I continued to dominate and the fact they had by the end of the interwar period 325,000 shareholders between them and an average shareholding of around £200 implies the pattern of dispersed share ownership they had developed by 1919 was sustained.[281]

---

[275] P. Sargant Florence, *The Logic of British and American Industry: A Realistic Analysis of Economic Structure and Government* (1953), 187–89. Three companies with special voting provisions were also excluded.

[276] *Ibid.*, 202.   [277] *Ibid.*, 190.

[278] *Ibid.*, 202–3.

[279] Railways Act 1921, 11 & 12 Geo. 5, c. 55; Derek H. Aldcroft, *British Railways in Transition: The Economic Problems of Britain's Railways Since 1914* (1968), 41.

[280] Parkinson, *supra* n. 71, 86, 122–23, 125.

[281] Ch. Seven, Pt V (position up to 1918); Monopolies Commission, *Barclays Bank Ltd, Lloyds Bank Ltd and Martins Bank Ltd: A Report on the Proposed Marger* (1968), 9–10 (Big Five); Ellinger, *supra* n. 5, 214 (share ownership).

Florence's sample also excluded, however, companies where blockholding was likely to be a hallmark. His decision to leave out oil producers meant that the UK government's majority stake in Anglo-Persian Oil was not taken into account (Chapter Four, Part I). Similarly, Florence's decision not to cover iron and steel companies served to exclude an industry traditionally characterized by family-dominated companies, complicated somewhat by a shift of influence to banks and insurance companies as a result of crisis-driven restructurings in the late 1920s and early 1930s.[282] More generally, the publicly available share registers Florence relied on could only provide minimum estimates of the voting power of blockholders because shares held by members of a blockholder's family, family trusts or in nominee accounts might well be untraceable.[283] On balance, then, while there were various examples of companies with widely dispersed shares during the interwar years, Florence's evidence suggests this was not the predominant pattern.

The 'two-thirds' rule Hannah has cited as a catalyst for dispersal of share ownership was in force during the interwar years.[284] Nevertheless, it was commonplace for companies to go public without a wholesale dispersion of share ownership, with one reason being the London Stock Exchange's rules on granting 'permission to deal' did not include a requirement akin to the two-thirds rule (Part II.B.3). As a 1935 study of capital issues said, 'The public provides the vendors with cash, acquires the assets, but more often than not leaves the original owners in control... To keep control in the vendor's hands, the public is invited to subscribe mainly to preference shares or debentures, and only to a small proportion of the ordinary, sufficient of these being retained by the financiers and vendors to give them a majority of the voting power.'[285] A 1936 study by the *Economist* of 20 engineering and manufacturing companies confirmed the pattern, finding that on average 'insiders' retained 42 per cent of the voting power, including a 50+ per cent stake in eight instances.[286] Hence, while the two-thirds rule plausibly fostered at least some dispersion of share ownership during the interwar years, as was the case before 1914 its presence in the London Stock Exchange's rulebook does not provide conclusive proof of a divorce between ownership and control.

* * *

During the interwar years there was continued momentum on both the sell side and buy side in favour of diffusion of share ownership. Nevertheless, a full

---

[282] Vaizey, *supra* n. 79, 65, 69, 77.

[283] J.R.S. Revell, 'Book Review: *Ownership, Control and Success of Large Companies*', (1961) 71 Economic Journal 825, 826.

[284] Code Holland and Werry, *supra* n. 152, 419, London Stock Exchange, Rules, Appendix 35A, para. 4; Leslie Hannah, 'The Divorce of Ownership from Control from 1900: Re-calibrating Imagined Global Historical Trends', (2007) 49 Business History 404, 414–17.

[285] Group of Cambridge, *supra* n. 6, 134, 135.

[286] 'Re-Armament Boom', *supra* n. 241.

divorce between ownership and control apparently remained the exception to the rule. As Chapter Nine discusses, the transformation to an outsider/arm's-length system of ownership and control only concluded after 1939. Even then there was a potential twist. The institutional investors that came to dominate the buy side after World War II were in various ways well suited to use share ownership to take a 'hands on' role with the companies in which they owned shares. Chapter Ten explains both why institutional shareholders moved to the forefront as buyers of shares and why they were not inclined to exercise control over the companies in which they invested.

NINE

1940–1990: The Sell Side

As Chapters Six through Eight have discussed, during the late 19th and early 20th centuries there was in the UK activity on both the sell side and the buy side that fostered a separation of ownership and control in various instances. However, by World War II Britain still lacked a fully fledged outsider/arm's-length system of ownership and control. Moreover, railway companies, the leading examples of dispersed share ownership since the mid-19th century, were removed from the equation in 1947 when the Labour government nationalized the railway industry (Chapter Three, Part X). Nevertheless, as Part II of this chapter describes, between 1940 and 1990 a separation of ownership and control became the norm in large business enterprises in the UK. Part I puts the transformation into context by indicating that in the decades following World War II fledgling companies rarely (if ever) offered shares to the public and provincial capital markets faded into insignificance. Part III explains from the perspective of the sell side why ownership split from control following World War II, discussing the incentives block-holders had to exit or consent to dilution of their holdings and showing that in various ways these were more potent than had been the case prior to 1940.

I. Reduced Variation in the Share Market

Most business enterprises start their life with high insider ownership and if ownership separates from control, this only occurs at some later stage. Geographically, since the London Stock Exchange has historically been the dominant securities market in Britain, one might assume this is where the action would be. However, in the UK there were numerous instances over time where founders of a business enterprise launched it without ever having a controlling stake, such as canals in the late 18th century, railways in the early 19th century and electricity ventures in the late 19th century (Chapter Three, Part I; Chapter Six, Part II.A). Likewise, while the London Stock Exchange was always pre-eminent, historically the British securities market had a multicentred aspect, with stock exchanges emerging in key provincial centres during the mid-19th century and with shares often being distributed exclusively on a local or regional basis (Chapter Five, Part V.A; Chapter Six, Part I, Part III.C.2).

Diversity on these counts largely disappeared from the 1940s through to the 1980s. During this period it was essentially unknown for a public offering of shares to be used to generate 'start up' capital for a newly launched enterprise. Only one in three of the public offerings carried out on the London Stock Exchange between 1959 and 1963 by companies without shares previously traded on the Exchange brought any new money to the firm.[1] The ratio was even lower—one out of five—for public offerings carried out on provincial stock exchanges between 1951 and 1960.[2] Those companies that carried out initial public offerings to raise fresh capital were in turn unlikely to be fledgling enterprises. Instead, as Paish said in 1968, '[A] company needs to have grown to a very considerable size before it is in a position to make an issue on the London, or even on one of the provincial capital markets.'[3]

London Stock Exchange listing rules help to explain the pattern. Beginning in 1947, auditors of companies seeking a quotation were obliged to report on 10 years' worth of profits and losses.[4] While matters could proceed when the track record was shorter, the Stock Exchange discouraged such applications, thus essentially excluding 'start up' firms from the London stock market.[5] A requirement introduced in 1966 that a company seeking a quotation have a minimum market value of £250,000 would have further discouraged fledgling enterprises from joining the stock market.[6]

As for the multicentred orientation of British securities markets, the local dimension was already on the wane in the interwar years (Chapter Eight, Part II.B.4). During World War II, new issues by companies came to a virtual standstill as the Treasury was given a *de facto* veto over capital raising to preserve demand for securities the government issued to finance the war effort.[7] After World War II, the London market dominated share trading. Whereas an average of 101 share offerings were carried out annually on the London Stock Exchange by previously unquoted companies between 1959 to 1963, not even 14 such transactions were carried out per year on provincial stock markets between 1951 and 1960.[8] The vast majority of companies with shares dealt on a provincial

---

[1] A.J. Merrett, M. Howe and G.D. Newbould, *Equity Issues and the London Capital Market* (1967), 84.

[2] J.K.S. Ghandhi, 'Some Aspects of the Provincial New Issue Market', (1963) 26 Bulletin of the Oxford University Institute of Economics and Statistics 239, 244.

[3] F.W. Paish, *Business Finance*, 4th edn (1968), 107.

[4] F.R. Randall, *Issue, Control and Regulation of Capital* (1951), 58 (reproducing Appendix 34A, Pt I, para. 18 *verbatim*); F.W. Paish, 'The London New Issue Market', (1951) 18 Economica 1, 4.

[5] David Chambers, 'New Issues, New Industries and Firm Survival in Interwar Britain' (2007), unpublished working paper, at 21; David Chambers and Elroy Dimson, 'IPO Underpricing Over the Very Long Run' (2006), unpublished working paper at 5.

[6] Merrett, Howe and Newbould, *supra* n. 1, 15, 92; Federation of Stock Exchanges in Great Britain and Ireland, *Admission of Securities to Quotation* (1966), The Admission of Securities to Quotation, para. 2; Appendix, Requirements for Quotation, Section A, Pt I, I.

[7] Ranald Michie, *The London Stock Exchange: A History* (2000), 314–15; W.A. Thomas, *The Provincial Stock Exchanges* (1973), 257.

[8] Merrett, Howe and Newbould, *supra* n. 1, 73, 75; Ghandhi, *supra* n. 2, 242, 244.

stock exchange also had a London quotation, with only 1.4 per cent of publicly traded ordinary shares not being quoted in London as of 1962.[9] The days of the autonomous provincial stock exchange, moreover, were numbered. The London Stock Exchange and the main provincial stock markets federated in 1965 and in 1973 merged as 'the Stock Exchange', giving the London Stock Exchange a *de facto* monopoly over the domestic securities market.[10]

II. Tracking the Unwinding of Control

A. Data

Research by Florence showing that only a small minority of Britain's 82 largest industrial and commercial companies as of 1936 had 'no dominant ownership of interest' indicates Britain lacked an outsider/arm's-length system of ownership and control prior to 1940 (Chapter Eight, Part III.B). His analysis as of 1951 revealed a different pattern. He examined the share ownership structure in the 98 'very large' companies (i.e. having an issued share capital, including preference shares, of over £3 million) in manufacturing (oil production and brewing excluded), distributive trades, entertainment and catering.[11] Florence's findings show 'core' shareholders were on the wane in big firms in the UK, even if they had not disappeared.

Using the categorization system Florence adopted for his study of share ownership as of 1936, as of 1951, 40 of Florence's 98 'very large' companies had a 'dominant ownership interest' (i.e. they had a majority shareholder, a single shareholder owning between 20 per cent and 50 per cent of the shares or the 20 biggest shareholders owning 30 per cent or more of the shares). Forty-one companies qualified as 'marginal' in that the largest 20 shareholders collectively owned between 10 per cent and 30 per cent of the shares. In the remaining 17 companies, there was no hint of a dominant ownership interest, since the largest 20 shareholders owned less than 10 per cent of the shares.[12] Only 35 of the companies had a single shareholder owning 10 per cent or more of the shares.

Florence concluded on the basis of his evidence that a 'managerial evolution, if not revolution' was taking place and said a trend towards a divorce between ownership and control 'was clear for very large companies'.[13] A couple of qualifications are in order. First, if Florence had included breweries among his 'very large' 98 companies this would have bolstered the percentage of companies with a dominant ownership interest or qualifying as a marginal case. While Florence

[9] Jack Revell, *The British Financial System* (1973), 62.

[10] Michie, *supra* n. 7, 459–60, 501–2, 578; Companies (Stock Exchange) Order 1973, S.I. 1973/482.

[11] P. Sargant Florence, *Ownership, Control and Success of Large Companies: An Analysis of English Industrial Structure and Policy 1936–1951* (1961), 3–6, 8, 36, 65.

[12] Derived from data *ibid.*, 114–15.   [13] *Ibid.*, 186–87.

did not offer any sort of detailed breakdown for breweries, he reported that of 10 qualifying as 'very large', one had a majority shareholder, one had a shareholder owning 20–49 per cent of the shares and in all eight of the others the top 20 shareholders collectively held a 20+ per cent stake.[14]

Second, the publicly available share registers on which Florence relied to investigate share ownership would not always draw attention to the true seat of control in a company (Chapter Eight, Part III.B). For instance, Florence indicates the largest shareholder of British American Tobacco was an institutional investor owning 1.1 per cent of the shares when it was well-known that Imperial Tobacco had a very large holding (28 per cent as of 1961, according to a government report).[15] Although Florence identified the largest single owner of Amalgamated Press as a nominee holding 5 per cent of the shares, until the company was sold in 1958 it was effectively controlled by Viscount Camrose (William Berry) and the Berry family.[16] Florence says that H. Davenport Price, chairman of Illustrated Newspapers, was the largest shareholder with 23 per cent of the shares but other sources suggest Davenport Price held 50 per cent.[17] Florence indicates J. Arthur Rank owned 0.1 per cent of the shares of Odeon Theatres and 38 per cent of the shares were held by a nominee company when it was well-known Rank and his allies held the bulk of the equity.[18] Florence reports the largest holding in Unilever Ltd was 4.3 per cent and the largest 20 holders owned collectively 7.6 per cent of the shares while through to the 1970s the Leverhulme Trust, established by virtue of a bequest of Lever Brothers' founder William Lever, owned nearly 20 per cent of the shares.[19] Finally, while all the ordinary shares of Union International were controlled by the Vestey family from before World War II until the company ended up in receivership in the mid-1990s, Florence does not list any member of the Vestey family among the 20 largest vote-holders.[20] The largest shareholding identified was a nominee stake of 17.5 per cent and the others named apparently were individuals who owned a category of preference shares vested with voting rights.

The limitations with Florence's research, combined with some other empirical data, suggest blockholders had not been fully marginalized at the beginning of

[14] *Ibid.*, 68.

[15] William Mennell, *Takeover: The Growth of Monopoly in Britain, 1951–61* (1962), 135.

[16] Florence, *supra* n. 11, 196; 'Daily Mirror Offer for Amalgamated Press', Times, November 28, 1958; Lord Hartwell, *William Camrose: Giant of Fleet Street* (1992), 128, 324.

[17] Mennell, *supra* n. 15, 84.

[18] 'The Odeon Affair', Economist, December 20, 1947, 1012, 1014.

[19] See <http://www.leverhulme.ac.uk/about/history/> (last visited January 24, 2008); Charles Wilson, *The History of Unilever: A Study in Economic Growth and Social Change*, vol. III (1968), 111–12; *The Times 1000: Leading Companies in Britain and Overseas 1972–73* (1972), 53.

[20] Ch. Three, Pt II; Phillip Knightley, *The Rise and Fall of the House of Vestey* (1993), 80; 'Ice Cream Merger', Times, October 6, 1962 (referring to 'the Vestey family's private Union International Company'); Martin C. Timball and Diana L. Tweedie (eds), *Stock Exchange Official Yearbook 1993–1994* (1994), 879 (all 'ordinary stock is owned by Western United Investment Co. Ltd, a company controlled by E.H. Vestey and Lord Vestey').

the 1950s. Franks, Mayer and Rossi report that in a random sample of 55 quoted companies as of 1950 the largest 10 shareholders collectively held, on average, 49 per cent of the shares, a slightly higher figure than they found for a similar 1920 sample.[21] Channon, as part of a study of the largest 100 manufacturing enterprises in the UK as of 1970, examined the ownership structure in the 92 firms carrying on business as of 1950. Sixty of the 92 were among the top 100 British manufacturers of the time, and 50 were controlled by families.[22] Also, as of 1948, 119 of the largest 200 British firms had family board members, down from 140 in 1930, but still a majority.[23] A caveat is that by 1950 it was common-place for the proportion of founding family members on boards to exceed the percentage of shares held, which implies the directorships were often in place to preserve continuity and permit family members to represent their interests as minority shareholders rather than to provide a 'hands on' role dictating corporate policy.[24]

Even if Florence's methodology suffered from some limitations he did use a consistent research strategy for both 1936 and 1951—examining the publicly available share registers of very large industrial and commercial companies—and found ownership was separating from control. The pattern continued throughout the 1950s and 1960s. A study of British business carried out in 1969 remarked upon the 'steady decline of family power in British industry' and suggested that 'the family empire' was 'being steadily swept away by the forces of nature'.[25] Sampson, in the 1962 instalment of his *Anatomy of Britain* series, asserted that '[A]mong the largest firms in the country, there is still often a family or an individual with a dominating influence on the board' and made his point by analyzing the 23 UK companies which had as of 1961 assets of over £100 million.[26] His characterization had changed substantially by 1971. He acknowledged there continued to be large companies built up by entrepreneurs or families who had kept effective control.[27] Generally, however, '[T]he big corporations are left, like perpetual clocks, to run themselves; and the effective power resides not with the shareholders but with the boards of directors...Most directors of boards of companies are no more and no less

---

[21] Julian Franks, Colin Mayer and Stefano Rossi, 'Ownership: Evolution and Regulation' (2006) ECGI Fin. Working Paper No. 09/2003, 19–20, Table 2.

[22] Derek F. Channon, *The Strategy and Structure of British Enterprise* (1973), 66, 75.

[23] Leslie Hannah, 'Visible and Invisible Hands in Great Britain' in Alfred D. Chandler and Herman Daems (eds), *Managerial Hierarchies: Comparative Perspectives on the Rise of the Modern Industrial Enterprise* (1980), 41, 53.

[24] *Ibid.*; Julian Franks, Colin Mayer and Stefano Rossi, 'Spending Less Time With the Family: The Decline of Family Ownership in the United Kingdom' in Randall K. Morck (ed.), *A History of Corporate Governance Around the World: Family Business Groups to Professional Managers* (2005), 581, 590–93.

[25] Graham Turner, *Business in Britain* (1969), 221, 239.

[26] Anthony Sampson, *The Anatomy of Britain* (1961), 478.

[27] Anthony Sampson, *The New Anatomy of Britain* (1971), 602.

than jumped-up managers, and the distinction between the board and the rest is often an artificial one.'[28]

The available empirical data corroborated what contemporaries were saying. Channon reported that as of 1970 only 30 of the UK's top 100 manufacturing companies were under family control.[29] An analysis of share ownership in the 86 largest companies in the food, electrical engineering and textile industries between 1957 and 1967 indicated a 'clear decline in vote and share concentration over the period'.[30] Prais, taking advantage of the fact that the Companies Act 1967 imposed a requirement on companies to maintain a public register of directors' interests in shares, ascertained the collective ownership stake of directors in Britain's 100 largest manufacturing companies and found that as of 1968 the directors held under ½ per cent of the voting shares in 52 companies (56 as of 1972) and owned more than 10 per cent in only 16 companies (14 as of 1972).[31]

Academic studies of ownership and control using 1970s data generally confirmed large ownership blocks had become the exception to the rule (Chapter One, Part V). Nyman and Silberston did find in a study of the largest UK companies by either net assets or sales as of 1975 that 56 per cent of the 224 they focused upon were 'owner-controlled'.[32] This evidence convinced some that 'the managerial revolution heralded by Berle and Means in 1932 has probably not yet happened'.[33] Nyman and Silberston, however, relied on an expansive definition of 'owner-controlled', bringing into this category not only any company with a shareholder having a stake of 5 per cent or more of the equity but also any firm with a family chairman or managing director.[34] According to the data they provide, if unquoted companies were excluded from consideration and 'owner-controlled' was defined simply on the basis of whether a company had a shareholder owning 10 per cent or more of the equity, only 37.5 per cent would have qualified, with the figure dropping to 23.7 per cent with a 20 per cent threshold.[35] This, together with other empirical evidence from the 1970s, indicates that blockholding had become the exception to the rule in large UK companies. Empirical

---

[28] *Ibid.*, 599.

[29] Channon, *supra* n. 22, 75.

[30] H.K. Radice, 'Control Type, Profitability and Growth in Large Firms: An Empirical Study', (1971) 81 Economic Journal 547, 551.

[31] S.J. Prais, *The Evolution of Giant Firms in Britain: A Study of the Growth of Concentration in Manufacturing Industry in Britain 1909–70* (1976), 88–89. On the change to the law, see Ch. One, Pt V.

[32] Steve Nyman and Aubrey Silberston, 'The Ownership and Control of Industry', (1978) 30 Oxford Economic Papers (N.S.), 74, 84–85.

[33] Arthur Francis, 'Families, Firms and Finance Capital: The Development of UK Industrial Firms with Particular Reference to Their Ownership and Control', (1980) 14 British Journal of Sociology 1, 1. See also Sam Aaronovitch and Ron Smith, *The Political Economy of British Capitalism* (1981), 249.

[34] Nyman and Silberston, *supra* n. 32, 84.

[35] *Ibid.*, 85.

studies carried out using data from the 1980s verified the point (Chapter One, Part V).

B. Paths to Dispersed Ownership: The Importance of Merger Activity

When a publicly traded company has a blockholder, control can be unwound when the blockholder sells shares on the stock market and when the company issues additional equity to finance expansion or buy another company. Alternatively, a blockholder can exit once and for all by selling out in a merger, which in turn will foster dispersed ownership if the buyer already has diffuse share ownership or has a blockholder experiencing dilution as a by-product of the acquisition (Chapter Three, Part VI). For instance, textile manufacturer Courtaulds, which was already widely held by 1951, carried out 44 acquisitions between 1957 and 1969.[36] To the extent the companies purchased were privately held or were publicly held with blockholders, these transactions would have promoted a divorce between ownership and control.

There is little data available on how often these various paths to divorcing ownership from control are followed.[37] A case study can provide a sense of how matters proceeded as the UK's outsider/arm's-length system of ownership and control crystallized following World War II. Florence provides a potentially instructive sample, this being a list of 30 'very large' firms he categorized as owner-controlled as of 1951 and for which he identified the largest 20 shareholders and the size of their ownership stakes.[38] These companies should have been at the centre of the action, because they had blockholders as of 1951 and there was considerable momentum in favour of dispersed ownership up to 1980. As a result, tracking what happened to these companies during this period should indicate how share blocks unwound as the UK experienced its decisive transition to outsider/arm's-length corporate governance.

---

[36] Florence, *supra* n. 11, 203; John Cubbin and Dennis Leech, 'The Effect of Shareholding Dispersion on the Degree of Control in British Companies: Theory and Measurement', (1983) 93 Economic Journal 351, 364 (ownership dispersion); Douglas Kuehn, *Takeovers and the Theory of the Firm* (1975), 22 (number of mergers).

[37] Jean Helwege, Christo Pirinsky and René Stulz, 'Why Do Firms Become Widely Held? An Analysis of the Dynamics of Corporate Ownership' (2007) 62 Journal of Finance 995, 995 (focusing on the US). With respect to Britain, an exception is Franks, Mayer and Rossi, *supra* note 21, but the results have to be treated with caution due to a survivorship bias among their sample companies—Ch. One, Pt V.

[38] Florence, *supra* n. 11, Appendix A. Florence did not provide a detailed breakdown of share ownership for Tobacco Securities Trust Co. but identified the three leading shareholders and indicated they each held 20 per cent or more of the shares.

There was indeed considerable change among the 30 companies up to 1980. There were only five where the *status quo* prevailed, in the sense there was no major transformation in ownership structure (Table I). Two of these companies did not have any ordinary shares traded on the stock market (John Lewis and Union International). One of the others (F.W. Woolworth) was soon to drop out of the *status quo* category, as it was bought in 1982 by a consortium of institutional investors.

In the 25 of the 30 companies that experienced a significant reconfiguration in ownership between 1951 and 1980, mergers were a crucial agent of change. In only three of the 25 was control unwound without merger activity (Table II). The decisive event in each instance was a decision to dismantle unequal share voting arrangements that favoured the incumbent blockholders.

Table I: *Status quo* Florence 'ownership-controlled' companies, 1951–80

Company	Industry	1951 ownership, according to Florence	Position as of *c.* 1980
John Lewis	Retail	Lewis family/trustees for employees.	Owned and operated by a trust on the employees' behalf.[39]
Odeon Theatres	Entertainment	38% of shares owned by a nominee company J. Arthur Rank presumably controlled.	Sold by the Rank Organisation in 2000.[40]
W.H. Smith	Retail and distribution	Viscountess Hambledon (i.e. the Smith family) owned 24+% of the votes.	Smith family owned 11% of the shares and 30% of the votes as of 1975.[41]
Union International	Food products	The leading shareholder, with 18%, was a nominee. E.H. Vestey was chairman of the board.	All ordinary shares were owned indirectly by the Vestey family until the company was put into receivership in 1995 (Part I).
F.W. Woolworth	Retail and distribution	Majority owned by US parent.	Sold in 1982 to Paternoster.[42]

[39] 'More Ways Than One to Share Out Profits', Economist, March 29, 1986, 19.
[40] 'Rank Sells Odeon Cinema Chain to Cinven for £280m', Independent, February 22, 2000.
[41] Francis, *supra* n. 33, 17.
[42] 'Consortium Bids £310m for Woolworth Stores', Times, October 1, 1982.

Table II: Florence 'ownership-controlled' companies, 1951–80 where ownership changed without merger activity

Company	Industry	1951 ownership, according to Florence	Transition prior to 1980
Burton (Montague) Ltd. (renamed Burton Group, 1969)	Tailors and clothing manufacturing	Burton family 69%.	Unequal voting scheme introduced in 1961 was dismantled in 1979, leaving the privileged shareholders with just over 10% of the capital.[43]
Marks & Spencer	Retailing	Marks, Sacher and Sieff families owned a substantial minority of the voting shares.	Enfranchising of non-voting shares in 1966 eliminated family control.[44]
Ranks	Entertainment	Rank family held a majority of the votes attached to shares.	Two Rank family charitable trusts owned a majority of the voting shares until Rank enfranchised its non-voting shares in 1976.[45]

The fact that merger activity constituted the catalyst for change in most of the Florence 'owner controlled' companies where a major ownership transition occurred reflected a more general trend among publicly traded companies. Prior to the middle of the 20th century mergers were of little significance among such companies. A study of 725 firms quoted on the London Stock Exchange as of 1924 revealed that over the next 15 years fewer than 5 per cent disappeared as a result of a merger.[46] In contrast, between 1957 and 1969, 43 per cent of publicly quoted commercial and industrial companies in the UK were taken over.[47] Moreover, large companies as well as small companies were disappearing as a result of mergers. A study of the biggest 120 firms in the UK as of 1954 found that a dozen years later 32 companies had disappeared from the list, with mergers

---

[43] 'Enfranchisement and Recovery', Times, November 22, 1979.

[44] 'Marks Enfranchises Voteless Thousands', Times, February 4, 1966; '£150,000 Donated to Charity by M & S, Times', May 9, 1968; Judi Bevan, *The Rise and Fall of Marks & Spencer* (2001), 48.

[45] 'Compensation for the Voters', Times, January 26, 1976.

[46] P.E. Hart and S.J. Prais, 'The Analysis of Business Concentration: A Statistical Approach', (1956) 119 Journal of the Royal Statistical Society 150, 166; see also Les Hannah, 'Takeover Bids in Britain Before 1950: An Exercise in Business "Pre-History"', (1974) 16 Business History 65, 67.

[47] Kuehn, *supra* n. 36, 9, 153.

accounting for 23 of the disappearances.[48] Mergers thus were a major agent of change. As Sampson said in 1971, 'In the last decade a hectic succession of mergers and takeovers have turned Britain, traditionally a country of small businesses, into a nation of big corporations.'[49]

Of the 22 Florence 'owner-controlled' companies where merger activity contributed to a major change in ownership structure, in only one instance was the dominant block of shares transferred from one party to a purchaser intact. This occurred when Swedish Match and its allies, which owned nearly 30 per cent of the shares of British Match (renamed Wilkinson Match in 1973), sold most of its shares to Allegheny Ludlum Industries, a US company.[50] Even this was a transitional phase, as in 1980 Allegheny Ludlum took British Match private by purchasing all of the outstanding shares.[51] In the case of Consolidated Tin Smelters (CTS), the controlling interest remained in the same hands as part of a corporate reorganization, as the Patino family dominated both CTS and Amalgamated Metal Corporation, the company that bought CTS in 1975.[52] In three instances Florence's 'owner-controlled' companies were taken private directly by their parent companies, these being Ford Motor Co. (bought up by its US parent in 1961), British United Shoe Machinery (transformed into a wholly owned subsidiary of United Shoe Machinery in 1969) and Tobacco Securities Trust (merged with British American Tobacco in 1978).[53]

Twelve of the 22 of Florence's owner-controlled companies that experienced a major change in ownership structure due to a merger were bought up in their entirety by a previously unrelated acquirer. One of these deals constituted only a brief respite before the break up of the business. In 1979 furniture maker Lebus (Harris) was bought by P.M.A. Holdings (PMA), a fellow furniture maker that carried out a flurry of acquisitions in the latter half of the 1970s. Hampered by a heavy debt load and a recession, PMA went into receivership in 1981.[54]

In four of Florence's owner-controlled companies acquired by a previously unrelated party, the buyout transaction did not result in a divorce between ownership and control because the acquirer itself had a major blockholder (Table III).

[48] M. Barratt Brown, 'The Controllers of British Industry' in Ken Coates (ed.), *Can the Workers Run Industry?* (1968), 36, 46–47.

[49] Sampson, *supra* n. 27, 570.

[50] 'Wilkinson Match Stake Sold at £17m', Times, December 20, 1977.

[51] 'Allegheny May Bid for Wilkinson', Times, July 4, 1980.

[52] 'The Amalgamated Metal Tail Wags Consolidated Tin', Times, September 19, 1970; 'What's Ours is Ours', Economist, December 11, 1971, 105; 'Patino Interests Merged', Times, April 26, 1975. Florence indicates that 50 per cent of the votes in CTS were held by a single nominee with another nominee holding 7 per cent (*supra* n. 11, 238). These would have represented the interests of the Patino family, which founded the company in 1929: Helmut Waszkis, *Mining in the Americas: Stories and History* (1993), 126.

[53] 'Ford Take-Over Successful', Times, January 12, 1961 (Ford); 'US Parent Bids for BUSM', Times, May 10, 1969, 'Sole Owner', Economist, May 17, 1969, 86 (British United Shoe Machinery); Ch. Four, Pt I (events affecting Tobacco Securities Trust in the 1970s).

[54] 'Are You Sitting Comfortably...?', Times, September 8, 1980; 'Why the Worst May be Over', Financial Times, April 20, 1985. Harris Lebus remained family-dominated at least through the 1960s: 'Tottenham, the Last Frontier', Economist, November 26, 1966, 948.

Table III: Florence 'ownership-controlled' companies bought by companies with a dominant shareholder

Company	Industry	1951 ownership, according to Florence	Acquisition Circumstances
Bovril	Food	Chairman of the board held 7% of the shares, a trust company affiliated with the chairman controlled 7% and the Lawson Johnston family held a 7% stake.[56]	Bought in 1971 by Cavenham, controlled by financier James Goldsmith.[55]
Carreras	Tobacco	The Baron family owned nearly 35% of the shares, two other individuals owned just over 40% between them.	Acquired in 1958 by Rembrandt Tobacco Corporation, a South African tobacco company controlled by South African Anton Rupert.[57]
Illustrated Newspapers	Publishing	23% shares owned by chairman of the board H. Davenport Price, 12% by A.C.S. Irwin.	Acquired in 1961 by the Thomson Organisation, which was majority owned by Lord (Roy) Thomson.[58]
Kemsley Newspapers	Publishing	Nearly 20% of the shares were owned by the Kemsley family; sizeable nominee holdings accounted for nearly 10%.	Bought by the Thomson Organisation in 1959.[59]

On the other hand, in six instances acquisition of Florence's owner-controlled companies by an unrelated party did imply the unwinding of control because the acquiring company lacked a dominant shareholder (Table IV).

[55] On Cavenham Foods buying Bovril, see Geoffrey Wansell, *Tycoon: The Life of James Goldsmith* (1987), 147–53. On control of Cavenham Foods, see Maurice Corina, 'Mr. Goldsmith Takes Paris by Storm', Times, April 14, 1972, 19; Ivan Fallon, *Billionaire: The Life and Times of Sir James Goldsmith* (1991), 212.

[56] The chairman, Lord Luke, was chairman of the trust company, Southern Cross Trust Co.: 'Sir Isaac Pitman & Sons—advertisement', Times, July 18, 1934, 19.

[57] 'Rembrandt's £5 10s Bid for Carreras Shares', Times , November 4, 1958; 'Carreras: the First Truly European Company or Dr. Rupert's Theocracy?', Times, September 4, 1972; Maurice Corina, *Trust in Tobacco: The Anglo-American Struggle for Power* (1975), 209, 268.

[58] 'Magazine Group Purchased by Mr. Thomson', Times, November 28, 1961. On the ownership structure of the Thomson Organisation, see Mennell, *supra* n. 15, 81–82; Monopolies Commission, *Thomson Newspapers Ltd. and Crusha & Son Ltd*, (1968), 7–8, Appendix 5.

[59] Monopolies Commission, *The Times Newspaper and The Sunday Times Newspaper: A Report on the Proposed Transfer to a Newspaper Proprietor* (1966), 9–10.

Table IV: Florence 'ownership-controlled' companies bought by companies lacking a dominant shareholder

Company	Industry	1951 ownership, according to Florence	Acquisition Circumstances
Albright & Wilson	Chemical manufacturing	Over 35% held by members of the Albright and Wilson families.	Tenneco, a widely held US company, bought a 50% stake in 1971 and all of the remaining shares by 1978.[60]
Associated British Pictures Corp.	Entertainment	25% of the shares held by a nominee; 13% held by chairman of the board.	Electrical & Music Industries (EMI), a widely held UK recording company, bought a 25% stake in 1968 and bought the rest of the shares in 1969.[61]
Bristol Aeroplane Company	Aeronautics	16% held by the managing director and his family; 8% held by the chairman and his family.	Joined in 1960 an amalgamation creating British Aircraft Corporation, which was 80% owned by widely held English Electric and Vickers.[62]
Crompton Parkinson Ltd.	Electrical engineering	Arthur Parkinson, chairman of the board, owned 35% of the shares.	Taken over in 1967 by widely held Hawker Siddely.[63]
Rootes Motors Ltd.	Automobile manufacturing	30% owned by Rootes family.	Widely held Chrysler bought a 30% stake in 1964 and bought out all shareholders by 1972.[64]

[60] 'Tenneco Bids for a Controlling Stake in Albright & Wilson', Times, March 31, 1971; 'US Bid for Albright Almost Clinched', Times, July 1, 1978. On Tenneco's ownership structure, see Robert J. Larner, *Management Control and the Large Corporation* (1970), 72–73 (categorizing what was then known as the Tennessee Gas Transmission Co. as 'management controlled' on the basis of 1964 securities filings).

[61] Anthony Vice, *The Strategy of Takeovers: A Casebook of International Practice* (1971), 86–94. On the ownership structure of EMI, see Francis, *supra* n. 33, 23.

[62] 'Three Aircraft Firms to Merge', Times, January 12, 1960; 'Sir Reginald Verdon-Smith to be the New Chairman of BAC', Times, October 4, 1968. On share ownership in English Electric, see Florence, *supra* n. 11, 205. On Vickers, see 'Who Holds Ordinary Shares in Britain?', Times, June 18, 1959, 16.

[63] 'Gloves Off in the Bids Game', Times, June 21, 1967. On share ownership in Hawker Siddeley see Florence, *supra* n. 11, 207.

[64] Turner, *supra* n. 25, 305, 395 (initial purchase by Chrysler), 'US Parent Will Pay £6m Cash for Full Control of Chrysler UK', Times, December 5, 1972 (buy-out of minority); Larner, *supra*

Table IV: (*Cont.*)

Company	Industry	1951 ownership, according to Florence	Acquisition Circumstances
Winterbottom Book Cloth Co.	Textiles (weaving, bleaching and dying)	10% stake held by the Magor family, 5% by the Winterbottom family.	Bought in 1960 as Winterbottom Industries by Venesta, which had sufficiently diffuse share ownership by 1971 to leave the company unable to fend off a hostile takeover bid.[65]

In the final of the twelve instances where a Florence owner-controlled business (Associated Electrical Industries—AEI) was bought by an unrelated party (General Electric—GEC), the acquirer had a shareholder owning a substantial stake but the transaction contributed to the dispersal of share ownership because the block in question was diluted as part of the transaction.[66] In 1961, GEC responded to a serious decline in profitability by drafting in new managerial talent, doing so by acquiring Radio and Allied, a successful smaller competitor run by Arnold Weinstock. Weinstock, who together with family members owned 14 per cent of GEC as a result of the merger, reversed GEC's declining fortunes, reflected in a share price that rose from 10s, 5p in 1962 to 91s, 6p in 1967. GEC, after a successful hostile takeover bid, acquired AEI in 1967 using a mixed offer of cash and GEC shares. AEI was vulnerable to a hostile bid because the block-holder Florence identified—General Electric, the US electricity giant[67]—had largely exited in the 1950s.

In 1968 GEC bought English Electric, another major competitor, using a combination of GEC shares and debentures. The GEC/AEI/English Electric merger was generally a success, with Weinstock ending up running a business that generated healthy profits and operated on a par with global leaders in heavy-scale electrical engineering.[68] However, the acquisition of AEI and English Electric

n. 60, 72–73 (categorizing Chrysler as 'management controlled' on the basis of 1964 securities filings).

[65] 'The Winterbottom Book Cloth Company Limited', Times, March 31, 1959; 'Terms of the Winterbottom Bid', Times, October 19, 1960; 'Venesta Rejects £9m Bid', Times, October 20, 1971; 'Williams Hudson Wins Control of Venesta', Times, December 18, 1971.

[66] On this and other aspects of GEC's involvement with of AEI, see Robert Jones and Oliver Marriott, *Anatomy of a Merger: A History of GEC, AEI and English Electric* (1972), 114–20, 182–83, 232–39, 245–46, 259, 323, 331, 367.

[67] Florence, *supra* n. 11, 226.

[68] John Williams, 'GEC: An Outstanding Success' in Karel Williams, John Williams and Dennis Thomas (eds), *Why Are the British Bad at Manufacturing?* (1983), 133, 140–53, 168–78;

apparently diluted Weinstock's shareholding dramatically. The *Times 1000* reported that as of 1972 Prudential Assurance was GEC's largest shareholder with 4.4 per cent of the shares.[69]

The final five of Florence's 'owner-controlled' companies affected by merger activity continued as going concerns throughout the 1950s, 1960s and 1970s but the merger activity in which they engaged helped to unwind the incumbent control blocks (Table V).

Table V: Florence 'ownership-controlled' companies where acquisitions helped to disperse share ownership

Company	Industry	1951 ownership, according to Florence	Transition prior to 1980
British Cocoa and Chocolate Ltd. (renamed Cadbury Ltd. 1968)	Food	Dominated by the Cadbury and Fry families; the company was not listed on the stock market until 1962.[70]	After a 50/50 merger with Schweppes in 1969, the Cadbury-Fry families and trusts owned 25% of Cadbury-Schweppes.[71] By the end of the 1970s, Cadbury-Schweppes was recognized as being an institutionally controlled company.[72]
J. & J. Colman Ltd., re-named Reckitt and Colman (R & C) after an alliance with Reckitt & Sons was formalized by merger in 1954.[73]	Food, consumer goods	Colman family owned 25% of the shares.	The merger with Reckitts would have diluted the Colman stake. R & C then employed an 'opportunist' acquisition strategy, often using shares as the currency.[74] By the early 1990s, R & C 'ha(d) not been a family business for 20 years or more'.[75]

Geoffrey Owen, *From Empire to Europe: The Decline and Revival of British Industry Since the Second World War* (1999), 196.

[69] Times 1000, *supra* n. 19, 53.

[70] 'Cadbury Shares to Come on Market', Times, May 26, 1962, 8.

[71] Carl Chinn, *The Cadbury Story: A Short History* (1998), 98 (nature of the merger); 'Cadbury Shares over 83s in Heavy Trading', Times, January 30, 1969, 17 (ownership).

[72] Francis, *supra* n. 33, 22–23.

[73] 'Putting a Polish on Reckitt and Colman', Times, May 22, 1970.

[74] 'Reckitt & Colman's Strong Overseas Bias', Times, March 20, 1969 (remarking on the company's 'opportunist philosophy'); 'Reckitt Acquire Carbic for £1.8m', Times, March 17, 1973; 'Reckitt Makes Offer Worth £4m for Reeves Dryad', Times, June 8, 1974.

[75] 'Cleaning Up With the Polished Mr. Colman', Evening Standard, October 3, 1994.

Table V: *(Cont.)*

Company	Industry	1951 ownership, according to Florence	Transition prior to 1980
Morgan Crucible	Manufacturing	Directors and ex-directors collectively owned approximately 25% of the shares (Chapter One, Part VII).	The company carried out numerous acquisitions, often using shares as the currency.[76] By the early 1970s, the largest share ownership block was under 5% and the largest five shareholders collectively owned under 15%.[77]
Robinson (E. S. & A.) Ltd.; merged in 1966 with John Dickinson Ltd. to form the Dickinson Robinson Group (DRG).[78]	Paper-making, stationery	Robinson family owned 25+% of the shares.	The 1966 merger, a share-for-share exchange, diluted the Robinson stake. DRG carried out a number of acquisitions in the 1970s using its shares as currency.[79] A failure to fend off a hostile takeover bid in 1989 and earlier speculation of possible unsolicited bids implies there was dispersed ownership by 1980.[80]
Rowntree & Co., merged with Mackintosh in 1969 to form Rowntree Mackintosh.	Food	Rowntree family and trusts owned a majority of the shares.	The merger with Mackintosh ultimately reduced the stake of Rowntree family trusts to 7%.[81]

---

[76] 'Morgan Crucible to Buy Rest of Bettix', Times, September 4, 1968; 'Instrument Firm Joins Morgan Crucible', Times, November 8, 1968; Peter Pugh, *A Global Presence: The Morgan Crucible Story* (2006), 186, 211.

[77] D. Collett and G. Yarrow, 'The Size Distribution of Large Shareholdings in Some Leading British Companies', (1976) 38 Oxford Bulletin of Economics and Statistics 249, 251 (providing data on Morgan Crucible permitting a reliable estimate of the size of share blocks).

[78] '£125m Step Towards Paper Rationalization', Times, April 22, 1966.

[79] 'Royal Sov Says "Yes" to £3.7m from DRG', Times, July 21, 1976; '1804–2004 The History of John Dickinson', <http://www.johndickinson.co.uk/bicent01.htm> (last visited January 28, 2008).

[80] 'DRG and Britannia Arrow Surge on Bid Speculation', Times, October 10, 1984; 'Franklin Unwraps DRG's Package', Times, May 12, 1990; David Kynaston, *The City of London, vol. IV: A Club No More, 1945–2000* (2001), 747.

[81] S.J. Gray and M.C. McDermott, *Mega-Merger Mayhem: Takeover Strategies, Battles and Controls* (1990), 144.

Acquisition-driven dilution of ownership stakes was by no means restricted to GEC and the five companies in Florence's owner-controlled list. A 1970 book on mergers said '[T]ycoons...have been quite willing to dilute their percentage holding in order to swallow another company through a substantial share exchange.'[82] This does not mean all blockholders in acquisitive companies succumbed, at least readily. Charles Clore, a pioneer of the hostile takeover bid, was a hold-out. He orchestrated a number of acquisitions through J. Sears and Co., a retailer he took over in 1952 and which remained publicly quoted, with the public owning 25 per cent of the equity.[83] Clore was able to retain control of Sears because the deals it carried out were financed primarily with Sears' cash flow and because outside investors generally held only non-voting shares.[84]

Similarly, Issac Wolfson, the dominant shareholder and driving force behind retailer Great Universal Stores (GUS), retained tight control even though the company carried out numerous post-World War II acquisitions. For smaller, privately owned companies GUS paid cash but for larger companies it offered shares as well as cash. As a 1961 book on takeovers pointed out, this posed a potential problem for Wolfson: 'To have taken companies over then by way of share exchanges could have endangered his own supremacy; and Mr Wolfson likes effective authority.'[85] The solution was non-voting 'A' ordinary shares, which GUS first issued in 1952. Over the next five years, GUS used the 'A' ordinary shares regularly to finance takeovers, to the point where by 1957 there were six times as many 'A' shares as voting ordinary shares.

The House of Fraser, another acquisitive retailer, adopted a similar strategy, at least for a while.[86] The firm, which went public in 1947 with the Fraser family continuing to own a little less than half the equity, carried out a number of acquisitions in the first half of the 1950s. To retain family control, Hugh Fraser, chairman of the board and the leading shareholder, arranged for the deals to be financed by selling assets (primarily property) owned by the targets. In 1956, House of Fraser adopted a new tactic designed to preserve control in the hands of the family, issuing 'A' ordinary shares with only 5 per cent of the voting power of the ordinary shares. A year later, House of Fraser used the 'A' ordinary shares as the medium of exchange to conclude a successful takeover of John Barker, a London-based retailing group.

Distrust of voteless (or largely voteless) shares was growing at the time of the John Barker bid, particularly on the part of institutional buyers, and the British

[82] William Davis, *Merger Mania* (1970), 27.
[83] *Ibid.*, 20–21; George Bull and Anthony Vice, *Bid for Power*, 3rd edn (1961), 119–22 (Clore's acquisition of Sears); David Clutterbuck and Marion Devine, *Clore: The Man and His Millions* (1987), 71–73, 78, 92–95 (Sears' acquisitions).
[84] Clutterbuck and Devine, *supra* n. 83, 96–97.
[85] Bull and Vice, *supra* n. 83, 96; for general background on GUS see at 83, 96–109.
[86] On House of Fraser takeover activity up to 1959, see *ibid.*, 40, 150–51, 153, 164, 169–72; Michael Moss and Alison Turton, *A Legend of Retailing: House of Fraser* (1989), 168, 178–79, 184–85.

Insurance Association advised its members not to purchase ordinary shares with inferior voting rights.[87] This forced the House of Fraser to change tactics in 1959 when it became involved in a bidding war for control of Harrods, owner of the famous London store and a number of department stores in other English cities. A pure cash offer was too expensive for the House of Fraser and the unpopularity of its low-voting 'A' shares meant the odds were against its bid prevailing.[88] Hugh Fraser responded by announcing the 'A' shares would be given full voting rights, a tactic that paved the way for a successful bid but also significantly diluted the Fraser family's stake in House of Fraser.[89]

The Birmingham Stock Exchange announced in 1959 that it would not grant a quotation in non-voting shares for companies whose principal share market was in Birmingham.[90] The London Stock Exchange never went this far.[91] However, in the late 1950s it issued a press notice saying it did not look with favour on non-voting shares and amended its Listing Rules to provide that non-voting and restricted voting ordinary shares had to be expressly designated as such.[92]

Institutional opposition also remained strong. The British Insurance Association said in 1962 that insurance companies, pension funds and investment trusts all held 'to the principle that control of any undertaking should not be divorced from financial interest and that the right of a holder of ordinary shares to a vote is fundamental'.[93] With institutional ownership of publicly traded companies growing rapidly in the 1950s and 1960s (Chapter Four, Part I), as the House of Fraser's experience illustrates, it became very difficult for companies carrying out acquisitions to make successful bids using ordinary shares lacking full voting rights. This meant dilution of existing control blocks was frequently inevitable for acquisitive companies, since shares were a mainstay in takeovers. Between 1955 and 1985, one in four successful UK takeovers involved 'all-equity' offers and in two out of three deals there was some form of equity component, with the general trend over time being to use shares instead of cash.[94]

The upshot is that takeovers were fostering considerable dilution of block-holding among companies carrying out acquisitions. As the *Times* said in 1969,

[87] Bull and Vice, *supra* n. 83, 86, 169; 181; 'Voteless Equities', Economist, November 3, 1956, 449; 'The Price of Votes', Economist, July 27, 1957, 328.

[88] Bull and Vice, *supra* n. 83, 176; 'House of Fraser's Next Move', Times, June 24, 1959, 15.

[89] Bull and Vice, *supra* n. 83, 151; Moss and Turton, *supra* n. 86, 195; Paul Ferris, *The City* (1960), 182–83; 'Full Voting Rights for House of Fraser "A" Shares', Times, June 29, 1959.

[90] John Littlewood, *The Stock Market: 50 Years of Capitalism at Work* (1998), 134.

[91] Ronald W. Moon, *Business Mergers and Take-Over Bids*, 5th edn (1976), 204.

[92] Ronald W. Moon, *Business Mergers and Take-Over Bids*, 2nd edn (1960), 166–67; *Report of the Company Law Committee* (Lord Jenkins, chairman) (hereinafter Jenkins Report), Cmnd. 1749 (1962), 48 (press notice); Federation of Stock Exchanges, *supra* n. 6, sch, VII, Pt A, K1–2; L.C.B. Gower, *The Principles of Modern Company Law*, 3rd edn (1969), 369 (listing rules).

[93] Frank H. Jones, *Guide to Company Balance Sheets and Profit & Loss Accounts*, 6th edn (1964), 226. See also Sampson, *supra* n. 26, 410.

[94] Julian R. Franks, Robert S. Harris and Colin Mayer, 'Means of Payment in Takeovers: Results for the United Kingdom and the United States' in Alan J. Auerbach (ed.), *Corporate Takeovers: Causes and Consequences* (1988), 221, 236.

'Mergers, such as Cadbury-Schweppes (Table V), reduce the big family holdings' proportionate importance, and takeovers of smaller groups mostly have the same effect now that non-voting shares cannot be issued.'[95] Even Clore loosened his grip on control of Sears in 1972 by enfranchising the non-voting shares.[96] Hence, the nature of acquisitions carried out by companies with blockholders helped to ensure mergers played an integral role in unwinding control in UK public companies following World War II.

III. Incentives to Exit

A. Market Forces

Earlier chapters have drawn attention to market forces that created incentives for blockholders to exit or accept dilution of their stake. These continued to operate in the decades following World War II, though the intensity varied. One market-oriented scenario where a blockholder will be tempted to exit partially or fully is where a company's shares are advantageously priced (Chapter Three, Part VII). A buoyant stock market is the most likely setting for this scenario, since the prices at which shares are trading can rise to levels substantially exceeding blockholders' private estimates of what their companies are worth. Following World War II, merger activity and public offerings of shares were both associated with rising stock prices, implying there were blockholders ready and willing to take the opportunity to exit in buoyant market conditions.[97] On the other hand, the bursts of exuberance that can characterize share trading were less conspicuous in the UK after World War II than in previous eras (Chapter Four, Part III.F). Hence, while there would have been instances where blockholders exited due to offers too good to refuse, this likely was not as important a trend as it had been previously.

Similarly, while dividend payouts create an incentive to exit by reducing the 'free cash flow' available for blockholders to exploit (Chapter Three, Part IX), the pressure dividends exerted was not as great after World War II as before. The vast majority of publicly quoted companies paid dividends to shareholders (90 per cent from the 1950s until the late 1980s).[98] However, publicly traded companies distributed a lower proportion of their earnings as dividends following World War II, with the payout ratio not reaching the 1919–39 average of 75 per cent (Chapter Eight, Part I.D) in any one year until 1992 (Figure I). The comparison

---

[95] 'The Wealth and Power in Britain's Top Boardrooms', Times, September 9, 1969.

[96] Clutterbuck and Devine, *supra* n. 83, 97.

[97] Merrett, Howe and Newbould, *supra* n. 1, 75; R.J. Briston, *The Stock Exchange and Investment Analysis*, 3rd edn (1975), 338–39 (public offerings); Alan Peacock and Graham Bannock, *Corporate Takeovers and the Public Interest* (1991), 21 (takeovers).

[98] Elroy Dimson, Paul Marsh and Mike Staunton, *Triumph of the Optimists: 101 Years of Global Investment Returns* (2002), 160.

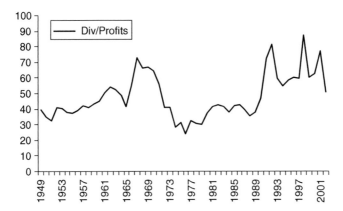

Figure I: Per cent of net profits distributed as dividends by UK industrial companies, 1949–2002

Source: Based on data compiled for Bank, Cheffins and Goergen, *supra* n. 100.

is not entirely fair, as companies reported profits more fully post-World War II.[99] Nevertheless, with tax rules in place that imposed a higher tax burden on distributed profits and with dividend controls operating for most years between the mid-1960s and the late 1970s,[100] it is not surprising that dividend payouts constituted a lower proportion of profits.

While the pressure companies were under to pay dividends likely did not prompt blockholder exit to the same extent after 1940 as before, competitive forces likely did more, at least in the 1960s and 1970s. UK companies generally prospered in the 1950s, which were characterized by a rapid acceleration of domestic demand, flourishing export markets and an ongoing expectation of rising living standards, exemplified by Prime Minister Harold Macmillan's famous statement 'you've never had it to so good'.[101]

The situation then changed. As Turner said in 1969, '[F]amily businesses face increasing pressures; tougher competition... (and) the need for expensive new investment. Many have disappeared under these pressures...'[102] Empirical data confirms times had become tougher. The net profit rate for the UK manufacturing and services sectors dropped steadily from 17 per cent in 1960 to 12 per cent in 1969.[103] The decline prompted talk of a profitability crisis in

[99] Brian R. Cheffins, 'Dividends as a Substitute for Corporate Law: The Separation of Ownership and Control in the United Kingdom', (2006) 63 Washington & Lee Law Review 1273, 1307.

[100] Pt III.B (tax); Steven Bank, Brian Cheffins and Marc Goergen, 'Dividends and Politics', (2004), ECGI working paper, No. 24/2004, Table 6 (dividend controls).

[101] Littlewood, *supra* n. 90, 122.

[102] Turner, *supra* n. 25, 239.

[103] Christine Oughton, 'Profitability of UK Firms' in Kirsty Hughes (ed.), *The Future of UK Competitiveness and the Role of Industrial Policy* (1993), 55, 58–59. For additional data on the 1960s,

British capitalism.[104] Matters, however, soon got worse, as the profit rate hovered between 10 and 11 per cent between 1970 and 1973 before falling below 8 per cent through the mid-1970s.[105]

Wage increases not matched by productivity improvements contributed to the 'profit squeeze' occurring in the 1960s and 1970s.[106] Demands by organized labour, buttressed by the bargaining power offered by low unemployment, were met with a weak response by employers and, as management struggled with obstructive industrial relations and restrictive practices by trade unions, productivity suffered.[107] Economic mismanagement at the state level also played a role. Ill-advised government subsidies, the imposition of price and profit controls and erratic macroeconomic 'demand management' all had a detrimental effect on business.[108] Finally, with European competitors benefiting from tariff cuts and falling transport costs, the 'soft' markets UK business had enjoyed in the 1950s disappeared, thus precluding companies from compensating for rising costs by putting up prices.[109]

Legal reforms carried out in the 1950s likely worked in tandem with evolving market conditions to make exit a more attractive option for blockholders. During the interwar years, anti-competitive alliances were a common response in industries afflicted by over-capacity (Chapter Eight, Part I.E.). Following World War II, UK businessmen were keen to return to their interwar cartels and at least initially collusive behaviour was commonplace.[110] Statutory reform helped, however, to curb this trend.

see Andrew Glyn and Bob Sutcliffe, *British Capitalism, Workers and the Profits Squeeze* (1972), 65–68; Brinley Davies, *Business Finance and the City of London* (1976), 86–87; Committee to Review the Functioning of Financial Institutions (Chairman, Sir Harold Wilson) (hereinafter Wilson Committee), *Evidence on the Financing of Trade and Industry*, vol. 3 (1977), 230.

[104] Glyn and Sutcliffe, *supra* n. 103, 10.

[105] Oughton, *supra* n. 103, 58–59. For additional data on the 1970s, see Littlewood, *supra* n. 90, 206, 250; Wilson Committee, *supra* n. 103, 230.

[106] Davies, *supra* n. 103, 87–89; Wilson Committee, *Evidence on the Financing of Trade and Industry*, vol. 2 (1977), 6–7; Wilson Committee, *Evidence on the Financing of Trade and Industry*, vol. 7 (1977), 72.

[107] Littlewood, *supra* n. 90, 95, 122, 136; Stephen Broadberry and Nicholas Crafts, 'UK Productivity Performance From 1950 to 1979: A Restatement of the Broadberry-Crafts View', (2003) 56 Economic History Review 718, 721–26; David M. Higgins, 'British Manufacturing Financial Performance, 1950–79: Implications for the Productivity Debate and the Post-War Consensus', (2003) 45(3) *Business History* 52, 57.

[108] Wilson Committee, *Evidence on the Financing of Trade and Industry*, vol. 1 (1977) 6, 8; Derek H. Aldcroft, 'Britain's Economic Decline 1870–1980' in Gordon Roderick and Michael Stephens (eds), *The British Malaise: Industrial Performance, Education & Training in Britain Today* (1982), 31, 41–52.

[109] Owen, *supra* n. 68, 422–23; Glyn and Sutcliffe, *supra* n. 103, 60–65, 69, 72; Charles More, *The Industrial Age: Economy and Society in Britain 1750–1995*, 2nd edn (1997), 347.

[110] Broadberry and Crafts, *supra* n. 107, 728–29; Higgins, *supra* n. 107, 57–58; A.A. Rogow, *The Labour Government and British Industry, 1945–1951* (1955), 85–89, 96–98 (focusing on activities of trade associations).

In 1948, the UK government enacted the first specific piece of British antitrust legislation in modern times but the new law did little more than generate evidence on cartels and their potential counterproductive effects.[111] The Restrictive Trade Practices Act 1956 toughened up the regulation of anti-competitive conduct, which encompassed for the purposes of the legislation collusive alliances between independent parties.[112] Restrictive practices governed by the regime were presumed to be against the public interest and, therefore, unenforceable and illegal.

The 1956 Act did not unleash vigorous competition throughout the economy.[113] Nevertheless, enforcement was sufficiently robust to cause companies to abandon overtly collusive practices and to deter firms from seeking to control markets through explicit anti-competitive alliances.[114] Since companies lacked a familiar defensive response when the profits squeeze hit in the 1960s and the 1970s, blockholders would have been compelled to consider exit more seriously than they would have in the absence of the 1956 legislation.

B. Taxation

During the interwar years taxation provided various incentives for blockholders to carry out public offerings and dilute their holdings (Chapter Eight, Part I.E, F). This remained the case following 1940. Interwar tax rules that protected shareholders of publicly traded companies against unfavourable share valuations for the purposes of calculating death duties and against a 'surtax direction' due to an excessive retention of earnings remained in place until the mid-1970s and the mid-1980s, respectively.[115] The primary rationale for the bias in favour of public companies continued to be that individuals with high incomes should not be able to sidestep taxation by carrying on trading activities under the cloak of a private company.[116]

Various tax regulations that did not specifically favour publicly traded companies also encouraged exit by blockholders from 1940 through to at least 1980. The taxation of corporate profits was one example. To help to pay for rearmament

---

[111] Monopolies and Restrictive Practices (Inquiry and Control) Act 1948, 11 & 12 Geo. 6, c. 66; Dennis Swann, Denis P. O'Brien, W. Peter J. Maunder and W. Stewart Howe, *Competition in British Industry: Restrictive Practices Legislation in Theory and Practice* (1974), 51; David Gerber, *Law and Competition in Twentieth Century Europe: Protecting Prometheus* (1998), 215–16.

[112] 4 & 5 Eliz. 2, c. 68.

[113] Higgins, *supra* n. 107, 64 (saying the effect of the legislation may have been cancelled out by increased industrial concentration caused by mergers).

[114] Gerald D. Newbould, *Management and Merger Activity* (1970), 218; George Symeonidis, *The Effects of Competition: Cartel Policy and the Evolution of Strategy and Structure in British Industry* (2002), 32–33, 41–44.

[115] Brian R. Cheffins and Steven A. Bank, 'Corporate Ownership and Control in the UK: The Tax Dimension', (2007) 70 Modern Law Review 778, 786, Table II.

[116] D.G. Rice, 'Small Business and its Problems in the United Kingdom', (1959) 24 Law and Contemporary Problems 222, 230.

in preparation for the looming war against Germany, Parliament introduced in 1937 a National Defence Contribution (NDC) that imposed a levy of 5 per cent on business profits.[117] Of greater practical significance was the Excess Profits Tax (EPT), introduced in 1939 to raise revenue for fighting World War II and to mute hostility towards anticipated wartime profiteering.[118] EPT constituted a levy on profits exceeding a benchmark fixed by reference to a company's profit levels in prescribed pre-war years, with the rate being 100 per cent, subject to a 20 per cent credit on tax paid when the war ended, from 1941 until the EPT's abolition in 1946.[119]

The EPT's 100 per cent tax hit, to quote the *Economist*, 'excluded increased profits from the investor's immediate horizon'.[120] Firms that could not take advantage of high pre-war profits to establish a favourable benchmark would have been particularly affected. Operating under the uncertainties created by World War II combined with this tax burden would have prompted at least some blockholders to think of exit. During the war, exiting by selling shares to outside investors was difficult but not impossible. Full-scale public offerings of shares were officially discouraged but stock market trading in a large block of shares that were tightly held (e.g. by a family) could be launched by the 'placing' of shares privately with a small syndicate of investors, followed by seeking permission for dealings to begin on the London Stock Exchange.[121] The Treasury largely closed off this exit route in 1944 by discouraging placings.[122] The backlog that ensued, combined with a partial relaxation of wartime capital market restrictions, contributed to a surge in public offerings by family-owned companies in the late 1940s.[123]

Immediately following the end of World War II the EPT was abolished but in 1947 the NDC became a permanent tax on profits. A feature of the new scheme borrowed from the EPT gave directors who collectively owned a majority interest in a company's shares an incentive to cut their stake. While remuneration paid to employees normally was deductible as an expense in calculating profits, the Finance Act 1947 stipulated 'director-controlled' companies (i.e. companies where the directors collectively owned 50 per cent or more of the votes) could not deduct remuneration paid to directors who owned more than 5 per cent of

---

[117] Martin Daunton, *Just Taxes: The Politics of Taxation in Britain, 1914–1979* (2002), 173; A. Farnsworth, 'Some Reflections upon the Finance Act 1937', (1938) 1 Modern Law Review 288, 290–91.

[118] Companies potentially liable for both the NDC and the EPT paid only the higher of the two: E.E. Spicer, *Excess Profits Tax and National Defence Contribution* (1940), 109. Due to high EPT rates it was usually the tax companies had to pay.

[119] R.S. Sayers, *Financial Policy 1939–45* (1956), 40, 86, 88–89, 118–19; Finance Act 1946, 9 & 10 Geo. 6, c. 64, s. 36 (abolition of EPT).

[120] 'Security Profits and Prejudice', Economist, December 8, 1946, 832, 833.

[121] Sayers, *supra* n. 119, 164, 172–74; David Kynaston, *The City of London: Volume III, Illusions of Gold 1914–1945* (1999), 421.

[122] Sayers, *supra* n. 119, 179–80.

[123] 'Fresh Ruling on New Issues' Times, April 5, 1945; 'New Issue Boom Goes On', Times, July 23, 1947; W.A. Thomas, *The Finance of British Industry* (1978), 146–48.

the shares.[124] There were some qualifications to the basic rule but these were 'unlikely to offset the penal effects of restricting the extent to which directors' remuneration is admissible as an expense for profits tax purposes'.[125] The restrictions on deductibility were abolished in 1969.[126]

The UK government, in addition to raising finance for World War II by imposing new taxes on corporate profits, also increased markedly taxation of personal income. From 1941 throughout the remainder of the war income above £2,000 (£68,000 in 2006 currency, using 1941 as the base year) was taxed at a rate of 60 per cent, as compared to 37 per cent in 1938.[127] The top rate of income tax throughout this period was 95 per cent for all taxable income above £20,000, which meant that a gross income of roughly £150,000 was required to yield a net income of £7,000, compared with £12,000 in 1938.[128]

The Labour government elected in 1945 reduced the 'standard rate' of income tax from 50 per cent to 40 per cent. At the same time, though, it increased surtax rates on higher levels of income, so there was no significant tax break for those with incomes of £12,000 or more annually.[129] During Labour's tenure (1945–51), the tax rate for income above £12,000 was set at 85 per cent and the top marginal rate of 90 per cent applied to income above £15,000. Labour's decision to tax heavily those with high incomes set the tone until the 1980s, with the top rate of income tax being 83 per cent or more until Margaret Thatcher's Conservative government made dramatic cuts.[130] The tax burden in the decades immediately following World War II was high in comparative as well as historical terms, with the UK having a higher top marginal income tax rate than other major industrialized countries and a top marginal rate that began to 'bite' at relatively modest income levels.[131]

For major shareholders who worked in a managerial capacity—typically the founder of a company and, in subsequent generations, members of a blockholding family deemed qualified—employment income was potentially a significant perk associated with blockholding. The punishing income tax rates in place

---

[124] Finance Act 1947, 10 & 11 Geo. 6, c. 35, s. 45, amending Finance Act 1937, 1 Edw. 8 & 1 Geo. 6, c. 54, sch. 4, para. 11. On the position under EPT, see Finance Act 1939 (No. 2), 2 & 3 Geo. 6, c. 109, Sch. 7, para. 10; Ronald Staples and Roy E. Borneman, *Excess Profits Tax: Law and Practice* (1945), 135–41.

[125] Rice, *supra* n. 116, 232. On the qualifications, see Roy Borneman and Percy F. Hughes, *The Profits Tax* (1953), 160–68.

[126] Derek E. Cox, 'The Use of Companies' in Oliver Stanley (ed.), *The Creation and Protection of Capital* (1974), 220, 224–25.

[127] Rogow, *supra* n. 110, 119; 'Proposed Changes in Taxation', Times, April 27, 1938.

[128] Sayers, *supra* n. 119, 49; G. Findlay Shirras and L. Rostas, *The Burden of British Taxation* (1942), 26–27, 72.

[129] 'Tax Changes', Times, October 24, 1945.

[130] See <http://www.ifs.org.uk/ff/income.xls> (individual tax rates, 1973–74 to 2005–2006). 1973 was the lone exception, when the top marginal rate was set at 75 per cent.

[131] E.B. Nortcliffe, 'Personal Income Tax in Nine Countries', [1957] British Tax Review 203, 206–7; 'Need for Incentives at the Top', Times, February 2, 1967; 'The Executive and British Tax', Times, August 25, 1970.

during World War II and the decades immediately following meant, however, that executives paid most of what they earned to the government. Hence, according to a 1958 book on British businessmen, 'big business may not look much better than the civil service or the professions in its top rewards.'[132]

The *Economist* said in 1946 of the rate of taxation on large incomes, 'There can be no doubt that progression has now reached the point at which additional leisure is often more attractive than additional income.'[133] Income tax therefore likely prompted at least some blockholders to exit who otherwise might have been inclined to stay on and run their companies. Certainly it was well known the tax regime discouraged those otherwise inclined to manage companies from doing so.[134] As the Federation of British Industries put it in 1951, 'If this situation continues that, to young men of character and ability, endeavour in this country does not offer the same rewards in others, then the spirit of enterprise which has been characteristic of British industry for so long must inevitably suffer.'[135]

The fact it was difficult to structure remuneration in a way that bypassed the heavy taxation of income compounded matters. So as to prevent the creation of a class of person immune from any increase in taxation the Companies Act 1948 prohibited companies from paying a director remuneration free of income tax.[136] In 1950, the government responded to the use of tax-friendly 'restrictive covenants' (lump sum payments made just before retirement to a senior director in exchange for an agreement not to compete in the same industry) by banning such schemes and taxing them retrospectively to 1948.[137]

Sidestepping income tax by disguising remuneration in the form of managerial 'perks' was unlikely to work either. The Finance Act 1948 deemed all 'benefits in kind' received by a director (or employee) with gross remuneration of £2,000 or more to be taxable in the hands of the director and stipulated that the onus was on the director to show that any payment made in respect of expenses covered genuine business expenditures.[138] The 1948 amendment worked sufficiently effectively to ensure neither a Royal Commission examining taxation of profits and income nor a 1961 review ordered by the Chancellor of the Exchequer recommended more than minor changes to the administration of the law.[139] Hence,

---

[132] Roy Lewis and Rosemary Stewart, *The Boss: The Life and Times of the British Business Man* (1958), 211.

[133] 'Taxation of the Rich', Economist, January 19, 1946, 101. See also 'The Toll Our Taxes Take', Times, January 12, 1968.

[134] Arnold A. Rogow, 'Taxation and 'Fair Shares' Under the Labour Government', (1955) 21 Canadian Journal of Economics and Political Science 204, 206.

[135] Quoted *ibid*.

[136] Companies Act 1948, 11 & 12 Geo. 6, c. 38, s. 189; *Report of the Committee on Company Law Amendment* (Mr. Justice Cohen, chairman) (hereinafter Cohen Report), Cmd. 6659 (1945), 46.

[137] Littlewood, *supra* n. 90, 71.

[138] Finance Act 1948, 11 & 12 Geo. 6, c. 49, ss. 38, 39, 41(3).

[139] Royal Commission on the Taxation of Profits and Income, *Final Report*, Cmd. 9474 (1955), 335 (recommended changes); Richard M. Titmuss, *Income Distribution and Social Change: A Study in Criticism* (1962), 174–75 (1961 review).

as the *Economist* said in 1979, 'For highly paid employees…there really is no choice but to resign oneself to paying one's pound of flesh, even if it amounts to 83 per cent.'[140]

The tax treatment of dividends also encouraged exit. Dividends can be a significant source of income for any blockholder but they can gain special importance when a successful business reaches its second and third generation. Under such circumstances, many of the shareholders within the company's founding family will lack an operational role with the company and the only ongoing source of return they will derive from the shares they own will be cash distributions the company makes to shareholders. UK company law prohibited companies from repurchasing shares until the early 1980s,[141] so, as a practical matter, dividends constituted the only regular cash flow shares generated for shareholders. Thus, to the extent the tax system was biased against the payment of dividends, this would have provided blockholders generally, and family owners particularly, with an incentive to sell out.

Tax rules in the UK indeed were dividend-unfriendly during the decades immediately following World War II, particularly when the recipients were individual shareholders. The profits tax that replaced the NDC was in place from 1947 to 1965 and up to 1957 a higher tax burden was imposed on distributed profits than retained profits.[142] A corporate tax bias against dividends then returned between 1965 and 1973. Contrary to the approach used both before and after, during these years Britain had in place a system of income tax where dividends were taxed at the shareholder level without any allowance being made for the fact that income was already taxed at the corporate level, so that dividends, unlike retained earnings, were subject to double taxation.[143] While this implicit bias against dividends was removed in 1973 for the decade following dividends were explicitly penalized since investment income above £2,000 was subject to a separate surcharge of 15 per cent.[144]

The overall extent of the tax bias against dividends can be illustrated by way of a 'tax preference ratio' that takes into account the relevant tax variables for an individual in the top marginal tax bracket (e.g. the tax treatment of corporate profits, investment income and capital gains) and assigns a score of less than 1 where retained earnings are tax preferred and greater than 1 where dividends

[140] 'Personal Finance' (Survey), Economist, March 24, 1979, 10.

[141] *Trevor v Whitworth* (1887) 12 App. Cas. 409 (repurchase of shares prohibited by common law); Companies Act 1981, c. 62, ss. 45–62 (authorizing share buy-backs under prescribed circumstances).

[142] For a year-by-year breakdown of the differential, see Thomas, *supra* n. 123, 230.

[143] Steven A. Bank, 'The Dividend Divide in Anglo-American Corporate Taxation', (2004) 30 Journal of Corporation Law 1, 42–47; on the position before 1965 and after 1973 see Ch. Three, Pt V, Ch. Eight, Pt II.B.7.

[144] Bank, Cheffins and Goergen, *supra* n. 100, Table 3; J.A. Kay and M.A. King, *The British Tax System* (1978), 24.

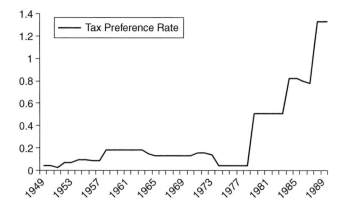

Figure II: 'Tax preference ratio', 1949–89

Source: Compiled from data from Bank, Cheffins and Goergen, *supra* n. 100, Table 3.

are taxed more favourably.[145] After World War II this 'tax preference ratio' never came anywhere near 1 (i.e. neutrality) until the late 1980s (Figure II). Empirical studies do not conclusively establish that the tax rules actually affected dividend levels.[146] Nevertheless, blockholders might reasonably have surmised that government policy would depress their after-tax return from dividends and thus treated tax policy as a cue to exit.

Estate tax also made exit attractive to families owning large stakes in publicly traded companies. As a 1953 letter to the *Times* bemoaning takeover activity put it, '[T]hose responsible for a business, and directing it, were usually the principal owners, but now that death duties make this almost impossible for the succeeding generation...family enterprises...are often at the mercy of the speculators.'[147] While estate taxes were first introduced in the UK in 1894,[148] their impact in this context was greatest from the end of World War II onwards. The Labour government of 1945–51 boosted the death duty rate for estates with a value of between £100,000 (£2.7 million in 2006 currency) to £150,000 from 27 per cent to 50 per cent, dropped the class of estate where the top rate applied from £2 million

---

[145] See James Poterba and Lawrence Summers, 'The Economics Effect of Dividend Taxation' in Edward Altman & Marti Subrahmanyam, (eds), *Recent Advances in Corporate Finance* (1985), 227.

[146] Martin Feldstein, 'Corporate Taxation and Dividend Behaviour', (1970) 37 Review of Economic Studies 57 (differential profits tax had an impact); Alex Rubner, 'The Irrelevance of the British Differential Profits Tax', (1964) 74 Economic Journal 347; (no impact); R.J. Briston and C.J. Tomkins, 'The Impact of the Introduction of Corporation Tax upon the Dividend Policies of United Kingdom Companies', (1970) 80 Economic Journal 617 (the introduction of new tax system in 1965 did not strongly influence dividend policy).

[147] 'Stock Market Rumours', Times, November 7, 1953.

[148] Finance Act 1894, 57 & 58 Vict., c. 30, s. 1.

to £1 million and increased the top rate from 65 per cent to 80 per cent.[149] Death duties remained the same until the introduction of capital transfer tax in 1975, which taxed transfers made under a will or within three years before death at 60 per cent for estates valued between £250,000 and £1 million and 65 per cent beyond that.[150] The relevant rates remained largely unchanged until 1988 when under the new label 'inheritance tax' bequests became taxed at a flat rate of 40 per cent above a threshold of £110,000.[151]

While death duties were high following World War II, with careful planning rich individuals could leave estates that for tax purposes bore little relation to their real wealth.[152] For blockholders in family companies, unwinding their ownership stake was often a key step in minimizing death duties. As the *Times* said in 1951, '[U]sually the disappearance of the family business as a result of death duties is due not so much to the actual breaking up of assets to meet death duties but to the practice—more provident but equally effective for the purpose—of selling in advance.'[153] A survey of firms that carried out new issues on provincial stock exchanges between 1951 and 1960 revealed a majority of respondents thought of provision for death duties as the main motive for going public.[154]

Given that, prior to the change from estate tax to the capital transfer tax in 1975, assets placed in trust a prescribed number of years before the settlor's death were exempt from tax, when the well-off structured their affairs to minimize death duties they often used trusts under which family members were the beneficiaries.[155] The proprietor of a family-dominated company minded to use this method of sidestepping estate taxes could try to ensure that control remained in the family's hands by transferring his shares to trusts under which family members were beneficiaries.[156] Death duties nevertheless put pressure on blockholders to exit. If the settlor died too early for the shares to be protected from estate tax, the beneficiaries would face what one tax advisor called 'the classic nightmare... (of) holding blocks of unsaleable shares and having no cash to pay the duty'.[157] Proprietors of family businesses thus had a strong incentive

[149] G.Z. Fijalkowsi-Bereday, 'The Equalizing Effect of the Death Duties', (1950) 2 Oxford Economic Papers (N.S.) 176, 182; D.J. Jeremy, *A Business History of Britain, 1900–1990s* (1998), 117.

[150] Kay and King, *supra* n. 144, 161 (capital transfer tax rates, 1977–78); Jeremy, supra n. 149, 118 (estate duty rates, 1894–1975).

[151] Finance Act 1986, c. 41, s. 100 (renaming the tax), on rates, see sch. 19, para. 36; Finance Act 1988, c. 39, s. 136.

[152] Kay and King, *supra* n. 144, 161.

[153] 'Family Firms and Death Duties', Times, July 16, 1951.

[154] Ghandhi, *supra* n. 2, 244.

[155] G.S.A. Wheatcroft, 'Settlements Inter Vivos' [1957] British Tax Review 61, 63–64; on the timing of gifts to avoid estate tax see Finance Act 1946, s. 47, sch. 11 (increasing the period from three to five years); Finance Act 1968, c. 44, s. 35, sch. 14 (increasing the period to seven years). Even after 1975, trusts could still operate as a partial shield against estate tax: Kay and King, *supra* n. 144, 55.

[156] David R. Stanford, *Tax Planning and the Family Company*, 2nd edn (1964), 136.

[157] Milton Grundy, *Tax and the Family Business*, 3rd edn (1966), 128.

to sell out to generate proceeds to buy liquid assets to transfer to the trusts they were establishing.

C. Company Law

Business historians frequently cite the Companies Act 1948 as a significant statutory measure.[158] However, with respect to the unwinding of control in large businesses, the legislation did not alter fundamentally the legal position of corporate insiders and minority shareholders. The Companies Act 1948 did increase regulation of periodic disclosure somewhat and prohibited for the first time loans to directors.[159] The legislation also created a statutory right for shareholders to vote by proxy, a change that increased from '2' to '3' out of '6' Britain's rating on the well-known 'anti-director' index La Porta, López-de-Silanes, Shleifer and Vishny constructed to measure corporate law across jurisdictions (Chapter Two, Part II.B).

On the other hand, the Companies Act 1948 did nothing to liberalize shareholder enforcement of breaches of duty by directors, leading one critic to say 'the individual shareholder is to all intents and purposes powerless'.[160] More broadly, it remained 'a cardinal rule of corporation law' that the majority 'is entitled to exercise the powers of the corporation, and generally to control its operations'.[161] Other than prohibiting loans, the 1948 Act failed to toughen up regulation of transactions between companies and their insiders.[162] Similarly, insider dealing remained largely unregulated. The Companies Act 1948 did oblige companies to prepare and have available for inspection information regarding share transactions of directors.[163] More generally, though, the legality of insider dealing remained unquestioned and trading on the basis of 'tips' reportedly was commonplace.[164]

The Companies Act 1967 ushered in the next significant set of amendments to UK company law, following on from a 1962 report on company law reform chaired by Lord Jenkins.[165] The legislation was referred to as a 'stop-gap

---

[158] Littlewood, *supra* n. 90, 13, 35–36; Leslie Hannah, *The Rise of the Corporate Economy*, 2nd edn (1983), 149–50; Andrea Colli and Mary B. Rose, 'Families and Firms: The Culture and Evolution of Family Firms in Britain and Italy in the Nineteenth and Twentieth Centuries', (1999) 47 Scandinavian Economic History Review 24, 41. The Companies Act 1948, which was a fresh consolidation of UK companies legislation, encompassed amendments made by the Companies Act 1947, 10 & 11 Geo. 6, c. 47.

[159] Ch. Ten, Pt IV.D (periodic disclosure); Companies Act 1948, s. 190 (director loans).

[160] Guy Naylor, *Company Law for Shareholders* (1960), 39.

[161] A.F. Topham, *Palmer's Company Law*, 19th edn (1949), 228; see also H.B. Rose, *The Economic Background to Investment* (1960), 157–58.

[162] See Naylor, *supra* n. 160, 30–32; L.C.B. Gower, *The Principles of Modern Company Law* (1954), 138.

[163] Companies Act 1948, s. 195.

[164] Gower, *supra* n. 162, 139; David Cohen, *Fear, Greed and Panic: The Psychology of the Stock Market* (2001), 105.

[165] Jenkins Report, *supra* n. 92.

measure' since it only implemented some of the Jenkins Committee recommendations and did not result in a new 1948-style consolidation of companies legislation.[166] The 1967 Act also did not change the UK's score on La Porta *et al*'s anti-director index.

Nevertheless, the 1967 Act did make various changes that potentially affected incentives concerning the unwinding of control. By imposing additional requirements to disclose financial data, the legislation might well have fortified the buy side (Chapter Ten, Part IV.D). The 1967 Act also compelled disclosure of various facts that blockholders would likely have preferred remained confidential. For instance, a company became obliged to identify publicly owners of 10 per cent or more of its shares and divulge material facts about transactions involving the company in which directors had a personal interest. These changes significantly boosted the UK's score on the index Djankov, La Porta, López-de-Silanes, Shleifer and Vishny constructed to measure protection against director self-dealing that is positively correlated with cross-country measures of share ownership dispersion (Chapter Two, Part II.B). Companies were also required to make available to shareholders service agreements between the directors and the company, to disclose the pay of the chairman of the board and to identify within a range of £2,500 the remuneration of other directors being paid more than £2,500 annually.[167] These reforms were enacted as a result of a scandal at the British Printing Corporation that revealed the chairman of the board was entitled to remuneration of £270,000 for 1964 under a service agreement some of his fellow directors did not know about.[168]

The UK currently scores '5' out of '6' on La Porta *et al*'s anti-director index and it was the Companies Act 1980 that moved the score from '3' to '5'. One change the Act made which bumped the score up was to require companies issuing new shares to make the equity available on a *pro rata* basis to existing shareholders in accordance with the percentage of shares already owned unless shareholders waived this protection.[169] Since neither case law nor companies legislation provided for such 'pre-emptive' rights previously, this change would have raised the UK's anti-director grade.[170]

The other change that bumped up the UK's anti-director index score was the creation of meaningful statutory protection for minority shareholders disadvantaged by a company's actions. In 1948, the UK Parliament expanded in a very tentative fashion the jurisdiction which courts had to provide relief to disgruntled shareholders and followed up in 1980 by authorizing the judiciary to

---

[166] Gower, *supra* n. 92, 55.

[167] Companies Act 1967, c. 81, s. 6.

[168] Briston, *supra* n. 97, 256; 'Mr. Harvey and His Board', Economist, July 10, 1965, 159; 'Second Bite', Economist, November 12, 1966, 736.

[169] Companies Act 1980, c. 22, s. 17.

[170] Iain MacNeil, 'Shareholders' Pre-emptive Rights', [2002] Journal of Business Law 78, 84–85.

grant a remedy to a shareholder who had been unfairly prejudiced by a company's actions.[171] The courts responded positively to the 1980 change and granted relief to aggrieved minority shareholders in numerous circumstances where no remedy would have been available under the common law or under the Companies Act 1948.[172] An anti-director index rating of '5' correspondingly became appropriate.

The Companies Act 1980 also criminalized insider dealing for the first time. The relevant provisions, which were transferred in 1985 to the Company Securities (Insider Dealing) Act 1985, stipulated that an individual committed an offence if he dealt in a company's shares while in possession of price sensitive, confidential information concerning the company received by virtue of a connection with the company.[173] Since blockholders frequently would have been directors and since the size of their ownership stake would have typically created a relationship where they might reasonably be expected to have access to price sensitive information, their share trading activity potentially fell within the parameters of the offence.[174]

Since an outsider/arm's-length system of ownership and control was well established in the UK by the end of the 1970s the 1980 amendments came too late to act as a catalyst for the divorce of ownership and control. Moreover, the 1980 changes were of limited practical significance, at least for publicly quoted companies. Some claimed the creation of pre-emption rights was an important change of principle.[175] However, as we will see in the next sub-section Stock Exchange listing rules introduced *de facto* pre-emptive rights in 1966, meaning that for quoted companies there already was a regulatory precedent for offering shares *pro rata*. The statutory provision introducing the 'unfair prejudice' remedy applied to all companies, including those with publicly traded shares, but judicial interpretation helped to ensure proceedings were extremely rare with publicly quoted companies.[176] Finally, there was minimal enforcement of the laws prohibiting insider dealing, with there only being a tiny number of convictions and guilty pleas (fewer than two a year up to 1994) and with judges refraining from imposing heavy fines or sending insider dealers to jail.[177] The upshot is that while outside investors in UK companies are currently well protected, contrary to the popular thesis that company law is a crucial determinant of ownership structure,

[171] Companies Act 1948, s. 210; Companies Act 1980, s. 75.

[172] Paul L. Davies, *Introduction to Company Law* (2002), 236–38.

[173] Companies Act 1980, ss. 68–73; Company Securities (Insider Dealing) Act 1985, c. 8.

[174] Companies Act 1980, s. 73(1)(b) (defining what constituted a connection with the company for the purposes of the relevant measures).

[175] Victor Joffe, *The Companies Act 1980: A Practical Guide* (1980), 3.202.

[176] Brian R. Cheffins, *Company Law: Theory, Structure and Operation* (1997), 464; Law Commission, *Shareholder Remedies: A Consultation Paper* (Law Commission Consultation Paper No. 142) (1996), ¶¶ 9.53–9.54, Appendix E.

[177] Brenda Hannigan, *Insider Dealing*, 2nd edn (1994), 118–22.

companies legislation apparently did little to prompt the separation of ownership and control in British public companies.

D. Stock Exchange Regulation

The London Stock Exchange and provincial stock exchanges each imposed requirements on companies seeking to list shares for trading, with the relevant regulations being unified after the exchanges federated in 1965.[178] The rules in question did not qualify as 'law' for the purposes of indices of corporate and securities law constructed by La Porta, López-de-Silanes, Shleifer and Vishny since the London Stock Exchange and other UK stock markets were purely private associations with rule books supported only by common law principles of contract and agency (Chapter Two, Part II.B; Chapter Three, Part VIII). Matters only changed on this count when Parliament gave the London Stock Exchange's listing rules direct statutory force in the mid-1980s (Chapter Ten, Part IV.D). Nevertheless, the listing rules were of substantial practical importance because the London Stock Exchange took seriously the need to regulate the market and because companies did not want to forfeit a listing due to non-compliance.[179] Hence, in the decades immediately following World War II stock exchange regulation bolstered the still modest incentives company law provided for blockholders to exit.

During the interwar years, companies seeking access to the Stock Exchange's trading facilities could opt for a full quotation and admission to the 'Official List' or seek 'permission to deal' and admission to the 'Supplementary List'. Companies seeking 'permission to deal' did not have to comply with the 'two-thirds' rule that applied to public offerings undertaken by quoted companies and otherwise generally faced few regulatory hurdles (Chapter Eight, Part II.B.3). However, the situation changed in the early 1940s in ways that imposed constraints on blockholders.

While directors relying on proxies might be tempted to downplay the fact that shareholders can use a proxy to oppose as well as support proposals, beginning in 1943 companies seeking permission to deal had to undertake to distribute proxy forms that made it clear shareholders could vote 'yes' or 'no' (Chapter Four, Part IV.B). Also, while corporate insiders can potentially extract private benefits of control from a public company by orchestrating one-sided transactions between the company and the insider, by 1945 companies seeking admission to the Supplementary List had to have a provision in their articles precluding directors from voting on contracts in which they had a personal interest.[180] The London Stock Exchange also began to require companies seeking permission

---

[178] Gower, *supra* n. 92, 291.

[179] *Ibid.*; Michie, *supra* n. 7, 567; James J. Fishman, *The Transformation of Threadneedle Street* (1993), 24–26.

[180] Cohen Report, *supra* n. 136, 50; 'Company Directors', Economist, September 15, 1945, 377.

to deal to notify the Stock Exchange immediately of any proposed change in the nature of the business of the company, any preliminary annual earnings figures and 'any...information necessary to enable the shareholders to appraise the position of the company and to avoid the establishment of a false market in the shares'.[181] The Stock Exchange was then in a position to publicize the information it received from the companies. The amendment would have curtailed to some degree the ability of corporate insiders to profit from insider dealing, since once information that can provide the basis for profitable share trading by those 'in the know' is in the public domain the potential to benefit disappears.

In 1947, the distinction between an application for an official quotation and an application for permission to deal was abolished (Chapter Eight, Part II.B.3), thus eliminating the parallel regulatory regimes that had built up. One by-product was that the two-thirds rule disappeared.[182] Also, all quoted companies were required to give the undertakings that had formerly been expected only of Supplementary List companies. As a result, the regulations concerning proxy voting and disclosure of preliminary annual earnings figures, etc. now applied universally.[183] In addition, consistent with requirements imposed on quoted companies prior to World War II, all companies applying for a listing had to include stipulated provisions in their articles of association.[184] Quoted companies, which became obliged at the beginning of the 20th century to preclude directors from voting on contracts in which they had a personal interest—a practice otherwise permissible—remained under an onus to do so.[185] Otherwise, the requirements were not particularly onerous, because on two key points (the right of shareholders to dismiss directors before the end of their term and the public dissemination of the balance sheet and profit and loss account) the Companies Act 1948 contained rules that were as strict or stricter.[186]

The regime governing quoted companies was toughened in 1966 when the newly established federation of UK stock exchanges published a revised set of listing rules.[187] One change related to the method already quoted companies were supposed to adopt in issuing additional shares. Pre-emptive rights, which

---

[181] 'New S.E. Rules for Companies', Times, January 23, 1945; 'S.E. Permission to Deal Regulations', Times, January 23, 1945.

[182] Beginning in 1966 Stock Exchange required companies seeking a quotation by way of a 'placing' (shares being 'placed' with selected investors rather being offered to the public generally) to ensure 35 per cent or more of the issued amount of the equity capital ended up in the public's hands: Federation of Stock Exchanges, *supra* n. 6, The Admission of Securities to Quotation, para. 13; Merrett, Howe and Newbould, *supra* n. 1, 7.

[183] See Randall, *supra* n. 4, 54.

[184] *Ibid.*, 75–77; on pre-World War II requirements for quoted companies, see Ch. Eight, Pt II.B.3.

[185] Gower, *supra* n. 162, 138; on the position at the beginning of the 20th century, see Ch. Six, Pt III.B.3.

[186] Companies Act 1948, ss. 127, 156, 158 (presentation and circulation of balance sheet and profit and loss account), s. 184 (removal of directors by ordinary resolution).

[187] Federation of Stock Exchanges, *supra* n. 6. On the extent to which the revised rules applied to companies quoted prior to 1966, see Ch. Ten, Pt IV.E.2.

can preclude a company's insiders from issuing shares to favoured parties on advantageous terms unavailable to other shareholders, were not provided for under UK company law until 1980, but the 1966 version of the listing rules provided some advance protection.[188] Specifically, listed companies were required to undertake to obtain the consent of their shareholders before issuing equity to any parties other than those already owning shares.

Transactions potentially tainted by self-interest also attracted tighter scrutiny. The 1966 listing rules, as part of new guidelines on acquisitions and realizations of assets by listed companies, required a quoted company to inform the Stock Exchange of any transfer of assets between the company and a director or a substantial shareholder. The Stock Exchange could then require that a circular be sent to the shareholders publicizing the relevant transaction and that the shareholders be given the opportunity to vote on the transaction.[189] This went beyond what the Companies Act 1948 required, which was simply disclosure to the company's directors.[190] The upshot is that from the 1940s through to the 1980s Stock Exchange 'self-regulation' imposed constraints on blockholders additional to company law and correspondingly would have enhanced incentives to exit.

E. Takeover Regulation

In the context of a takeover bid a shareholder (or a tight coalition of shareholders) owning a substantial minority of the shares in a target company stands in a potentially privileged position since a bidder could well offer advantageous terms to persuade such a key investor to sell. For example, when in 1972 Bowater, a papermaker, bought Ralli International, a commodity trading group, Slater Walker, the owner of a 12 per cent stake in Ralli and a 15 per cent stake in Bowater, pocketed £11 million after it, alone among Ralli shareholders, was paid in cash in a declining stock market.[191] If those owning large blocks of shares can routinely obtain highly advantageous terms when their companies are bought, this gives them a strong incentive to retain their dominant stake in readiness for such a windfall. In fact, due to growing extralegal regulation of takeovers between the late 1950s and early 1970s, there was increasingly little scope for blockholders to steal a march on their fellow shareholders.

Given that prior to the middle of the 20th century only a tiny minority of companies acquired were publicly traded (Part II.B), there were not many instances

---

[188] Federation of Stock Exchanges, *supra* n. 6, sch. VIIIA, General Undertaking (Companies), para. 15; R.R. Pennington, *The Investor and the Law* (1968), 635. On company law, see Pt III.C.

[189] Federation of Stock Exchanges, *supra* n. 6, Memoranda of Guidance, Acquisitions and Realisations of Subsidiary Companies, Businesses or Fixed Assets by Quoted Companies, and Bids and Offers for Securities of a Company, para. 6.

[190] Gower, *supra* n. 92, 529–31.

[191] 'Bowater in Surprise £82.5m Bid for Ralli', Times, September 27, 1972; 'Paper for Paper', Economist, September 30, 1972, 99; Robert Heller, *The Naked Investor* (1976), 206–7.

where the relative treatment of blockholders and minority shareholders would have been controversial. With it becoming more common in the 1950s for publicly traded companies to be acquired, the manner in which outside shareholders were treated in comparison with blockholders became an issue of greater practical importance. Consistent with the pre-World War II pattern, takeover offers were typically structured in accordance with what was well understood in the City of London to be 'best practice',[192] namely offering the same terms for all investors owning the same class of shares.[193] Equality of treatment in turn became a core feature of 'Notes on the Amalgamation of British Businesses', guidance on takeover practice issued in 1959 by the Bank of England in concert with the London Stock Exchange and representatives of leading issuing houses, clearing banks and key institutional investors.[194]

The 1959 Notes stipulated that a takeover offer should be for all of the shares of a company, meaning all shareholders should receive the same opportunity to sell as a blockholder.[195] If, under exceptional circumstances, there was a 'partial' bid for a mere controlling interest, the offer was to be extended to all shareholders on a strictly *pro rata* basis, meaning that a blockholder might well be unable to dispose of all of his shares and walk away from the company.[196] The equality of treatment issue was addressed more broadly in a 1963 revision of the 1959 Notes. The 1963 Notes stipulated that if an offeror acquired effective control of a company by buying outstanding shares of the target in the market or otherwise on terms different than in its formal offer, it should revise its existing offer or make a formal offer to all uncommitted shareholders at a 'fair price'. The purpose was to ensure similar treatment for the shareholders to whom a takeover bid was addressed.[197] Not all bidders in fact did make a practice of paying exactly the same price, but they nevertheless were under an onus to structure offers with the 'fair price' principle in mind.[198]

---

[192] Ch. Two, Pt III (pre-World War II pattern); Bull and Vice, *supra* n. 83, 287; Alexander Johnston, *The City Take-Over Code* (1980), 11.

[193] See description of buyout terms in Bull and Vice, *supra* n. 83, 160 (House of Fraser buying Binns); 'Multiple Tailors Share Deal', Times, July 8, 1953 (United Drapery Stores buying Prices, Tailors Limited); 'Bid for Tailors' Capital', Times, July 16, 1953 (Montague Burton Estates buying Jackson the Tailor Ltd.).

[194] John Armour and David A. Skeel, 'Who Writes the Rules for Hostile Takeovers and Why? The Peculiar Divergence of US and UK Takeover Regulation', (2007) 95 Georgetown Law Journal 1727, 1758–59.

[195] Johnston, *supra* n. 192, 20–21. From 1968 onwards, the consent of the Takeover Panel was required for partial bids to go forward: *ibid.*, 40, 56, 253–54.

[196] D.G. Rice, 'Good and Bad Take-over Bids', [1960] Journal of Business Law 308, 314.

[197] Edward Stamp and Christopher Marley, *Accounting Principles and the City Code: The Case for Reform* (1970), 10; Robert R. Pennington, 'Takeover Bids in the United Kingdom', (1969) 17 American Journal of Comparative Law 159, 171 (quoting the relevant provision).

[198] 'Should Shareholders Lose Out?', Times, June 10, 1967 (describing the structure of competing bids for a brewer).

The 1963 Notes addressed the position of shareholders owning large blocks of shares in a target company from an additional angle.[199] It was acknowledged that those with a controlling interest in a company were free to sell their stake at any time. On the other hand, the 1963 Notes stipulated that if the individuals in question were also directors of the company, they should consider carefully the position of other shareholders. The idea was to prompt the directors to use their influence to get the acquiring company to offer all shareholders an equivalent opportunity to sell.

The bias in favour of equality of treatment was fortified a few years later. With the Notes on Company Amalgamations drafted in 1959 and 1963, there was no organization charged with enforcement. This changed in 1968 when the Bank of England, the London Stock Exchange, leading issuing houses and major institutional investors sponsored the creation of the Takeover Panel, which was given responsibility for administering and enforcing a new body of rules referred to as the City Code on Take-Overs and Mergers.[200] The new Code addressed more directly equality of treatment in takeover bids than had either version of the Notes. The 1968 Code stipulated that a party who acquired a significant percentage of shares in a public company—an obvious way of doing so was to buy directly from a blockholder—had to make an offer on the same terms to all remaining shareholders unless the Panel otherwise agreed.[201] This principle was supplemented in 1971 by provisions designed to deal specifically with situations where a blockholder negotiated a deal with a bidder that conferred effective control of the company. Most important, a party who had acquired *de facto* control by purchasing shares was compelled to make an offer on the same terms to all shareholders.[202]

The new regime left little room for bidders to offer premium prices to blockholders. Instead, the Takeover Code in effect required a bidder to divide the consideration offered for shares rateably among all shareholders.[203] The notion of an equal opportunity to be bought out upon a change of control went far beyond shareholder protection offered by UK company law.[204] The sanctions available to the Takeover Panel were only reputational, such as offering the expression of views about the suitability for directorships.[205] Nevertheless, due to the respected

[199] Jones, *supra* n. 93, 561.

[200] Gower, *supra* n. 92, 627; Armour and Skeel, *supra* n. 194, 1760–61; Douglas M. Branson, 'Some Suggestions from a Comparison of British and American Tender Offer Regulation', (1971) 56 Cornell Law Review 685, 717–19.

[201] Johnston, *supra* n. 192, 68; Pennington, *supra* n. 197, 174.

[202] Johnston, *supra* n. 192, 78–79; D. Prentice, 'Take-Over Bids—The City Code on Take-Over and Mergers', (1972) 18 McGill Law Journal 385, 402–6. The minimum ownership threshold for a mandatory bid was reduced from 40 per cent to 30 per cent in 1974: Paul L. Davies, *The Regulation of Take-Overs and Mergers* (1976), 79.

[203] Deborah DeMott, 'Current Issues in Tender Offer Regulation: Lessons from the British', (1983) 58 New York University Law Review 945, 962; Paul L. Davies, *Gower and Davies' Principles of Modern Company Law*, 7th edn (2003), 731.

[204] Davies, *supra* n. 202, 82.

[205] Johnston, *supra* n. 192, 161.

status of the regulators and the ease with which market players could punish rule-breakers by way of a 'cold shoulder', compliance was taken seriously and the regulatory scheme was generally effective.[206] As a result, extralegal control of takeover bid terms diminished at least to some degree the private benefits of control of those owning large blocks of shares in UK public companies and thereby enhanced incentives to exit.

*　　*　　*

Britain's outsider/arm's-length system of ownership and control crystallized in the decades following World War II as family capitalism was largely sidelined in major public companies. Part of the explanation for this transformation was that in various ways the incentives for blockholders to exit were more potent than they had been previously. However, as has been stressed a number of times, a divorce between ownership and control can only occur if there is demand for shares. This could not be taken for granted, because individual investors, who had heretofore dominated the buy side, were net sellers of shares following World War II. Chapter Ten takes up this point, discussing how institutional shareholders—primarily pension funds and insurance companies—came to dominate the buy side and generated sufficient demand for equity to facilitate the unwinding of control.

[206]　*R. v Panel on Take-overs and Mergers ex p* [1987] 2 Q.B. 815, 824.

TEN

1940–1990: The Buy Side

Since the transformation to outsider/arm's-length corporate governance in Britain concluded between 1940 and 1990, one would anticipate matters were buoyant on the buy side during this period. However, as Part I of this chapter describes, there were various deterrents to investing in shares and individuals, who had previously dominated the buy side, were net sellers of equity. It fell, as Parts II to IV discuss, to institutional shareholders to fill the gap. The dramatic rise of institutional investment created theoretically hospitable conditions for 'hands on' involvement in the management of publicly traded companies. As Part V explains, however, the potential for institutional shareholder intervention went largely unfulfilled, thus ensuring a divorce between ownership and control was a hallmark of UK corporate governance.

I. Factors Discouraging Investment in Shares

A. Britain's Economic Decline

In various ways it is surprising there was sufficient demand for shares for the transformation in favour of outside/arm's-length corporate governance to conclude in the decades following World War II. One deterrent to investment in equities was that Britain's position relative to its national economic rivals implied investing elsewhere made good sense (Chapter Four, Part II.B). The UK expanded at what was, in historical terms, a solid rate from the late 1940s until the early 1970s, when a recession caused growth to stall until the early 1980s.[1] Nevertheless, Britain's economic performance lagged behind that of its peers, as measured by annual growth in GDP and annual growth in labour productivity (Figures I, II). Hence, whereas in 1950 the UK was the second richest economy in Europe in terms of GDP per capita, by 1973 she had slipped to seventh richest and by 1985 to ninth.[2]

---

[1] Andrew Gamble, *Britain in Decline: Economic Policy, Political Strategy and the British State*, 3rd edn (1990), 6, 14.

[2] Christine Oughton, 'Competitiveness Policy in the 1990s', (1997) 107 Economic Journal 1486, 1486. See also Gamble, *supra* n. 1, 13–15; Sam Aaronovitch and Ron Smith, *The Political Economy of British Capitalism* (1981), 57–58; Derek Matthews, 'The Performance of British Manufacturing in

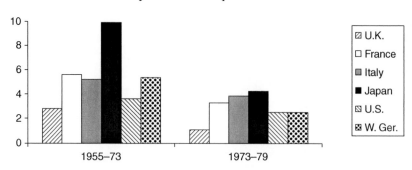

Figure I: Annual GDP growth rate (after inflation), 1955–73, 1973–79

Source: Derived from data from Aaronovitch and Smith, *supra* n. 2, 58 (based on OECD statistics).

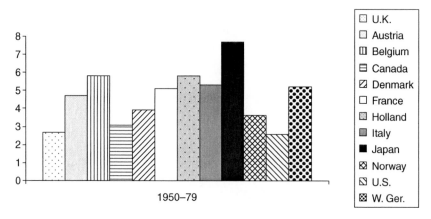

Figure II: Annual growth in labour productivity, 1950–79

Source: Derived from data from Matthews, *supra* n. 2, 767 (based on OECD statistics).

B. Managerial Quality

Since investors often take into account the calibre of executives when deciding whether to invest in companies, the fact managerial quality was widely regarded as sub-standard in the UK following World War II was another potential deterrent to investing in shares of public companies (Chapter Four, Part II.B). A 1956 report on management succession in British companies bemoaned '(t)he shortage of good managers, particularly at the top'.[3] A 1971 critic of British industry said it retained 'more of the characteristics of the Home Guard than of a professional

the Post-War Long Boom', (2007) 49 Business History 763 (providing data to refute a challenge to the conventional wisdom that British manufacturing faltered post-World War II).

[3] Acton Society Trust, *Management Succession* (1956), 1.

fighting force: in many parts it is poorly equipped and organized, and often indifferently led'.[4] A 1972 study of management in Britain, France, the Soviet Union and the United States alleged that 'suboptimization within individual British companies has a content similar to that within the Soviet economy as a whole'.[5]

Critics laid various charges against British executives. One was inadequate training. As a 1967 study argued, 'Too many of our managers simply don't know enough to do the job... They are among the worst educated and least trained of any advanced country.'[6] Executives also allegedly lacked the drive to maximize profits, to market aggressively and to foster innovation. Instead, there was 'a certain claret-grouse-and-port induced somnolence in British boardrooms',[7] with 'the unconscious ambition of most directors (being) to retire and become a country squire'.[8] British managers thus allegedly let 'sleeping dogs lie', as 'they ha(d) their own security and comfort at heart; and they hate(d) the psychological traumas of demanding good performance'.[9] The manner in which a leading executive characterized the lifestyle of senior managers in a 1951 conference speech suggests the critics might well have had a point. He said:

A top-level executive's life... (is) to apply himself a balanced cultivated life—about half his time should be spent directing his business and the other half in business activities outside, and he should, as far as his working life is concerned, confine that to the minimum. He should have long weekends... he should play golf... he should garden... he should play bridge, he should read, he should do something different.[10]

The incentive structure of British managers likely contributed to whatever complacency existed.[11] British executives were poorly paid compared to their peers in other industrialized countries.[12] High taxes on personal income further reduced the take-home pay of potential 'high-fliers' (Chapter Nine, Part III.B). Correspondingly, the remuneration packages on offer did little to motivate executives to work hard and generate value for shareholders. As the *Times* said in

---

[4] Quoted in C.J. Bartlett, *A History of Postwar Britain 1945–1974* (1977), 171.

[5] David Granick, *Managerial Comparisons of Four Developed Countries: France, Britain, United States and Russia* (1972), 55, 363.

[6] Glyn Jones, and Michael Barnes, *Britain on Borrowed Time* (1967), 222. See also John Constable and Roger McCormick, *The Making of British Managers* (1987), 16; David E. Hussey, *Management Training and Corporate Strategy: How to Improve Competitive Performance* (1988), 58.

[7] Charles Raw, *Slater Walker: An Investigation of a Financial Phenomenon* (1977), 170, quoting *Fortune*, June 1973.

[8] George Norman, 'The English Sickness', Bankers' Magazine, November, 1973, 192, 195.

[9] Robert Heller, *The Naked Manager* (1972), 46, 161. See also Granick, *supra* n. 5, 363–64; Graham Turner, *Business in Britain* (1969), 431–33; Robert Dubin, 'Management in Britain—Impressions of a Visiting Professor', (1970) 7 Journal of Management Studies 183.

[10] Quoted in Nicholas Faith, *A Very Different Country: A Typically English Revolution* (2002), 47–48.

[11] Derek F. Channon, *The Strategy and Structure of British Enterprise* (1973), 45; David Clutterbuck, and Stuart Crainer, *The Decline and Rise of British Industry* (1988), 238, 348.

[12] Granick, *supra* n. 5, 286–88; 'The Executive and British Tax', Times, August 25, 1970; Hugh Parker, 'The Effective Executive: What is He Worth?', McKinsey Quarterly, Winter 1976, 22, 27–28.

1970, '[M]anagers have little incentive for risk-taking, or even for a busier life at all when the net rewards are so small.'[13]

Executives were not just poorly paid. Instead, as Heller argued in 1972 '...they are paid in the wrong ways. Their take seldom has any true relation to their personal success or to the company's.'[14] For instance, UK public companies rarely used stock options to provide performance-related rewards.[15] This form of remuneration was first awarded to UK executives in 1950 due to perceived tax advantages but tax officials soon cracked down and between the mid-1960s and the mid-1980s tax rules effectively precluded stock option grants.[16] The fact that turnover in top managerial posts typically was minimal compounded the problem, since neither the fear of dismissal (other than by way of an exceptional event like a takeover) nor the prospect of being poached by another company did much to motivate incumbent executives.[17] Heller made the point forcefully:

> The real problem lies in the self-perpetuation of the mediocre: of managers who are never brilliant and never atrocious, but whose use of the assets is less effective than the dumbest shareholder could manage for himself. There is no easy escape...Pressure rarely comes from inside because of the rare emergence of individuals outstanding enough to apply it. It can only come from outside because of a change or incipient change in ownership—mostly in the form of a takeover bid... [18]

C. The Status of Shareholders

A further deterrent to investment in equities was that the status of shareholders in the economic system was open to doubt. Under UK company law, among constituencies associated with companies, shareholders occupy centre stage. The shareholders determine the content of a company's corporate constitution, the shareholders have the statutory right to dismiss incumbent directors by majority vote and the duties directors owe to promote a company's best interests generally equate 'the company' with the shareholders.[19] Correspondingly, there is a legal

---

[13] 'Executive and British', *supra* n. 12. See also Granick, *supra* n. 5, 273–76; Turner, *supra* n. 9, 434–37; Channon, *supra* n. 11, 45–46, 206, 210, 213, 232–33; 'Investment in Britain: A Survey', Economist, November 12, 1977, 25.

[14] Heller, *supra* n. 9, 85.

[15] Granick, *supra* n. 5, 274; Channon, *supra* n. 11, 46, 213; Theo Nichols, *Ownership Control and Ideology: An Enquiry into Certain Aspects of Modern Business Ideology* (1969), 76.

[16] Channon, *supra* n. 11, 46; 'Opinions About Options', Economist, August 7, 1954, 463; Don Egginton, John Forker and Paul Grout, 'Executive and Employee Share Options: Taxation, Dilution and Disclosure', (1993) 23 Accounting and Business Research 363, 363–64.

[17] Dubin, *supra* n. 9, 192–93; S.P. Keeble, *The Ability to Manage: A Study of British Management* (1992), 56–57; Brian R. Cheffins, *Company Law: Theory, Structure and Operation* (1997), 111–12.

[18] Heller, *supra* n. 9, 115.

[19] Companies Act 2006, c. 46, s. 21 (shareholders determining the content of the corporate constitution), s.168 (removal of directors), s. 172 (statutory duty to promote the success of the company is framed in a way that accords primacy to shareholders but also mandates that directors consider various stakeholder interests). On directors' duties at common law, see, for example, *Parke v Daily News* [1962] Ch. 927.

foundation for claims made in the context of present-day debates on corporate governance that, while directors of UK companies are responsible for relations with a range of 'stakeholder' groups, it is the shareholders to whom they are accountable.[20]

Matters were not so clear immediately following World War II. With social democracy being the dominant political ethos, it was not taken for granted directors were obliged to think of the company in terms of its shareholders.[21] The *Economist* argued in 1953 that shareholders 'rank well after the employees, the progress of "the company", and the wellbeing of the customer in the thoughts of the directors whom—in legal form—they appoint'.[22] Anthony Crosland, an influential Labour politician who served as the minister for trade and industry between 1967 and 1969, denounced in a 1954 article on takeovers as 'absurd' the notion that the purpose of companies was to make profits for their shareholders.[23] L.C.B. Gower, a leading academic expert on UK company law, said in 1955, '[I]t has become almost an accepted dogma that management owes duties to "the four parties to industry" (labour, capital, management and the community).'[24] The editor of the *Investor's Chronicle* said likewise in 1960 that the shareholders, employees and customers were 'co-equal interests to be served by companies'.[25] Given the tide of opinion, investors seemingly had little reason to expect directors would treat creation of shareholder value as a priority when deciding how to run companies.

D. Tax

Tax also provided a potent disincentive to buying shares, at least when investors owned the equity directly on their own behalf. The Labour government elected in 1945 launched a tax-driven attack on 'socially functionless wealth' and the Conservatives, who were in office from 1951 to 1964, did little to reverse the situation (Chapter Three, Part X). One result was a tax regime that provided strong incentives for blockholders to exit (Chapter Nine, Part III.B). At the same time, owning shares offered little attraction for retail investors. As the *Economist* explained in 1953 after declaring the private investor 'dead', 'he was crushed by high taxation'.[26]

---

[20] See, for example, Committee on Corporate Governance (Sir Ronald Hampel, chair), *Final Report* (1997), 12, 23. Some take issue with this characterization e.g. Paddy Ireland, 'Company Law and the Myth of Shareholder Ownership', (1999) 62 Modern Law Review 32.

[21] 'Reforming Company Law', (1960) 31 Political Quarterly 142, 145–46.

[22] 'The Shareholder Today', Economist, December 19, 1953, 903, 904.

[23] Anthony Crosland, 'The Case Against Take-over Bids', The Listener, September 2, 1954, 347, 347.

[24] L.C.B. Gower, 'Corporate Control: The Battle for the Berkeley', (1955) 68 Harvard Law Review 1176, 1190.

[25] Quoted in Lord Wedderburn, 'Trust, Corporation and the Worker', (1985) 23 Osgoode Hall Law Journal 203, 230.

[26] 'Corpse in the Capital Market', Economist, February 7, 1953, 375, 376. See also Richard Kellett, *Ordinary Shares for Ordinary Savers* (1962), 32–35; Adrienne Gleeson, *People and Their*

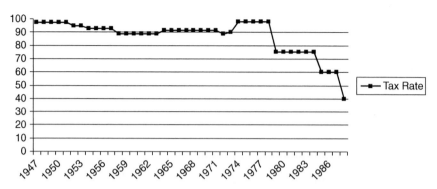

Figure III: Top marginal tax rate on dividends for individuals, 1947–88 (assuming full surcharge on investment income applied, 1973–83)

Source: Compiled from Steven Bank, Brian Cheffins and Marc Goergen, 'Dividends and Politics', (2004), ECGI working paper, No. 24/2004, Table 3.

Most striking was the tax burden on dividends. Due to high rates of tax imposed on dividends for those with large incomes (Figure III), the after-tax return from dividends was potentially negligible from World War II through until the early 1980s. The discrimination against dividends was compounded because certain deductions that were made available for 'earned' income were not available for investment income.[27] In addition, from 1973 to 1983, 'unearned' investment income, including dividends, exceeding £2,000 per annum was subject to a 15 per cent income tax surcharge (Chapter Nine, Part III.B). Most strikingly, between 1974 and 1978 those in the top marginal tax bracket could pay tax as high as 98 per cent on dividends.

Figure III exaggerates somewhat the impact the tax system had on the receipt of dividends by individual investors because numerous investors were not in the top income tax bracket and even for those in this position, only income above a specified level was taxed at the top rate. Even with these caveats, however, the tax hit was substantial. Statistics compiled on behalf of a royal commission studying the distribution of wealth and income indicate that in 1972/73 for those earning more than £12,000 (£109,000 in 2006 currency), post-tax net income from dividends and interest was a mere 28.5 per cent of the pre-tax figure.[28]

There were other tax-related constraints on direct investment in shares. From 1965 onwards, investors had to pay capital gains tax of 30 per cent on profits derived from selling shares, which, though lower than income tax, was high

Money: 50 Years of Private Investment (1981), 69; William M. Clarke, *Inside the City: A Guide to London as a Financial Centre* (1983), 93.

[27] H.G.S. Plunkett and Cecil A. Newport, *Income Tax: Law and Practice*, 29th edn (1961), 394–95.

[28] Derived from Royal Commission on the Distribution of Income and Wealth (Lord Diamond, chairman), *Report No. 2: Income from Companies and its Distribution*, Cmnd. 6172 (1975), 23, 27.

compared with rates in other countries.[29] Even without capital gains tax, an investor generally needed to make a profit of 10 per cent or more on the sale of shares to cover the attendant transaction costs, including stamp duty, a tax on share transactions.[30] Also, from 1962 to 1971 capital gains derived from 'short-term' dealings (buying and selling the same shares within a six-month period, extended to twelve in 1965) were deemed to constitute investment income and thus were subjected to taxation at the same punitive levels as dividends.[31]

E. Private Investor Exit

The fact the climate for investment in shares was chilly in various ways had a major impact on private investors, who had been prior to World War II the dominant force on the buy side (Chapter Four, Part I; Chapter Eight, Part II.A.2). There were individuals who bought shares following the war, but collectively retail investors were unloading equities faster than they were buying. As the London Stock Exchange said in 1977 to a committee struck to review the functioning of financial institutions and chaired by former Prime Minister Harold Wilson, 'The personal sector has been for over twenty years a consistent net seller of securities at a fairly steady rate in constant price terms.'[32] For instance, between 1966 and 1977 investment in shares by individuals declined each year, with the amounts involved varying between £1.22 billion in 1969 and £3.79 billion in 1973.[33] Correspondingly, while equities constituted 22 per cent of personal wealth in 1957, this figure dropped to 12 per cent by 1973 and 9 per cent in 1976.[34]

The trend was clearly evident to contemporaries. The *Economist* said in 1953 that 'In the last five years there has been no net personal investment on the Stock Exchange. Sales of securities from private portfolios seem to have clearly exceeded the purchases that individuals have made.'[35] Stock Exchange officials made the same point in 1975, saying 'In modern times, the great private capitalist responsible to himself exists, so far as the UK is concerned, only in the realms of fiction.'[36] A 1983 survey of London's financial district concurred, arguing 'The private investor has become a threatened species' and backed up

---

[29] Finance Act 1965, c. 25, ss. 19, 20, 22; 'Missed Opportunity', Economist, April 10, 1965, 210, 210.

[30] Gleeson, *supra* n. 26, 136; P.J. Naish, *The Complete Guide to Personal Investment* (1962), 25.

[31] Finance Act 1962, 10 & 11 Eliz. 2, c. 44, ss. 12–16, sch. 9; Finance Act 1965, s. 17.

[32] Committee to Review the Functioning of Financial Institutions (Chairman, Sir Harold Wilson) (hereinafter Wilson Committee), *Evidence on the Financing of Trade and Industry*, vol. 3 (1977), 208. See also *ibid.*, 142; A.G. Ellinger, *The Art of Investment*, 3rd edn (1971), 60.

[33] Marshall E. Blume, 'The Financial Markets' in Richard E. Caves and Lawrence B. Krause (eds), *Britain's Economic Performance* (1980), 261, 294.

[34] J.A. Kay and M.A. King, *The British Tax System* (1978), 65 (1957, 1973). The figures for 1976 are derived from Blume, *supra* n. 33, 292.

[35] 'Corpse in the Capital Market', *supra* n. 26, 375.

[36] Quoted in Ranald Michie, *The London Stock Exchange: A History* (2000), 536.

the point by noting individuals were net sellers of shares by more than £2 billion annually.[37]

If demand by private investors was the only variable governing the buy side, the final transition to outsider/arm's-length corporate governance that occurred in the decades following World War II might have never happened. Given retail investors were net sellers of equities, lack of demand could have undermined plans by companies intending to make public offerings of shares and by blockholders anticipating using the stock market to exit. Blockholding thus might have remained prevalent in Britain's publicly quoted companies well after World War II. However, the decline of the private investor was more than matched by the rise of institutional investors, ensuring conditions were hospitable on the buy side for the unwinding of control.

II. The Rise of Institutional Share Ownership

As of the early 1930s, private investors owned upwards of 80 per cent of the securities traded on the London Stock Exchange (Chapter Eight, Part II.A.1). As of 1957, the first year for which detailed statistics on share ownership are available, individuals, including executors, were the beneficial owners of 66 per cent of the shares of UK public companies. By 1969, retail investors no longer owned a majority of the shares of UK public companies and by 1991 they were no longer the most important single category of investor (Chapter Four, Part I).

Institutional shareholders stepped into the breach. Unlike in some countries (e.g. India and Norway), they were not confronted with any restrictions designed to reserve funds for government borrowing or projects approved by the government.[38] Among options available, shares of publicly quoted companies proved a popular choice. A 1955 survey of London's financial district observed that institutional shareholders had become 'the mainstay of the stock markets' as '(t)he rich and well-to-do who used to invest their savings through the Stock Exchange are not now able to save on any scale' and 'only the institutions...have "new money" to invest'.[39] Or as the *Economist* said in 1975, 'Usually in this London of the last days of the rich, private individuals are net sellers of stock which the institutions buy.'[40] The buy side for shares was duly transformed. As the Wilson Committee said of institutional shareholders in its 1980 report on the functioning of financial institutions, 'their increasing dominance of...equity markets was one of the most important developments in the financial system'.[41]

---

[37] Clarke, *supra* n. 26, 91.
[38] H.B. Rose, *The Economic Background to Investment* (1960), 286.
[39] Oscar R. Hobson, *How the City Works* (1955), 120.
[40] 'There is £3½ Billion on the Way, But Plenty to Buy', Economist, March 1, 1975, 84.
[41] Wilson Committee, *Report* (hereinafter Wilson Report), Cmnd 7937 (1980), 92.

Among institutional investors, pension funds and insurance companies were the dominant players, as the percentage of shares they owned collectively grew from 9 per cent in 1957 to 33 per cent in 1975 and 51 per cent in 1991 (Chapter Four, Part I). Investment trusts and unit trusts were of sufficient importance to qualify as the third and fourth legs of the institutional market.[42] Until just prior to World War II only investment trusts were significant players, since doubts about the legality of the unit trust arising in the latter part of the 19th century derailed its use as a vehicle for collective investment.[43] Following World War II, however, unit trusts did a great deal to catch up. Through to the 1980s, the only meaningful source of fresh demand for the services of investment trusts came from various insurance companies and pension funds lacking expertise to manage their own share portfolios, and even this faltered as the managing of investments in-house became more popular.[44] In contrast, investment in unit trusts grew smartly due to a combination of effective marketing, reliable price quotations, the pricing of units in small denominations that facilitated regular purchases by individuals and alertness to new areas of expansion (e.g. creating unit-linked life assurance schemes).[45]

Institutional shareholders built up their share portfolios in two basic ways. One was by buying up equities companies made available for sale.[46] For instance, in 1970 UK companies issued £87 million worth of shares to the public and institutional investors bought up £76 million.[47] Insurance companies and pension funds were particularly influential, not only because of their buying power but also because they often acted as underwriters of public offerings.[48] A potential constraint was that quoted companies seeking to raise equity capital typically did so by rights offerings, meaning shares were made available on a *pro rata* basis to existing shareholders in accordance with the percentage of shares they owned.[49] Institutional shareholders were nevertheless able to build up their stakes since they accepted not only their own allotments

---

[42] John Littlewood, *The Stock Market: 50 Years of Capitalism at Work* (1998), 262.

[43] L.C.B. Gower, J.B. Cronin, A.J. Easson and Lord Wedderburn of Charlton, *Gower's Principles of Modern Company Law*, 4th edn (1979), 266.

[44] E. Victor Morgan and W.A. Thomas, *The Stock Exchange: Its History and Functions* (1969), 178; Dominic Hobson, *The National Wealth: Who Gets What in Britain* (1999), 1035–36, 1039, 1042.

[45] Gleeson, *supra* n. 26, 92–95; Clarke, *supra* n. 26, 96–97; Littlewood, *supra* n. 42, 128, 255–56, 260, 441–42.

[46] Ellinger, *supra* n. 32, 60; 'Good Eye for a Gilt, But...', Economist, February 4, 1978, 115.

[47] Hamish McRae and Frances Cairncross, *Capital City: London as a Financial Centre* (1974), 121.

[48] Wilson Committee, *supra* n. 32, 112, 137; Committee on the Working of the Monetary System (Lord Radcliffe, Chairman) (hereinafter Radcliffe Committee), *Memoranda of Evidence*, vol. 2, (1960), 36, 73; W.A. Thomas, *The Finance of British Industry* (1978), 145, 178–9.

[49] Lewis G. Whyte, *Principles of Finance and Investment*, vol. I (1949), 101–2; A.J. Merrett, M. Howe and G.D. Newbould, *Equity Issues and the London Capital Market* (1967), 48, 75; Jerry Coakley and Laurence Harris, *The City of Capital: London's Role as a Financial Centre* (1983), 113.

but also took the place of personal investors who did not want to exercise their rights fully or in part.[50]

Private individuals, as persistent sellers of shares, constituted the second key source of supply of corporate equity.[51] For instance, while in 1963 new issues of ordinary shares totalled less than £200 million, institutional shareholders added some £400 million of corporate equity to their portfolios 'by buying existing issues, no doubt largely from private individuals or other estates'.[52] This reflected a more general trend. As the London Stock Exchange told the Wilson Committee in 1977, '(t)he institutions . . . have been absorbing the sales by the private individuals'.[53] Or as Plender said in 1982 '[I]n order to satisfy their voracious appetite for investments these institutions are today buying shares from private individuals at the rate of more than £20 million per week.'[54]

III. Tax and the Institutional 'Wall of Money'

The fact that institutional investors became the dominant buyers of shares following World War II while personal investors were persistent net sellers implies buy side factors unique to institutional investors were of considerable importance. This was indeed the case. Tax was of central importance in this context. As the *Economist* observed in 1979, 'Tax efficiency has replaced productive efficiency as the main criterion in many investment decisions because of tax rates that make the actual returns on capital almost irrelevant to personal investors.'[55] Tax rules, in addition to penalizing private investors who owned shares directly, provided them with strong incentives to invest through financial intermediaries. This contributed to a 'wall of money' in institutional hands that had to be invested and created demand by default for shares.

To elaborate, given the unfavourable climate for direct investment in shares, private investors turned to forms of savings that received more favourable tax treatment.[56] Home ownership was one tax-friendly option.[57] Pensions and insurance were other key beneficiaries. As Plender explained in 1982, 'Richer members of the older generation . . . with the help of ingenious accountants have

---

[50] Richard Stone, Jack Revell and John Moyle, *The Owners of Quoted Ordinary Shares: A Survey for 1963* (1966), 54.

[51] 'There is £3½ Billion', *supra* n. 40, 84; Richard J. Briston and Richard Dobbins, *The Growth and Impact of Institutional Investors* (1978), 11; John Plender, *That's the Way the Money Goes: The Financial Institutions and the Nation's Savings* (1982), 13, 35.

[52] 'The Financial Institutions', (1965) 5 Bank of England Quarterly Bulletin 132, 153.

[53] Wilson Committee, *supra* n. 32, 214.

[54] Plender, *supra* n. 51, 13.

[55] 'Personal Finance' (Survey), Economist, March 24, 1979, 22.

[56] Wilson Committee, *supra* n. 32, 269; Blume, *supra* n. 33, 317; 'Institutions and Tax', Economist, November 12, 1977, 44.

[57] Gleeson, *supra* n. 26, 101, 135; Kay and King, *supra* n. 34, 61–62; 'Personal Finance', *supra* n. 55, 2–3.

found that investment returns can perfectly legally be doubled, tripled or even quadrupled without risk to the investor. The trick is to make maximum use of tax reliefs available on institutional forms of saving...so that the government pays for part of the investment.'[58] The private investor responded accordingly, forsaking direct ownership of shares in favour of reliance on tax-favoured institutional investment. The *Economist* said in 1977 of the tax-driven hunt for investment options, 'The enormous advantages of institutional saving for the rich who might once have invested in equities but who are now prevented from doing so by tax, explains the overwhelming dominance the institutions have acquired in the stock market.'[59]

In 1974, an expert on UK pension funds acknowledged some advertisements for retirement savings plans were 'so absurdly generous that the reader must feel there must somehow be a snag' but assured readers that this was not the case due to the tax position.[60] To be more precise, assuming a pension fund was approved in the sense it met prescribed statutory criteria, all employer contributions were excluded from the recipient's income for tax purposes until withdrawal and employee contributions were deductible from employment income. Also, pension funds were 'gross funds', meaning that no tax was levied on their investment income or on capital gains.[61] Given this, so long as an approved scheme permitted voluntary contributions, a beneficiary could reap significant tax advantages by forgoing direct investment in shares or other financial assets in favour of making additional pension contributions.[62] Individuals who were not members of an approved pension fund lacked similar incentives until the mid-1950s. However, due to reforms carried out in 1956 and 1971, money they set aside in an approved form for retirement purposes received many of the same tax benefits as private contributions to an approved employer-established scheme.[63]

Life insurance was another example of a tax-advantaged investment vehicle that private investors relied upon in lieu of owning shares directly.[64] Up to 1984 an individual received a partial allowance against the basic rate of income tax

---

[58] Plender, *supra* n. 51, 26.   [59] 'Investment in Britain', *supra* n. 13, 49.

[60] D. Gilling-Smith, 'Pensions' in Oliver Stanley (ed.), *The Creation and Protection of Capital* (1974), 109, 110.

[61] Committee on the Taxation Treatment of Provisions for Retirement (James M. Tucker, chairman), *Report*, Cmd. 9063 (1954), 21; Gordon A. Hosking, *Pension Schemes and Retirement Benefits* (1956), 63–65, 72–75; David Blake, *Pension Schemes and Pension Funds in the United Kingdom*, 2nd edn, (2003), 38–40.

[62] On the possibility of voluntary contributions, see Michael Pilch and Victor Wood, *Pension Schemes* (1960), 59–60.

[63] See *ibid.*, 32–36, discussing reforms introduced by Finance Act 1956, 4 & 5 Eliz. 2, c. 54, ss. 22–24; Gilling-Smith, *supra* n. 60, 109–110 (discussing 1971 reforms).

[64] On the tax advantages life insurance traditionally offered, see Kay and King, *supra* n. 34, 62–63, 210; 'Personal Finance', *supra* n. 55, 9, 21–22; R.W. Simpson, 'Life Policies and Annuities' in Stanley, *supra* n. 60, 133. On the partial erosion of the tax-favoured status of insurance from the 1970s onwards, see T.C. Sole, 'The Puzzle of Life Office Tax', (1995) 1 British Actuaries Journal 79, 97; Seth Armitage, 'Returns After Personal Tax on UK Equity and Gilts, 1919–1998', (2004) 10 European Journal of Finance 23, 29, 32.

for life insurance premiums paid, generally in the neighbourhood of 15 per cent. Also, so long as certain statutory criteria were met, with life insurance policies structured so as to deliver an investment-driven return to beneficiaries on an ongoing basis, the amounts distributed were 'tax free' in the sense that they were not subject to income tax or capital gains tax. Insurance companies were liable to pay tax on the returns earned from invested funds but, as insurers were not taxed heavily, significant tax advantages remained for policyholders.

Life insurance companies exploited the tax rules to market life assurance policies that functioned more as investment vehicles for policyholders than financial protection for beneficiaries in the event of death or illness, usually in the form of 'with profits' policies that delivered bonuses based on insurance company investment returns and other criteria.[65] The marketing efforts were successful. The British public invested massively in life insurance during the decades following World War II and, as of the mid-1970s, life assurance premiums constituted a higher percentage of gross national product in the UK than they did in the US, Canada, Japan or any western European country.[66] The total financial holdings of insurance companies accordingly grew more than tenfold between 1952 and 1979, and more than doubled in real terms (1952: £4.0 billion/£79.5 billion in 2006 currency; 1979: £52.8 billion/£184.5 billion in 2006 terms).[67]

The trend was even more dramatic with pension funds. Their total financial assets grew 32 times between 1952 and 1979, or more than five times in inflation-adjusted terms (1952: £1.3 billion/£25.8 billion in 2006 currency; 1979: £41.0 billion/£143.3 billion).[68] By the 1970s, pension funds accounted for approximately one-third of the savings of the personal sector in the UK, a significantly higher fraction than the US, despite the countries sharing a tradition of private pension provision.[69]

Tax-driven decisions by individuals to 'top up' their employer-sponsored pension schemes or to establish their own retirement schemes contributed to the large growth in the size of pension assets.[70] Another important consideration was that the percentage of workers who were members of pension schemes rose from 13 per cent in 1936 to 33 per cent in 1956 and finally to 45 per cent in 1963, before levelling off at just short of half of the workforce through the remainder of the 1960s and the 1970s.[71] Also significant was that employers' pension contributions grew as a percentage of salary as employers that had established

---

[65] Kay and King, *supra* n. 34, 64; 'Personal Finance', *supra* n. 55, 13; A. Adams, *Investment* (1989), 207–12.

[66] Clarke, *supra* n. 26, 102; Wilson Committee, *supra* n. 32, 66.

[67] On the data, see S.J. Prais, *The Evolution of Giant Firms in Britain: A Study of the Growth of Concentration in Manufacturing Industry in Britain 1909–70* (1976), 116; Sidney Pollard, *The Development of the British Economy*, 4th edn (1992), 332.

[68] Prais, *supra* n. 67, 116 (1952, 1962, 1967, 1972); Coakley and Harris, *supra* n. 49, 96 (1979).

[69] Leslie Hannah, *Inventing Retirement: The Development of Occupational Pensions in Britain* (1986), 51, 66.

[70] *Ibid.*, 51.   [71] *Ibid.*, 66–67.

pension plans were under an onus to improve pension benefits for staff.[72] The final piece of puzzle was that with most schemes the average age of the members was well below the retirement age, resulting in a low ratio of benefiting to contributing members. This 'immaturity' of pension funds ensured that cash inflows greatly exceeded outflows, meaning in turn a rapid growth in funds available for investment.[73]

The institutional 'wall of money' implied substantial demand for shares existed by default. As the investment manager of the Legal and General Assurance Society said in 1959, 'Because of the very large sums which accrue for investment, aggregating well over £1 million per day, the offices are not always in a position to implement what might be described as a theoretical investment policy. Their decisions to some extent must be governed by what investments are available...'[74] The period between the mid-1960s and mid-1970s illustrates the point. During these years the percentage of total assets under management by key institutional investors allocated to shares was largely static.[75] Regardless, due to the rapid accumulation of funds to invest, collectively institutional investors were net purchasers of shares in each and every year throughout this period.[76] As a 1978 study on the rise of institutional investment said, 'The continuous net acquisitions of company ... securities by institutional investors is the result of the increased total assets held by financial institutions, the increase in total assets being financed by the contractual savings of the personal sector.'[77]

During the 1980s, matters began to change somewhat. The 1984 abolition of life assurance premium relief on income tax fostered greater emphasis on saving through unit trusts and personal pension plans at the expense of life insurance.[78] Some pension funds began to 'mature', which reduced the ability of fund managers to rebalance their portfolios simply by using new money.[79] Despite the new conditions, in the decades immediately following World War II an institutional wall of money attributable largely to tax fortified the buy side and accelerated the institutionalization of the market for shares in UK public companies.

---

[72] Littlewood, *supra* n. 42, 255; Richard Minns, *Pension Funds and British Capitalism: The Ownership and Control of Shareholdings* (1980), 5–7, 59; Hamish McRae and Frances Cairncross, *Capital City: London as a Financial Centre*, rev. edn (1991), 108.

[73] Littlewood, *supra* n. 42, 255; Radcliffe Committee, *Minutes of Evidence* (1960), 500.

[74] Quoted in Sam Aaronovitch, *The Ruling Class: A Study of British Finance Capital* (1961), 41–42.

[75] Blume, *supra* n. 33, 261, 279.

[76] Briston and Dobbins, *supra* n. 51, 189.

[77] *Ibid.*, 18.   [78] Adams, *supra* n. 65, 210.

[79] David Blake, *Pension Schemes and Pension Funds in the United Kingdom* (1995), 493–94; P.M. Greenwood, 'Pension Funding and Expensing in the Minimum Funding Requirement Environment', (1997) 3 British Actuarial Journal 497, 502; David Blake and J. Michael Orszag, 'The Impact of Pension Funds on Capital Markets', (1998) Pensions Institute, Birkbeck College, Discussion Paper PI–9803, 7–8.

IV. Factors Inducing Institutional Investors to Buy Shares

A. Asset Allocation by Insurance Companies and Pension Funds

An institutional wall of money could only fortify the buy side for shares if institutional investors were prepared to allocate at least some of the capital they had available for investment to equities. They were indeed inclined to do so. While overall asset allocations by key institutional shareholders remained largely unchanged between the mid-1960s and mid-1970s (Part III), prior to this both insurance companies and pension funds readjusted their investment portfolios in favour of equities, thus reinforcing institutional demand for shares.

Life insurance companies first began to treat UK equities as a serious investment option during the interwar years, with nearly 10 per cent of British life assurance assets being invested in ordinary shares by 1937 (Chapter Eight, Part II.A.1). This figure remained unchanged as of 1946 but rose to 12 per cent in 1951 and 16 per cent in 1956, by which point equities had become the single largest asset category on insurers' balance sheets.[80] After the proportion of insurance company assets invested in shares increased still further to 21 per cent at the beginning of the 1960s, insurance companies generally called a halt to the re-weighting of their investment portfolios, with the allocation to shares ranging between 20 per cent and 26 per cent between 1961 and 1976.[81] During the 1980s, insurers again reallocated their relative asset holdings in favour of equity, albeit partly due to growing overseas investment. This is reflected in an increase in the ratio of the value of quoted shares on their balance sheets as compared to total investments (Figure IV).[82]

With pension funds, during the opening decades of the 20th century the trust deeds governing permitted investments usually precluded the acquisition of shares and those trustees vested with wide discretion generally shunned 'risky' equities (Chapter Six, Part III.A.1; Chapter Eight, Part II.A.1). By the 1950s, the custom was for private pension funds to have the full investment powers of an

---

[80] Radcliffe Committee, *Report*, Cmnd. 827 (1959), 86; William Mennell, *Takeover: The Growth of Monopoly in Britain, 1951–61* (1962), 87–88; Mae Baker and Michael Collins, 'The Asset Portfolio Composition of British Life Insurance Firms, 1900–1965', (2003) 10 Financial History Review 137, 146, 149.

[81] J.C. Dodds, *The Investment Behaviour of British Life Insurance Companies* (1979), 49–50. See also J.G. Blease, 'Institutional Investors and the Stock Exchange', District Bank Review, September 1964, 38, 45–46; George Clayton and W.T. Osborn, *Insurance Company Investment: Principles and Policy* (1965), 135–36.

[82] National Statistics Online database, <http://www.statistics.gov.uk/statbase/TSDtables1.asp> (last visited January 25, 2008) Series RCKK RCKM, RCLP.

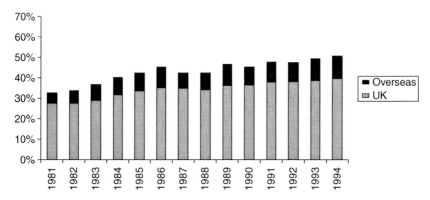

Figure IV: Value of UK/overseas quoted shares on insurance company balance sheets/ total investments, 1981–94

Source: Compiled with data from National Statistics Online, *supra* n. 82.

ordinary investor.[83] Investing in equity became fashionable as awareness grew among trustees that shares were steadily delivering better returns than fixed income securities (Chapter Four, Part III.E). By 1953 pension funds of commercial and industrial companies had 19 per cent of their assets invested in ordinary shares of companies, and this figure rose to 30 per cent by 1955 and 48 per cent by 1963.[84]

For pension funds the ratio of investments in UK shares to total investments continued to increase from the early 1960s until a stock market collapse in 1973/74 (Figure V). The fact that shares outperformed other investment alternatives (Part IV.C) meant that even if pension funds made no effort to readjust asset allocations, the value attributed to shares would have increased relative to other investments. Also significant was a process of 'catch up' by local authority pension funds that were precluded from investing in shares until the late 1950s.[85] By the early 1970s they had reallocated their investment portfolios so they had almost as high a proportion of shares in their portfolios as did private pension funds.[86]

A marked drop in the ratio of share values to total investments in 1974 reflected a steep decline in returns on shares, which was associated with a massive 'institutional vote of no confidence in equity shares'.[87] During 1973 and 1974, pension funds, insurance companies, unit trusts and investment trusts became increasingly wary of equities and in the fourth quarter of 1974, for the only time

---

[83] Radcliffe Committee, *supra* n. 80, 89.
[84] Radcliffe Committee, *supra* n. 73, 501; Blease, *supra* n. 81, 45.
[85] Blake, *supra* n. 79, 352; Radcliffe Committee, *supra* n. 80, 88.
[86] Kenneth Midgley and Ronald G. Burns, *Business Finance and the Capital Market*, 3rd edn (1979), 363.
[87] Plender, *supra* n. 51, 38.

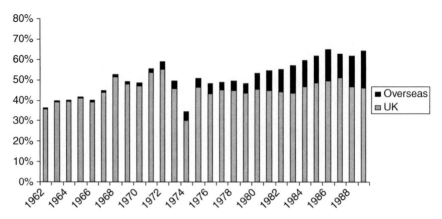

Figure V: Value of UK/overseas quoted shares on pension fund balance sheets/total investments, 1962–89

Source: Compiled with data from National Statistics Online, *supra* n. 82, series AHVA, AHVR, RHYD.

during the decade, the institutions sold more shares than they bought.[88] Matters reversed in 1975 as professional investors returned to the market to buy shares trading at deep discounts; private pension funds were among the quickest off the mark.[89] The ratio of investments in UK-quoted shares to total investments then remained largely static until 1980, when a bull market fostered a mild upward trajectory (Figure V).[90]

B. Trapped Capital

Due to the poor performance of the UK relative to its leading economic rivals, the frequent criticism of the quality of British managers and the hesitant commitment to shareholder value (Part I), it may seem surprising that following World War II pension funds and insurance companies reallocated assets available for investment in favour of shares. Various factors, however, helped to sustain institutional demand. One was that there was little scope to opt out of Britain by investing overseas.

While there is an inevitable 'home bias' with investment, British investors historically proved willing to allocate a sizeable proportion of capital to overseas assets, particularly in the late 19th and early 20th centuries (Chapter Six, Part III.B.1). Due to exchange controls there was little scope to adopt this strategy during the decades following World War II. The regulatory regime, which was initially introduced under the Exchange Control Act 1947 and was restructured

[88] *Ibid.*   [89] *Ibid.*, 55–56; Robert Heller, *The Naked Investor* (1976), 17, 107–8.
[90] Blake, *supra* n. 79, 354 (making this observation on the basis of similar but not identical data).

on various occasions before its abolition in 1979, worked essentially as follows.[91] All overseas portfolio investment had to occur through a pool of foreign 'investment currency', the size of which only increased when UK residents sold overseas investments. Thus, a new purchase of foreign securities by a British resident had to be financed by a sale by some other resident. While minor aggregate net fluctuations occurred, exchange controls tightly restricted overseas portfolio investment. Moreover, most overseas currencies were only available at a price above the official exchange rate due to the scarcity of foreign investment currency and the resulting 'investment currency premium' acted as an implicit tax on overseas portfolio investment. Turnover was further suppressed after 1965 by a 'surrender arrangement' which required those selling foreign securities to convert 25 per cent of the proceeds to pounds sterling at the less favourable official exchange rate.

The manner in which UK institutional investors conducted themselves after exchange controls were lifted in 1979 illustrates that regulation likely artificially boosted demand for domestic investment assets, including shares. By 1981, investors were supposedly 'falling over themselves to invest overseas... (T)he psychological dam built up during 40 years of exchange controls has finally burst.'[92] The statistical evidence does not support a verdict this decisive, but there clearly was pent-up demand for overseas equity. With pension funds, the ratio of overseas quoted shares to total balance sheet assets increased from 5 per cent in 1979 to 14 per cent in 1983 (Figure V). Likewise, British life insurance companies increased the proportion of the assets they held in foreign corporate securities (3 per cent in 1979; 9 per cent in 1985), as did unit trusts (20 per cent/34 per cent) and investment trusts (32 per cent/46 per cent).[93] These trends imply that in the decades immediately following World War II exchange controls trapped investment capital in the UK and thus helped to reinforce demand for shares in British-based companies.

C. Shares versus Other Domestic Options

Restrictions on foreign investment aside, institutional demand for shares was fortified by the returns shares were delivering relative to other major domestic options. Investors in the UK have a long tradition of comparing equity with obvious domestic alternatives, such as fixed income securities issued by the government, in determining whether to buy shares (Chapter Four, Part III.E.).

---

[91] Exchange Control Act 1947, 10 & 11 Geo. 6, c. 14. On aspects of the regime discussed here, see Blume, *supra* n. 33, 280; Benjamin J. Cohen, 'The United Kingdom as an Exporter of Capital', in Fritz Machlup, Walter S. Salant and Lorie Tarshis (eds), *International Mobility and Movement of Capital* (1972), 25, 37; Stephen Bond, Evan Davis and Michael Devereux, *Capital Controls: The Implications of Restricting Overseas Portfolio Capital* (1987), 18–23.

[92] Coakley and Harris, *supra* n. 49, 101–2 (quoting a 1981 article from the Financial Times).

[93] Bond *et al*, *supra* n. 91, 28–29.

Post-World War II institutional investors followed the pattern. According to a 1960 article on financial institutions, 'in practice investment managers are guided mainly by their assessment of relative yields on different classes of assets'.[94] Or as the Wilson Committee said about pension funds in a 1977 progress report, 'As with insurance funds, the yield on gilt-edged is taken as the yardstick against which other investments are judged'.[95]

Pension funds provided the most dramatic illustration of the process. A decision by the Imperial Tobacco pension fund in the late 1940s to switch heavily into equities on the basis gilts were a 'swindle' was soon widely imitated, thus launching what became known as the 'cult of the equity' (Chapter Four, Part III.E). Trends in the 1950s and early 1960s vindicated the switch, as shares outperformed both gilts and other fixed interest securities by a substantial margin (Figure VI).

In the mid-1960s, amidst growing pessimism about shares,[96] the institutional reallocation in favour of equity generally stalled (Part IV.A). Annual returns on shares justified the cautious approach, as they were considerably lower on average in the 1960s than the 1950s and were even negative during the 1970s (Chapter Four, Part III.E). Extrapolating from the poor results equities delivered in the 1970s, some even argued that 'The equity cult was well and truly dead.'[97] But matters need to be kept in perspective. Even though the holdings of UK equities as a percentage of total institutional investment assets were roughly the same in the mid-1970s as in the mid-1960s, institutional investors remained net purchasers each and every year (Part III). Most strikingly, while there was an 'institutional vote of no confidence in equity shares' in 1973/74 and major institutional investors were net sellers of shares during the final quarter of 1974, throughout 1974 as a whole they bought more shares than they sold.[98] Moreover, institutional shareholders returned to the market in 1975 and their buying contributed to a recovery in share prices running throughout much of 1977.[99]

The fact that in both the 1960s and the 1970s shares, despite lacklustre returns, managed to outperform government-fixed interest securities (Chapter Four, Part III.E) corroborated the decision not to reverse investment patterns developed as the 'cult of the equity' initially took hold. Institutional demand for shares was fortified further by the collapse of the market for corporate debt. There was during the 1950s and 1960s an active market in new issues of fixed-interest

[94] H.B. Rose, 'Financial Institutions and Monetary Policy', Bankers' Magazine, July 1960, 14, 23.

[95] Wilson Committee, *Progress Report on the Financing of Industry and Trade* (1977), 23. See also Clarke, *supra* n. 26, 103; G.H. Ross Goobey, 'The Use of Statistics in the Investment of Funds', (1956) 5 Applied Statistics 1, 2–3.

[96] 'Equity Investors Should Do Their Homework', Times, September 9, 1963.

[97] Plender, *supra* n. 51, 45; see also Wilson Report, *supra* n. 41, 140.

[98] 'There is £3½ Billion', *supra* n. 40; Briston and Dobbins, *supra* n. 51, 189.

[99] Pt IV.A; 'Good Eye', *supra* n. 46.

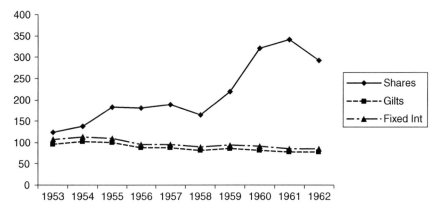

Figure VI: Market values of UK industrial shares, gilts and fixed interest investments, 1953–62

Source: Compiled with data from William G. Nursaw, *The Art and Practice of Investment* (1963), 2.

corporate bonds.[100] This market collapsed in the 1970s due to uncertainty about future interest rates in a volatile and inflation-ridden decade.[101] Hence, while as of 1970 14 per cent of pension fund assets were held in the form of corporate bonds, by 1980 this figure was 2 per cent.[102] Companies lost the appetite to borrow due to concerns about 'locking in' rates of interest of 15 per cent or more that would have imposed prohibitive borrowing costs if inflation, and thus long-term interest rates, came down.[103] Investors conversely did not want to be exposed to the threat of negative real returns in the event inflation got worse.[104] Thus, at least in the 1970s institutional investors that otherwise might have forsaken equity in favour of investing in corporate debt were precluded from following through.

Given Britain's relative decline in comparison to other major industrialized countries, the poor performance of shares in the 1970s relative to prior decades and the elimination of exchange controls, it might have been anticipated institutional investors would have reduced their exposure to the UK stock market in the 1980s. The reverse happened. While the foreign option proved popular, in the case of both insurance companies and pension funds the ratio of investments in UK quoted shares to total investment assets increased during the 1980s (Figures IV, V).

[100] Wilson Committee, *Evidence on the Financing of Trade and Industry*, vol. 1 (1977), 9; 'The UK Corporate Bond Market', Bank of England Quarterly Bulletin, March 1981, 54, 56.

[101] Blume, *supra* n. 33, 305; Wilson Report *supra* n. 41, 225.

[102] E. Philip Davis, *Pension Funds: Retirement-Income Security, and Capital Markets—An International Perspective* (1995), 137.

[103] Plender, *supra* n. 51, 187; Wilson Committee, *supra* n. 100, 9, 55–56; 'UK Corporate', *supra* n. 100, 57.

[104] Wilson Report, *supra* n. 41, 225; Lionel T. Anthony, 'Investment in Industry' in Alan Philipp (ed.), *A Background to Pension Fund Investment* (1980), 146, 147.

One explanation was a changed political climate. Soon after the 1979 election brought Margaret Thatcher's market-friendly Conservatives to power there were 'stories of leaner and fitter companies' confronting 'the long-neglected reality that we all have to earn our own living in a tough competitive world'.[105] Falling interest rates, combined with the end of a lengthy recession in 1982, also provided a good platform for recovery.[106] In this changed context, corporate profitability rebounded strongly after slumping in the 1960s and 1970s.[107] Shares duly performed very well, as returns for investors during the 1980s were higher than in any other decade during the 20th century (Chapter Four, Part III.E). Thus, despite the dismal performance of the stock market in the 1970s and the emergence of a wider range of foreign options, UK shares remained, relative to other investment options, a popular choice among institutional investors in the 1980s.

D. Company Law and Stock Exchange Regulation

The fact shares performed well relative to other investment alternatives was not the only reason there was in the decades following World War II a sufficiently robust institutional buy side to underpin a separation of ownership and control. Regulation also likely played a role. In the decades following World War II, amendments made to companies legislation, alterations made to stock exchange listing rules and the development of guidance on takeovers all served to reduce the scope for blockholders to secure benefits unavailable to other shareholders (Chapter Nine, Part III.C.,D.,E). Similar trends simultaneously reassured investors about decisions they were making about buying shares.

Investors potentially apprehensive about initial public offerings could draw comfort from the fact the London Stock Exchange continued its interwar practice of carefully scrutinizing companies that sought quotations.[108] Amendments made to companies legislation and stock exchange listing rules that enhanced disclosure requirements similarly should have fortified the buy side for shares. By virtue of the Companies Act 1948, companies that previously only had to make their annual profit and loss accounts available to shareholders became obliged to file such documentation publicly.[109] An additional 1948 departure from past practice was detailed regulation of the form and content of both the balance sheet and the profit and loss account.[110] Another innovation was to require company

---

[105] Anthony Sampson, *The Changing Anatomy of Britain* (1982), 342, 349; see also Michael Francis, 'Investing in Equities' in Alan Phillip (ed.), *A Background to Pension Fund Investment* (1980), 70, 73.

[106] 'Britain plc is Not in Such a Mess', Economist, November 20, 1982, 80.

[107] Christine Oughton, Probability of UK Firms' in Kirsty Hughes (ed.), *The Future of UK Competitiveness and the Role of Industrial Policy* (1993), 55, 58.

[108] Ch. Eight, Pt II.B.3; R.J. Briston, *The Stock Exchange and Investment Analysis*, 3rd edn (1975), 36.

[109] Ch. Eight, Pt II.B.2; Companies Act 1948, 11 & 12 Geo. 6, c. 38, ss. 126(1), 127(1), 156(1).

[110] Companies Act 1948, s. 149(2), sch. VIII.

accounts to be prepared so that they gave a 'true and fair view' of a company's financial position.[111]

Finally, the 1948 Act tightened up disclosure requirements for holding companies and their subsidiaries.[112] Under the new scheme, a holding company's balance sheet and profit and loss account had to be presented in the form of group accounts giving a true and fair view of the state of the affairs of the group as a whole. Normally, this meant consolidated accounts for the group had to be prepared. However, the directors could, if they provided figures on the aggregate profits (or losses), prepare accounts for each of the subsidiaries if they considered it more informative to do so.

The quality of corporate financial disclosure improved due to the Companies Act 1948.[113] Nevertheless, doubts continued to exist about the statutory regime, with soon-to-be Prime Minister Harold Wilson arguing in favour of company law reform in 1964 on the basis of 'the totally inadequate information directors are required to give to shareholders'.[114] A failure to require companies to divulge information concerning turnover and expenses of production was one oft-cited shortcoming.[115] Another was that companies failed to make adequate disclosure of their shareholdings in other companies.[116] Annual reports prepared by directors and circulated to shareholders were also criticized as being insufficiently informative, in part because of inadequate descriptions of the businesses in which companies were engaged.[117] Moreover, there were complaints that most UK public companies, even large ones, only published financial results on an annual basis, rather than quarterly, as was the practice in the US.[118] Some critics said the deficiencies with disclosure were sufficient to discourage further widening of share ownership in publicly traded companies.[119]

Changes to disclosure regulation occurring in the 1960s responded to these concerns to a significant degree. In 1963, washing machine retailers Rolls Razor Ltd collapsed with debts of over £4 million shortly after reporting annual profits

---

[111] Companies Act 1948, s. 149(1).

[112] Companies Act 1948, ss. 150–53, sch. VIII, Pt II.

[113] A.J. Arnold and D.R. Matthews, 'Corporate Financial Disclosures in the UK, 1920–50: The Effects of Legislative Change and Managerial Discretion', (2002) 32 Accounting and Business Research 3.

[114] 'Mr. Wilson's Company Law', Economist, April 25, 1964, 418.

[115] Guy Naylor, *Company Law for Shareholders* (1960), 22; 'Company Law: Some Questions for Review', Economist, September 24, 1960, 1211, 1213; Harold Rose, *Disclosure in Company Accounts*, 2nd edn (1965), 33, 35.

[116] 'Mr. Wilson's', *supra* n. 114; *Report of the Company Law Committee* (Lord Jenkins, chairman) (hereinafter Jenkins Report), Cmnd. 1749 (1962), 146.

[117] Rose, *supra* n. 115, 32–33; Jenkins Report, *supra* n. 116, 40; Anthony Sampson, *The Anatomy of Britain* (1961), 501.

[118] Naylor, *supra* n. 115, 22; Rose, *supra* n. 115, 41–42; C.D. Foster, 'Economic Policy' in Peter Hall (ed.), *Labour's New Frontiers* (1964) 17, 28.

[119] 'British Companies Urged to Disclose More', Times, February 11, 1964.

of nearly £900,000.[120] The scandal prompted the Stock Exchange to bolster the disclosure requirements in its Listing Rules, as in 1964/65 it compelled companies seeking a quotation to disclose annual turnover figures, issue quarterly or half-yearly interim financial reports and provide information on major interests in associated companies.[121] Following on from recommendations in a 1962 report on company law reform by a committee chaired by Lord Jenkins, the Companies Act 1967 required companies to publish annually information about sales, substantial shareholdings in other companies and the classes of business being carried on.[122] The amount of information to be disclosed remained modest compared to the US and was said by some to continue to be inadequate from an investment analysis perspective.[123] The changes were nevertheless credited with improving markedly the quality of investment research being carried out, a service those managing investments on behalf of pension funds and insurance companies were relying upon with greater frequency during the 1960s.[124]

Further changes were made to disclosure regulation in the 1980s. The Companies Act 1981 obliged companies for the first time to prepare their accounts in accordance with a standardized format.[125] The Financial Services Act 1986 deemed the London Stock Exchange to be the competent authority responsible for promulgating and enforcing listing requirements for companies with publicly traded shares, thereby vesting the Stock Exchange's listing rules with the status of subordinate legislation.[126] The Act also specified the Stock Exchange's enforcement powers, stipulating that the Exchange could suspend trading in a company's shares and publicize breaches of its listing rules.[127]

The 1986 formalization of the listing rules was only of limited practical significance since the Stock Exchange could already suspend or cancel dealings in shares of non-complying companies.[128] However, the change explains why the UK's score on an index of prospectus disclosure regulation constructed by La Porta, López-de-Silanes and Shleifer leapt from 0.33 to 0.75 in 1986, near its current level of 0.83 (Chapter Two, Table III). As of the mid-1980s, the Stock Exchange listing rules dealt with a series of variables La Porta *et al* relied on in

---

[120] Rose, *supra* n. 115, 59; 'Rolls Razor Deficiency Exceeds £4m', Times, August 28, 1964; 'The Doomsday Book', Times, September 4, 1964, 63.

[121] Charles Anderson, 'The Stock Exchange and Disclosure', The Banker, October 1964, 619; 'FBI and Stock Exchange', Economist, October 3, 1964, 76; 'Clearing Up the Details', Economist, February 27, 1965, 933.

[122] Jenkins Report, *supra* n. 116, 40–42, 144–54; Companies Act 1967, c. 81, ss. 3, 4, 17, sch. 1, para. 14.

[123] Brinley Davies, *Business Finance and the City of London* (1976), 71.

[124] Littlewood, *supra* n. 42, 160–61; Briston, *supra* n. 108, 270.

[125] Companies Act 1981, c. 62, s. 1, sch. 1.

[126] Financial Services Act 1986, c. 60, ss. 142(6), 143–44. See also Stock Exchange (Listing) Regulations 1984, S.I. 1984/716.

[127] Financial Services Act 1986, ss. 145(b), 153.

[128] Gower *et al*, *supra* n. 43, 349; Council of the Stock Exchange, *Rules and Regulations of the Stock Exchange* (1973), rule 165.

constructing the index which UK company law did not, such as director share ownership, executive compensation and disclosure of major share blocks.[129] In grading the quality of securities law, La Porta, López-de-Silanes and Shleifer focused on 'actual laws, statutes . . . and any other rule with force of law'.[130] While the Stock Exchange listing rules did not fall into this category before the mid-1980s, they did after the enactment of the Financial Services Act 1986, thus qualifying the relevant provisions for inclusion.

Extending back as far as the 18th century, investors in the UK have compensated for disclosure gaps by treating dividends as a signalling mechanism offering clues as to a company's future prospects (Chapter Four, Part III.D). The signalling effect of dividends generally diminishes as other sources of information on companies become available.[131] Hence, as post-World War II changes to company law and stock exchange regulation put the onus on quoted companies to disclose more information about their financial affairs, UK investors placed increasing emphasis on earnings data and profit forecasts when valuing shares and paid less attention to dividends. For instance, in 1992 the *Economist* acknowledged a dividend cut was taken far more seriously by the markets than 'glossy hand-outs and analysts' briefing', but said 'investors are increasingly clear-eyed . . . looking less to the dividend and more to the profits covering it'.[132]

Still, despite more detailed regulation of corporate disclosure, investors continued to treat dividend policy as an important barometer of corporate performance. A 1955 report issued by a royal commission investigating taxation of profits and income noted It is the distributed profits that tend most directly to influence the market value of a share.'[133] George Ross Goobey, the actuary credited with launching the UK's post-World War II 'cult of the equity' by way of investment decisions taken on behalf of Imperial Tobacco's pension fund, said in 1956 about reviewing investments in shares, '[C]ompanies with good results are passed over without further investigation, whereas any company that has reduced its profits, or worse still, reduced its dividend, is brought very forcibly to notice.'[134] King argued in 1977 'the payment of the dividend is the principal direct line of communication from management to shareholder'.[135] Marsh

---

[129] Brian R. Cheffins, 'Dividends as a Substitute for Corporate Law: The Separation of Ownership and Control in the United Kingdom', (2006) 63 Washington & Lee Law Review 1273, 1294–95.

[130] Rafael La Porta, Florencio López-de-Silanes and Andrei Shleifer, 'What Works in Securities Laws?', (2006) 61 Journal of Finance 1, 5.

[131] Nils H. Hakansson, 'To Pay or Not to Pay Dividend', (1982) 37 Journal of Finance 415.

[132] 'Dividend Dilemmas', Economist, August 15, 1992, 12. See also Littlewood, *supra* n. 42, 159; Heller, *supra* n. 89, 223–24; Janette Rutterford, 'From Dividend Yield to Discounted Cash Flow: A History of UK and US Equity Valuation Techniques', (2004) 14 Accounting, Business & Financial History 115, 138.

[133] Royal Commission on the Taxation of Profits and Income, *Final Report*, Cmd. 9474 (1955), 17, see also 386–87.

[134] Goobey, *supra* n. 95, 6. On Goobey and the cult of the equity, see Ch. Four, Pt III.E.

[135] Mervyn King, *Public Policy and the Corporation* (1977), 175.

found, based on 1989–92 data, that companies that announced a big dividend increase experienced a share price increase 1.7 per cent larger than those of otherwise similarly placed firms, that shares of companies that cut their dividends fell by a relative 4.3 per cent and that companies that omitted the dividend entirely plunged by 7.4 per cent.[136] Hence, to the extent there were gaps in disclosure, post-World War II investors, as with their pre-World War II predecessors, were relying on dividends to provide signals on the future prospects of publicly traded companies. Dividends therefore continued to play a significant, if somewhat diminished, role fortifying the buy side for shares.

E. Takeovers

1. Advantages for Institutional Shareholders

For institutional investors who might have refrained from investing in shares due to doubts about managerial quality, insufficient commitment to the promotion of shareholder value or other shortcomings concerning British publicly quoted companies (Part I), the manner in which the takeover transaction developed from the 1950s onwards would have been reassuring. One consideration was the windfall takeovers yielded for investors in target companies. During the 1950s, 1960s and 1970s, shareholders in publicly traded companies that were taken over received, on average, a 20 to 30 per cent premium on the pre-bid share price.[137] Goobey, the Imperial Tobacco actuary, characterized the situation after he retired: '(E)very now and again in the investment world we get a ruddy good takeover which bumps your performance up tremendously…I always liked a nice juicy takeover.'[138]

Takeover premium windfalls aside, merger and acquisition (M & A) activity was potentially appealing for investors because of anticipated economy-wide benefits. Harold Wilson said of the merger wave occurring during his 1964–70 tenure as Labour Prime Minister that it was doing more than anything else to drag Britain 'kicking and screaming into the twentieth century'.[139] This reflected a general consensus that the formation of large firms should be encouraged because UK industry was failing to take sufficient advantage of size-oriented opportunities for increased efficiencies.[140] As a government White Paper said in 1966 'The need for more concentration and rationalisation to promote the greater efficiency

---

[136] 'Revisiting the Dividend Controversy', Economist, August 15, 1992, 69, 'Why Dividend Cuts are a Last Resort', Financial Times, August 12, 1992, discussing Paul Marsh, 'Dividend Announcements and Stock Price Performance', (1992), unpublished working paper.

[137] Julian R. Franks and Robert S. Harris, 'Shareholder Wealth Effects of Corporate Takeovers: The UK Experience 1955–1985', (1989) 23 Journal of Financial Economics 225, 232.

[138] Hobson, *supra* n. 44, 1136.

[139] William Davis, *Merger Mania* (1970), 2.

[140] *Ibid.*, 234; George Bull, 'The Urge to Merge' in Andrew Robertson (ed.), *A Penguin Survey: Business & Industry 1967* (1967), 28, 35; J.D. Gribbin, 'The Post-War Revival of Competition as Industrial Policy', Government Economic Service Working Paper No. 19 (1978), 33–34.

and competitiveness of British industry ... is now widely recognised.'[141] Or as the *New York Times* said more colourfully in 1968, 'Britain's rundown economy has long been patched up with policies such as temporary tax changes and bank rate adjustments. But an industrial remodeling job is now under way in the form of giant mergers, suggesting more lasting improvement.'[142] In these circumstances, investors were prepared to accept that mergers—at least those that were well executed—could bring significant advantages to the firms involved and indeed to the national economy more generally.[143]

M & A activity was also potentially attractive to investors since mergers created the potential to fit the right managers into the right jobs.[144] As a US corporate law scholar observed in the mid-1980s, '[A] commonly noted function of the market for corporate control is to allow good managers to replace poor managers.'[145] Something of this appeared to be going on with mergers in the UK following World War II. Sampson said in 1962 of takeovers occurring over the previous few years, 'The raiders transformed whole areas of business: sleepy and comfortable firms have been rationalised, combed and costed ... their managers re-valued with unsuspected thrusting men emerging from the undergrowth.'[146] Companies carrying out mergers in the 1960s and the 1970s generally were bigger, faster-growing and more profitable than target companies and companies not carrying out acquisitions.[147] Investors thus might reasonably have inferred that M & A activity would yield benefits by expanding the influence of strong management more widely through the economy.

M & A activity would also have been encouraging to investors because takeovers can play a beneficial disciplinary role and place an onus on managers to focus on shareholders' interests. The theory is well known.[148] 'Hostile' bids, the thinking goes, occur when a bidder calculates managerial changes at a poorly run target company will generate enough additional profit to justify launching a takeover to acquire control. Once incumbent executives know this kind of bid can occur they have an incentive to fend off unwelcome suitors by running their companies in a manner that promotes shareholder value. Thus the mere threat of a takeover imposes beneficial discipline on corporate executives.

---

[141] *Industrial Reorganisation Corporation*, Cmnd 2889 (1966), 2.

[142] 'Britain and Mergers', New York Times, January 31, 1968.

[143] 'Company Mergers Need Greater Selectivity', Times, February 15, 1966.

[144] 'Britain and Mergers', *supra* n. 142, 'Should We Believe in Giants?', Economist, January 10, 1970, 12; F.R. Jervis, *The Economics of Mergers* (1971), 77.

[145] Bernard S. Black, 'Bidder Overpayment in Takeovers', (1989) 41 Stanford Law Review 597, 609.

[146] Sampson, *supra* n. 117, 495.

[147] Alan Hughes, 'Mergers and Economic Performance in the UK: A Survey of the Empirical Evidence 1950–1990' in James A. Fairburn, and John A. Kay (eds) *Mergers and Merger Policy* (1989), 9, 50–53 (summarizing the relevant studies).

[148] See, for example, Frank H. Easterbrook and Daniel R. Fischel, *The Economic Structure of Corporate Law* (1991) 171–73.

A poem entitled 'A Company Prayer' printed in the *Sunday Times* in 1970 illustrated takeover bids produced anxiety in British boardrooms:

Oh Lord watch o'er our costings,
And help us keep them down;
Give us sales beyond compare
And a name of great renown.
Oh save us from the revenue
From strikes do keep us rid:
But most of all, Almighty God
Please—no take-over bid.[149]

The nervousness of executives in turn helped to keep them focused on shareholder returns. As the London Stock Exchange told the Wilson Committee in 1977:

The stock market itself exercises a form of control in providing a spur to efficient management. The rating of a company's ordinary shares in the stockmarket (*sic*) provides a direct measure of a company's past and expected performance relative to other companies. Management is aware of this measure of its ability and, if its relative rating falls, strives to do better. Moreover, if management happens to be unaffected by the decline in its company's share price, the market provides a more dramatic incentive to efficiency—the prospect of a takeover.[150]

The Wilson Committee was more cautious in its assessment in its 1980 report, but nevertheless said the 'discipline being imposed on managements by the continued threat of a takeover...may be one of the more potent mechanisms whereby pressure towards efficiency is maintained'.[151]

The disciplinary aspect of takeovers was a new development in the post-World War II era. Until the early 1950s, mergers in the UK were almost invariably effected by mutual agreement between the boards of the companies involved.[152] Directors kept negotiations secret until a deal had been finalized, then got the shareholders to ratify the transaction.[153] Though the term 'takeover' soon became thought of more broadly, it was first used in the early 1950s to describe a new phenomenon, this being the acquisition of control of a publicly quoted company by the purchase of a majority of its shares without any prior consent from the directors.[154]

---

[149] ' "Prufrocks" ' Company Prayer Competition', Sunday Times, January 25, 1970, 35 (quoting a poem entered by Myer Robinson).

[150] Wilson Committee, *supra* n. 32, 215.

[151] Wilson Report, *supra* n. 41, 305.

[152] Frank H. Jones, *Guide to Company Balance Sheets and Profit & Loss Accounts*, 6th edn (1964), 535; Alexander Johnston, *The City Take-Over Code* (1980), 8.

[153] Jones, *supra* n. 152, 535; Les Hannah, 'Takeover Bids in Britain Before 1950: An Exercise in Business "Pre-History" ', (1974) 16 Business History 65, 68.

[154] Richard Roberts, 'Regulatory Responses to the Rise of the Market for Corporate Control in the 1950s', (1992) 34 Business History 183, 184.

One explanation for the emergence of this type of transaction in the 1950s was the unwinding of control blocks. There were more targets because there were fewer companies where a dominant coalition could in effect veto an unwelcome offer due to its voting power.[155] Legal reform also played a role. Tighter regulation of periodic disclosure under the Companies Act 1948 made it easier for potential bidders to rely on published financial data to find undervalued target companies.[156] The 1948 Act also increased the leverage bidders possessed by stipulating that incumbent directors could be removed at any time by way of a shareholder resolution passed by a simple majority vote (Chapter Four, Part IV.B).

Academics did not draw attention to the disciplinary aspect of takeover bids until the early 1960s.[157] However, as soon as hostile takeover offers began to occur in the UK in the early 1950s there was immediate recognition such bids provided directors with incentives to create value for shareholders.[158] As the *Economist* said in 1953, 'To claim that those who offer to buy shares at a premium are "attacking the independence" of the shareholders' business is an odd misconception indeed. The only "attack" that such bids involve is on the complacency of existing directors or managers—with results that neither the country nor the shareholders . . . seem to have any reason to rue.'[159]

Takeover bids were also reassuring for investors because they added to the power and status of shareholders by underscoring the value of voting rights attached to shares.[160] A much-publicized takeover battle known as 'the Aluminium War' illustrated how takeover activity provided shareholders of targets with leverage against incumbent directors.[161] In 1958 Tube Investments (TI), in association with Reynolds Metals, an American aluminium producer, began buying British Aluminium shares with a view to making a bid for control and launched a hostile bid after efforts to reach an agreement with British

---

[155] Hannah, *supra* n. 153, 67–68; Margaret Ackrill, 'Britain's Managers and the British Economy, 1870s to the 1980s', (1980) 4 Oxford Review of Economic Policy 59, 63, 65.

[156] Hannah, *supra* n. 153, 75; John F. Wilson, *British Business History, 1720–1994* (1995), 202; David J. Jeremy, *A Business History of Britain 1900–1990s* (1998), 212–13. On the 1948 reforms, see Pt IV.D.

[157] William J. Carney, 'The Legacy of "The Market for Corporate Control" and the Origins of the Theory of the Firm', (1999) 50 Case Western Reserve Law Review 215, 233.

[158] The explanation for the delayed academic response likely is that hostile takeovers became prominent in the US a decade later than in the UK. See John Pound, 'The Rise of the Political Model of Corporate Governance and Corporate Control', (1993) 68 New York University Law Review 1003, 1016 (US chronology); Robin Marris, 'A Model of the "Managerial Enterprise"', (1963) 78 Quarterly Journal of Economics 185, 189, n. 5 (citing the lengthy track record of takeover bids in Britain to justify the emphasis placed on the disciplinary role of takeover activity in modeling managerial behaviour).

[159] 'Shelter from Share Bids?,' Economist, February 14, 1953, 433.

[160] Jones, *supra* n. 152, 543.

[161] On the events involved, see Stephen Hatch and Michael Forbes, 'The Struggle for British Aluminium', (1960) 31 Political Quarterly 477; George Bull and Anthony Vice, *Bid for Power*, 3rd edn (1961), 43–69; David Kynaston, *The City of London, vol. IV: A Club No More, 1945–2000* (2001), 107–16.

Aluminium's directors failed. The British Aluminium board failed to disclose that, prior to meeting with representatives of TI and Reynolds Metals, it had agreed to issue to Reynolds' US rival Alcoa new shares sufficient to give Alcoa one-third voting control.

A consortium of City merchant banks, stockbrokers and investment trusts, led by British Aluminium's merchant bankers, secured the agreement of a number of big insurance companies to spurn the TI/Reynolds Metals offer and then made a rival bid. Warburgs, merchant bankers for TI/Reynolds Metals, responded with heavy buying in the market at a price above that offered by the City consortium. The insurance companies reasoned their undertaking to the City consortium did not preclude them from selling out on the stock market, and they did precisely that once Warburgs started buying shares. TI/Reynolds Metals, with their voting stake duly fortified, followed up with a formal offer that generated sufficient acceptances for a successful bid.

The price on offer was clearly one factor that motivated the insurance companies to sell out to Warburgs. However, they, together with various other institutional investors, objected to the heavy-handed manner in which the British Aluminium board had conducted itself.[162] One complaint was that the board had favoured a deal with Alcoa without seriously considering an offer from TI/Reynolds Metals that was potentially advantageous to British Aluminium's shareholders. Also, the consensus among key institutional investors was that the board should not have agreed to issue a large block of shares to affect control without first consulting the shareholders.

A key message arising from the British Aluminium affair was that directors who failed to take the shareholders seriously did so at their peril. As the *Times* said, 'That is the most important moral that emerges. Boards must get closer to their shareholders... The more that boards can improve "shareholder relations", in which the main ingredients are information, consultation, and adequate dividends, the fewer will be the occasions for heart-burning...'[163] Or, according to a 1959 memo prepared for the Governor of the Bank of England, 'Developments since 1953 have tended to support the view that take-over bidders generally perform a useful function... In present circumstances Directors generally have only themselves to blame if they are dispossessed by more enterprising rivals.'[164] Similarly, a 1960 survey of takeovers said, 'However unevenly, companies have largely adjusted themselves to the very different world economy of post-war Britain... In some cases bidders have directly brought about these healthy

---

[162] Sampson, *supra* n. 117, 388–89; Paul Ferris, *The City* (1960), 89; 'No Early Official Decision on British Aluminium', Times, December 5, 1958.

[163] 'The Price of Saying Too Little', Times, January 15, 1959. See also Davis, *supra* n. 139, 37; J.F. Wright, 'The Capital Market and the Finance of Industry' in G.D.N. Worswick and P.H. Ady (eds), *The British Economy in the Nineteen-Fifties* (1962), 461, 464.

[164] Quoted in Roberts, *supra* n. 154, 193.

changes; in many more it was their example that inspired boards of directors to bring policy into line with modern needs.'[165]

The lessons of British Aluminium generally endured. Littlewood observed 40 years after the fact 'British Aluminium was a landmark in post-war financial history...Above all, it was a victory for shareholders and displayed for the first time the power of shareholders to act against their directors and advisers.'[166] As such, the affair, together with other takeover bids occurring in the 1950s, would have offered a reassuring message to institutional investors deciding whether to buy equity in UK public companies.

Although takeover activity in the 1950s made directors more aware of the need to promote shareholder value, there remained numerous underperforming companies.[167] Jim Slater, chairman of Slater Walker Securities, argued in 1969 'many British managements forget their primary responsibility is to their shareholders' and 'are primarily concerned with making things, as opposed to making money'. Slater went on to say that when managers 'let their prepossession for making things conflict unduly with their duty to make money for their shareholders, an asset situation can be created...and the company becomes attractive to managements who are more concerned with making money for their shareholders'.[168] During the mid-1960s under Slater's chairmanship—he was labelled 'the trendiest man in takeovers' in 1967—Slater Walker put theory into practice.[169] Slater Walker's acquisitions department studied closely data on public companies available on cards prepared by the Exchange Telegraph statistical service and when the department was satisfied a company had saleable assets with a value significantly in excess of the share price, Slater Walker would carry out a takeover and seek to generate profits by promptly realizing unwanted assets and reorganizing other aspects of the business.[170]

James Goldsmith, a friend of Slater's, adopted a similar philosophy in running Cavenham Foods, a publicly traded company he controlled that carried out a series of acquisitions and restructurings in the food industry in the late 1960s and early 1970s.[171] Slater Walker's acquisition activity ranged more widely, as it executed deals in industries as diverse as rubber processing, window frame manufacturing, optical equipment, gas meters, water treatment and health

---

[165] Anthony Vice, *Balance Sheet for Take-overs* (1960), 14.

[166] Littlewood, *supra* n. 42, 104–5. See also B. Mark Smith, *The Equity Culture: The Story of the Global Stock Market* (2003), 161.

[167] Davis, *supra* n. 139 at 249; Ivan Fallon, *Billionaire: The Life and Times of Sir James Goldsmith* (1991), 153.

[168] 'The Role of Conglomerates in the British Economy', Times, April 9, 1969.

[169] Kynaston, *supra* n. 161, 353.

[170] 'Is This the Day of the Merger Specialists?', Times, March 4, 1968; 'Following, But Not Listening To, Mr. Jim Slater', Times, June 7, 1971.

[171] Fallon, *supra* n. 167, chs 10, 11, 14. On Goldsmith's control of Cavenham, see Ch. Nine, Pt II.B.

food.[172] Slater Walker initially had few buyout rivals, but due to its notoriety and popularity with investors, various other companies began imitating its business plan of buying companies and reshaping the assets to generate a profit.[173] None, however, stamped their financial philosophy on the markets in the same way as Slater Walker.[174]

According to a biography critical of Slater, 'By 1970, it was axiomatic that Slater and his imitators represented the white hope of the nation's industry—they were the men who could reconstruct old, tired companies and release under-used assets…'[175] The pronounced stock market slide in 1973/74 soon de-railed most of 'the Slater generation of whizzkids'.[176] Slater Walker, despite spending the start of the 1970s transforming itself from an acquisitive conglomerate to an investment bank with a portfolio of industrial investments, collapsed itself in 1975.[177] Goldsmith, discouraged by Britain's economic malaise and left-wing politics, withdrew to pursue opportunities elsewhere, taking Cavenham Foods private in 1977.[178] Nevertheless, the activities of Slater Walker, Cavenham Foods and various imitators meant takeovers continued to play a disciplinary role through the late 1960s and early 1970s, thus providing UK executives with a potent incentive to focus on using corporate assets to create value for shareholders.[179] Investors in turn could plausibly believe fear of a falling share price acted as a meaningful check on management.[180]

Slater Walker's mantle was taken up in the 1980s by Hanson Trust (known simply as Hanson after 1987), led by James (later Lord) Hanson and Gordon (later Lord) White.[181] Hanson and White, backed partly by Slater Walker, began in the late 1960s to buy up and restructure underperforming businesses, focusing particularly on companies in slow-growth sectors with mature technologies, strong market positions and loose profitability controls.[182] The 1970s were difficult for Hanson Trust, but it was 'just about the only survivor of the

---

[172] Raw, *supra* n. 7, 124–25, 201–5; Anthony Vice, *The Strategy of Takeovers: A Casebook of International Practice* (1971), 3, 9–10.

[173] On the initial lack of competition, see Jim Slater, *Return to Go: My Autobiography* (1978), 93–94. On imitators, see Fallon, *supra* n. 167, 226–27; Vice, *supra* n. 172, 1; 'A Dampener for Mr. Jessel's Fireworks Display', Times, October 16, 1974.

[174] Fallon, *supra* n. 167, 165, 216.

[175] Raw, *supra* n. 7, 191.

[176] Fallon, *supra* n. 167, 227–28; see also Raw, *supra* n. 7, 351–52.

[177] Slater, *supra* n. 173, 102–3, 113–14, 120–22, 149–50, 193–94, 210, 219–21, 236–37; 'Changing Camps', Economist, April 11, 1970, 76; 'To Saving Slater—£30 Million', Sunday Times, August 21, 1977.

[178] Fallon, *supra* n. 167, 332–35.

[179] Anthony Sampson, *The New Anatomy of Britain* (1971), 502; 'Rarely Will So Grand a Designer Have Had So Little Effect', Times, October 27, 1975; *cf.* Raw, *supra* n. 7, 353 (acknowledging the point but doubting whether takeovers had really made British management more efficient).

[180] Plender, *supra* n. 51, 61.

[181] On 'Trust' being dropped in 1987, see 'Conglomerate as Antique', Economist, March 11, 1989.

[182] Alex Brummer and Roger Cowe, *Hanson: A Biography* (1994), 70–80; 'An Endangered Species', Financial Times, August 3, 1996.

late-sixties generation of whizz-kids to weather the bleak days of the bear market and keep (its) reputation—if not share price—intact'.[183] Hanson Trust, fortified by market-friendly politics, an improving economy and share prices of potential targets still lagging due to a lengthy recession, carried out in the 1980s 'an astonishing charge through the British and American industrial hierarchy'.[184] By the end of the decade its annual pre-tax profits surpassed £1 billion and the company was valued at more than £8.6 billion, placing it third out of all FTSE 100 companies by gain in market value during the decade.[185] Various other companies, such as BTR (formerly British Tyre and Rubber), Tomkins and Williams Holdings, followed in Hanson footsteps, seeking to create value by acquiring underpriced companies and then either selling the assets or improving profits through tough fiscal discipline.[186]

Hanson and its fellow acquisitive conglomerates languished in the 1990s, ending up themselves restructured and streamlined.[187] However, in their 1980s heyday they had a significant disciplinary impact on British management. Executives, due to awareness of the threat of a potential takeover bid by Hanson or one of its peers, frequently took pre-emptive corrective action so as to make themselves less vulnerable, focusing on cash generation, selling peripheral assets and reducing costs.[188] As Lord Sterling, chairman of travel group P & O, explained in 2004, '[T]he effect was rather like a stone in a pond. Even companies that were not being targeted directly realised they could be targets of Hanson or someone else if they didn't do something about their use of assets and methods of operation.'[189] The disciplinary side-effects in turn would have made investing in public companies a more attractive proposition for institutional investors. As a business columnist observed in 1994, 'if Hanson did not exist it would be necessary to invent him'.[190]

2. Defensive Tactics

The reassurance M & A activity provided due to the disciplinary aspect of takeovers was contingent upon directors not having ample latitude to take decisions about changes of control out of the hands of shareholders. Between the

---

[183] Brummer and Cowe, *supra* n. 182, 113–14, quoting 'Questor Column', Telegraph, December 17, 1974.

[184] *Ibid.*, 132–33.   [185] 'Winners and Losers', Times, December 24, 1989.

[186] *Ibid.*; 'How the Superstars won City Support', Guardian, January 22, 1985; 'Racing with the Raiding Pack', Financial Times, October 13, 2000.

[187] 'Endangered Species', *supra* n. 182; 'End of Empires', Sunday Times, August 18, 1996; 'End of Guns-to-Buns Group Sounds Last Post for the Big Conglomerates', Independent, July 13, 1999.

[188] 'Merger Men Find Key to Success', Independent, February 3, 1991; 'Hanson: The End of an Era', Financial Times, January 31, 1996; 'Times Must Have Changed if Hanson Can Do No Right', Times, February 12, 1996.

[189] Quoted in 'Legacy of the Lord With the Midas Touch', Guardian, November 3, 2004. See also 'The Conglomerate as Antique Dealer', Economist, March 11, 1989, 83; 'Less of an Art and More of an Industry', Financial Times, May 4, 1995.

[190] 'Keep on Truckin'', Sunday Telegraph, August 28, 1994. See also 'Predator That Lost its Habitat', Financial Times, February 3/4, 1996.

mid-1950s and mid-1970s it became increasingly clear directors had little scope to take such defensive measures. A 1954 report, prepared for the Board of Trade on a takeover bid for the Savoy Hotel that failed because the board transferred the company's major hotel property to the Savoy hotel staff benevolent fund, suggested the action of the directors was invalid because they had not exercised their powers for the purposes intended.[191] The 'Aluminium War' indicated it was bad practice for directors of a publicly traded company to fail to consult with existing shareholders before issuing to a favoured party a block of shares large enough to dictate control.[192]

A 1963 decision of the Chancery Division affirmed the logic underlying the Savoy Hotel report, holding that directors who allotted shares with multiple voting rights attached to a friendly party to defeat an unwelcome takeover bid had used their powers to allot shares for a challengeable improper purpose, namely to affect control of the company.[193] 1966 amendments to the London Stock Exchange listing rules imposed further limits on this particular defensive tactic. Boards of listed companies became required to undertake not to issue shares for cash to parties other than existing shareholders without obtaining shareholder consent. Also, listed companies that wanted to increase their 'authorized capital' (the maximum number of shares a company was permitted to issue) by 25 per cent or more had to undertake the increased capital would not be issued so as to change control without prior approval of the shareholders.[194]

With companies quoted prior to 1966 the rule changes did not apply until a quotation of further securities was sought.[195] This loophole affected the outcome of a 1967 takeover bid by Aberdare Holdings for Metal Industries (MI).[196] As a result of the bid, a majority of MI shares was pledged to Aberdare. MI's board favoured a merger with Thorn Electrical Holdings and responded by allotting to Thorn, in exchange for a subsidiary of Thorn engaged in the manufacture of gas appliances, a sufficiently large block of MI shares to dilute Aberdare's stake to 32 per cent. MI was not governed by the 1966 listing rule amendments because it had not carried out a public offering after the amendments were made, so the ploy succeeded.

---

[191] E. Milner Holland, *The Savoy Hotel Limited and the Berkeley Hotel Limited: Investigation Under Section 165(b) of the Companies Act 1948: Report* (1954), 26.

[192] Davis, *supra* n. 139, 37; 'Take-over Memories', *Times*, July 18, 1967.

[193] *Hogg v Cramphorn* [1967] Ch. 254. On the link between the case and the Savoy Hotel report, see L.S. Sealy, 'Company—Directors' Powers—Proper Motive but Improper Purposes' [1967] Cambridge Law Journal 33, 33.

[194] Ch. Nine, Pt III.D; Federation of Stock Exchanges in Great Britain and Ireland, *Admission of Securities to Quotation* (1966), Admission of Securities to Quotation, para. 6.

[195] R.R. Pennington, *The Investor and the Law* (1968), 627–28 (saying the Stock Exchange indicated that it expected all issuers to be in compliance regardless within seven years).

[196] On the events involved, see Johnston, *supra* n. 152, 34; 'Time for a Tough Line in the City', *Times*, July 18, 1967; Edward Stamp and Christopher Marley, *Accounting Principles and the City Code: The Case for Reform* (1970), 16–17; Ronald W. Moon, *Business Mergers and Take-Over Bids*, 5th edn (1976), 136–37.

While MI was able to fend off its unwanted suitor, the strategy adopted prompted vigorous protests from institutional shareholders.[197] The controversy prompted the London Stock Exchange, acting in concert with the Bank of England, to announce an overhaul of the 'Notes on the Amalgamation of British Businesses' that had been prepared in 1959 and revised in 1963.[198] The resulting 1968 'City Code on Take-Overs and Mergers' set down as a general principle that the board of a target company should not frustrate a *bona fide* offer without first seeking the approval of the shareholders and introduced a rule precluding the board of a company subject to a takeover bid from issuing shares, disposing of assets or entering into material contracts out of the ordinary course of business without obtaining the prior approval of the shareholders.[199] The rules precluding managers of target companies from undertaking defensive measures without shareholder consent remained intact throughout the 1970s and beyond,[200] so that directors of UK quoted companies had little scope to derail the disciplinary impact of takeover bids.

While merger activity likely encouraged institutional investment in shares by providing a platform for potentially beneficial corporate restructuring and by providing directors with incentives to focus on shareholder value, mergers were no panacea. The *Times* observed in 1959 that takeovers 'tend often to throw up strangely assorted groups which put in question whether there is any point allying textiles with machine tools, paper with drop forgings or boots with shipyards'.[201] A 1970 study based on a survey of directors from 38 UK companies carrying out mergers in 1967 and 1968 found that many of the transactions were arranged hastily and most failed to yield any meaningful post-merger rationalization activity.[202] Davis said the same year 'there is more scepticism about the true value of bids and mergers than ever before' and suggested the ongoing merger boom had 'become a fever instead of a rational, well-planned move towards a healthier industrial structure'.[203] A series of studies published in the 1970s based on accounting data confirmed mergers were not an automatic recipe for success,

[197] 'Take-over Memories', *supra* n. 192.

[198] Stamp and Marley, *supra* n. 196, 18–19; 'A Momentous Stride Forward for the City', Times, March 27, 1968; D. Prentice, 'Take-Over Bids—The City Code on Take-Over and Mergers', (1972) 18 McGill Law Journal 385, 409. On the 1959 and 1963 Notes, see Ch. Nine, Pt III.E.

[199] *City Code on Take-overs and Mergers*, (1968), General Principle 3, Rule 34.

[200] Deborah A. De Mott, 'Current Issues in Tender Offer Regulation: Lessons from the British', (1983) 58 New York University Law Review 945, 1015–16; Andrew Johnston, 'Takeover Regulation: Historical and Theoretical Perspectives on the City Code', (2007) 66 Cambridge Law Journal 422, 443–44.

[201] 'Big Battalions', Times, August 14, 1959.

[202] Gerald D. Newbould, *Management and Merger Activity* (1970), 115, 164–69. Newbould's study received considerable attention in the press (e.g. 'Is Merger the Message?', Times, July 13, 1970; 'The Time to Make a Bid', Times, July 3, 1971).

[203] Davis, *supra* n. 139, 1, 3.

reporting that companies carrying out acquisitions frequently experienced a decline in profits.[204]

Though numerous corporate acquisitions failed to deliver anticipated benefits, from the perspective of investors deciding whether to buy shares, M & A activity should on balance have remained a lure. While studies based on accounting data suggested companies carrying out acquisitions did not fare particularly well, the share price performance of acquisitive companies was acceptable enough. Franks and Harris, in the most comprehensive study of share price reactions to mergers during the decades following World War II (almost 1,900 bids between 1955 and 1985) found a company executing a takeover on average added during the six months around the bid 2.4 per cent to its market value attributable to the merger. Companies carrying out mergers experienced a share price decline relative to the stock market during the two years following the acquisition but outperformed the market once firm-specific risk was taken into account.[205] Since shareholders in target companies received, on average, a sizeable bid premium, on a net basis mergers created value for investors.[206] Given this, and given that takeovers had from a shareholder perspective a beneficial disciplinary aspect, the manner in which M & A activity evolved from the 1950s onwards should have fortified demand for shares as the UK's outsider/arm's-length system of ownership and control took final shape.

V. Institutional Shareholder Passivity

A. The Potential for Intervention

If all shareholders in a publicly traded company have equal, tiny stakes, then the dominant strategy for each individual shareholder will be to decline to engage in any effort to influence or discipline management (Chapter Four, Part IV.B). Even if there is a good chance collective intervention would deliver net benefits for the shareholders, no one investor will step forward because the costs they will have to incur will in all likelihood exceed the gains attributable to the tiny percentage of shares they own. Those sufficiently uneasy with matters to take action will take advantage of the liquidity the stock market offers and sell rather than become entangled in a time-consuming turnaround effort. Dispersed share ownership

---

[204] Ajit Singh, *Take-Overs: Their Relevance to the Stock Market and the Theory of the Firm* (1971); M.A. Utton, 'On Measuring the Effects of Industrial Mergers', (1974) 21 Scottish Journal of Political Economy 13; G. Meeks, *Disappointing Marriage: A Study of the Gains from Merger* (1977).

[205] Franks and Harris, *supra* n. 137, 233, 244–45. Some other studies, using smaller samples, found acquiring companies experienced a share price decline (e.g. Michael Firth, 'Takeovers, Shareholder Returns, and the Theory of the Firm', (1980) 94 Quarterly Journal of Economics 235).

[206] Franks and Harris, *supra* n. 137, 247.

thus necessarily seems to go hand-in-hand with a separation of ownership and control.

The situation, however, can be different if a small group of otherwise unaffiliated shareholders owns enough equity to dominate the share register on an aggregate basis. Exit could create significant trading losses for this cohort since efforts to bail out over a short period might drive the share price down sharply. Conversely, a well-judged intervention could create a substantial uplift in the value of the shares these investors collectively hold. The small numbers also will facilitate negotiations about sharing the costs of engaging in a 'hands on' strategy. Moreover, if the same investors own similarly sized stakes in a wide range of companies, there will be potential for intervention to be supported by reciprocity, with an understanding developing that the shareholder with the largest holding in a particular company will take responsibility for coordinating engagement with the company. The upshot is that while dispersed share ownership normally should be synonymous with outsider/arm's-length corporate governance, the manner in which share ownership becomes configured can create the potential for control-oriented investment.

The institutionalization of share ownership that took place in Britain in the decades following World War II created in various ways a promising environment for collectively oriented intervention to occur. From a fairly early stage, major institutional stakes were becoming too large to unwind entirely at will, with the *Times* reporting in 1967 on institutional investments that were 'too big for the market to digest their selling', obliging institutions 'to sit tight, philosophically watching their holdings in badly managed companies slide in value'.[207] Moreover, the shift to institutional ownership created greater coherence on share registers than would have been the case with shares spread equally among hundreds or thousands of investors. By the early 1990s, the 25 largest institutional investors in a UK public company typically owned about one-half of the equity as compared with one-third in the US, meaning coalition formation was easier in Britain than in the US.[208] The tendency of UK pension funds to delegate responsibility for investment decisions to large external fund managers reinforced the coherence of institutional ownership, as the top 20 fund managers accounted for just over one-third of the market value of all quoted shares by the 1990s.[209] Stapledon even claimed in 1996 that the structure of investment in shares meant 'the highly diffuse ownership structure described by Berle and Means (Chapter Two, Part IV) (does) not exist in the vast majority of quoted UK...companies'.[210]

---

[207] 'Time for a Tough', *supra* n. 196.

[208] Cheffins, *supra* n. 17, 638–39.   [209] Hobson, *supra* n. 44, 984, 986.

[210] G.P. Stapledon, *Institutional Shareholders and Corporate Governance* (1996), 10; see also Minns, *supra* n. 72, 11; Paul Davies, 'Shareholder Value, Company Law, and Securities Markets Law: A British View' in Klaus J. Hopt and Eddy Wymeersch (eds), *Capital Markets and Company Law* (2003), 261, 271–72.

Also potentially important was a close-knit financial community. While US institutional shareholders have generally been spread out among various financial centres, most British institutional investors, including fund managers, have traditionally been based within a small area in the City of London or in Scotland's financial capital of Edinburgh, meaning communication between influential shareholders was potentially easy.[211] As a UK institutional investor said in the mid-1990s, 'One of the major advantages of the City (of London) is that there are a small number of professional financial institution bodies and they are all nearby and in close contact with each other. We think US pension funds and insurance companies are more fragmented both professionally and physically in the US financial system and this hinders coordination.'[212]

Contemporaries recognized the potential for institutional intervention in the UK. In 1960 Seldon urged pension funds 'to bring influence to bear on sluggish or reckless boards of directors'.[213] A 1965 paper in the Bank of England Quarterly Bulletin argued institutional investors 'are able to exercise the responsibilities of share-ownership more effectively than some private investors and, if grievances arise, they can more readily exert an influence upon boards of directors than a widely scattered body of private individuals can'.[214] A 1973 survey of London's financial district said of the surge of institutional investment in shares, '[I]t has conferred on the institutions... the right to control a huge slice of British business, by virtue of the fact that equities carry voting rights. More specifically it has conferred on the group of people who manage this money the almost uncontrolled power to intervene in the management of the companies in which they have invested.'[215] The Wilson Committee concurred, in its 1980 report, arguing the time was ripe for institutional shareholders to exercise a beneficial influence on corporate governance:

(T)here now exists a body of shareholders which collectively owns a significant proportion of the equity of many companies and which has the ability to mobilise the support of other shareholders... If a company gets into obvious difficulties institutions with substantial holdings can seldom dispose of them without realising a considerable financial loss... and this gives them a strong incentive to take action about weak or inadequate management. Even when difficulties are less evident it may well be in the interests of large institutional shareholders to commit time and effort to trying to improve a company's management, rather than simply disposing of their holdings.[216]

---

[211] Cheffins, *supra* n. 17, 639; Milford B. Green, 'A Geography of Institutional Stock Ownership in the United States', (1993) 83 Annals of the Association of American Geographers 66.

[212] Quoted in John Holland, *The Corporate Governance Role of Financial Institutions in Their Investee Companies* (1995), 38.

[213] Arthur Seldon, *Pensions for Prosperity* (1960), 20.

[214] 'Financial Institutions', *supra* n. 52, 153.

[215] Richard Spiegelberg, *The City: Power Without Accountability* (1973), 55.

[216] Wilson Report, *supra* n. 41, 250.

B. Reluctance to Step Forward

While the dramatic post-World War II shift in favour of institutional ownership in the UK created an environment that was congenial to collective intervention, the potential for control-oriented investment was not turned into reality through to the end of the 1980s.[217] Instead, for the most part institutional shareholders were 'the sleeping giants of British corporate life'.[218] As a result, the transition to an institutionally dominated stock market yielded a full-blown 'outsider/arm's-length' system of ownership and control.

In the mid-1950s, Prudential Assurance did offer crucial support to directors of the Birmingham Small Arms Company (BSA), a manufacturer of armaments, motorcycles and cars, in their successful campaign to oust the flamboyant and extravagant Sir Bernard Docker as chairman of the board and managing director.[219] Nevertheless, officials at the Prudential emphasized at that point 'our clear policy (is)...not to interfere in the management of industrial companies in which we invest' and characterized 'such incidents (as) essentially repugnant to the (Prudential) board'.[220] The Prudential put the policy into practice, as the BSA incident was one of only two instances of well-publicized involvement in company affairs by the insurer up to 1970.[221]

Other institutional investors shared Prudential Assurance's reluctance to engage with management. The *Economist* made the point in 1958, indicating that 'Those with the concentrated power—the institutional investors—are seen to use it only in extreme cases (as one did in the BSA argument)...'[222] A 1960 government committee report on the working of the monetary system said of insurance companies 'their policy is to avoid entanglement in the management of the companies' in which they invested.[223] As of the mid-1960s, it remained possible to count on one hand the number of instances where British institutions had publicly asked for the removal of a director of a large public company.[224] Hence, according to a 1967 article in the *Times* urging institutions 'to move in', '(t)he Prudential...and its fellow institutions have been deeply reluctant to show their power even in the indirect, indicative sense'.[225] Sampson said similarly in 1971 'Only in moments of extreme crisis...do shareholders sometimes

[217] On the distinction between potential and reality in this context, see Coakley and Harris, *supra* n. 49, 109, 112; Paul Davies, 'Institutional Investors in the United Kingdom' in D.D. Prentice and P.R.J. Holland, (eds) *Contemporary Issues in Corporate Governance* (1993), 69, 82.

[218] Kynaston, *supra* n. 161, 434.

[219] Sampson, *supra* n. 117, 409–10; 'Sir Bernard Docker's Waterloo', Economist, August 4, 1956, 425; R.P.T. Davenport-Hines, *Dudley Docker: The Life and Times of a Trade Warrior* (1984), 231–32. Docker was son of Dudley Docker (Ch. Seven, Pt IX, Ch. Eight, Pt I.H).

[220] Hobson, *supra* n. 44, 1014.

[221] 'Is the City in Need of a New Code?', Times, November 6, 1970.

[222] 'Shareholders and Directors', Economist, February 14, 1959, 612, 614.

[223] Radcliffe Committee, *supra* n. 80, 87.

[224] Alex Rubner, *The Ensnared Shareholder: Directors and the Modern Corporation* (1966), 151.

[225] 'Time for the Institutions to Move In', Times, February 13, 1967.

organise themselves to put pressure on management', citing as one example a 1970 campaign involving engineering company Vickers launched after 12 years of inept managerial performance.[226]

Matters changed as the 1970s progressed, but only slowly. It was increasingly recognized by insurance companies and pension funds holding shares in troubled companies that a 'gentle nudge' might be better than exit.[227] Nevertheless, shareholder power was not used with any enthusiasm by institutional investors, as there was a continuing tendency to believe their best option was to sell the shares.[228] Discussions of instances when institutional shareholders had prompted a successful public showdown with managers of public companies offered only a tiny handful of examples, involving companies such as retailers Debenhams and the textile group Coats Paton.[229] Hence, according to a 1978 report on institutional shareholders, 'institutional participation in managerial decision-making has been favoured generally (but)...(f)inancial institutions have generally been unwilling to act collectively in the use of their voting strength, or to accept those responsibilities which others would assign to them'.[230] Similarly, a 1981 analysis of institutional shareholder activism acknowledged there had been some instances of institutional intervention but concluded 'there have been too many cases where the institutions have stood aside, thereby giving ammunition to the City's critics who say they should be more robust'.[231]

During the 1980s, perhaps prompted by the Wilson Committee's plea to institutional shareholders to challenge weak or inadequate management, institutional shareholders raised their profile somewhat. As Coakley and Harris said in 1983, the 'sleeping giant' had 'one eye open'.[232] Nevertheless, in the early 1980s only a handful of interventions attracted any publicity, with prominent examples being the financing of a 1982 takeover bid of the UK arm of retailer Woolworths and a 1983 boardroom shake-up at the Rank Organisation.[233] Matters changed

---

[226] Sampson, *supra* n. 179, 598; see also Heller, *supra* n. 9, 23.

[227] McRae and Cairncross, *supra* n. 47, 165–66; 'Velvet Glove Without the Iron Hand?', Times, November 17, 1972.

[228] Briston, *supra* n. 108, 413; 'Velvet Glove', *supra* n. 227; Lord Carr of Hadley, 'The Function of Ownership and the Role of Institutional Shareholders' in Kenneth Midgley (ed.), *Management Accountability and Corporate Governance: Selected Readings* (1982), 91, 95.

[229] Plender, *supra* n. 51, 70; Steve Nyman and Aubrey Silberston, 'The Ownership and Control of Industry', (1978) 30 Oxford Economic Papers (N.S.), 74, 94–96.

[230] Briston and Dobbins, *supra* n. 51, 54.

[231] 'When Should Shareholders Intervene?', Times, January 28, 1981, 19. See also Prais, *supra* n. 67, 114.

[232] Coakley and Harris, *supra* n. 49, 115. See also 'Increasing Degree of Involvement', Financial Times, Survey of Corporate Finance, November 1, 1983.

[233] Bernard S. Black and John C. Coffee, 'Hail Britannia? Institutional Investor Behavior Under Limited Regulation', (1994) 92 Michigan Law Review 1997, 2042 ('The folklore of the City provides only a few well-known stories of such interventions through the early 1980s, notably the campaigns to change management at Rank and Woolworths'). See also McRae and Cairncross, *supra* n. 72, 130 (calling Woolworth 'the most radical example of the institutions taking the lead in sacking a management').

little in the remainder of the decade, as buoyant stock prices helped to ensure good returns for institutional shareholders even in companies being indifferently run. Data from the late 1980s and early 1990s confirms the point, indicating that the presence of institutional shareholders with high relative voting power generally did not accelerate executive turnover in poorly performing companies.[234]

It was widely acknowledged that institutional activism operated at a low level as the 1980s drew to a close and the 1990s began. In 1990 the chief investment manager of the Prudential, transformed by that point into one of the more active institutional investors, said, '(I)ntervention by shareholders does in fact occur from time to time, and we have been concerned with some well-known instances as well as many more less publicised cases. But the extent of such activity by shareholders in Britain does not remotely approach the level where it is an effective substitute for the involvement of the banks in Germany or the Kereitsu system in Japan.'[235] Charkham suggested in 1994 that most fund managers in Britain tended towards diversification, minimal communication with companies and low interest in corporate governance.[236] Black and Coffee noted the same year that 'the complete passivity announced by Berle and Means' was absent in the UK but remarked upon 'the reluctance of even large shareholders to intervene'.[237]

While UK institutional shareholders generally refrained from taking a hands on role in corporate governance in the closing decades of the 20th century, they never adopted a stance of complete passivity. Institutional hostility to non-voting shares in the 1950s and early 1960s helped to undermine their use (Chapter Nine, Part II.B). Institutional opposition to share issuances likely to influence a change of control prompted the introduction of Takeover Code reforms designed to discourage defensive action by directors of target companies (Part IV.E.2). Also, insurance companies, pension funds, investment trusts and unit trusts each had in the 1970s and 1980s investment protection committees that handled cases where institutions sought to deal collectively with a management problem by exercising joint pressure.[238] Much of the work done by these committees was, however, routine and technical in nature, such as addressing the accounting and legal issues associated with capital reconstruction schemes and reviewing amendments companies were proposing to their corporate constitutions.[239] As

---

[234] Rafel Crespi-Cladera & Luc Renneboog, 'Corporate Monitoring by Shareholder Coalitions in the UK' (2003), ECGI Working Paper in Finance, No. 12/2003.

[235] R.E. Artus, 'Tension to Continue' in National Association of Pension Funds, *Creative Tension* (1990), 12, 14. On the Prudential and activism, see 'An Outbreak of Virtue', Financial Times, December 15, 1995.

[236] Jonathan P. Charkham, *Keeping Good Company: A Study of Corporate Governance in Five Countries* (1994), 284.

[237] Black & Coffee, *supra* n. 233, 2086.

[238] Wilson Report, *supra* n. 41, 250–51.

[239] McRae and Cairncross, *supra* n. 72, 129; Spiegelberg, *supra* n. 215, 62–63; P.E. Moody, 'A More Active Role for Institutional Shareholders', Banker's Magazine, February 1979, 49, 52; When Should Shareholders Intervene?', Times, January 28, 1981.

the *Financial Times* said in 1987, '[I]nvestment institutions are well structured to respond to narrow investment issues through their investor protection committees, but are very poor at coping with broader corporate responsibilities.'[240]

The setting of dividend policy was a higher-profile scenario, where institutional shareholders exercised influence. The general policy of institutional shareholders was that dividend payouts should not be reduced or cancelled if there was merely a temporary fall in profits.[241] Pension funds had particular reason to oppose dividend cuts. In the mid-1960s pension fund actuaries began valuing shares held using a 'dividend discount model' based on dividend payouts, which put corporate employers under an unwelcome onus to increase pension contributions when dividend reductions or omissions drove down the actuarial valuation of shares.[242]

Events concerning Coats Paton illustrated how institutional shareholders could become proactive with dividend policy. In 1975, with financial results suffering due to recessionary conditions, the company announced that in order to preserve cash it would give shareholders new shares in lieu of the annual cash dividend. Institutional shareholders objected strongly and only backed off from voting down the adoption of the company's accounts on the understanding that such a policy would not be adopted again.[243] The incident underscored that companies that cut or passed on dividend payouts without a powerful excuse were likely to incur institutional wrath.[244]

Another area where institutional shareholders were prepared to depart from their typical pattern of passivity was where companies were seeking to raise fresh capital through the issuance of shares. Here the method by which publicly quoted companies typically proceeded reinforced the leverage institutional shareholders had. From at least the late 1950s onwards, a rights offering was the standard method UK public companies used when returning to the capital markets to obtain funding by issuing shares (Part II). Prior to 1980, there was no common law or statutory rule of pre-emption but from 1966 onwards stock exchange listing rules steered quoted companies towards using rights offerings unless the shareholders had otherwise agreed (Chapter Nine, Part III.C., D.).

Because individuals, as net sellers of shares, were unlikely candidates to subscribe for available equity, institutional shareholders necessarily became the investors at which rights offerings were targeted, and the underwriting role pension funds and insurance companies played further enhanced their influence (Part II). The view institutions took on the price and terms on which new

---

[240] 'The Rights of Shareholders', Financial Times, April 24, 1987; see also Wilson Report, *supra* n. 41, 251.

[241] Stapledon, *supra* n. 210, 225.

[242] Cheffins, *supra* n. 129, 1326–27.

[243] Kynaston, *supra* n. 161, 536; 'Why the Market Should Forget About Dividends for a While', Economist, June 14, 1975, 62; 'We Wuz Robbed—Oh Yeah?', Economist, July 5, 1975, 128.

[244] Plender, *supra* n. 51, 70; Kynaston, n. 161, 536–37; 'To Cut or Not to Cut?', Economist, June 9, 1979, 118.

shares were offered therefore generally had a decisive impact on the success or failure of a rights issue.[245] As Sampson said in 1971 of fund managers of insurance companies, 'a new issue of shares can depend on the raising of an eyebrow, or a twitch of a toothbrush moustache'.[246] Companies took their cue from this by structuring rights offerings so as to ensure the shares available would be taken up and by shying away from raising capital when they were underperforming.[247] Still, while institutional shareholders had considerable clout with rights offerings and dividends, a reluctance to step forward set the tone, thus ensuring UK corporate governance operated on an outsider/arm's-length basis.

C. Explanations

One explanation for the 'hands off' approach UK institutional investors adopted was a perception that market pressures imposed constraints on management that made intervention superfluous.[248] A number of insurance company associations made this point when giving evidence to the Wilson Committee in the late 1970s. Having acknowledged improvements in the standard of management could yield benefits for shareholders and the nation at large, they said detailed institutional monitoring of public companies was not the way forward. Instead, 'To a large degree reliance can be placed on the essentially competitive nature of the private enterprise system which imposes strong pressures and incentives on management, and the capital markets can play their part in this.'[249] The reference to capital markets encompassed the scrutiny to which public offerings of shares were subject as well as takeover bids, of which the insurance company associations said:

Poor management tends to lead to lower share prices, less ability to raise cash and more vulnerability to acquisition by successful competitors. For many years now industrial managements have shown themselves to be sensitive to the message of their relative ratings in the stock market. Far more managements of public companies have taken this message and put their houses in order than have ever been taken over . . . [250]

The fact that institutional shareholders functioned as investment intermediaries under an onus to maximize the risk-adjusted return of their beneficiaries (policyholders in the case of insurance companies, employees with pension funds, shareholders with investment trusts and unitholders with unit trusts) was another deterrent to activism.[251] Institutional investors, as custodians of others'

---

[245] Wilson Committee, *supra* n. 32, 113; Wilson Report, *supra* n. 41, 209; Coakley and Harris, *supra* n. 49, 113.

[246] Sampson, *supra* n. 179, 526.   [247] Wilson Committee, *supra* n. 32, 113, 276.

[248] Clarke, *supra* n. 26, 120.   [249] Wilson Committee, *supra* n. 32, 91.

[250] *Ibid.*, 71. See also at 111, 215.

[251] Briston and Dobbins, *supra* n. 51, 57; Prais, *supra* n. 67, 116; Sampson, *supra* n. 179, 526; Lord Carr of Hadley, *supra* n. 228, 94.

funds, wanted to be free to handle risk appropriately by diversifying widely their investment portfolios and by being able to sell underperforming assets when appropriate.[252] This created a bias against getting 'locked in' by virtue of having stakes in companies too large to unwind readily, thus obviating the need to intervene when an investment proved unsatisfactory. As the *Times* said in 1975 about insurance companies, 'they avoid concentrating their investments to a point where massive stakes in a few situations would force them, willy-nilly, into a semi-proprietorial role'.[253]

To maintain freedom of action, even the largest insurance companies and pension funds imposed upon themselves limits on the maximum percentage of shares they would own in any one company and on the proportion one company's shares could make up of their total asset portfolio.[254] Hence, a 1965 text on insurance company investment reported that of a sample of 326 quoted companies, there were 32 instances where an insurance company owned 5 per cent or more of the shares but none where an insurer owned more than 10 per cent.[255] Likewise, from the early 1970s to the early 1980s the *Times 1000* provided a list of investors owning stakes of 1 per cent or more in the UK's largest 50 companies and in only one instance did a particular institutional investor own more than 10 per cent of the shares, this being in 1975 when Royal London Mutual Insurance owned 12 per cent of Tozer, Kemsley & Millbourn, an Australian-focused trading group.[256]

Cost and inconvenience were further deterrents to institutional activism. A successful 1991 campaign by Norwich Union, a large insurance company, and Framlington Group, an institutional investor that worked closely with Norwich Union, to remove the incumbent management team of Tace plc, an environmental control equipment group, illustrates the point.[257] The Framlington Group and Norwich Union had to pay £60,000 in solicitors' fees, as none of the other shareholders that ultimately supported their campaign agreed to share the costs. Considerable staff time was consumed negotiating with the Tace management team and in recruiting other institutional investors to support the cause. At Norwich Union the Tace affair was a distraction because its chief investment officer had to face questioning by his board of directors as he was proceeding.

[252] McRae and Cairncross, *supra* n. 72, 119; Blake, *supra* n. 79, 487; Seldon, *supra* n. 213, 19.

[253] 'Finding a Formula in the City for Industry's Needs', Times, January 13, 1975. See also Briston and Dobbins, *supra* n. 51, 57–58; Spiegelberg, *supra* n. 215, 38; Mairi Maclean, 'Corporate Governance in France and the UK: Long-Term Perspectives on Contemporary Institutional Arrangements', (1999) 41 Business History, 88, 98.

[254] Plender, *supra* n. 51, 67; Minns, Pension, *supra* n. 72, 58; Seldon, *supra* n. 213, 19; Paul L. Davies, 'Institutional Investors: A UK View', (1991) 57 Brooklyn Law Review 129, 140.

[255] Clayton and Osborn, *supra* n. 81, 175.

[256] *The Times 1000: Leading Companies in Britain and Overseas, 1975–76* (1975), 68. On Tozer, Kemsley & Millbourn, see 'Injection of Cash by Australian Cash Could Solve Tozer Debt Worries', Guardian, June 29, 1985.

[257] Cheffins, *supra* n. 17, 633–34, 637.

Due to holding a sizeable combined stake—21 per cent—Framlington Group and Norwich Union proceeded regardless. In the vast majority of instances institutional shareholders would not have bothered, anticipating the hassle involved and fearing any benefits accruing would be tiny, relative to the size of their investment portfolio.[258]

Another cause for passivity was that the commencement of discussions about potential intervention could trigger a 'race to the exit'.[259] Matters might begin with a key institutional shareholder, such as the Prudential, asking other institutions to join with it in taking corrective action in relation to a particular company. An institution receiving such a request would assume the Prudential had reasonable grounds for dissatisfaction and/or would sell if satisfactory changes were not secured. There correspondingly would be a temptation to sell out immediately rather than waiting to see how things worked out. The danger that there would be such a reaction would in turn force the Prudential to be selective in approaching potential partners, thus complicating the process of coalition-building.

Concerns about insufficient resources and expertise also deterred institutional investor activism.[260] The fund managers that typically invested on behalf of institutional shareholders argued they were well placed to spot pricing anomalies and implement effective trading strategies but lacked the experience, training and specialized knowledge required to involve themselves in the management of public companies.[261] Others tended to concur. The *Times* said in 1972 'The obvious implication is that a lack of managerial expertise by fund managers makes them easy meat for fast-talking company chairmen who insist that things are coming right if institutional investors will have a little patience.'[262] The *Economist* offered a similar verdict nearly two decades later, saying 'Institutional shareholders are investment managers, not industrial ones; they are poorly equipped to steer boardrooms. Voting with their feet tends, unfortunately, to be a better way of exerting control.'[263] Even the Wilson Committee, which in its 1980 report urged institutional shareholders to be more activist, partially excused past passivity on the grounds 'The

---

[258] 'Punters or Proprietors: A Survey of Capitalism', Economist, May 5, 1990, 9.

[259] Cheffins, *supra* n. 17, 636.

[260] Wilson Committee, *supra* n. 32, 90, 122; 'Is the City', *supra* n. 221; Lord Carr of Hadley, *supra* n. 228, 95; 'The Unchanging City: A Survey of London's Financial Markets', Economist, October 9, 1976, 48, 51.

[261] Plender, *supra* n. 51, 65; Black and Coffee, *supra* n. 233, 2071–72; John Farrar and Mark Russell, 'The Impact of Institutional Investment on Company Law', (1985) 5 Company Lawyer 107, 109.

[262] 'Velvet Glove', *supra* n. 227, 21. See also 'The City on the Sidelines', Economist, July 1, 1978, 74.

[263] 'The End of the Beginning: A Survey of Business in Britain', Economist, May 20, 1989, 34.

institutions are still to some extent feeling their way, which may inhibit them intervening at an early enough stage.'[264]

Politics provided a final reason for institutional passivity. The financial intermediaries that dominated share ownership deliberately shunned any role in national politics and their desire to retain as low a profile as possible discouraged public interventions in the affairs of the companies in which they owned shares.[265] As an investment manager of an insurance company said in the early 1970s of General Electric's consolidation of the electrical engineering industry a few years earlier (Chapter Nine, Part II.B), 'If we had put Arnold Weinstock in as managing director...and he had closed down factories, it would have been us who got the blame from the unions.'[266] Fears that attempts to influence business policy might lead to greater interference by the government in turn meant the institutions were shy about showing their strength. As the *Times* said in 1975, 'The threat of some state direction of their investments is never far from the institutions' minds...'[267]

Insurance companies in particular feared that high-profile interventions could put their affairs on the political agenda and lead to detrimental and perhaps fundamentally crippling reform.[268] In 1949, Labour, which was in the midst of a campaign to nationalize key aspects of the British economy (Chapter Three, Part X), announced Britain's insurance companies were potential targets. The insurance industry launched a major anti-nationalization campaign and fended off the threat. Nevertheless, the episode had a considerable psychological impact on insurer behaviour as insurance companies realized their financial strength rendered them vulnerable. As the *Times* said in 1967, 'The insurance companies are terrified of a more open approach to their responsibilities. The Government might conceivably think more seriously about nationalizing insurance companies if they interfered more readily in industry.'[269]

The spectre of nationalization would continue to haunt insurance companies thereafter as the Labour Party remained formally committed to government ownership of the industry until the mid-1980s.[270] During the mid-1970s internal party support for the policy was sufficiently strong to help to prompt the Labour government to establish the Wilson Committee to investigate the

[264] Wilson Report, *supra* n. 41, 253; see also Wilson Committee, *supra* n. 95, 26.

[265] Plender, *supra* n. 51, 20; Sampson, *supra* n. 117, 412; Black and Coffee, *supra* n. 233, 2067; Kenneth Midgley, *Companies and Their Shareholders—The Uneasy Relationship* (1975), 77.

[266] Spiegelberg, *supra* n. 215, 56.

[267] 'Hopes for Industry-Institutions Investment Strategy as City Warms to Equity Bank', Times, November 25, 1975. See also Briston and Dobbins, *supra* n. 51, 57; Briston, *supra* n. 108, 413; Farrar and Russell, *supra* n. 261, 109.

[268] See generally Hobson, *supra* n. 44, 1005; Spiegelberg, *supra* n. 215, 56; Laurie Dennett, *A Sense of Security: 150 Years of Prudential* (1998), 298–301.

[269] 'Shot in the Arm for Shareholders', Times, April 29, 1967.

[270] Hobson, *supra* n. 44, 1005; Coakley and Harris, *supra* n. 49, 216.

operation of the UK's financial institutions.[271] Ironically, the report the Wilson Committee issued constituted an early example of a governmental effort to prod institutional shareholders into action on the corporate governance front.[272] Up to that point, however, politics was one of a variety of factors that deterred institutional investors from taking a hands on role with respect to the companies in which they owned shares and thereby ensured a divorce of ownership and control characterized UK corporate governance.

[271] Sampson, *supra* n. 105, 294; Trevor Smith, *The Politics of the Corporate Economy* (1979), 188; Peter Pugh, *Absolute Integrity: The Story of Royal Insurance 1845–1995* (1995), 203–4.

[272] Wilson Report *supra* n. 41, 255, 259–60; Plender, *supra* n. 51, 20–22.

ELEVEN

Epilogue: Challenges to the UK System of Ownership and Control

Chapters Five to Ten have outlined how the transformation to a divorce between ownership and control occurred in major UK business enterprises. Will the outsider/arm's-length system of corporate governance that is currently in place prove durable? Three trends emerging over the past fifteen years raise doubts: 1) increased activism by traditionally dominant institutional shareholders (pension funds and insurance companies); 2) the emergence of 'offensive' shareholder activism by a new breed of investor; and 3) 'public-to-private' buyouts carried out by private equity firms. This chapter argues these trends will not compromise the divorce of ownership and control that characterizes UK corporate governance and may indeed serve to reinforce current arrangements.

I. Increased Activism by 'Mainstream' Institutional Investors

The rise of institutional investment following World War II created promising conditions for collectively oriented intervention in the affairs of UK public companies. Regulation imposed few explicit restrictions on the building up of large stakes in particular companies and/or collaboration between institutions minded to intervene (Chapter Two, Part IV). Large institutional shareholders began almost in spite of themselves to accumulate holdings too sizeable to unwind readily and a cosy investment community oriented around London's financial district facilitated potential cooperation. Nevertheless, up to 1990 institutional engagement with investee companies was the exception to the rule (Chapter Ten, Parts III, V). Institutional activism then became more prevalent, but largely due to a 're-diffusion' of share ownership, intervention by 'mainstream' institutional investors is unlikely to result in control-oriented corporate governance for the foreseeable future.

Various observers remarked in the 1990s on the growth of institutional activism. When in 1991 the chief executive of British Aerospace departed after institutional shareholders indicated they would not support a proposed rights offering, the *Financial Times* observed, '[T]he big investment institutions are finally flexing their muscles after decades of complaining that it was not their job to act as productivity chasers by appointment to British industry.'[1] In 1993 the *Telegraph* explained the forced departure of chief executives of Granada, a media group, and a small handful of other companies on the basis of 'a group of fund managers setting a cracking pace in establishing long-neglected shareholders' rights'.[2] In 1996 the *Sunday Times* cited challenges to executive pay arrangements at United Utilities, a water and electricity group, and the removal of the chief executive of Eurotherm, a firm specializing in plant automation technologies, as 'the latest examples of a trend starting to revolutionise relations between the City and industry: shareholder power'.[3] Holland, in a 1995 study of institutional activism, referred to 'a partial reversal of Berle and Means' . . . observations about the separation of ownership and control' saying, 'Financial institutions invested in relationships with investee companies to increase their ability to influence the company.'[4]

One explanation for the increase in activism in the 1990s was the marginalization of the disciplinary takeover bid.[5] While during the 1980s a company unpopular with institutional shareholders would suffer a share price decline and become vulnerable to a takeover bid by 'raiders' such as Hanson or BTR, these acquisitive conglomerates languished in the 1990s. With the demise of this favoured method of sidelining unwanted executives, institutional investors knew that in instances where different managerial leadership was needed to get an underperforming company back on track they would likely have to take the initiative themselves.

Another catalyst was the 1993 introduction of a requirement in the London Stock Exchange listing rules that quoted companies report on compliance (or lack thereof) with a code of corporate governance best practice drafted by a committee sponsored by the Stock Exchange and the accountancy profession and chaired by Sir Adrian Cadbury.[6] The 'Cadbury Code'—subsequently relabelled the 'Combined Code'—expanded from 19 provisions in 1993 to 43 principles and 48 provisions in 2003 due to a 1995 report on executive pay, a 1998 review and a 2003 report on non-executive directors.[7] Quoted companies were not required to comply with the relevant guidelines. Instead, failures to observe the

---

[1] 'Tougher at the Top', Financial Times, September 28/29, 1991.

[2] 'Corporate Assassins', Sunday Telegraph, October 17/18, 1993.

[3] 'Investor Invasion', Sunday Times, July 21, 1996.

[4] John Holland, *The Corporate Governance Role of Financial Institutions in Their Investee Companies* (1995), 21.

[5] Ch. Ten, Pt IV.E.1; 'Corporate Assassins', *supra* n. 2; 'Investor Invasion', *supra* n. 3; G.P. Stapledon, *Institutional Shareholders and Corporate Governance* (1996), 128.

[6] London Stock Exchange, *Listing Rules* (1993), para. 12.43(j); *Report of the Committee on the Financial Aspects of Corporate Governance* (1992).

[7] *Tolley's Corporate Governance Handbook*, 2nd edn, (2003), 62 (number of provisions). The reports were *Directors' Remuneration: Report of a Study Group Chaired by Sir Richard Greenbury*

Code only had to be explained. However, adoption of the Cadbury Code under-scored the significance of shareholder rights and the disclosures quoted compa-nies had to carry out made it easier and cheaper for institutional shareholders to be proactive.[8] Over the longer haul, institutional shareholders were able to draw on the Combined Code to impose pressure on quoted companies that combined poor compliance and poor financial results.[9] One investment manager even char-acterized the Cadbury Code as 'the greatest constitutional change in the manage-ment of British public companies since the 19th century'.[10]

While activism increased in the 1990s, institutional investors' approach to corporate governance remained fundamentally 'arm's-length' in orientation. A study of non-financial companies quoted on the London Stock Exchange based on data from the mid-1990s reported that the presence or absence of a pension fund owning 3 per cent or more of a company's outstanding equity did not alter its financial performance in any meaningful way, implying a lack of influence over strategic or operational issues.[11] The *Financial Times* said in 1997 of the relationship between institutional shareholders and management, 'A certain very British reserve…unmistakably remains.'[12] A 1998 *Financial Times* survey of senior executives in the UK's 100 largest publicly traded companies backed up the claim, as 92 per cent of respondents said shareholders rarely or never sought to make changes behind the scenes.[13] Or as Hobson observed in 1999, 'Provided directors' greed is not too conspicuous, and they keep dividends up and the share price rising, the average board can do more or less what it likes.'[14]

A 2001 review of institutional investment by Paul Myners, acting under commission by the UK government, confirmed a continuing bias in favour of passivity. Myners acknowledged that in the previous few years institutional activ-ism had increased. Still, he argued the initiatives taken by those acting on behalf of the institutions left much to be desired: 'It remains widely acknowledged that concerns about the management and strategy of major companies can persist

---

(1995); *Report of the Committee on Corporate Governance* (chaired by Sir Ronald Hampel) (1998); Derek Higgs, *Review of the Role and Effectiveness of Non-Executive Directors* (2003).

   [8] 'Corporate Assassins', *supra* n. 2; Jane Simms, 'New System Puts Mouth Where Investors' Money Is', Independent on Sunday, November 22, 1992, 25 (quoting the chairman of the Institutional Shareholders' Committee); Stuart Bell, 'The Battle Against Cronyism is not Over', Financial Times, August 11, 2003.

   [9] Sridhar R. Arcot and Valentina G. Bruno, 'In Letter but not in Spirit: An Analysis of Corporate Governance in the UK' (2006), LSE/RICAFE 2, Working Paper No. 31, 32–33; Iain MacNeil and Xiao Li, ' "Comply or Explain": Market Discipline and Non-Compliance with the Combined Code', (2006) 14 Corporate Governance: An International Review 486, 492.

   [10] 'Value is the Acid Test of Good Governance', Financial Times, April 19, 2004.

   [11] Mara Faccio and M. Ameziane Lasfer, 'Do Occupational Pension Funds Monitor Companies in Which They Hold Large Stakes?', (2000) 6 Journal of Corporate Finance 71.

   [12] 'UK Institutions' (Lex Column), Financial Times, November 10, 1997.

   [13] 'Shares in the Action', Financial Times, April 27, 1998.

   [14] Dominic Hobson, *The National Wealth: Who Gets What in Britain* (1999), 1149.

among (company) analysts and fund managers for long periods of time before action is taken.'[15]

After the Myners Report institutional activism stepped up a gear, at least in the short term. The *Independent*, in an article entitled 'Where Will the Fur be Flying Next?' claimed that 'In terms of investor activism, 2003 was a watershed year.'[16] That year GlaxoSmithKline, the pharmaceuticals group, cut back its chief executive's pay and dismissed the directors primarily responsible for remuneration issues after institutional shareholders expressed their disapproval of the company's executive pay policies using a newly introduced right of shareholders to vote annually on an advisory basis on remuneration issues.[17] Fidelity International, the British arm of a large US fund management company, took the lead in a highly public confrontation with Carlton Communications and Granada, which were planning to merge as ITV plc, and forced the companies not to follow through on plans to appoint Carlton's executive chairman as chairman of ITV.[18] Institutional shareholders also publicly challenged the appointment of the chairman of the board proposed by J. Sainsbury plc, the supermarket chain, ultimately forcing the company to change its plans.[19]

Various factors precipitated the surge in public confrontations between managers and institutional shareholders. The new remuneration regulations created the potential for awkward confrontations about problematic executive pay schemes.[20] A prolonged stock market downturn (the benchmark FTSE 100 index fell from 6,930 in January 2000 to 3,567 in February 2003) served to expose underperforming companies and fostered impatience with mediocre management.[21] Some 'active' fund managers (those endeavouring to 'beat the market') rather than mimic a stock market index realized clients, disillusioned by poor returns, were increasingly shifting cash to passive 'index-tracking' funds and decided public confrontations with executives of underperforming companies could make good marketing sense.[22]

Above all, there was growing awareness that passivity could open the door for unwelcome legislation. The 2001 Myners Report expressed concern about the value lost through reluctance of institutional investors to engage actively with underperforming companies and the Labour government responded by saying on

---

[15] Paul Myners, *Institutional Investment in the U.K.: A Review* (2001), 89; see also at 91.

[16] Independent, May 16, 2004.

[17] Companies Act 1985, c. 6, s. 241A; Lee Roach, 'CEOs, Chairmen and Fat Cats: The Institutions are Watching You' (2006) 27 Company Lawyer 297, 302.

[18] 'Tip of the Iceberg', Sunday Times, October 26, 2003.

[19] 'Where Will the Fur', *supra* n. 16; 'Shareholder Revolution Spreads', Times, October 22, 2003.

[20] 'Institutions Crack Whip on Pay and Perks for Executives', Independent, April 23, 2003; 'Whose Army Rules in Britain's Boardrooms?', Business, October 26/27, 2003.

[21] 'Investors Bite Back', Financial Times, October 25/26, 2003; 'Not so Great Revolt', Financial Times, December 30, 2003, 14; 'Investors Should Not Be "Absentee Landlords"', Financial Times, January 5, 2004. On FTSE 100 share prices, see the link to historical prices on <http://uk.finance.yahoo.com/q/cp?s=%5EFTSE> (last visited January 21, 2008).

[22] 'Tip of the Iceberg', *supra* n. 18; 'Cold Wind of Democracy is Sharpening up the City', Financial Times, February 24, 2004; 'Gunning for the Board', Observer, April 4, 2004.

various occasions it would press ahead with legislation to compel shareholders to intervene on corporate governance issues if voluntary change was insufficient.[23] In a much-publicized 2003 report on non-executive directors commissioned by the government, Derek Higgs endorsed Labour's approach to more active engagement, thus adding credibility to the government's threats.[24] A desire to avoid intervention by compulsion prompted major institutional investors to bolster corporate governance operations and step up the level of engagement with their portfolio companies.[25]

If the trend in favour of activism had taken hold in a serious way in the UK this could have moved Britain towards the insider/control-oriented approach of corporate governance that prevails in most other industrialized countries (Chapter One, Part III). The *Business* newspaper suggested in 2003 that 'A series of corporate showdowns this year suggests that real power is shifting from Britain's boardrooms to an army of anonymous fund managers...'[26] Or as the *Independent* said in 2004, 'Many business leaders think the situation is already out of hand, with a small number of self-appointed City busy bodies playing the role of backseat driver among our biggest companies. In the old days it was the unions that would interfere with the right to manage. Now it seems to be the shareholders.'[27]

While the post-Myners Report surge in activism lent credibility to assertions that a fundamental reorientation of UK corporate governance was occurring, the momentum soon stalled. One reason for change was 'peace talks' held between senior executives of major UK public companies and leading fund managers to defuse the tensions that had led to the confrontations in 2003.[28] With executives having been shocked by the aggressive atmosphere and institutional investors having found matters hard to manage, both sides were receptive and a concerted shift to compromise-oriented behind-the-scenes dialogue ensued.[29] The chief executive of Hermes, asset manager for the British Telecom and Post Office pension schemes, captured the mood, saying, 'Shareholders and

---

[23] See, for example, 'Investors Face Pressure From Government', Financial Times, June 4, 2002; 'Shareholder Power Wins Government Backing', Times, March 16, 2003; 'Minister Issues Myners Warning', Financial Times, October 13, 2003.

[24] Higgs, *supra* n. 7, 70.

[25] 'The Activism Show', Financial Times, January 4/5, 2003; 'Regulator Ignores History', Financial Times, January 5, 2004; Cynthia A. Williams and John M. Conley, An Emerging Third Way?: The Erosion of the Anglo-American Shareholder Value Construct', (2005) 38 Cornell International Law Journal 493, 540–41 (summarizing results of interviews with various fund managers and pension fund trustees in London's financial district).

[26] 'Whose Army', *supra* n. 20.

[27] 'Fund Managers Should Stay Out of Boardrooms', Independent, March 2, 2004.

[28] 'Captains of Industry Summon Investors to Secret Peace Talks', Sunday Times, February 29, 2004; 'UK plc Takes on Fund Managers', Sunday Times, March 14, 2004; 'Time to Shake Hands and Work Together', Financial Times, April 5, 2004.

[29] 'Where Will the Fur', *supra* n. 16; 'Calm After the Storm in Pay Wars', Guardian, May 24, 2004, 22; 'Investors Discover They Have Real Power', Financial Times, December 30, 2004.

companies are doomed if they are set in an adversarial position.'[30] An improving stock market also helped to put investors in a more forgiving frame of mind.[31] Moreover, the threat of government regulation receded as Labour became pre-occupied with the Iraq war and sought to sooth increasingly strained relations between the government and the corporate sector.[32]

More fundamentally, changing share ownership patterns were undermining the unique position pension funds and insurance companies had to exercise influence in publicly traded UK companies. With their combined ownership stake rising from 16 per cent in 1963 to 52 per cent in 1993, they emerged as the obvious candidates to adopt a 'hands on' approach to investment in shares but generally retained their traditional bias towards passivity (Chapter Ten, Part V.B). By the 1990s, the reluctance to intervene had diminished. However, pension funds and insurance companies simultaneously began reducing their exposure to equities, and the coalescing of share ownership that provided the foundation for coordinated intervention began to unravel.

A combination of regulation and market factors contributed to the exit from UK shares. The position with life insurance companies was dictated by the accounting treatment of the many 'with profits' policies they had sold offering policyholders bonuses based on investment returns. Traditionally, when life insurers prepared their accounts, they valued investment assets in a manner that fluctuated with market value. Liabilities were not adjusted similarly, meaning that no provisions were made for implied future obligations to pay higher bonuses to policyholders when equity markets rose and for less onerous bonus obligations when markets fell.[33] One effect of this was that in a stock market downturn there was pressure on insurance companies to sell shares to shore up the 'free asset ratios' (the excess of capital after liabilities had been accounted for) they depended on to attract investors, protect themselves against fluctuations in investment performance and make acquisitions.[34] Insurers duly were net sellers of equity during the 2000–03 stock market downturn, reflected in a marked decline in the ratio of the value of UK shares on their balance sheets as compared to total investments (Figure I).[35]

Regulatory changes introduced in 2004 then helped to discourage insurance companies from reversing the sell-off of equities. The Financial Securities Authority, the UK regulator with responsibility for the insurance sector, required

---

[30] Quoted in 'UK plc', *supra* n. 28.

[31] 'Where Will the Fur', *supra* n. 16.

[32] 'Brown Plan to Cut Red Tape for Business Provokes Chorus of Disapproval', Guardian, November 29, 2005.

[33] 'Getting Real With Balance Sheets', Financial Adviser, April 15, 2004; Amanda Forsyth, 'Bringing Realism to Life Insurers' Balance Sheets', Finance Week, July 20, 2005, 19.

[34] 'Life's Tough in the Life Business', Guardian, July 17, 2002; David Rutter, 'It's No Longer an Equitable Life', Financial Adviser, August 7, 2002.

[35] National Statistics Online database: <http://www.statistics.gov.uk/statbase/TSDtables1.asp> (last visited January 25, 2008) series RCKK, RCKM, RCLD.

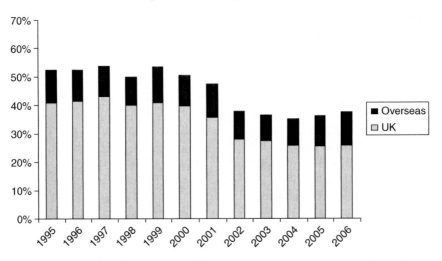

Figure I: Value of UK/overseas quoted shares on insurance company balance sheets/ total investments, 1995–2006

Source: Compiled with data from National Statistics Online, *supra* n. 35.

insurers reporting on their financial position to adopt the more pessimistic of two measures of assets versus liabilities, the traditional method described above, or a 'realistic' approach designed to reflect directly the impact of market fluctuations on liabilities. Insurers were also required to calculate a risk capital margin for a 'stressed scenario', this being the cover they would have in the event of a worst-case scenario for financial markets.[36] Though some major insurers continued to have substantial equity holdings in their investment portfolios, generally the new regulations encouraged insurers to invest in bonds rather than equities to bolster surpluses and achieve a higher degree of certainty with liabilities.[37] The fact that the ratio of the value of UK quoted shares to total investments fell as the FTSE 100 rose from 3,567 in February 2003 to 6,129 in November 2006 bears this out (Figure I).[38] Given the changes in the regulatory environment, a marked future upswing in investment in shares of domestic public companies by British insurers seems unlikely.

As for pension funds, a change in the taxation of dividends constituted one factor discouraging investment in UK shares. Beginning in 1921, pension funds meeting criteria stipulated by tax legislation were exempted from paying income

[36] 'Getting Real', *supra* n. 33; Forsyth, *supra* n. 33; 'Insurers Make "Major Progress" in Boosting Assets', Financial Times, July 9, 2005.
[37] Forsyth, *supra* n. 33; 'Secrets of Standard's £7.5bn Sale', Scotsman, August 19, 2004; 'A Swing Into Bonds: Why Equities are Losing Their Allure for Global Investors', Financial Times, October 10, 2005.
[38] On the source for FTSE 100 price trends, see *supra* n. 21.

tax on dividends they received.[39] As a result, when companies deducted at source income tax shareholders were obliged to pay on dividends (Chapter Three, Part V), pension funds could in effect demand from UK tax officials a refund for amounts notionally deducted on their behalf. By the 1990s, the rebates from the dividend tax credit amounted to around £5 billion annually.[40] In 1993, the size of the tax break was reduced and it was abolished entirely in 1997.[41] The cut in after-tax returns UK shares delivered duly provided pension funds with an incentive to switch out of equities.[42]

A radical change in the expectations of pension fund trustees also discouraged investment in shares. Until the mid-1990s pension fund trustees gave investment managers a generally open-ended mandate to invest in a range of assets with performance evaluated in terms of peer group benchmarks. Within a decade there had been a marked shift to 'liability-driven' investing, as trustees wanted investment managers to ensure there was a proper matching of assets with liabilities associated with the particular pension schemes for which the trustees were responsible.[43]

One reason for the switch was that many pension schemes were maturing, meaning outflows were growing relative to contributions as the average age of beneficiaries covered by plans grew.[44] Regulation affecting both pension fund trustees and the companies sponsoring pension plans was also pivotal. From 1995 onwards, trustees of pension schemes where beneficiaries were promised a specific monthly benefit ('defined benefit' plans) were placed under an onus to take liabilities into account by a regulatory benchmark governing the acceptable ratio of assets to liabilities, with the standard changing in 2005 from a 'minimum funding requirement' to a scheme-specific funding standard referred to as the 'statutory funding objective'.[45] As for the companies that sponsored pension plans, accounting regulations were introduced forcing them to account for pension liabilities on the balance sheet.[46] The Pension Protection Fund, a statutory corporation established under the Pensions Act 2004, has indicated that the levies it imposes on companies to finance the protection it offers will be

---

[39] David Blake, *Pension Schemes and Pension Funds in the United Kingdom*, 2nd edn, (2003), 38–39.

[40] S.R. Bond, M.P. Devereux and A. Klemm, 'The Effects of Dividend Taxes on Equity Prices: A Re-examination of the 1997 UK Tax Reform', IMF Working Paper 07/204, 5.

[41] *Ibid.*, 7, 19.

[42] *Ibid.*, 20–21; 'More Pension Funds Likely to Swap Gilts for Shares', Financial Times, October 14, 1997, 13; 'Seven Years on, Brown's Swoop on Pensions Looks Less Clever', Times, October 15, 2004.

[43] Nadine Wojakovski, 'Long-Term Liabilities—Think Outside the Box', Pensions Week, November 24, 2003; Nadine Wojakovski, 'Abandoning the Herd', Pensions Age, February, 2004; 'Shooting the Rapids of Pension Liabilities', Financial Times, December 12, 2005.

[44] 'UK Pensions to Off-Load Equities', Financial Times, June 21, 2004.

[45] 'More Power for Scheme Guardians to Ensure Solvency', Financial Times, June 12, 2006, 13; on the nature of the minimum funding requirement, see Blake, *supra* n. 39, 105–6.

[46] Accounting Standards Board, 'Retirement Benefits: F.R.S. 17', <http://www.frc.org.uk/asb/technical/standards/pub0206.html> (last visited January 16, 2008).

designed to 'tax' weakly funded schemes heavily.[47] Interest-bearing investments generate returns that match up well with liabilities associated with maturing pension schemes and yields on such instruments have been adopted by accounting regulators and the Pension Protection Fund as key benchmarks for assessing the financial health of pension funds.[48] The shift to liability-driven investing has therefore created momentum in favour of investment in fixed-interest securities rather than equities.[49]

The changes in the tax treatment of dividends received by pension funds and the shift to liability-driven investing prompted pension funds to reduce steadily their exposure to equities. Investment in UK shares was hit particularly hard as pension funds sought to increase global exposure.[50] A marked decline in the value of UK shares on pension fund balance sheets as compared to total investments illustrates the trend (Figure II).

As insurance companies and pension funds de-emphasized investment in shares of publicly traded UK companies, their combined ownership stake in such enterprises fell steadily from 52 per cent in 1993 to 41 per cent in 1999 and 26 per cent in 2006 (Chapter Four, Figure I). The gap was filled partly by 'other financial institutions' (e.g. investment vehicles, such as hedge funds, not structured to qualify as 'authorized' investment trusts under tax law), with the proportion of shares they held rising from 0.6 per cent in 1993 to 3 per cent in 1999 and 10 per cent in 2006. The rise of overseas investors was even more pronounced, with aggregate foreign holdings rising from 16 per cent in 1993 to 33 per cent in 1999 and 40 per cent in 2006 (Chapter Four, Figure II). The new foreign owners included mainstream institutional investors seeking to diversify, specialist investment funds focusing on 'active' investing strategies (e.g. 'value investing' involving the targeting of companies with under-priced shares), shareholders in companies based outside Britain obtaining a UK stock market listing and even an occasional foreign investor buying up sizeable stakes in publicly traded UK companies (e.g., Baugur, a privately owned Icelandic investment vehicle owned, as of 2008, large minority blocks in four quoted UK retailers).[51]

[47] Pensions Act 2004, c. 35, s. 107; 'Companies Face Up to the Real Costs of Pensions', *Financial Times*, February 18, 2008; 'Companies Face Bigger Pensions Risk Levy', *Financial Times*, March 7, 2008.

[48] Accounting Standards Board, 'Financial Reporting Standard 17: Pension Benefits' (2000), 18–19; Pensions Protection Fund, 'Guidance on Assumptions to Use When Undertaking a Valuation in Accordance With Section 179 of the Pension Act 2004', available at <http://www.pensionprotectionfund.org.uk/s179_assumptions_guidance_sep06.pdf> (last visited January 16, 2008).

[49] Blake, *supra* n. 39, 109–10; 'Putting in More But Getting Back Less', *Finance Week*, December 14, 2005; 'Regulation Killed the Pensions Industry', *Times*, October 16, 2006; 'It's Time to Get a Grip of the Pension Fund Mess', *Evening Standard*, March 3, 2006.

[50] 'Pension Funds Steadily Forsaking UK Equities', *Financial Times*, June 19/20, 2004.

[51] On Baugur, see 'Baugur Insists its Empire is not Unravelling', *Financial Times*, March 26, 2008. Otherwise see 'International Investors in the UK are Buying Up the Keys to Kingdom', *Financial Times*, June 22, 2005; 'Companies Feel the Impact of Pension Fund Share Selling',

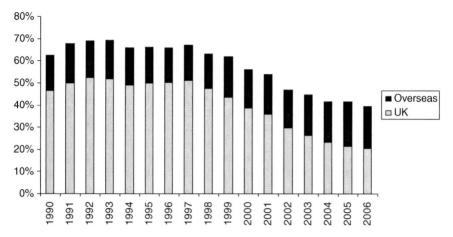

Figure II: Value of UK/overseas quoted shares on pension fund balance sheets/total investments, 1990–2006

Source: Compiled with data from National Statistics Online, *supra* n. 35, series AHVA, AHVR, RYHD.

The partial exit by domestic pension funds and insurance companies from the UK stock market has meant dispersion of share ownership has been on the increase. In the 1980s and 1990s, a small group of UK-based institutional investors owned collectively major stakes in large British companies and operated in a close-knit financial environment (Chapter Ten, Part V.A). The changes occurring to share ownership since the mid-1990s have diminished this coherence and reduced overlap on share registers. As the head of broking at the British arm of US investment bank Morgan Stanley said in 2006, 'There used to be a time when British chief executives could walk around the Square Mile (London's financial district) and bump into almost all their shareholders—when an investor roadshow meant going up to Edinburgh to see (Scottish-based insurers) Scottish Widows or Standard Life. Now there are not just foreign institutions but some that the company will have never heard of.'[52]

The increased dispersion of share ownership has reduced the potential for intervention by leading British pension funds, insurers and fund managers.[53] With major UK-based institutions holding smaller stakes than was the case formerly, exit is now easier for them to orchestrate without putting downward pressure on

---

Financial Times, December 10/11, 2005; 'Market Takes Stock to Find it's Not British', Birmingham Post, July 14, 2007.

[52] 'Americans Sweep Aside Blue-Blooded Britons', Sunday Times, August 27, 2006.

[53] 'Cross-Border Concerns for Governance Movement', Financial Times, June 28, 2004; 'Foreign Power', Financial Times, June 22, 2005; 'Power in Different Hands as City of London Goes Global', Business, August 11, 2007.

prices. Also, forming a coalition with sufficient clout to attract management's attention has become more costly, since tracking down and negotiating with foreign shareholders and 'other financial institutions' is more complicated than dealing with a small cohort of major UK-based pension funds, insurance companies and fund managers. In addition, the foreign investors that dominate the share register now are not promising candidates to back an insurgency campaign because they typically will have only a small investment in the UK stock market relative to their full investment portfolio and thus can lack whatever commitment to corporate governance they have at home.[54] Hence, while the rise of pension funds and insurance companies as shareholders in the decades following World War II created the potential for a shift towards control-oriented corporate governance in the UK, the window of opportunity now seems closed.

II. 'Offensive' Shareholder Activism

Open confrontations occurring between major UK institutional shareholders and corporate executives as the 20th century drew to a close can be characterized as 'defensive' shareholder activism. The standard pattern was that the proactive institution would be the largest institutional shareholder and would be 'overweight' in the shares, in the sense it owned a greater proportion of the equity than it owned of the market generally.[55] The proactive institution would have serious doubts about the capabilities of management, typically due to poor financial results, and thus was inclined to take the initiative to protect its investment. If the initial response by management proved unsatisfactory, the proactive institution's next step was to try to strengthen its hand by securing the backing of other major institutional shareholders, representing ideally 20 per cent or more of the equity.

What was largely absent in the 1980s and 1990s was 'offensive' shareholder activism, which occurs when an investor lacking a meaningful stake in a company builds up a sizeable holding with the intention of agitating for changes intended to boost the share price. This form of activism has long been a feature of stock market investing in the United States, extending back to Jay Gould, the notorious financier and 'robber baron'.[56] Gould, who has been labelled 'the consummate example of the active shareholder',[57] did not seek or obtain one-man

---

[54] 'Voting Habits', Financial Times, February 7, 2005 (indicating foreign institutional investors—North Americans excepted—rarely vote the shares they own in UK quoted companies).

[55] Stapledon, *supra* n. 5, 106, 123–27; Bernard S. Black and John C. Coffee, 'Hail Britannia? Institutional Investor Behavior Under Limited Regulation', (1994) 92 Michigan Law Review 1997, 2046–50.

[56] For an overview of the history, see John Armour and Brian R. Cheffins, 'The Market for Corporate Influence: Activist Hedge Funds and their Antecedents', (2007), unpublished working paper, Pt IV.

[57] Allen D. Boyer, 'Activist Shareholders, Corporate Directors, and Institutional Investment: Some Lessons from the Robber Barons', (1993) 50 Washington & Lee Law Review 977, 1009.

domination of the companies with which he became involved. Instead, he looked constantly for 'weak spots'—essentially undervalued companies—and with those he found, he would gain sufficient leverage to orchestrate changes designed to result in a rise in the share price then exit at a profit.[58] Moving rapidly from one situation to another, with interventions, negotiations and transactions following each other in rapid succession, he generally refrained from active participation in management and shied away from taking exclusive control. His business 'empire' thus was composed of minority holdings, fortified by aggressive trading strategies and carefully chosen allies.[59]

There have been in Britain parties whose business strategy was to profit by finding underperforming companies and orchestrating changes. Leading examples were the pioneering takeover raiders of the 1950s, Slater Walker during the late 1960s and Hanson in the 1980s (Chapter Ten, Part IV.E.1). Their method of operation, however, was to acquire a targeted company by way of a takeover, not to buy up a minority stake and agitate for change. There were isolated exceptions. In 1903 Owen Phillips (later the controversial Lord Kylsant) secured the chairmanship of Royal Mail Steam Packet Co. after investment trusts his brother operated bought a sizeable but not controlling stake and he and his brother successfully persuaded neutral shareholders to back their plan to introduce new management.[60] Slater Walker, as part of an unsuccessful attempt to transform itself from an acquisitive conglomerate to an investment bank, adopted a business strategy of holding significant but not controlling stakes in quoted companies.[61] Financier James Goldsmith bought up a 20 per cent stake in Procea Products in 1963, a small public company making slimming products, and did the same in 1989 with Ranks Hovis McDougall, a large diversified food group, in both instances intending to create value by recommending improvements to the company.[62] However, it was much more common for him, when dealing with UK companies, to pursue the more conventional strategy of a takeover bid.[63]

The nature of share ownership in Britain in the decades following World War II militated against offensive shareholder activism. For institutional investors who moved to the forefront as shareholders in publicly traded companies from the 1950s onwards, their traditional default rule was to back the

[58] Julius Grodinsky, *Jay Gould: His Business Career 1867–1892* (1957), 22–23.

[59] *Ibid.*, 318–21; Maury Klein, *Life and Legend of Jay Gould* (1986), 276–82.

[60] 'The Royal Mail Steam Packet Company', Economist, June 28, 1902, 1014; Edwin Green and Michael Moss, *A Business of National Importance: The Royal Mail Shipping Group 1902–1937* (1982), 19, 22. On subsequent events involving Lord Kylsant, see Ch. Seven, Pt VII; Ch. Eight, Pts I.D, II.B.2.

[61] Ch. Ten, Pt IV.E.1; Jim Slater, *Return to Go: My Autobiography* (1977), 120–21; Charles Raw, *Slater Walker: An Investigation of a Financial Phenomenon* (1977), 243–46, 249, 335, 347–48.

[62] Ivan Fallon, *Billionaire: The Life and Times of Sir James Goldsmith* (1991), 156, 453–55.

[63] *Ibid.*, 161; Geoffrey Wansell, *Tycoon: The Life of James Goldsmith* (1987), 119–20, 127–28, 151–52, 157, 159–60. Goldsmith's takeover vehicle, Cavenham Foods, took a different approach with companies in continental Europe, typically participating as a major shareholder rather than becoming the sole owner: Fallon, *op. cit.* at 244; Wansell, *op. cit.* at 168–69.

incumbent management team, giving the benefit of the doubt to directors who kept them informed and whom they trusted.[64] As a result, if a shareholder minded to agitate for change appeared on the share register, executives could generally be confident that, in the absence of a full-blown takeover bid, the proposals would receive a frosty reception.

For instance, Leslie Harris, an accountant who exceptionally did achieve some notoriety for his efforts as a shareholder to prod moribund or otherwise suspect directors, complained in a 1972 interview that it was virtually impossible to get any recognition from company management since efforts to make changes rarely drew any response from institutional shareholders.[65] Even an investor that built up a sizeable stake could struggle to prompt changes. In the late 1980s, General Cinema, a US cinema and retail group renowned for buying minority holdings in vulnerable companies and selling them on at a profit, built up an 18 per cent stake in Cadbury Schweppes, the confectionery and soft drinks company.[66] Though General Cinema did not declare publicly the strategy being adopted, the intent likely was to pressure Cadbury Schweppes to split its confectionery and soft drinks businesses or put the entire company in play. Cadbury Schweppes' chief executive Dominic Cadbury and chairman Adrian Cadbury said any attempt by General Cinema to interfere with the management of the business 'would be unwelcome and strongly resisted'.[67] Cadbury family holdings by that point were insufficient to veto any change in control (Chapter Nine, Table V) but the company's institutional investors never wavered. In 1990 General Cinemas quietly sold its stake to a consortium of institutional shareholders.[68]

In the 1990s offensive shareholder activism began to gain a foothold in Britain. The UK Active Fund, backed by a number of US pension funds and wealthy American and European families and managed by two South African entrepreneurs, Brian Myerson and Julian Treger, made a name for itself by taking sizeable stakes in companies that had fallen on hard times and agitating for change.[69] Initially, Myerson and Treger struggled to be taken seriously, labelled as 'fast-buck merchants' and perturbing many leading institutional shareholders with their tactics.[70] However, matters began to change, with some investing institutions being happy for the UK Active Fund 'to shake things up so they

[64] Jonathan P. Charkham, *Keeping Good Company: A Study of Corporate Governance in Five Countries* (1994), 310; 'Guardians of the Standards', Sunday Business, August 19, 2001; 'Investors Who Pack a Powerful Punch', Financial Times, September 26, 2007.

[65] 'Velvet Glove Without the Iron Hand?', Times, November 17, 1972. See also Alex Rubner, *The Ensnared Shareholder* (1966), 139 (activism having little impact); 'Standing up for Shareholders', Times, April 30, 1977 (Harris achieving some notoriety).

[66] 'Chewing into Cadbury', Times, June 5, 1988.

[67] 'Cadbury's Next for the Bite?', Guardian, April 28, 1988.

[68] 'First Taste of a Sweeter Life After Four Years of Siege', Financial Times, October 13, 1990.

[69] 'Scourges of the Poor Performers', Sunday Times, October 27, 1996; 'Raiders Cause a Stir at Kenwood', Guardian, October 29, 1996.

[70] 'Time to Put a Stop to the Fast Buck Merchants', Independent, October 22, 1995; 'An Offer That Can't Be Refused', Business, April 21, 2007.

didn't have to get their hands dirty'.[71] By 2001, Treger was saying of traditional UK institutional investors, 'They love the role we play because we set the stage for them. We do the hard work at the coal face.'[72]

When mainstream institutional shareholders began taking the proposals of offensive shareholder activists seriously this increased the leverage of the activists considerably, as executives at targeted companies could no longer take for granted institutional backing in the event the dissidents threatened to call a shareholder meeting to resolve matters. The reorientation of share ownership in favour of overseas investors compounded matters since executives increasingly had to deal with share registers populated with unfamiliar owners from whom no special loyalty could be anticipated. A practice engaged in with growing frequency by big institutional shareholders increased further the uncertainty for incumbent management teams, this being lending, for a fee, shares—and voting rights—to investment vehicles, such as hedge funds, specializing in aggressive trading strategies.[73] Further complicating matters were 'contracts for difference', derivatives sold by investment banks to hedge funds providing the option to convert positions into vote-bearing shares, with a bonus being that large stakes did not have to be disclosed until conversion took place.[74] This was unsettling for executives used to dealing with long-term institutional shareholders who typically welcomed establishing a communicative relationship.[75]

In this new environment, a growing number of investors emerged prepared to engage in offensive shareholder activism. In 1998, Hermes set up, with the support of several other institutional investors, the UK Focus Fund, which had a mandate to invest in companies that were underperforming, were susceptible to engagement and had considerable turnaround potential.[76] A few years later financier Edward Bramson began capturing headlines for taking up sizeable stakes in smaller quoted companies through investment vehicles he controlled and pressing for change, backed up by the threat of shareholder resolutions to dismiss recalcitrant incumbent directors.[77] UK Active Fund colleagues Myerson

[71] 'Active Duo Rough Up Boards But Are Not Always Able to Add Value', Times, November 1, 1997.

[72] 'Active Duo Who Arouse Strong Feelings in City and Boardroom', Financial Times, January 29, 2001.

[73] 'Uneasy Bedfellows With Money in Mind', Financial Times, April 19, 2004; 'Hedge Funds are Very Keen to Flex Their Secretive Shareholding Muscle', Financial Times, August 9, 2005; 'Little Money to be Made by Institutions Lending Stock', Financial Times, June 16/17, 2007.

[74] 'Follow the Smart Money', Investors Chronicle, September 29, 2006; 'Derivatives Stand in the Way of Equity', Financial Times, September 26, 2007; Financial Services Authority, *Disclosure and Transparency Rules*, para. 5.1.1, available at <http://fsahandbook.info/FSA/html/handbook/DTR> (last visited March 12, 2008).

[75] 'Transparency Finds a High-Level Champion', Financial Times, April 22, 2005.

[76] Marco Becht, Julian Franks, Colin Mayer and Stefano Rossi, 'Returns to Shareholder Activism: Evidence from a Clinical Study of the Hermes UK Focus Fund', (2006) ECGI Working Paper No. 138, 12–15.

[77] 'Follow the Smart', *supra* n. 74; 'Bramson Attracts Criticism as He Sets Sights on Spirent', Financial Times, November 22, 2006; 'Hanover Investors Forces Shake Up of Board at SMG', Financial Times, March 1, 2007.

and Treger parted ways in 2004 but each soon returned to the activism scene with their own investment vehicles.[78] Atticus Capital, a New York-based hedge fund, gained notoriety in Britain as an activist shareholder in 2007 by lobbying Barclays Bank to pull out of a contest to buy Dutch bank ABN Amro.[79] The same year, 3i, a publicly quoted investment firm, launched a fund with a mandate to buy sizeable but not controlling stakes in mid-sized publicly traded firms, but with the declared aim of working in cooperation with management rather than agitating for fundamental change.[80]

Events involving Cadbury Schweppes in 2007 implied to some that offensive shareholder activism had the potential to change markedly the balance of influence between managers and shareholders in UK public companies. In March of that year, Trian Funds, an investment vehicle of Nelson Peltz, a veteran US shareholder activist, bought a 3 per cent stake in Cadbury Schweppes amid speculation Peltz would press the company to split up its drinks and confectionary operations.[81] Two days later Cadbury Schweppes announced its plan to do precisely this.[82] A senior official at the British arm of Fidelity, the US fund manager, denounced Cadbury Schweppes' decision as 'a come-on to every corporate raider or activist investor' and 'an episode that alters the relationship between shareholders and the companies in which they invest'.[83] The financial press chimed in, suggesting that activism was 'the new game in town and it strikes at the very heart of that elite group of Footsie companies that were previously seen as untouchable' and 'the scrutiny goes right to the very top'.[84]

Matters looked much different over the course of the following year as activism efforts at other major British-based public companies fell flat. Shareholders at Vodafone, the global mobile phone operator, decisively rejected a shareholder resolution proposed by activist Efficient Capital Structures that the company spin off a major US operation.[85] Likewise, criticism of the corporate governance and spread of operations of banking giant HSBC by Knight Vinke, another activist investor, did not resonate with shareholders and failed to prompt any immediate changes.[86] The two incidents underscored the fact that for offensive shareholder

---

[78] 'Offer That Can't', *supra* n. 70; 'The Exec-Terminator', Financial Times, July 6, 2007.

[79] 'Activist Investors Flex Their Biceps', Sunday Times, June 17, 2007.

[80] '3i to Invest in Quoted Groups', Financial Times, November 30, 2006; '3i Plans to Float Stake-Building Funds', Financial Times, May 16, 2007.

[81] 'Cadbury's Bitter-Sweet Dilemma', Financial Times, March 14, 2007.

[82] 'Cadbury Bows to Pressure With Split Plan', Financial Times, March 16, 2007.

[83] 'Boards Must Stand Up to Minority Activists', Financial Times, June 11, 2007 (column by Anthony Bolton).

[84] 'Nowadays, Everyone is a Target', Telegraph, June 16, 2007; 'No Company is Out of Reach of Activists', Sunday Times, July 8, 2007.

[85] 'Vodafone Sees Off Rebel ECS', Financial Times, July 25, 2007.

[86] 'Critic of Bank's Incentive Plan Fails to Find Allies', Financial Times, November 27, 2007; 'HSBC Can Turn a Deaf Ear to This Talkative Activist', Evening Standard, December 17, 2007. HSBC did subsequently replace a number of non-executive directors after its share price took a major hit: 'Boardroom Shake-up Revealed', Financial Times, March 4, 2008.

activism to succeed, the activist needs good timing and a strong case that rallies larger investors to the cause.[87] Even if key shareholders were less inclined to give management the benefit of the doubt than was the case formerly, a sure-handed chief executive supported by the board of directors continues to hold the balance of power.

What of Cadbury Schweppes? In retrospect, management's assertions that it had been moving towards splitting the company for some time before the Peltz intervention and that the timing of the de-merger announcement was purely coincidental were increasingly plausible.[88] This all suggests that while offensive shareholder activism will be a catalyst for change in at least some companies going forward, it will not alter in any fundamental way the divorce of ownership and control that characterizes UK corporate governance.

III. Private Equity

Private equity funds are raised by firms that specialize in accumulating capital for deployment for a range of transactions. The capital is almost always generated privately rather than by a public offering (hence the label 'private equity') and will be allocated to funds created by the private equity house. Private equity transactions can include a range of different deals, including venture capital (the financing of 'start up' businesses) and management buyouts (the funding of purchases of divisions of publicly traded companies by incumbent managers).[89] In the 2000s, however, 'private equity' became popularly associated with deals involving the acquisition of publicly traded companies, followed by their removal from the stock market.[90]

'Public-to-private' buyouts are typically arranged in anticipation of improving the financial performance and growth profile of the acquired companies. Proponents of private equity claim a buyout is an optimal environment for such a value-enhancing transition to occur as companies taken private benefit from a more streamlined, efficient and effective system of corporate governance than a stock market company.[91] It is said, for instance, that private equity firms

---

[87] 'Knight's Tilt at HSBC Shows Activists are Still at Large', Financial Times, September 7, 2007; 'Fears Over Surge in Corporate Activism', Observer, October 14, 2007; 'Activists Flex Muscles as Markets Falter', Financial Times, January 8, 2008.

[88] 'Bolton Attacks Cadbury Split in Face of Activists', Financial Times, June 11, 2007; 'Informed Boards Can Still See Off the Activists', Financial Times, June 12, 2007.

[89] Simon Beddow and Karl Taylor, 'Private Equity Transactions: An Overview', Practical Law for Companies, July 2004, 15, 15; Walker Working Group, 'Disclosure and Transparency in Private Equity: Consultation Document July 2007', 11, 13.

[90] 'The Private Equity Boom', Washington Post, March 15, 2007.

[91] Michael C. Jensen, 'The Eclipse of the Public Corporation', Harvard Business Review, September/October 1989, 61; 'A Lesson in Governance from Private Equity Firms', Financial Times, November 30, 2006; 'Boardrooms Should Soak Up the Culture of Private Equity', Times,

orchestrating buyouts will be dedicated owners, able and willing to offer direction in a way that dispersed shareholders cannot. In addition, executives in charge of companies taken private reputedly are better incentivized than their counterparts in a public firm since they are major shareholders. Advocates of the private equity model also claim the board of directors works more effectively because it can focus purely on trading and strategy issues rather than becoming bogged down in corporate governance 'box ticking'.

As a public company director argued in 2007 in the *Financial Times*, '[I]f this "private is better" sales pitch is really true, we will inevitably condemn the public company to die as our dominant institution.'[92] A private equity boom in the mid-2000s indeed prompted speculation that the publicly listed company's days were numbered. The *Financial Times* asked in 2007, 'After 150 glorious years, is the limited liability company no longer fit for its purpose?'[93] The *Economist* similarly conjectured 'Could the private equity model become the norm, replacing the public company?'[94] Some, at least, were prepared to say yes. In 2006 the *Times* claimed that the 'Plc is Ready to Join Mutuals in Land of the Dodo' and said one could imagine within ten years 'a world where no company making real things or marketing real services is listed and stock exchanges trade only bonds, funds, high-tech start-ups and dodgy exploration outfits'.[95] A year later, the *Financial Times* suggested '(t)here seems to be a dreadful inevitability about the phenomenon of private equity at the moment'.[96] Economist Tim Jenkinson was more cautious, but only moderately so, saying in an article in The *Times* the same year, 'It's not quite a revolution, but it is certainly a challenge to the throne.'[97]

Despite the hyperbole, private equity is not a threat to the pre-eminence of the widely held public company in the UK. One reason is that private equity counts on having the option to take the companies they have bought public. Since private equity investment funds most often have a fixed duration (typically ten years) exit is a critical element of the private equity business model.[98] The three core exit options are carrying out a public offering, selling the company in a 'trade sale' to a corporate buyer and a 'secondary sale' to another private equity firm.[99]

February 1, 2007; Robert Easton, 'Developments and Challenges in Buy-outs' in *Private Equity in the UK: The First 25 Years* (2008), 91, 93.

[92] 'The Paradox Behind the Invasion of the Privateers', Financial Times, February 13, 2007.

[93] 'The Public Company is Battered But Not Broken', Financial Times, March 19, 2007.

[94] 'The Business of Making Money', Economist, July 7, 2007, 74, 76.

[95] 'Private Equity Takes Over the World', Times, January 27, 2006; 'Plc is Ready to Join Mutuals in Land of the Dodo', April 21, 2006, 71.

[96] 'Praise the Company that Stays Public, For it Does Good Work', Financial Times, January 23, 2007.

[97] 'The New Model Army is a Threat to the Stock Market's Throne', Times, March 5, 2007 (column by Tim Jenkinson).

[98] Walker Working Group, *supra* n. 89, 13; Financial Services Authority, 'Private Equity: A Discussion of Risk and Regulatory Engagement', (2006) Discussion Paper 06/6, 21, 50.

[99] Financial Services Authority, *supra* n. 98, 50.

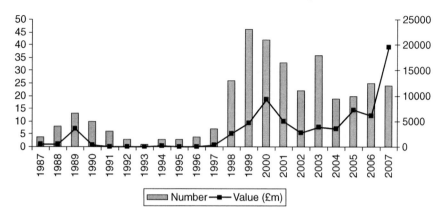

Figure III: UK public to private buyouts/Buy-ins 1987–2007, (£m)

Source: Centre for Management Buyout and Private Equity Research/Barclays Private Equity/Deloitte, provided by Rod Ball.

Companies that are subject to a secondary buyout may themselves come to the stock market in due course, so with publicly traded companies taken private in a buyout there is a decent chance that after restructuring they will return to the stock market, thus reducing any net loss to the population of publicly traded companies.[100]

Even assuming companies taken off the stock market often do not return, in Britain the private equity deal flow is too modest in relation to the population of publicly traded companies to pose a serious threat to the public company's dominance. As of 2008 there were nearly 1,300 UK-based companies quoted on the main market of the London Stock Exchange and almost 1,600 traded on the London Stock Exchange's Alternative Investment Market.[101] Compared to this sizeable cohort, the number of companies taken private is small, with the number of public-to-private buyout transactions carried out annually in the UK never exceeding 50 in any one year between 1987 and 2007 and only exceeding 25 five times (Figure III).[102]

---

[100] 'Private Equity Gets One Over the Stock Market Again', Financial Times, October 26, 2006 (saying secondary buyouts can lead to public offerings); 'The Benefit of Hindsight', Financial Times, March 12, 2007 (attributing a long queue of 'mid-cap' companies seeking to re-list on the London Stock Exchange partly to exits being required due to a wave of companies being taken private in 1999).

[101] See <http://www.londonstockexchange.com/en-gb/pricesnews/statistics/listcompanies/> (providing links to Excel spreadsheets, updated monthly, listing all UK-based companies traded on the two markets; last visited January 17, 2008).

[102] Buyout activity of any sort was rare prior to 1980 and was dominated by management buy outs until the end of the 1980s: Mike Wright, Ken Robbie, Brian Chiplin and Mark Albrighton, 'The Development of an Organisational Innovation: Management Buy-Outs in the UK, 1980–1997', (2000) 42 Business History, #4, 137, 149–56.

Public-to-private deals have also been too small-scale to have a significant impact on the large public companies where a divorce between ownership and control is particularly likely to be a hallmark. As of 2007, the average market capitalization of a company in the FTSE 100, the index of the UK's largest quoted companies, was £14.7 billion.[103] In only one year, 2007, did the aggregate value of all UK public-to-private buyouts exceed this amount, and this was primarily attributable to the first private equity acquisition of a FTSE 100 company, an £11.1 buyout of Alliance Boots, the wholesale and retail pharmacy group, by Kohlberg Kravis and Roberts, a US private equity house.[104]

The Alliance Boots buyout was labelled 'a milestone in British capitalism' amidst speculation numerous other UK 'going private' transactions of a similar scale would soon follow.[105] No such deals happened, and before long the consensus was that there would not be any for some time.[106] The change in mood was attributable primarily to a radical change in credit markets. Debt is an integral element of the private equity business model since public-to-private buyouts are typically highly leveraged and since the borrowing creates discipline for executives of the companies taken private by imposing an obligation to generate cash to meet interest payments.[107] Through the 2000s, credit spreads (the disparity between interest rates for low-risk and high-risk fixed income securities) fell and debt increasingly became available with few legal strings attached, creating a highly hospitable financial environment for private equity buyouts.[108] The party ended in the summer of 2007, with a 'credit crunch' causing credit spreads to rise dramatically and prompting banks to scale back high-risk lending and tighten up the terms on offer to private equity borrowers.[109]

The debt market chill aside, private equity in the UK was already somewhat on the back foot. Concerns that private equity firms were profiting by buying up iconic companies and carrying out job-threatening reorganizations out of the public gaze sparked Parliamentary hearings in the spring of 2007, which in turn

---

[103] 'FTSE 100 Index Factsheet 2007', available at <http://www.ftse.com/Indices/UK_Indices/Downloads/FTSE100_Index_Factsheet.pdf >(last visited January 18, 2008). The median market capitalization was £6.0 billion.

[104] 'Distasteful Alliance Overshadows Approach for Boots', Times, March 31, 2007; e-mail correspondence with Rod Ball confirming Alliance Boots' contribution to the aggregate value of public-to-private transactions for 2007.

[105] 'Distasteful Alliance', *supra* n. 104 ('milestone' quote); 'Everything in UK's Store is Available for Purchase', Times, February 3, 2007; 'Boots Likely to be the First in a String of Footsie Private Bids', Telegraph, April 25, 2007.

[106] 'Private Equity Groups Foresee Slowdown in Deals as Credit Sources Dry Up', Times, September 14, 2007; 'Private Equity Needs Tactical Changes', Financial Times, October 8, 2007; 'Credit Crunch Will Take its Toll on Private Equity Deals', Business, December 15, 2007.

[107] 'Business of Making', *supra* n. 94 (disciplinary aspect); Financial Services Authority, *supra* n. 98, 32–37 (use of debt).

[108] Financial Services Authority, *supra* n. 98, 59–61; 'Get-in-Get-Out Private Buyers are Damaging Good Companies', Telegraph, January 3, 2007; House of Commons Treasury Committee, *Private Equity: Tenth Report of Session 2006–07*, Volume I (2007), 22–25.

[109] 'Private Equity Groups', *supra* n. 106; 'Credit Crunch Will', *supra* n. 106; 'Tycoons Flying too Close to the Sun', Observer, November 18, 2007.

yielded recommendations of increased transparency and removal of tax loopholes that benefited private equity houses.[110] Even prior to the political controversy, deals were becoming increasingly difficult to pull off. Events concerning Debenhams, the retailer, constituted the catalyst. Debenhams was taken private in 2004 and returned to public markets in 2006 on terms that generated hundreds of millions of pounds in profits for the buyout team but left previous shareholders feeling badly short-changed.[111]

Thereafter, there was 'something of a seller's strike' as neither boards nor shareholders of UK public companies wanted to look foolish for accepting 'low ball' private equity bids.[112] Indeed, an investment banker specializing in buyouts said there was 'almost an automatic reaction...that if the bidder is a private equity firm, then investors will not sell it'.[113] Hence, during 2006 the value of withdrawn or failed private equity bids in the UK was nearly five times the value of completed deals.[114]

Given the political controversy private equity attracted and given investor scepticism concerning private equity buyouts, a return to benign credit conditions is unlikely to prompt a dramatic expansion in public-to-private deals in the UK. After all, even with credit markets that provided a highly congenial platform for buyout activity, public-to-private transactions only occurred on a modest scale in Britain, at least in relation to the number and size of companies currently publicly traded. A partner at Permira, a major UK private equity house, conceded the point in a post-credit crunch 2007 interview, saying, 'We were never quite as important as people thought we were.'[115] Correspondingly, with respect to the structure of ownership and control in large UK companies, the private equity business model is unlikely to offer a serious 'challenge to the throne' anytime soon, let alone prompt any sort of revolution.

IV. Why Recent Trends Will Reinforce the Separation of Ownership and Control

When assessing the buy side's contribution to the separation of ownership and control in large business enterprises, it is necessary to take into account not only

---

[110] On the political controversy, see House of Commons Treasury Committee, *supra* n. 108, 3, 5; 'Private Equity Faces its Critics', Sunday Times, February 18, 2007; 'Private Equity Cannot Escape the Public Eye', Financial Times, April 24, 2007. On the recommendations, see House of Commons Treasury Committee, *op. cit.*, 43–44.

[111] 'Pressure Building for Public Companies to Adopt Private Equity Tactics', Financial Times, August 12/13, 2006; 'Private Equity Beaten to the Punch', Financial Times, October 28/29, 2006.

[112] 'Private Equity Beaten', *supra* n. 111; 'Fund Managers Go For the Long Haul', Telegraph, April 30, 2006; 'Private Equity Barbarians Face Battle for the Throne', Financial Times, September 4, 2006.

[113] 'Public Companies in Fightback', Financial Times, March 17/18, 2007.

[114] 'Private Equity Beaten', *supra* n. 111; see also 'Companies Urged to Use Funds to Ward Off Private Equity Takeovers', Financial Times, January 24, 2007 (listing companies where private equity bids were rejected).

[115] 'Private Equity Needs', *supra* n. 106.

the factors that motivate investors to purchase shares but also the extent to which those buying equity will be minded to exercise control (Chapter One, Part IV). We have considered in this chapter three categories of investor where taking a 'hands on' approach to the running of businesses is an integral aspect of what they do (offensive-minded shareholder activists and private equity houses) or a habit they can acquire (pension funds and insurance companies engaging in defensive activism). We have seen that neither shareholder activism (defensive or offensive) nor private equity buyouts is likely to redefine British corporate governance in insider/control-oriented terms. Nevertheless, these strategies (or close substitutes) are likely to remain part of the corporate governance scene going forward and, if that turns out to be the case, the trends involved should serve to reinforce the division of ownership and control that currently constitutes a hallmark of UK corporate governance.

Publicly traded companies characterized by a separation of ownership and control derive powerful advantages through their ability to agglomerate large amounts of capital and to exploit the benefits of specialization of management and risk bearing (Chapter Two, Part I). Nevertheless, tension between shareholders and managers is inherent in the widely held firm. With executives owning only a small percentage of the equity, they necessarily have an incentive to exploit control to further their own interests at the expense of those who own equity.

Various constraints keep what is referred to as the agency cost problem within manageable bounds, but do not eliminate it completely (Chapter Two, Part I). This, in turn, creates the potential for shareholder activism and for private equity buyouts to generate value. With shareholder activism, the 'carrot' that potentially justifies the time and effort involved with cajoling or removing underperforming executives is that corrective action can improve shareholder returns, at least in well-chosen instances. As for private equity, an oft-cited rationale for public-to-private buyouts is that executives, mindful of careful monitoring by the private equity firm in charge, a large potential managerial 'upside' and the disciplinary effect of leverage, will adopt bold value-enhancing strategies they would be reluctant to implement in a public company context. Since the agency cost problem is not going away and since shareholder activism and private equity potentially create value by improving in particular contexts the alignment of interests between shareholders and managers, they (or close substitutes) are likely to remain part of corporate governance activity going forward.

There is not only 'room' for shareholder activism and private equity buyouts within the UK's current corporate governance system, but they in fact could fortify current arrangements. Between the 1950s and the 1980s the threat of a takeover bid placed an onus on managers to focus on shareholders' interests, thus offering a reassuring message to investors who otherwise might have hesitated to buy shares due to concerns about whether directors were sufficiently 'on message' (Chapter Ten, Part IV.E.1). When Hanson and its fellow takeover raiders languished in the 1990s, the next generation of public company executives showed no inclination to seek to profit by acquiring and turning around underperforming firms.[116] The sidelining of this disciplinary mechanism created the potential for the agency cost gap to widen. If this became a trend, investor confidence in publicly traded companies could have been shaken, at least to some degree. Shareholder activism and private equity have emerged, however, as substitutes that help to keep agency costs in check.

The point has already been made with defensive shareholder activism. Again, a catalyst for intervention during the 1990s was the realization among major institutional shareholders that a Hanson-style takeover bid was unlikely to supply a solution if a company was being badly mismanaged. In addition, the occurrence of periodic interventions by large institutional investors has potentially beneficial incentive effects because a desire on the part of executives to avoid awkward confrontations should encourage them not to go 'off message' in the first place.[117]

The situation is similar with offensive shareholder activism. With the disappearance of Hanson, BTR *et al* potentially weakening market discipline on underperforming companies, it likely was not a coincidence this form of intervention first emerged in Britain with regularity in the mid-1990s. Moreover, going forward the prospect of offensive intervention should help to keep executives in check. As the head of mergers of the London office of a financial advisory firm said in 2007, 'Activist shareholders are giving more confidence to those who felt in the past that they had no say and remind managers of their duties to account for shareholders' interests.'[118]

As far as private equity is concerned, to the extent dealmakers in the UK can generate profits nowadays by taking over and restructuring poorly run or underpriced public companies, private equity firms now stand out as the leading candidates to orchestrate the transactions. As the *Financial Times* said in 2002 of Hanson and its ilk, 'their bottom-fishing role has been institutionalised: private equity houses are the modern conglomerates, pouncing on market inefficiencies'.[119] Private equity bidders prefer to negotiate with incumbent executives rather than making 'hostile' bids.[120] Nevertheless, in buyout negotiations the bargaining position of the incumbent management team will be strengthened if the company is well run, and an underperforming chief executive could easily find himself (or herself) on the outside of a private equity restructuring looking in. Private equity thus has a disciplinary effect something akin to Hanson-style takeover bids. As the chief executive of Hermes said in 2007, '(Executives) can either implement good governance structures now, or they can run the risk

---

[116] 'Why We'll Not See the Likes of the Barnstorming Lord Hanson Again', Independent, November 3, 2004; Simon Dixon, 'Boardroom Girly-Men', Spectator, February 18, 2006.

[117] 'The New Activism', Financial Times, October 23, 2002.

[118] Quoted in 'Boards Feel the Heat as Investor Activists Speak Up', New York Times, May 23, 2007; see also 'Embrace the Activists', Telegraph, March 19, 2007.

[119] 'Why We'll Not', *supra* n. 116; see also 'The Buccaneers Who Go No More A'Roving', Financial Times, July 20, 2002; 'Lord of the Raiders', Economist, November 6, 2004.

[120] 'Watch Out for Bear Hugs and Cabbages', Financial Times, April 24, 2006.

of a private equity company buying the company, taking it private and implementing their own governance strategy—a strategy which may well exclude the incumbent chief executive. If chief executives have the fear of God put into them by private equity firms, that's a good thing for the shareholders.'[121]

Even aside from the disciplinary attributes of shareholder activism and private equity buyouts, a divorce between ownership and control is likely to remain the norm in UK public companies for some to time to come. Quantitative studies of company law suggest that in spite of a *laissez-faire* tradition extending back to the 19th century, the UK currently offers in comparative terms strong protection to shareholders.[122] This implies both that blockholders lack substantial scope to extract private benefits of control and that investors can buy shares with confidence corporate law offers significant protection against dishonest, self-serving uses of corporate control. Corporate governance norms also militate against charismatic founders (or their heirs) treating their companies as private fiefs. The Combined Code discourages blockholder-dominated board structures since it emphasizes publicly traded companies should have a strong independent element on the board and indicates that directors who represent a significant shareholder do not qualify as independent.[123] Moreover, an institutional backlash against BSkyB's 2003 decision to appoint James Murdoch, son of founder Rupert Murdoch, as chief executive illustrates that dynastically minded blockholders, no matter what their credentials, are unlikely to be given any sort of 'free pass'.[124]

Given past trends and present circumstances, in the absence of an unforeseen major disruption to corporate life in the UK, the outsider/arm's-length system of ownership and control that first emerged with railway companies in the 19th century and became predominant during the second half of the 20th century should survive well into the 21st century. This book has refrained from offering a normative assessment of the British system of corporate governance, so readers will need to refer elsewhere to assess whether this is a trend to be welcomed. However, the analysis provided here means they should be able to do so with a better sense of how and why the UK has ended up where it has.

---

[121] 'Why Directors Dance to the Activists' Tune', Telegraph, March 25, 2007.

[122] Ch. Two, Pt II.B. See also Mathias M. Siems, 'Shareholder Protection Around the World ("Leximetric II"),' (2008) 33 Delaware Journal of Corporate Law 111, 123 (awarding the UK the top score for corporate law among 20 countries as of 2005, based on ten variables).

[123] Combined Code on Corporate Governance (2006), available at <http://www.frc.org.uk/corporate/combinedcode.cfm> (last visited January 22, 2008), Code Provision A.3.1 (representing a significant shareholder can compromise independence), Code Provision A.3.2 (at least half of the board should be independent directors); 'Families Maintain a Firm Grip on Business Ownership', Financial Times, August 30, 2004, 3 (quoting economist Julian Franks as saying UK 'corporate governance rules militate against hereditary board control of publicly traded companies').

[124] 'Fretting Over BSkyB, But Aren't Investors Mainly to Blame?', Independent, November 5, 2003.

Index

Companies and Other Business Enterprises Referred to in the Text

Index of People (Other than Authors) Referred to in the Text

Authors, Journals cited in the Text